Contents

Contemporary Conflict Resolution

The prevention, management and transformation of deadly conflicts

Hugh Miall
Oliver Ramsbotham
Tom Woodhouse

Polity Press

First published in 1999 by Polity Press
in association with Blackwell Publishers Ltd

Reprinted 2000 (twice), 2001

Editorial office:
Polity Press
65 Bridge Street
Cambridge CB2 1UR, UK

Marketing and production:
Blackwell Publishers Ltd
108 Cowley Road
Oxford OX4 1JF, UK

Published in the USA by
Blackwell Publishers Inc.
350 Main Street
Malden, MA 02148, USA

A catalogue record for this book is available from the British Library.

Library of Congress Cataloging-in-Publication Data

Miall, Hugh.
  Contemporary conflict resolution : the prevention, management and transformation of deadly conflicts / Hugh Miall, Oliver Ramsbotham, Tom Woodhouse.
    p. cm.
  Includes bibliographical references and index.
  ISBN 0-7456-2034-5 (hb). — ISBN 0-7456-2035-3 (pb)
  1. Pacific settlement of international disputes. 2. Conflict management. 3. Peace. I. Ramsbotham, Oliver. II. Woodhouse, Tom.
III. Title.
JZ6010.M53   1999
327.1'7—dc21   98-52193
                                                                          CIP

Typeset in 10 on 11 pt Sabon by York House Typographic Ltd
Printed in Great Britain by TJ International, Padstow, Cornwall
This book is printed on acid-free paper.

List of Figures

List of Tables

List of Boxes

List of Maps

Preface

We wrote this book to meet the need for a single, comprehensive survey of contemporary conflict resolution and its contribution to the management of post-Cold War conflicts. Given the changing nature of conflict, we felt that the time was ripe for a reassessment of theory and practice. Since C. R. Mitchell wrote his survey on *The Structure of International Conflict*, there have been many edited volumes, but few authored books, which offer an overall satisfactory account.

Whether in Angola, Cambodia, Bosnia or Rwanda, people are struggling to cope with the consequences of destructive conflicts. Governments retain, in Anatol Rapoport's words, 'the ability to destroy all human life on this planet *at will*'. Unless humanity can find peaceful and just means of dealing with its differences without resort to violence, our collective survival remains in doubt. Our concentration on how conflict resolution is dealing with contemporary conflicts remains beset with difficulties and dilemmas, but in the progress it has made we find seeds of hope.

Many people have helped us in this work. We are particularly indebted to the scholars, mediators, thinkers and activists whose work we cite. We would like to thank Patricia Barandun, Gary Blythe, Andy Carl, Professor Christopher Clapham, Professor John Darby, Dr Gerd Nonneman, Sergei Khrychikov and members of the Conflict Resolution Research Seminar, Department of Peace Studies, University of Bradford, for their comments and suggested improvements. The Richardson Institute at Lancaster University and the School of Peace Studies at Bradford University gave us the time and facilities to do this work. We would also like to thank our partners, Claire, Meredith and Gill, for the perspective they brought and their tolerance and support. The authors, of course, are responsible for whatever errors and shortcomings remain.

Hugh Miall
Oliver Ramsbotham
Tom Woodhouse

Acknowledgements

The authors and publisher gratefully acknowledge permission to reproduce copyright material:

Boxes and tables

Ted Robert Gurr for box 4.2, 'Risk Factors for Ethnopolitical Rebellion', reprinted from T. R. Gurr, *Peoples versus States* (United States Institute of Peace, 1998).

MIT Press for table 3.5, reprinted from M. E. Brown, 'Causes and regional dimensions', in Michael E. Brown (ed.), *The International Dimensions of Internal Conflict* (CSIA Studies in International Security, MIT Press, Cambridge, MA, 1996).

Oxford University Press for table 1.5, reprinted from *World Disasters Report 1996* (OUP, 1996, for International Federation of Red Cross and Red Crescent Societies).

Sage Publications Ltd and the authors for table 4.1, reprinted from Peter Wallensteen, 'Universalism vs. particularism: on the limits of major power order', *Journal of Peace Research*, 21(3), 1984; and box 6.1, reprinted from Peter Wallensteen and Margareta Sollenberg, 'Armed conflicts, conflict termination and peace agreements, 1989–96', *Journal of Peace Research*, 34(3), 1997.

Extracts

Nicole Ball: extract reprinted from 'Rebuilding war-torn societies', in Chester A. Crocker, Fen Osler Hampson, with Pamela Aall (eds), *Managing Global Chaos: Sources of and Responses to International Conflict* (United States Institute of Peace Press, 1996), by permission of the United States Institute of Peace.

Kenneth Boulding: extracts reprinted from *Journal of Conflict Resolution* on publication of the first issue (1957) and in *Journal of Conflict Resolution*, 27(1), 1973, by permission of Sage Publications Ltd.

Albert Camus: extract from *The Plague* translated by Stuart Gilbert (Hamish Hamilton, 1944), translation copyright © 1948 by Stuart Gilbert, by permission of the publishers, Penguin Books Ltd and Random House, Inc.

Seamus Heaney: lines from 'The Cure at Troy', reprinted from *The Cure at Troy: A Version of Sophocles' Philoctetes*, copyright © 1990 by Seamus Heaney, by permission of the publishers, Faber & Faber Ltd and Farrar Straus & Giroux, Inc.

J. McConnell: extract from Dhammapada Commentary, Pali Text reprinted from *Mindful Meditation: A Handbook for Buddhist Peacemakers* (Buddhist Research Institute, Mahachula University, Bangkok, 1995), distributed by Wisdom Books, UK, by permission of the author.

Michael Renner: extract reprinted from Worldwatch Paper 114, *Critical Juncture: The Future of Peacekeeping* (1992), by permission of the Worldwatch Institute.

List of Abbreviations

ACCORD	African Centre for the Constructive Resolution of Disputes
ADFLCZ	Alliance of Democratic Forces for the Liberation of Congo-Zaire
ADR	Alternative Dispute Resolution
AFL	Armed Forces of Liberia
ANC	African National Congress
ARENA	Alianza Republicana Nacionalista (El Salvador)
ASEAN	Association of South-East Asian Nations
BRA	Bougainville Revolutionary Army (Papua New Guinea)
CCCRTE	Coordinating Committee for Conflict Resolution Training in Europe
CCF	Citizens' Constitutional Forum (Fiji)
CDGK	Coalition Government of Democratic Kampuchea (Cambodia)
CECORE	Center for Conflict Resolution (Uganda)
CFSP	Common Foreign and Security Policy
CIS	Commonwealth of Independent States
CMOC	Civil-Military Operation Centre
CODESA	Convention for a Democratic South Africa
CPP	Cambodian People's Party
CSCE	Conference on Security and Cooperation in Europe
CSNPD	Committee of National Revival for Peace and Democracy (Chad)
DHA	Department of Humanitarian Affairs (UN)
DPA	Department of Political Affairs (UN)
DPKO	Department of Peacekeeping Operations (UN)
DUP	Democratic Unionist Party (Northern Ireland)
EC	European Community
ECCP	European Centre for Conflict Prevention

ECHO	European Community Humanitarian Office
ECOMOG	Economic Community of West African States Ceasefire Monitoring Group
ECOWAS	Economic Community of West African States
ECPS	Executive Committee on Peace and Security (UN)
ECTF	European Community Task Force
ELN	Ejército de Liberación Nacional (Colombia)
EPL	Ejército Popular de Liberación (Colombia)
EPR	Ejército Popular Revolucionario (Mexico)
EZLN	Ejército Zapatista de Liberación National (Mexico)
FAFO	Institute for Applied Social Sciences (Norway)
FARC	Fuerzas Armados Revolucionarias Colombianas
FBH	Federation of Bosnia-Herzegovina
FIS	Front Islamique du Salut (Algeria)
FMNL	Farabundo Marti Front for National Liberation (El Salvador)
FRELIMO	Frente para a Libertaçâo de Moçambique
FRETILIN	Frente Revolucionario Timorense de Libertaçâo e Independência (Timor)
FRY	Federal Republic of Yugoslavia
FSU	Former Soviet Union
FUNCINPEC	Front Uni National pour un Camboge Indépendent, Neutre, Pacifique et Coopératif
FYROM	Former Yugoslav Republic of Macedonia
GEDS	Global Event-Data System
GIA	Groupe Islamique Armée (Algeria)
GRIT	Graduated and Reciprocated Initiatives in Tension Reduction
HCNM	High Commissioner on National Minorities
ICRC	International Committee of the Red Cross
IFI	International Financial Institution
IFOR	Implementation Force (Bosnia)
IFP	Inkatha Freedom Party
IISS	International Institute for Strategic Studies
IMF	International Monetary Fund
INCORE	Initiative on Conflict Resolution and Ethnicity
INGO	International Non-governmental Organization
IPRA	International Peace Research Association
ISC	'international social conflicts'
JCR	*Journal of Conflict Resolution*
JKLF	Jammu and Kashmir Liberation Front (India)
JNA	Yugoslav National Army
KDP	Kurdistan Democratic Party (Iraq)
KDPI	Kurdish Democratic Party of Iran
KLA	Kosovo Liberation Army
KLF/KCF	Khalistan Liberation Force/Khalistan Commando

	Force (India)
KNU	Karen National Union (Myanmar)
KPNLF	Khmer People's National Liberation Front
LRA	Lord's Resistance Army (Uganda)
LTTE	Liberation Tigers of Tamil Eelam (Sri Lanka)
MCPMR	Mechanism for Conflict Prevention, Management and Resolution
MDD	Movement for Democracy and Development (Chad)
MILF	Moro Islamic Liberation Front (Philippines)
MISAB	Inter-Africa Mission to Monitor the Implementation of the Bangui Agreements
MNLF	Moro National Liberation Front (Philippines)
MONUA	UN Observer Mission in Angola
MPLA	Movimento Popular de Libertaçâo de Angola
MQM	Mohajir National Movement (Pakistan)
MRTA	Movimento Revolucionario Tupac Amaru (Peru)
NATO	North Atlantic Treaty Organization
NDA	National Democratic Alliance (Sudan)
NGO	Non-governmental Organization
NP	National Party (South Africa)
NPFL	National Patriotic Front of Liberia
NPT	Non-Proliferation Treaty
OAS	Organization of American States
OAU	Organization of African Unity
OECD	Organization for Economic Cooperation and Development
ONUCA	UN Observer Mission in Central America
ONUMOZ	UN Operation in Mozambique
ONUSAL	UN Observer Mission in El Salvador
OPM	Organisasi Papua Merdeka (Indonesia)
OSCE	Organization for Security and Cooperation in Europe
PDK	Party of Democratic Kampuchea
PFLP	Popular Front for the Liberation of Palestine (Israel)
PIOOM	Interdisciplinary Research Program on Causes of Human Rights Violations
PISGA	Palestinian Interim Self-Governing Authority
PKK	Kurdistan Workers' Party (Turkey)
PLO	Palestine Liberation Organization
PNG	Papua New Guinea
POLISARIO	Popular Front for the Liberation of Saguia, El-Hamra and Rio de Oro (Western Sahara)
PRIO	Peace Research Institute Oslo
PSC	'protracted social conflict'
PTSD	post-traumatic stress disorder
PUK	Patriotic Union of Kurdistan (Iraq)
RBH	Republic of Bosnia–Herzegovina

RENAMO	Resistência Nacional Moçambicana
RPF	Rwanda Patriotic Front
RS	Republika Srpska (Serb Republic)
RUC	Royal Ulster Constabulary
RUF	Revolutionary United Front (Sierra Leone)
SADC	South African Development Community
SAIRI	Supreme Assembly for the Islamic Revolution in Iraq
SALT	Strategic Arms Limitation Talks
SB	Shanti Bahina (Army of Peace) (Bangladesh)
SDLP	Social Democratic and Labour Party (Northern Ireland)
SFOR	Stabilization Force (Bosnia)
SIPRI	Stockholm International Peace Research Institute
SLA	South Lebanon Army
SNC	Supreme National Council (Cambodia)
SOC	State of Cambodia
SOP	'standard operating procedure'
SPLA	Sudanese People's Liberation Army
SRSG	Special Representative of the Secretary-General
SWAPO	South-West Africa People's Organization
SWAPOL	South-West Africa Police
TFF	Transnational Foundation for Peace and Future Research
UKUP	UK Unionist Party (Northern Ireland)
ULFA	United Liberation Force of Assam
ULIMO	United Liberation Movement for Democracy (Liberia)
UNAMIR	UN Assistance Mission for Rwanda
UNAVEM	UN Angola Verification Mission
UNCRO	UN Confidence Restoration Operation (Croatia)
UNDP	UN Development Programme
UNESCO	UN Educational, Scientific and Cultural Organization
UNFICYP	UN Peacekeeping Force in Cyprus
UNHCR	UN High Commissioner for Refugees
UNICEF	UN Children's Fund
UNITA	Uniâo Nacional para a Independência Total de Angola
UNITAR	UN Institute for Training and Research
UNMIBH	UN Mission in Bosnia and Herzegovina
UNMIH	UN Mission in Haiti
UNMOP	UN Mission of Observers in Prevlaka
UNOMIL	UN Observer Mission in Liberia
UNOSOM	UN Operation in Somalia
UNPREDEP	UN Preventive Deployment Force (Macedonia)
UNPROFOR	UN Protection Force (Former Yugoslavia)
UNTAC	UN Transitional Authority in Cambodia
UNTAES	UN Transitional Administration for Eastern Slavonia, Baranja and Western Sirmium (Croatia)

UNTAG	UN Transition Assistance Group (Namibia)
URNG	Unidad Revolucionaria Nacional Guatemalteca
USAID	US Agency for International Development
USC	United Somali Congress
USC/SNA	United Somali Congress/Somali National Alliance
UTO	United Tajik Opposition

1

Introduction

The international community is faced with a wave of new conflicts. Taken together they amount to nothing less than an epochal watershed: a time that future historians may describe as the moment when humanity seized – or failed to seize – the opportunity to replace obsolescent mechanisms for resolving human conflict.

Michael Renner

Conflict resolution as a defined specialist field has come of age in the post-Cold War era. It has also come face to face with fundamental new challenges.

It started in the 1950s and 1960s, at the height of the Cold War, when the development of nuclear weapons and the conflict between the superpowers seemed to threaten human survival. A group of pioneers from different disciplines saw the value of studying conflict as a general phenomenon, with similar properties whether it occurs in international relations, domestic politics, industrial relations, communities, families or between individuals. They saw the potential of applying approaches that were evolving in industrial relations and community mediation settings to conflicts in general, including civil and international conflicts.

A handful of people in North America and Europe began to establish research groups to develop these new ideas. They were not taken very seriously. The international relations profession had its own categories for understanding international conflict, and did not welcome the interlopers. Nor was the combination of analysis and practice implicit in the new ideas easy to reconcile with traditional scholarly institutions or the traditions of practitioners such as diplomats and politicians.

Nevertheless, the new ideas attracted interest, and the field began to grow and spread. Scholarly journals in conflict resolution were created. Institutions to study the field were established, and their number rapidly increased. The field developed its own subdivisions, with different groups studying international crises, internal wars, social conflicts and approaches ranging from negotiations and mediation to experimental games.

By the 1980s, conflict resolution ideas were increasingly making a difference in real conflicts. In South Africa, for example, the Centre for Intergroup Studies was applying the approaches that had developed in the field to the developing confrontation between apartheid and its challengers, with impressive results. In the Middle East, a peace process was getting under way in which negotiators on both sides were gaining experience of each other and of conflict resolution through problem-solving workshops. In Northern Ireland, groups inspired by the new approach had set up community relations initiatives that were not only reaching across community divides but were also becoming an accepted responsibility of local government. In war-torn regions of Africa and South-East Asia, development workers and humanitarian agencies were seeing the need to take account of conflict and conflict resolution as an integral part of their activities.

By the closing years of the Cold War, the climate for conflict resolution was changing radically. With relations between the superpowers improving, the ideological and military competition that had fuelled many regional conflicts was fading away. Protracted regional conflicts in Southern Africa, Central America, and East Asia moved towards settlements. It seemed that the UN could return to play the role its founders expected.

The dissolution of the Soviet Union brought to a close the long period in which a single international conflict dominated the international system. Instead, internal conflicts, ethnic conflicts, conflicts over secession and power struggles within countries became the norm. These reflected not so much struggles between competing centres of power, of the kind that had characterized international conflict for most of the 350 years since the peace of Westphalia, but the fragmentation and breakdown of state structures, economies and whole societies. At their extreme, in parts of Africa, the new wars witnessed the return of mercenary armies and underpaid militias which preyed on civilian populations in a manner reminiscent of medieval times.

In this new climate, the attention of scholars of international relations and comparative politics turned to exactly the type of conflict that had preoccupied the conflict resolution thinkers for many years. A richer cross-fertilization of ideas developed between conflict resolution and these traditional fields. At the same time, practitioners from various backgrounds were attracted to conflict resolution. International statesmen began to use the language, international organizations set up Conflict Resolution Mechanisms and Conflict Prevention Centres. A former President of the United States, Jimmy Carter, became one of the most active leaders of a conflict resolution non-governmental organization (NGO). A former Foreign Minister of the USSR, Eduard Shevardnadze, set up an organization to address ethnic conflicts in the former Soviet Union. The

Nyerere Foundation was established with comparable aims for Africa. Overseas development ministries in several countries set up conflict units and began funding conflict prevention and resolution initiatives on a significant scale. How to achieve a peaceful settlement of disputes between states was a familiar theme in the international relations and strategic studies literature and had always been part of the stock-in-trade of international diplomacy. Less familiar was the challenge to statist international organizations of managing non-state conflicts.

A greater degree of impact, however, also brought greater scrutiny, and the development of searching critiques from different quarters. Conflict resolution had always been controversial, both in relation to outside disciplines, and internally amongst its different protagonists and schools. It also drew persistent fire from critics at different points on the political and intellectual spectrum. On the one hand, realists saw conflict resolution as soft-headed and unrealistic, since in their view international politics is a struggle between antagonistic and irreconcilable groups, in which power and coercion were the only ultimate currency. Might not lasting peace more often result from decisive military victory than from negotiated settlement? And might not third party intervention merely prolong the misery? The ideological preconceptions of some of those working in the peace research and conflict resolution field were regarded as compromising, and the attempt to combine 'scientific' academic analysis with a normative political agenda as intellectually suspect. From a different angle, neo-Marxists and radical thinkers from development studies saw the whole conflict resolution enterprise as misconceived, since it attempted to reconcile interests that should not be reconciled, failed to take sides in unequal and unjust struggles, and lacked an analysis within a properly global perspective of the forces of exploitation and oppression. Beneath this lay the fundamental question whether any value is worth fighting for at all. Other critics were less prepared to reject conflict resolution outright, but were sceptical of overblown claims made for the field, and unconvinced that methods developed within a western setting could overcome their cultural boundaries and offer useful tools in very different cultures and political systems. They also questioned whether the models of conflict resolution that were developed during the Cold War still have application to post-Cold War conflicts.

This last criticism was the most searching. Are we witnessing a fundamentally new kind of conflict, to which previous ideas do not apply? If modern conflicts are becoming neo-medieval struggles between warlords, drug barons, mercenaries and militias who benefit from war and have found it their only means of making a living, of what value will be efforts to resolve conflicts between them peacefully? Can conflict resolution apply in situations such as those that have prevailed in Bosnia, where ethnonationalist leaders whipped up ethnic hatred and courted war in order to serve their own political purposes? Is conflict resolution based on values of liberal internationalism which fail to grasp that the new conflicts

are a by-product of the impact of westernization and liberal internationalism on the rest of the world?

This book argues that, on the contrary, the developing tradition of
thinking about conflict and conflict resolution is all the more relevant as
the fixed structures of sovereignty and governance break down. All over
the world, societies are facing stresses from population growth, structural
change in the world economy, migration into cities, environmental degradation and rapid social change. Societies with institutions, rules or norms
for managing conflict and well-established traditions of governance are
generally better able to accommodate peacefully to change; those with
weaker governance, fragile social bonds and little consensus on values or
traditions are more likely to buckle. Strengthening the capacity of conflict
resolution within societies and political institutions, especially preventa-
tively, is a vital part of the response to the phenomena of warlordism and
ethnonationalism. We argue that conflict resolution has a role to play,
even in war zones, since building peace constituencies and understandings
across divided communities is an essential element of humanitarian
engagement. We argue that conflict resolution is an integral part of the
work towards development, social justice and social transformation,
which aims to tackle the problems of which mercenaries and child soldiers
are symptoms. We argue for a broad understanding of conflict resolution,
to include not only mediation between the parties but efforts to address
the wider context in which international actors, domestic constituencies
and intra-party relationships sustain violent conflicts. Finally, we argue
that although the theories and practices of conflict resolution we deal with
spring from western roots, every culture and society has its own version of
what is, after all, a general social and political need. The point is not to
abandon conflict resolution because it is western, but to find ways to
enrich western and non-western traditions through their mutual
encounter.

In making these arguments, we recognize that conflict resolution itself is
changing and developing, as it must, to deal with the changing nature of
conflict. Our main purpose is to foster an understanding of contemporary
conflicts and to indicate how the practice and thinking of contemporary
conflict resolution is changing in response. In doing so, we aim to offer a
picture of the range of organizations and individuals that are involved in
the field, not only in international organizations and NGOs but also in
political parties and at grass-roots level in societies in conflict. We will
review the theories and practices of conflict resolution, pointing to the
new methods and approaches, the difficulties and dilemmas they face, and
the broadening scope of their application.

Introduction to Conflict Resolution

First, we briefly introduce some of the classical ideas that have shaped conflict resolution thinking and practice and are still foundations of the field. We give a fuller account of their development in chapter 2.

Classical ideas

Conflict is an intrinsic and inevitable aspect of social change. It is an expression of the heterogeneity of interests, values and beliefs that arise as new formations generated by social change come up against inherited constraints. But the way we deal with conflict is a matter of habit and choice. It is possible to change habitual responses and exercise intelligent choices.

Conflict approaches

One typical habit in conflict is to give very high priority to defending one's own interests. If Cain's interests clash with Abel's, Cain is inclined to ignore Abel's interests or actively to damage them. Leaders of nations are expected to defend the national interest and to defeat the interests of others if they come into conflict. But this is not the only possible response.

Figure 1.1 illustrates five approaches to conflict, distinguished by whether concern for Self and concern for Other are high or low. Cain has high concern for Self and low concern for Other: this is a 'contending' style. Another alternative is to yield: this implies more concern for the interests of Other than Self. Another is to avoid conflict and withdraw: this suggests low concern for both Self and Other. Another is to balance concern for the interests of Self and Other, leading to a search for accommodation and compromise. And there is a fifth alternative, seen by many in the conflict resolution field as the one to be recommended where possible – high regard for the interests both of Self and Other. This implies strong assertion of one's own interest, but equal awareness of the aspirations and needs of the other, generating energy to search for a creative problem-solving outcome.

Win–lose, lose–lose, win–win outcomes

What happens when the conflict approaches of two parties are considered together? Parties to conflicts are usually inclined to see their interests as diametrically opposed. The possible outcomes are seen to be win–lose (one wins, the other loses) or compromise (they split their difference). But there is a much more common outcome in violent conflicts: both lose. If neither is able to impose an outcome or is prepared to compromise, the

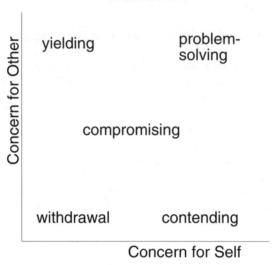

Figure 1.1   Five approaches to conflict

conflictants may impose such massive costs on each other that all of the parties end up worse off than they would have been had another strategy been adopted. In conflict resolution analysis this is found to be a much more common outcome than is generally supposed. When this becomes clear to the parties (often regrettably late in the day), there is a strong motive based on self-interest for moving towards other outcomes, such as compromise or win–win. The spectrum of such outcomes may well be wider than conflictants suppose.

Traditionally, the task of conflict resolution has been seen as helping parties who perceive their situation as zero-sum[1] (Self's gain is Other's loss) to reperceive it as a non-zero-sum conflict (in which both may gain or both may lose) and then to assist parties to move in the positive-sum direction. Figure 1.2 shows various possible outcomes of the conflict between Cain and Abel. Any point towards the right is better for Abel, any point towards the top is better for Cain. In the Bible, the prize is the Lord's favour. Cain sees the situation as a zero-sum conflict: at point 1 (his best outcome) he gets the Lord's favour, at 2 (his worst) the Lord favours Abel. All the other possibilities lie on the line from 1 to 2 in which the Lord divides his favour, more or less equally, between the two brothers. Point 3 represents a possible compromise position. But it is the other diagonal, representing the non-zero-sum outcomes, that is the more interesting from a conflict resolution perspective: the mutual loss that actually occurred, at 0, when Abel was slain and Cain lost the Lord's favour, and the mutual gain that they missed, at 4, if each had been his brother's keeper.

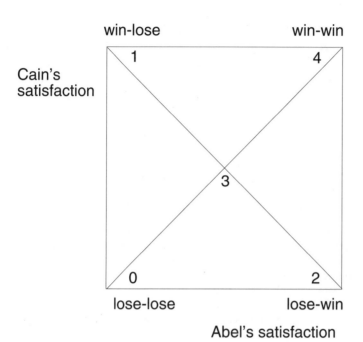

Figure 1.2 Zero-sum and non-zero-sum outcomes

Prisoner's Dilemma and the evolution of cooperation

Prisoner's Dilemma is a simple representation in game theory, which clearly illustrates the tendency for contending strategies to end in lose–lose outcomes. Two players (prisoners accused of crime) each have two choices: to cooperate with each other (remain silent) or to defect (inform on the other). The choices must be made in ignorance of what the other will do (they are kept in separate cells). The possible pay-offs are given in table 1.1. It can be seen that, whatever choice the other may make, each player considered singly gains a higher pay-off by choosing to defect (if the other cooperates, defection earns 5 points rather than 3; if the other defects, defection earns 1 point rather than 0). So the only rational course is to defect. But this is not the best outcome for either, since, whereas mutual defection earns 1 point each, mutual cooperation would have earned both of them 3 points. So the individually rational choice turns out to deliver a mutual lose–lose outcome. The collectively rational choice is for both to cooperate, reaching the elusive win–win outcome (point 4 in figure 1.2). But if both could communicate and agree to go for mutual cooperation, how can each guarantee that the other will not subsequently

Table 1.1   Prisoner's Dilemma

	Cooperate	Defect
Cooperate	3, 3	5, 0
Defect	0, 5	1, 1

defect, tempted by the 5-point prize? In this kind of social trap, self-interested parties can readily get stuck at lose–lose outcomes.

The trap depends on the game being played only once. If each move is part of a sequence of repeated games, there are possibilities for cooperative behaviour to evolve. In a well-known series of experiments, Axelrod (1984) invited experts to submit programs for a Prisoner's Dilemma competition run on computer. A spectrum of 'nice' and 'nasty' strategies was submitted and each was tested in pairs against all the others in repeated interactions. The surprise clear overall winner was a simple strategy called 'Tit-for-Tat' (submitted by the conflict resolution analyst Anatol Rapaport), which began by cooperating on the first move, and thereafter copied what the other had done on the previous move. The repeated overall success of Tit-for-Tat shows, in Dawkins's phrase, that, contrary to a widely held view about competitive environments of this kind (including Darwinian natural selection), 'nice guys finish first' (1989, 202–33). Tit-for-Tat is not a push-over. It hits back when the other defects. But, crucially, it initially cooperates (it is 'generous'), and it bears no grudges (it is 'forgiving'). Its responses are also predictable and reliable (it has 'clarity of behaviour'). For the 'evolution of cooperation' to get going in a mêlée of competing strategies, there must be a critical if at first quite small number of initially cooperating strategies, and the 'shadow of the future' must be a long one: interaction must not be confined to just one game (for example, with one player able to wipe out another in one go). But, so long as these conditions operate, even though 'nasty guys' may seem to do well at first, 'nice guys' come out on top in the end.[2] Natural selection favours cooperation.

So taking account of the future relationship (for example, between two communities which will have to live together) is one way out of the trap. Another is to take the social context into account. Imagine, for example, that the prisoners know that there is a gang outside, who will punish them if they defect and reward them if they cooperate. This can change their pay-offs and hence the outcome. A similar change occurs if instead of considering only their own interests, the parties also attach value to the interests of each other: social players are not trapped.

Positions, interests and needs

How can the parties reframe their positions if they are diametrically opposed, as they often are? One of the classical ideas in conflict resolution is to distinguish between the positions held by the parties and their underlying interests and needs. For example, two neighbours quarrel over a tree. Each neighbour claims that the tree is on his land. No compromise is possible: the tree cannot be sawn in half. But it turns out that the interest of one neighbour is in using the fruit of the tree, and the interest of the other is in having the shade. So the interests are not irreconcilable after all. Interests are also often easier to reconcile than positions, since there are usually several positions that might satisfy underlying interests and some of these positions may be mutually compatible. Matters may be more difficult if the conflict is over values (which are often non-negotiable) or relationships, which may need to be changed to resolve the conflict, although the same principle of looking for a deeper level of compatible underlying motives applies. Some analysts take this to the limit by identifying basic human needs (for example, identity, security, survival) as lying at the roots of other motives. Intractable conflicts are seen to result from the denial of such needs, and conflict can only be resolved when such needs are satisfied. The hopeful argument of these analysts is that whereas interests may be subject to relative scarcity, basic needs are not (for example, security for one party is reinforced by security for the other). As long as the conflict is translated into the language of needs, an outcome that satisfies both sides' needs can be found.

For example, Woodhouse is aggrieved that, although he is the author with the best ideas, his name comes only third on the list of authors. He therefore demands that Miall and Ramsbotham change their names to Woodhouse by deed poll. But they refuse to do so, because of their interest in personal glory and fame (see figure 1.3). Enter Woodhouse's daughter. She points out that if the deadlock persists, they will be unable to publish a book together, which is a common underlying need. They must find a way to acknowledge their equal participation in the text. By shifting to a new position that reflects their underlying needs, the conflict is resolved.

Third party intervention

In the previous example, Woodhouse's daughter plays the role of a third party, and her intervention changes the dynamics of the conflict. Where two parties are reacting to one another's actions, it is easy for a spiral of hostility and escalation to develop through positive feedback. The entry of the third party changes the conflict structure and allows a different pattern of communications, enabling the third party to filter or reflect back the messages, attitudes and behaviour of the conflictants. This intervention may dampen the feedback spiral.

Woodhouse's daughter is an example of a 'powerless' mediator – her

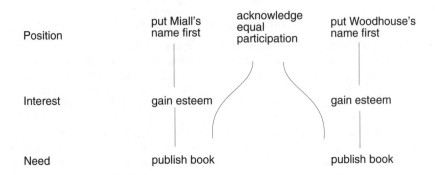

Figure 1.3   Positions, interests and needs

communications are powerful, but she herself brings to bear no power resources of her own. In other situations there may also be powerful third parties whose entry alters not only the communication structure but also the power balance. Such third parties may alter the parties' behaviour as well as their communications by judicious use of the carrot and the stick (positive and negative inducement); and they may support one outcome rather than another. Of course, by taking action, powerful third parties may find themselves sucked into the conflict as a full party. Figure 1.4 illustrates how third parties may act as arbiters (with or without the consent of the conflict parties), or may try to facilitate negotiations or mediate between the parties (coercively or non-coercively).

Three faces of power

It may seem strange to call Woodhouse's daughter 'powerless', when she has provided the impetus to resolve the conflict. This is because the term 'power' is ambiguous. On the one hand it means the power to command, order, enforce – coercive or 'hard' power. On the other, it means the power to induce cooperation, to legitimize, to inspire – persuasive or 'soft' power. Hard power has always been important in violent conflict, but soft power may be more important in conflicts managed peacefully. Kenneth Boulding (1989) calls the former 'threat power' ('do what I want or I will do what you don't want'). Following earlier theorists of management-labour negotiations, he then further distinguishes between two forms of soft power: 'exchange power', associated with bargaining and the compromising approach ('do what I want and I will do what you want'), and 'integrative power' associated with persuasion and transformative long-term problem-solving ('together we can do something that is better for both of us'). Conflict resolvers try to shift emphasis away from the use of threat power and towards the use of exchange and integrative power (see table 1.2).

Third parties such as politicians and governments may use all these

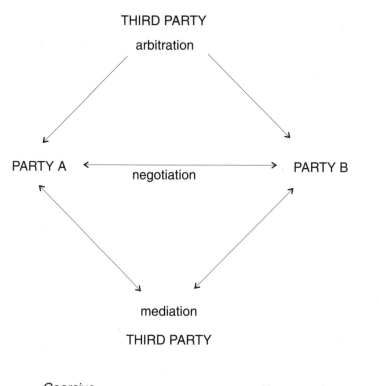

THIRD PARTY
arbitration

PARTY A ⟷ negotiation ⟶ PARTY B

mediation

THIRD PARTY

Coercive   *Non-coercive*

Enforcement   Pure mediation
Non-forcible coercion   Conciliation/problem-solving
Mediation with muscle   Good offices

Figure 1.4   Coercive and non-coercive third party intervention

forms of power. In terms of third party intervention (see figure 1.4) it is helpful to distinguish between powerful mediators, or 'mediators with muscle', who bring their power resources to bear, and powerless mediators, whose role is confined to communication and facilitation. Track I diplomacy involves official governmental or inter-governmental representatives, who may use good offices, mediation, and sticks and carrots to seek or force an outcome, typically along the win–lose or 'bargaining' line (between the points 1, 3 and 2 in figure 1.2). Track II diplomacy, in contrast, involves unofficial mediators who do not have carrots or sticks,

Table 1.2   Three faces of power

Threat power	Exchange power	Integrative power
Destructive	Productive	Creative
productive	destructive	productive
creative	creative	destructive

The entries in the bottom two rows indicate that, in Boulding's words, 'None of these categories will be perfectly clear. They are what all mathematicians call 'fuzzy sets', so that each contains elements of the other two types of power.'
Source: from Boulding, 1989, 25

They work with the parties or their constituencies to facilitate agreements, encouraging the parties to see their predicament as lying along the lose–lose to win–win line (between points 0, 3 and 4 in figure 1.2) and to find mutually satisfactory outcomes.

Symmetric and asymmetric conflicts

So far we have been considering conflicts of interest between relatively similar parties. These are examples of *symmetric* conflicts. Conflict may also arise between dissimilar parties such as a majority and a minority, an established government and a group of rebels, a master and his servant, an employer and her employees, a publisher and his authors. These are *asymmetric* conflicts. Here the root of the conflict lies not in particular issues or interests that may divide the parties, but in the very structure of who they are and the relationship between them. It may be that this structure of roles and relationships cannot be changed without conflict.

Classical conflict resolution, in some views, applies only to symmetric conflicts. In asymmetric conflicts the structure is such that the top dog always wins, the underdog always loses. The only way to resolve the conflict is to change the structure, but this can never be in the interests of the top dog. So there are no win–win outcomes, and the third party has to join forces with the underdog to bring about a resolution.

From another point of view, however, even asymmetric conflicts impose costs on both parties. It is oppressive to be an oppressor, even if not so oppressive as to be oppressed. There are costs for the top dogs in sustaining themselves in power and keeping the underdogs down. In severe asymmetric conflicts the cost of the relationship becomes unbearable for both sides. This then opens the possibility for conflict resolution through a shift from the existing structure of relationships to another.

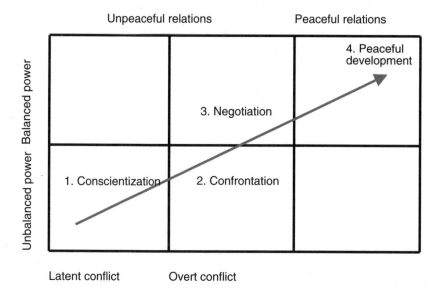

Source: from Curle, 1971 and Lederach, 1995

Figure 1.5 Transforming asymmetric conflicts (I)

The role of the third party is to assist with this transformation, if necessary confronting the top dog. This means transforming what were unpeaceful, unbalanced relationships into peaceful and dynamic ones. Figure 1.5 illustrates how the passage from unpeaceful to peaceful relationships may involve a temporary increase in overt conflict as people become aware of imbalances of power and injustice affecting them (stage 1, education or 'conscientization'), organize themselves and articulate their grievances (stage 2, confrontation), come to terms in a more equal way with those who held a preponderance of power over them (stage 3, negotiation) and finally join in restructuring a more equitable and just relationship (stage 4, resolution). There are many ways in which this can be approached without using coercion. There is the Gandhian tactic of 'speaking truth to power', influencing and persuading the power-holders. Then there are the tactics of mobilizing popular movements, increasing solidarity, making demonstrations of resolve, establishing a demand for change. Raising awareness of the conflict among those who are external or internal supporters of the top dog may start to weaken the regime (as did for example the opponents of apartheid in South Africa). The unequal power structure is unbalanced; it is held up by props of various kinds; removing the props may make the unbalanced structure collapse. Another tactic is to strengthen and empower the underdogs. The underdogs may

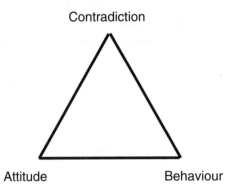

Source: Galtung, 1969

Figure 1.6   The conflict triangle

withdraw from the unbalanced relationship and start building anew: the parallel institutions approach. Non-violence uses soft power to move towards a more balanced relationship.

The conflict triangle

In the late 1960s Galtung (1969; 1996, 72) proposed an influential model of conflict, that encompasses both symmetric and asymmetric conflicts. He suggested that conflict could be viewed as a triangle, with contradiction (C), attitude (A) and behaviour (B) at its vertices (see figure 1.6). Here the contradiction refers to the underlying conflict situation, which includes the actual or perceived 'incompatibility of goals' between the conflict parties generated by what Mitchell calls a 'mis-match between social values and social structure' (1981, 18). In a symmetric conflict, the contradiction is defined by the parties, their interests and the clash of interests between them. In an asymmetric conflict, it is defined by the parties, their relationship and the conflict of interests inherent in the relationship. Attitude includes the parties' perceptions and misperceptions of each other and of themselves. These can be positive or negative, but in violent conflicts parties tend to develop demeaning stereotypes of each other, and attitudes are often influenced by emotions such as fear, anger, bitterness and hatred. Attitude includes emotive (feeling), cognitive (belief) and conative (will) elements. Analysts who emphasize these subjective aspects are said to have an expressive view of the sources of conflict. Behaviour is the third component. It can include cooperation or coercion, gestures signifying conciliation or hostility. Violent conflict behaviour is characterized by threats, coercion and destructive attacks. Analysts who emphasize objective aspects such as structural relationships, competing material interests or behaviours are said to have an instrumental view of the sources of conflict.[3]

Galtung argues that all three components have to be present together in a full conflict. A conflict structure without conflictual attitudes or behaviour is a latent (or structural) conflict. Galtung sees conflict as a dynamic process in which structure, attitudes and behaviour are constantly changing and influencing one another. As a conflict emerges, it becomes a conflict formation as parties' interests come into conflict or the relationship they are in becomes oppressive. Conflict parties then organize around this structure to pursue their interests. They develop hostile attitudes and conflictual behaviour. And so the conflict formation starts to grow and develop. As it does so, it may widen, drawing in other parties, deepen and spread, generating secondary conflicts within the main parties or among outsiders who get sucked in. This often considerably complicates the task of addressing the original, core conflict. Eventually, however, resolving the conflict must involve a set of dynamic changes that involve a de-escalation of conflict behaviour, a change in attitudes, and transforming the relationships or clashing interests that are at the core of the conflict structure.

A related idea due to Galtung (1981) is the distinction between direct violence (children are murdered), structural violence (children die through poverty) and cultural violence (whatever blinds us to this or seeks to justify it). We end direct violence by changing conflict behaviours, structural violence by removing structural contradictions and injustices, and cultural violence by changing attitudes.

Conflict dynamics

This model then sees conflict formations arising out of social change, leading to a process of violent or non-violent conflict transformation, and resulting in further social change in which hitherto suppressed or marginalized individuals or groups come to articulate their interests and challenge existing norms and power structures. Figure 1.7 shows a schematic illustration of phases of conflict, and forms of intervention that may be feasible at different stages. A schematic life-cycle of conflict sees a progression from peaceful social change to conflict formation to violent conflict and then to conflict transformation and back to peaceful social change. But this is not the only path. The sequence can go from conflict formation to conflict transformation and back to social change, avoiding violence. Or it can go from conflict formation to violent conflict back to the creation of fresh conflicts.[4]

New developments in conflict resolution theory and practice

A new pattern of conflicts is prevailing in the post-Cold War period, which is evoking a fresh pattern of responses. The main focus used to be on international wars; now it is on internal conflicts. Much of the theory of conflict resolution developed in response to symmetric conflicts; now

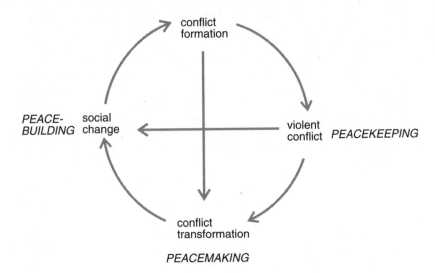

PREVENTION

PEACE-BUILDING

PEACEKEEPING

PEACEMAKING

Figure 1.7   Conflict dynamics and conflict resolution

asymmetric conflicts are dominant. International wars have typically been Clausewitzean affairs, fought out by power centres which use organized force directed against enemy forces in order to break the opponent's will to continue. But many post-Cold War conflicts are post-Clausewitzean, involving fragmented decision-making and disorganized forces directed against civilian populations. International conflicts were conducted between sovereign states; internal conflicts reflect breakdowns in states, which implies the disappearance of the structures through which internal power balances are organized and the appearance of 'holes' in the international fabric of sovereign states.

In response there has been a differentiation and broadening in the scope of third party intervention. Whereas classical conflict resolution was mainly concerned with entry into the conflict itself and with how to enable parties to violent conflict to resolve the issues between them in non-violent ways, the contemporary approach is to take a wider view of the timing of intervention. It suggests that efforts to resolve conflict should begin before armed conflict has broken out. They should be maintained even in the heat of battle and are applicable to peacekeeping and humanitarian intervention. They are still needed to assist parties to settle violent conflicts. And they continue to be relevant into the post-settlement phase, when peacebuilding must address the continuing issues in conflict (see figure 1.7).

In response to these prevailing patterns of asymmetric conflict, Curle's

Unbalanced power

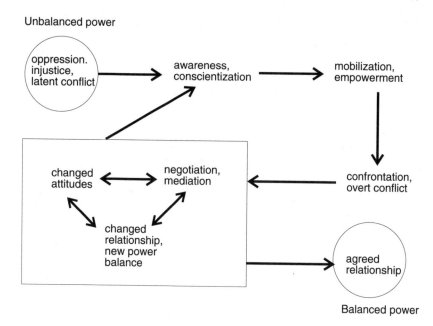

Source: from Francis, 1994

Figure 1.8 Transforming asymmetric conflicts (II)

original model of conflict transformation (figure 1.5) has been further developed (see figure 1.8). The asymmetry inherent in situations of unbalanced power and unsatisfied needs is reduced by increased awareness, mobilization and empowerment, leading to open confrontation where necessary before moving on to the negotiation of a new relationship and changed attitudes. Further mobilization and confrontation may follow, or the transformation of conflict resolution capacities may have reached far enough to accommodate future social and political change peacefully within agreed institutionalized processes. The elements bounded by the large box in figure 1.8 are those that are traditionally seen as conflict resolution, but they can be seen to play a complementary part in a larger process of transforming asymmetric relationships (van der Merwe, 1989, 1–8).

Moreover, given the varied sources of contemporary conflicts and complex political emergencies, responses are required at different levels. Changes in the context of conflict may depend on international and regional arrangements, conflicts within or over the state may demand structural change at state level, the conflict between the parties will still require resolution at the relational level, and cultural change at all levels may be necessary for the transformation of discourses and institutions

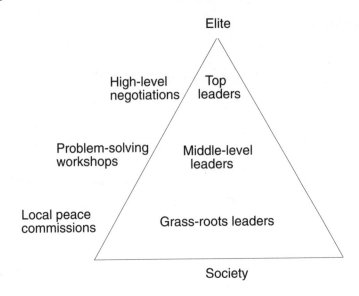

Source: from Lederach, 1997

Figure 1.9   Actors and approaches to peacebuilding

which sustain and reproduce violence. Greater emphasis is now placed on integrating the different levels at which peacebuilding and conflict resolution need to work within affected countries, with particular emphasis on the significance of 'bottom-up' processes (see figure 1.9).

Linked to this, there has been a shift from seeing third party intervention as the primary responsibility of external agencies towards appreciating the role of internal third parties or indigenous peacemakers. Instead of outsiders offering the fora for addressing conflicts in one-shot mediation efforts, the emphasis is on the need to build constituencies and capacity within societies and to learn from domestic cultures how to manage conflicts in a sustained way over time. This implies supporting domestic peace constituencies, developing domestic institutions and eliciting from those in conflict what approaches are socially and culturally acceptable. Encarnacion et al. (1990) have suggested a helpful model here. Instead of using the blanket term 'third parties', with its implication of externality and detachment, they distinguish a spectrum of agents ranging from 'uninvolved parties', through 'marginal concerned parties' to 'actively influential concerned parties'. The further a party is placed from the centre of the conflict, the lower will be its interest and commitment (see figure 1.10). Uninvolved outsiders may become progressively more involved and finally become core parties themselves in a widening of the conflict. Conversely, Encarnacion et al. introduce the idea of 'embedded parties', that is to say, individuals or groups who may emerge from within

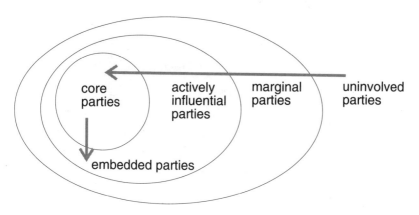

Source: from Encarnacion et al., 1990, 45

Figure 1.10   The gradient of conflict involvement

the situation (from the core parties) but wish to play the role of a concerned party in facilitating or expediting moves towards conflict resolution.

Behind all this lies an increased sensitivity to the culture question in general, as discussed briefly at the beginning of this section, and the hope that if the conflict resolution field has in the past been too narrowly western, it may in future become the truly cooperative cross-cultural venture that its founders conceived it to be.

The implication of this broadening in the scope and application of conflict resolution approaches has been to see the need for a complementary range of third party interventions. They should be multitrack instead of either Track I or Track II, addressing elites and grass roots, operating at structural-constitutional as well as at relational-community levels, with cooperation between involved international and internal agencies and a sustained commitment to the conflict in question over time. The increased emphasis on the importance of indigenous resources and local actors suggests the addition of what might be termed Track III peacemaking (see figure 1.11).

Terminology

Before we introduce the conflicts that we are concerned with in this book and the types of agent capable of responding creatively to them, we need to clarify how we are using the terms 'conflict' and 'conflict resolution'. The terminology is often confusing, with the same terms used in different ways both within the academic literature and in general usage.

By *conflict* we mean the pursuit of incompatible goals by different

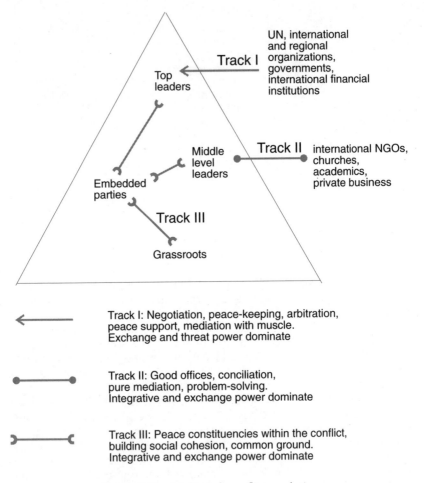

Figure 1.11   Multitrack conflict resolution

groups. This suggests a broader span of time and a wider class of struggle than armed conflict. We intend our usage here to apply to any political conflict, whether it is pursued by peaceful means or by the use of force. (Some theorists have distinguished between disputes about negotiable interests that can be settled by compromise, and more deep-seated conflicts that involve human needs and can only be resolved by removing underlying causes.)

Armed conflict is a narrower category, denoting conflicts where parties on both sides resort to the use of force. It is notoriously difficult to define, since it can encompass a continuum of situations ranging from a military overflight or an attack on a civilian by a single soldier to an all-out war with massive casualties. The research community has identified a number of thresholds and rules for deciding what to count. We will consider these definitions in the next section of this chapter.

Violent conflict, or *deadly conflict*, is similar to armed conflict, but also includes one-sided violence such as genocides against unarmed civilians. We mean direct, physical violence. We acknowledge the strong argument in peace research for broadening the concept of violence to include exploitative social relations that cause unnecessary suffering, but prefer to use the now well-known term 'structural violence' for this.

Contemporary conflict refers to the prevailing pattern of political and violent conflicts in the post-Cold War world; *contemporary armed conflicts* refer only to those that involve the use of force.

Conflict settlement means the reaching of an agreement between the parties which enables them to end an armed conflict. It puts to an end the violent stage of conflict behaviour. This suggests finality, but in practice conflicts that have reached settlements are often reopened later. Conflict attitudes and underlying structural contradictions may not have been addressed.

Conflict management, like the associated term *conflict regulation*, is sometimes used as a generic term to cover the whole gamut of positive conflict handling, but is used here to refer to the limitation, mitigation and containment of violent conflict.

Conflict resolution is a more comprehensive term which implies that the deep-rooted sources of conflict are addressed, and resolved. This implies that behaviour is no longer violent, attitudes are no longer hostile, and the structure of the conflict has been changed. It is difficult to avoid ambiguity since the term is used to refer both to the process (or the intention) to bring about these changes, and to the completion of the process. A further ambiguity is that conflict resolution refers to a particular defined specialist field (as in 'conflict resolution journals'), as well as to an activity carried on by people who may or may not use the term or even be aware of it (as in 'conflict resolution in Central America'). Nevertheless, these two senses of the term are tending to merge.

Conflict transformation is a term which for some analysts is a significant step beyond conflict resolution, but which in our view is a development of it. It has particular salience in asymmetric conflicts, where the aim is to transform unjust social relationships. It is also used in the understanding of peace processes, where transformation denotes a sequence of necessary transitional steps. It implies a deep transformation in the parties and their relationships and in the situation that created the conflict. As was indicated in figure 1.7, we see conflict transformation as the deepest level of change in the conflict resolution process.

Negotiation is the process whereby the parties within the conflict seek to settle or resolve their conflicts. *Mediation* involves the intervention of a third party; it is a voluntary process in which the parties retain control over the outcome (pure mediation), although it may include positive and negative inducements (mediation with muscle). *Conciliation* or *facilitation* is close in meaning to pure mediation, and refers to intermediary efforts to encourage the parties to move towards negotiations, as does the more minimalist role of providing good offices. *Problem-solving* is a more ambitious undertaking in which conflict parties are invited to reconceptualize the conflict with a view to finding creative, win–win outcomes. *Reconciliation* is a longer-term process of overcoming hostility and mistrust between divided peoples.

We use *peacemaking* in the sense of moving towards settlement of armed conflict, where conflict parties are induced to reach agreement voluntarily, for example as envisaged in Chapter VI of the UN Charter on the 'Pacific Settlement of Disputes' (Article 33). *Peacekeeping* (traditionally with the consent of the conflict parties) refers to the interposition of international armed forces to separate the armed forces of belligerents, often now associated with civil tasks such as monitoring and policing and supporting humanitarian intervention. *Peace-enforcement* is the imposition of a settlement by a powerful third party. *Peacebuilding* underpins the work of peacemaking and peacekeeping by addressing structural issues and the long-term relationships between conflictants. With reference to the conflict triangle (see figure 1.6), it can be suggested that peacemaking aims to change the attitudes of the main protagonists, peacekeeping lowers the level of destructive behaviour, and peacebuilding tries to overcome the contradictions which lie at the root of the conflict (Galtung, 1996, 112).

Finally, it is worth noting that the aim of conflict resolution is not the elimination of conflict, which would be both impossible and, as is made clear in Curle's model of the transformation of asymmetric conflicts (see figure 1.5), sometimes undesirable. Rather, the aim of conflict resolution is to transform actually or potentially violent conflict into peaceful (nonviolent) processes of social and political change. This is an unending task as new forms and sources of conflict arise.

Statistics of Deadly Quarrels

Having outlined some of the ideas that continue to shape the conflict resolution field, our second task in this introduction is to familiarize ourselves with the 'statistics of deadly quarrels', to borrow the title of Richardson's posthumously published seminal study (1960b).

The conflict domain

What are to count as the relevant conflicts? Conflict resolution analysts have traditionally included all levels of conflict, from intrapersonal conflict through to international conflict, and all stages of conflict escalation and de-escalation. In this book we restrict our focus to actual or potentially violent conflicts, ranging from domestic conflict situations which threaten to become militarized beyond the capacity of domestic civil police to control, through to full-scale interstate war. The Interdisciplinary Research Program on Causes of Human Rights Violations (PIOOM) at Leiden University includes five 'stages of conflict' in its annual review of international conflict. These begin with (1) 'peaceful stable situations' which are defined as a 'high degree of political stability and regime legitimacy', and move on to (2) 'political tension situations' defined as 'growing levels of systemic strain and increasing social and political cleavages, often along factional lines' (these cases are not included in their statistics). At stage (3), 'violent political conflict', tension has escalated to 'political crisis' inasmuch as there has been 'an erosion of political legitimacy of the national government' and / or a 'rising acceptance of violent factional politics', which is roughly quantified in terms of the number of people killed in any one calendar year up to but not including 100 (in 1998 PIOOM listed 114 such conflicts). At stage (4), 'low-intensity conflict', there is 'open hostility and armed conflict among factional groups, regime repression and insurgency' with 100–999 people killed in any one year (42 such conflicts listed for 1998), and at stage (5), 'high-intensity conflict', there is 'open warfare among rival groups and / or mass destruction and displacement of sectors of the civilian population' with 1,000 or more people killed (16 such conflicts listed for 1998) (Jongman and Schmid, 1998). The striking assumption here is that late twentieth-century conflicts will be mainly 'internally' generated and that interstate war of the classic kind can be virtually ignored. This is in marked contrast to most quantitative studies of major armed conflict and war since 1945, and is an eloquent testimony to the transformation in conflict studies which has taken place in recent years.

Richardson included both international and domestic conflicts in his dataset of 'deadly quarrels' between 1820 and 1949. By deadly quarrel he meant 'any quarrel which caused death to humans. The term thus includes murders, banditries, mutinies, insurrections, and wars small and large' (1960b). Sorokin included revolutions as well as wars in his study (1937). Most studies since the 1950s in the 'classical' phase of the statistical study of international conflict, however, confined the field to interstate and related wars above a certain measurable threshold. The best-known study is Singer and Small's Correlates of War Project. They counted 'interstate wars', which were defined as armed conflict 'involving at least one member of the interstate system on each side of the war, resulting in a total of 1,000 or more battle-deaths', and 'extra-systemic' wars (e.g. imperial war, colonial war and internationalized civil war), which were defined as international wars 'in which there was a member of the interstate system on only one side of the war, resulting in an average of 1,000 battle deaths per year for system member participants' (1972, 381–2).[5] In more recent

Map 1 Countries with major armed conflicts in progress, 1995–7

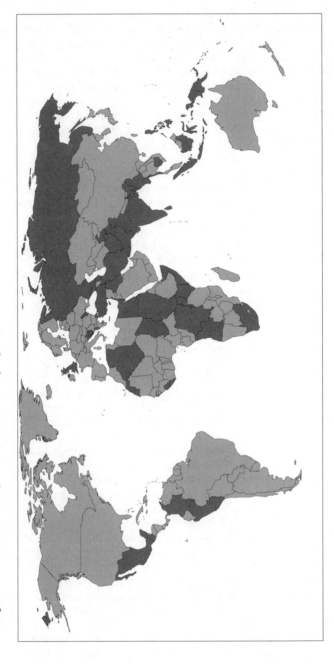

studies, however, these restrictive definitions have been progressively relaxed in a partial return to Richardson's original wide canvas.

A comparison of conflict datalists in the 1990s reveals a wide discrepancy both in criteria for inclusion and in reliable figures for what are often chaotic and politically contested war zones. Despite considerable effort, we have found no way of definitively reconciling these discrepancies, so that the composite list of major deadly conflicts in progress in 1995–7, given in table 1.3, represents a series of compromises between competing datasets.[6]

Table 1.3   Countries with major armed conflicts in progress, 1995–7. Major armed conflicts with a cumulative total of 1,000 or more conflict-related deaths since fighting began.[7]

Location	Inception	Principal conflictants	Deaths
Afghanistan	1978	Rabbani vs. Hekmatyar Taleban vs. Dostum / Masood	1–2m.
Albania	1997	Govt of Albania vs. rebels	> 1,500
Algeria	1992	Govt of Algeria vs. FIS, GIA etc. (Islamic)	> 60,000
Angola	1975/1992	Govt of Angola vs. UNITA	> 500,000
Azerbaijan	1988	Govt of Azerbaijan vs. Armenia (Nagorno-Karabakh)	> 50,000
Bangladesh	1973	Govt of Bangladesh vs. SB (Chittagong)	> 3,000
Bosnia–Herzegovina	1992	Govt of Bosnia–Herzegovina vs. Bosnian Croats (Croatia) vs. Bosnian Serbs (FRY)	> 100,000
Burundi	1993	Govt of Burundi vs. Hutu etc. militia	> 100,000
Cambodia	1975	Govt of Cambodia vs. PDK (Khmer Rouge)	> 2m.
Chad	1966	Govt of Chad vs. CSNPD, MDD	> 100,000
Colombia	1978	Govt of Colombia vs. FARC, ELN, EPL (cocaine drug barons)	> 30,000
Croatia	1991	Govt of Croatia vs. Croatian Serbs (FRY)	> 10,000
Cyprus	1964	Cyprus National Guard vs. Turkish and Turkish Cypriot forces	> 5,000
Egypt	1992	Govt of Egypt vs. Gamaat Islamiya	> 1,000

Georgia	1991	Govt of Georgia vs. Abkhazian rebels and South Ossetian rebels	> 17,000
Guatemala	1968	Govt of Guatemala vs. URNG	> 45,000
India		Govt of India vs.	
	1979	ULFA (Assam)	> 5,000
	1981	KLF/KCF (Sikh)	> 20,000
	1989	JKLF etc. (Kashmir)	> 15,000
	1992	BdSF (Bodo)	> 1,000
Indonesia	1975	Govt of Indonesia vs. Fretilin (E. Timor)	> 100,000
	1984	OPM (Irian Jaya)	> 10,000
Iraq	1980	Govt of Iraq vs. KDP, PUK (Kurds), Shi'a, SAIRI etc.	> 500,000
Iran	1979	Govt of Iran vs. Mujahideen e-Khalq, KDPI (Kurds)	> 5,000
Israel	1948	Govt of Israel vs. PLO, Hamas, Hezbollah, Islamic Jihad, PFLP	> 13,000
Kenya	1992	Govt of Kenya vs. tribal resistance	> 1,500
Lebanon	1976	Govt of Lebanon vs. Hezbollah, SLA	> 15,000
Liberia	1989	Govt of Liberia/ECOWAS vs. NPFL, Krahn factions etc.	> 200,000
Mexico	1994	Govt of Mexico vs. EZLN, EPR	> 1,000
Moldova	1992	Govt of Moldova vs. Trans-Dniestr rebels	> 1,000
Myanmar	1948	Govt of Myanmar vs. KNU (Karen) etc.	> 14,000
Pakistan	1986	Govt of Pakistan vs. MQM	> 1,500
Papua New Guinea	1989	Govt of PNG vs. BRA	> 15,000
Peru	1980	Govt of Peru vs. Sendero Luminoso MRTA (Tupac Amaru)	> 28,000
Philippines	1968	Govt of Philippines vs. NPA, MNLF, MILF	> 30,000
Russia	1991	Govt of Russia vs. Chechen rebels	> 20,000
Rwanda	1990	Govt of Rwanda vs. Hutu death squads	> 800,000

Sierra Leone	1989	Govt of Sierra Leone vs. (Executive outcomes), RUF	> 20,000
Somalia	1991	USC (Mahdi) vs. USC (Aidid) etc.	> 400,000
South Africa	1996	ANC vs. IFP	> 15,000
Sri Lanka	1983	Govt of Sri Lanka vs. LTTE (Tamils)	> 35,000
Sudan	1983	Govt of Sudan vs. SPLA, NDA	> 1.5m
Tajikistan	1992	Govt of Tajikistan/CIS vs. UTO	> 30,000
Turkey	1983	Govt of Turkey vs. PKK (Kurds)	> 20,000
Uganda	1994	Govt of Uganda vs. LRA, etc.	> 1,000
United Kingdom	1969	UK govt vs. Provisional IRA, etc.	> 3,000
Western Sahara	1973	Govt of Morocco vs. POLISARIO	> 15,000
Zaire	1993	Govt of Zaire vs. ADFLCZ, etc.	> 20,000

Source: Data has been compiled using datasets in the Centre for Conflict Resolution, University of Bradford, and the Richardson Institute, University of Lancaster, as well as the annual conflict lists produced by Wallensteen et al. at Uppsala University, the PIOOM programme at Leiden University, the International Institute of Strategic Studies *Military Balance*, the US Committee of Refugees *World Refugee Survey*, Human Rights Watch *World Wide Report*, the ICRC *World Disasters Reports*, the Minorities at Risk programme at the University of Maryland, Brown (1996, 4–7), Holsti (1996, 210–24), Weiss and Collins (1996, 5–7), and King (1997, 84–7).

Conflict trends

Given the discrepancies noted above over which conflicts to include in datasets, it has proved difficult to establish significant trends in post-Cold War conflict. For example, comparing data over the period 1993–6, the PIOOM programme at Leiden University conclude that the number of high-intensity conflicts and low-intensity conflicts has remained at a 'relatively constant level' (Jongman and Schmid, 1998), whereas, according to the Uppsala University data used by SIPRI, over the period 1989–96 'there was an almost constant decline in the number of major armed conflicts worldwide' (1997, 20). More specifically, in 1995 Wallensteen and Axell reported a 'new pattern of conflict' in the 1990s in which the prime emphasis is on 'challenges to existing state authority', including secessionist movements which threaten the territorial integrity of the state (former Yugoslavia, Chechnya) and challenges to central control which may also end in fragmentation with no one actor in overall command

(Liberia, Somalia) (1995, 345). There have been attempts to find quantitative measures for conflict escalation and de-escalation from year to year (PIOOM uses thirteen variables, and the Stockholm International Peace Research Institute (SIPRI) uses a five-level numerical scale), and to note regional variations and changes in the incidence of different conflict types (see next section). One of the most hopeful findings at the time of writing is Gurr's conclusion, based on twelve years of research at the Minorities at Risk Programme, that, although there were eleven 'new ethnonational wars of autonomy and independence' in 1991–3, there were no new ethnonational wars in 1994–6, suggesting that the turbulence following the collapse of the Soviet Union and the end of the Cold War may now be dying away. Moreover, whereas at the end of each five-year period between 1971 and 1990 there had been between twenty-two and twenty-five ongoing ethnonational wars, in 1996 there were eleven. Of the twenty-four wars ongoing in 1993, eight had been contained or suppressed and five settled through accommodation three years later (Gurr, 1998). Clearly, though, these suggested recent trends may be a poor basis for future prediction. A violent response to rapid economic change in China or uncontrollable intercommunal conflict in India might swiftly trigger a huge increase in regional turbulence.

One major trend, however, shows through in almost all accounts, and that is a decline in the number of interstate wars. Over a longer-term time-frame, according to Holsti, the number of interstate wars per year per state has gone down from 0.036 for the period 1918–41 to 0.005 for the period 1945–95 (1996, 24).[8] In chapter 3 we will suggest that the key transition here came earlier rather than at the end of the Cold War, but since 1989 the decline in the number of interstate wars has approached its limit. There were no interstate wars in 1993 and 1994, and only a minor border altercation between Peru and Ecuador in 1995 and a flare-up in the long-running dispute between India and Pakistan over Kashmir in 1996 (Wallensteen and Sollenberg 1996; SIPRI 1997, 17). We must no doubt hesitate before celebrating 'the end of international war'. Nevertheless, given the data to hand, the main thrust in this book must clearly be to discuss conflict resolution in relation to non-interstate rather than to interstate war.

Conflict distribution

Many commentators agree that with the ending of the Cold War regional patterns of conflict have become all the more significant. There have, therefore, been efforts to compare characteristics of conflict from region to region.[9] At the heart of such studies lies the attempt to provide a reliable statistical basis for distinctions such as those between 'zones of peace' and 'zones of war' (Kacowicz, 1995). There are many variations here. For example, Holsti (1996, chapter 7), following Deutsch (1954), Jervis

(1982), Vayrynen (1984) and Buzan (1991), distinguishes 'pluralistic security communities', in which no serious provisions are made for war between member states, such as North America, the Antipodes, Western Europe; 'zones of peace', between states such as the Caribbean and the South Pacific; 'no-war zones', such as South-East Asia and (perhaps) East Asia; and 'zones of war' such as Africa, some former Soviet republics, the Middle East, Central America, South Asia and the Balkans.

It is clearly relevant to conflict resolution to understand the distinctions between regional 'security regimes' with relatively stable interstate relations, such as the Association for South-East Asian Nations (ASEAN), 'security communities' which avoid large-scale violence, as in Western Europe and North America, and more volatile and conflict-prone regions. There are several quite striking regional variations here, such as the surprising absence of interstate war in South America since 1941, despite its famously turbulent past (Holsti, 1996, 150–82). More recently, SIPRI sees a declining number and intensity of conflicts in Central and South America but little change in the Middle East (1997, 20–1). The level of violent conflict in Southern Africa in the 1990s has been going down, but not in sub-Saharan West Africa or the Great Lakes region. Why is this? Setting geographical location aside, is there a quantitative and qualitative difference in the incidence and nature of armed conflict between and within developed countries in comparison with so-called Third World or post-colonial countries? And do different types of conflict predominate in different regions?

Conflict types

This leads to one of the most testing questions in conflict analysis. Are there different types of conflict which need to be distinguished from each other if effective and discriminate conflict resolution is to be undertaken? Unfortunately, the overall state of current conflict typology is in a state of confusion. There are as many typologies as analysts, and the criteria employed not only vary, but are often mutually incompatible. A compilation of some of the different labels used in well-known analyses from the 1990s soon runs to well over a hundred. Some differentiate in terms of conflict parties,[10] others in terms of conflict issues,[11] others in terms of conflict causes,[12] but most do so in terms of hybrid lists that seem to muddle diverse categories. Some have two types, others run to more than twenty. The field is littered with typologies suggested by particular authors but discarded by others. In order to clarify our discussion, we offer our own working typology in table 1.4.

First, it may be helpful to think more in terms of historically and geographically based 'generations' of conflict rather than in terms of blanket typologies. After all, the roots of all major conflicts reach back into the historical past – often several centuries back. Superimposed on this are clusters of enduring rivalries, many still unresolved, going back

Table 1.4   A working conflict typology

Conflict	Type	Example
Interstate	1	Gulf war 1991
Non-interstate		
revolution/ideology	2	Algeria
identity/secession	3	Sri Lanka
factional	4	Liberia

respectively to the time of: the break-up of the Russian, Austro-Hungarian and Ottoman empires at the end of the First World War (we might add Northern Ireland to this list); the political settlements at the end of the Second World War; the period of decolonization (1950s, 1960s); the post-colonial period (1970s, 1980s); and, finally, the break-up of the Soviet bloc (1990s). Some analysts anticipate future generations of conflict fuelled by environmental deterioration, north–south tensions, weapons proliferation, and the collapse of weak states under the twin pressures of globalization and fragmentation (see chapter 3).

Second, we would do well to heed Singer's advice that a classificatory system should 'remain as atheoretical as possible' lest 'by accepting conventional labels of certain armed conflicts, we buy into simplistic interpretations, and ultimately embrace disastrous reactions and responses' – although it is unlikely that we will succeed in finding a typology which is 'logically exhaustive, mutually exclusive, operationally explicit, semantically consistent, and substantively comparable' (1996, 40, 48). Box 1 compares Singer's conflict typology with that of Holsti (1996). The two seem more or less to coincide. Omitting Singer's 'extra-systemic wars' and Holsti's 'decolonizing wars' on the grounds that the era of decolonization is all but over, there seems to be rough agreement about a distinction between type 1 interstate conflict, and two types of non-interstate conflict, type 2 revolution/ideology conflict (Singer's and Holsti's type (c)) and type 3 identity/secession conflict (Singer's and Holsti's type (d)).[13] Finally, we are also tempted to distinguish revolution-ideology and identity-secession conflicts in turn from a third class of non-interstate conflict, type 4 factional conflict, in which the fighting is not about revolutionary-ideological issues, nor about identity-secessionist issues, but solely about the competing interests or power-struggles of political or criminal factions.[14]

This line of enquiry, therefore, suggests that provisional distinctions may usefully be made between three types of non-interstate conflict. The term 'factional conflict' covers *coups d'état*, intra-elite power-struggles, brigandage, criminality and warlordism, where the aim is to usurp, seize

---

BOX 1.1   Conflict typologies: a comparison

Singer's conflict typology (1996, 43–7) is based on the political status of conflict parties. He retains his original distinction between (a) interstate wars and (b) extra-systemic (mainly colonial) wars, but now adds two further classes of non-interstate conflict: (c) 'civil' conflicts, in which, unlike (b), one protagonist may be 'an insurgent or revolutionary group within the recognised territorial boundaries of the state', and (d) the 'increasingly complex intra-state wars' in former colonial states, where the challenge may come from 'culturally defined groups whose members identify with one another and with the group on the basis of shared racial, ethnic, linguistic, religious, or kinship characteristics'. Holsti (1996, 21) has also adapted Singer's typology. He earlier categorized international (interstate) conflict up to 1989 in terms of twenty-four issues, grouped into five composite sets: conflict over territory, economics, nation-state creation, ideology, and 'human sympathy' (i.e. ethnicity/religion). He concluded that the incidence of the first two had been declining, but that of the last three had, if anything, been increasing (1991, 306–34). He later focused on non-interstate war, basing his typology on 'types of actors and/or objectives', ending up with four categories of conflict: 'standard state versus state wars (e.g., China and India in 1962) and armed interventions involving significant loss of life (the United States in Vietnam, the Soviet Union in Afghanistan)'; 'decolonizing wars of "national liberation"'; 'internal wars based on ideological goals' (e.g., the Senderoso Luminoso in Peru, the Monteneros in Uruguay); and 'state-nation wars including armed resistance by ethnic, language and/or religious groups, often with the purpose of secession or separation from the state' (e.g., the Tamils in Sri Lanka, the Ibos in Nigeria).

---

or retain state power merely to further particular interests. The term 'revolution/ideology conflict' includes the more ambitious aim of changing the nature of government in a state, for example by (a) changing the system from capitalist to socialist, or (b) changing the form of government from dictatorship to democracy, or (c) changing the religious orientation of the state from secular to Islamic. In the post-Cold War world it is possible to discern a decline in the incidence of (a) but not in the incidence of (b) and particularly not of (c). The term 'identity/secession conflict' involves the relative status of communities or 'communal groups', however defined, in relation to the state. Depending upon the nature of the group and the contextual situation, this includes struggles for access, for autonomy, for secession or for control.[15] In brief, a factional conflict is merely a struggle to control the state or part of the state, a revolution/

ideology conflict is, in addition, a struggle to change the nature of the state, and an identity/secession conflict may well be a threat to the integrity of the state (see table 1.4).

Needless to say, specific conflicts elude neat pigeon-holing of this kind on closer inspection. Scholars disagree about categorization, as seen, for example, in the elaborate attempts by Marxist analysts in the 1960s and 1970s to interpret type 3 ethnic conflict as type 2 class conflict (Munck, 1986), in contrast to the reverse trend on the part of many analysts in the 1990s. Moreover, the conflicts themselves often change character over time, and are interpreted in different ways by the conflict parties.[16] As John Darby notes with regard to type 3 'ethnic' conflicts: '[e]thnicity is often situationally determined and may wax or wane according to circumstances', so that it 'may be acquired or divested according to the extent to which it aligns with, or becomes dissociated from, other grievances' (1998, 3–4). It may also be invoked by unscrupulous political leaders in what would otherwise be classed as type 4 factional conflict. The same elasticity is found in other categories of conflict. Singer's ideal of an 'atheoretical' taxonomy, therefore, proves to be a chimera. For this reason we do not rest much weight on conflict typologies in this book, apart from the broad distinction between type 1 interstate conflict and various forms of non-interstate or 'international-social' conflict, as further elaborated in chapter 3.

Returning to the question posed at the end of the last section, according to the Uppsala classification system used by SIPRI, it is striking that in the Americas there have been no major 'territorial' (identity/secession) conflicts in the early 1990s, whereas in Europe there have been no 'government' (revolution/ideology) conflicts (see table 1.5).

Conflict costs

Before concluding this section on quantitative data we must briefly note the significance of the voluminous data on the material and human cost of contemporary violent conflict. Some 28 million people may have been killed in more than 150 major armed conflicts fought mainly in the Third World since 1945 (IISS, 1997). According to UNICEF figures, whereas only 5 per cent of the casualties in the First World War were civilians, by the Second World War the proportion had risen to 50 per cent, while 'as the century ends, the civilian share is normally about 80 per cent – most of them women and children' (Grant, 1992, 26). Others put the figure as high as 90 per cent (Lake, 1990, 4). This is a reversion to older types of warfare. To this must be added UNHCR's estimate of the primary role of vicious internal conflict in generating 18.2 million refugees and 24 million internally displaced people in 1993 (Ogata, 1993, iii). In African countries like Angola, Eritrea, Liberia, Mozambique, Rwanda, Somalia and Sudan, up to half or more of the total population has been forced to flee at some

Table 1.5 Uppsala regional table of conflict types, 1990–5

	1990		1991		1992		1993		1994		1995	
	G	T	G	T	G	T	G	T	G	T	G	T
Europe	–	1	–	2	–	4	–	6	–	5	–	3
Middle East	1	4	2	5	2	3	2	4	2	4	2	4
Asia	5	10	3	8	4	9	4	7	4	7	4	8
Africa	8	3	8	3	6	1	6	1	6	1	5	1
America	4	–	4	–	3	–	3	–	3	–	3	–

G = government (type of political system, change of central government or its composition)

T = territory (control of territory (interstate), secession or autonomy)

Source: IFRCRCS, 1996, 138

point. All of this is compounded by the length of time that certain classes of conflict last – in some cases an average of twenty-five years (Gurr, 1995, 52). Whole generations have no other experience than war. The resultant size of the cumulative death toll is difficult to comprehend (see the death figures in table 1.3), while the overall tally of material destruction, psychological suffering and human misery – what Cranna calls 'the true cost of conflict' (1994) – dwarfs any gains by particular conflict parties. This provides the main impetus for the central aim of conflict resolution as outlined in the previous section: to find alternative non-violent ways of achieving structural and political goals.

Conflict Resolution and the International Community

Having identified the 'statistics' of deadly conflicts, we comment briefly on how the conflict resolution capacities of the international community are beginning to evolve in response to these problems.

The primary responsibility for responding to contemporary conflict no doubt lies within the affected states. Nevertheless, four factors dictate that outsiders are inevitably involved and often play a vital role. First, as noted more fully in chapter 3, the sources of many contemporary conflicts lie as much outside as inside the state. The international community in its various guises is often responsible for the conflict in the first place. Second, increasing interdependence means that contemporary conflicts affect the interests of regional neighbours and beyond. Third, the combination of human suffering and media transparency makes it difficult for outside governments to persist in doing nothing. Fourth, nearly all studies agree that many protracted conflicts can only be resolved when outside resources are brought to bear. In short, nearly all these conflicts can in one way or another be classed as 'international-social' conflicts.

Turning to the role of outsiders in attempting to resolve conflict, there has been a long tradition of third party mediation in international relations, documented since the time of the Greek city states and the Roman Empire in the West, and evolving into a recognizable pattern of interstate diplomacy in the early modern period (Mitchell and Webb, eds, 1988). The leading role was played in somewhat ad hoc fashion by neighbouring states and great powers, mainly in their own interests. In the nineteenth century attempts were made to construct more formal restraints on war, for example through the Congress system and the Concert of Europe. In the twentieth century, in the aftermath of the two world wars, these attempts were further systematized through the League of Nations and the United Nations (UN). Since 1945, under Chapter VI of its charter the UN has been provided with a set of techniques which it can use in order to secure the peaceful settlement of disputes, including fact-finding, good offices, conciliation, mediation and negotiation. Under Chapter VII of the charter, the Security Council was given power to use coercion and armed force if necessary to maintain or restore international peace and security. Under Chapter VIII of the charter, regional organizations were encouraged to play an active role in furthering its aims.

All the contemporary conflicts in the forty-four countries identified in table 1.3, however, are non-interstate or international-social conflicts, many of which reflect a weakening of state structures, the collapse of sovereignty and a local breakdown in the state system. It is ironic that the task of managing such conflicts has fallen primarily to international institutions which are still based on precisely the system of sovereignty and non-interference that the new conflicts undermine; it is not surprising that the international community struggles to find effective means of response. This also has a marked effect on what kinds of solution are seen as acceptable by those organizations.

Non-interstate conflicts are not obviously the responsibility of any international institution. Governments of major states are reluctant to get involved with internal conflicts when they do not concern their own state interests. And when they do get involved, governments and international agencies frequently act at cross purposes, on account of differences in their interests and mandates. At the same time, governments of states which are on the receiving end of international interventions have considerable misgivings about what they perceive as unwarranted meddling from the outside. Where the authority of the state has broken down altogether, a whole range of difficult questions arises. With whom should the international community negotiate, when the state has collapsed and the use of force is in the hands of local leaders commanding paramilitary militias? Should the international community negotiate with those in power, even if they have no legitimacy, and are in power only because of

their ruthlessness and rapacity? Does the international community legitimize and even preserve such power-holders by negotiating with them?
Should it negotiate with representatives of civil society even if these
representatives hold no power? Satisfactory answers have yet to emerge in
international practice.

Moreover, non-interstate conflicts impinge on the work of a range of
organizations which have not previously seen their mission in terms of
conflict management: organizations concerned with refugees, humanitarian assistance, development and human rights. Many of these agencies
find themselves caught up in attempts to manage internal conflicts. At the
same time, non-governmental agencies, which in some cases might have
better entry into the conflict than state authorities, are also making their
mark. In practice, a redistribution of tasks and mandates is under way, but
it remains incomplete and uncoordinated. It is not surprising that, all too
often, the international response to contemporary conflict has been mar-
red by confusion, hesitancy and a lack of clear direction.

Apart from states, three main types of agent now play an enhanced role
in the resolution of contemporary conflict: the UN, regional organizations
and NGOs. Each has strengths and weaknesses.

The UN and its agencies remain central to the international community's response to conflict. During the Cold War, the overall effectiveness
of the UN in settling international disputes was mixed. The UN did,
however, become a prime instrument through which the international
community attempted to defuse crises and de-escalate disputes, arrange
ceasefires, organize peacekeeping, facilitate elections and monitor disengagement and demilitarization. It has an acknowledged corpus of
knowledge and experience in these fields. With the end of the Cold War,
it was hoped that the UN would for the first time be able to take up the
role that was intended for it. In practice, the post-Cold War experience,
too, has been mixed, with notable successes (Namibia, Cambodia, El
Salvador, Mozambique) alongside dismal failures (Somalia, Bosnia,
Rwanda). The vital factor distinguishing success from failure has usually
been not so much the UN institutions, but rather the policies of the major
powers on the Security Council and the intractability of the conflicts
themselves. Where parties have consented to a UN mandate and have
wished to settle, and where adequate finances and personnel have been
available, orders have been clear, chains of command and communication
have been straightforward, and the UN has been able to play a remarkable
and useful role; but when the parties have been unwilling to accept a UN
role, the UN has not been able to impose settlements.

In his ambitious *Agenda for Peace*, the UN Secretary-General Boutros
Boutros-Ghali proposed that the UN should be involved in peacekeeping,
peacemaking and peacebuilding from the earliest stage of conflict prevention to the stage of post-conflict reconstruction. He was forced to retract
some of his proposals, notably his advocacy of coercive peacemaking, one
year later. Nevertheless, the scope of UN action has certainly enlarged. It

now ranges from conflict prevention (chapter 4, pp. 111–16), peacekeeping and humanitarian action, as well as crisis management in war zones (chapter 5), through conflict settlements (chapter 6, pp. 158–62) to post-settlement peacebuilding (chapter 7). Unfortunately, combined with the organization's global mandate and a severe financial crisis, this expansion of tasks has resulted in chronic overload for the secretariat, resulting in inevitable degrading of performance and a sometimes slow response.

The principal agency of the UN is the office of the Secretary-General and his political arm, the Department of Political Affairs (DPA). The Department of Peacekeeping Operations oversees the political and operational side of peacekeeping. The Secretary-General is assisted by Special Representatives and Envoys, who frequently play an important role in the UN's practical conflict resolution activities. In addition, the UN is equipped with procedures and agencies in the humanitarian and human rights fields which are now seen to be increasingly relevant to conflict resolution. When it comes to the use of coercion or force in responding to threats to international peace and security, there are the Chapter VII powers available to the Security Council.

For all its weaknesses, the UN remains the 'only existing framework for building the institutions of a global society' (Ogata and Volcker, 1993) and is thus the only institutional expression of the international community as a whole in its conflict resolution capacity.

Regional organizations make up the second tier of external agents in contemporary conflict resolution. In an effort to shed part of the UN's load, Boutros-Ghali proposed that regional organizations should take on the primary responsibility for conflict management, leaving the UN to pick up cases only if they had failed. Such a division of labour has yet to appear, however, in part because the member states of regional organizations do not always accept that these groups have a legitimate role in their internal affairs. The regional organizations have developed widely varying mandates, which reflect the very different characteristics and historical experience of states in the different regions.

The members of the Organization for Security and Cooperation in Europe (OSCE) have gone farthest in accepting a role for their regional organization in reviewing the human rights and security practices of member states. They have accepted a common set of wide-ranging norms affecting the human dimension, and have created new institutions for conflict management (including the High Commissioner on National Minorities (HCNM), the Long Term Missions, the Office for Democratic Institutions and Human Rights). Within Europe, other regional organizations such as NATO, the Council of Europe and, of course, the European Union also play significant roles in conflict management.

The Organization of African Unity (OAU) was established in 1963 with the aim of preserving the territorial independence and sovereign equality of the post-colonial African states. Its charter precludes interference in the internal affairs of member states. It has therefore been reluctant to involve itself in internal conflicts, although in 1993 it set up the OAU Mechanism for Conflict Prevention, Management and Resolution (MCPMR) to provide assistance to states affected by war. In practice the most important interventions in Africa have generally been taken by leaders from neighbouring states. Other bodies with relevant roles include the Economic Community of West African States (ECOWAS), which has had a role in dispute resolution in West Africa, and the South African Development Community (SADC), which has agreed a regional peacekeeping role. The Commonwealth also plays a significant role in certain cases.

The Organization of American States (OAS) also operates a norm of non-interference in internal affairs. However, the member states undertook to act against violations of democracy, through the Santiago Commitment (1991), and have promoted conflict resolution in partnership with the UN, for example in Central America, and through the Secretary-General's Unit for the Promotion of Democracy.

The Association of South-East Asian Nations (ASEAN) has been concerned to avoid involvement in member states' internal affairs; indeed, one of its main functions has been to regulate interstate disputes between the members lest they spill over into internal challenges to regimes. The ASEAN Regional Forum has developed as a means for building consensus over security challenges in the region, and it has been used as an umbrella for Track II initiatives and cooperation with the UN.

One region which strikingly lacks a comprehensive organization is the Middle East, where the Arab League and the Gulf Cooperation Council represent the interests of their members, but no regional organization spans the region's political fault lines. South Asia also lacks a forum similar to those mentioned above. The coverage of the regional organizations is therefore patchy, and their scope in internal conflict remains limited by concerns for sovereignty.

For conflict resolution, regional organizations have the advantage of proximity to the source of conflict and familiarity with the main actors, cultural values and local conditions. On the other hand, the interests of local actors and, in particular, those of regional hegemons may make regional organizations unsuitable fora for conflict resolution, and in most parts of the world they are also chronically short of financial and other resources.

Finally, the gaps in the coverage of internal conflicts by the official arms of the international community have left a space for humanitarian agencies and non-governmental agencies to play a larger role. Agencies such as the International Committee of the Red Cross (ICRC) have taken on an enhanced profile in internal conflicts. NGOs have also become more important. The number of NGOs involved with conflict resolution increased rapidly in the 1980s, as development agencies, aid donors and governments became willing to fund their activities. The European Centre for Conflict Prevention (ECCP) lists more than five hundred organizations which define themselves as being concerned in some way with conflict prevention and management (ECCP, 1998), although the number of organizations which can sustain interventions for some time and in more than one location remains quite limited (see chapter 6, pp. 158–62). Whatever the constraints on individual NGOs, as a whole, given their multiplicity and variety, they have the advantage of flexibility and adaptability. They are able to work with local protagonists without the worry of thereby conferring official recognition, and can operate at the middle and grass-roots end of Lederach's peacebuilding pyramid (see figure 1.9). As described in later chapters, they have played a significant role in a number of peacemaking breakthroughs, although in individual cases the appropriateness and effectiveness of particular NGO initiatives have been criticized.

We do not, however, wish to give the impression that external parties are the most important agents. It is usually the parties themselves that are the key actors for managing their own conflicts. Domestic conflict management capacity is crucial, since it is likely to be culturally appropriate and sustained. Indigenous political parties, institutions, business organizations, church groups and third parties of all kinds play important and often undocumented roles. For example, most of the new entries in the ECCP survey noted above (for example the African Centre for the Constructive Resolution of Disputes (ACCORD) in South Africa and CECORE in Uganda) are indigenous conflict resolution organizations.

Structure of the Book

The structure of the book is based on the idea that, having described the evolution of the conflict resolution field (chapter 2) and characterized the nature of contemporary conflict (chapter 3), broad distinctions can then be made between the tasks of preventing violent conflict (chapter 4), mitigating or alleviating violent conflict once it has broken out while at the same time searching for ways of terminating it (chapter 5), ending violent conflict (chapter 6), and ensuring that conflict does not subsequently regress to violence but is lastingly transformed into peaceful processes of political and social change (chapter 7). We are not suggesting that conflicts necessarily go through these phases, but think that this is the simplest expository structure to adopt.

2

Conflict Resolution: Foundations, Constructions and Reconstructions

The reasons which have led us to this enterprise may be summed up in two propositions. The first is that by far the most important practical problem facing the world today is that of international relations – more specifically the prevention of global war. The second is that if intellectual progress is to be made in this area, the study of international relations must be made an interdisciplinary enterprise, drawing its discourse from all the social sciences and even further.

Kenneth Boulding on the publication of the first issue of the
Journal of Conflict Resolution, 1957

The threat of nuclear holocaust remains with us and may well continue to do so for centuries, but other problems are competing with deterrence and disarmament studies for our attention. The journal must also attend to international conflict over justice, equality and human dignity; problems of conflict resolution for ecological balance and control are within our proper scope and especially suited for interdisciplinary attention.

Journal of Conflict Resolution, 1973, 27(1), 5

The two extracts from the *Journal of Conflict Resolution* quoted above give a good idea of the way in which conflict resolution, constituted as a distinct field of study through the setting up of formal centres in academic institutions and the publication of professional journals, first defined itself and then expanded its remit during what we are calling its foundational period in the 1950s and 1960s and its period of further construction and expansion in the 1970s and 1980s. In this chapter we describe the historical evolution of the field, some of whose classic concepts we have already outlined in chapter 1. We do so mainly by identifying individuals who have contributed strategically to the subject, whom we take as exemplars of key developments in order to avoid giving a dry list of institutions and publications. They include Mary Parker Follett among the precursors; Kenneth Boulding, Johan Galtung and John Burton among the founders; and Herbert Kelman, Roger Fisher, William Ury, William Zartman, Adam Curle and Elise Boulding among those who carried the subject forward thereafter. Needless to say, many others also played important roles. Any selection will be indicative rather than comprehensive and will reflect authorial perceptions. When we reach the 1990s, what we call the period of 'reconstruction', we encounter further creative inputs, critical as well as constructive, including perspectives from development theory and practice, from critical social theory, from gender and cultural analysis and, not least, from the voices and experiences of individuals and frequently small groups of people who have struggled in conflict-affected communities to affirm values of justice, peace and reconciliation.

Precursors

The failure of the variety of peace, socialist and liberal internationalist movements to prevent the outbreak of the First World War motivated many people in the years that followed to develop a 'science' of peace which would provide a firmer basis for preventing future wars than what were regarded as the frequently sentimental and simplistically moral responses of pacifism. Early attempts were made in France, Germany, Holland, Czechoslovakia, Switzerland, the United States and other countries, as described by van den Dungen (1996). However, most proposals in this period were isolated and individualistic, where, in van den Dungen's words, 'exhortations far outnumbered realisations' (p. 27), and the sustained development of peace and conflict research in the form of institutional growth had to wait until the post-1945 world, when the added threat of nuclear weapons created a new urgency.

Meanwhile, although not known to many of those calling for a new science of peace, some of the necessary empirical evidence was already being gathered and analysed. Prominent here were the early empirical studies of war and conflict conducted in the interwar years by the Russian Pitirim Sorokin, the Englishman Lewis Fry Richardson, and the American Quincy Wright.[1]

In related but as yet unintegrated fields other important pioneering work was being done which would later be drawn upon to enrich the conflict resolution field. Prominent here was the thinking of Follett (1942) in the field of organizational behaviour and labour-management relations. Advocating a 'mutual gains' approach to negotiation associated with what would be called 'integrative bargaining', as against the traditional concession/convergence approach associated with 'distributive bargaining', she anticipated much of the later problem-solving agenda as outlined in chapter 1. Whereas distributive bargaining assumes concealment, inflated initial demands and zero-sum contexts, the integrative bargaining advocated in the mutual gains approach tries to redefine the negotiation as a shared problem to be resolved. Pooling knowledge and resources and looking to maximize mutual gain is seen to yield greater pay-offs to all parties.

Initiatives in three other fields would also prove of importance to the future interdisciplinary study of conflict resolution – psychology, politics and international studies. For example, in the field of psychology, frustration-aggression theories of human conflict (Dollard et al., 1939) and work on the social psychology of group conflict conducted by Lewin (1948) would be influential in future conflict resolution studies. Similarly, in the field of political studies, Brinton's approach to the analysis of political revolution (1938) – that revolution takes place when the gap between distributed social power and distributed political power reaches a critical point – can be taken as exemplary of what was to prove another significant strand (carried forward later in Dahrendorf (1957), Gurr (1970) and Tilly (1978)). In international studies, Mitrany's (1943) functionalist approach to overcoming the win–lose dynamic inherent in realist analyses of competitive interstate relations via a progressively denser network of cooperative cross-border frameworks made necessary by the advance of technology – seen by some to have previsaged the evolution of the European Union – would inspire similar ideas for sustaining peace through cross-border institution-building in future conflict resolution circles (complemented by Deutsch et al.'s analysis of the development of 'political community' in the North Atlantic area (1957)).

Finally, despite some of the criticisms of peace researchers, accounts and analyses of pacifist and non-violent objectives and strategies are clearly of relevance to conflict resolution, and have done much to influence and define the formation of the academic field. The work of non-violent theorists such as Sharp (1973), and the persistence of historical traditions and practices of pacifism such as those contained in the beliefs of Quakers and Mennonites, or in the ideas of Gandhi, have cross-fertilized with academic enterprise to enhance understanding of violent political conflict and alternatives to it. The objectives of Gandhi's *satyagraha* ('struggle for truth') were to make latent conflict manifest by challenging social structures that were harmful because they were highly inequitable, but to do this without setting off a spiral of violence. In the Gandhian model of conflict, which contains within it built-in inhibitors of violence, the objective is not to win but, through what Bondurant called the Gandhian dialectic, 'to achieve a fresh level of social truth and a healthier relationship between antagonists' (Wehr, 1979, 64). In the teachings of Buddha (the Dhamma), on the other hand, McConnell (1995) has shown how the doctrine of the middle way and the four noble truths locate the deepest roots of conflict in the perceptions, values and attitudes of conflictants: while this does not ignore what Gandhi would have seen as oppressive structures, it does direct the peacemaker to focus on changes in self-awareness and the development of self-knowledge.

Foundations: the 1950s and 1960s

The first institutions of peace and conflict research appeared in the twenty-year period between 1945 and 1965. The Peace Research Laboratory was founded by Theodore F. Lentz at St Louis, Missouri, after the bombing of Hiroshima and Nagasaki in 1945. Science, according to Lentz, 'did increase physical power but science did not increase physical harmony ... the power–harmony imbalance has been brought about by science in misorder' (Lentz, 1955, 52–3). Lentz argued not only that people had a capacity to live in harmony, but that 'humatriotism' was a value which would emerge from rigorous research into human attitudes and personality. One of the first attempts to follow up this lead was taken by a group of pioneers of the new conflict resolution field at the University of Michigan.

Kenneth Boulding, Michigan and the Journal of Conflict Resolution

Kenneth Boulding was born in Liverpool in the north of England in 1910. Motivated personally and spiritually as a member of the Society of Friends (Quakers), and professionally as an economist, he moved to America in 1937, married Elise Bjorn-Hansen in 1941, and began with her a partnership which was to make a seminal contribution to the formation of peace and conflict research. After the war he was appointed as Professor of Economics at the University of Michigan. Here, with a small group of academics, which included the mathematician-biologist Anatol Rapoport, the social psychologist Herbert Kelman and the sociologist Robert Cooley Angell, he initiated the *Journal of Conflict Resolution* (JCR) in 1957, and set up the Center for Research on Conflict Resolution in 1959. Inspirational to what Boulding called the 'Early Church' of the peace research movement (Kerman, 1974, 48) was the work of Lewis Richardson, brought over on microfilm by his son Stephen, and not yet published at that time.

Boulding's publications focused firmly on the issue of preventing war, because, partly as a result of the failures of the discipline of international relations, 'the international system is by far the most pathological and costly segment of the total social system' (Kerman, 1974, 83). *Conflict and Defense* advanced the thesis of the decline or obsolescence of the nation state, while *Perspectives on the Economics of Peace* argued that conventional prescriptions from international relations were unable even to recognize, let alone analyse, the consequences of this obsolescence. If war was the outcome of inherent characteristics in the sovereign state system then it might be prevented, in Boulding's view, by a reform of international organization, and by the development of a research and information capability. From this capability, data collection and processing could enable the advance of scientific knowledge about the build-up of conflicts, to replace the inadequate insights available through standard diplomacy. In the first issue of the JCR in March 1957 Wright had an article proposing a 'project on a world intelligence centre', which showed the influence of Richardson from the past, while anticipating what has more recently come to be called early warning and conflict prevention. For Boulding, in these formative years of conflict theory, conflict resolution meant the development of a knowledge base in which 'social data stations' would emerge, forming a system analogous to a network of weather stations which would gather a range of social, political and economic data to produce indicators 'to identify social temperature and pressure and predict cold or warm fronts' (Kerman, 1974, 82).

Johan Galtung and conflict resolution in Northern Europe

While the developments at Michigan and the interest of the Bouldings in peace as well as conflict research provided one polar point for the emergence of peace research, its main elaboration was to be defined in developments in Europe. Lawler makes a distinction between the more limited agenda of conflict research (seeking to reduce the incidence and extent of war) and the emergence of peace research whose origins were not in North America but in Scandinavia, and most remarkably in the work of Johan Galtung (Lawler, 1995). We have already introduced Galtung's concept of the conflict triangle, and his distinction between direct violence, structural violence and cultural violence, in chapter 1. To this can be added his further distinction between negative and positive peace, the former characterized by the absence of direct violence, the latter by the overcoming of structural and cultural violence as well. Negative peace can be associated with the more limited but better defined 'minimalist' agenda of preventing war, and in particular nuclear war, as advocated by what might be called the North American pragmatist school. Positive peace encompasses the broader but vaguer 'maximalist' agenda insisted upon by the European structuralists.

The medical analogy, which seems to have occurred to so many of the peace science pioneers, was also at work in Galtung's background. His father was a physician and Galtung absorbed the ethic, transforming it into the notion of the peace researcher as a 'social physician' guided by a body of scientific knowledge. He studied philosophy, sociology and mathematics, and as early as 1951, at the age of 21, he became influenced by Gandhian ideas, which formed a persistent theme in his peace research.

In 1958 he became visiting professor of sociology at Columbia University, returning to Oslo in 1960 to help found a unit for research into conflict and peace, based within the Institute for Social Research at the University of Oslo and the precursor to the International Peace Research Institute Oslo (PRIO). The further development of peace research institutions in Europe in the 1960s was vigorous: in 1962 the Polemological Institute was formed in Groningen, Holland; in 1966 the Stockholm International Peace Research Institute (SIPRI) was opened to commemorate Sweden's 150 years of peace; and in 1969 the Tampere Peace Research Institute was formed in Finland. Galtung was also the founding editor of the *Journal of Peace Research*, which was launched in 1964.

This is not the place to attempt a summary of Galtung's work. His output since the early 1960s has been phenomenal and his influence on the institutionalization and ideas of peace research seminal. He saw the range of peace research reaching out far beyond the enterprise of war prevention to encompass study of the conditions for peaceful relations between the dominant and the exploited, rulers and ruled, men and women, western and non-western cultures, humankind and nature. Central here was the search for positive peace in the form of human empathy, solidarity and community, the priority of addressing 'structural violence' by unveiling and transforming structures of imperialism and oppression, and the importance of searching for alternative values in non-western cosmologies such as Buddhism.[2]

The struggle between European structuralists and North American pragmatists to define the peace research and conflict resolution agenda was at times hard-hitting. In an article in the *Journal of Peace Research* in 1968, for example, Schmid castigated many of those working in the field for failing to engage critically with issues of social justice. Absence of war on its own (negative peace) can obscure deep injustices which make a mockery of peace, and, if unaddressed, contain the seeds of future violent conflict (217–32). On the other hand, as Lawler's conclusion to his study of Galtung's ideas suggests, although the constant expansion of the peace research and conflict resolution agenda may be seen as a sign of its dynamism, 'it may also be seen as acquiring the qualities of an intellectual black hole wherein something vital, a praxeological edge or purpose, is lost' (1995, 237). This was a criticism made, among others, by Boulding.[3] The second quotation from the *Journal of Conflict Resolution* (1973) cited at the head of this chapter may be seen to represent an uneasy compromise between the maximalist and minimalist poles, which has more or less persisted to this day. In our view, the central core of the conflict resolution approach described in this book does represent the 'praxeological edge or purpose' of peace research. As both an analytic and normative field, conflict resolution takes violent or destructive conflict as its topic, and aims to gain an accurate understanding of its nature and aetiology in order to learn how it can best be overcome. This implies not only the treatment of symptoms, but work on conflict causes as well.

John Burton and a new paradigm in international studies

At this point we can review the contribution of our third 'founder-figure', John Burton. Burton was born in Australia in 1915. He studied at the London School of Economics from 1938, gained a Masters degree and, in 1942, a doctorate. He joined the Australian civil service, attended the foundation conference of the United Nations in San Francisco, served in the Australian Department of External Affairs and as High Commissioner in Ceylon. He was appointed to a post at University College London in 1963, following a period on a research fellowship at the Australian National University in Canberra. His appointment coincided with the formation of the Conflict Research Society in London, of which he became the first Honorary Secretary. An early product of this initiative was the publication of *Conflict in Society* (de Reuck and Knight, eds, 1966) with contributions from Boulding, Rapoport and Burton. Following soon after the appearance of other important studies of social conflict as a generic phenomenon, whether at community, industrial or other levels (Coser, 1956; Coleman, 1957) and coinciding with a rediscovery of Simmel's pioneering work (1902), this represented a significant step in the drawing together of multidisciplinary insights for the study of conflict at international level from a much broader perspective than was current in the formal international relations field. Whereas some earlier social scientists, such as the Chicago School, regarded conflict as dysfunctional and the job of the sociologist to remove it, most analysts in the conflict resolution tradition saw conflict as intrinsic in human relationships, so that the task became one of handling it better.

This was linked to attempts to coordinate international study through the formation of an International Peace Research Association (IPRA), which held its first conference at Groningen in Holland in 1965. At the same time, during 1965 and 1966, Burton organized the meetings which were to result in the use of controlled communication, or the problem-solving method, in international conflict, to be outlined further in the next section. These meetings were sufficiently impressive for both the Provost of University College London and the British Social Science Research Council to support and develop the theoretical and applied techniques which Burton and his group were pioneering. The result was the formation in 1966 of the Centre for the Analysis of Conflict, established under the Directorship of Burton and based at University College London.

Burton later spent a period in the mid-1980s at the University of Maryland, where he assisted Azar with the formation of the Center for International Development and Conflict Management and where he worked on the concept of protracted social conflict, which became an important part of an emerging overall theory of international conflict, combining both domestic-social and international dimensions and focused at a hybrid level between interstate war and purely domestic unrest. This model, described more fully through an outline of Azar's analysis in chapter 3, in our view anticipated much of the revaluation of international relations thinking that has taken place since the end of the Cold War. Burton himself did not hold back from making extravagant claims for this new approach in conflict analysis and conflict resolution, describing it as a decisive paradigm shift.

Burton finished his formal academic career as professor at the Institute for Conflict Analysis and Resolution at George Mason University in Virginia, and as a Fellow at the United States Institute of Peace in the late 1980s. Here he produced four volumes of the Conflict Series (1990), which offer a good summation of his own work and that of colleagues, associates and others working with him in the field.

Early influences on Burton's intellectual journey away from the conventional wisdom of international relations traditions were systems theory as a new vocabulary and set of explanations for the cooperative and competitive behaviour of social organisms, and game theory as a means of analysing the variety of options and orientations available to the conflict parties. The work of Schelling (1960) on irrationality in competitive strategies and Rapoport (Rapoport and Chammah, 1965) on the self-defeating logic of win–lose approaches were influential here. As Rapoport put it: 'the illusion that increasing losses for the other side is equivalent to winning is *the* reason that the struggles are so prolonged and the conflicting parties play the game to a lose/lose end' (1986, 441). We have introduced some of these ideas in chapter 1.

Another source of inspiration for Burton were the insights drawn from industrial relations, organizational theory and client-centred social work. Here, the legacy of Follett's 'mutual gains' approach was being vigorously carried forward (Blake et al., 1963; Walton and McKersie, 1965), and applied further afield in family conciliation work, community mediation and the rapidly expanding arena of Alternative Dispute Resolution (ADR) in general, which sought less costly alternatives to formal litigation. Much of this literature, and related literatures on, for example, race and ethnic relations, was based on studies in social psychology and social identity theory, which examined the dynamics of intergroup cooperation and conflict through field-based surveys and small group experimentation. The work of Kurt Lewin was further developed to show how group affiliation and pressure to gain distinctiveness by comparison with other groups can lead to intergroup conflict, and how positive relations can be restored or new relationships negotiated between groups in conflict. Deutsch was amongst the first to apply this kind of research explicitly to conflict resolution (1949, 1973). Useful recent surveys of a wide field include Fisher (1990) and Larsen, ed. (1993). This research has explored both the negative and positive aspects. Negatively, it has concentrated on processes of selective perception through forms of tunnel vision, prejudice and stereotyping, on malign perceptions of the 'other', on dehumanization and the formation of enemy images, on the displacement of feelings of fear and hostility through suppression and projection. Positively, it has focused on changing attitudes, on developing mutual understanding and trust, on the development of common or 'superordinate goals' and on the general identification of conditions which promote positive intergroup contact (Sherif, 1966; Deutsch, 1973). These insights were at the same time applied to international conflict, as later summed up in Mitchell (1981). Linked to this were studies of 'perception and misperception' among decision-makers in international politics, to borrow Jervis's 1976 title. Burton drew on this material in a series of books published in the late 1960s and early 1970s, including: *Systems, States, Diplomacy and Rules* (1968), *Conflict and Communication* (1969) and *World Society* (1972).

What made it possible to unlock these intractable conflicts for Burton was above all the application of needs theory (Maslow, 1954; Sites, 1990) through a 'controlled communication' or problem-solving approach. As already indicated in chapter 1, the positing of a universal drive to satisfy basic needs such as security, identity and recognition provided Burton with the link between causal analysis and modes of resolution precisely because of the differences between interests and needs. Interests, being primarily about material 'goods', can be traded, bargained and nego-tiated. Needs, being non-material, cannot be traded or satisfied by power bargaining. However, crucially, non-material human needs are not scarce resources (as territory or oil or minerals might be) and are not necessarily in short supply. With proper understanding, therefore, conflicts based on unsatisfied needs can be resolved. It is possible (in theory) to meet the needs of both parties to a conflict, because 'the more security and recognition one party to a relationship experiences, the more others are likely to experience' (Burton, 1990, 242). For example, although the question of sovereignty in Northern Ireland or Jerusalem may appear to be intractable, if the conflict can be translated into the underlying basic needs of the conflict parties for security, recognition and development, a space is opened up for the possibility of resolution.

But the problem-solving approach was seen as more than a conflict resolution technique by Burton. It was to become a central concept in his idea of the paradigm shift in thinking about behaviour and conflict in general that he believed was essential if humankind was to avoid future disaster. He was again influenced by some of the concepts in general systems theory here, and in particular the idea of first order and second order learning. In systems theory attention is given to the role of social learning and culture in the way in which social systems change. The theory holds that although social systems 'learn' through their members, who individually adjust their world views according to experience, socio-cultural systems also have underlying assumptions which make the system as a whole more resistant to change than their individual members. These underlying assumptions are defined by Rapoport as 'default values' (1986), which, because they are so commonly used, become regarded as immutable, and actors in the system tend to forget that they can exercise choices in order to attain goals. When problems occur, they are addressed by reference to the 'default values' and this kind of reaction is termed first order learning. Orderly and creative transformation of social systems, however, depends upon a capacity for second order learning, which requires a willingness and capacity for challenging assumptions. Ideological orientations to social change are regarded as the antithesis of second order learning, because ideologies are claims to ultimate truth achieved with a predefined set of ends and means, the challenging of which is seen as heretical. For systems theorists such as Rapoport, 'the critical issue of peace and the need to convert conflict to co-operation demand incorporation of second order learning in social systems, and the most effective way to produce social learning is through a participative design process' (Rapoport, 1986, 442).

This idea of second order learning, or second order change, is further developed by Burton and Dukes in the third volume of the Conflict Series (1990), where it is seen to be essential for human survival. The problem-solving approach, given philosophical depth through Charles Sanders Peirce's 'logic of abduction' (1958), is the means of overcoming blockages to second order learning, thereby becoming a central element in what Burton saw as a new political philosophy, which moves beyond episodic conflict resolution to a new order marked by 'provention' (a neologism that has not been widely adopted): 'conflict provention means deducing from an adequate explanation of the phenomenon of conflict, including its human dimensions, not merely the conditions that create an environment of conflict, and the structural changes required to remove it, but more importantly, the promotion of conditions that create cooperative relationships' (Burton and Dukes, eds, 1990, 2). It connotes, in other words, a proactive capability within societies to predict and avoid destructive conflict by the spread of the problem-solving method and philosophy throughout all relevant institutions, discourses and practices.

Constructions: the 1970s and 1980s

By the early 1970s, as suggested in the second quotation at the head of this chapter, conflict resolution, drawing from a wide range of disciplines and with a reasonably sound institutional base, had defined its specific subject area in relation to the three great projects of avoiding nuclear war, removing glaring inequalities and injustices in the global system, and achieving ecological balance and control. It was attempting to formulate a theoretical understanding of destructive conflict at three levels, with a view to refining the most appropriate practical responses. First, there was the interstate level, where the main effort went into translating détente between the superpowers into formal win–win agreements. Here, the processes which produced the 1963 Limited Test Ban Treaty and later Strategic Arms Limitation Talks and Non-Proliferation Treaty negotiations were seen to vindicate Osgood's 'graduated reciprocation in tension-reduction' (GRIT) approach (1962) and to exemplify Axelrod's analysis of the 'evolution of cooperation' described in chapter 1. Similar work went into the formulation of alternative defence strategies in the 1980s. The expansion of the European Economic Community and of the North Atlantic security area were seen as further confirmation of the ideas of Mitrany and Karl Deutsch. Second, at the level of domestic politics, a great deal of conflict resolution work, particularly in the United States, went into the building up of expertise in family conciliation, labour and community mediation, and ADR. An important new initiative here was in public policy disputes in general (Susskind, 1987). Third, between the two, and for this book the most significant development in the 1970s and 1980s, was the definition, analysis and prescriptive thinking about what were variously described as 'deep-rooted conflicts' (Burton, 1987), 'intractable conflicts' (Kriesberg et al., eds, 1989) or 'protracted social conflicts' (Azar, 1990), in which the distinction between international and domestic level causes was seen to be elided. Here the emphasis was on defining the elements of 'good governance' at constitutional level, and of intergroup relations at community level. Since we will be outlining Azar's thinking about protracted social conflict in chapter 3, we will not elaborate on these concepts here. They seem to us to have constituted a significant advance in thinking about what has since become the prevailing pattern of contemporary conflict (see chapter 1, pp. 22–33). These levels of analysis were brought together from a conflict resolution perspective in studies such as Kriesberg's *The Sociology of Social Conflicts* (1973) and Mitchell's *The Structure of International Conflict* (1981).

In what follows we select for attention the first systematic attempts to apply the problem-solving approach to real conflicts, and the major advances in the analysis of the negotiation and mediation processes which took place in this period. We end the section by noting the concomitant expansion of the conflict resolution institutional base worldwide, and pay tribute to the role of Elise Boulding both in encouraging it and in articulating its wider significance.

The Harvard School: problem-solving and principled negotiation

One of the most sustained attempts to wed theory to practice was the attempt to set up problem-solving workshops to tackle the more intractable conflicts of the day. Initially referred to as 'controlled communication', the first two workshops were set up in 1965 and 1966, and were designed to address aspects of the conflict between Malaysia, Singapore and Indonesia, and between the Greek and Turkish communities in Cyprus. The London Group, whose members included Michael Banks, Anthony de Reuck, Chris Mitchell and Michael Nicholson as well as John Burton, were joined for the second workshop in 1966 by Herbert Kelman and Chad Alger from America. Kelman, who formed at Harvard the Program on International Conflict Analysis and Resolution, and who had already been a significant influence in the emergence of conflict resolution research in the pioneering initiatives at the University of Michigan, went on to become perhaps the leading practitioner-scholar of the problem-solving method over the following thirty years, specializing in the Israeli–Palestinian conflict (Doob, ed., 1970; Kelman, 1996). To anticipate events in the 1990s, Kelman's long-standing 1974–91 'pre-negotiation' Arab–Israeli interactive problem-solving workshops, followed by the 1991–93 'para-negotiation' workshops, and post-1993 'post-negotiation' workshops (fifty-four workshops in all by 1998), involved many of the chief negotiators of the 1993 agreement on both sides. Participants were influential, but non-official figures; meetings were held in private academic environments, encouraged by third party facilitation but only in an enabling capacity inasmuch as ground rules were explained and a problem-solving agenda followed. Information was shared, participants were encouraged to listen without judgement to each others' needs, concerns and perspectives, there was then joint exploration of options, joint analysis of likely constraints and a joint search for ways of overcoming those constraints. These were seen as non-binding non-official micro-processes, which, it was hoped, would contribute to macro-level negotiations but in no way substitute for them. One of the chief ways in which they might do this was through the building of new relationships.

As experience developed amongst a growing circle of scholar-practitioners in the 1970s and 1980s, problem-solving workshops were used to pursue a variety of goals – for example, in some cases they performed a research and educational or training role – and it became clear that each workshop had to be designed with some reference to the specific characteristics of the particular conflict. A universal model for the ideal problem-solving process did not emerge. Nevertheless, there now exists a whole cluster of approaches known variously as interactive conflict resolution, third party consultation, process-promoting workshops, facilitated dialogues, all of which use many of the essential characteristics of the problem-solving approach. This is well explained and illustrated in Mitchell and Banks's *Handbook of Conflict Resolution: The Analytical Problem-Solving Approach* (1996). The difficult questions of methodology and evaluation have been much discussed (Mitchell, 1993), with a view to enhancing the process of hypothesis-generation, theory-testing and theory-use.

By the 1980s the study of negotiation in international conflict had also taken on the win–win, problem-solving and mutual gain vocabulary of conflict resolution, particularly through the work of Roger Fisher and William Ury at the Harvard Program on Negotiation, popularized through their best-selling title *Getting to Yes* (1981), and later through the quarterly *Negotiation Journal*. We noted in chapter 1 the distinction between positions and interests, which is central in the 'principled negotiation' approach. The Harvard Program involves a consortium of academic centres and, in authentic conflict resolution vein, draws from a range of disciplines including politics, psychology, anthropology, sociology and international relations, as well as labour relations, community negotiations and public planning. A number of systematic analyses and comparative studies of successful and unsuccessful negotiation approaches and styles are now available, including Druckman, ed. (1977), Zartman, ed. (1978), Raiffa (1982), Hall, ed. (1993), and Zartman and Rubin (1996).

Adam Curle: the theory and practice of mediation

We noted in chapter 1 how the practice of mediation has a long history, traceable to Greek and Roman times in the West. By 1945 there were critical studies of state level diplomacy and international mediation to complement the day-to-day experience acquired by professional diplomats and negotiators (Mitchell and Webb, eds, 1988). The attempt by the international community to convert this into a more formal institutionalized practice following the call in Chapter VI of the UN Charter for agreed mechanisms for the peaceful settlement of disputes, inspired studies such as that by Young, which included an assessment of the role of the UN and its agencies (1967). Nevertheless, a number of scholars in the conflict resolution tradition in the early 1980s agreed with Pruitt that there was a deficit in critical studies of mediation which still lacked systematic analysis (Pruitt and Rubin, 1986, 237). Since then much of the deficit has been made up. In addition to Mitchell and Webb, the literature now includes Touval and Zartman (1985), Bercovitch and Rubin (1992), as well as Kressell and Pruitt, eds (1989), Bercovitch, ed. (1996) and a host of individual studies of particular mediations in specific conflicts. Quite sophisticated comparisons are now being made of different types of mediation, with or without 'muscle', by different types of mediator (official and unofficial, from the UN to individual governments, insider-partial or outsider-neutral) and in different types of conflict situation. A special issue of the *Journal of Peace Research* published in February 1991 encouraged critical comparison of the efficacy of new paradigm approaches (non-coercive and based broadly on problem-solving) in relation to power–coercion–reward models. Coming out of this have been attempts to suggest that different types of third party intervention are effective at different stages of the conflict process, that they can be seen as complementary, and that the type of appropriate intervention is contingent upon the nature and stage of the conflict. In one well-known model, for example, stages of conflict are related to optimal conflict resolution interventions (Fisher and Keashly, 1991). The argument is that softer forms of intervention are more appropriate when miscommunication and mistrust is high (when the subjective elements are strong), whereas harder forms of intervention are more successful when substantive interests are at the forefront. All of this is considered more fully in chapter 6, as is the question whether there are 'ripe moments' for the resolution of conflicts (Zartman, 1985). Relating all of this to the 'conflict triangle' (see figure 1.6), it is possible to see the structural approach exemplified by Galtung as addressing the 'contradiction' apex of the triangle, the controlled communications approach of Burton and Kelman as addressing the 'attitude' apex, and the analytic study of various types of bargaining/negotiation, mediation/conciliation and (less usual) arbitration/adjudication approaches exemplified by Zartman, Bercovitch, Druckman, Pruitt and Rubin as addressing the 'behaviour' apex.

As a complement to the emphasis on Track I mediation in many of the studies noted above, we take Curle as our exemplar for the development of 'soft' mediation in the conflict resolution field, particularly what McDonald and Bendahmane (1987) christened Track II mediation. Coming from an academic background in anthropology, psychology and development education, Curle moved from Harvard to take up the first Chair of Peace Studies at the University of Bradford, which, together with the Richardson Institute for Conflict and Peace Research at the University of Lancaster and the Centre for the Analysis of Conflict at the University of Kent (a relocation of the original 1966 Centre based at University College London) was to become a focal point for conflict resolution in the UK.

Curle's academic interest in peace was a product of front-line experiences of conflict in Pakistan and in Africa, where he not only witnessed the threats to development from the eruption of violent conflicts, but was increasingly drawn into the practice of peacemaking, especially as a mediator. Most importantly, during the intensive and searing experiences of the Biafran War he felt a compelling need to understand more about why these conflicts happened (Yarrow 1978: Curle, 1971 and 1986). Violence, conflict, processes of social change and the goals of development began to be seen as linked themes. Curle's *Making Peace* (1971) defines peace and conflict as a set of peaceful and unpeaceful relationships, so that 'the process of peacemaking consists in making changes to relationships so that they may be brought to a point where development can occur'. Given his academic background, it was natural that he should see peace broadly in terms of human development, rather than as a set of 'peace-enforcing' rules and organizations. And the purpose of studying social structures was to identify those that enhanced rather than restrained or even suppressed human potential.

In the Middle (1986) points to the importance of mediation and reconciliation themes in peace research and practice in the conflict-ridden world of the late twentieth century. Curle identified four elements to his mediation process: first, the mediator acts to build, maintain and improve communications; second, to provide information to and between the conflict parties; third, to 'befriend' the conflict parties; and, fourth, to encourage what he refers to as active mediation, that is to say to cultivate a willingness to engage in cooperative negotiation. His philosophy of mediation is essentially a blend of values and experiences from Quaker practice[4] with the knowledge of humanistic psychology absorbed in his early professional career, with both of these influences tempered and modified by his experiences in the field.

Curle's work is an illustration both of the applied nature of conflict resolution and its stress on the crucial link between academic theory and practice. It also provides one example of an approach to Track II or citizens' diplomacy, and a number of studies have contributed to a fuller understanding of the methods and approaches of mediation and third party intervention in conflicts at both official-governmental and at unofficial-citizens' diplomacy levels activity. A good general account of unofficial diplomacy is provided by Berman and Johnson in the introduction to their book, which includes a definition of citizens' diplomacy and a classification of the types of citizens' organizations that conduct it (Berman and Johnson, eds, 1977; MacDonald and Bendahmane, eds, 1987; Aall, 1996; Anderson, 1996b).

Elise Boulding: new voices in conflict resolution

During the 1970s and 1980s the number of peace researchers and conflict resolution specialists worldwide continued to grow from a few hundred to perhaps thousands, and the institutional bases for conflict resolution expanded accordingly, mainly in Western Europe, North America and Japan, but also increasingly in other parts of the world. Notable centres were established in areas of protracted conflict, such as South Africa, Northern Ireland, the Spanish Basque country and Sri Lanka. Some indication of this institutional expansion is given in box 2.1, albeit unavoidably selective. In this section we take the work of Elise Boulding as exemplary of this process of expansion and of the development of thinking that has accompanied it.

Elise Boulding trained as a sociologist and was involved in the early work of the Michigan Centre outlined above. She began the IPRA News-letter as a project of the Women's International League for Peace and Freedom, of which she was subsequently international chair. This News-letter, with the help of UNESCO, developed the network which facilitated the formulation of IPRA, and Elise continued to serve as its editor for a number of years. After her retirement from teaching, she also served as Secretary-General of IPRA. In order to encourage wider participation in peace and conflict resolution processes, she introduced the idea of 'imaging the future' as a powerful way of enabling people to break out of the defensive private shells into which they retreated, often out of fear

---

BOX 2.1   The growth of the conflict resolution field, 1975–96

1976: Consejo Latinoamericano de Investigacion para la Paz (Latin American Council for Peace Investigation), Latin American regional affiliate of IPRA Guatemala

1979: University of Ulster, Centre for the Study of Conflict (Northern Ireland)

1980: University for Peace, UN University, Costa Rica

1982: Carter Center: International Negotiation Network

1984: Nairobi Peace Group (from 1990, Nairobi Peace Initiative)

1984: United States Institute of Peace, Washington

1985: International Alert, United Kingdom

1986: Conflict Resolution Network, Australia

1986: Harvard Law School, Program on Negotiation

1986: Jean B. Kroc Institute for International Peace Studies, University of Notre Dame, USA

1988: Institute for Conflict Resolution and Analysis, George Mason University, USA

1988: Austrian Study Centre for Peace and Conflict Resolution/ European Peace University

1990: Centre for Conflict Resolution, University of Bradford

1991: First European Conference on Peacemaking and Conflict Resolution, Istanbul

1991: Gaston Z. Ortigas Peace Institute, Philippines

1992: Centre for Conflict Resolution, University of Cape Town, South Africa

1992: Academic Associates PeaceWorks, Nigeria

1992: Institute for Multi-Track Diplomacy, Washington

1992: Instituto Peruano de Resolución de Conflictos, Negociación, y Mediación, Peru

1993: Berghof Research Centre for Constructive Conflict Management, Berlin

1993: Organization of African Unity, Mechanism for Conflict Prevention, Management and Resolution

1993: University of Ulster/United Nations University: Initiative on Conflict Resolution and Ethnicity (INCORE)

1994: The Conference for Security and Cooperation in Europe becomes the Organization for Security and Cooperation in Europe, (OSCE), containing High Commissioner on National Minorities

1994: Conferencias Iberoamericanas de Paz 7 Tratamineto de Conflictos (Ibero-American Conferences on Peace and the Treatment of Conflicts), Chile

1994: Institute for the Prevention of International Conflict, Japan

1994: International Resource Group (Somalia, Kenya, Horn of Africa)

1994: UNESCO's Culture of Peace Programme

1995: Kazakhstan Centre for Conflict Management

1996: European Centre for Conflict Prevention, Holland

1996: Forum on Early Warning and Early Response, London

The above list makes no claim to be comprehensive. In particular, many organizations in Africa, Asia and Latin America might be added. It is intended to indicate the institutional development of the field since the late 1970s. Fuller information on all of the organizations listed above can be obtained from *Prevention and Management of Violent Conflicts: An International Directory* (European Platform for Conflict Prevention and Transformation), 1998 edition. The Directory has profiles of 475 organizations worldwide, and is also available on-line at http;//www.euconflict.org

of what was happening in the public world, and encouraging them to participate in the construction of a peaceful and tolerant global culture. The use of social imagination and the idea of imaging the future was placed within the context of what she called the '200-year present', that is, the idea that we must understand that we live in a social space which reaches into the past and into the future: 'it is our space, one that we can move around directly in our own lives and indirectly by touching the lives of the young and old around us' (Boulding, E., 1990, 4). She was also an early exponent of the idea of civil society, of opening up new possibilities for a global civic culture which was receptive to the voices of people who were not part of the traditional discourses of nation-state politics, and in this anticipated many of the preoccupations of conflict resolution workers today. Women and children were obviously excluded groups, but she added to these the idea that globalism and global civic culture needed to accommodate the many culture communities which were not heard in the existing international order. For Elise Boulding, the next half of our '200-year present', that is, the next one hundred years from the 1980s, contains within it the basis for a world civic culture and peaceful problem-solving among nations, but also for the possibility of Armageddon. She saw the development of indigenous and international citizens' networks as one way of ensuring that the former prevailed. For Elise Boulding, peacemaking demands specific 'craft and skills', a peace praxis encompassing 'all those activities in which conflict is dealt with in an integrative mode – as choices that lie at the heart of all human interaction' (1990, 140). In the intersubjective relationships that make up social and political life, as also in the structures and institutions within which they are embedded, the success with which this is inculcated and encouraged will determine whether, in the end, we are peacemakers or warmakers.

Reconstructions: the 1990s

As suggested in chapter 1, the 1990s have offered students of conflict resolution unexpected opportunities to make effective contributions to the resolution of contemporary deadly conflicts, as the international community, through the UN and regional organizations, as well as through sympathetic governments, has come to adopt many of the approaches pioneered by those whose work has been described above. With greater opportunity has come greater critical scrutiny, however, as those working in related fields, from military peacekeeping to aid and development work, have become more interested in conflict resolution techniques and principles, particularly in what came to be called 'complex political emergencies'. From prevention to post-settlement peacebuilding, conflict resolution ideas are being tested both at local and governmental levels. Since the rest of the book is about these issues, we will comment quite briefly here. We conclude this chapter, first, by noting one way in which new technology may open new possibilities for conflict resolution (see Box 2.2), and then by looking at four linked areas where there has been innovative constructive criticism, and where conflict resolution work is being adapted accordingly. These tend to be critiques from the radical left. We postpone engagement with critiques from the radical right to later chapters – for example, the criticism that there is no room for conflict resolution in disputes between irreconcilable interests where power and coercion are the name of the game, and a questioning of the role of well-meaning outsiders whose interference may prolong the fighting and prevent a more secure peace following a clear-cut military victory.

Peacebuilding from below

One of the origins of the term 'peacebuilding' was in the peace research and conflict resolution literature. We have defined it in chapter 1 as the attempt to overcome the structural, relational and cultural contradictions

---

BOX 2.2   Virtual diplomacy

In the 1990s an emerging world of cyberspace is 'compressing time and space, flattening the traditional bureaucratic structures of governance and building "virtual" or electronically linked coalitions . . . that are the structures of a global civil society' (Solomon, 1997). For some observers these networks and coalitions are producing new opportunities for peacemaking and democracy, eroding traditional notions of national sovereignty and making national frontiers more permeable than they have ever been before. There are dangers as well as opportunities here. But, in addition to greater capacity to update information and link humanitarian and conflict resolution agencies, as shown in the UN's Department of Humanitarian Affairs' ReliefWeb there are also possibilities for overcoming the baleful effects of media manipulation, such as that perpetrated on behalf of genocidal political programmes by the radio station Radio-Télévision Libre des Milles Collines in Rwanda and state-controlled media in Serbia. For example, late in 1996 there were mass protests against the decision of President Milosevic's government not to accept the result of local elections which gave power to opposition groups in many of the cities of the Republic of Serbia. The demonstrators were using an independent radio station, 'B92', to spread and coordinate their protests, with the result that the station was cut off by the government. In response, the leaders of the protest put the B92 broadcasts onto the internet, where they were picked up by both the BBC and Voice of America and retransmitted to Serbia. The protests continued and in February 1997 the government was pressurized into accepting the result of the elections. For Solomon this is a good illustration of 'cyber-democracy', in which 'networked international communications empower people to act against government authority' and 'the Internet can build coalitions that are unconstrained by physical or political frontiers' (1997, 3–4).

---

which lie at the root of conflict in order to underpin the processes of peacemaking and peacekeeping. In the 1990s there has been a significant shift of emphasis away from the idea of 'top-down' peacebuilding in which powerful outsiders act as experts, importing their own conceptions and ignoring local cultures and capacities, and in favour of a cluster of practices and principles referred to collectively as 'peacebuilding from below'. The conflict resolution and development fields have come together in this shared enterprise. John Paul Lederach, working as a scholar-practitioner within a Mennonite tradition which shares many of the values and ideas of the Quakers, and with practical experience in Central America, is one of the chief exponents of this approach:

> The principle of indigenous empowerment suggests that conflict transformation must actively envision, include, respect, and promote the human and cultural resources from within a given setting. This involves a new set of lenses through which we do not primarily 'see' the setting and the people in it as the 'problem' and the outsider as the 'answer'. Rather, we understand the long-term goal of transformation as validating and building on people and resources within the setting. (*Lederach, 1995*)

In chapter 1 we illustrated Lederach's idea of the 'pyramid' of levels of leadership in societies in conflict (see figure 1.9). While recognizing the significance of initiatives at all three levels for peacemaking and peacebuilding, his particular stress is on 'bottom-up' processes: 'One could argue that virtually all of the recent transitions toward peace – such as those in El Salvador and Ethiopia, as well as the earlier one in the Philippines – were driven largely by the pressure for change that was bubbling up from the grassroots' (1997, 52). More will be said about this in chapter 7.

Power, participation and transformation

A second area of constructive criticism is found at the interface between traditional conflict resolution approaches and critical social theory. We will take Vivienne Jabri's *Discourses on Violence* (1996) as exemplary here. As both a sociologist and conflict resolution specialist, she can be taken as representative of a younger generation of critical conflict resolution theorists, which includes Mark Hoffman, Betts Fetherston and Caroline Nordstrom. Critical of the empirical and comparative tradition in conflict studies with its emphasis on purposive agents and utility-maximizing decision-makers, Jabri views violent conflict as a social product and militarism as 'a deeply embedded continuity reinforced through dominant discursive and institutional frameworks' (p. 150). Neither the 'objectivist' (rational actor/bargaining) approach nor the 'subjectivist' (communications/problem-solving) approach is seen to do justice to this, since each is, in its different way, individualistic. Nor is what we have earlier in this chapter called the European 'structuralist' approach adequate, since it fails to account for the way social contradiction transmutes into violent conflict.

Instead, Jabri looks to structurationist theory (Giddens, 1979; Bhaskar, 1989), with its recognition of the mutual dependency of agency and structure, to bridge the ontological gap between the individualist and structuralist approaches. Violent conflict is seen to 'generate a hegemonic discourse which seeks to subsume subjectivity and its multiple forms of representation into a singular entity involved in a confrontational inter-action with another assumed/constructed monolithic entity'. The problem with traditional conflict resolution approaches for Jabri is that these monolithic entities may also be reproduced 'through the representation of observers, conflict researchers and third parties attempting mediation', especially when and if such third parties interpret the conflict through the definitions of its leading actors, in which case conflict resolution may merely 'reproduce the exclusionist, violent discourses and practices which perpetuate it' (180–1).

Behind this lies Cox's distinction (1981) between problem-solving theory and critical theory. In Fetherston's words:

> Problem-solving theory focuses on existing frameworks of institutions, social relations and social meaning which are often taken for granted, with the goal of sustaining this order to make it work efficiently. Critical theory starts by problematizing this given framework or social order with the aim of con-sidering its origins and how it might be changed, clarifying possible alternatives, and providing insights into ways of transforming it. (*1998, 2*)

The danger of failing to incorporate a critical-theoretical approach for Fetherston is that attempts at conflict resolution will once again simply reinforce the unchallenged order which generated the conflict in the first place. The result will be that we are 'continually re-solving conflicts' instead of developing a 'solution that will not reappear again in another time or place to demand solutions or re-solutions that did not work the first time' (Nordstrom, 1995, 106).

The implications of this for conflict resolution are extensive, leading to a radical questioning of much of the UN's approach to peacebuilding, to be considered in chapter 7, including the suitability of military peace-keepers, on the grounds that it reinforces existing patterns of exclusion and domination. Similar criticisms are made of the impact of much international aid and development work. In more positive vein, in chapter 7 we will also note some of the ways in which, in Fetherston's terminol-ogy, conceptions of power and dominance taken from Foucault, Gramsci and Habermas suggest, respectively, anti-hegemonic, counter-hegemonic and post-hegemonic peacebuilding projects. Jabri similarly emphasizes the importance of transformative counter-discourses in challenging the dominance of public space by exclusionist hegemonic discourses which legitimate violence and war. She locates a 'discourse of peace' in an emancipatory politics, which celebrates dominance-free participation and difference (individuality, nonconformity, dissent), as defined through Habermas's conception of communicative action. This idea of the creative possibilities for the production of new meaning inherent in the encounter between the Self and the Other is reminiscent of the writing of Martin Buber. It also echoes what Broome, in the tradition of Gadamer (1975), calls relational empathy in 'managing differences in conflict resolution'

(1993) – the move away from individual-centred resolution to the creation of a 'third culture', which is not just the result of fusion but the generation of a new possibility-space for the flourishing of difference:

> This third culture can only develop through interaction in which participants are willing to open themselves to new meanings, to engage in genuine dialogue, and to constantly respond to the new demands emanating from the situation. The emergence of this third culture is the essence of relational empathy and is essential for successful conflict resolution. (*p. 104*)

At this point we will sidestep a terminological dispute in which some theorists prefer the term 'conflict transformation' for what we are calling the longer-term and deeper structural, relational and cultural dimensions of conflict resolution (Rupesinghe, ed., 1995). Like all terminological issues, this is a matter of preference. As suggested in chapter 1, we will go with the majority in seeing transformation as the ultimate goal of the conflict resolution enterprise.[5]

A gendered critique of conflict resolution

We noted in chapter 1 that conflict resolution has meanings in three dimensions: as a specialist academic and practical field; as an objective and an activity that is universal and practised by people throughout the world who may or may not be aware of the term; and prescriptively, as a description of a successful outcome to peacemaking and peacebuilding processes. All three are relevant to a gendered critique.

We have seen in this chapter how conflict resolution as an academic project was created and institutionalized in a small number of centres, most of them set up by men, who consequently constitute a majority among our exemplars. This fact of male dominance, however, did not go unnoticed, as shown in Elise Boulding's 1976 book, *The Underside of History: A View of Women Through Time*. The significance of early theorists like Mary Parker Follett has been recognized, and today the gender proportions may well be more equal (the 100 per cent male authorship of this book notwithstanding).

Number-counting is of far less significance, however, than the fact that, in our second grouping, women are pre-eminently the silenced victims of violent conflict throughout the world, and also often the main creators of new modes of survival and conflict resolution, usually at local level and nearly always unrecorded. This is, for obvious reasons, much more difficult to chronicle – as also in the case of male victims and unsung peacemakers. Attempts have been made to compare the effectiveness of men and women as mediators, with mixed results (Maxwell and Maxwell, 1989; Stamato, 1992). Some see Track I conflict resolution approaches based on diplomacy and military power as male-dominated, and Track II citizen peacemaking as associated more with women (Stiehm, 1995). A number of social anthropological studies of peacemaking practices in different parts of the world have emphasized the key role played by women (Duffey, 1998).

The third dimension introduces the most difficult and contested conceptual question: whether the discourses and institutions that reproduce militarism and violence are themselves gendered so that successful long-term conflict resolution requires a radical transformation here as well (Taylor and Miller, 1994). Duffey (1998) has pointed out that the involvement of women in formal peace processes has been very limited and that they are largely excluded from high-level negotiations, despite their active participation in local peace movements and peacemaking initiatives. The exclusion of women from the discourse about new political structures defined in peace agreements, and the political process of negotiations determined at international level, may well be factors which perpetuate the exclusionist and violent discourses and institutions which contribute to the conflict in the first place. Byrne (1996) has noted that, despite the many local organizations which represented women's interests in former Yugoslavia, there were no women representatives involved in the Dayton peace talks in 1995. Similarly, Duffey (1998) has demonstrated that the exclusion of women from the UN-sponsored peace conferences in Somalia served to increase the legitimacy and power of the warlords, who were frequently unaccountable to the local community. When women are excluded from contributing to peace negotiations, the realities of a conflict in terms of its impact on communities may not be fully comprehended. For this reason, Berhane-Selassie (1994) argues that the international community should consult and involve women in order to understand more about the root causes of conflict, to understand how obstacles to peace processes can be removed and to gain insight about how traditional practices can offer alternative ways of ending conflicts.

The culture question

In our fourth area of constructive criticism we have to ask the question whether the conflict resolution field constitutes a truly global enterprise, as its founders assumed, or whether it is based upon hidden cultural specifics which are not universal. If it turns out that the latter is irrevocably the case, then many of the hopes of those who have devoted their lives to the project will have been proved vain.

We noted earlier in this chapter the seminal influence of Gandhian and Buddhist approaches to peacemaking on the nascent conflict resolution scene. The same continues to be the case, as also with other cultural traditions, both Christian and non-Christian. Nevertheless, the unexpected expansion in peacemaking, peacekeeping and peacebuilding work in areas of conflict in the 1990s, through the UN, regional organizations,

or a multiplicity of INGOs and NGOs, has propelled the 'culture question' in conflict resolution to the top of the agenda. The presence of
thousands of military and civilian personnel from numerous countries in
conflict zones in all parts of the world, attempting to achieve common
conflict resolution goals, has shown up glaring cultural discontinuities, as
indicated later in this book. There is no doubt about the depth of
ignorance and misunderstanding, or the inappropriateness of attempted
conflict resolution approaches, in many cases. But the important question
is: can this be corrected? In other words, can conflict resolution as a
specialist field be made more culturally sensitive, enriched by hitherto
neglected insights and traditions from all over the world, while retaining
its defining principles? Or does the entire enterprise amount to no more
than a specific localized cultural moment, unrecognized in other reaches
of an irreducible global multiplicity?

In fact, these questions have long been anticipated within the conflict
resolution community, beginning with the influx of anthropological studies of diverse conflict and conflict resolution practice in the 1960s (LeVine,
1961; Gulliver, 1979; Ross, 1993). They then erupted into a major
controversy in the 1980s in the form of an explicit critique of Burton's
universalist human needs theory, and the argument that culturally diverse
ethnoconflict theories (derived from locally constructed common-sense
views of conflict) and ethnopraxis (techniques and customs for dealing
with conflict derived from these understandings) need to be developed and
incorporated into the construction of general conflict resolution approaches (Avruch et al., 1991). In similar vein, Lederach and Wehr, reflecting
on their work in Central America, found that the western model of
outsider neutral mediators was not understood or trusted in many Central
American settings where the idea of insider partial peacemaking was the
norm (Lederach and Wehr, 1991). In South-East Asia some westerners
have been critical of the conflict management approach of ASEAN, seeing
it as an arrangement between governments to 'brush problems under the
carpet' and crush internal dissent, against the western conflict resolution
assumption that latent conflict must be brought out into the open if it is to
be resolved. ASEAN members have responded by rejecting such assumptions and contrasting them with the 'Asian way' of handling conflict
(Askandar, 1997). Cohen gives examples of the way in which 'cross-
cultural dissonances' (different interpretations of roles, motivations and
behaviours which are culturally constructed) can significantly inhibit
conflict resolution – or enhance it if appropriate adjustments are made, as
when US President Carter's personal intervention in 1978 to secure
agreement between President Sadat of Egypt and President Begin of Israel
(the Camp David Accords) mirrored a traditional practice of Egyptian
village conflict resolution (the *mulakah*, or getting together) designed to
avoid personal embarrassment or public retreat (Cohen, 1996, 125). At
an even more fundamental level, Salem questions some of the 'hidden
assumptions in the Western approach to conflict resolution' from an Arab

Muslim perspective (1993; 1997, 11). Whereas in the western imperialist tradition, according to Salem, the ideology of peace and order has precedence over the ideology of struggle and conflict, this is not the case in the nationalist, Marxist and Islamic fundamentalist ideologies that have shaped the modern Arab world (1997, 14). Similarly, the 'focus of Western conflict resolution theorists on the suffering generated by conflict rather than on the justice or morality of the cause may not strike resonant philosophical chords in other cultures' (p. 15). In fact, we have noted earlier how some of these themes are also found in western critiques of early conflict resolution assumptions about 'symmetric' conflicts. Salem's conclusion would probably be echoed by most conflict resolution specialists: 'The conclusion to be drawn from this is not that the Arab world, for example, is more conflict-prone or less conflict resolution-oriented than the West but that in transporting western conflict resolution theories and techniques to the Arab world or elsewhere, they must undergo considerable cultural adaptation' (p. 23). In our view, this task has only just begun and is the most important single challenge facing the conflict resolution field today.

Conclusion

In this chapter we have noted the diverse nature of the conflict resolution tradition, rooted in different disciplines and encompassing the 'subjectivist' controlled communication and problem-solving approach, the 'objectivist' rational negotiation/ mediation approach, and the 'structuralist' social justice approach. We have tentatively suggested that these correspond to attempts to address the 'attitude', 'behaviour' and 'contradiction' vertices of the conflict triangle. We have also noted criticism of all three approaches from a critical social theory perspective. Nevertheless, despite this diversity, quite a simple central commitment may still be said to prevail. Having grown in a number of centres through the pioneering work of a small group of individuals, the enterprise of conflict resolution is now conducted across an international network where scholars and practitioners from many countries share in the common objective of formulating, applying and testing structures and practices for preventing, managing, ending and transforming violent and destructive conflict. Conflict resolution does not prescribe specific solutions or end goals for society, beyond a commitment to the core assumption that aggressive win–lose styles of engagement in violent conflict usually incur costs that are not only unacceptably high for the conflict parties, but also for world society in general. This does not mean endorsing the status quo, since unjust and oppressive systems are seen as some of the chief sources of violence and war. What it does entail, as chapter 1 suggests, is a search for ways of transforming actually or potentially violent conflict into peaceful processes of political and social change. Whatever the differences and controversies within the conflict resolution field, this remains its defining goal.

In the next chapter we turn to an examination of the nature and sources of contemporary conflict. This will serve as an analytic foundation for the chapters that follow.

3

Understanding
Contemporary Conflict

Said the Teacher to his kinsman: 'what is all this quarrel about, Great King?'
'We do not know, Reverend Sir.'
'Who then would be likely to know?'
'The Commander-in-Chief of the army would be likely to know.'
The Commander-in-Chief of the army said, 'The Viceroy would be likely to know.'
Thus the Teacher put the question first to one and then to another, asking the slave labourers last of all. The slave labourers replied, 'The quarrel is about water, Sir.'
Then the Teacher asked the King, 'How much is water worth, Great King?'
'Very little, Reverend Sir.'
'How much are Khattiyas (warriors) worth, Great King?'
'Khattiyas are beyond price, Reverend Sir.'
'It is not fitting that because of a little water you should destroy Khattiyas who are beyond price.'

Dhammapada Commentary, Pali text: McConnell (1995)

Having introduced some of the main concepts in conflict resolution theory in chapter 1, and described the evolution of the field in chapter 2, we begin our survey of conflict resolution in the late twentieth century by looking at the way in which major armed conflict has been analysed within the conflict resolution tradition. Adequate conflict analysis – *polémologie*, to borrow the French terminology – has, from the start, been seen as the essential prerequisite for normative conflict resolution. This chapter, therefore, provides the necessary conceptual basis for those that follow.

Our starting point is the dataset of major deadly conflicts listed in table 1.3. In chapter 1, pp. 22–33, using this dataset, we commented upon contemporary conflict trends, distribution, types and costs. These statistically derived conclusions form the empirical basis from which our analysis begins. What are we to call these conflicts? Current terminology includes 'internal conflicts' (Brown, ed., 1996), 'new wars' (Kaldor and Vashee, eds, 1997), 'small wars' (Harding, 1994), 'civil wars' (King, 1997), 'ethnic conflicts' (Stavenhagen, 1996), 'conflict in post-colonial states' (van de Goor et al., eds, 1996) and so on, as well as varying expressions used by humanitarian and development NGOs and inter-national agencies, such as 'complex human emergencies' and 'complex political emergencies'. We have no particular quarrel with these or similar labels, though they all require some qualification. 'Internal conflicts', for example, often have external causes and attract outside interventions, and when states collapse the international system is affected: these are 'international-social conflicts'. As a more neutral, yet for our purposes more precise term, we prefer 'prevailing patterns of post-Cold War conflict' – or 'contemporary conflict' for short.

Theories and Frameworks

In chapter 1 we introduced some well-known theories of conflict from the conflict resolution tradition. These generic models are intended to apply, with variations, to all human conflicts and at all levels of conflict (from interpersonal level upwards). At the other end of the spectrum are a mass of specific political and historical explanations of particular conflicts. But at the intermediate level, between generic models and individual explana-tions, is it possible to find what John Vasquez calls a 'unified theory of conflict' (1995, 137), sufficient to account for the prevailing patterns of post-Cold War conflict with which we are concerned?

It seems unlikely on the face of it that a single all-encompassing explanation will be adequate for conflicts of different types with different starting points in forty-four countries that have different histories and cultures and are at different stages of economic and political development. Apart from anything else, since the time when systematic studies were first undertaken in the conflict resolution field, it has been recognized that there are apparently irreducible discrepancies between major schools of analysis, including, for example, the 'seven main approaches' listed by Paul Wehr in terms of the central propositions: that conflict is innate in social animals; that it is generated by the nature of societies and the way they are structured; that it is dysfunctional in social systems and a symptom of pathological strain; that it is functional in social systems and necessary for social development; that it is an inevitable feature of competing state interests in conditions of international anarchy; that it is a result of misperception, miscalculation and poor communication; that it is a natural process common to all societies (1979, 1–8). We have seen how some locate the sources of conflict in the nature of the protagonists (e.g., certain ethnological and anthropological theories), some in relations

---

BOX 3.1 Interpretations of the Northern Ireland conflict

1 The traditional nationalist interpretation: Britain v. Ireland

   The Irish people form a single nation and the fault for keeping Ireland divided lies with Britain.

2 The traditional unionist interpretation: Southern Ireland v. Northern Ireland

   There are two peoples in Ireland who have an equal right to self-determination, Protestant (unionist/loyalist) and Catholic (nationalist/republican), and the fault for perpetuating the conflict lies with the refusal of nationalists to recognize this.

3 Marxist interpretations: capitalist v. worker

   The cause of the conflict lies in the combination of an unresolved imperial legacy and the attempt by a governing capitalist class to keep the working class repressed and divided.

4 Internal-conflict interpretations: Protestant v. Catholic within Northern Ireland

   The cause of the conflict lies in the incompatibility between the aspirations of the two divided communities in Northern Ireland.

Source: from Whyte, 1990, 113–205

---

between conflict parties (e.g., certain theories in behavioural sociology and social psychology), and some in the conditioning contexts which structure the conflict and, in some versions, also generate the conflict parties themselves (e.g., certain neo-realist and Marxist theories).[1]

Moreover, different types of explanation are more often than not politically compromised, whether propounded by conflict protagonists or by third parties. This was the case during the Cold War,[2] and is a common feature of post-Cold War conflicts. For example, in box 3.1, we may note the discrepancy between third party relational interpretations of the Northern Ireland conflict such as the internal-conflict model, and the traditional nationalist and traditional unionist interpretations historically espoused by the main conflict parties. This also shows how neutral outside views, including academic theories of various kinds, can become as politically implicated in the struggle as any others.[3]

Nevertheless, there are explanations of conflict at the intermediate level which offer insight into contemporary conflict and help to situate it in the context of social and international conditions. Here, we will focus on the late Edward Azar's theory of 'protracted social conflict' (PSC) as an example of conflict resolution analysis from the late 1970s and 1980s, which anticipated much of the current preoccupation with the domestic social roots of conflict and failures of governance. We will then bring Azar's ideas up to date by relating them to the literature on the nature and sources of contemporary conflict through to 1997 by way of a proposed general framework for the analysis of prevailing patterns of post-Cold War conflict.

Edward Azar's Theory of Protracted Social Conflict (PSC)

In the view of Kalevi Holsti, wars of the late twentieth century 'are not about foreign policy, security, honor, or status; they are about statehood, governance, and the role and status of nations and communities within states' (1996, 20–1). It may seem strange, therefore, that '[u]ntil recently, international relations theorists and strategic studies analysts paid comparatively little attention to the causes, effects and international implications of ethnic and other forms of communal conflict' (Brown , ed., 1993, vii). In this section we would like to pay tribute to an analyst who was arguing in much this way twenty years ago, but whose pioneering work has received scant acknowledgement since then. We should point out that Azar's analysis of PSC was heavily indebted to others, notably John Burton with whom he co-published, but we will not try to disentangle credit for contributory ideas here. In order to explain and evaluate Azar's interpretation we need first to take note of the prevailing thinking in the period in which he developed it.

It has become popular in recent years for analysts to relate accounts of the evolution of modern warfare to accounts of the evolution of the modern state. The key qualitative turning points are seen to be, first, the emergence of the so-called sovereign dynastic state in Europe, heralded by Machiavelli, Bodin and Hobbes from the sixteenth and seventeenth centuries, second, the coming of the principle of popular sovereignty and national self-determination from the time of the American and French Revolutions, and, third, the bipolar stand-off at great power level after 1945. The first is associated with the domestic monopolization and reorganization of military force by sovereigns and its projection outwards to create the relatively formal patterns of early modern interstate warfare in place of previous more sporadic, localized and ill-disciplined manifestations of organized violence. The second heralded the transition to mass national armies and 'total war' accompanying the first industrial revolution and the romantic movement and reaching its climax in the First and Second World Wars. The advent of nuclear weapons and the military stand-off between the Soviet and Western blocs rendered major interstate war unviable (with a few exceptions at lower levels). Instead, the prevailing patterns of armed conflict in the 1950s and 1960 became wars of national independence associated with decolonization, and those of the 1970s and 1980s were post-colonial civil wars in which the great powers intervened as part of a continuing geopolitical struggle for power and influence (Howard, 1976; Giddens, 1987; Keegan, 1993). For this reason Edward Rice (1988) has called the prevailing pattern of post-1945 wars 'wars of the third kind' (in contrast to the two earlier Clausewitzean phases), a term subsequently endorsed by Holsti (1996) and others. These are conflicts in which communities seek to create their own states in wars of 'national liberation', or which 'involve resistance by various peoples against domination, exclusion, persecution, or dispossession of lands and resources, by the post-colonial state' (Holsti, 1996, 27).

Some detect a further evolution in prevailing patterns of conflict in the 1990s – as it were, a third phase of 'wars of the third kind', namely a pattern of post-Cold War conflict which is seen to bear little resemblance to European wars in the era of the dynastic state or to the 'total wars' of the first half of the twentieth century. If anything, they resemble earlier medieval wars in their lack of differentiation between state and society, soldier and civilian, internal and external transactions across frontiers, war and organized crime (van Creveld, 1991). Mary Kaldor characterizes these 'new wars' in terms of: political goals (no longer the foreign policy interests of states, but the consolidation of new forms of power based on ethnic homogeneity); ideologies (no longer universal principles such as democracy, fascism or socialism, but tribalist and communalist identity politics); forms of mobilization (no longer conscription or appeals to patriotism, but fear, corruption, religion, magic and the media); external support (no longer superpowers or ex-colonial powers, but diaspora, foreign mercenaries, criminal mafia, regional powers); mode of warfare (no longer formal and organized campaigns with demarcated front-lines, bases and heavy weapons, but fragmented and dispersed, involving para-military and criminal groups, child soldiers, light weapons, and the use of atrocity, famine, rape and siege); and the war economy (no longer funded by taxation and generated by state mobilization, but sustained by outside emergency assistance and the parallel economy including unofficial export of timber and precious metals, drug-trafficking, criminal rackets, plunder) (Kaldor and Vashee, eds, 1997, 7–19).

In fact, both Kaldor and Holsti follow Rice in suggesting that the key turning point in all this was not so much 1989 or 1990, as 1945. For Kaldor '[f]ew conflicts since 1945 have corresponded to the Clause-witzean model' (1997, 3), while for Holsti:

[T]he problem is that the Clausewitzean image of war, as well as its theoretical accoutrements, has become increasingly divorced from the characteristics and sources of most armed conflicts since 1945. The key question is: given that most wars since 1945 have been *within* states, of what intellectual and policy relevance are concepts and practices derived from the European and Cold War experiences that diagnosed or prescribed solutions for the problem of war *between* states? (*1996, 14; italics in the original*)

This suggestion that the whole paraphernalia of the mainstream analysis of interstate war, the great bulk of which has been produced since 1945, has been largely irrelevant to the actuality of most post-1945 conflict is sweeping. Entire tracts of quantitative research over the postwar decades have been devoted to the search for correlates of interstate war which might give a clue to its sources and nature. Analysts have sought to align measurable features of interstate and related wars, such as its incidence, frequency, duration, magnitude, severity, intensity and costs, with empirically verifiable variables, such as structures (e.g., whether the hegemonic system is unipolar, bipolar, multipolar), relations (e.g., patterns of alliances, distribution of relative capabilities, configurations of power and power transition, arms races), national attributes (e.g., levels of domestic unrest, types of domestic regime, levels of economic development), and other aspects of what Mansbach and Vasquez (1981) call the 'paths to war' (e.g., the positive expected utility for decision-makers in initiating hostilities).[4] This vast enterprise has produced mixed results.[5] But is it possible that, in terms of prevailing patterns of post-1945 conflict, most international relations and strategic studies experts were looking in the wrong direction? Could it be that, mesmerized by the bipolar stand-off at great power level, analysts subsumed both decolonizing wars of national liberation and post-colonial civil wars into traditional Europeanized conceptual categories, failing to notice the qualitative change that had taken place when prevailing patterns of major armed conflict ceased being intra-European interstate wars after 1945? And was it only with the collapse of the Soviet Union that analysts belatedly realized that the 'new' patterns of post-Cold War conflict were in fact not so new, but had been prevalent, albeit under different geopolitical conditions, for nearly half a century?

We do not want to pronounce on these large questions here, beyond noting that this is the context within which Azar's work should be evaluated, because he had been arguing for a radical revision of prevailing Clausewitzean ideas since the 1970s. It should be acknowledged, however, that, even if it is accepted that 'wars of the third kind' have been prevalent since 1945, the post-Cold War phase is different from what has gone before if only because superpower rivalries no longer structure and partially shape them. For this reason, although some conflicts may have been formally brought to an end over the past decade by the withdrawal of outside support for war parties and pressure for peace settlements (see chapters 6 and 7), others have flared up, changed character or become more chaotic in the subsequent power vacuum (Rufin, 1993, 112–13). The former may be seen as the tail end of the phase of post-colonial civil wars fuelled by superpower rivalries and ideology; the latter as a further phase of post-Cold War conflict associated with regional instability, political fragmentation and fragile state structures. During the 1950s and 1960s decolonizing wars of national liberation were mainly nationalist and ideological in character, often characterized by relatively disciplined national liberation forces (such as the Vietcong), and, although often hitting civilians hard, rarely targeting them in the ethnic-cleansing or predatory way seen latterly in former Yugoslavia, Algeria or Sierra Leone. In the 1970s and 1980s, when the main wave of decolonization was largely over, there was a gradual shift to post-colonial civil wars with the emergence of internal wars in successor states, a pattern recognized by analysts such as Moore at the time, who distinguished six categories of prevailing internal war: non-authority-oriented, anti-colonial, secessionist, indigenous control of authority structures, external imposition of authority structures, and Cold War sponsored (1972). Only anti-colonial and Cold War sponsored conflicts have since dropped out of this list: the rest still constitutes quite a reasonable typology for major armed conflict in the 1990s.

A marked increase in the number of refugees in the 1970s was another indicator of changing patterns of conflict which is still prevalent and has since accelerated. Moore distinguished international wars, civil wars and mixed civil-international wars, and noted how 'since World War II civil wars and mixed civil-international conflicts have replaced the more conventional international wars as the principal forms of violence in the international system' (1974). In short, a number of features of the 'new wars' of the 1990s were already evident from the 1970s. Nevertheless, throughout this period there were still Clausewitzean wars going on (between India and Pakistan, Israel and her neighbours, China and Vietnam, Iraq and Iran), 'mixed civil-international wars' were largely structured by Cold War geopolitics, and at great power level the two main alliances were still strenuously preparing for the possibility, if not likelihood, of a thoroughly Clausewitzean military encounter, despite the nuclear stalemate. It was the latter which largely preoccupied international relations and strategic studies analysts at the time, so that the reconceptualization of prevailing patterns of conflict offered by Azar and other conflict resolution analysts was hardly noticed in the conventional literature.

For Edward Azar, in a sustained sequence of studies published from the late 1970s, the critical factor in protracted social conflict (PSC), such as persisted in Lebanon (his own particular field of study), Sri Lanka, the Philippines, Northern Ireland, Ethiopia, Israel, Sudan, Cyprus, Iran, Nigeria or South Africa, was that it represented 'the prolonged and often violent struggle by communal groups for such basic needs as security, recognition and acceptance, fair access to political institutions and economic participation' (1991, 93). Traditional preoccupation with relations between states was seen to have obscured a proper understanding of these dynamics. Indeed, in radical contrast to the concerns of international law, the distinction between domestic and international politics was rejected as 'artificial': 'there is really only one social environment and its domestic face is the more compelling' (Azar and Burton, 1986, 33). The role of the state (as also linkages with other states) was to satisfy or frustrate basic communal needs, thus preventing or promoting conflict (Azar, 1990, 10–12).

Drawing upon datasets of PSC compiled at the University of Maryland from the mid-1970s, with an original main base conflict set for the period 1978–84, Azar systematically developed and refined his understanding of the dynamics which generated violent and persistent conflict of this kind (see Azar et al., 1978; Azar and Cohen, 1981; Azar, 1986). At the time of his last writings in the early 1990s he identified more than sixty examples of this 'new type of conflict', which, 'distinct from traditional disputes over territory, economic resources, or East-West rivalry ... revolves around questions of communal identity' (1991, 93). In the opening chapter of what is perhaps his most succinct summation of a decade and a half's work, *The Management of Protracted Social Conflict: Theory and Cases* (1990), Azar contrasts three aspects of what up until then had been a prevailing orthodoxy in war studies with his own approach. First, there had been a tendency 'to understand conflicts through a rather rigid dichotomy of internal and external dimensions' with sociologists, anthropologists and psychologists preoccupied with the former ('civil wars, insurgencies, revolts, coups, protests, riots, revolutions etc.') and international relations scholars with the latter ('interstate wars, crises, invasions, border conflicts, blockades, etc.'). Second, prevailing frameworks of analysis had often been based on the functional differentiation of conflict aspects and types into sub-categories of psychological, social, political, economic and military conflicts, and into different 'levels of analysis'. Third, there had been a tendency to focus on overt and violent conflict while ignoring covert, latent or non-violent conflict, and on an approach to conflict dynamics in terms of conflict cycles in which the 'termination of violent acts is often equated with the state of peace'. In contrast, a study of PSC suggested that:

> many conflicts currently active in the underdeveloped parts of the world are characterized by a blurred demarcation between internal and external sources and actors. Moreover, there are multiple causal factors and dynamics, reflected in changing goals, actors and targets. Finally, these conflicts do not show clear starting and terminating points. (*p. 6*)

The term PSC emphasized that the sources of such conflicts lay predominantly within rather than between states, with four clusters of variables identified as preconditions for their transformation to high levels of intensity.

First, there was the 'communal content', the fact that the 'most useful unit of analysis in PSC situations is the identity group – racial, religious, ethnic, cultural and others' (Azar, 1986, 31). In contrast to the well-known 'levels of analysis' framework popularized by Kenneth Waltz (1959), which in its classic form distinguished system, state and individual levels, PSC analysis focuses in the first instance on identity groups, however defined, noting that it is the relationship between identity groups and states which is at the core of the problem (what Azar called the 'disarticulation between the state and society as a whole', 1990, 7), and that individual interests and needs are mediated through membership of social groups ('what is of concern are the *societal needs* of the individual – security, identity, recognition and others', 1986, 31). Azar links the disjunction between state and society in many parts of the world to a colonial legacy which artificially imposed European ideas of territorial statehood onto 'a multitude of communal groups' on the principle of 'divide and rule'. As a result, in many post-colonial multicommunal societies the state machinery comes to be 'dominated by a single communal group or a coalition of a few communal groups that are unresponsive to the needs of other groups in the society', which 'strains the social fabric and eventually breeds fragmentation and protracted social conflict' (1990, 7). As to the formation of identity groups themselves, as noted in chapter 2, Azar, like other conflict resolution theorists, drew on a rich tradition of research in social psychology and social anthropology to sketch the various ways in which individual needs come to be mediated and articulated through processes of socialization and group identity, themselves culturally conditioned (Lewin, 1948; Kelly, 1955; Sherif, 1966; Tajfel, 1978; Deutsch, 1973).

Second, following other conflict resolution analysts as described in earlier chapters, Azar identified deprivation of human needs as the underlying source of PSC ('Grievances resulting from need deprivation are usually expressed collectively. Failure to redress these grievances by the authority cultivates a niche for a protracted social conflict', 1990, 9). Unlike interests, needs are ontological and non-negotiable, so that, if conflict comes, it is likely to be intense, vicious and, from a traditional Clausewitzean perspective, 'irrational'. In particular, Azar cites security needs, development needs, political access needs, and identity needs (cultural and religious expression), the first three corresponding to Henry Shue's three 'basic rights' of security, subsistence and freedom (Shue, 1980). Arguing for a broader understanding of 'security' than was usual in academic circles at the time, Azar linked this to an equally broad understanding of 'development' and 'political access':

> Reducing overt conflict requires reduction in levels of underdevelopment. Groups which seek to satisfy their identity and security needs through conflict are in effect seeking change in the structure of their society. Conflict resolution can truly occur and last if satisfactory amelioration of underdevelopment occurs as well. Studying protracted conflict leads one to conclude that peace is development in the broadest sense of the term. (*1990, 155*)

Third, in a world in which the state has been 'endowed with authority to govern and use force where necessary to regulate society, to protect citizens, and to provide collective goods', Azar cited 'governance and the state's role' as the critical factor in the satisfaction or frustration of individual and identity group needs: 'Most states which experience protracted social conflict tend to be characterised by incompetent, parochial, fragile, and authoritarian governments that fail to satisfy basic human needs' (1990, 10). Here, he made three main points. Whereas in western liberal theory the state 'is an aggregate of individuals entrusted to govern effectively and to act as an impartial arbiter of conflicts among the constituent parts', treating all members of the political community as legally equal citizens, this is not empirically what happens in most parts of the world, particularly in newer and less stable states where political authority 'tends to be monopolized by the dominant identity group or a coalition of hegemonic groups' which use the state to maximize their interests at the expense of others. Both through the mobilization of group interests and identities by ruling elites, and through the reactive counter-identification of excluded 'minorities' the 'communal content of the state' becomes basic to the study of PSC. Next, the monopolizing of power by dominant individuals and groups and the limiting of access to other groups precipitates a 'crisis of legitimacy', so that 'regime type and the level of legitimacy' come to be seen as 'important linkage variables between needs and protracted social conflict'. Finally, Azar notes how PSCs tend to be concentrated in developing countries which are typically characterized by 'rapid population growth and limited resource base' and also have restricted 'political capacity' often linked to a colonial legacy of weak participatory institutions, a hierarchical tradition of imposed bureaucratic rule from metropolitan centres, and inherited instruments of political repression: 'In most protracted social conflict-laden countries, political capacity is limited by a rigid or fragile authority structure which prevents the state from responding to, and meeting, the needs of various constituents'.

Finally, there is the role of what Azar called 'international linkages', in particular political-economic relations of economic dependency within the international economic system, and the network of political-military linkages constituting regional and global patterns of clientage and cross-border interest. Modern states, particularly weak states, are porous to the international forces operating within the wider global community: the '[f]ormation of domestic social and political institutions and their impact on the role of the state are greatly influenced by the patterns of linkage within the international system' (1990, 11).

Whether or not in any one case these four clusters of preconditions for PSC in the event activate overt conflict will depend upon the more contingent actions and events of 'process dynamics', which Azar analyses into three groups of determinants: 'communal actions and strategies', 'state actions and strategies' and 'built-in mechanisms of conflict' (1990,

12–15). The first of these involves the various processes of identity group formation, organization and mobilization, the emergence and nature of leadership, the choice of political goals (access, autonomy, secession, revolutionary political programme) and tactics (civil disobedience, guerrilla war), and the scope and nature of external ties. State actions and strategies form the second main element, with governing individuals and elites at any one time theoretically facing an array of policy choices running from different forms of political accommodation at one end of the spectrum to 'coercive repression' or 'instrumental co-option' at the other. In Azar's view, given the perceived political and economic costs involved in weak and fragmented polities and because of the 'winner-takes-all' norm 'which still prevails in multicommunal societies', it is much more likely to be repression than accommodation. Finally, there are the various self-reinforcing 'built-in mechanisms of conflict', exhaustively studied by conflict resolution analysts once the malign spiral of conflict escalation is triggered. In chapter 1 we related these to the 'conflict triangle' (see figure 1.6):

> A contradiction [C] may be experienced as a *frustration*, where a goal is being blocked by something, leading to aggressiveness as an attitude [A] and to aggressive behavior [B] ... Aggressive behavior may be incompatible with the other party's concept of happiness ... leading to a new contradiction on top of the old one, possibly stimulating more aggressiveness and aggression in all parties concerned. Violence breeds violence, the triangle becomes the projection of a spiral that may run its course the same way as a fire: stopping when the house is burnt down. (*Galtung, 1996, 72*)

Azar draws on the work of Sumner (1906), Gurr (1970), Mitchell (1981) and others to trace the process by which mutually exclusionary 'experiences, fears and belief systems' generate 'reciprocal negative images which perpetuate communal antagonisms and solidify protracted social conflict'. Antagonistic group histories, exclusionist myths, demonizing propaganda and dehumanizing ideologies serve to justify discriminatory policies and legitimize atrocities. In these circumstances, in a dynamic familiar to students of international relations as the 'security dilemma', actions are mutually interpreted in the most threatening light, 'the worst motivations tend to be attributed to the other side', the space for compromise and accommodation shrinks and 'proposals for political solutions become rare, and tend to be perceived on all sides as mechanisms for gaining relative power and control' (1990, 15). All of this intensifies further as political crisis spirals into war, where new vested interests emerge dependent upon the political economy of the war itself, the most violent and unruly elements in society appear in leadership roles and criminality becomes a political norm. At the limit, disintegration follows. With sustained attrition, political structures buckle and collapse, creating a social implosion which subsequently sucks everything else in.

Table 3.1   Azar's preconditions for protracted social conflict (PSC)

Relevant discipline	Preconditions for PSC	Correlates
Anthropology, history, sociology	Communal content	Degree of ethnic heterogeneity
Psychology, biology, development studies	Needs	Levels of human development
Politics, political economy	Governance	Scales of political repression
International relations, strategic studies	International linkages	Volume of arms exports and imports

Azar saw PSC analysis as an attempt to 'synthesize the realist and structuralist paradigms into a pluralist framework' more suitable for explaining prevalent patterns of conflict than the more limited alternatives (1991, 95). We are not claiming here that Azar's analysis is the last word on the subject, nor that he was alone in pointing to the significance of mobilized identities, exclusionist ideologies, fragile and authoritarian governance, and disputed sovereignty as chief sources of major armed conflict. We contend only that his approach anticipated many aspects of what has since become orthodoxy, and that his ideas deserve more recognition than they have been given.

In terms of correlates of war, Azar's ideas can also be seen to offer a framework for the analysis of prevailing patterns of non-interstate war. For example, in one study, where 113 instances of civil wars, crises and state failures were checked against a list of 75 political, leadership, demographic, social, economic and environmental factors, three elements in particular were seen to be associated with the highest correlations: the size of the infant mortality rate, the level of development of democratic institutions and processes, and the extent of trade with neighbouring states (Esty et al., 1995). These correspond to the second, third and fourth of Azar's four preconditions for PSC. Taking the same four preconditions in order, others (Miall, 1991; UNDP, 1996; PIOOM, 1997; Ploughshares, 1995) have similarly attempted to test correlations between the incidence of non-interstate conflict and quantitatively measurable variables, such as those shown in table 3.1. Such statistical studies of non-interstate war are still in their infancy, but Azar's model offers a hopeful beginning.

Table 3.2 Sources of contemporary conflict: a framework

Level	Example
Global	Geopolitical transition, North–South divide
Regional	Clientage patterns, cross-border social demography
State	
social	Weak society: cultural divisions, ethnic imbalance
economic	Weak economy: poor resource base, relative deprivation
political	Weak polity: partisan government, regime illegitimacy
Conflict party	Group mobilization, inter-group dynamics
Elite/individual	Exclusionist policies, factional interest, rapacious leadership

Sources of Contemporary International-Social Conflict

A survey of the literature on contemporary conflict analysis written since Azar's death suggests that there is a considerable difference of opinion on how to set about the task. This can be illustrated with reference to works published in 1996 and to the array of different analytical frameworks employed. For example, referring to interstate war, Levy (1996) uses a traditional 'levels-of-analysis' approach in his review of 'contending theories of international conflict'; and Suganami (1996) uses a 'levels-of-causation' model in his analysis of the causes of war. Van de Goor et al. (1996) base their 'enquiry into the causes of conflict in post-colonial states' on a fourfold functional or sectoral model reminiscent of Azar. Ramsbotham and Woodhouse (1996) use a 'dimensions-of-conflict' approach, which distinguishes structural, relational and cultural features. Here, we suggest that an adapted 'levels-of-analysis' approach offers an acceptable overall framework for the explanation of contemporary conflict, inasmuch as it lays bare the complex and controversial relationships between international, state and societal sources of conflict, all of which are prominent in the recent literature and none of which is reducible to the others. Adapting Azar's terminology, we refer to these as 'international social conflicts' (ISCs), that is conflicts that are neither pure international (interstate) conflicts, nor pure social (domestic) conflicts, but sprawl somewhere between the two. The framework can also be seen as a location for different theoretical explanations (see table 3.2). Azar's 'international linkages' can be recognized at global and regional levels, his 'communal content', 'deprivation of needs' and 'governance' at state level (social, economic, political), and his 'process dynamics' at conflict party and elite/individual levels.

Global sources of contemporary conflict

Azar, as we have noted, saw 'international linkages' as one of the four main clusters of variables making PSC likely, as well as playing a key role in the 'process dynamics' of conflict escalation. What he did not address directly, not surprisingly given the period during which most of his seminal work was done, was the whole discourse of globalization and its connection with prevailing patterns of contemporary conflict. Clearly, this is a vast and contested subject. We will return briefly to the question of the relationship between states and the twin pressures of international globalization and social domestic resistance (fragmentation) under the section 'The role of the state' below. Here, we simply note how a number of analysts locate the sources of contemporary conflict at global level and regard particular conflicts as local manifestations of systemic processes. Two main points are made.

First, much of the turbulence in Africa, the Balkans and along the borders of the former Soviet Union in the 1990s is attributed to the end of the Cold War. Although some conflicts which had been fuelled by East–West rivalry were wound down (see chapters 6 and 7), others were precipitated, as authoritarian systems were weakened by the withdrawal of external subsidies and support, and international financial pressures for economic and political liberalization intensified. As many commentators have observed, periods of transition tend to be unstable. Moreover, with the ending of the Cold War the rules and boundaries of the old order were rescinded, and it was not clear where the new ones lay. Political interests of all kinds were testing the limits of the new system: 'More than anything else, it is the uncertainty following the passing of the old order that allows conflict to break out with such abandon at the end of the millennium' (Zartman, 1997, 6). These global pressures exposed fundamental weaknesses of post-colonial states in many areas, and contributed to a crisis of the state, of which contemporary conflicts have been a symptom.

Second, there are analyses of the systemic sources of conflict themselves. Setting aside the 'clash of civilizations' hypothesis which predicts future conflict across the fault lines between civilizations and, in particular, a geopolitical struggle between 'the West and the rest' (Huntington, 1997), the main focus is on three interlinked trends: deep and enduring inequalities in the global distribution of wealth and economic power;[6] human-induced environmental constraints exacerbated by excessive energy consumption in the developed world and population growth in the undeveloped world, making it difficult for human well-being to be improved by conventional economic growth; and continuing militariza-

BOX 3.2   Arms exports and conflict

Some $176 billions-worth of weaponry was exported to the Third World between 1987 and 1991. Keith Krause notes three theoretical models of the relation between arms exports and conflict, each of which carries a different policy prescription. Weapon availability can be seen as: an independent variable causing conflict, a dependent variable following conflict, or an intervening variable acting as a catalyst in conflicts caused by deeper factors. He favours the third alternative (Krause, 1996). Whichever view is taken, the belated arms embargoes placed by major weapons suppliers on countries like Somalia (January 1992) or Liberia (November 1992) when violent conflict finally erupts seems at best inadequate, at worst hypocritical.

In fact, many post-Cold War conflicts have been fought with small arms rather than heavy weapons (Boutwell et al., eds, 1995). Moreover, the recipients have increasingly been sub-state groups (Karp, 1994). On one estimate, the trade in small arms has been worth some $10 billion a year (*The Economist*, 12 February 1994, 19–21). Indeed, in many cases, as in Rwanda in 1994, the worst massacres have been perpetrated with machetes.

tion of security relations, including the further proliferation of lethal weaponry (Rogers and Ramsbotham, 1999). As a result, 'the combination of wealth–poverty disparities and limits to growth is likely to lead to a crisis of unsatisfied expectations within an increasingly informed global majority of the disempowered'. The probable outcome of this, argues Homer-Dixon, will be three kinds of conflict: scarcity conflicts mainly at interstate level over oil, water, fish, land; group-identity conflict exacerbated by large-scale population movements; and relative-deprivation conflicts mainly at domestic level as the gap between expectation and achievement widens (Homer-Dixon, 1995). With the demise of the second world after the collapse of the Soviet bloc, the first and third worlds are seen to be confronting each other all the more starkly (Chubin, 1993). This is said to be already evident in voting patterns in the UN General Assembly (Kim and Russett, 1996). At the moment one-seventh of the world's population controls three-quarters of its wealth, and three-quarters of humanity live in developing countries, a proportion likely to go on rising:

> Were all humanity a single nation-state, the present North–South divide would make it an unviable, semi-feudal entity, split by internal conflicts. Its small part is advanced, prosperous, powerful; its much bigger part is under-developed, poor, powerless. A nation so divided within itself would be

Table 3.3   Major deadly conflicts by region and type, in progress
1995–7

	Interstate	*Revolution/ ideology*	*Identity/ secession*	*Factional*	*Total*
Africa	0	3	8	2	13
Asia	0	4	10	2	16
Europe	0	0	7	1	8
Latin America	0	3	0	1	4
Middle East	0	3	4	0	7

Source: Authors' classification of table 1.3

recognized as unstable. A world so divided within itself should likewise be recognized as inherently unstable. And the position is worsening, not improving. (*South Commission, 1990, quoted in Peck, 1998, 10*)

Grandiose global-level conflict theories of this kind are impressive but difficult to substantiate in particular cases. Nevertheless, predictions of a coming generation of conflicts fuelled by global economic turbulence, environmental deterioration, North–South (and other) political tensions, weapons proliferation and international crime impacting on 'weak states' seem ominously persuasive. As traditional patterns of authority and order are weakened, exclusionist policies allied to ethnic and religious identities emerge as alternative sources of loyalty (Darby, 1998, 4). It is worth noting here that, once again, much of this can be seen to have been foreshadowed in the 1970s and 1980s, when the same phenomena that were bringing stability to 'zones of peace' in the North and West – strong nationally based states, liberal trading economies, international inter-dependence, new phases of globalization – were bringing instability and war to areas in the third world where western-type states were ill-adapted, where contact with the international economy brought mal-development and economic dislocation, and where fragile states were struggling for survival or becoming prizes for competing armed groups.

Regional sources of contemporary conflict

The end of the Cold War and the regionalization of world politics have highlighted the importance of the regional level of explanation.

Our data in table 1.3, when classified by the typology in table 1.4, show clear regional differences in contemporary conflicts (see tables 3.3 and

Table 3.4   Major deadly conflicts by region and start date, in progress
1995–7

Start dates of contemporary conflicts

Africa	1966, 1973, 1975, 1983, 1989, 1989, 1990, 1991, 1992, 1993, 1993, 1994, 1996
Asia	1948, 1968, 1975, 1975, 1978, 1979, 1981, 1982, 1983, 1984, 1986, 1989, 1990, 1992, 1992, 1997
Europe	1964, 1969, 1991, 1991, 1991, 1992, 1992, 1997
Latin America	1964, 1968, 1980, 1994
Middle East	1948, 1976, 1979, 1980, 1983, 1992, 1992

Source: Authors' classification of table 1.3

3.4). Confirming the Uppsala pattern (table 1.5), none of the conflicts in
Latin America was over identity/secession, while all of those in Europe
(bar the Albanian rebellion) were. In Latin America the dates for the
origins of conflicts do not cluster together, and in both Latin America and
Asia the starting date of most of the conflicts still under way precedes the
end of the Cold War. In Europe and Africa, however, there are distinct
clusters of conflict with close start dates in the post-Cold War period,
suggesting a process of regional overspill or diffusion in these regions.
Moreover, in both continents the clusters are of type 3 identity/secession
conflicts. Previous studies of pre-1989 conflicts have also found evidence
of regional diffusion (Geller and Singer, 1998, 105–8), but because of
incommensurable datasets we are unable to assess whether this effect has
grown stronger after 1989. We can identify a number of regions where
fighting has spilled over from one area to another, or where a common
precipitating factor has generated violent conflicts in a vulnerable area, for
example: the Great Lakes area of Africa (identity/secession conflicts and
refugee movements); West Africa (factional conflicts following the breakdown of post-colonial states); the Caucasus (identity/secession conflicts
following the collapse of the Soviet Union); Central Asia (identity/
secession and factional conflicts following the collapse of the Soviet
Union).

The regional effects are both outwards – 'spill-over', 'contagion', 'diffusion' – and inwards – 'influence', 'interference', 'intervention' (Lake and
Rothchild, eds, 1997). Internal wars have external effects on the region,
resulting from the spread of weaponry, economic dislocation, links with
terrorism and disruptive floods of refugees, and spill over into regional
politics when neighbouring states are dragged in or when one ethnic
group straddles several states. Conversely, regional instability affects the
internal politics of states through patterns of clientage, the actions of

---

BOX 3.3   A regional pattern of conflict interventions

A number of Tutsi exiles from Rwanda helped President Museveni of Uganda in his successful bid for power, were integrated into the Ugandan army after 1986, and subsequently defected with their weapons to the mainly Tutsi-led Rwanda Patriotic Front forces which eventually seized control of Rwanda in 1994. This led to a consolidation of Tutsi control in Burundi and, in the autumn of 1996, to cross-border action in what was then Zaire against the Hutu militia responsible for the 1994 Rwanda massacres, who were being sheltered by President Mobutu. With enthusiastic backing from the Zairean Tutsi Banyamulenge, who had been discriminated against by Mobutu's Western Zairean-based regime, this swelled into concerted military support for Laurent Kabila in his march on Kinshasa and eventual deposition of Mobutu. This in turn had a knock-on effect in Angola by depriving UNITA's (the National Union for the Total Independence of Angola) Jonas Savimbi of Mobutu's support, and encouraging the sending in of Angolan troops to Congo-Brazzaville to help reinstall Denis Sassou-Nguesso as President in October 1997. Meanwhile, similar incursions were beginning to tip the scale in the long-standing conflict in Sudan. In 1998 renewed fighting in former Zaire threatened further inter-nationalization of the conflict, as Angola, Namibia and Zimbabwe were drawn in on the side of Kabila, and Rwanda and Uganda on the side of the rebels.

---

outside governments, cross-border movements of people and ideas, black market activities, criminal networks and the spread of small arms. In some cases the challenge to an incumbent government may be almost entirely initiated from outside, as when Rhodesia set up Resistência Nacional Moçambicana (RENAMO) in Mozambique after 1975. In others there may be a more complex pattern of causes and effects, as in the Great Lakes region (see box 3.3). There are also evident sources of regional conflict where river basins extend across state boundaries (Gleick, 1995),[7] or where a regional mismatch between state borders and the distribution of peoples (usually as a result of the perpetuation of former colonial boundaries) lays states open to the destabilizing effects of large-scale population movements (Gurr, 1993; Gurr and Harff, 1994).

On the other hand, regional security arrangements and regional integration can contribute to the containment and limitation of internal conflicts. Cross-border cooperation and the reduced significance of borders has clearly had this effect in Europe. Latin America, as Holsti (1996, 150–82) has pointed out, has had very few interstate wars or armed conflicts over secession, a phenomenon he attributes to the strength of the

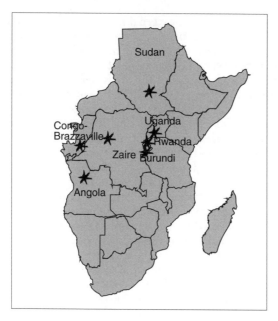

Map 2 Regional conflicts in Africa: spillover effects

state. Elsewhere, as in South-East Asia, regional security arrangements have (for better or worse) dampened interstate instability for many years through the non-intervention principle, while allowing governments to continue to suppress internal insurrections, as in East Timor. Whether this state of affairs will survive the economic shock-waves in the region and the consequent pressures on minorities and migration remains to be seen.

Others attribute the contrast between zones of war and zones of peace to the stability of power structures in the various regions. Barry Buzan and his associates studied 'regional security complexes' in the 1980s (that is, groups of states with interconnected security concerns). They found a spectrum ranging from regions in turmoil (marked by numerous conflict formations), through security regimes (where member states remain potential threats to each other but have reduced mutual insecurity by formal and informal arrangements), to pluralistic security communities (where member states no longer feel that they need to make serious provision for a mutual use of force against each other). They located the main determinants of regional stability in interstate factors: the number of state players within a given security complex, the patterns of amity and hostility and the distributions of power (Buzan, 1991, chapter 5). Change within a security complex could thus be measured in terms of four quite simple structural parameters: the maintenance of the status quo, internal change within the complex, external boundary change (states entering or leaving the complex) and 'overlay' – the dominant intrusion of an outside power. As with almost all classical or neoclassical approaches in the security field, however, the theory has been substantially adapted in the 1990s in an attempt to account for the wider range of determinants now seen to be relevant (Buzan et al., 1997). In particular: the emphasis on the military and political sectors has been expanded to include environmental, economic and societal sectors (introducing the concept of cross-sectoral heterogeneous security complexes); local causes are seen to have global effects and vice versa; states are no longer regarded as necessarily the main referents with 'societal security' introduced as a major theme (1997, chapter 6); and 'microregions' are recognized as sub-units within the boundaries of a state. The concept of security itself is taken to be intersubjective and socially constructed (1997, chapter 2). It remains to be seen whether greater sophistication has been bought at the expense of conceptual clarity and predictive power.

The global and regional levels together comprise the international dimension of contemporary conflict. Azar was right to call the distinction between international and domestic-social politics 'artificial' in these cases. International sources impacting on weak states have a dynamic effect on internal politics; internal sources of conflict have international repercussions when they escalate to the point that they become a crisis of the state. Either way, it is at state level that international-social conflict is defined as such.

The role of the state

At this point we move from a consideration of contextual factors at international level to structural factors at state level. Here we agree with Azar that, at whatever level the main sources of contemporary conflict may be seen to reside, it is at the level of the state that the critical struggle is, in the end, played out. Despite predictions of the 'end of the state' under the twin pressures of globalization and what Richard Falk calls 'the local realities of community and sentiment' (1985, 690), the state is nevertheless seen to remain 'the primary locus of identity for most people' (Kennedy, 1993, 134). Ian Clark agrees that it is still the key mediator in the continuously oscillating balance between forces of globalization – 'increasingly potent international pressures' – and fragmentation – 'the heightened levels of domestic discontent that will inevitably be brought in their wake' – (1997, 202). Given the juridical monopoly on sovereignty still formally accorded to the state within the current international system, all conflict parties are in the end, in any case, driven to compete for state control if they want to institute revolutionary programmes (type 2 conflict), safeguard communal needs (type 3 conflict) or merely secure factional interests (type 4 conflict). Even in 'failed' states this still remains the prize for the warring elements. Unlike classic interstate wars, or lower levels of domestic unrest, therefore, the major deadly conflicts with which this book deals are defined as such through their becoming integral crises of the state itself, problematically cast as it still is as chief actor on the international stage and chief satisfier of domestic needs.

At state level it may seem that Azar parts company with a number of contemporary conflict analysts. Although issues of state legitimacy and governance were central to his analysis of PSC, he viewed the post-Westphalian state as more part of the problem than the solution: 'Since Westphalia, nation-states have been legal fictions of the international system. They perpetuate the myth of sovereignty and independence as instruments of control' (1986, 32). A number of other scholars writing at the same time, such as Anthony Smith, agreed that there was 'an inherent instability in the very concept of the nation, which appears to be driven, as it were, back and forth between the two poles of *ethnie* [community/people] and state which it seeks to subsume and transcend', a task which few of today's nations have succeeded in doing (Smith, 1986, 150). Robert Jackson has made a similar point about ex-colonial states which 'have been internationally enfranchised and possess the same external rights and responsibilities as all other sovereign states: juridical statehood', but at the same time 'have not been authorised and empowered democratically and consequently lack the institutional features of sovereign states' (1990, 21). Following Bull and Watson (1984, 430), Jackson called these 'quasi-states', while Buzan (1991) referred to them as 'weak states'.[8] Azar went further, however, and concluded that, since in PSCs 'highly centralized political structures are sources of conflict' because they 'reduce the opportunity for a sense of community among groups', increase alienation and 'tend to deny to groups the means to accomplish their needs', the solution was to hasten the demise of the centralized sovereign state and foster decentralized political systems: 'For conflicts to be enduringly resolved, appropriate decentralized structures are needed', designed to 'serve the psychological, economic and relational needs of groups and individuals within nation-states' (1986, 33–4). Here, Azar appears to be at odds with the recommendations of analysts such as Holsti, who have concluded that, on the contrary, the best solution to the problem is 'the strengthening of states' (1996, xii). The discrepancy may not be as stark as it at first appears, however, since Holsti agrees with Azar that 'vertical legitimacy' (political consensus between governors and governed about the institutional 'rules of the game') and 'horizontal legitimacy' (inclusive political community in which all individuals and groups have equal access to decisions and allocations) are what ultimately underpin 'the strength of states' (Holsti, 1996, 82–98).

Among those analysts who locate the key sources of contemporary conflict at state level, emphasis varies in the relative weight given to social, economic and political factors. In the social sphere there seems to be some agreement with Azar's general proposition that 'weak societies' (his 'disarticulation between state and society') are associated with the prevalence of conflict, particularly in heterogeneous states where no overarching tradition of common and juridically egalitarian citizenship prevails. But there is little agreement about the psycho-social underpinnings of contemporary conflict in general. The debate between those who emphasize the 'vertical' (ethnic) roots of conflict and those who emphasize the 'horizontal' (class) roots (Munck, 1986) has been further complicated by the advent of other revolutionary ideologies such as Islamist and Hindu nationalist movements. On the other hand, others again have noted the inadequacy of western preoccupations with class and ethnicity in determining the social roots of conflict in parts of the world, such as Africa, where social life 'revolves, in the first instance, around a medley of more compact organizations, networks, groupings, associations, and movements that have evolved over the centuries in response to changing circumstances' (Chazan et al., 1992, 73–103). According to the Commonwealth Secretary-General, forty-nine of the fifty-three Commonwealth states are ethnically heterogeneous, and, as John Darby notes, given complex settlement patterns and the mismatch between state borders and the distribution of peoples, 'ethnic homogeneity, on past evidence, is almost always unattainable' (1998, 2).

In the economic sphere, once again few would dispute Azar's contention that PSC tends to be associated with patterns of underdevelopment or uneven development. This is a much discussed topic, with some evidence, first, that, contra certain traditional theories of social and political revolution, there is a correlation between absolute levels of economic underdevelopment and violent conflict (Jongman and Schmid, 1997);[9] second, that conflict is associated with over-fast or uneven development where modernization disrupts traditional patterns, for example through rapid urbanization, but does not as yet deliver adequate or expected rewards – as in a number of countries from Eastern Europe to China attempting a swift transition from command to market economies (Newman, 1991); and, third, that, even where there are reasonable levels of development in absolute terms, conflict may still be generated where there is actual or perceived inequity in the distribution of benefits (Lichbach, 1989) – for example, in the former Yugoslavia (Woodward, 1995). In all three cases mounting discontent offers fertile recruiting ground for ideological extremism and racial exclusionism.

In the political sphere, Azar's identification of conflict prevalence with 'incompetent, parochial, fragile, and authoritarian governments' (1990, 10) is also borne out. For many analysts who take a governance-oriented view of the sources of contemporary conflict this is the key sector, since social and economic grievances are in the end expressed in political form. Three main patterns may be discerned here. First, conflict can become endemic, even in established liberal democratic states, when party politics become ascriptively based and one community perceives that state power has been permanently 'captured' by another, and is therefore driven to challenge the legitimacy of the state in order to change the situation, as in Canada, Belgium, Spain (Basques) or Northern Ireland (Lijphart, 1977; Gurr and Harff, 1994, chapter 5). This has also been a feature in a number of non-western countries, such as Sri Lanka (Horowitz, 1991). Second, conflict is likely in countries where authoritarian regimes successfully manipulate the state apparatus in order to cling to power and block political access to all those not part of their own narrow patronage network, eventually becoming little more than exploitative 'klepto-cracies', as in Mobutu's Zaire. Here, politics has indeed become zero-sum and change can only be effected through a direct challenge to the incumbent regime. Third, there is what seems to be the growing phenomenon of 'failed' or 'collapsed' states (Helman and Ratner, 1992; Zartman, ed., 1995), which, in the absence of adequate means for raising revenue or keeping order, succumb to endemic and chaotic violence. Snow notes that whereas during the Cold War there was a greater incidence of violent conflict in 'strong, coercive states', albeit with 'weak societies', now it is more prevalent in 'weak, failed states' (1996, 38). Here, violent conflict is simply an expression of politics itself. In a report on Africa presented to the UN Security Council in April 1998, Secretary-General Kofi Annan noted:

> The nature of political power in many African states, together with the real and perceived consequences of capturing and maintaining power, is a key source of conflict across the continent. It is frequently the case that political victory assumes a winner-takes-all form with respect to wealth and resources, patronage, and the prestige and prerogatives of office. Where there is insufficient accountability of leaders, lack of transparency in regimes, inadequate checks and balances, non-adherence to the rule of law, absence of peaceful means to change or replace leadership, or lack of respect for human rights, political control becomes excessively important, and the stakes become dangerously high.

There are no simple remedies for any of these three clusters of challenges. Liberal democracies are themselves a prey to the first; a number of commentators have pointed out with regard to the second that transitions to democracy may exacerbate rather than dampen down conflict (de Nevers, 1993; Mansfield and Snyder, 1995); while Mohammed Ayoob notes how 'norms of civilised state behavior' in the West, such as principles of individual and minority rights, are 'often in contradiction with the imperatives of state making' elsewhere (1996, 43). Established western states are only able to indulge in such sentiments because of earlier success in crushing internal dissent and forcibly assimilating minorities at a time when there were no such international human rights regimes.

A brief comment should be added on the military/security aspect at this point, since this suddenly becomes the critical arena at the moment when domestic conflict crosses the Rubicon and becomes a violent struggle for the state itself. Taking a narrower meaning of security than that used by

Azar, the key points come, first, when civilian police are identified by sectors of the community with particular political interests and are no longer seen to represent legitimate authority in upholding law and order (as, for example, in Northern Ireland); and, second, when civil unrest can no longer be controlled by non-military means. At this stage, as Barry Posen has noted, the 'security dilemma', familiar to analysts of international relations, now impacts with devastating effect on the inchoate social-state-international scene (1993). Once this genie is out of the bottle and armed factions are organized and active, it is very difficult to put it back again.

Group mobilization and inter-party dynamics

Having outlined some of the contextual and structural sources of contemporary conflict, we move on to consider relational sources at conflict party level. As we have seen, this is the dimension where Azar placed his main emphasis, tracing the deepest source of PSC to the societal (sub-state) level and locating it in the unsatisfied human needs of identity groups. And this is the level where he found the main locus for 'process dynamics', attributing it to 'communal actions and strategies', 'state actions and strategies' and 'built-in mechanisms of conflict'.

First, on 'communal actions and strategies', important further work has been done in tracing the ways in which dissatisfied groups come to articulate grievances, mobilize, specify goals and strategies and, eventually, mount a militarized challenge to existing state power-holders. This is clearly integral to the process of conflict formation. Gurr (1993; 1994) shows how national peoples, regional autonomists, communal contenders, indigenous peoples, militant sects, ethnoclasses and other groups tend to move from non-violent protest, through violent protest, to outright rebellion in an uneven escalation that takes many years in most cases. This is the time-lag that gives major incentives for the proactive prevention of violent conflict, as discussed in the next chapter. Goals variously include demands for political access, autonomy, secession or control, triggered by historical grievances and contemporary resentments against the socio-cultural, economic and political constraints outlined in the previous section. New threats to security, such as those felt by constituent groups in the break-up of former Yugoslavia, and new opportunities, often encouraged by similar demands elsewhere, will encourage mobilization, and the nature of the emergent leadership will often be decisive in determining degrees of militancy. When it comes to demands for secession, usually the most explosive issue, a history of past political autonomy, however long ago, is often critical.

Second, 'state actions and strategies' in response are also clearly crucial. Here, Azar's conclusions as outlined earlier in this chapter are confirmed by most conflict resolution analysts, with 'coercive repression' in the long run seen to be a decreasingly effective strategy, as missed opportunities for earlier accommodation in Sri Lanka and the failure of Milosevic's post-1989 policies in Kosovo are taken to show.

Third, there is what Azar called 'built-in mechanisms of conflict', that is to say the mutually reinforcing dynamics of intergroup conflict escalation and de-escalation captured through the three vertices of the conflict triangle, this is seen to lead to 'conflictual interactions such as premature closure, misattribution of motives, stereotyping, tunnel vision, bolstering and polarization' (1990, 15). Here again, much was written in the 1990s (Northrup, 1989; Deutsch, 1990; Fein, 1990; Fisher, 1990; Larsen, ed., 1993).

At this point we should note that Azar's use of the term 'communal groups' may open him to criticism from some quarters. For example, there is disagreement about the extent to which various group identities are 'primordial' and pre-date the conflict situation as 'perennialists' argue, or are 'imagined' and manufactured by political interests as 'social constructionists' claim (Anderson, 1983; Smith 1995, 51–84). We need not enter this debate here. Azar himself never intended his analysis to be seen as primordialist, rejecting the tendency to subsume social difference under the blanket label 'ethnicity' and using the term 'identity group' as no more than an indicator for whoever the disadvantaged, marginalized and repressed people were whose unsatisfied needs he saw as the main source of PSC. In any case, students of identity formation in intense conflict situations note how previously indeterminate or cross-cutting identities are often melted down into what Glazer calls 'terminal loyalties' in the crucible of conflict (1983, 244). Ascriptive, and sometimes mutually incompatible, identities are imposed on individuals both by 'friendly' and 'hostile' parties, and, more often than not, by unwitting third parties as well.

Elites and individuals

Turning, finally, to the elite/individual level, we encounter another major criticism of the kind of conflict analysis that Azar's theory of PSC represents. Behind this lie complex arguments about agency and structure (the latter a lineal descendant of earlier debate about the relative roles of 'great men' and 'vast impersonal forces' in history), which we need not pursue here. The gist of the critique is that a focus on international level (contextual), state level (structural) and conflict party level (relational) types of analysis may make conflict appear to be a natural or even inevitable process, and fails to lay the blame squarely on the shoulders of the individuals and elites who are usually responsible – along the lines of Lord Acton's observation a century ago with reference to 'morally neutral' accounts of historical events that 'too much explaining leads to too much forgiving'. A comparison between the leadership roles of Slobodan

Milosevic and Franjo Tudjman in Yugoslavia and those of F. W. de Klerk and Nelson Mandela in South Africa may demonstrate the force of this point. In fact, Azar himself can be largely exonerated from this criticism, given his emphasis on the significance of government actions and strategies in generating PSC, and his observation that this is likely to veer in the direction of coercive repression or instrumental co-option. But others are not let off so lightly. For Human Rights Watch, for example, it is the elite/individual level of analysis that is usually the critical one: 'Communal violence is often seen simply as the product of "deep-seated hatreds" or "ancient animosities" that have been unleashed by the collapse of the authoritarian structures that had contained them', a view which is promoted by those with an interest in doing so, including culpable governments and third parties wanting to turn a blind eye. As a result, the impression is given that these are 'natural processes' about which little can be done:

> But the extensive Human Rights Watch field research summarized here shows that communal tensions per se are not the immediate cause of many violent and persistent communal conflicts. While communal tensions are obviously a necessary ingredient of an explosive mix, they alone are not sufficient to unleash widespread violence. Rather, time after time the proximate cause of communal violence is governmental exploitation of communal differences. (*Human Rights Watch, 1995, 1–2*)

Government incitement is seen to take different forms, including discrimination which favours a dominant group and marginalizes a minority, the defining of political rights in terms of ethnic rather than civic nationalism, the fanning of communal hatreds through the media, and deliberate organization of murder squads, as in the case of the *interahamwe* (lit. 'those who work together') in Rwanda in 1994. Brown agrees that the academic literature 'places great emphasis on mass-level factors', but is 'weak in understanding the role played by elites and leaders in instigating violence'. The result is a ' "no-fault" history that leaves out the pernicious effects of influential individuals'. Instead, Brown's 'main argument with respect to the causes of internal conflict is that most major conflicts are triggered by internal, elite-level activities – to put it simply, bad leaders – contrary to what one would gather from reviewing the scholarly literature on the subject' (Brown, ed., 1996, 22–3). Similarly, the main external problems are due to 'bad neighbours' rather than 'bad neighbourhoods' (see table 3.5). Why do individuals and elites behave in this way? Brown suggests three variations here: genuine ideological struggles over how the state should be organized, criminal assaults on state sovereignty to secure control of assets, and factional power struggles when elites lacking legitimacy and threatened by loss of power play the 'communal card' and appeal to ethnic or nationalist rhetoric. And why do followers follow? He gives two reasons: 'the existence of antagonistic group histories' and 'mounting economic problems'. We can recognize

Table 3.5 Proximate causes of internal conflict

	Internally driven	*Externally driven*
Elite-triggered	bad leaders (23)	bad neighbours (3)
Mass-triggered	bad domestic problems (7)	bad neighbourhoods (1)

Source: from Brown, ed., 1996, 597, 582. Figures in brackets allocate numbers from Brown's list of 'major active conflicts'

explanations at elite/individual level, conflict party level and state level here: 'It appears that all three factors – irresponsible leaders driven by intensifying elite competitions; problematic group histories; and economic problems – must be present for this kind of conflict to explode' (Brown, ed., 1996, 597).

Conflict Mapping and Conflict Tracking

Most of this chapter has been concerned with seeking explanations for contemporary conflicts taken as a group. But there is also a vast literature about particular conflicts, where the appropriate form of explanation focuses on their specific origins (e.g., Suganami, 1996). Without going into such detail here, we conclude the chapter with a brief note on 'conflict mapping' and 'conflict tracking'.

Conflict mapping, in Wehr's words, is 'a first step in intervening to manage a particular conflict. It gives both the intervenor and the conflict parties a clearer understanding of the origins, nature, dynamics and possibilities for resolution of the conflict' (1979, 18). It is a method of presenting a structured analysis of a particular conflict at a given moment in time. It is used by analysts to give a quick picture of their view of the conflict situation, and is also widely used in conflict resolution workshops to provide participants with a snapshot of the conflict under consideration. Any particular map should be understood to represent the views of the author(s), and, as a schematic, to be indicative rather than comprehensive.

Adapting Wehr's conflict mapping guide (1979, 18–22),[10] we suggest the steps outlined in box 3.4 for the initial conflict analysis. This is then followed up by further analysis using the information in the map to identify the scope for conflict resolution, preferably carried out with the help of the parties or embedded third parties. This would identify: changes in the context which could alter the conflict situation, including the interests and capacities of third parties to influence it; changes within and

---

BOX 3.4   A conflict mapping guide: conflict analysis

A   Background
  1   Map of the area
  2   Brief description of the country
  3   Outline history of the conflict

B   The conflict parties and issues
  1   Who are the core conflict parties?
      What are their internal sub-groups and on what constitu-
      encies do they depend (see pp. 88–9)?
  2   What are the conflict issues?
      Is it possible to distinguish between positions, interests
      (material interests, values, relationships) and needs (see
      p. 9)?
  3   What are the relationships between the conflict parties?
      Are there qualitative and quantitative asymmetries (see pp.
      12–14)?
  4   What are the different perceptions of the causes and nature
      of the conflict among the conflict parties (see, for example,
      box 3.1)?
  5   What is the current behaviour of the parties (is the conflict in
      an 'escalatory' or 'de-escalatory' phase?) (see p. 16)?
  6   Who are the leaders of the parties? At the elite/individual
      level, what are their objectives, policies, interests, and rela-
      tive strengths and weaknesses (see pp. 89–91)?

C   The context: global, regional and state-level factors
  1   At the state level (see pp. 84–8): is the nature of the state
      contested? How open and accessible is the state apparatus?
      Are there institutions or fora which could serve as legitimate
      channels for managing the conflict? How even is economic
      development and are there economic policies that can have a
      positive impact?
  2   At the regional level (see pp. 80– 4): how do relations with
      neighbouring states and societies affect the conflict? Do the
      parties have external regional supporters? Which regional
      actors might be trusted by the parties?
  3   At the global level (see pp. 78–80): are there outside geopo-
      litical interests in the conflict? What are the external factors
      that fuel the conflict and what could change them?

A conflict map is an initial snapshot. Analysts may then want to keep
updating it by regular conflict tracking. This can now be done
increasingly efficiently through the internet, using information from

sources such as ReliefWeb, INCORE, the UN, the International
Conflict Initiatives Clearinghouse and news pages and conferences
on particular conflicts. Amongst the most useful website resources
are:

The Carter Centre	http://www.emory.edu/carter_center
Center for Refugee Studies, York	http://www.yorku.ca/research/crs/
ConflictNet	http://www.igc.org/igc/peacenet/
Contemporary Conflicts in Africa	http://www.synapse.net/ ~ acdi20/welcome.html
Creative Associates International	http://www.cali-dc.com/ghai
ICRC (Red Cross)	http://www.icrc/ch/
INCORE	http://www.incore.ulst.ac.uk/cds/
International Crisis Group	http://www.intl-crisis-group.org
Minorities at Risk	http://www.bsos.umd.edu/cidcm/mar
Open Media Research Institute (OMRI)	http://www.omri.cz/omri.htm
ReliefWeb	http://www.reliefweb.int/
Yahoo World Headlines	http://www.headlines.yahoo.com/Full_Coverage/World/

The European Platform for Conflict Prevention and Transformation
produces an international directory describing the activities of 475
organizations working in the field of the prevention, management
and resolution of conflict. The directory also contains profiles of
current conflicts, along with sources of further information about
them. The Directory (ECCP, 1998) is available on-line at:
http://www.euconflict@antenna.nl

between the conflict parties, including internal leadership struggles, varying prospects for military success and the readiness of general populations
to express support for a settlement; possible ways of redefining goals and
finding alternative means of resolving differences, including suggested
steps towards settlement and eventual transformation; likely constraints
on these; and how these might be overcome. These issues are considered
further in the chapters that follow.

Conclusion

This chapter has outlined a framework for the analysis of contemporary conflict that draws on Edward Azar's account of PSC, and then updates it via a levels-of-analysis approach at international, state and sub-state levels. This is not a theory of conflict, but a model for locating the chief sources of contemporary conflict. The main conclusion to be taken from this chapter for the rest of the book is that, given the complexity of much contemporary conflict, attempts at conflict resolution have to be equally comprehensive. Although peacemakers striving to maximize humanitarian space and the scope for peace initiatives in the middle of ongoing wars (chapter 5) or aiming to bring the violent phase of conflict to an end (chapter 6) usually have to work within quite narrow power constraints, long-term peacebuilders who aspire to prevent violent conflict (chapter 4) or to ensure that settlements are transformed into lasting peace (chapter 7) have to address the deeper sources of conflict. This may involve contextual change at international level (for example, via more equitable and accountable global and regional arrangements), structural change at state level (for example, via appropriate constitutional adaptations and the promotion of good governance), relational change at conflict party level (for example, via community relations and reconciliation work) and cultural change at all levels (for example, via the transformation of discourses and institutions which sustain and reproduce violence). It is to these broad themes that we now turn.

4

Preventing Violent Conflict

Conflict, including ethnic conflict, is not unavoidable but can indeed be prevented. This requires, however, that the necessary efforts are made. Potential sources of conflict need to be identified and analysed with a view to their early resolution, and concrete steps must be taken to forestall armed confrontation. If these preventive measures are superseded by a sharpening of the conflict, then an early warning must be given in time for more rigorous conflict containment to take place.

Max van der Stoel (1994), OSCE High Commissioner on National Minorities

Preventing violent conflict has been a central aim of the conflict resolution enterprise from its start in the late 1950s, as illustrated in chapter 2 through Kenneth Boulding's early ambition to create early warning conflict 'data stations' with a view to timely preventive action, and Quincy Wright's proposed project for a 'world intelligence centre' in the first issue of the *Journal of Conflict Resolution*. A remarkable feature of the post-Cold War era forty years later has been the growing consensus on the importance of prevention in the UN and among many international organizations, governments and NGOs. This is partly a reaction to the catastrophes in Rwanda, Yugoslavia and elsewhere, and partly a realization that it may be easier to tackle conflicts early, before they reach the point of armed conflict or mass violence. Major-General Romeo Dallaire's assertion that a mechanized brigade group of five thousand soldiers could have saved hundreds of thousands of lives in Rwanda in the spring and summer of 1994 has reverberated through the international community. So has a realization of the cost-effectiveness of prevention when compared with the exorbitant bill for subsequent relief, protection and reconstruction if prevention fails. The new preoccupation with prevention is also a response to the globalization of contemporary conflicts. Not only do 'wars of the third kind' have causes related to the global system, as the previous chapter noted; they also have global effects, through worldwide media coverage, refugee flows, the impact of diasporas and the destabilization of surrounding regions. At the same time, the weakening of the norms of sovereignty and non-interference is beginning to open space for international interventions. In the late 1980s many were predicting catastrophe for South Africa, while few foresaw calamity in Yugoslavia. The dramatic contrast in their subsequent fates underlines the case for prevention. If violent conflict has so far been minimized in the former, could this not also have been achieved in the latter?

This chapter explores how conflicts can be prevented from becoming violent. It first examines the epistemological issues involved in prevention and how we can know that prevention has worked. It then looks at the factors that contribute to the prevention of interstate and non-interstate wars. This leads to a review of possible policy measures and to discussion of the roles of the various agencies involved in conflict prevention. The chapter ends with some examples. The question that underlies the analysis is this: what forms of prevention are effective, and what are the circumstances under which they can work?

We noted earlier how 'conflict prevention' is a misnomer, since it is clearly impossible to prevent conflict from taking place. It would also be undesirable, for conflict is a creative and necessary means of bringing about social change. Here, we restrict our definition of conflict prevention to those factors or actions which prevent *armed* conflicts or mass violence from breaking out.[1]

Causes and Preventors of War

Wars are much like road accidents. They have a general and a particular cause at the same time. Every road accident is caused in the last resort by the invention of the internal combustion engine ... [But] the police and the courts do not weigh profound causes. They seek a specific cause for each accident – driver's error, excessive speed, drunkenness, faulty brakes, bad road surface. So it is with wars. (A.J.P. Taylor, quoted in Davies, 1996, 896)

If Taylor is right, perhaps we can learn something about the prevention of wars from the prevention of traffic accidents. It is usually possible to point to particular factors that might have prevented an individual accident. If the driver had not been inebriated, if the weather had not been foggy, if the road had been better lit, the accident might not have happened. But it is hard to be sure of the influence of any particular cause in a single incident. Only when we have a large number of traffic accidents to study can we hope to establish a relationship between accidents and the factors associated with them. This may suggest generic measures that can make roads in general safer. For example, when driving tests were introduced in Britain, there was a measurable impact on the number of accidents per driver per year. Better lighting on roads has also reduced accident figures.

The prevention of fires is similar. Managers of buildings hope that the occupants will not start fires. But they do not place all their trust on the good sense of the occupants. Instead they invest in sprinklers, fire alarms, fire extinguishers and other measures designed to prevent the risk of fires getting out of control. They introduce 'preventors' of fire.[2]

There is a case, similarly, for introducing preventors of war. This is not entirely new: there are already preventors at work, present alongside causes of war.

Light and deep prevention

Active measures to prevent conflict can be divided into two types. One is aimed at preventing situations with a clear capacity for violence from degenerating into armed conflict. This is called 'light prevention'. Its practitioners do not necessarily concern themselves with the root causes of the conflict, or with remedying the situation which led to the crisis which the measures address. Their aim is to prevent latent or threshold conflicts from becoming severe armed conflicts. Examples of such action are diplomatic interventions, long-term missions and private mediation efforts. 'Deep prevention', in contrast, aims to address the root causes, including underlying conflicts of interest and relationships. At the international level this may mean addressing recurrent issues and problems in the international system, or a particular international relationship which lies at the root of conflict. Within societies, it may mean engaging with issues of development, political culture and community relations. In the context of post-Cold War conflicts, light prevention generally means improving the international capacity to intervene in conflicts before they become violent; deep prevention means building domestic, regional or international capacity to manage conflict. This distinction between light and deep prevention can be related, in turn, to the immediate and more profound causes of war as discussed in the previous chapter.

Causality and prevention

Suganami (1996, 6) distinguishes three levels on which the causes of war can be explained: first, 'What are the conditions which must be present for wars to occur?'; second, 'Under what sorts of circumstances have wars occurred most frequently?'; and, third, 'How did this particular war come about?' The first is a question about the necessary causes of wars, the second about the correlates of war, the third about the antecedents of particular wars. We can reformulate the further question, 'what prevents violent conflicts?' in a similar way: first, can war be prevented by removing its necessary conditions? second, can the incidence of wars be reduced by controlling the circumstances under which they arise? and, third, how can this particular conflict be prevented from becoming violent?

Suganami (1996, 62) identifies three conditions that are logically necessary for war: the 'capacity of human beings to kill members of their own species'; 'sufficient prevalence of the belief among a number of societies, in particular the states, that there are circumstances under which it is their function to resort to arms against one another, and in doing so demand the co-operation of society members (without which no organized armed conflict could take place between societies)'; and 'the absence from the international system of a perfectly effective anti-war device'. Surprisingly, he ignores a further necessary condition which has been pointed to by many students of war: the existence of weapons.

It is clear that if any of these necessary conditions could be removed, war as an organized activity would be prevented. Following the order of Suganami's conditions, war could be prevented by changing human nature, by reducing the prevalence of the belief that resort to arms is a legitimate function of the state or by introducing a perfectly effective anti-war device, although all of these face serious practical difficulties, as does achieving general disarmament. The difficulty lies in the fact that war is an institution, and, as such, it is rooted in the social systems which give rise to it (Rapoport, 1992). So long as the belief that states can legitimately order people to participate in war is prevalent and preparations for war are made, the likelihood of war remains a possibility. For practical reasons, then, most effort has been concentrated on searching for ways to prevent some wars, or to prevent a specific war.

In the last chapter we noted attempts to identify correlates of war: factors related to the incidence of war, which might be suggestive about both the causes and the preventors of certain types of war. This has stimulated an immense literature. Pioneers such as Wright (1942) and Richardson (1960b) undertook systematic examinations of war incidence in history and attempted to discover causal factors, and many others have followed them. We have seen how these efforts have produced modest results in the case of interstate war, and how the analysis of correlates of non-interstate war is still in its infancy, although a promising start has been made. Suganami's third approach, of identifying the causes of a particular war, has its parallels in efforts to prevent a particular conflict from becoming violent. If we could know the causes of a particular war, then we should be able to intervene to prevent it, to 'choke off' a causal sequence.

In the 1990s success in the prevention of imminent armed conflict has been claimed in Macedonia (1992), Guatemala (1993), Fiji (1996) and other places. The Organization for Security and Cooperation in Europe (OSCE) set up the office of the High Commissioner on National Minorities (HCNM) with a mandate to identify situations which might become violent and to seek ways of preventing this from happening. This innovation has been widely praised, and has been believed to have been effective

BOX 4.1   The prevention of armed conflict in Estonia, 1993–4

In 1993 the citizens of Narva voted by an overwhelming majority to secede from Estonia. They were almost all Russians who had been dismayed to become what they saw as second-class citizens in their own country. The Estonian government declared that the referendum was illegal and threatened to use force if necessary to prevent the break-up of Estonia. Russian vigilante groups began to arm themselves and in Russia the President warned that he would intervene if necessary to protect the rights of Russian speakers. At a time when it appeared that this deadlock could lead to the outbreak of fighting, Max van der Stoel, the OSCE High Commissioner on National Minorities, interceded. After meeting with representatives of the Narva city council and President Meri of Estonia, he suggested that the Narva council should regard the referendum as a declaration of aspiration without immediate effect. At the same time he suggested to the Estonian government that they abandon their threat to use force against the city. His suggestions were adopted and a potential armed conflict was avoided.

in the prevention of armed conflict in the OSCE region. The question arises, however, how one can assess whether a particular armed conflict has been prevented? This raises epistemological issues about how we understand causation and prevention. What do we mean by the prevention of armed conflict, and how can we know when it has worked? We illustrate this question with reference to the case of the apparently prevented conflict in Estonia in 1993–4 (see box 4.1). Was the intervention of the HCNM responsible for preventing the armed conflict? To answer this question, we have to enter a difficult field much disputed by historians, philosophers and philosophers of science, namely the issue of causation and counter-factuals.

In order to attribute the non-occurrence of armed conflict to the presence of the HCNM, we have to know, first, that the non-event could not be attributed to other preventive factors; second, that in the absence of the HCNM the causative factors would have resulted in a violent conflict; and third, that the intervention of the HCNM not only preceded and was associated with the avoidance of conflict, but is also sufficient to explain it.

These are, of course, demanding requirements. Even in retrospect, historians have great difficulty in agreeing how particular wars have been caused or how much importance to place on any one causal factor. We can rarely be sure that a particular cause would have had a particular effect, or that it was the agent for a particular effect. The clock cannot be turned back and the sequence of events rerun with the factor in question removed. In history, causes operate together and in combination. The effect of a cause is dependent upon other background conditions. Nor are events in history simply linked by predictable linear effects like physical laws, which can suggest, given a first event, a sequence of knock-on effects.[3] Rather, history is intrinsically made up of events that are connected by *meaning*, by the purposes and thoughts of those who act in history. This is what Pitirim Sorokin called the 'logico-meaningful' dynamics of history. Wars often arise from the juxtaposition and combination of previously unrelated chains of events. At the same time, what matters most is not the juxtaposition in time of different chains of events, but the meaning these events have for those who are responsible for taking decisions. We cannot properly explain their occurrence unless we understand not only the chain of events which led to them and the connections between them, but also the mental world of the participants and the connections *they* made. It is this which makes wars particularly difficult to predict and sometimes gives them their surprising and dramatic quality.

We should also note that different levels of explanation are usually deployed in explaining wars: there are immediate triggering factors, underlying sources of tension and deeper structural conditions which shape events (Nye, 1993). The longer-term and the immediate causes work together to bring about war. Neither by itself can satisfactorily explain war. The great catastrophes of history are 'a fatal combination of general and specific causes' (Davies, 1996, 896). If light conflict prevention addresses only the trigger causes, deeper causes may produce a new and slightly different configuration for violent conflict. To be satisfactory, conflict prevention must be about preventing not only particular possible wars, but a family of possible wars.

Because we cannot know in advance how different causal sequences will combine, it is difficult to establish the impact of prevention in advance. Conflict prevention is therefore concerned with war-prone situations. If deep conflict prevention measures make a situation less war-prone, then we can argue that they have been effective even if we have no direct evidence that a particular potential war has been prevented. If we have some knowledge or measure of the factors that make a situation war-prone, then we do not need to know the probability of a particular war to know that policy measures have done some good.

Early warning

With these general and epistemological considerations in mind, let us now turn to consider the drive in the late 1980s and 1990s to establish an early warning system for violent political conflict, along the lines of Boulding's proposed 'social data stations', which he saw as analogous to networks of weather stations in the identification of 'social temperature and pressure' and the prediction of 'cold or warm fronts' (see Kerman, 1974, 82). This is widely seen as essential for monitoring particular areas of potential conflict, and seeking ways to act early enough to nip a potential conflict in the bud where this is feasible and appropriate. There are two tasks involved here: first, identification of the type of conflicts and location of the conflicts that could become violent; second, monitoring and appraising their progress with a view to assessing how close to violence they are.

One line of approach, which addresses Suganami's second question, aims to establish the circumstances under which wars are likely to take place. We can take Ted Gurr's work as an example of this approach. Using data from his 'Minorities at Risk' project, he identifies three factors that affect the proneness of a communal group to rebel: collective incentives, capacity for joint action, and external opportunities (see box 4.2, below). Each concept is represented by indicators constructed from data coded for the project, and justified by correlations with the magnitude of ethnic rebellions in previous years. The resulting table makes it possible to rank the minorities according to their risk-proneness (Gurr, 1998b). The assumption is that the more risk-prone are those with high scores on both incentives for rebellion and capacity/opportunity. The table shows, for example, that the Kosovo Albanians at that time had high incentives to rebel but a lack of capacity and opportunity; the East Timorese, on the other hand, had both incentives and capacity.

This is a political science version of the methods used in econometric forecasting. Like them, it may yield results in the short term, though the technique obviously blurs the case-specific and context-specific information which area experts would use. If it turns out that this approach yields acceptably good forecasts, it may be possible to offer conflict prevention agencies useful information about where to concentrate their efforts. Variations in Gurr's indices could also be used as indicators of effectiveness of conflict prevention policies.

A similar approach, using a different starting-point, is taken by the Dutch conflict monitoring organization, PIOOM. Their studies assess risk of armed conflict using indicators of human rights violations and poor governance. As described in chapter 1, p. 23, they use a five-phase model to classify countries on a scale ranging from a peaceful stable situation, through political tension, violent political conflict, low-intensity conflict and high-intensity conflict, and thirteen indicators of conflict escalation (Schmid, 1997, 74). For forecasting purposes, their work is trend-based, in that the countries with current political tension or violent political conflict are expected to be sources of armed conflicts in the future.

Barbara Harff examined a number of post-Cold War conflicts, including some in countries that have experienced political violence, and 'controls' in countries with similar ethnic situations that did not experience violence (Davies et al., 1997). Her study used the concept of 'accelerators' and 'decelerators': accelerators are events that escalate the conflict, decelerators events that dampen it, although the study under discussion only reports accelerators. Based on a coding of events reported in *Reuters World Service*, she plots the number of accelerator events per month before war for each of the ethnic conflicts, with a comparison for the control over a similar period. In each case of conflict that led to a war, there was an intensification of the number of accelerator events in the three months preceding the war. The implication is that similar coding schemes might offer an early warning of conflict, by reporting on the intensity of events. The basic assumption is that trend extrapolation can be used to measure the intensity of political conflict. An ambitious version of this approach is the Global Event-Data System (GEDS) project which aims to provide near-real-time automated coding and monitoring of on-line news services, yielding a quantitative trace of the level of tension in ongoing conflicts.[4]

Enduring rivalries, that is, protracted disputes between pairs of states or peoples, have accounted for half the wars between 1816 and 1992. These may be expected to be sources of further disputes. It is not difficult to point to regions – such as West Africa, the Great Lakes region of Africa, the Caucasus, the India–Pakistan border, parts of Indonesia – where future violent conflicts can be expected. It is less easy, however, to anticipate wholly new conflicts, still less new types of conflict.

Turning from quantitative to qualitative conflict monitoring, a mass of information is available on particular societies and situations. It includes the reports of humanitarian agencies (now linked together on the Relief-Web site on the internet), e-mail early warning networks of conflict monitors (for example, in the former Soviet Union), analyses by the media and by the academic community and, of course, the diplomatic and intelligence activities of states. Efforts are under way to improve and systematize these qualitative sources of information and to make them available to those who could undertake a response. Qualitative monitoring offers vastly more content-rich and contextual information than quantitative statistical analysis, but presents the problems of noise and information overload. Given the current state of the art, qualitative monitoring is likely to be most useful for gaining early warning of conflict in particular cases: the expertise of the area scholar and the local observer, steeped in situational knowledge, is difficult to beat. In some cases, observers clearly realized that violent conflicts were coming well before they occurred: for example, in former Yugoslavia and Rwanda. In others they were taken by surprise. Even when observers have issued early warnings, it is by no means certain that they will be heard, or that there will be a response. Governments and international organizations may be distracted by other crises (as in the case of Yugoslavia), or unwilling to change existing policies (as in the case of Rwanda). Given the unpredictability of human decision-making, no system of forecasting is likely to give certain results. Nevertheless, there is already sufficient knowledge of situations where there is proneness to war to justify perseverance in international efforts to provide data which might enable early and timely preventive response.

Preventors of Interstate and Non-Interstate War

Preventors of armed conflict, like causes of armed conflict, operate on a number of levels. In chapter 3 we identified sources of contemporary violent conflict at five levels, from systemic global factors to the policies and actions of individuals and elites. Preventors of violent conflict are likely to be similarly located. We begin by considering preventors of interstate war.

Interstate war

If we look first at the pattern of war and peace in the international system over the last two centuries, there is a clear variation between periods of general war and periods when there was no general war, even if conflicts occurred in specific regions. The periods of general war were the Napoleonic Wars, the First World War and the Second World War and, arguably, Bismarck's wars from 1862 to 1871. Following each general war, the major powers created a new system of international politics that was, at least temporarily, stable. After 1815, it was the Concert of Europe; after 1918, the order based on the League of Nations and the Versailles Settlement; after 1945, the order based on the Security Council and the victors of the Second World War, which soon broke down into the armed stand-off of the Cold War. On each occasion, except the last, the temporarily stable system broke down when a rising power challenged the old order – Napoleonic France in the 1790s, Prussia in 1854, Germany in 1914 and Hitler against the Versailles system in 1939. The Cold War, however, ended anomalously with the collapse of one of the major powers, the Soviet Union, without a general war (Hinsley, 1963; 1987).

Similarly, Wallensteen identifies a fluctuation between what he calls 'universalist' periods, where 'policies are understood to be concerted among major powers to organize relations between themselves to work out acceptable rules of behaviour (general standards)' and 'particularist periods' which in contrast are 'marked by policies which emphasize the special interest of a given power, even at the price of disrupting existing organizations or power relationships' (1984, 243; also see table 4.1). Focusing on only one of these periods of universalism and non-general war, namely the Concert of Europe, the preventors can be seen to have lain, first, in a rough balance of power between a number of more or less equal states, which gave none of them an overwhelming opportunity to make unilateral gains; second, in a political order maintained through diplomacy and on effective diplomatic policies that could deliver the kind

Table 4.1 Wallensteen's table of 'universalist' and 'particularist' periods

Classification	Historical label	Period	Years	Major powers
Universalist	Concert of Europe	1816–48	33	5–6
Particularist		1849–70	22	5–6
Universalist	Bismarck's order	1871–95	25	6
Particularist		1896–1918	23	8
Universalist	League of Nations	1919–32	14	7
Particularist		1933–44	12	7
Particularist	Cold War	1945–62	18	5
Universalist	Détente	1963–76	14	5

Source: Wallensteen, 1984, 245

of stability their architects desired; and third, in a loose form of governance between states, which involved them in consultation and a limited degree of cooperation (Medlicott, 1956, 18; Holsti, 1991; 1992). The system was not proof against the larger conflicts that developed when nationalism grew stronger. It was an order defined for a particular time: a time of relatively stable empires, which could govern their relations by diplomacy. As the world began to change, the system could no longer cope. The preventors began to break down (they had largely broken down by the early twentieth century); meanwhile, the causes of war were intensifying. As crisis followed crisis in the early 1900s, it was evident that the European system was becoming more war-prone, although no one could clearly anticipate the likely specific source of a war.

We have seen that so far the post-Cold War period is another marked by relatively little international war. As suggested in chapter 3, the explanation for the high level of internal violence lies in the failure of existing states to provide legitimate and accepted governance responsive to human needs; hence, state failure, ethnic conflict and struggles to control government. But what is the explanation for the low level of interstate war?

A number of partly competing, partly overlapping explanations are available. Mueller (1989), for example, has argued that war is becoming obsolescent between major states because it is too destructive to be a usable policy instrument, and irrelevant to the real conflicts of interest that divide major states. Keohane and Nye (1986) stress the role of interdependence in transforming relations between states: when states' interests are tied together in a web of interrelated issue areas, governments tend to move towards bargaining as the main instrument for resolving conflicts of interest. Others stress the importance of international institutions and regimes, which have become more universal with the end of the

Cold War. For example, Axelrod and Keohane (1986) argue that institutions strengthen contacts between governments, make their actions more transparent, diminish security dilemmas and create a basis for reciprocation and mutual gains. Besides these changes in the structure of relations between states, the nature and importance of the state itself is changing, through globalization. Non-militarized economic power is seen to bring a greater enhancement of influence and ability to defend interests than investment in military power. As major states pool more of their powers and delegate others downwards, their role is changing; and interstate wars of the old kind, between adjoining states disputing territory and power, may be becoming anomalies.[5]

If we turn to preventors at the regional level, more specific explanations come into view. We have noted in chapter 2 the long-standing interest of conflict resolution scholars in the regional dimension of war prevention, citing David Mitrany's functionalist approach and Karl Deutsch's analysis of the 'pluralistic security community' in the Euro-Atlantic region as particularly influential. We have also mentioned the formation of ASEAN in South-East Asia by a number of states with similar internal problems, a regime that is intended to prevent interstate disputes and at the same time avoid rocking the boat of member states' internal arrangements. The essence of the system is *mushuwara*, the Malaysian village system for consensual decision-making, which has been applied to the international level (Askandar, 1997). In Latin America, an unusually low level of interstate wars has prevailed since 1945, without the existence of a security community of the kind Deutsch describes or strong bonds of interdependence. The explanation is unclear, although, as in the South-East Asian case, there is a common preoccupation with internal challenges (Holsti, 1996, 150–82).

At the level of individual pairs of states, explanations become more specific still. The European Coal and Steel Community (established 1952), for example, helped to seal the end of the protracted military rivalry between France and Germany, putting economic integration in the place of competition for power, resources and territory. Since recurrent armed conflicts are frequently the product of enduring rivalries between pairs of hostile states, addressing and resolving animosities and problems in particular relationships is clearly a way to avert violent conflicts.

The most striking result to emerge from statistical research on war and peace is the relationship between peace and democratic government. Pairs of states that are both democracies are less likely to fight one another than pairs made up of non-democracies, or a democracy and a non-democracy, although democracies are as prone to engage in war as any other type of regime. This finding is partly accounted for by the fact that democracies tend to join in wars on the side of other democracies once they have begun. There is no compelling theoretical explanation for why pairs of democracies are less war-prone, and it is possible that other conditions may account for both democratic governance and the absence of war.[6]

Nevertheless, the implication of the finding is that the increasing number of democracies (twenty-nine in 1920, thirty-six in 1945, sixty-six in 1990: see Schmid 1997, 55, quoting Huntington, 1991) should be associated with a decreasing number of interstate wars. According to the UN Secretary-General, 'some 120 countries now hold generally free and fair elections, the highest total in history' (Annan, 1997, 7).

While it is important to recognize that a range of preventors is already in existence, it cannot be assumed that they are robust enough to deal with the emergent twenty-first-century conflicts. Many states remain outside the interdependent 'centre' of the international system and resist its values. Communities and populations are facing increasing difficulty in meeting basic needs, and more and more people are on the move. Notwithstanding current financial problems in Asia, demographic and economic weight is shifting from the West to the formerly developing countries in the South and the East. Conflicts of interest are developing over the management of resources, trade and the environment. Borders and state structures are under pressure; and more of them are failing. Although the immediate post-Cold War period has seen a respite in interstate conflict, we cannot be sanguine about the adequacy of the existing preventors, at international, regional and national levels. In internal conflicts, they are already clearly failing.

Non-interstate war

The literature on the correlates and preventors of non-interstate wars is less extensive than that on interstate conflicts, but it is growing rapidly. For example, Gurr (1993; 1998b) offers a comprehensive survey of minorities at risk and ethnopolitical rebellions. Esty et al. (1995) carried out a survey of state failures and potential state failures, using data on forty revolutionary wars, seventy-five ethnic wars, forty-six genocides, and eighty-two abrupt changes of regime. Schmid and Joongman (1996, 1997; Schmid, 1997) have collected data on low-intensity conflicts and violent political conflicts, and looked for indicators in human rights abuses, the human development index and domestic political catalysts. Bloomfield and Leiss (1969), Bloomfield and Moulton (1997) and Sherman (1987) have classified interstate and non-interstate disputes into phases, and examined factors that are associated with transitions from political disputes to armed conflicts.

The literature is more concerned with tracing causes than establishing preventors. Nevertheless, some findings are appearing. We have seen how the Esty study correlated a large number of variables with state failure and identified three that appeared to be associated with a low risk of state failure: openness to international trade, low infant mortality, and democratic governance (Esty et al., 1995). Gurr found seven risk factors which had significant positive correlations with ethnopolitical rebellions in 1995

BOX 4.2   Risk factors for ethnopolitical rebellion

Group incentives for initiating collective action
   history of lost political autonomy;
   active economic and political discrimination against the group;
   history of state repression.

Group capacity for sustained collective action
   strength of group identity;
   extent of militant group mobilization.

Group opportunities for collective action
   number of adjacent countries in which armed conflicts are under
   way;
   active support from kindred groups in neighbouring countries.

Source: Gurr, 1998b

(Gurr, 1998b). These are listed in box 4.2. With reference to the frame-work for conflict analysis given in chapter 3 (see table 3.2), we may recognize risk factors at state level, conflict group level and regional level here. In a study of Asian states, Gurr and Harff found that the factors associated with ethnic accommodation are regime democracy, regime durability and resource base of the regime, while involvement in the society's politics, the absence of a history of armed rebellion and group cohesion were indicators that ethnic groups were more likely to pursue their interests by political than by military means (Gurr and Harff, 1996).

Most of the work on preventors of internal conflict, however, is more qualitative in nature, based in part on surveys of different types of conflict, in part on policy prescriptions for development and good governance. Table 4.2 gives examples of preventive policies that have been proposed for contemporary conflicts, though it is not suggested that the factors generating conflict should necessarily be matched by preventors at the same level: the causes of conflict are often deep-rooted and cannot easily be remedied without wide-ranging structural change.

Suggested 'light' preventors of non-interstate war roughly correspond to Azar's 'process dynamic' variables in protracted social conflict, includ-ing flexible and accommodating state actions and strategies, moderate communal actions and strategies on the part of the leaders of challenging groups, and mutually de-escalatory built-in mechanisms of conflict management.

'Deep' preventors correspond to Azar's four 'preconditions' for pro-tracted social conflict (see pp. 71–6), and include adequate political

Table 4.2 Preventors of non-interstate conflict

Factors generating conflict	Possible preventors
Global level	
inappropriate systemic structures	changes in international order
Regional level	
regional diasporas	regional security arrangements
State level	
ethnic stratification	consociational politics/federalism/ autonomies
weak economies	development
authoritarian rule	legitimacy, democratization
human rights abuse	rule of law, human rights monitoring/ protection
Societal level	
weak societies	strengthening civic society, institutions
weak communications	Round Tables, workshops, community relations
polarized attitudes	cross-cultural work
Elite/individual level	
exclusionist policies	stronger moderates

institutions and good governance, cohesive social structures, opportunities for groups to develop economically and culturally, and the presence of accepted legal or social norms capable of accommodating and peacefully transforming these formations. For example, research on ethnicity suggests that preventors of ethnic conflict include, among others, federal structures, consociational systems, multiculturalism, elite accommodation and other structural arrangements for improving governance (Horowitz, 1985; McGarry and O'Leary, eds, 1993). Preventors of violent social conflict include social mobility and policies of social inclusion. Different cultures have their own traditions for regulating and preventing conflict peaceably (Cohen, 1991; Gulliver, 1979), including traditional law-codes, informal methods of consensus-building, deference to arbiters. Western methods which stress formal institutions, written agreements and democratic accountability are obviously not the only methods available. Coercive or authoritative conflict prevention by rulers or ruling classes has also been common.[7]

The Prevention of Violent Conflict

Having looked at preventors of war, we can move on to discuss what scope there is for the prevention of violent conflict in the post-Cold War world. The aim of prevention is to strengthen likely preventors and reduce likely causes of war or mass violence. While recognizing that the prevention of violent conflict is primarily a matter for indigenous peacemakers and peacebuilders within the potential conflict area, we are particularly concerned in this chapter with the possible role that outsiders can play in support. A difficult underlying question here is whether it is a good thing to try to prevent violent conflict in the first place; may violence not be the only way to remedy injustice? We have addressed this question in general terms in earlier chapters, where we argued, first, that degeneration into violent protracted social conflict usually results in a lose–lose outcome for all main parties and for the population at large, and, second, that attempts to prevent violence should be accompanied by (and may be conditional on) strenuous efforts to ensure that human needs are satisfied, legitimate aspirations accommodated and manifest injustices remedied.

As suggested in chapter 3, the international environment strongly affects proneness to conflict, both negatively and positively. Yugoslavia provides an unhappy example: the austerity programmes imposed by western financial institutions in the 1990s contributed to reduced public services and employment and increased competition among the republics for a shrinking federal budget, and weakened the state's capacity to manage conflicts and maintain civic order (Woodward, 1995). In other cases interventions by external regional powers precipitated or exacerbated conflicts – for example, Israel in Lebanon, the United States in Cambodia, or South Africa in Angola and Mozambique. However, there is a great deal of scope for positive interventions by outside governments, international organizations and non-state actors to support and develop conflict prevention capacity. The need for this has been recognized broadly, although it is sometimes stated in terms of global governance, peacebuilding or more general terms (Brundtland, 1987; Evans, 1993; Aspen Institute, 1997; Carnegie Commission on Preventing Deadly Conflict, 1997). International agencies have recognized the need and are beginning to take steps to create preventive capacity.

An example of where the international environment has had positive effects on proneness to violent conflict has been the citizenship conflicts in the Baltic States. The secession of Lithuania, Estonia and Latvia might well have given rise to armed conflicts, both between the new states and Russia (or the former Soviet Union), and between the Baltic and Russian citizens in the Baltic States. We have already noted the intervention of the OSCE High Commissioner, Max van der Stoel, over the threatened secession of Narva in Estonia (see box 4.1). He was supported by an OSCE long-duration mission based in three cities, which held extensive

Map 3   The Baltic States

consultations with a wide range of parties. Western governments, the OSCE and the Council of Europe called for amendments to the contested citizenship law, and the EC called for consultation and restraint. In response, President Meri submitted the Estonian legislation to the OSCE and the Council of Europe for comments, and he forwarded the proposed amendments to the Estonian parliament. He also set up a Round Table to promote dialogue between the ethnic groups, and made it clear that there was no intention of expelling non-citizens. He went on to co-opt members of the Russian elite by granting citizenship to industrial and political leaders, and allowed non-Estonians to vote in local elections. These de-escalatory steps proved sufficient to defuse the crisis. The Russian-speakers remained divided, but the majority of them saw their best hopes for the future in participating in the Estonian economy which had better prospects of development and trade with the West than that of Russia. The modified Law on Aliens was adopted and gradually attention shifted from citizenship to economic issues.

In Latvia, a similar crisis over citizenship quotas blew up in 1994, and also became serious as the Russian government refused to withdraw its troops from the country. It was eventually defused a few months later after a visit by President Clinton to Riga, a US–Russian summit, a Russian agreement to withdraw its troops and Western pressure on Latvia to revise its citizenship quotas.

The Estonian outcome can be attributed to a combination of light and deep prevention. On the light side, the effective diplomatic interventions of Max van der Stoel and others, combined with the moderate positions taken by the Estonian President, de-escalated the crisis. At a deeper level, the membership of all the concerned parties in the OSCE, and their acceptance of OSCE standards on citizenship and minority rights, created a legitimate framework for consultation and mediation. Both the Baltic States and the Russian Federation sought entry into European institutions; this gave European institutions some weight in the conflict. Crucially, the West, the Baltic States and the Russian government were all keen to avoid an armed conflict, but to be effective this wish had to be translated into practical measures and bridge-building institutions in the Baltic States. Even then, the Latvia case demonstrated that the OSCE could still fail to prevent escalation, and that high-level diplomatic interventions and bargaining would sometimes be needed.

In both cases, powerful third parties transformed an asymmetric conflict by balancing the relationship between the two sides, introducing a measure of restraint and facilitating negotiation.[8] The intervention of the OSCE High Commissioner was well timed, creating time and political space for political movement.[9] Finally, the compromise over the central issue of citizenship allowed the situation to be redefined in terms of access to economic opportunities instead of as an ethnopolitical struggle for control of the state.

Successful cases of conflict prevention are by no means confined to Europe. Box 4.3 gives an example from Fiji.

Policy measures

Gurr's study of minorities at risk shows how long the time-lag usually is between the first manifestations of organized protest and the onset of violent action, a matter of years in most cases, with an average of thirteen years in liberal democracies. There is clearly plenty of time for remedial action if it is seriously undertaken. It is once again helpful to distinguish light preventive intervention from deep preventive intervention.

Light intervention: crisis management and preventive diplomacy

A wide range of policy options is, in principle, available for light prevention (Creative Associates 1997, 3–6). They range from official diplomacy (mediation, conciliation, fact-finding, good offices, peace conferences, envoys, conflict prevention centres, hot lines) through non-official diplomacy (private mediation, message-carrying and creation of back-channels, peace commissions, problem-solving workshops, conflict resolution training, Round Tables) to peacemaking efforts by local actors (church-facilitated talks, debates between politicians, cross-party discussions). Powerful states are also able to apply positive and negative inducements in an effort to twist the arms of governments, strengthen moderate leaders and counteract the influence of extremists. This includes a range of political measures (mediation with muscle, mobilization through regional and global organizations, attempts to influence the

BOX 4.3   Conflict prevention in Fiji

A civic forum, the Citizens' Constitutional Forum (CCF), has recently made a significant contribution to a new constitutional settlement in Fiji. This offers a peaceful way out of the acute ethnic conflict that developed following the military coup of 1987.

The ethnic division in Fiji originates from the colonial period. The indigenous Fijians, who make up 50 per cent of the population of 772,000, are descendants of Pacific island-dwelling Polynesians and Melanesians. The Indo-Fijians, who constitute about 45 per cent, are descendants of indentured Indian labourers who were brought to work in sugar plantations by the British, who colonized Fiji in 1874. In the colonial period the British cooperated with the indigenous Fijian chiefs and sometimes used the indigenous Fijian police force to put down revolts against low wages by the Indo-Fijians. In the post-colonial period the Indo-Fijians became the better educated group, dominating trade and the private sector. A segmented labour market developed, with the indigenous Fijians working on traditional smallholdings and owning most of the land, while the Indo-Fijians were either tenant farmers growing sugar, or miners or wage-earners. The two groups have different religious affiliations, as well as different cultural traditions (the indigenous Fijians favouring communal and collective ways of life, while the Indo-Fijians are more individualistic). The contemporary conflict has revolved around land ownership, employment, access to public sector jobs, and the relative power of the two groups.

The largest political parties have been ethnically based. The Alliance Party, dominated by indigenous Fijians, won most of the elections of the post-independence period until 1987, its rule strengthened by a winner-take-all majority voting system based on the Westminster model. In 1987 it was defeated by a coalition of the National Federation Party, which represented Indo-Fijians, and a multi-ethnic Labour Party. In May 1987 Lieutenant-Colonel Rabuka staged a coup against the government and attempted to establish the paramountcy of indigenous Fijians. In 1990 the military stepped down, but set up a new constitution that entrenched a Fijian majority and gave the Council of Chiefs and the military special powers. This led to a sharply divided society, increased emigration by Indo-Fijians and economic decline.

By 1995 the economic downturn was so serious that international financial assistance was essential. This could not be obtained without political stability and reform. This opened an opportunity for the non-ethnic CCF. Working with advice from the international NGO Conciliation Resources and others, the CCF proposed a new forum for debates of national problems from a non-ethnic, national perspective. It sought support for a new constitution amongst the people, rather than the political parties and elites, and held wide-ranging consultations to frame a new constitution. These discussions, which started in 1993, were the first time that the contestants had engaged in a prolonged dialogue. They resulted in agreement on a new constitution in 1996, which would embrace proportional representation through an alternative-vote (AV) system, and power-sharing in government. The aim was to overcome the winner-takes-all basis of politics, and offer incentives to parties to win votes across the ethnic divide. In turn, it was expected that this would lead to new approaches to the contested economic issues. The new constitution was adopted in 1997 and was to form the basis for the 1999 elections.

media), economic measures (sanctions, emergency aid, conditional offers of financial support) and military measures (preventive peacekeeping, arms embargoes, demilitarization).

The scope for and effectiveness of these measures in practice depends on circumstances, and preventive diplomacy remains controversial (see box 4.4). Nevertheless, an increasing weight of opinion supports the contention that informed, sensitive and well-judged intervention early in a violence-prone situation is likely to be more beneficial to all parties than inaction and neglect.

Deep intervention: promoting good governance

Turning to the task of addressing the deeper causes of violent conflict and war, we have said that at interstate level this means addressing recurrent problems in the international system or in particular interstate relationships, and that at non-interstate level it means building domestic, regional and international capacity to manage conflict peacefully. For the latter, relevant policy instruments include measures to strengthen or restore governance (national conferences, constitutional commissions), to assist in holding elections (election-monitoring), to support fair trials (monitoring human rights abuses, supporting judicial independence) and to promote independent media. Connie Peck characterizes the 'building-blocks of sustainable peace and security' as 'well-functioning local, state, regional and international systems of governance, which are responsive to human needs' (1998, 45). This accurately reflects the main thrust of conflict resolution analyses of protracted social conflict, as outlined in chapter 3.

The international community cannot avoid questions of governance within societies when issues of self-determination arise. The problems associated with this claim are notorious (Hannum, 1990). Since secession is rarely conducive to peaceful outcomes, a range of political forms has

BOX 4.4 The Stedman–Lund debate

In a sharp attack published in *Foreign Affairs*, Stephen Stedman argued that the concept of preventive diplomacy is oversold. Social scientists can pinpoint situations of risk, he argued, but not when they will become violent. Actions designed to prevent conflict may trigger it; prevention is risky and costly; talking will achieve nothing. Only the threat or use of massive force, which risks prolonged intervention, will convince individuals such as Savimbi (the leader of UNITA) and Karadzic (the leader of the Bosnian Serbs). And it is unlikely that western leaders will be able to mobilize force before the pictures of violence are shown on television. Providing aid and long-term development can, of itself, do nothing to prevent genocides such as that in Rwanda, which was perpetrated by a group that refused to cede power. To focus on prevention ignores the role that conflict plays in driving political change. Some conflicts have to be intensified before they are resolved. Without well-defined interests, clear goals and a judgement about costs and risks, conflict prevention will mean that 'one simply founders earlier in a crisis instead of later' (Stedman, 1995).

Michael Lund responded by arguing that Stedman had caricatured the arguments of proponents of preventive diplomacy and chosen examples to overestimate the obstacles. Social scientists make useful prognostications of probable precipitants of violence, and this work should not be ignored. Where early warnings have been taken seriously, they have enabled conflicts to be prevented. Although the consequences of actions cannot always be predicted and may turn out to be harmful, there are cases where preventive actions have been beneficial. There is a range of intermediate actions between talking and use of massive force, which Stedman ignores: for example US warnings to Milosevic were effective in preventing a spread of the Balkan wars through to the end of 1997. Although early intervention has costs, they should be compared with the costs of non-intervention and late intervention, which may be higher. The public is not necessarily unwilling to endorse preventive diplomacy: the dispatch of US soldiers to join the UN Preventive Deployment Force (UNPREDEP) in Macedonia in 1993 passed largely without comment. If existing ambassadors and field staff were to turn their efforts to proactive responses to conflict, the issues might not even come to the attention of the crisis decision-makers. The stakes in potential crises are too high to be approached 'with cavalier analyses' of a few unfortunate cases (Lund, 1995).

been explored to accommodate the mismatch between state borders and the distribution of peoples. Peaceful secession/separation, as in former Czechoslovakia, is rare. Usually there is no alternative to various forms of multi-group accommodation, including different degrees of regional, federalist or confederalist autonomy within the state (Gurr, 1993) and/or widened political access (McGarry and O'Leary, eds, 1993). There is a consensus that winner-takes-all systems are dangerous when allied with an ascriptive politics in which parties are aligned along the boundaries of social division. But there is still disagreement about preferred forms of power-sharing to overcome this, with some advocating consociational accommodation through elite agreement (Lijphart, 1977; 1995) and others recommending electoral incentives which favour multi-ethnic coalitions (Horowitz, 1985; 1991; 1993). Sisk (1996) helpfully disaggregates such approaches into ten component 'situational variables', and argues for a nuanced and informed response which is sensitive to variations in the local situation.

In the West, well-established institutions, a law-governed society and organizations capable of representing interests have become the basis for legitimate government and the regulation of conflict. They reflect a long history of accommodation and evolution of competing political interests, and the development of procedures to regulate conflict. They include:

- effective law courts, an independent judiciary and a clear rule of law;
- independent institutions, which are not tied to particular political parties, such as an independent civil service, police, media, etc.;
- independent media, capable of criticizing and debating matters of public policy without fear of intimidation or closure, and able to report freely on events of concern to society;
- a vigorous civil society, containing professional organizations, representatives of a wide range of interest groups (unions, minority organizations, etc.) and NGOs;
- a political system that institutionalizes and regulates political conflict;
- accepted procedures for popular participation (such as various forms of elections and democratic governance);
- rule-based methods of settling disputes, e.g. majority voting, consensus decision-making, etc.

Where these characteristics are absent, as in parts of Central and Eastern Europe, Africa and elsewhere, capacity to manage conflict may be poor. In these situations there may be a case for external support for establishing preventive capacity. We need to be sensitive to the charge that imposing these particular methods may amount to westernization, especially when conditionality is imposed. Where there are indigenous methods of prevention, there is a strong case for respecting and developing them.[10] Cultural sensitivity is crucial in conflict prevention, as it is in conflict resolution generally. Intervention raises a host of difficult questions, which two of the authors have dealt with elsewhere (Ramsbotham and Woodhouse, 1996). However, as we have argued, given the level of internationalization, interdependence and interpenetration of societies that exists today, non-intervention is rarely an option. The question is how to bring international influence to bear in a way that strengthens, rather than weakens, domestic preventors.

International organizations and conflict prevention

As will be elaborated in chapter 8, the international collectivity is best seen under different aspects which coexist uneasily: as an international system of states governed by power and individual state interest; as an international society of states cooperating for mutual advantage; as an international community with shared values and aspirations; and perhaps as a potential universalist world community of peoples. All of these aspects are relevant to the enterprise of preventing violent conflict. Although the main responsibilities for preventing internal violent conflict lie within the country in question, international organizations have developed a significant role in conflict prevention, as several studies attest (Brauwens and Reychler, 1994; Siccama, 1996; Peck, 1998).

The OSCE is perhaps the best example of a cooperative security order that combines elements of deep and light prevention.[11] On the one hand, it is a regime with wide geographical coverage, based on a common set of principles and norms, including recognition of state sovereignty and minority rights. What makes it remarkable is the agreement of member states that 'the commitments undertaken in the field of the human dimension ... are matters of direct and legitimate concern to all participating states and do not belong exclusively to the internal affairs of the state concerned'.[12] By this agreement member states accepted a *droit de regard*, and gave the OSCE a legitimate basis to involve itself in ethnic and minority disputes.

At their conference in Helsinki in 1992 the OSCE states also committed themselves to 'identify the root causes of tension' and 'provide for more flexible and active dialogue and better early warning and dispute settlement'. These commitments have been institutionalized in powers delegated to the Chairman-in-Office, the Committee of Senior Officials, the Conflict Prevention Centre in Vienna (which manages long-duration missions) and the HCNM and staff. The HCNM has been involved in a preventive role in many disputes involving minorities (Foundation on Inter-Ethnic Relations, 1996; Lund, 1996, 63–4, 68–9; Zaagman and Thorburn, 1997).

The EU and the Council of Europe are also deeply involved in policies which impact on conflict prevention, even if they are not specifically designed for the purpose. The EU at its Lisbon Council proposed improving its capacity 'to tackle problems at their roots in order to anticipate the outbreak of crises' and 'contributing to the prevention and settlement of conflicts' (Keukeleire, 1994). The EU has undertaken 'deep' measures through, first, support for economic infrastructure and economic development, measures to strengthen democracy and the rule of law, and, second, its structured Europe, Partnership and Cooperation Agreements and the Stability Pact. It is also involved, with mixed results, in light conflict prevention through the Common Foreign and Security Policy (CFSP), the International Conference on the former Yugoslavia, economic sanctions, policy on recognition, and its diplomatic presence in Africa, the Mediterranean littoral and the Middle East (Rummell 1996).

The UN and several of the major regional organizations are also committed to conflict prevention (Brauwens and Reychler, 1994; Siccama, 1996). The UN Secretary-General has powers under Article 99 to 'bring to the attention of the Security Council any matter which in his opinion may threaten the maintenance of international peace and security'.[13] The Secretary-General frequently operates through Special Representatives (SRSG); one notable example has been Ahmedou Ould Abdullah's work in Burundi, which facilitated power-sharing arrangements and helped to calm the situation after the death of the Hutu president, Ntarymira, in an air crash in 1994 (Creative Associates 1997, 3–15). Although some steps to establish a capacity for prevention have been taken, the attention of the Secretary-General and the Security Council is mainly focused on conflicts that are already violent (Parsons, 1995), and the UN system's capacity is still regarded as weak – for example only forty officials in the UN secretariat were involved with prevention in 1995 (Peck, 1993; Findlay, 1996).[14] The UN lacks sufficient institutional machinery and personnel to turn its rhetorical commitment to preventive diplomacy into an effective reality (Evans 1993; Rupesinghe 1996b). Moreover, a significant number of states hold serious reservations about an international prevention regime, on the grounds of state sovereignty and non-intervention.[15] International financial institutions such as the International Monetary Fund and the World Bank are now playing an increasingly central role in deep prevention by linking financial assistance to conditionalities of good governance.

Several regional organizations have committed themselves to prevention in principle, although in each case local regional politics and political culture have influenced how the concept is interpreted. ASEAN, for example, has set up a Regional Security Forum, which aims to preserve the consensus of the South-East Asian governments and prevent interstate conflicts; implicit in the agreement is the understanding that the states do not involve themselves in one another's internal conflicts. The organization set the terms at an early stage for the Paris Agreements, which settled the Cambodia conflict in 1990 and sponsored Track II diplomacy on the Spratly Islands dispute in 1991 and thereafter; however, when conflicts have concerned separatism, there has been more inclination to avoid involvement than to address or resolve them (Siccama, 1996, 59–69).

The OAU introduced the African Mechanism Apparatus for Preventing, Managing and Resolving African Crises at its 1993 summit; the procedure allows the OAU Secretary-General to undertake mediation and fact-finding missions and to send special envoys. It was activated in the same year in Brazzaville-Congo, where an ethnically based post-election conflict had broken out, already with some violence. Secretary-General Salim appointed Mahmoud Sahnoun as Special Representative to mediate between the parties, with the agreement of the Congo government. Lund describes how Sahnoun's intervention led to negotiations in Gabon, a ceasefire, disarmament of militias and an agreement on fresh elections over disputed seats (Lund, 1996, 74). The mechanism has yet to be invoked in a situation where some violence has not broken out.

In Latin America, the OAS set up machinery to support democracies threatened with military coups (Lund, 1996, 74–8), to protect human rights and to monitor elections. This can be seen as a form of preventive diplomacy, although the strong consensus on non-intervention has limited the institutionalization of an explicit conflict prevention policy (Siccama, 1996, 39–42).

Successes and failures

It is easy to point to the major failures of conflict prevention; indeed, they have provided much of the stimulus for developing and enhancing a conflict prevention regime. Rwanda, which we deal with in the next chapter, is one dreadful example.[16] In Yugoslavia in the 1990s, both the CSCE and the EC suffered damage to their political credibility from their failure to prevent or contain the conflict. It was already clear in 1990 that conflict was brewing, after the first free elections that year had given victories to nationalist leaders. Tensions were rising between Slovenia and Croatia, on the one hand, which favoured a confederal association between the republics based on the EC model and a rapid transition to a market society, and Serbia, Montenegro and the Jugoslav National Army (JNA) which favoured maintaining the federal constitution and retaining central planning. The federal presidency was deadlocked, unable to resolve the conflict. It was at this stage, before the Slovenian secession, that light prevention was needed. Prime Minister Markovic was trying desperately to hold Yugoslavia together and bring about economic reform; but he did not receive enough support either from the international community, or from within Yugoslavia. The deteriorating situation within Croatia, and Milosevic's determination to assert his own and Serbia's interests at the expense of the rest of the federation, made any effort at prevention difficult. Unfortunately, the EC made a difficult situation worse, by first insisting on Yugoslavia's territorial integrity, at a time when this course played into Milosevic's hands, and then abruptly changing direction after the Slovenian and Croatian secessions and supporting them against Serbia, despite the recommendations of the Badinter Commission and the danger to Bosnia. The international community failed either to slow the process of disintegration or to provide sufficient support to those within Yugoslavia who were looking for a new political and economic dispensation preserving a multicultural state. Whether or not the tragedy could have been prevented, the West's policies, both before and during the conflict, were soon to be seen as a failure (Bennett, 1995; Woodward, 1995).

Measures intended to prevent conflict or, more broadly, to assist with development and good governance frequently overlap and duplicate one another, and at the same time large gaps are left. Among NGOs, which are playing an increasingly active role in this field (Rotberg, ed., 1996; van Tongeren, 1996),[17] a consensus is emerging that conflict prevention is more likely to be effective when it relies not upon a single but on a multi-track approach, in which interventions by local actors, external NGOs, governments and international organizations complement one another (Diamond and McDonald, 1996; Rupesinghe, 1996). Many representatives of governments and international organizations also accept the principle of multi-track approaches, though others remain reluctant to allow NGOs any role in matters that are perceived to touch on state security. The multi-track approach raises difficulties for NGOs, especially over autonomy, independence and impartiality. Critics have attacked both governments and NGOs for failure to sustain initiatives, a tendency to be led by media attention and volatile funding priorities, and a continuing low priority on pre-violence as opposed to post-violence interventions.

But a number of cases are candidates for successful conflict prevention. We have already referred to Estonia (1993), Latvia (1994), Guatemala (1993) and Fiji (1996). Other cases in the 1990s where violence has been averted even if the conflicts were not necessarily resolved include the dispute between the government of Ukraine and Russia and Russians in the Crimea, ethnic issues involving Hungarians outside Hungary, the Macedonian secession from Yugoslavia, and the Czech–Slovak divorce, the elections in South Africa and the Quebec issue. The former Soviet Union and the transitions in East Central Europe provide a veritable laboratory of different responses to conflict (table 4.3).

We have to be careful about what we mean by 'success'. There are many cases of conflict where violence has not yet broken out, but still may; others where a lull in the manifestations of conflict may be a temporary respite; and still others where a political conflict or a situation of inequality persists without physical violence, not because of agreement or consent, but because parties lack the means, opportunity or capacity to bring about change. We take as a crude measure of success in light conflict prevention the conjunction of a de-escalation of political tensions and steps towards addressing and transforming the issues in the conflict. More sophisticated measures should be based on systematic monitoring that, as

Table 4.3   The variety of response to the break-up of communist rule in Eastern Europe and the former Soviet Union

Response	Cases
Non-violent revolutions	the 'Velvet Revolution' in Czechoslovakia; the peaceful fall of the regime in East Germany; the change of government in Hungary
Peaceful transitions to elected systems	Bulgaria
Violent revolutions	Romania
Peaceful secessions	Russian and other newly independent states from the Soviet Union, in 1991; the Czech–Slovak divorce
Mainly peaceful secessions	Estonia, Latvia, Lithuania from the Soviet Union
Attempted secessions leading to violence	Chechnya from Russia; Slovenia, Croatia, Bosnia from Yugoslavia; Moldova (Trans-Dnestr), Nagorno-Karabakh, Georgia (after March 1998)
Ethnic issues that have remained largely non-violent	Hungarians outside Hungary; Russians outside Russia in Kazakhstan, Uzbekistan, Turkmenistan, Ukraine, Estonia, Latvia, Lithuania; ethnic groups within Ukraine; FYROM; Pomaks in Bulgaria; Greeks in Albania; Slav Macedonians in Greece
Crises which did not become violent	Crimea, Ukraine
Ethnic violence	Tajikistan
Suppressed non-violence	Kosovo (up to March 1998)

argued above, can be seen as a continuation of early warning research. Theory suggests that conflict transformation can be assessed by changes in the conflict structure, attitudes and behaviour captured in the conflict triangle. Translating this into a practical programme for monitoring, however, remains a task for research.

There is no doubt that there are real constraints which make internal conflicts, especially those involving ethnonational aspirations, difficult to deal with. Prevention may be politically and logistically hardest in societies which are most in need of it. There may well be situations where light prevention cannot be effective, especially if deep preventors are absent. Nevertheless, there is little question that conflict prevention is possible, under appropriate circumstances. The issue is what these circumstances are, and what approaches to conflict prevention are effective? The early studies suggest that important conditions include early and rapid implementation of policies; coordination among the actors involved in conflict prevention; a permissive approach from the government of the country or countries concerned; a long-term approach; and the involvement of the national interest of one of the intervening powers (Ugglas, 1994; Jentleson, 1996; Lund, 1996, 83–105). A comprehensive treatment of the question will require a comparative examination of deep and light preventors in both violent and averted conflicts.

Case Studies: Macedonia, Albania, Kosovo

To illustrate contemporary approaches to ongoing conflicts, we close this chapter with a look at efforts to prevent violent conflict in Macedonia, Albania and Kosovo during the 1990s.

After the war broke out in Yugoslavia in 1991, there were good grounds for fearing that it could spread to the southern Balkans. This was an area of mixed peoples, weak states and contested governments (see map 4). The Kosovo conflict, which had triggered the disintegration of Yugoslavia in 1987, remained acute; Macedonia was a weak state, of doubtful viability; and Albania's chaotic transition from communism gave many grounds for concern.[18] In Kosovo, the Albanian community (90 per cent of the population) had been living under Serb police rule since the revocation of autonomy in 1989. It was feared that an ignition of the ethnonational conflict could lead to a domino effect, destabilizing Macedonia, drawing in Albania and, at the worst, starting a new Balkan war in which Greece and Turkey might enter on opposite sides (Pettifer, 1992).[19] It was a sign of the seriousness with which this was taken that President Bush warned President Milosevic in 1992 that the USA was prepared to use force against Serbian troops in the event of any conflict caused by Serbian action; and President Clinton repeated the warning in 1993.

In response to these warning signs, the UN deployed its first ever preventive peacekeeping operation, UNPREDEP, in Macedonia in January 1993, consisting initially of five hundred Canadians, later replaced by seven hundred Scandinavians. In July 1993, the USA sent three hundred of its own troops (Lund 1996b). Whether Milosevic ever intended to threaten Macedonia is unclear; UNPREDEP did at least check a number of probes by Serbian forces along the Macedonian border. UNPREDEP also became involved, indirectly, in the internal ethnic relations of Macedonia. A UN Special Representative attached to the force held regular meetings with the political parties, convened national youth

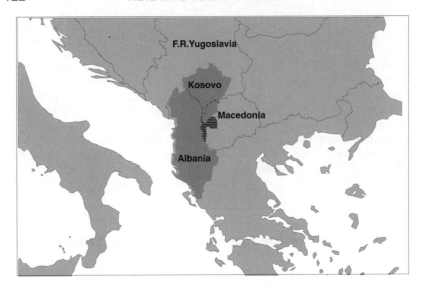

Albanian majority

No absolute majority; Albanians a large group

Map 4   The Southern Balkans

meetings and undertook a number of projects to encourage bridge-building, formation of NGOs and awareness of international human rights instruments. The government also invited an OSCE Mission to participate in these meetings and monitor the internal as well as the regional political situation. The HCNM frequently visited Macedonia to discuss educational and employment policies, citizenship and local government; and the government has adopted some of his suggestions. His visit in February 1995, after lives were lost in a demonstration over the unauthorized Albanian university at Tetovo, reduced tensions. He also contributed to an inter-ethnic Round Table (Zaagman and Thorburn, 1997, 56–9). NGOs, such as the Catholic Relief Services, the Center for Inter Ethnic Relations and Search for Common Ground, have initiated educational projects, problem-solving workshops, conflict resolution training and media projects designed to build bridges. All these measures have helped to an extent to build cross-community relations and some prevention capacity, although their breadth of coverage is inevitably limited. As we write, ethnic relations remain tense, and society remains polarized along ethnic lines. The violence in Kosovo in 1998 certainly increased the risk of spillover into Macedonia, and KLA members and stolen weapons from Albania appeared in Macedonia in 1998. But while the Albanian Party of Democratic Prosperity (PDP) remains part of the government coalition and the Gligorov government continues to pursue policies of relative moderation, major internal violence has been averted, even if the long-term future remains unresolved.

The Macedonian government has incurred political debts to the international community which has protected its interests in relation to Yugoslavia and Greece. While the Macedonian government and the international community continue to perceive a community of interest, it is likely that they will both continue with policies designed to avert conflict. But state-building remains difficult, for the Albanian population considers its treatment in the new state to be discriminatory and unequal, and on the Macedonian side there is a fear of including on equal terms a large national minority whose loyalty is conditional. This is a situation that will require continuing prevention efforts.

The second situation we will consider is that of Albania itself, which emerged from the harshest communist regime in Eastern Europe in a state of poverty and distress. The Albanian case illustrates how it is possible to identify deep-rooted sources of instability and potential conflicts of interest, and yet how hard it is to predict the actual combination of events that trigger violence. In 1995 it was possible to identify a number of important cleavages in Albanian society. There was a deep political polarization between the Democratic Party, which won the 1992 elections, and the Socialist Party. The transition to a market economy had resulted in a rapid process of social stratification, with winners and losers emerging from the transition. There were also potential conflicts between Albania's government and its ethnic minorities, and between the regional (Gheg and Tosk) and religious (Orthodox, Catholic, Muslim) identity groups. The capacity for managing or preventing conflict was very weak, although a number of bodies, including the Soros Foundation, the Council of Europe, development agencies and the churches, were making efforts to improve it (Miall, 1995). Although small-scale conflicts were rife, it did not seem likely that the major cleavages would lead to a civil war. Yet in early 1997 the Albanian state partly collapsed, armed rebels ransacked the government armouries in the south of the country and 1,800 people were killed in the ensuing anarchy. It was the coincidence of two unexpected events that caused the rebellion: President Berisha's decision to conduct the 1996 elections in a manner that international observers condemned as neither fair nor free, and the extraordinary growth and collapse of the Albanian pyramid schemes. The result was that Berisha, who had removed almost all legitimate sources of opposition, faced a revolt that was personally directed against himself, and found his army and police force melting away. Clearly, this was a failure for conflict prevention. Nevertheless, the intervention of the Operation Alba that followed, directed by the Italian government on the basis of a UN mandate, was a remarkable success (Miall, 1997). It halted the slide into further violence; it laid the way for fresh elections; and it provided a path out of the crisis which gained international and domestic legitimacy. Franz Vranitzky, the Personal Representative of the OSCE Chair-in-Office, played an important role by mediating between the Albanian politicians on several occasions, and the Italian NGO Comunità di Sant'Egidio helped to broker an agreement on a transitional government. The new government was more broadly based, and began to undertake some measures to reduce political polarization and stabilize the economy. However, it still faced continued widespread disorder and crime, and was not wholly in control of all parts of the country. As we write, Albanian politics remain highly charged, but the protracted violent conflicts that have been seen elsewhere have not occurred.

In Kosovo, a much more intractable conflict between the large Albanian community and the government of Serbia remains, in the late 1990s, unresolved. The Albanian side sought to balance the asymmetric conflict by internationalizing it and by withdrawing from a state it does not accept; hence its 'shadow state' policy and the non-participation in Serbian elections. The Serbian side, in contrast, treated the conflict as an internal security matter. The recent historical relationship was bitter, and hostility and mistrust high. Police repression on the Serb side, and demonstrations and occasional terrorist incidents on the Albanian side, served to sustain a highly charged and volatile situation. The failure of the Dayton Agreement to offer any framework for tackling the problem led the Albanians to begin to despair of international help, and to turn away from the patient policy of non-violence, advocated by the Kosovo Albanian leader Ibrahim Rugova, to more militant solutions, such as those offered by the Kosovo Liberation Army (KLA) (see box 4.5).

By 1998 the KLA, acting on its own initiative, managed to seize large parts of rural Kosovo, including areas near the Albanian border. It also won widespread support among the Kosovo Albanian population. But by August a strong force of Serbian military and police units dislodged the KLA from most of the areas they held, causing the Albanian population to flee from towns and villages affected by the crackdown. By September 1998 some 240,000 people had been displaced, and a humanitarian disaster was in the making.

The responsibility for the violence in Kosovo must be attributed primarily to President Milosevic, who had deprived the Kosovo Albanians of their autonomy, their jobs and their schools, and whose security forces suppressed dissent with great brutality. The leaders of the KLA and the Serbian security forces were the agents who actually triggered the fighting which occurred in 1998.

The international community deplored these events, but international efforts to prevent them had little success; nor did the conditions for successful conflict prevention obtain (see p. 121). The international community was divided and its actions were not always consistent. It maintained an 'outer wall of sanctions' against the Federal Republic of

BOX 4.5 A conflict resolution approach to Kosovo

On the Serbian side:
The position is that Kosovo must remain part of Serbia.

Underlying Serbian interests include:

* the identification of Kosovo with 'old Serbia' and its central importance in the Serbian national consciousness;
* the Serbian churches and historical sites associated with this;
* the Serbian community in Kosovo;
* the mines and mineral resources;
* the strategic protection of the mountains around Kosovo.

There are also significant fears of accepting Kosovo's independence:

* fear of a Greater Albania;
* fear of Serbia fragmenting along ethnic lines.

A   The question to be asked from a conflict resolution point of view is whether the underlying needs of the Serbian people (for security, identity and development) are best served by Kosovo remaining part of Serbia on existing terms, or whether the costs are likely to be too high and there are other ways in which these needs can be sustained.

On the Albanian side:
The position is that Kosovo must be independent.

Underlying Albanian interests include:

* the identification of Kosovo with ancient Illyria before the Slav migrations;
* affinity with Albanian peoples in neighbouring countries;
* resentment at being treated as second-class citizens in their own country;
* a growing conviction that full human rights and control over their own economic development can only come with complete political self-determination.

There are fears of mounting Serbian use of force if the status quo is maintained.

B   The questions to be asked from a conflict resolution point of view are whether the underlying needs of the Albanians can be met only by full independence, or whether there are other alternatives; and whether there are more productive ways of satisfying those needs than the use of violence.

For third parties seeking to encourage a win–win outcome, the aim is to use available influence to persuade key constituencies on both sides to give mutually compatible answers to questions (A) and (B), so that sufficient political space is opened up for a possible agreement.

Yugoslavia (FRY) – the rump state consisting of Serbia and Montenegro, and called for a settlement based on enhanced autonomy. This solution, however, was rejected out of hand by Milosevic, and gave the Albanians little incentive to negotiate, since it ruled out independence. During 1995 and 1996 the West courted Milosevic in order to gain a settlement to the Bosnia issue, in effect sacrificing conflict prevention in Kosovo in order to achieve a war ending in Bosnia. The Peace Agreement which brought the fighting in Bosnia to an end (signed in Paris in December 1996 after talks in Dayton, Ohio) mentioned Kosovo only once, to the bitter disappointment of the Kosovo Albanians. Soon afterwards the EU unconditionally recognized the FRY. It was after these developments that the Albanians in Kosovo turned away from Rugova's non-violent approach toward the KLA.

A number of Track II initiatives were undertaken, both by international NGOs and embedded parties (for example, a significant dialogue developed among student groups in Belgrade and Pristina). The Comunità di Sant'Egidio mediated an education agreement in 1996 between Milosevic and Rugova (though Milosevic failed to implement it) and the Bertelsmann Foundation hosted a series of high-level Round Tables that explored several possible outcomes and transitional strategies, some of which reappeared in the parties' negotiating positions (Troebst, 1998). Despite the apparent intractability of the conflict, it does not appear that the interests of the Serbian and Albanian communities are necessarily incompatible (see box 4.5).

At the time of writing, NATO was preparing air strikes to punish Milosevic for failing to observe a UN resolution requiring him to withdraw Serbian forces. It seemed clear that the KLA was not strong enough to take Kosovo, and also that the Serbian government was unable to hold it securely. This deadlock could foster either a negotiated settlement, or continued fighting. By September 1998 both sides had made moves away from their original positions in response to the violence. Milosevic said that a form of autonomy was negotiable. The Albanian side said that it was prepared to accept a republic within the FRY on a transitional basis.

Table 4.4   Success and failure in conflict prevention

	Success	*Failure*
Light measures	armed conflict averted	armed conflict
Deep measures	peaceful change	conflict-prone situation

But with many killed and hundreds of thousands displaced, the conflict had reached a level of intensity and bitterness which would make a settlement difficult to achieve. It had gone well past the stage of conflict prevention.

Conclusion

In this chapter we have looked at the causes and preventors of contemporary armed conflicts. If, as A. J. P. Taylor suggests, wars have both general and specific causes, then systems of conflict prevention should address both the generic conditions which make societies prone to armed conflicts, and the potential triggers which translate war-proneness into armed conflict. If deep conflict prevention is successful in providing capacity to manage emergent conflicts peacefully at an early stage, it should make societies less conflict-prone. If light conflict prevention is successful, it should avert armed conflicts, without necessarily removing the underlying conditions of proneness to armed conflict (see table 4.4). Both light and deep approaches to conflict prevention are clearly necessary.

The cases we have quoted suggest that conflict prevention is not easy. It is difficult for the preventors to gain a purchase in situations of violence or chaotic change, and episodes of violence can readily overwhelm them. Nevertheless, where preventive measures have begun, and where circumstances are propitious, a cumulative process of peacebuilding can be seen. The challenge is gradually to introduce and strengthen the preventors, and to foster a culture of prevention, with early identification, discussion and transformation of emergent conflicts.

The next chapter turns to the daunting challenge of introducing conflict resolution in war zones, where violence is ongoing.

5

Working in War Zones

Passing over heaps of dead and dying, he came to a neighbouring village. It was in ashes, having been an Abarian village and therefore burnt, in accordance with the laws of war, by the Bulgarians. Old men mangled by bayonets watched their wives lying with gashes in their throats, clasping their children to their blood-stained breasts. Amongst the dying were girls who had been used to satisfy a number of heroes' natural needs, and had afterwards been disembowelled. Other women, half burnt alive, begged to be put out of their pain. The ground was covered with brains, arms and legs.

As fast as he could, Candide made off to another village. This one was Bulgarian, and the Abarian heroes had treated it in the same way.

Voltaire, Candide, 1759

We have been angry for a long time . . . We all wear masks. Behind these masks is a mad, horrified people.

NGO worker, Liberia

When drums beat hard soft voices are not heard.

Francis Quarles, 1642

This chapter addresses the issues of conflict mitigation, alleviation and containment where prevention has failed and conflict has become severe. These wars, as we have seen, often persist for years, causing untold human suffering, but only sporadically catching the attention of the international community at large. In the next chapter we look at the way wars end. Here, we ask if there can be a role for conflict resolution in the most unpropitious of environments – active war zones where violent conflict continues to rage unabated.

We begin by looking at the behaviours which seem to characterize many contemporary, i.e. post-Cold War, international-social conflicts, especially the targeting of civilians and the destruction of social and cultural institutions. We then examine one of the most extreme manifestations of this kind of emergency, the crisis which overwhelmed Rwanda in 1994. After a brief discussion of the spectrum of intervention options for the international community in active war zones from abstention to peace enforcement, we then focus on the changing role of UN peacekeepers in these situations (creating security space), and the role of NGOs, UN civil agencies and aid agencies in responding to humanitarian needs (creating humanitarian space). There is a growing recognition that these agencies need to work together to link mitigation and relief to the political tasks that are necessary to settle the conflict and resolve it within a sustainable peace process (creating political space). The central argument in this chapter is that peacekeepers and the various humanitarian and development agencies working in war zones need to be aware of the conflict resolution dimension of their work.

War Zones, War Economies and Cultures of Violence

In this section, we will look at some of the hardest contemporary situations with which conflict resolution has to deal: those where warlords and militias have come to establish their power over civilian populations. In such situations, 'not only is there little recognition of the distinction between combatant and civilian, or of any obligation to spare women, children and the elderly, but the valued institutions and way of life of a whole population can be targeted', with the objective of creating 'states of terror which penetrate the entire fabric of grassroots social relations . . . as a means of social control' (Summerfield, 1996, 1). The academic community, humanitarian workers, UN policy staff and military planners often refer to these as 'complex emergencies', or 'complex political emergencies' to differentiate them from traditional interstate territorial and resource conflicts on the one hand, and natural disasters on the other:

> A complex emergency is a humanitarian disaster that occurs in a conflict zone and is complicated by, or results from, the conflicting interests of warring parties. Its causes are seldom exclusively natural or military: in many cases a marginally subsistent population is precipitated toward disaster by the consequences of militia action or a natural occurrence such as earthquake or drought. The presence of militias and their interest in controlling and extorting the local population will impede and in some cases seriously threaten relief efforts. In addition to violence against the civilian populations, civilian installations such as hospitals, schools, refugee centers, and cultural sites will become war objectives and may be looted frequently or destroyed. (*Mackinlay, ed., 1996, 14–15*)

Civilians are the targets in these wars, not accidental victims. In the First World War, over 80 per cent of battlefield deaths were combatants; by the 1990s over 90 per cent of war-related deaths are civilians, killed in their own homes and communities, which have become the battlefields of international-social wars. As Nordstrom has remarked, the least dangerous place to be in most contemporary wars is in the military (Nordstrom, 1992, 271), and 'dirty war' strategies, originally identified with state-sponsored terrorism, are now a feature of a widening band of militias, paramilitaries, warlords and armies seeking control of resources through depredation, terror and force. In chapters 1 and 2 we argued that new thinking was needed within conflict resolution in order to respond to the embedded cultures and economies of violence which were emerging and which provided more formidable barriers against constructive intervention than were originally assumed in early conflict theory. In order to understand why this is so we need to look more closely at the political economy and the culture and psychology of war zones.

Some analysts have argued that these behaviours in contemporary wars are senseless and irrational convulsions of violence, expressions of ancient hatreds and regressions to tribal war and neo-medieval warlordism (Kaplan, 1994). Others, including those writing from an anthropological and radical political economy perspective, offer more systematic explanations. In a pattern that has been well documented in the 1990s, for example in parts of Africa such as Tigray, Eritrea, Southern Sudan, Northern Uganda, Angola and Somalia (Macrae and Zwi, 1994, 13–20), but also elsewhere, scorched earth tactics are common, with livestock seized, grain stores attacked and looted, wells and watering places poisoned. Forced population movements are engineered to perpetuate dependency and control. Duffield speculates that rather than being an aberrant and irrational phenomenon, contemporary internal wars may represent 'the emergence of entirely new types of social formation adapted for survival on the margins of the global economy' (Duffield, 1997, 100). Actors like the international drug cartels in Central and South America, the Taliban in Afghanistan and rebel groups in West Africa have effectively set up parallel economies, trading in precious resources such as hardwoods, diamonds, drugs and so on. In Cambodia the Khmer Rouge leadership profited so much from the smuggling of timber and gems across the Thai border that it saw little incentive to demobilize its forces as agreed under the Paris Peace Accords of 1991, while there is evidence of some collusion between the Khmer Rouge and the Cambodian Army in mutual profiteering from this trade (Keen, 1998). Although this does not apply to all internal conflicts, there are war zone economies where civilians are seen as 'a resource base to be either corralled, plundered, or cleansed' (Duffield, 1997, 103). Humanitarian and development aid is captured, and humanitarian workers kidnapped, held hostage and killed. These wars can be seen to be both lucrative and rational for those who can take the advantage and are prepared to act violently to gain power.

In our view this kind of rapacious behaviour is often as much an effect of the disintegration of order in internal conflicts as a cause of it. Conflicts which may have been initiated for political-ideological (type 2) or ethno-national (type 3) reasons may subsequently disintegrate into purely factional conflict (type 4). A summary of Outram's analysis (1997) of the conflict in Liberia highlights this point. A series of wars since 1989 have reduced Liberia, a potentially prosperous African country, to a state of chaos and aid dependency. At least six factions have been vying for power, while a regional peacekeeping force, ECOMOG, has attempted to enforce a series of short-lived peace agreements. Historically, Liberia was divided between the dominant 'Americos', descendants of freed American slaves who created the Liberian state, and the indigenous peoples, themselves ethnically divided into at least sixteen different ethnic groups. From the mid-1980s President Doe attempted to consolidate his power base by favouring the Krahn ethnic group with economic and educational advantages, and by promoting them in the army and police force. When Charles Taylor's National Patriotic Front of Liberia (NPFL) started the First War in 1989, its declared objective was to liberate all of the people from Doe's regime, but it was clear that both sides (Doe's national army, the Armed Forces of Liberia (AFL) and Taylor's NPFL) were killing those who were perceived to be enemies, the test of which was ethnicity. The AFL targeted Gio and Mano peoples; the NPFL killed Krahn. After a stalemate, Taylor launched the Second War late in 1992. By the time of the Third War of 1994–5 the violence was no longer inter-ethnic but factional, and driven by general economic predation. This predation operated at two levels. First, the faction leaders built up power and wealth by dealing in the exploitation of the country's considerable natural resources. Taylor gained from the timber, rubber and mineral resources, while two factions (ULIMO-J and ULIMO-K) fought over the diamonds and gold resources. Second, because none of this wealth was used to pay the rank-and-file faction fighters, they were left to fend for themselves by theft and robbery. In doing so, there were widespread violations of human rights, as people were terrorized to part with their goods and property or to prevent them escaping from conscription and forced labour. This type of behaviour can best be described as warlordism, which is characterized by a 'ruthless and extractive attitude towards society and the economy' and by reliance on military force and violence (Outram, 1997, 363). This analysis helps to explain a good deal about behaviours in war zones in general. But for Outram this does not go far enough, because it does not explain the extent and absurdity of the violence involved. The violence goes beyond rational expectations of what can be gained economically, for a rational warlord would not kill the goose that lays the golden egg. To explain it, we have to take into account socio-psychological considerations as well as economic motivations. In Liberia, accumulated fears have driven people beyond killing the 'ethnic enemy' into factions which practise a general and undirected vengeance (Outram, 1997, 368).

We can understand this phenomenon further by considering the work of Nordstrom. While Outram concentrated on the experience of the warring factions and the political economy which they constructed, Nordstrom has worked on the experiences of the victims of the violence. Following field research in Mozambique and Sri Lanka, she explained the many stories of absurd destruction and the use of terror in warfare as deliberate efforts to destroy the normal meanings that define and guide daily life (Nordstrom, 1992, 269). This is the process whereby dirty war becomes the means through which economies of violence merge with what Nordstrom calls 'cultures of violence'. As she puts it, 'violence parallels power' and people come to have no alternative but to accept 'fundamental knowledge constructs that are based on force' (Nordstrom, 1992, 269).

At this point we must address one of the most difficult challenges for conflict resolution. Can there be any role for it in these circumstances? May it not even be counter-productive? For Duffield, for example, one consequence of this kind of analysis is to cast doubt on the validity of conflict resolution approaches to internal wars (1997, 100). Indeed, he suggests that just as aid capture can be used to serve the developments of parallel economies in war zones, conflict resolution interventions can be similarly incorporated and manipulated. In our view, part of his argument is based on a partial misunderstanding of the conflict resolution approach, which he misleadingly identifies with a purely 'social-psychological model'. Nevertheless, working in war zones clearly does create serious challenges for conflict resolution, and requires the analyst or intervener to be aware of their particular dynamics. We have commented elsewhere with reference to humanitarian intervention how principles of humanity, impartiality, neutrality and universality are unavoidably compromised in the intensely politicized environment of active conflict (Ramsbotham and Woodhouse, 1996). Interveners are confronted with agonizing dilemmas and difficult choices as a result (Slim, 1997; Weiss and Collins, 1996). The same applies to conflict resolution. But abstention involves equally difficult choices. There are no 'quick fixes'. What is required is patient and sensitive efforts to maximize help where most effective, fully mindful of the unpredictability of unforeseen consequences.

To take one contemporary conflict resolution approach as an example, Nordstrom argues that there is a 'need to create a counter-life world construct to challenge the politico-military one'. Evidently, it is very difficult for civilians wishing to seek an alternative to 'the dirty war paradigm as a survival mechanism' to find one in the vicious and dangerous environment of an active war zone (Nordstrom, 1992, 270). Nevertheless, there are innumerable examples of resistance to the rationality and culture of the war zone to set beside the otherwise overwhelming catalogue of brutalization and atrocity. These are the usually unsung heroes of conflict resolution and peacemaking in the midst of violence, often at great personal risk. In Burundi's capital, Bujumbura, for example, residents in two neighbourhoods, one Hutu and one Tutsi, formed a mixed committee of fifty-five men and women to try to protect each other from attack. In Colombia there has been the growth of 'communities of peace', many of them developed by Colombia's indigenous Indians, declaring themselves neutral in the fighting between the military and guerrillas. Many have been killed for taking this position, but they persist with the help of an organization, the Antioquia Indigenous Organization, supported by Oxfam, to help provide food, shelter and medicine, and to publicize their situation. In Liberia some communities have formed community watch teams to protect themselves against armed groups which threaten their communities (Cairns, 1997, 85–6). During the wars in former Yugoslavia, groups such as the Osijek Peace Centre in Croatia worked to counter ethnic hatred and maintain cultures of peace (Curle, 1994).

Before going on to consider what scope there is for conflict resolution approaches in general in war zones, however, we first acknowledge the scale of the obstacles in their way by citing the disastrous events in Rwanda between 1993 and 1996 as an illustration of the difficulties which the international community and indigenous organizations face when a systematized culture of violence sweeps across a whole country. Rwanda was not like Liberia. It was not fragmented into warlord-run areas, without social, economic or political programmes, but provides a chilling example of what can happen when a ruling faction turns its political and military energies to keeping power and to wrecking a peace agreement by violence. The enormity of what happened there, under the gaze of the international community, resulted in comprehensive reflections on how to respond more effectively in the future.

Case Study: Rwanda

During a three-month period in 1994 hundreds of thousands of civilians were killed in the course of a deliberately organized genocide in Rwanda, following an internationally brokered and supported peace under the aegis of the UN. How did this come about?

The peace agreement

In June 1993 both main parties to the conflict, the Tutsi-led Rwanda Patriotic Front (RPF) forces that had invaded in 1990 and the Hutu-dominated government, had asked the UN to be prepared for the quick deployment of a peacekeeping force as soon as the peace talks which were conducted at Arusha in Tanzania were concluded.[1] Following a year of negotiations, agreement was reached on a set of protocols covering human rights issues, power-sharing in a transitional government and parliament, the resettlement of refugees and internally displaced persons (who by February 1993 numbered one million) and the creation of a unified national army. Presidential and parliamentary elections were to be organized at the end of the period of transition, and a commission would be appointed to draft a new constitution which would then be put to a referendum. Nine months after the inauguration of the transitional government, the first groups of refugees would be allowed to resettle in a number of repatriation areas. This followed the classic lines of what in chapter 7 we will call the UN's 'post-settlement peacebuilding standard operating procedure'.

In August 1993, following the signing of the Arusha Agreement, the Security Council approved the establishment of a United Nations Assistance Mission for Rwanda (UNAMIR), with a peacekeeping force under the command of Brigadier-General Dallaire. The two-year UNAMIR operation was planned in four phases: phase one would end when the transitional government was established (anticipated to be late 1993); phase two would involve the demobilization of armed forces and the integration of a new national army; phase three would include the establishment of a new demilitarized zone and the integration of the gendarmerie; and phase four would cover supervision of the final stages leading up to the elections. Throughout all four phases the mission would assist in ensuring security in the capital, Kigali, and provide protection for the repatriation of refugees and displaced persons. It would also assist in the coordination of humanitarian relief operations. Mission strength would build up to 2,548 in phase two and decline to 930 by phase four.

Breakdown and genocide

A major obstacle to progress with the plan was the failure to install the transitional government. UNAMIR's deployment was delayed and it never received all the equipment it required. Despite this, and while expressing concern at the lack of progress, in April 1994 the Security Council extended the mandate of UNAMIR for a further six months, until July 1994. The next day witnessed the event that was to project the war into a vicious and decisive phase, the shooting down of the presidential aircraft at Kigali, killing President Habyarimana of Rwanda and the President of Burundi.

On the same evening of the crash what appeared to be a planned programme of killing began, directed from the highest level. Prunier's authoritative study identified the main perpetrators of the genocide as: the core group of Habyarimana's closest advisers; the leaders of the local communes, numbering up to three hundred; the *interahamwe* militias, possibly numbering up to 30,000, who carried out most of the killing; and members of the military elite and the Presidential Guard, which provided support to local *interahamwe*. The first act was the killing of opposition politicians, mostly moderate Hutu, followed by civilians who supported the peace process, including journalists, civil servants and human rights activists. One of the early victims was the Prime Minister Agathe Uwi-lingiyimana, who was killed along with the UN peacekeepers from Belgium acting as her bodyguards (Prunier, 1995). After the annihilation of the political opposition, the minority Tutsi community in general became the target. In the three months from April to June 1994 between 500,000 and 800,000 people were killed, two million fled to neighbouring countries, and one million were displaced within Rwanda.

Following the killing of ten of its peacekeepers, in deliberately brutal fashion, the Belgian government withdrew its battalion from UNAMIR. On 20 April the Secretary-General informed the UN Security Council that in the new situation UNAMIR could not carry out the tasks for which it had been deployed. Three options were offered: to reinforce UNAMIR; to reduce it to a small group in the capital acting as an intermediary in attempts to secure a ceasefire; or to withdraw altogether. General Dallaire said that with a brigade of 5,000 soldiers he could stop most of the killing, but the Security Council took the second option and decided to reduce the UNAMIR forces. With massacres continuing on a large scale in Kigali and especially in the south of the country, the UN had run down its peace-keeping force at precisely the time when such a force was most needed.

By the end of April pressure on the UN to act was increasing, especially from African countries. The Secretary-General urged the Security Council to re-engage. On 18 May, the Security Council belatedly imposed an arms embargo on Rwanda and expanded UNAMIR's mandate to provide for the security and protection of refugees through the establishment of secure areas, and to provide security for relief operations. Authorization was granted to expand the force from 540 to 5,500 troops (UNAMIR II), although it took six months before this larger force was in place. Because of the delays in deploying UNAMIR II, the Security Council authorized a French proposal to deploy a force under Chapter VII of the charter (Operation Turquoise), tasked to establish a humanitarian protected zone in south-west Rwanda, where an estimated two million people were internally displaced. The priority was to attempt to deal with the unprece-dented humanitarian crisis principally in the north-west and south-west of the country. The French troops withdrew in August, amidst criticism that the force's effect had been to protect those responsible for the genocide for national-political reasons.

Despite the alarming instability and violence which still continued, the context in which UNAMIR was operating had changed. The full-scale war and the genocide were finally ended, not by international inter-vention, but by the military victory of the RPF. The new Tutsi-dominated government asserted its own responsibility for security and questioned the role of UNAMIR. UNAMIR's mandate was extended for six months from June 1995, but with reduced troop numbers, and it was withdrawn in April 1996. A small Human Rights Field Operation remained, and the

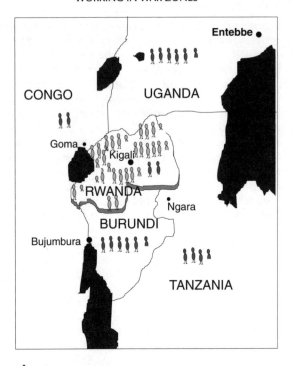

☙ 100,000 refugees/displaced people

☙ 100,000 returnees

Map 5   Rwanda and surrounding countries: refugees and returnees, February
1998

Sources: ReliefWeb, UNHCR

government agreed to the establishment of a UN office in Rwanda to
support the processes of reconciliation, the return of refugees, the
strengthening of the judicial system and the rehabilitation of the country's
infrastructure.

Lessons learned

The effectiveness of the UNAMIR mission, and the response of the
international community in general to the crisis, was inhibited from the
beginning by a number of factors. It has been suggested that an increasing
feeling of 'Africa fatigue' and 'compassion fatigue' was beginning to affect
the judgements and motivations of the main powers in the Security
Council, and that this produced a failure of political will to provide the

mandate and the resources which an effective peacekeeping operation would require. The débâcle in Somalia also induced a more cautious attitude, particularly on the part of US politicians and policy-makers after the much publicized deaths of eighteen US Rangers on 3 October 1993. This was to have a paralysing effect in Rwanda, leading to the UN ignoring warnings of the impending disaster, which came from NGOs and from the UNAMIR commander – on 11 January 1994 Dallaire had warned the UN Secretariat of the Hutu extremists' plans to assassinate politicians at the swearing-in of the transitional government, and also of plans to kill Belgian soldiers in an effort to force the withdrawal of the peacekeeping force. His warning was set aside, and other requests for reinforcements and authority to seize arms being delivered in violation of the ceasefire were refused. The UN's failure to take the early warning seriously was due partly to overload, and partly to the Secretariat's assessment that the Security Council would refuse any more proactive proposals (Adelman and Suhrke, 1996, 28–40). It was also clear that the humanitarian agencies of the international community were poorly pre-pared to respond to emergencies on the scale of Goma, when one million refugees crossed the border into Zaire in the space of a few days. This case study does not extend to the complex politics of the refugee camps over the next two years (1994–6), but here, too, a series of reforms was called for, causing much soul-searching among the humanitarian agencies.

Amongst the most comprehensive assessments of the 1994 catastrophe has been the Joint Evaluation conducted at the instigation of the Danish Ministry of Foreign Affairs and its development wing, Danida (Eriksson, 1996). Oxfam has also produced a concise and carefully focused analysis of the response of the international community to the Rwanda crisis (Vassall Adams, 1994). For example, Vassall Adams concludes that, while primary responsibility for the genocide lay with extremist groups inside Rwanda, the international community (specifically the major powers) was culpable by failing to respond effectively. These and other evaluations suggested that a major reform of the UN, both in its peacekeeping role and in its humanitarian capacity, was needed (Whitman and Pocock, eds, 1996; United Nations, 1996). For the future, Vassall Adams suggests, *inter alia*, that the UN form an Office of Preventive Diplomacy in order to be better able to respond to emerging conflicts; that UN peacekeeping be reformed, including better preparation for early and rapid deployment of forces; that the efforts of civilian/humanitarian agencies be better coordi-nated both among themselves and with the military; and that arms flows to conflict areas should be much more strictly controlled and regulated through the UN's Register of Conventional Arms (and should cover small arms and land mines, in particular to governments or groups which violate the basic human rights of their citizens). The Joint Evaluation study found that the NGO response to the crisis was mixed, with criti-cisms directed at the duplication and waste of resources and at some examples of unprofessional and irresponsible conduct (Eriksson, 1996,

59–60, 152–3). From this array of suggestions, two points in particular can be seen as significant from a conflict resolution perspective.

First, the decision by the Security Council to reduce its peacekeeping force to a minimum once the Belgian contingent was withdrawn is seen to be precisely the reverse of what should have been done. The ability of the small rump force left behind in Kigali to protect thousands of civilians during the period of the genocide indicates that the caution about peace-keeping, which resulted from experience in Somalia, should be reviewed and a renewed commitment to peacekeeping made. UN peacekeeping forces, mandated to protect civilians and to provide the security necessary for the delivery of humanitarian aid, are an important part of the conflict resolution process in war zones, providing the platform from which political and humanitarian spaces can be maintained even under the most extreme pressures. In practical terms this means, in the short term, much more positive support by those UN member states with the greatest military capacity to provide expertise, training, logistical support and finance for deploying UN peacekeepers under existing stand-by arrange-ments. In the longer term both the Oxfam study and the Joint Evaluation recommended that UN peacekeeping capability should be strengthened by the creation of a rapid deployment force, either directly under UN control or, with UN support, under the control of regional organizations such as the OAU and the OAS (Vassall Adams, 1994, 60; Eriksson, 1996, 48). Both reports also called for a 'harder' concept of peacekeeping, which nevertheless belongs within the category of non-coercive forms of conflict management, through the definition of standard operating procedures for UN peacekeeping missions, enabling and resourcing them to protect civilians threatened by political violence.

Second, and perhaps most significant, was the failure to act on warnings about the situation coming from indigenous human rights NGOs. As repression of political opponents and of Tutsi mounted after the invasion of Rwanda by the RPF in 1990, a group of Rwandan human rights NGOs was formed. It created a coalition within Rwanda, the Comité de Liaison des Associations de Défense des Droits de l'Homme au Rwanda, and made links with international organizations. Their warnings prompted an international commission to report in March 1993 that the Habyarimana regime had already engaged in acts of genocide against Tutsi, that further killings were threatened and that the militias (who later carried out the April 1994 genocide) should be disbanded. One Kigali-based NGO leader, Monique Mujyawamariya, was very active through 1993 and up to March 1994, warning foreign governments and international organiza-tions. One fax in particular revealed extensive preparations for systematic killings. Most of these warnings were ignored, or not acted on effectively. After its military victory the RPF and the government it installed removed the UN and most NGOs from the country, and, although human rights NGOs have remained active and important, others have not been able to sustain a significant role in peacebuilding. While reconstruction proceeds slowly, repatriation and reintegration of Hutu refugees has been slow and reconciliation at best a distant aspiration (Des Forges, 1996).

Preparing the Ground for Conflict Resolution

The Rwanda case illustrates a failure of early warning and prevention, and inadequate engagement by the international community. How, then, should the international community respond better, not only in the extreme situation of war zones, but also in other cases where divided societies fall into violent political conflict? What measures can be taken by the international community to prepare the ground for conflict resolution, after violence has broken out but before the parties reach the stage of active negotiations?

Azar and others in the conflict resolution field have been highly critical of many of the ways in which states and international organizations actually do intervene. Galtung, for example, criticizes 'conflict dictators', who impose settlements in their own interests. Burton urges that the parties must be encouraged to analyse their underlying needs in an open, exploratory process. The approaches they advocate are at odds with the stock-in-trade of international diplomats, for whom sticks and carrots are an essential means of inducing or forcing parties towards a settlement, for which an international third party provides the framework. Nevertheless, Azar recognized the importance of a positive international role, which he especially relates to 'development diplomacy'. He argued that 'the nature and direction of interventionist diplomacy must be shaped in such a manner as to reduce the severity of deep-rooted causes of social conflict' (Azar, 1990: 133). It follows from our updating of Azar that if contemporary conflicts increasingly have global sources and involve international or regional actors, then their management must also include an international dimension.

First, it is important to be aware of the role of international agencies in fuelling internal conflicts. Part of the task of conflict analysis (especially in asymmetric conflicts, as chapter 1 indicated) is to identify the external props by which the conflict is sustained. Outside parties may be supporting the contending parties, militarily or economically. Arms traders or mercenaries may fuel the conflict by directly supplying the means of war. International financial organizations may impose policies which precipitate conflict, and companies may make investments that sustain it. The same is true, as we have seen, in the case of humanitarian and development aid. Where this is the case, measures to influence these parties are required, often outside the war zone. There is now a good deal of auditing of the activities of states and companies and international financial organizations from the point of view of human rights, but, as yet, inadequate monitoring of their impact on internal conflicts.

Second, the international community has a powerful role to play in legitimating procedures and proposals for outcomes. UN resolutions, for example, may play a critical role in setting the parameters for a peace process, as did Resolutions 242 and 338 over the Middle East, and 435 which laid the groundwork for the eventual settlement in Namibia. Legitimation, of course, is a two-edged sword. The international community was criticized for conferring legitimacy on the ethnonationalist parties in Bosnia by including them in international negotiations, while excluding the moderates. Recognition policy is another crucial legitimating function, with a powerful impact on secessionist conflicts. This is the province of states, but non-state actors play a role by their contribution to the climate of opinion in which conflicts and responses to conflict are discussed. Analysts and journalists have a clear role here.

Third, the policies of states and international organizations bear directly on the prospects of conflict management, for better or worse (see Brown, 1996, 128; Crocker, 1996, 235). There are critical controversies here about the extent of intervention that is justified or required, the purposes to which it is directed and the 'softness' or 'hardness' with which it is delivered. In extreme situations, such as in Rwanda or the sieges witnessed in Sarajevo, Gorazde, Tuzla and Srebrenica, the presence or absence of forcible intervention becomes a life and death issue for the victims, and takes on huge political, emotional and ethical significance. We will not rehearse the debate over forcible intervention here, but restrict ourselves to the implications for conflict resolution. Soft measures, such as good offices, mediation, negotiation of ceasefires and launching of internationally supported peace processes, may lead to agreements (as in Mozambique, Moldova, El Salvador, Nicaragua), but they depend on creating a sufficient consensus among the parties. Hard measures ranging from the stick and carrot method to large-scale military intervention may force recalcitrant parties to stop fighting or desist from aggression. Political pressure of a sharp kind is usually required to induce parties to conflict to move positions. However, coercive measures may end the fighting (as in Dayton), but also run the risk of widening the conflict, intensifying it and imposing settlements that are not agreed and may not stick. Conflict resolution practitioners have usually advocated longer-term approaches, including empowering embedded parties, changing the regional context, building coalitions in favour of conflict resolution and setting up multiple tracks of dialogue and influence through which a peace process can be approached.

The actual practice of post-Cold War conflict management has exposed deep divisions within and between the major states. The United States is a decisive conflict manager in many regions of the world, but there is limited domestic support for foreign interventions, and Congress remains suspicious of multilateral diplomacy and UN action. In particular, the US military is committed to a doctrine that entertains military intervention only when a massive preponderance of force can be brought to bear with clear political objectives and a defined endpoint. The Clinton administration formally enunciated its limited willingness to intervene in Presidential Directive 25 (PDD-25) in 1994: 'it is not US policy to seek to expand either the number of UN peace operations or US involvement in such operations'. Nor has the US been alone in its reluctance to become involved: Britain and the major European states have experienced similar reservations, and Russia has had a sharp internal debate, in a different context. The unwillingness to intervene has been compounded when Contact Groups are formed to coordinate international conflict management, but in fact contain sharp divisions among their members, which the conflict parties can exploit.

In public, the debate over intervention has often been polarized between 'doing nothing' (abstention) and 'forcible military intervention' (peace enforcement), and the considerable range of intermediate possibilities is not always explored. Some argue for minimal intervention, on the grounds that violent conflicts will eventually burn themselves out and it is futile, imprudent or illegal to intervene. Others argue for containment (such as the placement of UNPREDEP in Macedonia) as a more active but still limited policy. For similar reasons the international community has sometimes favoured mitigation or alleviation as an alternative to extensive involvement (e.g. emergency assistance after the genocide in Rwanda). More active management involves separating the combatants (the traditional role of peacekeeping), bringing them together in the search for a settlement (peacemaking), confidence-building and trust-building (peacebuilding), and active measures to manage the political context.

In the next chapter we will look at processes of ending violent conflict. In the rest of this chapter we focus on conflict resolution options in ongoing war zones at the intermediate level. We consider overlapping clusters of options in three areas, which we differentiate under the labels 'creating security space', 'creating humanitarian space' and 'creating political space'. We argue that conflict resolution approaches are relevant to all three, above all in helping to nurture peace constituencies even in the midst of war.

Creating security space: peacekeeping and conflict resolution

UN peacekeeping in its classic guise, as defined in the Hammarskjöld/ Pearson principles in the 1950s, entailed impartial non-forcible deployment with the consent of the conflict parties in order to help maintain international peace and security in areas of conflict (White, 1993, 183; Fetherston, 1994, 1–12). The usual (although not universal) expectation was that there already was an agreed peace to be kept in these cases. These principles came under severe strain in the immediate post-Cold War years, as UN peacekeeping unexpectedly became central to the response of the international community to an array of complex international-social conflicts, taking on unfamiliar roles in prevention

(UNPREDEP in Macedonia), and intervention in active war zones (UNO-MIL in Liberia, UNPROFOR in Bosnia, UNOSOM in Somalia), as well as in post-settlement peacebuilding (ONUSAL in El Salvador, UNTAC in Cambodia, ONUMOZ in Mozambique). Prevention was the theme in chapter 4. Post-settlement peacebuilding will be the theme in chapter 7. Here, we are concerned with intervention in active war zones. The difficulty of intervening in ongoing wars is exemplified in the ambivalent roles of UN peacekeepers in Bosnia and Somalia, the former tasked with protecting safe areas without being given the means to do so, the latter sucked into a factional conflict as one of the warring parties. As a result, in Bosnia the UN was accused of doing too little, in Somalia of doing too much. In this section we do not debate the pros and cons of forcible and non-forcible military options along what is now often described as the spectrum of 'peace support operations'. These usually depend upon a number of variables, ranging from the willingness of contributing countries to provide troops and equipment to the amenability of the conflict in question to different forms of intervention. Instead, we underline how, whichever part of the spectrum is employed, conflict resolution concepts and techniques are now widely seen to be of increasing relevance to peacekeeping.

In the late twentieth century we can observe a tendency by experienced peacekeepers to call for the integration of conflict resolution mechanisms in their policy-making and operational practices. It is noticeable, for example, how much of the peacekeeping doctrine of the British Army, elaborated in *Wider Peacekeeping*, is suffused with the language of conflict resolution (*Wider Peacekeeping*, 1995). The same approach is taken in American doctrine covering peace support operations (Chayes and Raach, 1995). Here, the managing of consent (based on the principles of impartiality, legitimacy, mutual respect, minimum force, credibility and transparency) is related to the techniques of promoting good communication, of negotiation and mediation and of positive approaches to community relations through an active civil affairs programme, which is amply resourced to win 'hearts and minds'.

Mackinlay (1996) sees the concepts and doctrine which defined classical peacekeeping as no longer adequate to cope with the demands placed on peacekeepers in the civil wars into which they have been drawn in the 1990s. Nevertheless, while he argues for broadened and strengthened forms of peacekeeping, he still maintains that consent is the major precondition for the success of peace support operations. In a redefinition of British peacekeeping doctrine that goes beyond *Wider Peacekeeping*, Wilkinson (1996) also expands the range of action to include a possible greater use of force, citing impartiality rather than consent as the key determinant in distinguishing forcible peacekeeping from war. But he, too, continues to see the nurturing and building of consent within the wider peace constituency as an essential aim. In particular, he identifies six different sets of techniques designed to maintain consent in conflict areas where peacekeepers are deployed and which are particularly important because 'the military element's presence in the operational area does not always inspire local support for them. For this reason, land forces will have to spend more time and effort, down to the individual level, in consent promoting activity' (Wilkinson, 1996, 168). The six techniques are related to: negotiation and mediation; liaison; civilian affairs; community information; public information; and community relations. Much of the objective of these kinds of activity is to provide good information in order to reduce rumour, uncertainty and prejudice on the one hand, and to foster trust and stability in the area of conflict and positive perceptions of the role of peacekeepers and the nature of the peace process on the other.

A further example of the use of conflict resolution theory in relation to peacekeeping is in the work of David Last, a Canadian officer with experience in the UNFICYP (Cyprus) and UNPROFOR operations. Last set out to review the contribution of peacekeeping to conflict resolution as practised in the past; he also wished to identify 'what new techniques may be used to help peacekeepers work more actively with civilians to eliminate violent conflict':

> To argue by analogy, I believe the situation of peacekeepers today is much like the situation of commanders on the Western Front in 1916, who were bogged down in defensive operations. To push the analogy somewhat, new tools of war were becoming available to commanders in 1916 that would permit them to take the offensive if they could only adjust their thinking about how to use their forces. In the same way, new techniques of peacekeeping, taken from conflict resolution theory and civilian experience, now permit peacekeepers to take the offensive to restore peace. (*Last, 1997, 129*)

The integration of the operational and practical aspects of approaches from conflict resolution, and at this level of detail, into the processes of peacekeeping in the field is still at a somewhat unsystematic and rudimentary stage, but the requirement is now quite widely recognized.

Finally, the UN Secretary-General Kofi Annan has pointed to the need for peacekeeping forces to find new capabilities for what he refers to as positive inducements to gain support for peacekeeping mandates amongst populations in conflict zones. Reliance on coercion alone is insufficient, he argues, because, while peacekeeping forces in the future will need to have a greater coercive capacity, the effect of coercion will erode over time, and it is better to attempt to influence the behaviour of people in conflict situations by the use of the carrot rather than the stick. Thus while coercion can restrain violence at least temporarily, it cannot promote lasting peace; a durable peace and a lasting solution require not only stopping the violence but, crucially, 'taking the next step'. For Annan, taking the next step means offering positive incentives or inducements. Peacekeeping forces, in other words, need to be able to make available rewards in the mission area. Annan defines two broad categories of reward:

> The first is what some military establishments have called 'civic action'. Its purpose is limited, namely to gain the good will and consequent cooperation of the population. The second, which might be termed 'peace incentives', is more ambitious. It is intended as leverage to further the reconciliation process. It provides incentives – a structure of rewards – for erstwhile antagonists to cooperate with each other on some endeavour, usually a limited one at first, which has the potential for expansion if all goes well. (1997b, 28)

This concept, which Annan sees as absolutely essential for the future effectiveness of peacekeeping operations brings peacekeeping squarely into the realm of conflict resolution as defined above:

> To employ them [positive inducements/rewards] effectively as tools of conflict resolution requires understanding peoples' problems in their complexity and being able to respond at several levels simultaneously and with a certain amount of flexibility . . .
>
> Civic action, in short, is neither charity nor luxury but, in the types of conflicts we have been discussing, an essential requirement for operational effectiveness that requires a line item of its own in the peace operation's budget. Peace incentives, similarly, are rewards-cum-leverage rather than assistance for its own sake. (1997b, 28–9)

Working in conflict zones thus becomes a complex process of balancing coercive inducements with positive inducements, of supplementing military containment and humanitarian relief roles and of promoting civic action to rebuild communities economically, politically and socially. A wide range of actors and agencies, military and civilian, governmental and non-governmental, indigenous and external, therefore constitute the conflict resolution capability in war zones. Simultaneous activities are targeted on broadening the security, humanitarian, political and development spaces in which peace processes can take root. In such a complicated arena the issue of the coordination of multi-agency activity becomes paramount. Assessments following the 1994 Rwanda crisis agreed in essence on the nature of the required reforms: the Joint Evaluation report recommended the formation of a Humanitarian Subcommittee of the Security Council, tasked to synthesize crisis information, to oversee the integration of political, military and humanitarian objectives and to create an integrated UN line of command between UN headquarters and the field, and within the field. Vassall Adams suggests that this coordination might be secured by the creation of a new UN department which would incorporate the Department of Humanitarian Affairs (DHA) and all the disparate agencies involved in responding to emergencies (Eriksson, 1996, 47–8: Vassall Adams, 1994, 66). At the field level, post-conflict evaluations have also been yielding consistent recommendations. Dallaire, the

UNAMIR force commander in Rwanda, was adamant that coordination mechanisms be improved by the creation of a UN multidisciplinary team of senior crisis managers, and that there should be regular meetings between the UN and NGOs through civil–military operations centres (CMOCs). From this should emerge a culture of understanding between the various agencies, leading in turn to better-defined standard operating procedures. In Dallaire's view, too, an interdisciplinary UN-led crisis management and humanitarian assistance centre is needed (Dallaire, 1996, 216). Speaking of the various agencies of the international community, whether they are primarily concerned with opening up security, humanitarian, or political spaces, Dallaire argues: 'we are intertwined by the very nature of the crisis . . . Clearly, peacekeeping cannot be an end in itself – it only buys time. In its goals and its design, it must always be a part of the larger continuum of peace-making, that is to say conflict avoidance, resolution, rehabilitation and development' (Dallaire, 1996, 217).

Creating humanitarian space: humanitarian agencies and conflict resolution

As with so many other aspects of international action, the strategy for delivering aid to victims of armed conflict has undergone significant change in the 1990s. During the Cold War aid was rendered on the periphery, with victims sometimes trekking hundreds of miles to reach relief. Refugee problems then were seen as long term, often lasting up to twenty years and longer, with no immediate solution being sought. The emphasis now, post-Cold War, has shifted from a concern for refugee relief to a broader concern for humanitarian aid, which includes a preoccupation not only with provision of relief for physical deprivations, but incorporates the objective of empowering and resettling displaced populations and rebuilding structures of civil society. The changing concern has meant a radical adjustment for the UN in particular, which now plays a central coordinating role in the effort to move beyond relief to the stabilization of conflict and the progression to post-conflict development and reconstruction. This transition has not been unproblematic, and experiences in Cambodia, Bosnia, Somalia, Rwanda and elsewhere continue to be examined in a debate, the outcome of which is crucial for the effective development of conflict resolution. The central question is to what extent can a coherent and effective practice of humanitarianism, containing an integral conflict resolution process, prevail as a viable response to human suffering in war zones?

Given the complexity of much contemporary conflict, it has been realized that the international response needs to embody a range of capabilities which cannot normally be provided by any one nation or agency. Adequate humanitarian response must involve a truly international array of agencies at international, national and non-governmental levels. For example, the SRSG and the UN's Department of Political Affairs (DPA) may be involved to facilitate political negotiations and arrangements which may lead to peace agreements. The UN High Commissioner for Refugees (UNHCR), the World Food Programme, the UN Development Programme (UNDP) and UNICEF are likely to be present as supranational humanitarian agencies; multinational military peacekeeping forces may be on the ground supported by the UN Department of Peacekeeping Operations (DPKO), or purely national forces might be deployed; national aid and development agencies, such as the US Agency for International Development (USAID), are likely to be present, along with other aid agencies sponsored by national governments. Besides these, there will be the International Committee of the Red Cross (ICRC), and a host of NGOs, both external and indigenous.

Associated with this array of actors is a multiplicity of humanitarian and related roles, which now characteristically ramify beyond a simple focus on immediate relief, including the gaining of access, the negotiation of protection and local ceasefires, the settlement of displaced persons, the rebuilding of local trust within and across affected communities, the restoration of essential services and, in general, accommodation to fluctuating threats and opportunities from the war zone, while at the same time handling sensitive relations with other interveners. Many of these roles and activities have not been seen conventionally as humanitarian, and nearly all of them call for some understanding and skill in conflict resolution capabilities. In other words, the short-term humanitarian enterprise of providing emergency relief (creating humanitarian space) has become part of the process both of conceptualizing and practising conflict resolution (creating security, political and development space). While established aid donors will still respond to conflict-generated disasters conventionally and correctly with the provision of basic relief supplies such as food aid, shelter and medicine, criticisms of this narrow approach have led to a significant expansion of what is entailed in the concept of emergency relief. Thus, in 1995 the Development Assistant Committee of the Organization for Economic Cooperation and Development (OECD) included in its strategy guidelines for emergency aid: 'greater emphasis on development; local/regional ownership of the aid intervention; improved co-ordination of the international response; and greater integration of diplomatic, humanitarian and economic strategies' (Mackinlay, ed., 1996, 45).

In short, humanitarian intervention in ongoing war zones is unavoidably politicized. In the volatile and conflictual political environment of a complex political emergency, the status and impartiality of peacekeeping forces, aid agencies and NGOs comes under pressure, because the services they provide, intentionally or unintentionally, may be seen to be for or against the interests of one side or the other in the war. They became very much a part of the process of conflict itself, since their objectives are often defined in such a way as to involve them with the radical alteration of relationships (and therefore of power and its resources) within the affected society. NGOs, such as Médecins Sans Frontières, CARE and Oxfam engage in economic and social activity in the sense that they will bring in materials and resources and professional expertise (food aid, medicine, construction and technical skills to help rebuild ruined infrastructures), either as participating partners of the UN agencies or autonomously. In all these ways they come to be integrally involved in the nexus of conflict and need to be aware of the conflict resolution dimension of their activities.

Finally, although the majority of NGOs are of the kind just described, a significant minority combine relief work with explicit Track II conflict resolution roles, including human rights monitoring, education in the skills of conflict resolution, and direct attempts to achieve conflict resolution in the form of capacity-building for reconciliation projects between divided communities. Relief work has often created possibilities for mediation, as humanitarian agencies develop contacts across the conflict lines (Bailey, 1995). The Carter Center, the American Friends Service Committee, the Comunità di Sant'Egidio in Italy, or Quaker Peace and Service from the UK have combined these roles. Short-term relief for the victims of complex emergencies is a necessary first step in the humanitarian response. But humanitarian assistance must be linked to reducing future vulnerability. This means that it supports the longer-term objective of sustaining peace processes; and it connects peacekeeping to peace-building. The goal of humanitarian intervention is, in this sense, the resolution of conflict as well as the relief of suffering. Conflict resolution (including prevention or mitigation) is usually accepted now as a universal goal or value which should permeate the whole humanitarian system.

Creating political space: committed third parties and local empowerment

The various activities of military peacekeepers and of the diverse civilian agencies in war zones will, therefore, be fruitless unless their activities are informed by political solutions and underpinned by political will. Brigadier-General Dallaire emphasized the inadequacies of responding with 'a political theory with no capability, military operations with no political aim, [and] humanitarian missions without the necessary means' (1996, 216–17). The objectives of third party intervention and support of local actors in war zones in the security and humanitarian dimensions which we have considered in this chapter need, therefore, to be understood within the overall context of creating the political will and capacities for a peace process to emerge, however unpromising the immediate circumstances or distant the apparent goal.

In the war zone, negotiation and mediation (or, more frequently, shuttle mediation) are likely to be ongoing if at times sporadic. The whole process, from the initiation of contacts and the first indications of a readiness to settle to the eventual formal agreement, may take two or more years – as in Cambodia or Mozambique. Representatives of concerned states and of the UN undertake mediation and negotiation activities, seek to secure a ceasefire and then encourage a peace agreement between the parties. In the case of Rwanda, the Joint Evaluation found that one of the positive lessons emerging from the conflict was the consistent support for mediation efforts provided by Tanzania and the OAU, which led to the negotiation of the Arusha Accords (Eriksson, 1996, 45).

We have noted the failure to prevent the massacres in Rwanda, despite the efforts of a small number of indigenous NGOs to warn the international community what was about to happen. In Burundi in the late 1990s, many of the same problems and dangers exist. Burundi has a similar ethnic mix and witnessed mass killings in the autumn of 1993 when the Hutu leader, President Ndadye, was assassinated. The situation remains volatile as we write, but despite the frequent outbreak of violence, it has not reached the level seen in Rwanda in 1994. With an eye on what happened in Rwanda, and in an effort to prevent a similar disaster befalling Burundi, the UN and the OAU appointed SRSGs to Burundi and a large number of international organizations, bilateral donors and NGOs have projects and observers in the country. A number of appraisals have concluded that the fact that a genocidal war has been avoided is at least in part the result of the concern and attention of these agencies, and in particular of SRSG Ahmedon Ould Abdallah, in 1994 and 1995 (Christian Michelsen Institute (CMI), 1997; Sollom and Kew, 1996). At the suggestion of SRSG Abdallah, the London-based conflict resolution NGO, International Alert, began to work early in 1995 with other NGOs on a programme of cooperation to help prevent an escalation of the Burundi conflict. This work has been evaluated independently. Although there has been no major breakthrough in efforts to reach a sustainable peace, the evaluators concluded that the work of International Alert, in cooperation with other partners and with the SRSG, and as a result of 'listening and learning', is 'accepted and appreciated by all main actors on the Burundi scene, internal as well as external' (CMI, 1997, 55).

The programme involved a series of study tours to South Africa to see what could be learned from the peace process there, as a result of which a support group to promote peace by influential Burundi leaders was established (the Compagnie des Apôtres de la Paix). The work of International Alert in Burundi is summarized in box 5.1. A further example of such an approach is Conciliation Resources' programme in Sierra Leone. Empowerment of local communities and a shared analysis of the conflict are seen as crucial starting points for supporting indigenous conciliation work.[2]

A major lesson from all of the conflict interventions we have been considering is not to expect dramatic or rapid progress. However, when circumstances are favourable (see chapter 6), real political changes can occur quickly. In Mozambique the long-term commitment and mediation

---

BOX 5.1 International Alert: programme in Burundi, 1995 onwards

Goal of the programme:

'Helping to prevent escalation of the conflict, and contributing effectively to a process of achieving a just and peaceful resolution of the crisis in Burundi . . . There are no quick fixes. The strategy has to be one of process. A primary mechanism for catalysing and sustaining the process is the encouragement and facilitation of dialogue.'

Elements of the programme:

- international information exchange and a capacity for facilitation and advocacy initiatives (mainly at international and regional levels);
- an enabling partnership with the Compagnie des Apôtres de la Paix (mainly at the national elite level);
- a multifaceted programme to strengthen the peacebuilding capacity of the Burundian Women's Movement (at both national elite and grass-roots level);
- finite projects such as Peace Radio support, and Schools Peace Education Support

Source: CMI, 1997, 52–3

---

of the Italian NGO, the Comunità di Sant'Egidio, was a major factor in the formal launching of the peace process in 1990, which was concluded in the Rome Accords of October 1992. In a remarkable analysis of the peace process in Mozambique, Hume shows how the peace agreement there was the product of a system of multitrack diplomacy, as outlined above: while Sant'Egidio provided soft mediation and helped to build up a basic level of trust between FRELIMO and RENAMO leaders at various stages, church leaders, Italian parliamentarians, diplomats from ten governments, the UN Secretary-General and a number of concerned businessmen were all involved in bringing the two sides to the negotiating table (Hume, 1994). It should be recognized that even when the violence is at its worst, long-term low-profile mediatory initiatives will be taking place, often invisibly, to be revealed only after a formal agreement has eventually been made.

Conclusion

Violent civil wars are not amenable to quick-fix solutions or surgical military strikes. The challenge is to find ways and means of harnessing the mutual gain that ending the fighting can offer to the building of a peace process. By the time conflicts become war zones, the majority of the population is usually suffering massive mutual losses. Warlords and militias, who may make temporary gains in the fighting, as often as not end up as victims too. Eventually, almost all wars impose such dreadful costs that there is mutual advantage in ending them. The question is how this ending can be brought forward when calculations of advantage by the conflict parties may differ and various key constituencies are locked in to ongoing violence, and how those who represent the middle ground in their societies can be empowered to exert pressure in a search for alternatives. This question – how to end violent conflict – is the theme of the next chapter.

In the interim it is clear that the severe conditions in war zones create the most formidable difficulties for conflict resolution. Nevertheless, this chapter has pointed to ways in which peacekeeping, humanitarian intervention and work with committed third parties can prepare the ground for an eventual cessation of hostilities, while in the meantime helping to mitigate, alleviate or in some measure contain the ongoing conflict. The institutional development and coordination of such efforts is still weak, but there is scope to develop it further. Drawing on his experience as SRSG in Somalia, and as Deputy Secretary-General of the OAU, for example, Mohamed Sahnoun has proposed a new international institution for conflict management. Its role would be to 'mobilise all approaches to conflict resolution and ... increase communications and networks among different communities in local conflict areas through the integrated efforts of NGOs and the United Nations' (Aall, 1996, 441). The main challenge for such an institution would be to overcome well-founded objections to 'interventionary humanitarianism' from countries of the South, on the one hand, and reluctance to be drawn into conflict zones unless clear national interests were involved on the part of powerful, mainly western, governments, on the other. This ambivalence is reflected in the recognition in the OAU's 1993 *Declaration on the Establishment of a Mechanism for Conflict Prevention, Management and Resolution* that, with its burdensome debt and economic problems, Africa was not in a position to undertake a regional initiative to restore peace in Somalia, but, at the same time, 'Africa believes that regional actors, with a better understanding of local and regional issues, are better placed to handle local conflicts than more distant participants' (Ramsbotham and Woodhouse, 1996, 164). Western governments are often similarly ambivalent. Either way, as Trachtenberg puts it:

> For an interventionist system to be viable, it needs in particular to have a general aura of legitimacy. In the case of intervention in the Third World, the system needs to be supported especially by the major Third World countries that can be expected to be very suspicious of it. This means more than just solving the tactical problems of getting Third World governments to vote for interventionist actions in the UN and various regional bodies, or

even to send their own military contingents. It means figuring out how whole populations, or at least their politically active components, react to intervention – what excites hostility, which aspects of an interventionary policy can generate support – and then framing one's policy with this understanding in mind. It means listening to people we are not used to listening to, and understanding the limits on our own power and, especially, on our own wisdom. (*1993, 32*)

In this wider enterprise, conflict resolution approaches, understandings and techniques can play a significant role.

6

Ending Violent Conflict

Friends, comrades, and fellow South Africans. I greet you all, in the name of peace, democracy and freedom for all.
Nelson Mandela on his release from prison, 11 February 1990

On my knees I beg you to turn away from the paths of violence and return to the ways of peace. You may claim to seek justice. I too believe in justice and seek justice. But violence only delays the day of justice. Violence destroys the work of justice. Do not follow any leaders who train you in the ways of inflicting death. Those who resort to violence always claim that only violence brings change. You must know that there is a political peaceful way to justice.
The Pope, Drogheda, Ireland, 29 September 1979

Central to the problems obstructing any lasting resolution of the Israeli-Palestinian conflict are the profound asymmetries between Israelis and Palestinians.
Boutwell et al., 1995

In this chapter we turn from the question of the role of conflict resolution in ongoing wars to the question of war endings. We have seen how the conflict resolution approach addresses the root causes of violent conflict within a framework and a process that enables hostile parties with sharply opposed interests to transform their situation without the use of violence. It takes a deliberately broad and ambitious agenda, embracing efforts to transform injustice as well as to bridge opposing positions. It is not restricted to third party intervention, but includes the parties' own moves towards peace and the development of peacemaking capacity within societies. It is, in short, a radical programme for the non-violent transformation of societies in violent conflict. Conceived of in this way, therefore, conflict resolution is broader than conflict termination, and the relationship between conflict resolution and the ending of violent conflict is not necessarily direct. The root causes may persist without either war or a peace settlement doing anything to address them. More often than not, war generates additional conflicts, which add to and confuse the original issues. It is quite possible that efforts to resolve a conflict may not end a war, and efforts to end a war may not resolve the underlying conflict.

This chapter first examines the nature and difficulties of ending violent conflict in the post-Cold War world. It then moves on to explore 'transformers' of conflict and the process of ending violent conflict and restoring peace. The third section explores how conflict transformations have worked, and failed to work, in three contemporary peace processes: South Africa, Israel–Palestine and Northern Ireland.

The Challenge of Ending Violent Conflict

How have major post-Cold War armed conflicts ended, and what are the obstacles to conflict resolution?

How major post-Cold War conflicts have ended

Wallensteen and Sollenberg count a total of 101 armed conflicts being fought between 1989 and 1996 (1997, 357). Of these, 68 had come to an end (as armed conflicts) during the period. Only 19 ended in a peace agreement (see box 6.1); in 23 there was victory to one side or another, and some other outcome obtained in the remaining 24 terminated conflicts.[1] These findings accord with earlier ones that point to the intractability of internal conflicts. Only a quarter to a third of modern civil wars have been negotiated, whereas more than half of interstate wars have been (Licklider, 1995; Pillar, 1983).[2]

What constitutes a war ending is itself a tricky question. Wallensteen and Sollenberg use a minimal definition that no armed violence occurred in the following year; but peace settlements often break down, and further violence occurs. Cambodia, which produced a 'comprehensive political settlement' in 1990, was again a high-intensity conflict in late 1996 (Schmid, 1997, 79). The peace agreement in Sierra Leone has broken down, and a low-intensity conflict was under way in Guatemala in 1996/7.[3] A war ending is not usually a precise moment in time but a process, which is over when a new political dispensation prevails, or the parties become reconciled, or a new conflict eclipses the first. However, armed conflicts *do* end eventually, if we take a long enough time period (Licklider, 1995).

A conventional view is that a war ends when one side or the other wins a military victory, or when both sides agree to a draw. But, more often,

---

BOX 6.1   Armed conflicts terminated by peace agreement, 1989–96

Bosnia–Herzegovina (war with Serbs)
Bosnia–Herzegovina (war with Croats)
Russia (Chechnya)**
Lebanon
India (Jharkand)
Angola
Chad*
Djibouti*
Liberia
Mali
Morocco (Western Sahara)**
Mozambique
Niger*
Sierra Leone
South Africa
Ecuador–Peru**
El Salvador
Guatemala
Nicaragua

* Partial peace agreement, not necessarily including all protagonists
** Agreement to establish a peace process

Source: Wallensteen and Sollenberg, 1997

---

armed conflicts fizzle out without either a military victory or a settlement, simply because the parties no longer wish to or are able to continue the fight. There may be a ceasefire but the parties remain unable to agree on terms (as in Nagorno-Karabakh). Of Wallensteen and Sollenberg's 68 endings, 24 come in this category.

Licklider (1995) finds that civil wars ended by negotiated settlements are more likely to lead to the recurrence of armed conflicts than those ended by military victories. On the other hand, those ended by military victories are more likely to lead to genocide. His findings point to the need for continuing peacebuilding efforts to resolve the underlying conflicts.[4]

Obstacles to conflict resolution

Chapter 3 has indicated some of the reasons why contemporary international-social conflicts are so hard to end. Sources of conflict, which usually persist in intensified form into the ensuing war, were identified at international, state and societal levels, and were also located in the factional interests of elites and individuals. To these are added the destructive processes and vested interests engendered by the war itself, as described in chapter 5. Violence spawns a host of groups who benefit directly from its continuation. Soldiers become dependent on warfare as a way of life, and warlords on the economic resources and revenue they can control (Berdal and Keen, 1998; King, 1997, 37). Even in low-intensity conflicts, protagonists may depend, economically or psychologically, on the continuation of the conflict, such as those in Belfast who sustain paramilitary operations through protection rackets. Leaders who have become closely identified with pursuing the conflict may risk prosecution, overthrow or even death once the war is over, and have strong incentives for intransigence (for example, Karadzic in Bosnia, Savimbi in Angola, Vellupillai Probhakaran in Sri Lanka). Local and regional party officials or military officers who have made their careers in the conflict may develop a stake in its continuation (Sisk, 1996, 84). For such protagonists, peace may bring loss of role and status, and thus directly threaten their interests (King, 1997).

It would be easy to draw the conclusion that conflict resolution is not possible, and that political groups, like nations, will fight to the death to achieve their ends. However, we need to keep the obstacles in proportion. Most violent conflicts impose massive costs on the societies concerned, so there is a usually a large segment of the population which will benefit from the conflict ending. This is a shared interest across the conflicting communities, affecting security and economic welfare. Moderate politicians and constituencies, who may have been silenced or displaced by the climate of violence, will be keen to re-establish normal politics. Ordinary people will welcome a return to peace and wish to put the distress of war behind them. There is, therefore, a large reservoir of potential support that peacemakers should be able to foster.

We can point to a number of cases where conflicts have been settled by negotiation: examples include the ending of apartheid in South Africa, the ending of the internal conflicts in Nicaragua, El Salvador and Guatemala, the settlements in Mozambique and Namibia, and in Ethiopia and Eritrea. Given political vision, engaged peacemakers, moderation and the right conditions, conflicts can be brought to a negotiated end. It is, therefore, worth trying to identify the ingredients of an effective conflict resolution approach, and the conditions under which attempts to end conflict are likely to succeed.

Conflict Resolution and War Ending

In looking at the scope for conflict resolution in ending violent conflict, we will follow Vayrynen in adopting a broad approach which recognizes the fluidity of the conflict process. Conflicts are inherently dynamic and conflict resolution has to engage with a complex of shifting relations:

> The bulk of conflict theory regards the issues, actors and interests as given and on that basis makes efforts to find a solution to mitigate or eliminate contradictions between them. Yet the issues, actors and interests change over time as a consequence of the social, economic and political dynamics of societies. Even if we deal with non-structural aspects of conflicts, such as actor preferences, the assumption of stability, usually made in the game theoretic approach to conflict studies, is unwarranted. New situational factors, learning experiences, interaction with the adversary and other influences caution against taking actor preferences as given. (*Vayrynen, ed., 1991*)

The requirements are best seen as a series of necessary transformations in the elements which would otherwise sustain ongoing violence and war.

Transformers of conflict: a generic framework

Vayrynen (ed., 1991) identifies a number of ways in which conflict transformation takes place. His ideas complement those of Galtung (1984; 1989; 1996), who has developed his views on the resolution of inter-party and intra-party conflicts, in their structural, attitudinal and behavioural aspects, into a full theory of non-violent conflict transformation. From these sources, and informed by Burton, Azar, Curle and the related theorists mentioned at the start of chapter 2, we outline five generic transformers of protracted conflict which correspond to the outline framework for the analysis of contemporary conflict offered in chapter 3.

First, *context transformation*. Conflicts are embedded in a social, regional and international context, which is often critical to their continuation. Changes in the context may sometimes have more dramatic effects than changes within the parties or in their relationships. The end of the Cold War is the prime recent context transformation which has unlocked protracted conflicts in Southern Africa, Central America and elsewhere.[5]

Second, *structural transformation*. The conflict structure is the set of actors, issues and incompatible goals or relationships which constitutes the conflict. If the root causes of the conflict lie in the structure of relationships within which the parties operate, then a transformation of this structure is necessary to resolve the conflict. In asymmetric conflicts, for example, structural transformation entails a change in the relationship between the dominant and the weaker party. Empowerment of the weaker side (for example, through international support or recognition or mediation) is one way this can be achieved. Another is dissociation – withdrawal from unbalanced relationships, as for example in the Kosovar Albanians' decision to boycott the elections in Serbia and set up a 'shadow state'.

Third, *actor transformation*. Parties may have to redefine directions, abandon or modify cherished goals and adopt radically different perspectives. This may come about through a change of actor, a change of leadership, a change in the constituency of the leader or adoption of new goals, values or beliefs. It may involve intra-party conflicts, which is often crucial to the resolution of inter-party conflict. Changes of leadership are common as precipitators of change in protracted conflicts. Changes in the circumstances and interests of the constituency a party represents also transform conflicts, even if such changes in the constituency often take place gradually and out of view. Splitting of parties and integration of parties are important forms of change.

Fourth, *issue transformation*. Conflicts are defined by the conflicting positions parties take on issues. When they change their positions, or when issues lose salience or new ones arise, the conflict is transformed. Changes of position are closely related to changes of interest and changes of goals, and hence to actor transformation, and also to the context and structure of the conflict. Reframing of issues may open the way to settlements.

Fifth, *personal and group transformation*. For Curle, this is at the heart of change.[6] If we accept the Buddhist view that conflict is in the hearts and minds of people, then it is in hearts and minds that change comes about. John McConnell has shown how an understanding of Buddhist psychology sheds light on the processes involved. Conflict arises from *loba* (craving for fixed goals, striving for mastery), *dosa* (hatred, or generalized suspicion) and *moha* (self-distorted perceptions). It can be transformed by being transmuted into *aloba* (reconciliation), *adosa* (mutual acceptance) and *amoha* (broad vision and clarity) (McConnell, 1995). The former guerrilla leader, committed to victory through any means, becomes the unifying national leader, offering reconciliation; the leader of an oppressive government decides to accept his opponents into the government. Excruciating suffering leads in time through mourning and healing to new life (Montville, 1993).

Transformations such as the five just described do not necessarily move in a benign direction. It is characteristic of conflicts that they intensify and widen, that power passes from moderate to more extreme leaders, that violence intensifies and that restraint and moderation wither. The classification is useful, however, as a framework for analysing steps towards conflict resolution and for thinking about interventions in conflict. The second, third and fourth transformers (structure, actor, issue) correspond to the conflict party level identified in chapter 3 (see table 3.2); context transformation corresponds to the global, regional and state levels; and individual and group transformation to the elite/individual level.

In many cultures conflicts are explained as 'tangles' of contradictory claims that must be unravelled. In Central America the phrase 'we are all entangled', as in a fisherman's net, best describes the concept of conflict, and the experience of conflict is '*enredado*' ('tangled or caught in a net')

(Duffey, 1998). At the root of conflict is a knot of problematic relationships, conflicting interests and differing world-views. Undoing this knot is a painstaking process. Success depends on how the knot has been tied and the sequencing of the untying. The timing and coordination of the transformers is crucial (Fisher and Keashly 1991). They need to develop sufficient energy and momentum to overcome the conflict's resistance.

This broad view of conflict transformation is necessary to correct the misperception that conflict resolution rests on an assumption of harmony of interests between actors, and that third party mediators can settle conflicts by appealing to the reason or underlying humanity of the parties. On the contrary, conflict transformation requires real changes in parties' interests, goals or self-definitions. These may be forced by the conflict itself, or may come about because of intra-party changes, shifts in the constituencies of the parties or changes in the context in which the conflict is situated. Conflict resolution must therefore concern itself not only with the issues that divide the main parties, but also with the social, psychological and political changes that are necessary to address root causes, the intra-party conflicts that may inhibit acceptance of a settlement, the context which affects the incentives of the parties and the social and institutional capacity that determines whether a settlement can be made acceptable and workable. As we argued in chapter 5, a multitrack approach is necessary, relying on interventions by different actors at different levels (see also Rupesinghe, 1996).

Having outlined the main general requirements for ending violent conflicts in terms of conflict transformers, we now apply this in more detail, first to the issue of the role of mediation and third party intervention in war ending, second to the question whether there are ripe moments for peacemaking as determined by the conflict itself, and third to the nature of successful peace processes including the significance of turning points and sticking points and the threat from spoilers who want to wreck the prospects for settlement.

Mediation and third party intervention

As the concept of conflict resolution has gained currency, many more conflict resolution attempts are being made. They involve different kinds of agency (international organizations, states, NGOs, individuals), address different groups (party leaders, elites, grass-roots), and vary in form, duration and purpose. We have referred to this developing practice in earlier chapters, including the use of Track I, Track II, Track III and multitrack diplomacy, employing a spectrum of soft and hard intervention approaches, ranging from good offices, conciliation, quiet or 'pure' mediation at one end, through various modes of more muscled mediation and peacekeeping, to peace enforcement at the other. Much of this has been controversial. There have been fierce debates over whether third party intervention should be impartial or partial, coercive or non-coercive, state-based or non-state-based, carried out by outsiders or insiders (Touval and Zartman, eds, 1985; Curle, 1986; Mitchell and Webb, eds, 1988; van der Merwe, 1989; Lederach, 1995; Bercovitch, 1996). Attempts to integrate different approaches, such as Fisher and Keashly's (1991) 'contingency model'[7] and life-cycle models of conflict (Creative Associates, 1997, 3–4) suggest appropriate responses at different phases of conflict, though such models do not resolve the ethical issues involved, or the practical issues of coordination (Webb et al., 1996). They do, however, point to the conclusion that third party interventions usually need to be continued over an extended period, and that 'third parties need other third parties' (Hampson, 1996, 233).

At the softer end of the spectrum third parties are often essential in contributing to issue transformations. They typically help the conflicting parties by putting them in contact with one another, gaining their trust and confidence, setting agendas, clarifying issues and formulating agreements. They can facilitate meetings by arranging venues, reducing tensions, exploring the interests of the parties and sometimes guiding the parties to unrealized possibilities. These are tasks that are usually contentious and even dangerous for the conflictants to perform themselves. By allowing the parties to present their cases, by exploring them in depth, framing and ordering the discussion, and questioning the advantages and disadvantages of different options before the parties have to make a commitment to them, mediation can sometimes perform a valuable role in opening up new political space.

Mediation is especially important at a stage when at least some of the conflicting parties have come to accept that pursuing the conflict is unlikely to achieve their goals, but before they have reached the stage of accepting formal negotiations. At this point, face-to-face meetings may be very difficult to arrange, and mediation and 'back-channels' become important. They played a large role in the peace processes in Northern Ireland, South Africa and the Israel–Palestine conflict. In the Northern Ireland case, for example, the Social Democratic and Labour Party (SDLP), Sinn Fein, and the Irish government established communications by sending secret messages through representatives of the Clonard monastery, a religious community which ministers to Republican families living on the 'front line' in Belfast; this prepared the ground for the Hume–Adams proposals (Coogan, 1995). The back-channel between the Israeli government and the Palestinian leadership, established through the good offices of the Norwegian NGO FAFO, has become justly famous; it broke the impasse in the Madrid talks and led to the Oslo accords. Corbin (1994) tells the story of how it developed out of informal contacts between academics on the two sides, built around the formula of 'Gaza first' – and rapidly developed into informal and then formal negotiations between the two sides. The Norwegian government assisted by providing confidential meeting places and skilled facilitators to maintain a constructive atmosphere, in which unexpected breakthroughs became possible. In the South African case, the contacts arranged between the African National Congress (ANC) and the government by third parties enabled preliminary communication between the two sides, before they were ready to negotiate openly.

International organizations, governments and NGOs can all play a role at this stage. Although they usually have limited resources, NGOs may be able to enter conflicts that are barred to international organizations and governments on grounds of sovereignty. A growing number of NGOs have gained experience of working in conflict (Serbe et al., 1997; van Tongeren, 1996).[8] They use a variety of approaches, including facilitation (Fisher and Ury, 1981), problem-solving workshops (de Reuck, 1984; Burton, 1978; Kelman, 1992; Mitchell and Banks, 1996) and sustained mediation. It is possible to point to a number of cases where mediators from NGOs have contributed to transformation at key moments, usually in conjunction with governments and international organizations. For example, the Comunità di Sant'Egidio in Mozambique (Hume, 1994; Msabaha, 1995, 221), Jimmy Carter in Ethiopia/Eritrea (Ottoway, 1995, 117), the Moravians and the Mennonites in Central America (Wehr and Lederach, 1996, 65, 69), FAFO in the Oslo talks between Israel and the PLO (Corbin, 1994) and the Conflict Analysis Centre in Moldova.

NGOs have sometimes been able to adapt their methods to the local culture, and can work usefully with one or several parties rather than with all. Lederach, for example, found in his work in Central America that the parties look for *confianza* (trust) rather than neutrality in third parties, and that an 'insider-partial' would be more acceptable than impartial outsiders (Lederach, 1995; Wehr and Lederach, 1996).

The current trend in NGO interventions is away from entry into conflict situations by outsiders towards training people inside the society in conflict in the skills of conflict resolution, and combining these with indigenous traditions. We noted in chapter 2 how the constructions and reconstructions which took place in conflict resolution thinking placed great stress on the need to bring into the discourse the ideal of a global civic culture which was receptive and responsive to the voices often left out of the politics of international order. We saw how Elise Boulding envisaged the evolution of a problem-solving *modus operandi* for civil society, and how Curle and Lederach defined the priorities and modalities of indigenous empowerment and peacebuilding from below. Indeed, it is in the encounter with local traditions that important lessons about conflict resolution are being learned, particularly about the limitations of the dominantly Euro-American model defined in chapter 2. In his study of the Arab Middle East, Salem has noted a 'rich tradition of tribal conflict management [which] has thousands of years of experience and wisdom behind it' (Salem, 1997, xi). Such perspectives are now beginning to emerge in late twentieth-century understandings and practices of conflict resolution. Rupesinghe emphasizes the importance of building capacity to manage conflict within the affected society, a process which will necessarily involve the need for knowledge about the traditions of conflict management to which Salem referred. Kelman, Rothman and others have used an 'elicitive' model in their workshops in the Middle East, drawing on the wisdom of local cultures to stimulate creative dialogue and new thinking at elite or grass-roots levels. Participants in their workshops have gone on to play significant decision-making roles in the Israeli–Palestinian peace process (Rothman, 1992; Kelman, 1997). Similarly, community relations organizations in Northern Ireland have built networks of people across the communities which function as a long-term resource for peacebuilding, and which are changing both the society and the actors. It is in this way that the encounter between conflict resolution ideas and social and political forces can subtly transform the context of conflict. NGOs also work towards structural transformation, for example by acting to empower the weaker side (van der Merwe, 1989; Lederach, 1995; Curle, 1996).

Of course, international organizations and governments still play much the largest role in managing conflicts in the post-Cold War world. The UN Secretary-General and his representatives exercise good offices in many parts of the world (Findlay, 1996), and made important contributions to the settlements in El Salvador, Cambodia, Mozambique and Namibia. The UN's legitimacy contributes to its special responsibility, and its resolutions sometimes play a defining role in setting out principles for settlements (as in the case of Resolutions 242 and 338). It is true that the UN has also faced some dreadful failures in the post-Cold War world, including those in Bosnia, Rwanda and Somalia.[9] Nevertheless, as the instrument through which the international community arranges cease-fires, organizes peacekeeping, facilitates elections and monitors disengagement and demilitarization, the UN has an acknowledged corpus of knowledge and experience to bring to bear.[10]

Governments also play a prominent role as mediators. For example, Portugal (with the UN) facilitated the Bicesse Accord in Angola (Hampson, 1996, 87–127), the ASEAN countries took a leading role in Cambodia, and the United States in Central America. The United States is especially significant in post-Cold War conflicts, given its unique international position. However, governments are not always willing to shoulder a mediating role when their national interests are not at stake, and, where they are, mediation readily blurs into traditional diplomacy and statecraft.

When governments bring coercion to bear to try to force parties to change position, they become actors in the conflict. Forceful interventions clearly can bring forward war endings in some circumstances, as in the case of Bosnia, where after many months of abstention the USA tacitly built up the Croatian armed forces and sanctioned NATO air-strikes on Serb positions in order to force the Dayton Settlement. The question is whether such interventions can lead to a stable ending of conflict, and whether imposed settlements stick.[11] We have discussed the dilemmas involved briefly in the previous chapter, and elsewhere (Ramsbotham and Woodhouse, 1996).

The timing of mediation is a delicate issue, which depends on the particular conflict. On the one hand, mediation can only be successful if the parties are willing to explore a settlement, or can be induced to consider one. On the other, it is impossible to know whether the parties are ready without making the attempt. Zartman (1985) has argued that it is only when a conflict is 'ripe' for settlement that negotiations can succeed; by implication premature mediation is a waste of effort. What is 'ripeness' and how useful is this concept for conflict resolution?

Ripe moments

Many conflict resolution attempts are made, but only a few succeed. Zartman (ed., 1996, 18) argues that conflicts are ripe for negotiated settlements only under certain conditions; the main condition is a 'mutually hurting stalemate'. Both sides must realize that they cannot achieve their aims by further violence and that it is costly to go on:

> Where both sides perceived themselves to be in a stalemate that was painful to each of them and they saw a better alternative through negotiation (as in Sudan in 1972, Mozambique, South Africa, Colombia, and possibly Angola and Sri Lanka in the mid-1990s), they negotiated an agreement; and where the pain of the stalemate was bearable or justified (as in Angola, Afghanistan and Sri Lanka, and among the Colombian extremists), no settlement was negotiated. Stalemate was absent in cases where negotiations took place and then collapsed; in such cases parties often negotiated for other reasons, as in the Philippines, the Basque country, Afghanistan in the 1990s, and Eritrea. In some conflicts where stalemate did appear, as in Angola, Lebanon and Sudan in the 1980s, it became a way of life that buried talks, not a deadlock that promoted them. (*Zartman, ed., 1996, 334*)

The concept of 'hurting stalemate' is widely accepted in policy-making circles, and some diplomats, such as Chester Crocker, have deliberately attempted to bring about a 'hurting stalemate' in order to foster a settlement. Others refer to the need for a 'ripening process' to foster 'ripe moments' (Druckman, 1986).

Zartman (ed., 1996) argues that for negotiations to succeed there must also be valid spokespersons for the parties, a deadline and a vision of an acceptable compromise. Recognition and dialogue are preconditions, and for these to take place both parties have to be accepted as legitimate. In conflicts between a government and an insurgency, for example, the government must reach the point where it recognizes the insurgency as a negotiating partner. Similarly, a more equal power balance between the parties is held to favour negotiation: when the asymmetry is reduced, negotiations may become possible. Druckman and Green (1995) suggest that changes in relative legitimacy as well as relative power between regimes and insurgents affect the propensity to negotiate (Druckman and Green, 1995).

The 'ripeness' idea has the attraction of simplicity, but a number of authors have suggested modifications or criticisms. C. Mitchell (1995) distinguishes four different models of the 'ripe moment': the original 'hurting stalemate' suggested by Zartman; the idea of 'imminent mutual catastrophe', also due to Zartman; the rival model suggested by games of entrapment, such as the 'dollar auction' (Rapoport, 1989), where a 'hurting stalemate' leads to even greater commitment by the parties; and the idea of an enticing opportunity, or conjunction of favourable circumstances (such as, for example, the conjunction of conditions which encouraged the first IRA ceasefire in Northern Ireland in 1995: a Fianna Fáil Taoiseach, a Democratic President with strong American Irish support and an understanding between the Northern Irish Nationalists and Republicans). Others argue that the concept is tautological, since we cannot know whether there is a hurting stalemate until the actions that it is supposed to trigger takes place (Licklider, ed., 1993, 309; Hampson, 1996, 210–14). If a stalemate that hurts the parties persists for a long time before negotiations, as it often does, the value of the concept as an explanation for negotiated settlements must be qualified.

It has been argued that the simple 'hurting stalemate' model gives too much weight to the power relationship between the parties, and fails sufficiently to take account of changes within the parties or changes in the context which may also foster a propensity to negotiate (Stedman 1991). Moreover, although it is possible to point to cases of successful negotiations which have followed hurting stalemates, it is also possible to point to hurting stalemates which do not lead to successful negotiations – for example, Cyprus. It may be argued in these cases that the stalemate is not hurting enough; but then there is no clear evidence from case studies as to how long a stalemate has to last or how much it has to hurt before it triggers successful negotiations. We should distinguish, too, between ripeness for negotiations to start and ripeness for negotiations to succeed; in Angola and Cambodia, for example, the conditions for settlement 'unripened' after negotiated agreements had been made, because one or other of the parties was unwilling to accept the settlement terms, even though the condition of 'hurting stalemate' still obtained. A model that sees conflicts moving from 'unripeness', through a ripe moment to resolution, is perhaps too coarse-grained to take account of the many changes that come together over time and result in a settlement: redefinitions of parties' goals, changes in the parties' constituencies, contextual changes, shifts in perceptions, attitudes and behaviour patterns. Ripeness is not sudden, but rather a complex process of transformations in the situation, shifts in public attitudes and new perceptions and visions among decision-makers.

Peace processes: turning points, sticking points and spoilers

Conflict transformation may be gradual or abrupt; perhaps, more typically, a series of rapid shifts is punctuated by longer periods of inertia and
stalemate. If this process is to go forward, the parties and third parties
must identify an acceptable formula for negotiation, commit themselves
politically to a process of peaceful settlement, manage spoilers who seek
to block the process, and return after each setback to fresh mediation or
negotiation.

This suggests that there is a range of appropriate actions and interventions at different stages of the conflict, depending on the situation. If
the parties are not ready for mediation or negotiations, it may still be
possible to support constituencies which favour peacemaking, to work for
changes in actors' policies and to influence the context that sustains the
conflict. The international anti-apartheid campaign, for example, gradually increased the pressure on international businesses involved in South
Africa, to the point where sanctions and disinvestment became a significant factor. External and internal parties can contribute to the
structural transformations which enable parties to break out of asymmetrical relationships, by the process of conscientization, gathering external
support and legitimacy, and dissociation as a prelude to negotiation and
conflict resolution on a more symmetrical basis (see chapter 1, figure
1.8).

Once a peace process has begun, a dilemma arises as to whether first to
address the core issues in the conflict, which tend to be the most difficult,
or to concentrate on the peripheral issues in the hope of making early
agreements and establishing momentum. A step-by-step approach offers
the parties the opportunity to test each other's good faith and allows for
reciprocation (see box 6.2), in line with the finding from experimental
studies of conflict and cooperation that small tension-reducing steps are
easier to sustain than one-off solutions in two-party conflict (Osgood,
1962; Axelrod, 1984).[12] Since durable and comprehensive agreements are
difficult to establish all at once, interim agreements are usually necessary
in practice. They do need to address core issues, however, if the parties are
to have confidence that the process can deliver an acceptable outcome.
Interim agreements raise risks that parties may renege, or refuse to
reciprocate after obtaining concessions. Agreements that give the parties
some incentives to stay in the process (for example, transitional power-
sharing arrangements), that are supported by external guarantors and
that mobilize domestic support are therefore more likely to succeed
(Hampson, 1996; Sisk, 1996).

The fate of the Oslo agreement in the Israel–Palestine conflict illustrates
that both turning points and sticking points are characteristic of peace
processes. 'Turning points' occur not only at single ripe moments, but at
critical points when parties see a way forward through negotiations, either

BOX 6.2   Strategic dilemmas in peace processes

The obstacles to a peace process are almost always formidable. The parties to a violent conflict aim to win, and so they are locked in a process of strategic interaction which makes them acutely sensitive to prospects for gain and loss. Any concession that involves abandoning political ground, any withdrawal from a long-held position, is therefore resisted bitterly. This is reminiscent of aspects of Prisoner's Dilemma, described in chapter 1.

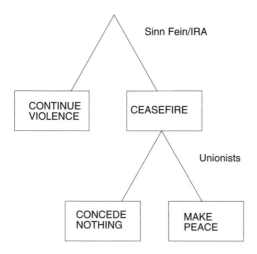

The strategic risks inherent in peacemaking can be illustrated in the tableau above, which is based on a simplified view of the Northern Ireland situation before the IRA ceasefire, but could apply to many other conflicts. Sinn Fein/IRA face a choice between declaring a ceasefire or continuing the violence. We assume they prefer a peace settlement to continuing the violence, but prefer to continue the violence than to stop if the Unionists hold out. The Unionists, too, we assume, prefer a settlement to a continuing conflict, but prefer holding out to settling. Sinn Fein/IRA have to choose first whether to cease fire, then the Northern Ireland Unionists choose between agreeing a settlement and holding out. Sinn Fein/IRA's dilemma is that if they declare a ceasefire the Unionists will continue to concede nothing; so the 'rational' strategy for the Sinn Fein/IRA is to continue to fight.

The way out of this dilemma is for both parties to agree to move together to the option of peaceful settlement and so reach an option they each prefer to continued conflict. In order to do this, the parties have to create sufficient trust, or guarantees, that they will commit themselves to what they promise. For both sides, the risk that the other will renege is ever present. One way of making the commitment is for leaders on both sides to lock their personal political fortunes so strongly to one option that they could not go down the other path without resigning. (This is an equivalent of throwing away the steering wheel in the game of Chicken.) Another method is to divide the number of 'moves' available to the parties into many steps, so that both parties can have confidence that each is taking the agreed route. In real peace processes, confidence-building measures, agreement on procedures or a timetable for moving forward, and public commitments by leaders are among the methods of building and sustaining a peace process.

by redefining their goals, opening new political space, finding a new basis for agreement or because the conjunction of political leaders and circumstances is favourable. Sticking points develop when elites are unfavourable to the process (as in Israel), when parties to agreements defect (as in Angola, Cambodia, Sri Lanka), or when political space is closed or conditions are attached to negotiations which prevent forward movement. At turning points, the aim must be to find ways to capitalize on the momentum of agreement and the changed relationships that have led to it, building up the constituency of support, attempting to persuade the critics and establishing a process with a clear goal and signposts to guide the way towards further agreements and anticipate disputes. At sticking points, the aim is to find ways around the obstacles, drawing on internal and external support, establishing procedures and learning from the flaws of previous agreements.

As a negotiated agreement comes into sight, or after it has been negotiated, spoilers, whose interests are threatened, step up efforts to wreck it. Stedman (1997) classifies spoilers into those with limited aims, who wish to improve their own position in an eventual settlement, and those who are totally opposed to agreement. He suggests the former may be managed by offering inducements and incentives to include them in the agreement, or by offering means to socialize them. The latter, he argues, have to be marginalized, rendered illegitimate or undermined. It may be necessary to accelerate a process, for example by a 'departing train' strategy, which sets a timetable on negotiations and hence limits the time for spoilers to work. In successful peace processes, the moderate parties come to defend the emerging agreement, and spoilers can even serve to consolidate a consensus in the middle ground.

Peace processes involve learning (and second-order learning), with the parties gradually discovering what they are prepared to accept and accommodate. Elements of an agreement may surface in early talks, but they may be insufficiently comprehensive or sufficiently inclusive to hold. They then fall apart; but the main principles and formulas of agreement remain, and can be refined or simplified, until a final agreement is devised. Negotiators and mediators learn from each other and from previous attempts and other peace processes.[13] Eventually they may reach fruition in a negotiated settlement; but even this is only a step, and not the last one, in the conflict resolution process.

Negotiations and settlements

What types of negotiated outcome are likely to resolve protracted conflicts? It is difficult to generalize here, since different types of conflict are associated with different families of outcomes (Horowitz, 1985; Falkenmark, 1990; Montville, ed., 1991; Miall, 1992, 131–63; McGarry and O'Leary, eds, 1993; Sisk, 1996).

As we noted in chapter 1, theorists of negotiation and conflict resolution distinguish integrative (or positive-sum) from bargaining (or zero-sum) approaches. Integrative approaches attempt to find ways, if not to reconcile the conflicting positions, then to meet the underlying interests, values or needs (Fisher and Ury, 1981; Galtung, 1984; Pruitt and Rubin, 1986; Burton, 1987). Examples of integrative approaches are: setting the issue into a wider context or redefining the parties' interests in such a way that they can be made compatible, sharing sovereignty or access to the contested resource, increasing the size of the cake, offering compensation for concessions or trading concessions in other areas and managing the contested resources on a functional rather than a territorial or sovereign basis. Bargaining divides a fixed cake, sometimes with compensations by linkage to other issues. In practice, negotiations combine both approaches.

Albin (1997) offers examples of several of these approaches in her study of options for settling the status of Jerusalem. Both Israelis and Palestinians agree that the city is indivisible, but the dispute over control remains at the core of their long-standing conflict. Both parties claim control over the holy places and claim the city as their capital. Proposals for settling the conflict have included suggestions for increasing the city boundaries of Jerusalem and dividing the enlarged area between two states, each with a capital inside it (resource expansion), establishing decentralized boroughs within a Greater Jerusalem authority elected by proportional representation (no single authority: delegation of power to a lower level), Israeli sovereignty in return for Palestinian autonomy (compensation), dual capitals and shared access to the holy sites (joint sovereignty), or their internationalization, return to a federated one-state solution with Jerusalem as the joint capital (unification of actors) and transfer of control to a city authority representing both communities but organized on functional rather than ethnic or national lines (functional).

In ethnic conflicts, integrative solutions are especially clusive (Zartman, ed., 1996); nevertheless consociationalism, federalism, autonomy, power-sharing, dispersal of power and electoral systems that give incentives to inter-ethnic coalitions offer ways out of conflict in some circumstances (Lijphart, 1968; Horowitz, 1985, 597–600; Sisk, 1996).

Some negotiated settlements are more robust than others. Although generalization is treacherous, successful settlements are thought to have the following characteristics (see Hampson, 1996, 217–21): first, they should include the affected parties, and the parties are more likely to accept them if they have been involved in the process that reaches them – this argues for inclusiveness and against imposed settlements. Second, they need to be well crafted and precise, especially as regards details over transitional arrangements, for example, demobilization assembly points, ceasefire details, voting rules. Third, they should offer a balance between clear commitments and flexibility. Fourth, they should offer incentives for parties to sustain the process and to participate in politics, for example through power-sharing rather than winner-take-all elections. Fifth, they should provide for dispute settlement, mediation and, if necessary, rene-gotiation in case of disagreement. And, sixth, they should deal with the core issues in the conflict and bring about a real transformation, incorpo-rating norms and principles to which the parties subscribe, such as equity and democracy, and at the same time creating political space for further negotiations and political accommodation.

Case Studies: South Africa, Israel–Palestine, Northern Ireland

We now turn to examine three of the major peace processes which have been central stories in post-Cold War conflict resolution. The uneven progress and dramatic reversals in the three peace processes offer insights into the difficulties encountered in ending protracted conflicts, and the various kinds of transformations that shape their course.

The transition from apartheid to multi-party elections in South Africa was one of the most remarkable cases of conflict resolution in the post-Cold War period. How did the white minority, which had been so determined to hold on to power, come to agree to majority rule? How was this extraordinary reversal in government achieved without a bloodbath?

The peace process in Northern Ireland reached a climax in 1995 with the IRA ceasefire, which ushered in the first year of peace in the troubled province since 1969. A year of stalling, in which talks were blocked by preconditions, then led to the resumption of violence with a massive explosion in London's Canary Wharf. Following the election of a new British government, multi-party talks resumed. The British–Irish Agree-ment reached at Easter 1998 brought the protracted peace process in Northern Ireland to an agreed settlement.

When Israel's Prime Minister Yitzhak Rabin shook the hand of the Palestine Liberation Organization (PLO) leader Yassir Arafat on 13

September 1993 to seal the signing of the Oslo Accords, it seemed that they were celebrating a historic breakthrough in the protracted conflict. The accords opened the way to a self-governing Palestinian authority, mutual recognition of Israel and the PLO, and final-status talks on other dividing issues. However, incomplete implementation of the accords and continuing violence by spoilers on both sides subsequently threatened to derail the process.

South Africa

The structure of the conflict lay in the incompatibility between the National Party (NP) government, which was determined to uphold white power and privileges through the apartheid system, and the black majority which sought radical change and a non-racial, equal society based on one-person one-vote. Transforming this conflict involved the empowerment of the majority through political mobilization and the campaign of resistance against the apartheid laws. The revolt in the townships, political mobilization and movements like Steve Biko's 'Black Consciousness' all expressed the refusal of the majority to acquiesce in a racially dominated society. Externally, the international pressure on the South African regime partly offset the internal imbalance of power, through the anti-apartheid campaign, international isolation, sporting bans, partial sanctions and disinvestment.

Changes in the context cleared significant obstacles. While South Africa had been involved in wars in Southern Africa with Cuban-supported and Soviet-supplied regimes, it had been possible for white South Africans to believe that their regime was a bastion against international communist penetration, and for the ANC to believe that a war of liberation based in the front-line states might eventually succeed. With the waning of the Cold War and changes in the region, these views became unsustainable. This separated the question of apartheid from ideological conflicts, and concentrated the struggle in South Africa itself.

Another crucial contextual factor was economic change. It had been possible to run an agricultural and mining economy profitably with poorly paid black labour. But as the economy diversified and modernized, a more educated and skilled labour force was necessary. The demands of the cities for labour created huge townships, such as Soweto, which became a focus for opposition to the regime. The more the government relied on repression to control the situation, the more exposed it became to international sanctions and disinvestment.

Significant changes of actors also made a crucial impact in the process of change. On the side of the National Party, the change in leadership from Vorster to P. W. Botha brought a shift from an unyielding defence of apartheid to a willingness to contemplate reform, so long as it preserved the power and privileges of the white minority. The change in leadership

---

BOX 6.3   South Africa: a chronology of transition

1985   Township rebellion
        State of Emergency
1987   Botha's reforms falter
        NP majority reduced
        Dakar talks (white liberals meet ANC)
1989   F. W. de Klerk replaces Botha
        Economy suffering from sanctions
1990   Mandela released
1991   Apartheid laws repealed
1992   Constitutional negotiations stall
        ANC calls general strike
        Demonstrators killed
        Talks resume
1993   ANC and government agree on 5-year power-sharing
        government
        Violence between Inkatha and ANC rises
1994   Free elections
        Government of National Unity
1995   Reduced political violence
        Threat of right-wing backlash recedes

---

from Botha to F. W. de Klerk heralded a more radical reform policy and the willingness to abandon many aspects of apartheid. Changes at constituency level supported these shifts. For example, the businessmen in South Africa were among the first to see the need for a change in the policy of apartheid, and took a leading role in maintaining contacts with the ANC at a time when the peace process seemed to have reached a sticking point, for example in 1985–6. The bulk of the white population gradually came to accept the inevitability of change, and this influenced the result of the 1988 elections and the referendum in favour of reform in March 1992. The split in the white majority in 1992 created an intra-party conflict between white extremists and the National Party.

On the side of the black majority, the most important actor change was the split that developed between the ANC and the Zulu-dominated Inkatha Freedom Party (IFP), starting in 1976 and growing gradually more serious, until it became a new source of internal armed conflict that threatened the peace process in 1992–4. It seemed that Inkatha and the white extremists might prevent a settlement, but in the end they helped to cement the alliance of the government and the ANC behind negotiated change. We return to this below.

With regard to the issues, both parties in the conflict made significant changes in their positions and goals.[14] On the NP side, a series of shifts can be identified in the mid- and late 1980s. First, there was Botha's shift from the defence of apartheid to the pursuit of limited reforms. He proposed a tricameral parliament which would include whites, Indian and coloured people, but exclude blacks. Botha also sought negotiations with Mandela, but Mandela refused to negotiate until he was released. The reforms failed in their intention to broaden the base of the government's support, and instead led to intensified opposition in the townships. This led to the government's decision to declare the State of Emergency, which contributed in turn to further international pressure and disinvestment. By 1985 the process had reached a sticking point, with the government unwilling to make further reforms, and the black population unwilling to accept the status quo.

It was at this point, with confrontation and no talks between the two sides, that third party mediators made an important contribution.[15] A group of businessmen met with ANC leaders in Zambia, and afterwards issued a call for political negotiations and the abandonment of apartheid. Botha made a new shift in September 1986, offering blacks resident outside the homelands a vote on township councils, but the elections were boycotted. Botha's reforms had stalled. By 1987–8 the situation had reached a second sticking point. The white electorate now showed in the 1988 elections that it was unhappy with the slow pace of change, and F. W. de Klerk's win in the election for the leadership of the National Party brought a change of direction.

On the ANC side, too, there was change. Before 1985, the ANC saw itself as a national liberation movement and expected to establish a socialist government by seizing power after a successful armed struggle. By 1985 it had begun to accept that this goal was unrealistic, and that a compromise was necessary.

A turning-point came in 1989–90. De Klerk shifted decisively towards a policy of negotiations: he began to end segregation, he lifted the ban on the ANC and, finally, he released Mandela on 11 February 1990. By the Groote Schuur Minute of May 1990, the government agreed to 'work toward lifting the state of emergency', while the ANC agreed to 'curb violence'. The ANC had now accepted that the National Party would remain in power while negotiations were carried out, and the National Party that it would have to give up its monopoly of power. The government's aim was now a power-sharing agreement, in which its future role in a multiracial government would be guaranteed. In February 1991 the parties took a further step towards each other's positions when the government agreed to tolerate the continued existence of an ANC militia force and, in return, the ANC agreed not to activate it. The government released political prisoners in April 1991 and in September the parties signed the National Peace Accord, which set up a code of conduct for the security forces and mechanisms for dispute settlement during the course of negotiations. This was followed by the establishment of the Convention for a Democratic South Africa (CODESA), which agreed on a list of

principles for a new constitution and set up working groups to work out
the details.

There was still a wide gulf between the parties' positions. The National
Party sought to sustain white power by arriving at a federal constitution
based on power-sharing, a bicameral parliament, proportional representation, protection of group rights and strong regional governments.
The ANC, in contrast, wanted to see a short-lived interim government of
national unity followed by elections based on one-person one-vote, and a
constitution based on individual rights and a centralized government.
After further negotiations the parties compromised on a Transitional
Executive Council, which would oversee the government, and an elected
constituent assembly, which would produce a new constitution. But they
could not agree on the proportion of votes which would be required for a
majority in the constituent assembly.

Meanwhile, the spoilers were becoming active at both extremes. White
extremists, who regarded the National Party's position as an unacceptable
compromise, and the IFP, which feared that an ANC-dominated government would override the Zulu regional power-base, found a shared
interest in wrecking the negotiations. At first, their pressure caused a
hardening of positions. After winning a referendum among the whites
approving his conduct of the negotiations, de Klerk refused to make
concessions on the voting issue. The ANC, facing escalating violence in
the townships, which Inkatha was suspected of fomenting with the
connivance of the police, decided to break off negotiations.

This was the third and most dangerous sticking point. Violence was
rising and the threat of breakdown was clear. The ANC called a general
strike and mass demonstrations. The police cracked down and twenty-
eight marchers were killed in Bisho, Ciskei in September 1992. This
disaster reminded both sides of the bloodbath that seemed likely if
negotiations failed. Roelf Meyer, the Minister of Constitutional Development, and Cyril Ramaphosa, the ANC's lead negotiator, continued to
meet unofficially in hotel rooms as violence rose. In September 1992 the
parties returned decisively to negotiations when de Klerk and Mandela
agreed a 'Record of Understanding'. This spelt out the basis on which
power would eventually be transferred: an interim, elected parliament to
agree a new constitution, and an interim power-sharing government of
national unity, to be composed of parties winning more than 5 per cent of
the vote, to last for five years. The ANC had shifted to accept power-
sharing and a long transition; the National Party had shifted to accept that
the continuation of white power would not be guaranteed. By now the
National Party was fearful of losing support to the right unless it acted
quickly, and it stepped up progress, accepting a deadline for elections in
April 1994. The Transitional Executive Council, set up in September
1993, gradually took on more and more of the key political functions of
government, and the National Party and the ANC found themselves
jointly defending the settlement against Inkatha and the white extremists,

who now supported a confederal alternative providing autonomy for the regions in which they lived.

The six months leading up to the elections were thus a struggle between the NP–ANC coalition and the spoilers, with the conduct of the elections as the prize. Inkatha left the Transitional Executive Council, and violence against ANC supporters in Natal intensified. Negotiations between the ANC and Chief Buthelezi, leader of the IFP, came to nothing and Buthelezi prepared to exercise his threat of boycotting the elections. At the last moment the ANC offered King Goodwill of the Zulus a major concession over the trusteeship of land in Natal. Buthelezi's followers refused to follow him into the wilderness, and he was forced to accept a last-minute deal and participate in the elections. The elections thus proceeded legitimately, and returned a parliament in which the ANC fell just below the two-thirds majority required to pass laws. Power-sharing would be a fact. Mandela became president of the government of national unity, with De Klerk and Buthelezi as ministers.

In the end, a process of negotiations and elections had replaced apartheid and white power. The legitimation of the black opposition had transformed the structure of the conflict, turning an asymmetrical relationship between minority and majority into a symmetrical relationship between parties and their followers. Though many tensions remained, and real socio-economic transformation was slow to come, the elections conveyed 'participation, legitimation and allocation, the three elements necessary to the settlement of internal conflicts' (Zartman, ed., 1995b, 339). The parties in South Africa had achieved an agreed and legitimate constitutional settlement in a situation so unfavourable that many observers had previously judged it to be impossible.

Israel–Palestine

The Israeli–Palestinian conflict, by contrast, offers a case of a peace process which reached a dramatic transformation, only to return to deadlock and violence through failure to carry the process forward.

Two changes in the international context led to decisive changes to Middle Eastern politics (Shlaim, 1995; Smith, 1996). First, the end of the Cold War meant the end of Soviet military and financial aid for the radical Arab states, and undermined any residual doubts about Israel's survival. The PLO reflected the new realism when it decided in 1988 to recognize Israel and pursue a two-state solution. Second, the Gulf War brought US pressure on Israel to seek a settlement and a disastrous cut in support for the PLO. These changes, combined, brought the parties to a point at which they were prepared to consider a negotiated settlement.[16]

Structurally, however, the asymmetry between the Palestinians and the Israelis appeared to be growing even worse. The intifada demonstrated it: the Palestinians threw stones, the Israelis replied by blowing up houses.

BOX 6.4   The Israeli–Palestinian peace process

1991 October	Madrid peace conference opens
1993 September	Declaration of Principles (Oslo I); Arafat and Rabin shake hands
1994 February	Hebron massacre
May	Parts of Gaza and Jericho handed over to Palestinians
1995 September	Oslo II – six other West Bank towns handed over
November	Rabin assassinated
1996 March	Hamas suicide bombs in Jerusalem and Tel Aviv
June	Netanyahu wins Israeli elections
December	Israel approves Jewish building projects in Arab parts of Jerusalem
1998 May	London talks fail

The PLO was in a particularly weak position, politically and financially, after being expelled from Lebanon and siding with Iraq in the Gulf War. The intifada put pressure on both Israel and the PLO leadership in far-away Tunis. It demonstrated that the status quo was unsustainable; Palestinians would not accept Israeli rule and the cost to Israel was becoming unacceptably high. On the other hand, it shifted the centre of Palestinian resistance to the people living in the occupied territories, and made their plight the most urgent priority. Reluctantly and slowly, the PLO changed position from seeking to supplant a Jewish Israel to accepting the idea of a Palestinian state based on Gaza and the West Bank side by side with Israel. And as a step towards this, the PLO was willing to accept 'Gaza and Jericho first' (Rubin, 1994).

Changes in actors were critical to both the successes and failures of the peace process. The election victory of the Labour Party in the Israeli election of June 1992 brought into power an Israeli government that was prepared to deal with the PLO. Shimon Peres, Foreign Minister during the negotiation of the Oslo accords, and his deputy Yossi Beilin, were both advocates of talking with the PLO, and represented the Ashkenazi, secular, middle-class stream of Israeli society. Personally, Rabin, the Prime Minister, wanted a success to crown his career, and he had promised to deliver an autonomy agreement. He was opposed to a Palestinian state, but was keen to rid Israel of the burden of policing Gaza and sought a settlement that would permit Israel to develop as a secure democracy. Under this leadership, Israel was able to reach a settlement. However, divisions within Israel have always been wide. There has never been a consensus on the peace process. Labour met bitter opposition from

Likud, which represented the Sephardim, the working class, and recent immigrants. The Likud leader Benjamin Netanyahu had campaigned against the peace process, and his narrow victory in the 1996 elections brought the process (which was already faltering) to a halt. On the Palestinian side, Arafat was ageing and losing political ground to Hamas and the Islamic Jihad, so he, like Rabin, had an individual motive to settle. But the accords led to open conflict between the rejectionists and the PLO, which was now forced into the opprobrious role of policing dissent itself. Externally, US pressure on Israel weakened as the Clinton administration courted the domestic Zionist lobby. All these changes worked against the completion of the peace process.

We have to trace two sets of shifts of position: first, towards the signature of the Oslo Accords; second, away from their implementation. Before September 1993, the key steps were: the PLO's recognition of Israel, and its acceptance of a two-state solution in 1988; the willingness of Syria and Jordan to consider a peace deal with Israel; the convening of peace talks in Madrid, which, however, made little progress; President Bush's insistence in February 1992 that loans to Israel would be conditional on a freeze in settlements; Rabin's agreement to halt new settlement-building (excluding 'security settlements') in September 1992; and the Israeli shift from refusal to talk with the PLO to a willingness to explore the Oslo back-channel.

Further shifts were made during the eight months of intensive negotiation in secret in Norway, although all of them were provisional up to the signing of the accords – as the key players insisted, they could never have reached the accords if the negotiations had been in public (Corbin, 1994). The Israelis moved a long way from their previous positions by recognizing the PLO as 'the representative of the Palestinian people' and as the authority in the autonomous Palestinian Interim Self-Governing Authority (PISGA) that was to be set up in Gaza and Jericho. The PLO also moved a long way, in formally recognizing 'the right of Israel to exist in peace and security', in renouncing armed struggle and accepting an autonomy arrangement that gave them less than a state. The agreement set out a five-year timetable for Israeli withdrawals and troop redeployments, and for further negotiations on permanent status. From the Palestinian point of view, this was an unequal agreement, acceptable only on an interim basis. It left PISGA with no authority over Israeli settlements, external relations, resident rights or lines of communication between the autonomous enclaves. The agreement deferred the so-called 'future status' issues, which lay at the root of the conflict, including the right of return of Palestinian refugees, the future borders of the Palestinian entity, the future of settlements in occupied territory and the question of Jerusalem. The Declaration of Principles was a historic development in the long conflict. But it was not a full peace settlement, only a step towards one.

Differences between the parties over the accords arose immediately, and the implementation of its measures were delayed. Extremists on both sides carried out bloody attacks directed against the peace process, such as the Hebron massacre and the suicide bombings by Hamas. Israel responded by sealing off the Palestinian enclaves, resulting in a sharp fall in living standards and undermining the ideas of economic cooperation on which the Oslo process had been based. Israeli troops did withdraw from the Gaza strip, Jericho and six other West Bank towns, albeit later than scheduled. The Taba or Oslo II agreement in 1995 left the West Bank as a patchwork of Palestinian areas scattered in the Israeli-occupied zone. But the planned negotiations on permanent status did not occur. Israel also continued building settlements in the occupied territories.

These problems arose primarily from the intra-party differences. On the Palestinian side, while the majority of those living in the Gaza strip and the West Bank were in favour of the deal, Palestinians outside Palestine and those in the refugee camps rejected it, as did the Islamic militant groups. On the Israeli side, an acute and bitter debate developed over the accords, marked bloodily by the assassination of Rabin by a Jewish extremist. Netanyahu's campaign against the peace process resulted in his narrow victory in the subsequent 1996 elections. With a Likud government in power, determined to maintain and extend Israeli control in the occupied territories, the peace process almost ground to a halt. The combination of a spoiler in power on one side and active spoilers in opposition on the other was devastating for further progress. Yet, for domestic and international reasons, neither side was willing wholly to reject the Oslo accords. A considerable part of the public on both sides still supported the process, and the violence that might accompany a complete breakdown was a chilling prospect. As in the South African case, therefore, the process created its own momentum, although in the Israeli–Palestinian case it had reached a sticking point so formidable that many judged it had altogether broken down.

On the one hand, some of the factors that had precipitated the peace process were still in place. The changes in the international context were such that the Arab states and the Palestinians still had an incentive to settle, if the terms were acceptable. Third parties also had a strong incentive to assist a settlement. The structure of the conflict had shifted with the mutual recognition and the creation of autonomous enclaves. On the other hand, the conflict still remained highly asymmetric. In this situation, the implementation of the agreement and of confidence-building measures by the stronger party was especially important. These proved insufficient. Given intra-party conflicts on both sides, and a lack of strong external pressure on the parties, the non-implementation of the agreement increased Palestinian frustration and violence, and this in turn reduced support for the agreement in Israel. The interpretation of the agreement by one side as a legal contract, and by the other as a first step in a changing political relationship, further highlighted the asymmetry that remained. While this and other major issues remained unresolved, the conflict was likely to continue.

BOX 6.5   The Northern Ireland peace process

1985	Anglo-Irish agreement
1988	First round of Hume–Adams talks
1989–91	Brooke talks
1990	Secret UK government–Sinn Fein contacts
1993 October	Hume presents Adams–Hume document to Dublin
November	Downing Street Declaration
1995 February	Framework Documents
August	IRA ceasefire
1996 January	Mitchell Commission reports; Major opts for an elected assembly
February	IRA ends ceasefire and bombs Canary Wharf
July	Drumcree confrontation
1996–7	All-party talks (without Sinn Fein) make little progress
1997 May	Labour government elected
June	Blair announces 'settlement train', setting a deadline of May 1998
July	Second IRA ceasefire
September	Sinn Fein accepts Mitchell principles and joins talks
December	Renewed sectarian violence in Belfast
1998 April	Good Friday Agreement

Northern Ireland

In April 1998 the parties to the conflict in Northern Ireland finally reached an agreement on a new political settlement. Although there will clearly be many difficulties ahead, the agreement marks a decisive stage in the long conflict.

During most of Northern Ireland's history, the structure of the conflict lay in the asymmetrical relationship between the Protestant and Unionist majority, backed by the British state, and the Catholic and nationalist minority. Three factors helped to change this asymmetry. First, the British government became increasingly impatient with the Unionists' handling of the situation, leading ultimately to the suspending of Stormont and the imposition of direct rule, which put the Unionists in the same position of exclusion as the Nationalists. Second, the agreement of the UK and Irish governments to work together through the Anglo-Irish Agreement transformed the structure of the conflict, which could no longer be seen as the UK and Northern Ireland Unionists against the Republic and Northern

Ireland Nationalists. Third, the pan-Nationalist coalition and the support of Irish Americans for the Nationalists helped to level the playing field.

The ending of the Cold War also contributed to the change of context in which it was seen as more politically sensible to engage in a peace process than a national liberation war. It had a clear impact on the Republican political analysis (Cox, 1997). Meanwhile, the growing political significance of the EU contributed to enhanced cooperation between the Irish and British governments and gave credibility to the idea of a European dimension and a reduced significance for the border, which played an especially important part in the thinking of the SDLP. Another contextual change was the relative improvement in the Irish Republic's economic fortunes, which made the Protestant stereotype of the 'backward, papist' South difficult to sustain.

Significant changes in actors included the change in the Republican leadership when Adams reached the top, the coming to power of Albert Reynolds in the Republic, and the election of a Labour government in Britain under Tony Blair.

The Northern Ireland peace process, which dates from the Hume–Adams meetings of 1988, can be divided into a series of phases punctuated by sticking points and turning points (see Coogan, 1995; Bew, 1996; O'Leary and McGarry, 1996). We start from the deadlock reached after the breakdown of the Sunningdale agreement in 1974. The British government was seeking an internal settlement among the constitutional parties in Northern Ireland, but failed to find a sufficient basis of agreement. The two communities in Northern Ireland remained divided. The Ulster Unionist Party demanded a return to devolved government and was unwilling to negotiate with either the Irish government or with Sinn Fein. And in the absence of a political agreement, paramilitaries on both sides pursued political violence.

Two shifts of position led to a change in the stalemate. The first was the switch by the British government from relying on an internal settlement to greater cooperation with Dublin. The Anglo-Irish Agreement gave the Irish government the right to be consulted over Northern Ireland's affairs, set up an intergovernmental conference, and affirmed that any changes in the status of Northern Ireland would depend on the consent of a majority there. For its part, the British government made clear that it was not committed to indefinite sovereignty when Peter Brooke, the then Northern Ireland Secretary, declared in 1990 that Britain had no 'selfish, strategic or economic interest' for being in Ireland.

The second shift was a gradual change in Republican thinking about the conflict. Having failed to force a British withdrawal by violence, the Republicans pursued a revised strategy of relying on both 'the Armalite and the ballot box'. By the late 1980s, this strategy too was perceived to be failing, and the idea of a purely political campaign was mooted. As Republicans became more engaged in politics, they could see the possibilities that a political route offered them, especially given Sinn Fein's strong performance in the polls.

The next key development was the decision of John Hume, the SDLP leader, to pursue a basis for a ceasefire and inclusive talks, by opening a controversial dialogue with Sinn Fein. These talks, facilitated by the mediation of the Clonard monks, led eventually to a suggested set of principles for a settlement. Aware of the possibility this agreement opened for a ceasefire, the Irish and British prime ministers then issued a joint statement which included some of the principles reached by Hume and Adams.[17]

The Downing Street Declaration was a turning point, since it lay down principles drawn from both sides which offered a reasonably comprehensive framework for a resolution. It reiterated the principle of consent, but also accepted the right of self-determination of the people of Ireland, 'by agreement between the two parts respectively' (North and South), including their right to bring about a united Ireland if that was their wish. It was followed up later by the Framework Documents, in which the two governments set out detailed proposals for a settlement, based on the three-strand framework that had emerged from the Brooke talks of 1989–91: a North–North strand, with provision for a devolved assembly, proportional representation and power-sharing in the North, a North–South strand, in which a new body would emerge to take on functions to be decided later, and an East–West strand, with the UK–Irish intergovernmental council underwriting the settlement and the interests of both communities. The proposals emphasized the importance of parity of esteem, in keeping with the recognition of cultural traditions which had emerged from community relations work. They received a cautious welcome from the public, and were close to nationalist proposals; the Unionists, having played little part in the peace process to date, rejected them, especially the provisions for a North–South body which they feared would be a slippery slope to unification. They were, however, prepared to accept internal power-sharing in the North.

The twin task of the peace process was to reach a broadly acceptable political settlement and to end political violence; both were clearly interdependent. The IRA ceasefire in August 1995 raised hopes that a rapid movement to all-party talks would follow, but instead, with deep mistrust on all sides, the process reached a sticking point over decommissioning of paramilitary weapons, which the Unionists and the government required as a precondition to talks. The British government agreed to accept a third party, US presence to resolve this impasse, in the form of the Mitchell Commission. The Mitchell Commission's five principles of non-violence and democratic methods were later to govern entry into the talks, but the then prime minister, John Major, rejected its proposal for simultaneous decommissioning and negotiations, and instead announced elections to a body to carry out negotiations the following May. The IRA, which made it clear that it would refuse to decommission weapons before negotiations, then ended its ceasefire.

The following summer saw some of the worst violence for years in Northern Ireland after the confrontation between the Orangemen and the Royal Ulster Constabulary (RUC) in Drumcree. On the ground, the communities were increasingly polarized, and intimidation on both sides drove Catholics out of Protestant areas and vice versa. Sinn Fein and the Democratic Unionist Party (DUP) both did well in the May elections to the negotiating body, at the expense of the more moderate parties.

It took an actor transformation, in the shape of the election of a new British government led by Tony Blair (and a new Irish one at the same time) to break this logjam. Blair announced a 'departing train' strategy, setting a deadline for the talks to end in May 1998. He also made it clear that he would not allow the deadlock over decommissioning to hold up the talks. Under the inducement of this new approach, the IRA declared a second ceasefire, Sinn Fein accepted the Mitchell Principles, and Sinn Fein entered the talks. Two of the Unionist parties dropped out – Ian Paisley's DUP and the smaller UK Unionist Party (UKUP) – but the Official Unionists remained, persuaded to pigeonhole the decommissioning issue, partly inspired by the South African example. The talks proceeded on the basis of sufficient consent: if parties representing a majority of the majority community and a majority of the minority community accepted the settlement, it would be considered as acceptable. It would then be put to a simultaneous referendum in the North and South, thereby meeting the requirement for self-determination of all the people of Ireland.

Characteristically, the spoilers stepped up their violence as the talks moved towards the deadline. A splinter group of the IRA, the Continuity Army Council, exploded bombs, while a similar loyalist group started a new round of sectarian killings. At different stages these violent incidents forced the removal of political parties from the talks to sustain the Mitchell Principles. But, despite the obstacles, the talks continued.

The parties all made significant movements over the course of the peace process. The Official Unionists had demonstrated that they were willing to negotiate, even with Sinn Fein in the talks. Sinn Fein was prepared to consider a long transition before unification. The SDLP accepted a framework based on consent. The British government had made it clear that it was prepared to withdraw, if that was agreed by the people of Ireland, and that its primary aim was to find a settlement. The Irish government had declared that it would amend the Irish constitution to remove the territorial claim to the North. The discussion in the three strands, in the context of the totality of relationships in the islands of Britain and Ireland, created space for negotiations, even though the detail (especially of arrangements for the crucial North–South strand) led to deadlocks. Despite the serious intra-party divisions and the deep divisions and mistrust on the ground, there were signs of rethinking and reframing of perspectives. Some Unionists were prepared to move towards a more inclusive approach that saw the need both to accommodate the two Irish traditions in the institutions of the North, and to build cooperation between North and South.[18] Some Republicans were clearly prepared to accept a political road towards their aspiration to unification. These transformations were significant. But the final issue, of whether the parties, especially the Unionists and Sinn Fein, would be able to sign up to a common document, remained in doubt up to the last moment.

The crucial issue of North–South institutions still seemed to be a major obstacle until the final stages, with Sinn Fein unwilling to accept any settlement that did not allow for movement towards a united Ireland, and the Unionists unwilling to accept a settlement that did allow such movement. The SDLP and the Unionists also remained divided over the details of a power-sharing agreement for Northern Ireland. Nevertheless, the willingness of the parties to remain in the talks indicated that all of them were seriously interested in a deal. As the deadline of 10 April neared, the pace intensified. George Mitchell, who chaired the talks, used his authority to propose a draft agreement. This was welcomed by the Nationalists but rejected by Unionists. The British and Irish prime ministers then arrived and in further all-night negotiations the final elements of the deal were put in place. The power-sharing assembly and the North–South Ministerial Council were locked together, so that neither could work without the other, and agreement in the North–South body would be subject to agreement of both the Irish government and the Northern Ireland assembly. A new British–Irish Council and a British–Irish Inter-governmental Conference replaced the Anglo-Irish Agreement, balancing the North–South arrangements, but also holding open the possibility of a new set of relationships emerging across the British Isles. The agreement met the demand of the Unionists that the Union should continue while it had majority consent. It met the demand of the nationalists for power-sharing, a commitment to equal rights and an expression of self-determination, North and South. It met the demand of the Republicans for some element of all-Ireland arrangements, which could be built on by agreement, and for an acceptance of Irish unity should it be agreed by a majority North and South.

On 22 May, the people of Northern Ireland endorsed the agreement in a referendum with 71 per cent voting 'yes' and 29 per cent 'no'; in the Republic 94 per cent voted 'yes'. This popular endorsement was a major achievement for the peace process, though it followed a bitter campaign which had divided the Unionist community. On 25 June the elections for the new Assembly at Stormont returned a working majority for parties which favoured the agreement, although among the Unionists the leader of the Ulster Unionist Party, David Trimble, held a slim majority and was threatened by Unionist defections amidst continuing Unionist unease about the course the peace process was taking.

Two violent incidents on both sides did much to discredit the spoilers. The defiance of the police by Orange Order loyalists at Drumcree in 1998 ended following an incident in which three children of a Catholic mother were burnt to death by fire-bombs thrown by loyalist militants in the small Protestant town of Ballymoney; and the Republican groups who had splintered from the IRA were forced to declare a ceasefire after one of the worst bombings of the Troubles in Omagh was perpetrated by the Real IRA, killing twenty-eight people (all but five of whom were women or children).

In Northern Ireland, as in South Africa and Israel–Palestine, the structural, issue and actor transformations which we have noted were in turn affected by subtle but significant personal and group transformations. In all three cases the work of third parties was in parallel with indigenous groups and projects, and with Track II NGOs, working though education, training and social capacity-building to foster the personal and communal changes of heart which make peace agreements thinkable in the first place. In South Africa the Centre for Conflict Resolution, based at the University of Cape Town, worked over many years to cultivate the skills and confidence in communities to promote the processes of the peaceful transformation of apartheid, and Centre staff were deeply involved as mediators, monitors, trainers and advisers on the Peace Accord Structures which guided the transition to a democratic South Africa. In the peace process between Israel and the PLO, in addition to the third party work of the Norwegians, there had been a generation of efforts in problem-solving workshops to promote dialogue and understanding, typified in the work of the reconciliation community Neve Shalom. In Northern Ireland, Mari Fitzduff, a conflict resolution trainer and researcher, proposed a strategy (see box 6.6) which was subsequently incorporated in the work of the Community Relations Council of Northern Ireland. The work of academic centres such as the Centre for the Study of Conflict, and the Initiative on Conflict Resolution and Ethnicity, both at the University of Ulster, deepened understandings of the conflict. The strategy was based on the assessment, central to conflict resolution theory, that structural, issue, and actor transformations interact in a complicated but dynamic way with personal and group perceptions and processes:

> A satisfactory constitutional settlement is dependent upon group relations within the community ... To leave the problem of improving community relations until one has finally solved the constitutional issue may merely exacerbate not only the problem of relationships between the communities but also the task of finding an acceptable constitutional settlement. (*Bloomfield, 1997, 134*)

The strategy which resulted from this assessment has guided a good deal of the grass-roots Track III peacemaking activities which have occurred in Northern Ireland. If the people there do finally accept the agreement made by the political parties in April 1998, then some at least of the will and motivation to take such a step will have come from the energy and desire

---

BOX 6.6 Northern Ireland community relations

1 MUTUAL UNDERSTANDING WORK: to increase dialogue and reduce ignorance, suspicion and prejudice

2 ANTI-SECTARIAN and ANTI-INTIMIDATION WORK: to transfer improved understanding into structural changes

3 CULTURAL TRADITIONS WORK: to affirm and develop cultural confidence that is not exclusive

4 POLITICAL OPTIONS WORK: to facilitate political discussion within and between communities, including developing agreed principles of justice and rights

5 CONFLICT RESOLUTION WORK: to develop skills and knowledge which will increase possibilities for greater social and political cooperation

Source: from Fitzduff, 1989

---

for peace liberated by such strategies. Perhaps because of its protracted conflict, Northern Ireland has developed one of the most impressive capacities for peacebuilding work and for ethnic conflict resolution research of any conflict arena (Darby, 1998, chs 8 and 9).

Conclusion

We have identified the characteristics of a conflict resolution approach to ending conflicts, while acknowledging that in many contemporary conflicts such an approach is not applied. We argued that conflict resolution is more than a simple matter of mediating between parties and reaching an integrative agreement on the issues that divide them. It must also touch on the context of the conflict, the conflict structure, the intra-party as well as the inter-party divisions and the broader system of society and governance within which the conflict is embedded. This suggests that interventions should not be confined to the 'ripe moment'. Peace processes, we argued, are a complex succession of transformations, punctuated by several turning points and sticking points. At different stages in this process, transformations in the context, the actors, the issues, the people involved and the structure of the conflict may be vital to move the conflict resolution process forward.

Even when settlements are reached, the best-engineered political arrangements can collapse again later, if new life is not breathed in to them by the will of the parties, their constituencies and external supporters to make them work. For this reason, peacebuilding remains a constant priority, especially in the post-settlement phase. The next chapter tackles the question of how settlements can be sustained without a return to fresh violence.

7

Post-Settlement Peacebuilding

Peace agreements provide a framework for ending hostilities and a guide to the initial stages of postconflict reform. They do not create conditions under which the deep cleavages that produced the war are automatically surmounted. Successfully ending the divisions that lead to war, healing the social wounds created by war, and creating a society where the differences among social groups are resolved through compromise rather than violent conflict requires that conflict resolution and consensus building shape all interactions among citizens and between citizens and the state.

Nicole Ball (1996, 619)

This chapter completes our review of the contribution that the conflict resolution field can make at the various stages of conflict escalation and de-escalation by focusing on post-settlement peacebuilding. In particular, we look at cases of post-Cold War settlements in which the UN has played a major interventionary role, covering conflicts in four continents (see table 7.1): Asia (Cambodia), South America (El Salvador), Africa (Namibia, Angola, Mozambique) and – albeit not primarily a UN operation – Europe (post-Dayton Bosnia).[1] There are many other examples of attempts at post-war peacebuilding in the absence of formal peace agreements – for example, after military victory for one side, or when the fighting reaches a stalemate or peters out into a precarious stand-off punctuated by sporadic localized violence. There are also examples of post-settlement peacebuilding unmediated by the UN, such as the South African, Israeli–Palestinian and Northern Ireland cases considered in chapter 6. Nevertheless, the cluster of examples which we look at here, taken together, make up a remarkable experiment in post-Cold War politics which will serve to sum up the main themes of this book.

It is an experiment which began with the UN's intervention in Namibia to help implement the December 1988 Namibia Accords, and then

Table 7.1 Six UN post-settlement peacebuilding missions, 1988–98

Country	Government	Opposition	UN intervention force
Namibia	South Africa	SWAPO	UNTAG
Angola	MPLA	UNITA	UNAVEM
El Salvador	ARENA	FMNL	ONUSAL
Cambodia	SOC	CDGK	UNTAC
Mozambique	FRELIMO	RENAMO	ONUMOZ
Bosnia–Herzegovina	Govt. of RBH	(FBH)/RS	IFOR/SFOR etc.

expanded unexpectedly into a global effort to bring a number of prolonged and vicious internal wars to an end by securing and consolidating peace agreements between the warring parties. What Clapham (1998) calls 'a fairly standardised conflict resolution mechanism' derived from this was applied like a template to a wide range of disparate conflicts. This is reminiscent of Wittgenstein's locomotive cabin in which a uniform-looking set of handles in fact fulfils a number of diverse functions. We call this the UN's post-settlement peacebuilding 'standard operating procedure' (SOP).

Post-Settlement Peacebuilding Defined

We noted in chapter 2 how the concept of conflict resolution was broadened in the 1990s to enable both a variety of support to local peacemakers in conflicts and better understanding of the process of post-conflict peacebuilding. If peace agreements are the point at which conflicts are terminated formally, the process of resolution in attending to root causes is crucial in the post-agreement, or post-settlement, phase. When the UN Secretary-General was asked by Security Council heads of government meeting on 31 January 1992 to draft general principles that would 'guide decisions on when a domestic situation warrants international action' (UN Doc. S/PV. 3046, 1F31), he based his response in part on distinctions that had long been current in the peace research and conflict resolution field, and in part on ideas drawn from the disaster relief and sustainable development literature (Pugh, 1995). So far as concerns the former, Galtung distinguished 'three approaches' to peace in the 1960s: peacekeeping which aimed 'to halt and reduce the manifest violence of the conflict through the intervention of military forces in an interpository role'; peacemaking which was 'directed at reconciling political and strategical attitudes through mediation, negotiation, arbitration and conciliation' mainly at elite level; and peacebuilding which addressed 'the practical implementation of peaceful social change through socio-economic reconstruction and development' (1975, 282–304). Ryan, critical of the neglect of the relational dimension in Galtung's characterization of peacebuilding, put his emphasis on changing mutually negative conflict attitudes at grass-roots level (1990, 50). With reference to Galtung's 'conflict triangle', Ryan contrasted it with peacekeeping, which aims for a reduction in violent conflict behaviour, and peacemaking, which aims to resolve conflicting interests. All of this has been recently brought together within the conflict resolution field in Lederach's characterization of peacebuilding as the attempt to address the underlying structural, relational and cultural roots of conflict: 'I am suggesting that "peacebuilding" be understood as a comprehensive term that encompasses the full array of stages and approaches needed to transform conflict towards sustainable, peaceful relations and outcomes' (1994, 14).

Drawing on this tradition, but narrowing it so that it applied specifically to postwar reconstruction, the UN Secretary-General distinguished 'post-conflict peacebuilding' from pre-conflict 'preventive diplomacy' in his June 1992 *Agenda for Peace*, while retaining the original contrast between peacebuilding, peacekeeping and peacemaking. He defined post-conflict peacebuilding as 'actions to identify and support structures which will tend to strengthen and solidify peace in order to avoid a relapse into conflict' (Boutros-Ghali, 1992, 11). This was at first largely identified with military demobilization and the political transition to participatory electoral democracy, which remains the core of the UN's post-settlement peacebuilding SOP. In the 1995 *Supplement to An Agenda for Peace* it was envisaged that post-conflict peacebuilding would initially be undertaken by multifunctional UN operations, then handed over to civilian agencies under a resident coordinator, and finally transferred entirely to local agents (Boutros-Ghali, 1995). Since *Agenda for Peace* the concept has been progressively expanded in subsequent versions (Boutros-Ghali, 1993; 1994; 1995b) to include a broader agenda aimed at alleviating the worst effects of war on the population and promoting what Michael Pugh calls 'a sustainable development approach which tackles the root causes of emergencies'. He sums this up as follows:

> [I]n the context of UN-authorized peace support measures, peacebuilding can be defined as a policy of external international help for developing countries designed to support indigenous social, cultural and economic development and self-reliance, by aiding recovery from war and reducing or eliminating resort to future violence. (*1995, 328*)

In order to clarify what is at issue here, it is helpful to refer again to the distinction made in the peace research and conflict resolution literature between 'negative' and 'positive' peace, where the former is defined as the cessation of 'direct' violence and the latter as the removal of 'structural' and 'cultural' violence (Galtung, 1990). From this viewpoint, post-settlement peacebuilding can be said to be made up of (a) the 'negative' task of preventing a relapse into overt violence and (b) the 'positive' tasks of aiding national recovery and expediting the eventual removal of the underlying causes of internal war. The distinctive but close relationship between these two complementary sets of tasks is indicated (albeit in reverse order) in the UN Secretary-General's definition of 'post-conflict peacebuilding' as 'the various concurrent and integrated actions undertaken at the end of a conflict to consolidate peace and prevent a recurrence of armed confrontation' (Annan, 1997c). Peacebuilding is distinguished here from ongoing humanitarian and development activities in 'countries emerging from crisis' in so far as it has the specific political aims of reducing 'the risk of resumption of conflict' and contributing to the creation of 'conditions most conducive to reconciliation, reconstruction and recovery'. We will call the first task 'preventing a relapse into war' and the second task 'constructing a self-sustaining peace'. Some of the most testing challenges in post-settlement peacebuilding concern the relationship between the two. In chapter 5 we saw how, in response to this challenge, UN peacekeeping doctrine was being developed around the idea of peace support operations, which aimed to link the task of military containment of conflict with the long-term goals of rehabilitation and the rebuilding of communities economically, politically and socially.

The Challenge of Post-Settlement Peacebuilding

A brief look at the situation in the six cases under scrutiny gives an idea of the scale of the challenge facing peacebuilders after long periods of war. In each instance the original causes of the war, themselves often deep-rooted and difficult to eradicate, had been overlaid by the traumatic experience of many years of intense fighting, as described in general terms in chapter 5. Compared with the tasks facing those attempting prewar conflict prevention, discussed in chapter 4, post-settlement peacebuilders may in some senses have an easier job, in so far as the main conflict parties have at least been induced to reach an agreement, outside governments may be exerting concerted pressure to sustain the settlement and war-weariness, if not war-revulsion, may predominate within the population at large. In most other respects, however, the tasks confronting postwar peacebuilders are much more demanding. We look first at the challenge of preventing a relapse into war, then at the challenge of constructing a self-sustaining peace and, finally, at the relationship between the two.

Task (a): preventing a relapse into war

Preventing a relapse into war means confronting what we might call the challenge of 'Clausewitz in reverse' – the continuation of the politics of war into the ensuing peace. This is the most immediate and urgent political task facing post-settlement peacebuilders. Clausewitz's insight that war is the 'continuation of political intercourse with the addition of other means',[2] also implies the reverse – that postwar politics is a continuation of the conflict, albeit transmuted into non-military mode. In fact, Clausewitz himself, prescient as ever, anticipated this observation in a continuation of the passage cited in endnote 2: 'The main lines along which military events progress, and to which they are restricted, are political lines that continue throughout the war *into the subsequent peace*' (italics added). The 'additional means' which characterize war will also have left their mark on the post-settlement process in the form of broken lives and shattered communities, as well as new actors, interests and political agendas spawned by what has usually been a prolonged period of fighting. The term 'post-conflict peacebuilding', therefore, despite its UN imprimatur, is a misnomer (hence the use of the term 'post-settlement peacebuilding' in this chapter). 'Post-conflict' is precisely what it is not. On the contrary, the peace agreement is not the end of the conflict, but, in Ball's phrase, 'the means through which the parties hope to resolve the unfinished business of war' (1996, 608) – or, rather, the means through which they hope to win, albeit no longer by military force. Nor is this an accidental feature of the postwar political situation. It is its very essence, as is made plain in recent analyses of internal war endings as described in chapter 6, where it is shown that the most difficult task facing those trying to bring about a lasting peace agreement is to persuade the conflict parties that their continuing interests will now be better served by entering the peace process than by continuing to fight (Haass, 1990; Licklider, ed., 1993; Smith, J., 1995; Hampson, 1996b, 13–16; Zartman, 1996).

For Licklider, for example, this is seen to underlie all three of the 'intrinsic' features regarded as critical to the ending of violent internal conflict: first, a shift in the way conflict issues are perceived by conflict parties so that interests seem better served by settlement than by fighting; second, the internal politics of the conflict parties themselves so that 'peace constituencies' come to predominate over 'war constituencies', or 'peace lords' over 'warlords'; and, third, the military power balance in the field, so that a 'mutually hurting stalemate' precipitates accommodation. Two 'extrinsic' factors are also closely related to it: the 'terms of the settlement', which need both to mirror and to reinforce those factors, and the 'activities of third parties', which need to help sustain them through the uncertain vicissitudes of the postwar period (Licklider, ed., 1993, 14–17). In other words, it is exactly because they are persuaded that the continuing interests for which they have been waging intense and prolonged war are now more likely to be served by transmuting the struggle into non-forcible politics that undefeated belligerents are induced to go along with the peace process in the first place. This feature subsequently constitutes the core of the settlement itself, which thereby, as it were, projects the politics of war forward, albeit transmuted, into the politics of peace.

Two additional points can be made about the nature of post-settlement politics in the light of this. First, that most of these instances involve asymmetric conflicts in which a government is fighting a rebel force: the South African government against the South-West Africa People's Organization (SWAPO) in Namibia; the State of Cambodia (SOC) regime against the allied Coalition Government of Democratic Kampuchea (CGDK) forces in Cambodia; the government-led Popular Movement for the Liberation of Angola (MPLA) against the National Union for the Total Independence of Angola (UNITA) in Angola; the Alianza Republicana Nacionalista (ARENA) government against the Farabundo Marti Front for National Liberation (FMNL) in El Salvador; the Front for the Liberation of Mozambique (FRELIMO) government against the Mozambican National Resistance (RENAMO) in Mozambique. Anatol Rapoport describes the crux of the problem:

> In asymmetric conflict, the systems may be widely disparate or may perceive each other in different ways. A revolt or a revolution is an example of an asymmetric conflict. The system revolted against 'perceives' itself as defending order and legitimacy; the insurgents 'perceive' themselves as an instrument of social change or of bringing new systems into being. Asymmetric conflicts [are those] whose genesis is not 'issues' to be 'settled' but the very structure of a situation that cannot be eliminated or modified without conflict. Indeed, the suspension of conflict or making conflict impossible is in these instances entirely in the interests of one of the parties – the dominant one. (*1971*)[3]

Second, that the general context for post-settlement peacebuilding is what Grenier and Daudelin call the 'peacebuilding market-place' in which 'peace' (the cessation of violence) is traded for other commodities such as political opportunity (elections) and economic advantage (land): '[e]xchanging resources of violence against other resources is arguably the pivotal type of "trade" in peacebuilding' (1995, 350). The key bargain in qualitatively asymmetric conflicts, therefore, is between governments asked to surrender their claim to a permanent monopoly of political power (they are asked to accept a democratic process in which they may lose), and opposition groups asked to give up the threat or use of violence (they are asked to submit to a process of disarmament which may be irreversible). Each is required voluntarily to cede its main power asset and risks having to accept an outcome equivalent to military defeat. Needless to say, these are highly precarious processes to deliver when there is an atmosphere of intense mistrust and leaders are not only negotiating with opponents but also struggling to satisfy disparate demands from factions within their own ranks or even beyond their control. It is difficult to ensure that the cards remain stacked against a resumption of hostilities in the eyes of erstwhile belligerents during the inevitably unstable, precarious and unpredictable jockeying for power which constitutes post-settlement politics. Box 7.1 outlines some of the difficulties facing

Map 6   Cambodia

peacebuilders in Cambodia. Similar challenges were posed in the other five countries.

Task (b): creating a self-sustaining peace

The second cluster of tasks which make up the composite process of post-settlement peacebuilding is 'constructing a self-sustaining peace'. This is the positive aspect of the enterprise. The aim is to underpin task (a) with a view to long-term sustainability by constitutional and institutional reform, social reconstruction and reconciliation, and the rebuilding of shattered polities, economies and communities. It is a colossal undertaking, merging as it does into longer-term processes that at a certain point can no longer be clearly related to the post-settlement scenario. Perhaps it is best described as an attempt to make up three interlinked deficits which characteristically afflict countries after prolonged internal war and hamper the consolidation of peace: political/constitutional incapacity, economic/social debilitation, and psycho/social trauma (together with an initial critical deficit in the military/security sphere). All three deficits must be made up if peace is to be permanently sustained.

The immediate challenge here is the sheer destructiveness of modern warfare. We would agree with Nordstrom that, although specific histories, cultures and political situations can be seen to be strikingly different from case to case, yet what she calls the 'field reality' of patterns of domination, terror and war, and their impact on local populations when sporadic but intense violence is sustained over a period of years, is depressingly similar (Nordstrom and Martin, eds, 1992, 3–17). Whole civilian populations have become direct targets as well as involuntary victims of a brutalized political economy of abuse, exploitation and force, as described in chapter 5. In Cambodia, in addition to the unimaginable human cost of more than twenty years of fighting and political extremism, pre-existing political structures had been largely obliterated, the per

BOX 7.1 The challenge of post-settlement peacebuilding in Cambodia

At the time of the 23 October 1991 Paris Peace Accords major armed conflict had been going on almost continuously for more than twenty years in Cambodia. In its most recent phase, between January 1980, when the Vietnamese-backed regime of Heng Samrin and Hun Sen drove Pol Pot from Phnom Penh, and the Paris Accords of 1991, the Soviet Union had supported Hun Sen's incumbent SOC regime, and China, the United States and the ASEAN countries had backed the opposition CGDK made up of the Khmer Rouge Party of Democratic Kampuchea (PDK), Sihanouk's United National Front for an Independent, Neutral, Peaceful and Cooperative Cambodia (FUNCINPEC) and the right-wing Khmer People's National Liberation Front (KPNLF) under Lon Nol's former Prime Minister, Son Sann. A number of factors seem to have come together to persuade the conflict parties to embark seriously on the peace process after earlier abortive efforts during the 1980s. Of these, the most important were probably external forces, as was fitting in a conflict so largely precipitated by them. At national level a 'mutually hurting' military stalemate eventually induced the SOC and the three factions in the CGDK to be more amenable to outside pressure for a settlement. The SOC was progressively weakened by the withdrawal of Vietnamese military support in 1989 and the shutting off of Soviet aid, while FUNCINPEC and the KPNLF had weak military forces and the PDK perhaps decided that negotiation and outside intervention which included China would be the best way to weaken the SOC. At great power level Soviet–US cooperation and Chinese acquiescence helped to sustain pressure through the UN Security Council (China only abstained on one Security Council Resolution on Cambodia during this period). All of this was reflected in the two treaties, declaration and final act that made up the October 1991 Paris Accords, or Paris Agreements. The Paris Accords were remarkable in two main ways. First, for their comprehensiveness, based as they were on an original Australian plan subsequently elaborated through the Security Council during a two-year negotiating process, and then reflected in the structure of the UN Transitional Authority in Cambodia (UNTAC) to be detailed below. Second, because of the role of UNTAC itself and its relationship with the new Supreme National Council (SNC), which was to be the 'unique legitimate body and source of authority' during the transition period until a Constituent Assembly could be elected to approve a Cambodian constitution, to transform itself into a legislative assembly and to create a new Cambodian government.

An incumbent government (SOC) was being asked to surrender

power, an armed insurgency (in particular the PDK) was being asked to disarm itself, and both were being asked to take part in what for most Cambodians were novel democratic processes. All of this was to be overseen by more than 16,000 troops and 7,000 civilian personnel from more than 100 countries (34 troop providers) at an estimated cost of some $3 billion. In the process, the UN was expected to demobilize and disarm more than 200,000 soldiers in some 650 locations (with a further 250,000 militia operating in almost every village), begin clearing between 6 million and 10 million landmines, supervise the existing administration (including the 50,000-strong police force) to ensure 'free and fair elections', repatriate more than 360,000 refugees, register 4.7 million voters, oversee the elections at some 1,400 polling stations, instil civic values and a respect for human rights and begin 'the enormous task of reconstruction and rehabilitation' (Doyle, 1995, 45). Many of these were new undertakings for the UN, and all had to be accomplished within an 18-month period. It is not surprising, then, that, in retrospect, Gareth Evans, Australian Foreign Minister and one of the main initiators of the peace plan, should describe the mandate as 'overly ambitious and in some respects clearly not achievable' (1994, 27).

capita GDP, which in 1969 had been higher than that of neighbouring Thailand, was by 1991 only one-sixth, and over two-thirds of the population were women, while the psycho-social effects of protracted violence on this scale meant that the war zone was not just the battlefield but extended into the most intimate parts of what Martin has termed a 'shattered society' (1994). By the end of the 1980s the *International Index of Human Suffering* rated Mozambique 'the most unhappy nation on earth', nearly one million having died in the fighting and associated deprivation, a quarter of the population having been displaced, and 1.5 million having fled abroad. In Angola, what had been the second largest oil exporter in Africa, and the fourth largest coffee and diamond exporter in the world, with ample maize production and Atlantic fisheries, was reduced to penury with a budget deficit 23 per cent of GDP, a $10 billion external debt, 3,700 per cent inflation and 30–55 per cent unemployment by the mid-1990s. In El Salvador, perhaps 75,000 out of a population of little more than 5 million had been killed since 1979. By the end of the 1980s per capita income had been reduced to 38 per cent of that of 1980, half the annual budget was being spent on war, economic targets had been repeatedly damaged and destroyed, foreign business had largely left, a tenth of the population had fled abroad and another tenth was internally displaced. The poor peasants, the *campesinos*, were the main victims of the war, as they had been of the 'centuries of exclusion, contempt, and exploitation' that preceded it (Grenier and Daudelin, 1995, 358). The misery of daily existence for the urban and rural poor remained unaddressed, perhaps the deepest challenge for peacebuilders aspiring to convert a precarious ceasefire into a lasting peace. In Bosnia, what had been an apparently civilized cosmopolitan society was systematically destroyed in the protracted intensity of the April 1992–December 1995 war, with hundreds of thousands of innocent victims subjected to extremities of siege, bombardment, summary expulsion, rape and mass murder.

The relationship between task (a) and task (b)

In addition to the difficulties inherent in these two sets of complementary challenges taken separately, there are also unavoidable tensions between them when they are taken together. The challenge of managing 'Clausewitz in reverse' – task (a) – predominates in the immediate aftermath of a peace settlement. Without it, almost nothing else can subsequently be achieved. The more ambitious challenge of building capacities for a 'self-sustaining peace' – task (b) – is more significant over the longer term. Without it, the cessation of overt violence is likely to prove little more than temporary. Each presupposes the other, yet, as a number of commentators have observed, the logic inherent in task (a) is at odds with important elements in task (b), while key assumptions behind task (b) are often at cross purposes with the more pressing short-term priorities involved in task (a). For example, the negative task of preventing a relapse into war demands uncomfortable trade-offs and compromises which may jeopardize the longer-term goal of sustainable peace. Conversely, measures adopted on the assumption that it is market democracy that best sustains peace in the long term, may en route increase the risk of a reversion to war. On the political/constitutional front it is pointed out how conflictual electoral processes may exacerbate political differences and increase conflict in certain circumstances (De Nevers, 1993, 61–78; Mansfield and Snyder, 1995). On the economic/social front the competitive nature of free market capitalism is also seen to engender instability and conflict (Jung et al., 1996, 50–63).[4] On the psycho/social front there are well-known tensions between the priorities of peace, reconciliation and justice (Baker, 1996, 563–72).

The UN's Post-Settlement Peacebuilding SOP

The UN's continuous involvement in post-settlement peacebuilding of this kind goes back at least as far as the 1978 Settlement Proposal in Namibia, devised by the Contact Group of Western States, where UNTAG's mandate under Security Council Resolution 435 was to assist a Special Representative appointed by the UN Secretary-General 'to ensure the early independence of Namibia through free and fair elections under the supervision and control of the United Nations'. The transition phase was to last a year. This unexceptionable formula for expediting the withdrawal of a former colonial master and its replacement by a fledgling independent state, put into practice in the interim in Southern Rhodesia/ Zimbabwe, was revived ten years later in very different circumstances and immediately, and surprisingly, became the main model for the UN's new post-settlement peacebuilding efforts in a number of long-standing internal wars (see table 7.2). In a sharp break with earlier international practice, rebel forces were now to be accorded equal status with governments, and both were to be regarded as proto-political parties deserving of equal access to a new UN-sanctioned reformed political process. The ending of the Cold War drew a line under what had been an almost automatic backing of rival sides by the superpowers, opened up the possibility of concerted action through the Security Council and ushered in the apparent global triumph of what Paris terms 'liberal internationalism' in its twin manifestations as liberal parliamentary democracy and liberal market capitalism (1997). With reference to post-settlement peacebuilding, in Paris's words: 'The central tenet of this paradigm is the assumption that the surest foundation for peace . . . is market democracy, that is, a liberal democratic polity and a market-oriented economy.'

> Peacebuilding is in effect an enormous experiment in social engineering – an experiment that involves transplanting western models of social, political, and economic organization into war-shattered states in order to control civil conflict: in other words, pacification through political and economic liberalization. (*1997, 56*)

The individual elements in the UN's post-settlement peacebuilding SOP have varied in detail from case to case, but within a recognizable overall pattern. In 1992 the UN Secretary-General described the main tasks as:

> disarming the previously warring parties and the restoration of order, the custody and possible destruction of weapons, repatriating refugees, advisory and training support for security personnel, monitoring elections, advancing efforts to protect human rights, reforming or strengthening governmental institutions and promoting formal and informal processes of political participation. (*Boutros-Ghali, 1992, 32*)

Three years later he described the key elements of peacebuilding in similar if expanded terms as demilitarization, the control of small arms, institutional reform, improved police and judicial systems, the monitoring of human rights, electoral reform and social and economic development (1995, paragraph 47), while in 1997 post-conflict peacebuilding was seen to involve 'the creation or strengthening of national institutions, the monitoring of elections, the promotion of human rights, the provision of reintegration and rehabilitation programmes and the creation of conditions for resumed development' (Annan, 1997c). UNTAG's five main

Table 7.2 Major UN post-settlement peacebuilding missions, 1988–98

Date	Namibia	Angola	El Salvador	Cambodia	Mozambique	Bosnia
1988 Dec	Namibia Accords					
1989 April	UNTAG					
1990 March						
1991 May July		UNAVEM II	ONUSAL			
1992 March Dec				UNTAC	ONUMOZ	
1993 Sept						
1994 Dec						
1995 Feb April Dec		UNAVEM III				IFOR
1996 Dec						SFOR
1997 July		MONUA				
1998						

tasks in Namibia were: the separation of military forces and demobilization of those not needed in the new national army; the demilitarization of
the South West Africa Police (SWAPOL); supervision of the interim
Administrator-General's government and repeal of discriminatory laws;
return of refugees; and electoral registration and monitoring. In El
Salvador ONUSAL's original human rights division was subsequently

---

BOX 7.2   Components of the UN Transition Authority in Cambodia

1 Military component: verify withdrawal of foreign forces; monitor ceasefire violations; organize cantonment and disarming of factions; assist mine-clearance.

2 Civilian police component: supervise local civilian police; training.

3 Human rights component: secure signing of human rights conventions by SNC; oversee human rights record of administration; investigate alleged human rights violations; initiate education and training programmes.

4 Civil administration component: supervise administration to ensure neutral environment for election in five areas – foreign affairs, national defence, finance, public security, information.

5 Electoral component: conduct demographic survey; register and educate voters; draft electoral law; supervise and verify election process.

6 Repatriation component: repatriate 360,000 refugees.

7 Rehabilitation component: see to immediate food, health and housing needs; begin essential restoration work on infrastructure; development work in villages with returnees.

In addition, there was an information division.

Source: United Nations, 1996, 447–84

---

supplemented by a military division, a police division and an electoral division. UNAVEM III's five main mission components in Angola were political, military, police, humanitarian and electoral, while in Mozambique ONUMOZ's original mandate included four interrelated components: political, military, electoral and humanitarian – a civilian police component was later added. Although post-Dayton Bosnian arrangements were different, given the central role of IFOR/SFOR, similar elements can be discerned.[5] For the seven components of UNTAC in Cambodia see Box 7.2. Taken together with UN peacebuilding work elsewhere, this is seen to be an integrated programme, with the Department of Political Affairs (DPA), in its capacity as current convenor of the Executive Committee on Peace and Security (ECPS), as coordinator of a joint enterprise involving the Office of the High Commissioner for Human Rights, the Department of Peacekeeping Operations (DPKO), the United

Nations High Commissioner for Refugees (UNHCR), the United Nations Development Programme (UNDP) and the World Bank. As the 'focal point' of this vast enterprise, the convenor of ECPS would also support and reinforce the individual task forces established 'to ensure integrated action by the entire United Nations system' in each case. In all this the planners were to bear in mind in particular 'the point at which the emphasis on the peacebuilding role will give way to full-fledged recon-struction and development activities' (Annan, 1997c).

Reflections on UN Post-Settlement Peacebuilding, 1988–98

It is now ten years since this ambitious experiment in post-settlement 'social engineering' was initiated with the reanimation of UNTAG after the December 1988 Namibia Accords. At the time of writing it seems that most of the large-scale missions will have wound down by 1999 and there is little prospect of comparable new ones being undertaken.[6] What, therefore, is the overall verdict on what may prove to have been a unique ten-year venture? Is it as a result of evident shortcomings in individual missions, or of a general rejection of the liberal universalist assumptions upon which the whole experiment has been based, that it now seems to be coming to an end? What is the verdict so far within the conflict resolution field?

Much has been written about the six cases under review,[7] and about peacebuilding in general.[8] Opinions have ranged from what are in effect official UN apologiae,[9] through accounts which accept the overall enter-prise but are critical of aspects of particular missions,[10] to others which criticize the means by which the UN's liberal internationalist agenda has been promoted but nevertheless accept it as a long-term aspiration,[11] and yet others which reject the whole attempt to universalize what are seen as inappropriate western models in this way.[12] Within this spectrum, six main types of criticism are made in the conflict resolution literature.

First, there is an emphasis on the importance of distinguishing different levels of application and of agency in peacebuilding. We saw in chapter 1, figure 1.9, how Lederach differentiates between the levels of national leadership (including leaders of rebel factions), of middle-range ethnic, religious and regional leadership and of local leadership and grass-roots groups and communities (1994, 16). This relates to what is seen as the importance of peacebuilding from below as described in chapter 2 and to criticism of the tendency of major actors, including the UN, to adopt a state-centric top-down approach to post-settlement peacebuilding which neglects smaller NGOs, local agents and indigenous resources (Lederach, 1995; Curle, 1994; Woodhouse, 1996). From this perspective much more emphasis should be placed on the lower levels, more resources should be concentrated here, and interveners should make sure that their activities serve to support indigenous practices and initiatives, rather than ignoring or overwhelming them.

Second, so far as concerns the different types of deficit to be made up, there are arguments for more emphasis to be put on aspects of the economic/social dimension and the relatively neglected psycho/social dimension.[13] On the former, the logic of 'local empowerment' is often a radical one and may imply deep involvement in indigenous struggles for social justice. On the latter, further comments are made below.

Third, there is criticism of the foreshortened time-frame within which most missions have been put together and propelled into the conflict arena, to be as abruptly removed a few months later after a frenetic period of activity largely dictated by the interests of powerful donor governments and the blueprints of planners in national capitals or the UN. Conflict parties are seen to have been frogmarched towards elections and then abandoned. Some have contrasted the two–five years needed to stabilize the military and political situation, the five–ten years needed to rebuild infrastructures and start to regenerate the economy, and the generation or so needed to reconcile formerly warring parties and communities.

Fourth, there is an argument that the nature of the third party intervention should be more consciously questioned, both because of the disproportionate power/interest relations of intervening states and because of the need to embed the peacebuilding process in the larger context of regional and global politics. External peacebuilders should see themselves as one further element in the situation, not some *deus ex machina* immune to criticism, accountability or control.[14]

Fifth, related to this is the so-called culture question, which challenges the applicability of what are seen as essentially western approaches in peacebuilding to the non-western countries which are their usual targets. Criticism ranges here from sharp exception taken to particular examples of cultural insensitivity in individual UN missions to a more radical wholesale rejection of what is seen as the westernized liberal internationalist model. This is part of a long-standing internal debate between those who advocate universal or 'generic' approaches to conflict intervention and those who argue for radical cultural pluralism and difference.[15]

Sixth, there is the question of the use of force and, more broadly, the suitability of what are seen as predominantly military operations in terms of numbers of personnel deployed for what are mainly non-military tasks in post-settlement peacebuilding.[16]

These criticisms, taken together, do not in our view amount for the most part to a wholesale rejection of the UN's post-settlement peacebuilding SOP. Rather, they suggest a substantial revision of it, which builds on successes, learns from failures and, if anything, envisages longer-term and more committed engagement, not a diminution and withdrawal of concern and support. Although there are some within the conflict resolution field, as elsewhere, who are more radical in rejecting the liberal

universalist assumptions behind the whole undertaking, this is a debate
that has yet to be properly argued out. At the moment, despite current
crises in global markets, it is not clear what the alternatives are, and,
above all, views from the non-western world are not nearly as prominent
in the English-speaking literature as they should be. Until they are, we
cannot say that an overall verdict has been reached. One of the main
arguments in this chapter, therefore, is that, if the ten-year experiment in
post-settlement peacebuilding by the UN is indeed drawing to a close,
then this is not because the experiment has been generally shown to have
failed. A few further comments on the two main post-settlement peacebuilding tasks may help to clarify this.

Task (a): preventing a relapse into war

Can it be said in the six cases under consideration here that the international community has succeeded in task (a) – that is to say, in helping to
make the settlement stick and preventing a relapse into war? And could
this have been achieved without such outside intervention? Clearly, these
are counter-factual questions which cannot be finally determined one way
or the other. Nevertheless, a number of commentators who are prepared
to pronounce relative success in some cases see the UN intervention as
essential to it. For example, in El Salvador Hampson concludes that
'without ONUSAL's active and constructive involvement in the implementation, the peace process would surely have come unstuck' (1996,
169), while Grenier and Daudelin agree that '[l]eft alone, El Salvador
could not have generated the necessary political guarantees and economic
compensations to make peace and democratization possible' (1995, 360).
Similarly, in Namibia UNTAG is seen to have played a critical role in
monitoring and pressuring the South African Administrator-General,
who, in contrast to 1978 intentions, remained in charge of the government during the transition phase, thus keeping SWAPO on board the
peace process. In Mozambique the RENAMO leader, Afonso Dhlakama,
announced his decision to withdraw from the election on 26 October
1994, the day before polling was due to begin. It took concerted pressure
from the international community and an extension of the voting period
being run by ONUMOZ to persuade him to change his mind. In Cambodia, where the Khmer Rouge defected and Phase II of the cantonment and
demobilization plan was abandoned in November 1992, UNTAC nevertheless succeeded against the odds in sustaining the peace process with the
remaining parties through to the May 1993 elections. In Angola, it is the
opinion of UN Special Representative Margaret Anstee that a key reason
for the failure of UNAVEM II in preventing the defection of the UNITA
leader, Jonas Savimbi, after the September 1992 elections, followed by a
resumption of war, was the fact that the UN had not played a lead role in
the May 1991 Bicesse Accords and was not properly resourced to oversee

implementation (Anstee, 1996). These shortcomings were largely reme-died in UNAVEM III's much larger role in the implementation of the November 1994 Lusaka Protocol.

Task (a) is still not securely achieved, however, because thus far only in Namibia of the six cases under review has an incumbent government (Pretoria) peacefully handed over power, and this had already been agreed in the peace settlement as part of the independence process, unlike the other five cases which were civil wars. In El Salvador, Mozambique and Angola the governing party retained power after the first elections, while in Cambodia the evergreen Hun Sen managed to survive yet again by joining a coalition government despite losing the election and subse-quently ousting his FUNCINPEC coalition partner. The 'Clausewitz in reverse' factor makes national and local elections the vital arena for the continuing conflict, and it will be the second election, or the first time an incumbent government peacefully hands over power having lost an elec-tion, that will be the significant watershed. This has not happened yet in any of our six cases, so task (a) remains uncompleted. Angola offers an example of the way in which the challenge of 'Clausewitz in reverse' demands uncomfortable trade-offs which compromise the underlying liberal universalist principles. Since Savimbi has been determined not to lose control of the diamond mines in Lunda Sul and Lunda Norte provinces, the power-sharing approach central to the 1994 agreement has accommodated a bargain whereby UNITA has been allowed a provincial governorship in Lunda Sul, even though the MPLA had comfortably won the local elections. Meanwhile two UNITA-controlled companies were set up as concessionaries in the diamond fields (Saferworld, 1996). Thus was democracy sacrificed to expediency in order to buy peace. In Bosnia the slow and painful business of implementing the December 1995 General Framework Agreement for Peace (Dayton Agreement) is still in train, underpinned by SFOR. The forcible component marks this out as distinc-tive among the six cases. It remains to be seen whether the greater scope for driving through implementation which force allows thereby compli-cates the task of leaving a stable balance of power when the force is removed. The return of ethnic hardliners to the most senior government positions both in Bosnian Serb territory and in the Muslim–Croat Federa-tion in the September 1998 elections does not augur well for the peace process.

In conclusion, therefore, so far as concerns task (a), the jury is still out, but there is a strong body of informed opinion which agrees with Hamp-son that:

> In general, our findings lend support to the proposition that external third-party involvement in all phases of the peace process does indeed matter to political outcomes, and that success and failure are indeed linked to the quality and level of support given by third parties to the peace process, especially during implementation of an agreement. (1996, 210)

Task (b): creating a self-sustaining peace

Turning to the broader aims embodied in task (b), the positive task of creating a self-sustaining peace, we may note that the tough bargaining process at the heart of task (a) involves securing the key interests of elites on both sides. The rank and file, as well as the dispossessed in whose name rebel factions have often purportedly been fighting, tend to lose out. The euphoria which accompanies the early stages of the post-settlement period, therefore, easily turns to disillusionment as what are often unrealistic hopes subsequently evaporate. The crime rate soars as the peacetime economy is unable to absorb large numbers of unemployed ex-soldiers and their families as well as hundreds of thousands of returning refugees, while a continuing wartime black economy, a ready availability of weaponry and the destabilizing effects of what has usually been abrupt introduction of free market conditionalities further destabilize the situation. Erstwhile heroes of the revolution lose touch with their followers and join the establishment. This clearly provides fuel for future conflict unless the basic needs of individuals and groups are satisfied. The making up of the three major deficits in war-shattered countries, political/ constitutional incapacity, economic/social debilitation, psycho/social trauma (in addition to the military/security problems left by the war), noted above as the key components of task (b), is an enormous undertaking. It is also a long-term project upon which it is difficult to pronounce with any confidence so soon after the ending of hostilities. Some idea of the vastness of the post-settlement peacebuilding project may be conveyed by a conceptual framework (see table 7.3).

Given limited space, we comment briefly on the military/security, political/constitutional and economic/social aspects, and focus mainly on the psycho/social aspect, which is where conflict resolution analysts have traditionally made their most distinctive contribution. The latter has also been relatively neglected hitherto within the UN's overall approach. We defer comment on the international aspect to the conclusion. In each case, what was required was a highly complex interlocking of different aspects of the peacebuilding process at different levels of society and over different time-frames (Dugan, 1996; Lederach, 1997). It can be seen from what follows that each element depends integrally upon the others.

Making up the military/security deficit

The usual pattern here was for the cantonment, disarmament and demobilization of rival regular and irregular forces, and the reconstitution of the remainder into a national army and civil police force. The varying success of this process in different cases, together with debates about preferred timings, modes and sequences, lie beyond the scope of this chapter. One of the most acute short- and middle-term problems here is the rise in the

Table 7.3 Post-settlement peacebuilding: a framework

	Interim/short-term measures	Medium-term measures	Long-term measures
Military/security[17]	Disarmament, demobilization of factions, separation of army/police	Consolidation of new national army, integration of national police	Demilitarization of politics, transformation of cultures of violence
Political/ constitutional[17]	Manage problems of transitional government, constitutional reform	Overcome the challenge of the second election	Establish tradition of good governance including respect for democracy, human rights, rule of law, development of civil society within genuine political community
Economic/social[18]	Humanitarian relief, essential services, communications	Rehabilitation of resettled population and demobilized soldiers, progress in rebuilding infrastructure and demining	Stable long-term macro-economic policies and economic management, locally sustainable community development, distributional justice
Psycho/social[19]	Overcoming initial distrust	Managing conflicting priorities of peace and justice	Healing psychological wounds, long-term reconciliation
International	Direct, culturally sensitive support for the peace process	Transference to local control avoiding undue interference or neglect	Integration into cooperative and equitable regional and global structures

crime rate that habitually accompanies the enterprise, as undisciplined former combatants retain weapons and fail to find alternative employment in shattered economies in a continuing culture of violence (Adeyemi, 1997). In Latin America, where 210 million (30 per cent of the population) still live in poverty and polls suggest that 65 per cent are dissatisfied with existing democratic processes, the murder rate is three times that in the United States (*The Times*, 29 April 1998). The rate is higher in El Salvador than in Colombia, with more killings per year in 1998 than during the war. Violent crime saps 14 per cent of the region's GDP. In these circumstances, the long-term prospect of demilitarizing politics and transforming cultures of violence seems remote.

Making up the political/constitutional deficit

In making up the political/constitutional deficit the UN template prescribes power-sharing arrangements and a new constitution underpinned by regular free and fair national and local elections – in short, liberal democracy.[20] A surprising number of commentators, not only in the West but also elsewhere, seem to accept this principle. Paris, mindful of what he describes as the 'tumultuous' effect of the raw democratic process on vulnerable war-shattered countries, while accepting the principle, advocates a longer period of adjustment in which the international community would be more active, among other things, in excluding extremists and controlling the media (1997, 82–3). This implies deeper involvement and more intimate embroilment in local politics than was attempted in five of our six cases. For example, it implies a considerable use of military force where extremists are major players like Pol Pot in Cambodia, Savimbi in Angola or Karadzic in Bosnia. Only in the latter case has the international community intervened along the lines advocated by Paris. Control of the media also implies a use of force, as shown, for example, in Somalia in the incident on 5 June 1993, when General Aidid's USC/SNA forces ambushed UN Pakistani troops in Southern Mogadishu purportedly in retaliation for UN attempts to close down Radio Mogadishu. In chapter 5 we noted how a hardened doctrine of peacekeeping is being fashioned in order to be able to enforce compliance with peace agreements by the ability to take action against spoilers, or those who try to wreck peace processes by the use of violence. The growing support for a UN rapid reaction stand-by force is a further example of the recognition to consider the use of force in response to threats to peace.

Opinions vary radically about the programme of participatory politics and constitutional and electoral reform which is at the heart of the UN's post-settlement peacebuilding SOP. For Yasushi Akashi, UN Special Representative in Cambodia, for example, witnessing the 89.6 per cent turnout for the polls was an emotional moment:

> If people ask me what was the best day of my life, I would say, without hesitation, that it was 23 May 1993 ... Only people who have experienced more than two decades of incessant fighting and the ravages of war can show this degree of thirst for peace ... Voters of both sexes and all ages at the polling stations told me, in simple words, that they were voting because of their interest in the future of their country or just for peace. (*1994, 204, 208*)

Others take an opposite line, although those who reject the liberal democratic principle behind the UN's SOP are seldom clear about what the alternative would be. Some form of traditional hierarchical author-itarianism seems to be in mind. We noted in chapter 3 how some commentators see a tension, if not contradiction, between current western notions of individual and minority rights and the priorities of third world nation-building (Ayoob, 1996). Others find the UN assumption that peacebuilding means introducing western liberal democratic political institutions and ideas of civil society unsuitable for cultural reasons. For example, Lizee concludes that the western democratic model just does not fit some non-Western cultures, such as the pyramidal Brahmanic and fatalistic Buddhist social system in Cambodia sustained by traditional patronage structures not popular consent:

> To put it simply, the UN hoped to impose a liberal political process in a society where this concept remains unclear. It could not work. The resulting lack of confidence in the ability of the UN to carry out its peace plan led to the spiral of violence which can now be witnessed in Cambodia. (1994, 143)

In any case, it seems likely that, no matter what UN framework is applied, local politics will develop idiosyncratically in different parts of the world, as can be seen to be already the case by those who look beneath the democratic surface elsewhere. Elections or no elections, Mozambique and Angola may evolve along the lines of neighbouring Zimbabwe, where President Mugabe has presided continuously since independence. In Cam-bodia the loser in the 1993 election, Hun Sen (CPP), has subsequently succeeded in ousting the winner, Prince Ranariddh (FUNCINPEC), by force, yet seems likely both to retain international legitimacy and to be able to use control of the state machinery to guarantee victory in future polls, in the past tradition of Suharto in Indonesia and others.

Similar 'minimalist' notions apply to the administration of justice in all its ramifications, where lack of an independent judiciary, and in some cases the basic infrastructure of a judicial system, dictate that the bare minimum of some measure of personal security is all that can be hoped for in the foreseeable future in some cases (Mani, 1997). Once again, the long-term liberal democratic ideals expressed in the right-hand column in table 7.3 do not correspond with current realities.

Making up the economic/social deficit

In making up the economic/social deficit the UN has applied a liberal market economy template, underpinned by conditionalities determined by International Financial Institutions (IFIs), although there has been a notable lack of coordination between the two in a number of instances. Here there is some agreement that IMF stringency was damaging in cases such as Mozambique in 1995, where an already struggling government was initially required to make further cutbacks likely to undermine the peace process. Similar consequences are seen in Cambodia and El Salvador, where initial increased growth rates have slowed and widening economic inequalities and a growth in crime threaten stability. Paris recommends a shift of priorities within the UN's SOP towards 'peace-oriented adjustment policies', which recognize the priority of stimulating rapid economic growth even at the risk of higher inflation, and target resources at supporting those hardest hit during the transition period (1997, 85–6).

Others place their emphasis on enabling indigenous economic systems to flourish protected from the harsh climate of international capital, controlled and manipulated as it is seen to be by the economic interests of the developed world. Most of those working in the conflict resolution field would agree with Smock that the main aim must be 'local empowerment', which he sees as the only alternative to what seems like an unending process of foreigners parachuting in to each new crisis spot (Smock and Crocker, 1995). Two further observations may be made here, however. First, as noted by Williams and Young (1994), the more radical NGO discourse about grass-roots participation – a terminology which they see 'to be entirely understood within western preoccupations' – is itself rooted in western conceptions of 'the state, "civil society", and the self' which may not be appropriate in non-western cultures (p. 98). Second, the logic of local empowerment may also imply deep involvement in indigenous struggles for social justice. Where structural inequalities are seen to lie at the root of the conflict, as, for example, in El Salvador, the only long-term remedy may be 'an agrarian reform carried out within a broad process of radical social transformation' (Pearce, 1986, 303). Beyond this lie questions about the nature and fairness of the international economic system into which postwar states are expected to integrate. As we saw in chapter 3, a number of analysts trace the roots of violent conflict back in the first place to the travails of societies on the exploited peripheries of the global economy.

Making up the psycho/social deficit

Healing the psycho/social scars of war has always been central to the work of those working in the conflict resolution field. This task is not an optional extra or an idealistic aspiration separate from the other more pragmatic aspects of post-settlement peacebuilding, as it is often seen to be. It is integral to every other enterprise, as Ball (1996) notes with regard to economic/social projects in Cambodia, where, for example, in community development work 'it took a year or two to reestablish a sufficient level of trust among community members to enable collaborative projects to be implemented' (p. 616). The same applies in the military/security and political/constitutional fields. Legitimacy, acceptance and trust (Boulding's 'integrative power') are integral to the functioning of any reasonably stable socio-political system, invisible and often taken for granted when differences are being settled relatively peacefully, but palpably lacking when they are not.

Evidently, one of the main obstacles to social and psychological healing is the accumulated hurt and hatred suffered by hundreds of thousands if not millions of victims, as described in chapter 5:

> People know if they are from a war-torn country how difficult it is to sit down across the table in the same room with an adversary. Just think about the Israelis negotiating with the PLO. It is likely that adversaries will say: 'we cannot negotiate because we despise the other side too much. They have killed our children, they have raped our women, they have devastated our villages'. (*Carter, 1992, 24*)

Two contrasting responses to this have been to argue, on the one hand that the best long-term solution is permanent separation (Kaufmann, 1996)[21] and, on the other, that what is required is an eventual redefinition of the Self/Other identity constructs themselves so that a sense of 'we' replaces the 'us/them' split (Northrup, 1989, 80). Given the complex geographical distribution of peoples in nearly all cases, territorial partition is rarely feasible, while most of the problems of mutual accommodation lie this side of a final transformation in basic identities.

At this point we encounter a complex set of relations and trade-offs. For example, in the general framework for post-settlement peacebuilding in table 7.3, we identified 'managing conflicting priorities of peace and justice' as a representative medium-term goal in the psycho/social field. Pauline Baker poses the question like this:

> Should peace be sought at any price to end the bloodshed, even if power-sharing arrangements fail to uphold basic human rights and democratic principles? Or should the objective be a democratic peace that respects human rights, a goal that might prolong the fighting and risk more atrocities in the time that it takes to reach a negotiated solution? (*1996, 564*)

She somewhat starkly contrasts 'conflict managers', for whom the goal is peace, with 'democratizers', whose goal is justice.[22] In our sample of six conflicts, we may see Angola, Cambodia and Mozambique as cases in which a conflict managers' approach was uppermost inasmuch as there has so far been little or no attempt to bring war criminals and perpetrators of atrocities to account; while in Namibia, El Salvador and Bosnia a democratizers' approach is more in evidence. In El Salvador, for example, the Commission on the Truth set up on 5 May 1992 reported back to the UN Secretary-General and President Cristiani on 22 September with a 200-page assessment of 22,000 complaints received of violations perpetrated since 1980. Direct evidence was confirmed in 7,312 cases, and indirect evidence in a further 13,562, with 97 per cent of the human rights violations attributed to the 'rightist military, paramilitary, security forces,

Table 7.4   From negative to positive peace, via justice

Negative Peace ⟶	Justice ⟶	Positive Peace
Absence of violence	Truth/ acknowledgement Reparation/ rehabilitation Punishment/pardon	Long-term reconciliation

and death squads' and 3 per cent to the FMNL (UN Doc. S/25500; Hampson, 1996, 156–7). Perpetrators were named, despite requests both from ARENA leader Cristiani and FMNL leader Joaquin Villalobos that they should not be, and 103 army officers were dismissed, but an amnesty was granted by the ARENA-controlled National Assembly and recommendations for a purge of the Supreme Court of Justice was obstructed. We will not pursue these issues further here, beyond noting that the relationship between peace and justice is a complicated one, inasmuch as, without a cessation of violence, there is usually no hope of bringing perpetrators of atrocities to justice, while, as Richard Goldstone, former Chief Prosecutor for the ex-Yugoslavia and Rwanda International Criminal Tribunals notes: 'Without establishing a culture of law and order, and without satisfying the very deep need of victims for acknowledgement and retribution, there is little hope of escaping future cyclical outbreaks of violence' (1997, 107).[23]

Turning, finally, to what we described in table 7.3 as the longer-term goals of reconciliation and psycho-social healing, we find that the peace and justice debate is further complicated as a result. Although the negative peace of order and the cessation of direct violence may in some situations appear to be incompatible with the requirements of justice, the positive peace of reconciliation and psycho/social healing largely presupposes it. In other words, the passage from negative to positive peace runs through justice (see table 7.4). But 'justice' itself is no longer necessarily synonymous with retribution and punishment here.[24] For example, the Truth and Reconciliation Commission in South Africa hopes that full public disclosure of human rights violations since 1960 and an attempt to harmonize competing versions of the past within what Lyn Graybill calls 'a single universe of comprehensibility' (1998, 49), together with some acknowledgement of responsibility, if not expression of regret (Commission on Human Rights Violations), as well as some measure of reparation for the victims (Commission on Reparations and Rehabilitation), will open up an emotional space sufficient for accommodation if not forgiveness, with the question of punishment or amnesty abstracted or postponed (Commission on Amnesty) (Asmal et al., 1996; Boraine et al., 1997). This mirrors Montville's work on reconciliation and healing in political conflict resolution, in which he outlines a comparable three-stage 'conflict resolution strategy' for reconciliation through a process of 'transactional contrition and forgiveness' based on the problem-solving approach (1993, 122–8). Kriesberg sees the stages as truth (revelation, transparency, acknowledgement), justice (restitution) and mercy (acceptance, forgiveness, compassion, healing) leading to peace (security, respect, harmony, well-being) (1998).

These are highly controversial issues. For example, in the wake of the 1993 Truth Commission Report in El Salvador, perpetrators of atrocities were given an amnesty without any private or public acknowledgement or expression of remorse, so that the healing process was incomplete and had to be carried further in some instances by Catholic priests who acted as intermediaries between perpetrators and victims and extracted information about the whereabouts of bodies in exchange for absolution. Needless to say, the South African Truth and Reconciliation Commission has been criticized from opposite directions, by those arguing that the country should not look back and risk causing new wounds, and by others (for example, Steve Biko's family) arguing that human rights violations should be tried and punished in courts of law. Supporters of the Commission nevertheless argue that:

> To close our eyes and pretend none of this ever happened would be to maintain at the core of our society a source of pain, division, hatred and violence. Only the disclosure of the truth and the search for justice can create the moral climate in which reconciliation and peace will flourish. (*Boraine et al., 1997*)

The term 'reconciliation', therefore, has at least three meanings here, all of which are relevant: the harmonizing of divergent stories, acquiescence in a given situation (perhaps reluctantly) and the restoration of friendly relations (Pankhurst, 1998).

There is only space to refer briefly here to the related enterprise of psycho/social healing. The 'invisible effects' of war are often harder to treat than the physical effects:

> The first victims of war are often women and children. Even though they do not lose life or limbs, they are often deeply traumatised in ways not visible to the naked eye. Victims of violence and rape cannot just walk back into everyday life as if nothing happened. As we all know, in the former Yugoslavia, peace has yet to break out for many of the victims. That is why psycho-social work deserves to be a high priority in our emergency aid programmes. (*Emma Bonino, European Commissioner with Responsibility for Humanitarian Aid, in Agger, 1995, foreword*)

Agger and Mimica, in an evaluation of psycho/social assistance to victims of war in Bosnia–Herzegovina and Croatia sponsored by the European Community Humanitarian Office (ECHO) and the European Community Task Force (ECTF) Psycho-Social Unit, conclude that outside help is needed at five psycho/social levels: emotional/survival interventions, task-oriented interventions, psychologically oriented group interventions, counselling and intensive psychotherapy (1996, 27).

Taking the long-term peacebuilding goals of reconciliation and psycho/social healing together, two final points can be made. First, there is a great deal of discussion at the moment about how culturally dependent these processes are. The core of the debate in psycho/social healing seems to focus on the appropriateness of western post-traumatic stress disorder (PTSD) approaches in non-western cultures (Parker, 1996; Petty and Campbell, 1996). Agger (1995), cited above, is an assessment of current work in Bosnia–Herzegovina and Croatia along traditional PTSD lines. Summerfield (1996) is critical of these approaches because they are often predicated on the individual, isolated from social and cultural contexts. Similarly, in the reconciliation and community relations field, there is debate about the resources and capacities for this work in local cultures, with Nordstrom emphasizing the role of traditional healers in Mozambique (1995), and Farah noting the significance of reconciliation through 'grassroots peace conferences' and the 'peace-making endeavours of contemporary lineage leaders' in 'Somaliland' (1993). In some cultures (for example, Mozambique), where misfortune and violence is often attributed to possession by bad spirits, there is scope for remarkably swift reconciliation through public cleansing ceremonies. In these cases the war is seen as a calamity imposed from outside, the fault of no single individual or group. One of the criticisms of the Regional and Local Dispute Resolution Committees, set up in South Africa after the 14 September 1991 National Peace Convention, has been that this was an elitist enterprise dominated by predominantly white business and legal, political and church leaders out of touch with grass-roots cultures, which is where the deepest sufferings have been felt (Gastrow, 1995, 70–1). On the other hand, there are pertinent warnings against indiscriminately resourcing 'indigenous processes' which may turn out to represent transparent mechanisms for perpetuating local systems of oppression, exclusion and exploitation (Pankhurst, 1998).

Second, there is the question of the relationship between community relations and reconciliation work, and the peacemaking process at state-constitutional level. It seems that the former is much easier to effect if the question 'who rules?' has been effectively settled, as in Namibia with the end of colonial rule, or in South Africa with the end of white minority rule, than where the sovereignty issue is still being contested, as in Bosnia, Northern Ireland or Rwanda. In the latter cases, issues of truth and acknowledgement of responsibility for past actions are still part of what is being disputed and questions of justice are still deeply contested and politicized. To this extent, decisive military victory for one side, as in 1945 Germany and Japan or in 1970 Nigeria, may in some cases, ironically, offer more propitious grounds for subsequent healing than post-settlement politics of the kind we have been considering here.

Peacebuilding from below revisited: an example

In earlier chapters we have referred to conflict resolution projects that support conflict-affected communities in designing their own peace processes, predicated on the principle of peacebuilding from below. One of these projects is the Osijek Peace Centre in Eastern Slavonia, Croatia, which set out in 1992 'to mitigate the fever of violence in one small area'. By 1993 the Centre had a core group of about fifty people (mostly, though not exclusively, women) and served 'as a repository for all those attitudes, so damaged in the fury of militarism, upon which peace depends'. Large, who became involved in supporting the Osijek Centre through the conflict resolution NGO network Coordinating Committee for Conflict Resolution Training in Europe (CCCRTE), describes Eastern Slavonia as 'a crossroads for the cooperative initiatives of local actors and interveners' and 'a major experiment in peacebuilding and peaceful "reintegration"' (1997, 152). We conclude this chapter with an account, given in box 7.3, of this experiment in peacebuilding and peaceful integration, involving local groups such as the Osijek Peace Centre, Track II organizations and networks such as the CCCRTE and the Swedish-based Transnational Foundation, Quaker Peace and Service, and many others. International and regional organizations, such as the UN Transitional Administration in Eastern Slavonia (UNTAES), UNHCR, OSCE and the Council of Europe, all combined in a complementary process of Track I, II and III conflict resolution.

Commenting on the many examples of local-level cross-community peacebuilding work in Eastern Croatia as a complement to the 1995 political-constitutional level settlement, Large concludes that, although it is easy for outside critics to be dismissive of these small-scale and usually unpublicized initiatives, this is not how things look from the inside. Here, it is the practical transformative work of all those who oppose the 'discourses of violence' noted in chapter 2, pp. 58–60, that is cumulatively crucial: 'for activists inside, it mattered too much not to try' (Large, 1997, 4). This represents what Fetherston (1998) calls anti-hegemonic, counter-hegemonic and post-hegemonic peacebuilding projects, and what Nordstrom refers to as 'counter-lifeworld constructs' that challenge the cultures of violence (1992, 270). In endorsing Large's conclusion, and applying it to the innumerable indigenous peacebuilding enterprises that go on all over the world, we are put in mind of Edmund Burke's dictum: 'it is only necessary for the good man to do nothing for evil to triumph'.

Conclusion

In summing up what we are calling the UN's ten-year experiment in post settlement peacebuilding, we have acknowledged the criticisms of the

BOX 7.3 Complementarity in post-settlement peacebuilding: Eastern Slavonia, Croatia, 1995–8

At the time of the 1995 Dayton peace agreement, the Croatian territories of Eastern Slavonia, Baranja and Western Sirmium were still occupied by the Serbs and had large long-standing Serb settlements. Throughout 1995 Eastern Slavonia was regarded as an area which was a potential flashpoint for reigniting the war between Serbs and Croats. In the event, a combination of Track I (official), Track II (non-official) and Track III (indigenous) initiatives have combined to defuse the tension and have begun the process of long-term reconciliation and sustained peacebuilding.

Track I level talks resulted in the signing by Presidents Tudjman of Croatia and Milosevic of Serbia of the Basic Agreement on the Region of Eastern Slavonia, Baranja and Western Sirmium on 12 November 1995, which envisaged a staged handover to Croatia. At the political and security levels this was to be supervised by UNTAES, a post-settlement peacebuilding operation established on 15 January 1996 by UN Security Council Resolution 1037. The characteristic mandate of UNTAES included: demilitarization to be completed on 20 June 1996; a transitional police force to be established by July 1996; local and regional elections to be held in April 1997; and displaced Croat and Serb residents to be returned to their homes. The UN saw the success of UNTAES as a precedent for peace throughout the former Yugoslavia, providing positive precedents for post-settlement peacebuilding in Bosnia and Herzegovina. The mandate of UNTAES was terminated in January 1998, its political and demilitarization tasks having been largely successfully achieved, leaving a post-UNTAES Civilian Police Support Group to liaise closely with the OSCE in supervising the continuing resettlement of returnees and other residual arrangements. By the end of 1997 6,000 Croats and 9,000 Serbs had returned, although continuing harassment induced large numbers of Serbs to cross into Serb-held territory, leaving 12,900 displaced Serbs still in the region in early 1998.

This was the context within which local peace groups in Osijek, Baranja and elsewhere, which had struggled to resist the cultures of violence, hatred and war which had swept over the region in the previous years, were now able to capitalize on their existing cross-community work and contribute to the longer-term processes of peacebuilding. These areas were only returned to Croatian control in the summer of 1997, having been Serb-occupied since 1991. Given the levels of mistrust and need for reassurance on the part of local Serbs, the support of international and local NGOs was essential for lasting peaceful reintegration. The Basic Agreement of

1995 and the work of UNTAES meant that Croats who fled the area from 1991, as well as Serbs who colonized it, could now return to their original homes. However, many of these homes had been destroyed and many people were wary of returning to live with former neighbours who had since become bitter enemies. According to Curle (1994), coping with such issues is not a matter of rebuilding the societies which originally spawned the horrors of war, but of creating values and attitudes which mean that war is unlikely to recur.

One aspect of this work is educational. For example, the Transnational Foundation for Peace and Future Research (TFF), an NGO based in Sweden, was invited by UNTAES to report on educational policy in relation to conflict and reconciliation in Eastern Slavonia. It concluded that, while UNTAES had achieved impressive results, particularly at military and political levels, at the local level 'there are very few signs of forgiveness. There is a serious feeling of frustration, insecurity and hurt among Serb teachers, students and their parents that urgently needs to be addressed' (TFF Pressinfo 1997). The nationally agreed Programme on the Re-establishment of Trust in War-Affected Regions was not very effective at the local level. In order to rectify this, TFF, amongst many other proposals, recommended that assistance should be given to the Croatian government on practical ways to implement a policy of trust-building and reconciliation. Relevant programmes would include training in conflict management and problem-solving skills, and in the skills and approaches of healing inter-ethnic relations after violent conflict. These programmes could be offered through schools, higher education and the media. Finally, TFF recommended that an inter-ethnic council of national reconciliation and trust-building should be established. The educational objective of the whole programme was to provide an opportunity for students all over Croatia 'to experience what conflict resolution and reconciliation means. A winner mentality is incompatible with reconciliation' (TFF Pressinfo November 1997).

---

cultural insensitivity and distortive effects of particular missions. In Cambodia, for example, Evans deplores 'the unacceptable behaviour of some military personnel' (1994, 26), while for Prasso the spending power of UNTAC created a warped economy and spawned a 'free-for-all crime wave' (1995). More generally, we have also noted the questioning of the assumptions behind the whole enterprise, although it seems that few have come up with alternatives:

> [P]eace building involves more than the physical separation of formerly fighting forces. It requires the nurturing of the institutions that are at the

> heart of a civil society. In some cases, those institutions have been com-
> pletely destroyed; in others, they may never have existed. In the latter case,
> peace building requires the United Nations to walk a fine line as it imposes
> values on a society for which that society may have no historical tradition or
> no understanding by the norms of the local culture. (*Heininger, 1994,
> 138*)

Nevertheless, we conclude overall that the experiment has not been shown
to have failed, and that premature abandonment, particularly in the light
of the difficulties encountered by UNPROFOR in Bosnia and UNOSOM
in Somalia which were not post-settlement peacebuilding operations,
would be profoundly retrogressive. Post-settlement peacebuilding is still
in its early stages in all six of the cases considered in this chapter, and what
is needed is more thorough analysis of the ongoing experience, particularly from non-western countries, accompanied by continuous adaptation in the light of this.

Hampson (1997) has distinguished four third party approaches to
ending violent conflict: 'hard realism', in which great powers use force and
coercion to manipulate balances of power; 'soft realism', in which the
emphasis shifts to constitutional power-sharing and confidence-building
measures at national level; 'governance-based approaches', where democracy, human rights, participatory politics and the rule of law are seen as
the critical determinants and in which international organizations and
NGOs have a greater role; and 'psychological approaches', in which the
stress is on attitudinal change and inter-party reconciliation mainly at
community and grass-roots levels. If the UN's post-settlement peacebuilding experiment is now being revised, this chapter has suggested that
conflict resolution approaches have something to contribute to perspectives from all except the hard realist programme. Some of the lessons
learned about responding to conflict-generated emergencies, or complex
political emergencies, were considered in chapter 5, where the case of
Rwanda was used to show how the international community was ill-
prepared to act when a post-settlement conflict phase, where a peace
agreement was being monitored by the UN, spiralled into a frenzied
genocide. Some of that learning resulted in the recognition of a need for
more decisive action and capability to stop extremists abusing human
rights, ignoring ceasefires and breaking internationally recognized peace
agreements. Such decisive action and capability is being defined within
emerging doctrines of peace support operations, where stronger or wider
concepts of peacekeeping are being considered to provide military-
security capabilities to protect civilians in areas of conflict. However, it is
recognized that wider peacekeeping, or peace support, has to be seen
within the context of a broader coordinated programme which links
emergency relief and rehabilitation with clear political goals, with social
and economic reconstruction (development), and with peace (cooperation
and reconciliation).

In general, we have seen how conflict resolution makes its most distinctive contributions as we move progressively from the military/security towards the psycho/social dimensions of post-settlement peacebuilding, from the short term towards the longer term, and from state-centric towards societal levels. In addition, conflict resolution offers: an understanding of the nature of the conflict environment and consequent appreciation of the scale of the challenge facing would-be peacebuilders; a resultant salutary lowering of unrealistic expectations and appreciation of the patience, flexibility and commitment required to accommodate the many setbacks to be anticipated along the way; and a holistic approach in which no one remedy is seen to be a panacea but different tasks are best performed by different actors at different stages in the conflict cycle under principles of contingency and complementarity. Above all, there is the insistence from almost all analysts and practitioners in the field that the goal of peacebuilding is the empowerment of local communities, so that the benefits of positive peace – the chance for development in ways they think best – are open to as many individuals and groups within the affected countries as possible. The implication here is that much greater cultural sensitivity is needed on the part of interveners than has often been shown in the past, so that what is attempted is seen to be legitimate and to be consonant with local tradition.

Lederach sums up the goal of cross-community reconciliation within a broad peacebuilding agenda of this kind:

> Reconciliation as a concept and a praxis endeavors to reframe the conflict so that the parties are no longer preoccupied with focusing on the issues in a direct, cognitive manner. Its primary goal and key contribution is to seek innovative ways to create a time and a place, within various levels of the affected population, to address, integrate, and embrace the painful past and the necessary shared future as a means of dealing with the present. (1997, 35)

8

Conclusion

[H]e knew that the tale he had to tell could not be one of final victory. It could be only the record of what had to be done, and what assuredly would have to be done again in the never-ending fight against terror and its relentless onslaughts, despite their personal afflictions, by all who, while unable to be saints but refusing to bow down to pestilences, strive their utmost to be healers.

Albert Camus, *The Plague*

History says, Don't hope
On this side of the grave
But then, once in a lifetime
The longed for tidal wave
Of justice can rise up
And hope and history rhyme

So hope for a great sea-change
On the far side of revenge
Believe that a further shore
Is reachable from here
Believe in miracles
And cures and healing wells.

Seamus Heaney, extract from *The Cure at Troy*

Hope and History

In this book we set out to consider how conflict resolution has risen to the challenge of post-Cold War conflicts, both as a body of theory and a developing practice. We examined the nature of contemporary conflicts, the formulation and reformulation of the key theoretical ideas and the elaboration and extension of practice. The conflict resolution enterprise can be seen as a continuing process of dialogue and reflection between these three elements: the context which shapes the conflicts with which we have to deal, the theories which frame how we understand them and the practical experience of those who struggle for peaceful outcomes.

In the decade after 1989 violent conflict was fought out primarily in non-interstate settings. While the trend to non-interstate warfare can be traced back to earlier decades, the post-Cold War pattern is distinctive in that it has involved, instead of conventional wars between nation-states, protracted and often unconventional deadly conflicts arising from divided societies, secessionist movements, the dissolution of states, and factional or revolutionary struggles for control of government. It is, indeed, precisely conflicts of this kind that have been analysed by theorists such as Azar, and in which experience of a range of conflict interventions and peace processes has developed – in some cases with successful outcomes. We, in our turn, reject the conclusion arrived at by those who argue that conflict resolution cannot be applied in contemporary conditions.

It is certainly possible to imagine worlds in which conflict resolution would make little headway. In a Hobbesian world, in which every individual was engaged in a power struggle with every other, and states 'have no permanent friends, only permanent interests', conflict resolution would have little to build on. Similarly, in a totally hierarchical world, in which classes or castes were immutably divided by relations of dominance, there would be nothing to mitigate the permanent conflict of interests between the dominant and the dominated. It is not surprising, therefore, that those who see the world in strict realist terms or strict Marxist terms reject the conflict resolution approach. But in the complexities of the real world, where people, communities and states have interests in common and in conflict, shared values and divergent values, relations of dominance and of mutual development, where parties are trapped by conflict dynamics into lose–lose outcomes, there are both private and social interests in making conflict resolution work. The purchase it has gained in the post-Cold War environment, not only in liberal agencies of the West but in a variety of social and cultural settings, suggests that it does have something significant to offer. Moreover, it not only adapts to developing social conditions, but aims to shape them. If it is seen merely as a palliative for permanent, festering, untreatable violent conflicts, it risks doing little more than sustaining existing power structures and legitimating existing authorities. But in the tradition from which it has developed, conflict resolution is much more than this. It is a transformative programme, which points with hope towards radical change in the context in which it operates.

We have argued that the theoretical insights of conflict resolution are relevant to contemporary conflicts, because scholars in the conflict resolution tradition had a pioneering role in theorizing the type of conflicts that have become predominant in the post-Cold War period. But we should acknowledge that there are, and remain, significant differences in the theoretical traditions on which this school of thought and practice draws.

For example, Zartman's work has emphasized means of addressing the strategic calculations of parties which are conceived primarily as rational actors using violence for instrumental purposes; his work fits most closely with Track I approaches. Burton's work puts more emphasis on means of creatively reperceiving conflict and redefining the interests involved; he emphasizes values, perceptions and needs; his work has inspired the Track II approach. The work of Elise Boulding, Curle, Lederach and others emphasizes the possibility for transformative change among the actors and in the societies involved, seeing the conflict resolution approach as a reflexive, elicitive dialogue with actors who may not play a current role in power structures, but are agents of personal and social change. This corresponds to the Track III approach. Finally, Galtung and others have continued to reflect an integrated approach, which stresses a holistic process of conflict formation and transformation, linking the subjective and objective approaches. The newer theorists are moving beyond the disjunction between subjectivist and objectivist (or relational and structural) thinking by exploring ways in which both subjective and objective views are interpreted intersubjectively within a culture of shared meaning, in which the discourse of theorists and of participants in conflict plays a crucial role. This line of thought, which is exploring new territory, links closely with the emphasis on the cultural context of conflict, and the appreciation that both perception of basic human needs, and of acceptable methods of transformation, are culturally bound.

We have also shown that the practice of conflict resolution has expanded and evolved. This has come, in part, through the increasing range of actors involved in the three tracks, in part through the extension and differentiation of conflict resolution to cover the range from prevention to post-settlement peacebuilding. In chapters 4–7 (while mindful of the danger of pigeon-holing 'phases of conflict' too rigidly), we have explored the potential for preventing violent conflict before it has broken out, working in war zones to mitigate and limit violent conflict while it is raging, and bringing violent conflict to a sustainable end with a view to long-term reconciliation and peacebuilding. We have shown that in all these circumstances the developing discipline of conflict resolution has something to contribute.

In chapter 4, we argued that conflict prevention must address the deep roots of conflict, and therefore that deep as well as light preventors are necessary. We claimed that the creation of domestic capacity is a crucial aspect of conflict prevention, and that this requires cooperation between international institutions and local actors. In chapter 5, our contention was that a conflict resolution approach is vital for those who are working in war zones, including peacekeepers and providers of humanitarian relief. At the micro-level, for example, the delivery of relief supplies may be impossible without effective negotiations between the conflicting parties on the ground. More importantly, at the macro-level, relationships made through relief work may become the foundation for moving into a process of conflict resolution and political negotiations to end the fighting. In chapter 6, we have seen that although most post-Cold War conflicts have not been ended through a conflict resolution approach, there have been significant successes for conflict resolution. The ideas of the founders and reformulators continued to be applicable – and applied – in contemporary peace processes. It is possible, we argued, to learn from different cases and identify some generic transformers of conflict, which may suggest approaches to existing and future conflicts. In chapter 7, we showed how a sustained effort to address the deep roots of conflict, and transform them, remains crucial in the phase of post-settlement peacebuilding, and that it is only when the different dimensions of this task are addressed, relationships are changed, institutions and economic structures rebuilt, and the psychological traumas of conflict are faced, that societies can move beyond conflict into peaceful change.

The primary and main responsibility for preventing, managing and transforming violent internal conflict lies with the domestic populations of the countries in question, above all national, regional and local leaders. But, as we have seen, many of these conflicts have external as well as internal causes, and in protracted wars indigenous resources for peacemaking are often much debilitated, if not deliberately targeted, by those with an interest in prolonging the violence. Nearly all commentators agree that outside assistance is usually essential for bringing the fighting to an end and ensuring that there is no subsequent relapse into war, and is more often than not also necessary for helping to prevent the slide into war in the first place. The idea that the international community has the option of staying uninvolved and doing nothing is an illusion. In the international society of states, those who can do something and choose not to are materially affecting the situation, and their actions and inactions have consequences like any others. Outsiders are, in any case, already caught up as a result of direct or indirect prior responsibility, and are more often than not blamed by interested parties whether they think that they are involved or not. If outside interests are not coordinated through regional organizations or the UN, then sooner or later, if not already implicated, a regional or global great power is likely to intervene unilaterally.

There seems to be general agreement, therefore, that the international community has a legitimate interest in intervening in one way or another to help prevent, mitigate or end internal wars. But, as this book has shown, there is as yet no agreement about when and how the international community should act – nor even about what it is.

We find the most helpful way to conceptualize the problem is to acknowledge at the outset that the international collectivity is many things at the same time. Seen from the realist perspective of anarchy, interest and power, it is an international system which presupposes little more than bare contact between states. Seen from the pluralist perspective of international order, it is an international society of states which includes a spectrum of mutual obligations, reciprocal arrangements and common interests between states. Seen from the solidarist perspective of international legitimacy, it is an international community which holds shared values and commitments. Seen from the universalist perspective of international justice, it is a world society which already constitutes a global community of humankind. Some of these aspects are all too actual, some are aspirational. None can be reduced to the others. In responding to the challenge of contemporary conflict, all four aspects of the international collectivity are in evidence, albeit as yet confused, disorganized and mal-coordinated. When it comes to the use of inducement, coercion and force, it is the first aspect that is to the fore. Here only great powers have the requisite resources, but by the same token are likely to act mainly out of self-interest. When it is a question of coordinating state action through regional or global institutions, for example with a view to confidence-building or constitutional guarantees, then the second aspect is more prominent and states are more ready to act through international organizations. When it is a matter of governance-based approaches, in which democracy, human rights, participatory politics and the rule of law are regarded as the pivotal determinants, then NGOs join international organizations as key actors. Finally, when what is at issue are universal cross-cultural principles and standards, or all-human appeals for attitudinal change and transformation, then it is at community and grass-roots levels that this may best be effected, with outside support from those elements within the international collectivity which genuinely aspire to represent universal values.

In view of the multiplicity of agencies involved in the three tracks of conflict resolution activity, and disagreements about appropriate and legitimate roles, it is not surprising that the multifaceted approaches necessary for the prevention, management and transformation of deadly conflict remain difficult to agree and to coordinate.

Difficult Questions

The struggle against violent conflict throws up difficult questions to which there seem to be no uncontroversial answers. Some of these take the form of hard choices, and some take the form of inescapable dilemmas, with resulting action or inaction hotly contested by conflict parties and challenged within the wider international community. In concluding the book, therefore, we will comment briefly on the clusters of issues that have troubled us most.

Coercion and force

The first cluster of issues to worry us has been the question of coercion and force in contemporary conflict and conflict resolution. As chapter 2 has shown, the main purpose of the new venture called conflict resolution in the eyes of many of its founders was to find an alternative to coercion and force in managing social conflict at all levels. Violence was seen to breed violence, and in any case to be ineffective in the long run as an instrument of social control. Particularly at the highest level of all – interstate conflict – continued reliance on force and the threat of force to settle quarrels was regarded as no longer rational in the nuclear age. In chapter 3 we cited the analysis of Edward Azar as an example of the way similar conclusions were reached about protracted social conflict. So it is certainly true to say that the conflict resolution tradition has from the beginning sought non-coercive and non-forcible means of conflict transformation. This invites the realist criticism that it is soft-headed and unrealistic, since, for realists, coercion and force are seen as the ultimate currency in the power struggle between antagonistic and irreconcilable groups which makes up inter-national politics. If, when it comes to it, the strong win and the weak have to accept such terms as they can get, then third parties are likely to influence the outcome of conflicts to the extent that they have the capacity to exert pressure on conflictants and alter the power balance through positive and negative inducements. It is the major players, therefore, who are likely to be most effective in preventing, containing and ending violent conflict, and they are seen to do this by power-political means. Others argue that outsiders should stay clear and let violent conflicts 'burn themselves out', or help to ensure victory for one side as the most decisive and probably least costly outcome.

In response to the realist critique, this book has shown how conflict resolution approaches do not neglect 'threat power', as Boulding (1989) called it, but recognize its limitation as an instrument for the prevention, management and transformation of deadly conflict. There is rarely a quick military fix in the kinds of conflict studied here, either in the form of swift victory for one side, or in the form of decisive outside intervention. These are not classic Clausewitzean wars. There may be occasions when force has to be applied within what remains an overall conflict resolution approach, for example, as part of a peace support operation in order to neutralize those who themselves use force to perpetrate atrocities, prey on civilian populations or prevent an otherwise peaceful settlement which has majority support. But, beyond that, the main message from this book is that, within the panoply of contingent and complementary instruments of conflict resolution, force has a strictly limited role to play and only as part of a wider conflict resolution process.

The same applies more broadly to coercion in general. Although a measure of coercion may help to bring conflict parties to the negotiating table, major conflictants cannot in the end be intimidated into agreement or bludgeoned into reconciliation. Nor can the deeper causes of violence such as disputed sovereignty, mobilized identity or struggles for social justice be coerced away. Coercion may keep a lid on violence, but this is likely to erode over time.

We are still left with unavoidable dilemmas in terms of what to do about force and coercion when attempting conflict resolution in violent and often chaotic wars. This includes, perhaps most critically, how to respond to demagogues and warlords with a continuing interest in prolonging the war, and whose bargaining strength in any eventual settlement is based on demonization of target populations, spoliation and the deliberate application of terror. We have seen how difficult it is to be consistent here, with mediators in most cases ready to include protagonists in negotiations who have made themselves too powerful to ignore, and only prepared to declare those beyond the pale who refuse to compromise or are seen to be weak enough to brush aside.

Inequality and oppression

We hope that this book has shown that the founders of the conflict resolution approach did not ignore the problems posed by structural inequalities or the deeper causes of conflict. The challenge of what to do about quantitatively and qualitatively asymmetric conflicts has tested conflict resolution analysts from the start, as described in chapter 2. They were well aware that suspension of conflict in cases of structural asymmetry was in the interests of the dominant party. The fundamental point here is that, in the peace research tradition, it is violence, not conflict, that is seen as the antithesis of peace. Gandhi was passionately opposed to all forms of direct violence through the doctrine of non-violence (*ahimsa*), but was at the same time equally passionate in pursuing an unrelenting struggle against injustice and oppression (*satyagraha*). In order to attain positive peace, overt levels of conflict may have to be raised. The aim of conflict resolution is not to suppress conflict, but to transform potentially or actually violent conflict into peaceful processes of political and social change. And this, as chapters 4, 6 and 7 have shown, involves not just the removal of symptoms, but engagement with what the UN Secretary-General called the 'deepest causes of conflict' – 'economic despair, social injustice and political oppression' (Boutros-Ghali, 1992, 8).

Nor is it true to say that the conflict resolution tradition has lacked self-criticism. As in all study fields, individuals have varied in this respect, with some of the more creative not hesitating to be forthright in the advocacy of particular approaches and leaving it to others to do the criticizing. Within the field as a whole, however, as chapter 2 has shown, continuous critical feedback was built in to the methodology from the beginning, for example through the constant scrutiny of 'default values' advocated in the social learning approach of second-order learning theory. And most of the more cogent criticisms of specific aspects of existing theory and practice have come from within the field itself, for example in the 1990s in the form of the 'culture question' and the 'conflict transformation' debate, as well as from critical theoretical and feminist perspectives.

Nevertheless, the dilemmas remain. Not to engage with the structural and cultural roots of violence is to ignore the requirements for deep prevention and lasting settlement and to risk reinforcing existing unpeaceful practice. It is to abandon the quest for positive peace (peace with justice). But to refuse to attempt conflict resolution before the vast agenda of exploitation and inequality at global, regional and state levels is addressed is to risk losing opportunities for immediate gain that may also provide scope for further development in future. It is to risk losing the chance of negative peace (the prevention or cessation of direct violence). Suffering populations cry out for peace with justice, but we should not underestimate the blessings that come with the prevention or ending of war.

Intervention and autonomy

Our third cluster of issues, closely linked to the others, is the whole question of intervention and autonomy. That is to say, the question of the relationship between third parties and indigenous resources in conflict resolution. We have seen how some of the most cogent criticisms of existing practice, as also of much traditional conflict resolution theory, has been of the idea of outsiders as 'experts' best placed to take the lead in resolving intractable conflicts. It is true, as noted particularly in chapters 6 and 7, that third parties are often needed to help free deadlocks when communications have broken down and to bring new resources to the marketplace of peacebuilding to increase the scope for bargaining, but the whole tenor of recent thinking in the field has been towards empowering indigenous actors to find the solutions that they want and to help them to build capacity to manage continuing conflict peacefully in ways of their own devising.

Nevertheless, difficult judgements and hard choices abound. Foremost come the general questions: who are the outside interveners and what are their capacities and interests? to whom are they answerable? how do their actions relate to the capacities, interests, understandings and needs of indigenous actors? and how successfully does all of this work together to promote lasting conflict resolution? Once again, there are no easy answers. The critical balance to be struck is no doubt between the need for a favourable international context and continuing outside support for peace processes, and the priority of not only preserving but strengthening local autonomy and capacities for indigenous conflict resolution.

A Further Shore

As we face forward to the twenty-first century it is easy to be fearful and despondent. The post-1989 euphoria has evaporated. Unresolved internal conflict in Kashmir, Afghanistan, Kosovo, the Democratic Republic of Congo and elsewhere threatens to spawn renewed interstate war. The situation in Southern Africa is precarious. Internal stability in populous countries such as Indonesia and Pakistan is at risk. Future interstate war – for example, between Greece and Turkey, Croatia and the Federal Republic of Yugoslavia, Iran and Afghanistan, Ethiopia and Eritrea, Armenia and Azerbaijan, India and Pakistan, Peru and Ecuador, China and Taiwan, North and South Korea – remains a possibility in nearly every continent. The long agony of the Middle East remains dangerously unresolved. The political fall-out from economic crises in Asia and Russia has hardly begun to feed through. At global level, deep and enduring inequalities in the distribution of wealth and economic power, coupled with tightening environmental constraints and continuing proliferation of lethal weaponry, provide potent soil for future conflict. As states come under mounting pressure from mass human migration, from the radicalization and criminalization of national and regional politics, and from recurrent crises of unsatisfied expectation from an increasingly informed majority of the disempowered, the international community may find it even more difficult to resolve the resulting conflicts. Certainly, if those countries, particularly in Europe and North America, which have the wealth and resources to help reshape the global political economy, fail to rise to the challenge and turn their backs on these problems, there is little hope of progress. To think that future security challenges can be permanently ring-fenced or controlled by force is a short-sighted delusion.

So it is, that, in conclusion, we suggest that the broad conflict resolution approach to the prevention, management and transformation of deadly conflicts outlined in this book offers the safest and most realistic way ahead. Although we have noted the new scope for benign intervention and community-building across international frontiers, the key goal is to strengthen the conflict resolution capacity of societies and communities. In doing this, the essential challenge will be to continue to broaden the agenda so that it truly represents a coming together of conflict resolution traditions from all parts of the world.

We would like to end the book by paying tribute to all those, usually anonymous and unheralded, who continue to search for peaceful outcomes even when the rising tides of intolerance, intransigence and hatred threaten to engulf them. Violent conflict, like disease, is an ancient and resourceful enemy. But it can be overcome. Despite the many difficulties acknowledged in this book, there are times, to borrow Seamus Heaney's words at the head of this chapter, when 'once in a lifetime the longed for tidal wave of justice can rise up and hope and history rhyme' and a confluence of aspiration and actuality can make the benign transformation of deadly conflict possible. If the story of conflict resolution is, in the end, 'the record of what had to be done, and would assuredly have to be done again in the never-ending fight against terror and its relentless onslaughts', then, to adapt Camus, its unsung heroines and heroes are all those who, often in the middle of destruction and war and despite repeated discouragement, 'refuse to bow down' to intimidation and violence or to be corrupted by bitterness, hatred and prejudice, but strive their utmost, despite great risk to themselves and often against all the odds, to be peacemakers. It is to them that we dedicate this book.

Notes

Chapter 1   Introduction

1 Technically, where one party's gain is the other's loss we should refer to constant-sum conflicts, and where both can lose or both can gain, to non-constant-sum. Unfortunately the zero-sum and non-zero-sum language has passed into general usage, although it is less precise.

2 This has not been the end of the story. Further competitions have been held with slight variations in the conditions, allowing for the possibilities that players might make mistakes in detecting another player's move. Here, a population of Tit-for-Tat players do badly because after making a mistake they get locked into mutual defection, and a somewhat nicer strategy, called 'Generous', which forgives the first defection and then retaliates, outperforms Tit-for-Tat. Generous, in turn, allows even nicer strategies to spread, reaching at the limit the ultra-nice 'Always Cooperate', which, however, can then be invaded by the ultra-nasty 'Always Defect'. If the players are allowed to remember the outcomes of previous moves, other strategies do well, especially one called 'Simpleton', which sticks to the same strategy if it did well last time and changes if it did badly.

3 This can be seen in the different ways conflict is defined. For example, most social scientists define conflict in behavioural terms, as here: there is conflict 'whenever incompatible activities occur' and 'an action that is incompatible with another action prevents, obstructs, interferes, injures or in some way makes the latter less likely to be effective' (Deutsch, 1973, 10). But some define conflict in attitudinal terms, as here: 'A social conflict exists when two or more parties believe they have incompatible objectives' (Kriesberg, 1982, 17).

4 The literature has many different examples of life-cycle or phase models of conflict, which suggest schematic sequences of conflict going from peace through unstable peace, crisis and war, and back down the escalation ladder. To avoid the impression of a linear sequence, we have chosen a circular representation here.

5 This research was regularly updated: see Vasquez, 1987, for a useful review.

For a more comprehensive idea of the range of empirical data available during the Cold War, see Cioffi-Revilla, 1990.

6 For example, in contrast to the PIOOM programme, Wallensteen et al. of the Conflict Data Project of the Department of Peace and Conflict Research, Uppsala University, define 'major armed conflicts' as 'prolonged combat between the military forces of two or more governments, or of one government and at least one organized armed group [thus ruling out spontaneous violence and massacres of unarmed civilians], and incurring the battle-related deaths of at least 1,000 people for the duration of the conflict [not just for one calendar year as in the PIOOM figures]' (SIPRI, 1997, 17). Major armed conflicts are subdivided into 'intermediate conflicts' and 'wars'. A minor armed conflict is one in which overall deaths are fewer than 1,000. On the other hand, the Minorities at Risk Project at Maryland University, initiated in 1986, compares data on the political aspirations of some 250 minority communal groups worldwide and includes measures taken short of the use of armed force. Within this brief, lists are drawn up of 'ethno-nationalist peoples' who have fought 'sustained or recurrent campaigns of armed force aimed at least in part at securing national independence for a communal group, or their unification with kindred groups in adjoining states' between 1945 and the 1990s. Terrorist and guerrilla strategies are also counted (Gurr, 1995, 5). In contrast, the Humanitarianism and War Project at Brown University is more concerned with data for 'populations at risk' in 'complex humanitarian emergencies' (Weiss and Collins, 1996).

7 See List of Abbreviations for all acronyms. There are inconsistencies between different datasets under each of the heads used here. For example, under 'location' some sources list countries, some conflicts, and there are discrepancies in the counting of separate conflicts; under 'inception' different dates are given for when conflicts began, depending upon which thresholds are taken and how interruptions to the fighting are interpreted; under 'principal conflictants' there are problems over splinter groups, over breakdown of organized control in disintegrated war zones, over whether a conflict is a proxy war sustained by another government – the impression given in this table that most wars were between government and rebel forces is often misleading; figures in the 'deaths' column are wildly discrepant partly because of different counting criteria (PIOOM figures are higher than those of SIPRI), partly because of the problem of finding reliable data in confused war zones and partly because the figures are politically disputed by propagandists on all sides. For example, figures for deaths in Bosnia between 1992 and 1995 given in reputable publications range between 25,000 and 250,000 – in this case we have followed a somewhat conservative norm.

8 We should note, however, that the overall number of interstate wars in the two periods went up from 25 to 38, although there was only an average of 30 states in the earlier period compared with 140 in the latter.

9 One of the problems here is defining regions in the first place. Geographical regions do not always coincide with the most important political groupings (for example, Arab North Africa is often included in the Middle East), some countries are difficult to 'place' (is Turkey in the Middle East? is Greece in the Balkans? is Afghanistan in Central or South Asia?), and sub-regions often emerge as the most significant loci for analysis (the Caucasus, the Greater Horn of Africa).

10 For example, Chazan et al.'s list of 'types of domestic political conflict' in Africa is organized in terms of whether they are elite, factional, communal, mass, or popular, (1992, 189–210).

11 For example, Holsti, 1991, 306–34.

12 For example, Furley groups twenty-nine conflict causes suggested by Timour Dmitrichev (1992) into four somewhat confusing categories: military causes, political/international causes, political/domestic causes and persecution causes (1995, 3–4).

13 This is also partially mirrored in the Uppsala typology used by SIPRI (1997, 23), which is based on 'conflict causes' and sees major armed conflict as caused by 'two types of incompatibilities': 'government conflicts', which are contested incompatibilities concerning 'government (type of political system, a change of central government or in its composition)', and 'territory conflicts', which are contested incompatibilities concerning 'control of territory (interstate conflict), secession or autonomy'. These two types of conflict again coincide quite closely with our revolution-ideology and identity-secession conflicts – except that interstate conflict and non-interstate identity-secession conflict are conflated in the Uppsala typology under the heading 'territory conflict'. We will follow Singer and Holsti in distinguishing between them. A number of conflict resolution analysts also recognize the distinction between revolution-ideology and identity-secession conflicts. For example, Mitchell (1991, 25) contrasts 'internal regime wars' which involve 'struggles over the control of a polity's state apparatus and the form of underlying economic and social systems', with 'ethnonational conflicts' which involve 'struggles to defend – and promote – identity on behalf of ethnolinguistic or ethnoreligious communities', while Rothman (1992, 38) distinguishes between 'interest-based intra-state conflicts', and 'needs-based communal conflicts'. We class Gurr's ethnonationalist wars as identity-secession conflicts.

14 Holsti implicitly acknowledges a sub-category of factional conflict inasmuch as his shorthand designation for his type (c) conflicts is 'internal factional/ ideological'.

15 Gurr distinguishes seven types of politically active communal group (national peoples, regional autonomists, communal contenders, indigenous peoples, militant sects, ethnoclasses, dominant minorities) which have four 'general orientations to, and demands on, the state' which may lead to conflict: access, autonomy, exit and control (1995, 3–5). All of these can be distinguished from the 'irredentist' claims of one state on territory beyond its borders on the basis of identity (e.g. Pakistan's claims in Kashmir), which would be classed as a form of interstate conflict.

16 For example, in 1996 the conflict in Afghanistan could be interpreted as a revolution-ideology conflict to the extent that it was identified with Taleban's drive to create an Islamic state; or as an identity-secession conflict to the extent that it was seen as a struggle between Pashtuns (Taleban), Uzbeks (Dostum) and Tajiks (Masood); or as a merely factional conflict if the fighting was seen to be perpetuated simply by the interests of rival warlords and their clients; or even as an interstate conflict by proxy if the war was seen to be little more than the playing out on Afghan soil of what were essentially rivalries between outside states such as Pakistan, Uzbekistan and Iran.

Chapter 2   Conflict Resolution: Foundations, Constructions and Reconstructions

1   Sorokin was a professor of sociology in Russia, but left for the USA in 1922 following a dispute with Lenin. He founded the Department of Sociology at Harvard in 1930 and the third volume of his four-volume *Social and Cultural Dynamics*, published in the late 1930s, contained an analysis of war, including a statistical survey of warfare since the sixth century BC. Both Wright and Richardson referred to Sorokin's work, but he had a limited influence otherwise. Richardson was born into a prominent Quaker family in Newcastle in the north of England in 1881. He worked for the Meteorological Office, but served from 1913 to the end of the war with the Friends' Ambulance Unit in France. His experience in the war, his background in science and mathematics and his growing interest in the new field of psychology all combined to lead him to research into the causes of war. He took a second degree in psychology in the late 1920s and he spent much time in the 1930s developing his arms race model. During the Second World War he decided to retire from his post as Principal of Paisley Technical College in order to devote his time to peace research. He compiled a catalogue of all conflicts he could find information on since 1820 and by the middle of the 1940s he had collated his various studies, which were not published, however, until after his death, when Wright (with whom Richardson had entered into correspondence in his later years) and other academics succeeded in having them issued in two volumes (*Arms and Insecurity* and *Statistics of Deadly Quarrels*) in 1960. Philip Quincy Wright (1890–1970) was a professor of political science at the University of Chicago from 1923, becoming professor of international law from 1931. He produced his monumental *A Study of War* after sixteen years of comprehensive research, which was initiated in 1926.

2   *Essays in Peace Research*, published in six volumes between 1977 and 1988, and *Papers in English*, published in seven volumes in 1980, represent the main body of Galtung's thinking. Early publications which indicated his distinctive contribution include 'Pacifism from a sociological point of view', in the *Journal of Conflict Resolution* in 1959, and his editorial statement in the first issue of the *Journal of Peace Research* in 1964. Good synthetic statements by Galtung about his general view of the scope and priorities for peace research appear in 'Twenty-five years of peace research: ten challenges and some responses' (1985). *Peace by Peaceful Means* (1996) and the timely and critical assessment of Galtung by Peter Lawler provide the most up-to-date accounts.

3   See, for example, Boulding (1977) and Galtung's reply (1987).

4   The best general account of Quaker mediation remains Yarrow (1978). See also the work of other Quakers who have worked in the Quaker tradition or who applied and developed Curle's approach: Bailey (1985); Williams (1996); McConnell (1995); Curle (1981).

5   Thus Vayrynen (1991) sees settlement and transformation as minimalist and maximalist perspectives in conflict resolution (pp. 1–25); Dukes (1993) sees 'transformative conflict resolution' as aligned with a 'larger ongoing movement within our society to reconstitute, where appropriate, and otherwise create, nurture, and sustain a life-affirming and democratic public domain' (p. 48); Zartman (Zartman and Rasmussen, eds, 1997), says that the book is

about 'international conflict resolution' and that it 'presents ways in which . . . conflict can be first managed, moving it from violent to political manifestations, and then resolved, transforming it and removing its causes' (p. 3).

Chapter 3   Understanding Contemporary Conflict

1 Needless to say, most theories escape such neat classification. For example, twentieth-century realist theories of interstate war have tended to combine explanations in terms of the international anarchy (structural) and the security dilemma (relational), whereas classical realists emphasized 'fallen' human nature (cultural). Frustration-aggression theories, on the other hand, have usually combined scarce resources (structural) and a tendency to aggression in some/all individuals or societies when frustrated (cultural).

2 For example, compare the orthodox western view that the Cold War was caused by Soviet aggression and the revisionist view that attributed it to the global ambitions of capitalist imperialism, with the neo-realist view that interpreted it in terms of normal inter-power rivalry in a bipolar world, the neo-liberal view that saw it as a dangerous dynamic generated by mutual worst case security preoccupations and the 'radical' view that it was an 'imaginary war' generated by the interest of elites on either side in maintaining control within their own blocs (Kaldor, 1991).

3 The same is true of the Bosnian conflict, where the common outside view that this was a three-way squabble between Croat, Serb and Muslim factions was passionately rejected, albeit on very different grounds, by most of those directly involved.

4 For example, Richardson compared the frequency, duration and costs of wars between dyads of states with such variables as alliance groupings, geographical proximity, population and culture. Since then a flood of material has been produced. Helpful contributions include: Luard (1986), Levy (1989), Midlarsky, ed. (1989), Holsti (1991), Vasquez (1993).

5 A number of commentators have concluded that the overall results of attempts at statistical analysis of interstate conflict have been disappointing. After a careful survey of some of the main hypotheses, for example, Holsti finds that '[i]n a significant proportion of the systemic studies of war, there is no verdict' (1991, 5), while for Dougherty and Pfalzgraff '[u]p to the present time, the statistical techniques have produced no startling surprises, and few conclusive or unambiguous results' (1990, 347). Many of the claimed positive 'external' correlations have been challenged, such as whether rigid alliance systems produce war (Singer and Small, 1968), whether bipolar or multipolar balances of power are more stable (Waltz, 1979), at what point in a transition of power between a rising and falling hegemon war is most likely (Organsky, 1958), or whether arms races increase the probability of war (Wallace, 1977). The same is true of 'internal' correlations, such as those said to support the theory that 'lateral pressure' from population and economic growth breeds war (Choucri and North, 1975), or that democracies do not fight wars. In an elaborate study of 236 variables relating to internal attributes of 82 nations, Rummell found no significant quantitative correlation with foreign conflict behaviour (1970). In addition, some of the more generally accepted conclusions seem rather obvious, such as that great powers fight more wars, or that alliance membership increases the chance that a state will become involved in war if its partner does.

6 Only 4 per cent of global direct foreign investment goes to Africa. By 1990 Africa's foreign debt, almost double the 1980 level, amounted to more than 90 per cent of annual production (in sub-Saharan Africa 112 per cent): 'Africa paid back to the IMF more than it gained in new resources in all but one year in the 1986–90 period' (Chazan et al., 1992, 310). Dramatic figures like this are persuasively taken as evidence of the devastating effect on poorer countries of unfair international terms of trade structured to reflect the interests of the rich. Others, however, attribute economic failure to 'bad governance' and regard fuller integration into the existing system as the best way to reverse it.

7 For example, the Tigris (Iran, Iraq, Syria, Turkey), the Jordan (Israel, Jordan, Saudi Arabia, Syria) and the Nile (Burundi, Democratic Republic of the Congo (Zaire), Egypt, Eritrea, Ethiopia, Kenya, Rwanda, Sudan, Tanzania, Uganda).

8 For Buzan, strong and weak states are defined as such, first, in affective terms with reference to the level of accepted legitimacy of the idea of the state, second, in concrete terms with reference to its physical basis (territory, resources) and third, in organizational terms with reference to its institutions (1991).

9 For example, most major armed conflicts are found in countries low down on the UN Development Programme's (UNDP) annual *Human Development Index* (which measures education, health and standard of living) or the World Bank's *World Development Report* – only one country (Colombia) in PIOOM's 1996 list of high-intensity conflicts was among the top fifty countries in the UNDP *Human Development Index* for that year, whereas seven were amongst the lowest twenty-five (Jongman and Schmid, 1997).

10 Wehr (1979) suggested that what was necessary in conflict mapping was: a short summary description (one page maximum); a conflict history; conflict context (geographical boundaries, political structures, communications networks etc.); conflict parties (primary, secondary, interested third parties) including power relations (symmetrical or asymmetrical), main goals, potential for coalitions; conflict issues (facts-based, values-based, interests-based, non-realistic); conflict dynamics (precipitating events, issue emergence, polarization, spiralling, stereotyping); alternative routes to a solution of the problem(s); and conflict regulation or resolution potential (internal limiting factors, external limiting factors, interested or neutral third parties, techniques of conflict management). Wehr's conflict mapping guide was to be applicable to 'the full range of conflict types from interpersonal to international levels'.

Chapter 4   Preventing Violent Conflict

1 This is a narrower definition than that of Boutros-Ghali, who included under the rubric of conflict prevention measures taken to forestall violence, to limit the spread of violence and to prevent the recurrence of violence after a settlement (Boutros-Ghali, 1992). Lund confines his definition of preventive diplomacy to preventing peaceable disputes from escalating into violence by 'action taken in vulnerable places and times to avoid the threat or use of armed force' (Lund, 1996, 37). His definition is somewhat narrower than ours, as it focuses on actions rather than other categories of preventors.

2 'Preventor' is spelt thus to suggest an active factor or actor.

3 As Suganami points out, explanation is a more rigorous requirement than prediction. (Suganami, 1996). We may note that one event follows another in a regular sequence, but this does not explain the second event. Ancient Chinese astronomers found a correspondence between supernovae and social disasters, but in the absence of any adequate explanation we are now inclined to dismiss their observations. More interestingly, the Chinese detected a link between unusual animal behaviour and subsequent earthquakes. Contemporary naturalists suspect that some animals may be able to sense earth tremors below the level of human sensitivity – we can accept an explanation linking the animal behaviour and the earthquake, through the tremors that induce them both.

4 The GEDS project is based at the Center for International Development and Conflict Management at the University of Maryland. Efforts to link up and integrate quantitative approaches such as these are under way, but problems posed by disparate coding schemes, purposes and assumptions make a cumulative research programme difficult.

5 Of course, there remain important major powers that are not tied in to the dominant political and economic institutions (e.g. China), governments that perceive their interests as threatened by the dominant system and which are willing to fight against it (Iraq), and many minor states in the global periphery that are less interlocked into interdependent relationships with each other than they are with the major capital and trading systems of the centre.

6 For introductions to the literature on democracy and war, see Doyle, 1986; Russett, 1993; Gleditsch and Hegre, 1997; Raknerund and Herge, 1997; and the special edition of the *European Journal of International Relations*, 1995, 1, 4. For a critique, see Cohen, 1994.

7 For example, the English monarchy quelled the quarrels among its nobles by establishing overlordship and 'the king's peace'; and it prevented rebellions in Wales by assimilating the Welsh nobility and absorbing or suppressing Welsh customs.

8 For a discussion of conflict resolution and prevention in asymmetric conflicts, see Curle, 1971; Galtung, 1996; International Alert, 1996.

9 The HCNM consulted with NGOs and academic experts in conflict management before his intervention in Estonia. Their recommendations, which have been published by the Conflict Management Group at Harvard, offer a good insight into contemporary NGO approaches to mediation in prevention situations. They urged an impartial and non-coercive approach, with more emphasis on establishing a framework within which constructive engagement between minority and government could take place, rather than proposing substantive recommendations; the HCNM should commit himself to an ongoing process, in which he would develop good personal relations with the parties, acting as a facilitator; he could spell out to parties the implications of unilateral actions and outline options which would incorporate the interests of both parties; the dialogue should be conceived as the start of a long-term process between the parties, and it should address the root causes of the dispute (Conflict Management Group, 1993).

10 Attempts to modernize northern Albania illustrate the dilemmas involved here. Traditional Gheg society in northern Albania has its own code regulating conflict, hospitality, the role of the household and relations between

households, and, to an extent, this code, the *Kanuni i Leke Dukagjinit*, is still respected; but it was suppressed by communism and is also in conflict with modern European legal codes which are the basis of Albanian law. Unsympathetic attempts to impose modernization, combined with economic deprivation and mal-development, have contributed to a return to old methods, including blood feuds, and a breakdown in social cohesion (Miall, 1995).

11 For the definitive work on the OSCE, see Bloed, 1993.

12 Preamble to the Document of the Moscow Meeting of the Conference on the Human Dimension of the CSCE, October 1991.

13 These are little used; see Travers, 1993.

14 For reviews of the Secretary-General's and the UN's roles in conflict management generally, see Sherman, 1987; Skjelsbaek, 1991; Dedring, 1994; Parsons, 1995.

15 As one example to illustrate the position of many, India opposed any measures that could suggest outside involvement in Kashmir (Findlay, 1996, 35).

16 Adelman and Surkhe (1996) identified three stages at which opportunities for prevention in Rwanda were missed: in 1989–90, when initiatives by the OAU and UNHCR to tackle the refugee problem failed through lack of US and European support; in 1992–3, when the international community failed to defend the Arusha Accords against violations; and at the onset of the crisis. See the case study in chapter 5.

17 For a directory of NGOs involved in conflict prevention, see ECCP, 1998.

18 For the history and political background of Kosovo, see Magas, 1993; Vickers, 1998; on Albania, see Vickers, 1995; Vickers and Pettifer, 1997; on Macedonia, see Pettifer, 1992; Mickey and Albion, 1993; Poulton, 1995. Mickey's study of Albanian-Macedonian tensions in FYROM is a fine example of one approach to mapping a contemporary conflict.

19 A number of high-level study panels, including the Carnegie Commission on Preventing Deadly Conflict (International Commission on the Balkans 1996), the Council on Foreign Relations (Rubin, 1996) and the Bertelsmann Foundation (Janning and Brusis, 1997), turned their attention to the area, which has become something of a test case for preventive diplomacy.

Chapter 5   Working in War Zones

1 The Arusha talks in Tanzania between the RPF and the Rwandan government began on 10 August 1992, facilitated especially by Tanzania but with the involvement of Burundi, Zaire, Belgium, France, Germany, the USA, Senegal and the OAU.

2 Andy Carl, one of the directors of Conciliation Resources, writes: 'Conflict analysis, in one form or another, is absolutely central to conflict prevention and transformation activities. An example is drawn from Sierra Leone where Conciliation Resources (CR) is pursuing a strategy of supporting community peacebuilding. In this acutely violent situation, the primary concerns of many civilians are for security and survival. Rural communities are seeking to make themselves less vulnerable to the violence by attempting to understand the conflict better and thus develop strategies to defend themselves and cope with its consequences. As with many violent conflicts, civilian populations are at

the mercy of rumour. The parties to the conflict deliberately use misinformation to mobilise support, confuse opponents, and create environments of
chaos and panic to dehumanise their enemies. Information and analysis,
however, can be a potent instrument of peace, reconciliation, justice and
reconstruction. A shared or consensual analysis of a conflict, and the process
by which consensus is reached, can help overcome social barriers, rehumanise
former opponents, and identify alternative avenues to violent conflict. CR is
supporting this through a series of workshops, seminars, international
exchanges, and sponsored studies with local civil groups, including the
churches, a women's movement, journalists and the Sierra Leone diaspora'
(Carl, Conciliation Resources, http://www.c-r.org/cr/).

Chapter 6   Ending Violent Conflict

1 Two were excluded for reasons of definition: one because the Soviet Union
   was dissolved, another because of the shift from one warring party to another.
   Darby, in work to be published, identifies 35 peace accords since 1989.
2 In his study of 91 civil wars in the period 1945–92, Licklider finds 57 that had
   ended; of these, 14 ended in negotiation and the other 43 in military victory
   (Licklider, 1995). Heraclides, in a study of the endings of 70 separatist armed
   conflicts of the period 1945–96 found outright victory by the incumbent state
   in 16 cases, outright victory by the separatist movement in 5 cases, some form
   of accommodation in 18 cases, of which two broke down, ongoing violence in
   29 cases and an unresolved or frozen conflict in 8 cases (Heraclides, 1998).
3 Even major international wars may be episodes in long-term violent conflicts:
   about half of the international conflicts that occurred between 1816 and 1992
   were the result of enduring rivalries between sides which constituted only 5
   per cent of the dyads in conflict; civil conflicts, too, may have an episodic
   character.
4 The study of the means by which internal and mixed internal-international
   conflicts terminate is still relatively new, and we cannot cite many systematic
   studies of the field. There is agreement that there are no simple patterns in why
   civil wars end (Licklider, 1993; King, 1997). Licklider suggests that in order to
   reach an ending it is necessary to obtain political change in the losing side, if
   there is one, or otherwise on both sides; that both sides must see the military
   situation as unstable and unlikely to improve; that the weaker side should not
   be helped by an external government; that 'quiet mediation' and 'mediation
   with muscle' can both facilitate endings (Licklider, ed., 1993).
5 Although such massive changes are difficult for agents to bring about deliberately, they illustrate the links between conflict resolution and the wider issues
   of international governance, international economic and political relationships, and the international, regional and economic orders.
6 Curle makes this personal change the basis for his theory of peacemaking: see
   Curle, 1971; 1986.
7 Fisher and Keashly suggested that conflict resolution attempts should be
   appropriate to the stage of a conflict, and argued for a 'contingency
   approach', in which the attempt suited the conflict stage (Fisher and Keashly,
   1991); for example, conciliation at an early stage where communications are
   poor, consultation when the conflict has escalated and relationships are
   breaking down, arbitration or power mediation when hostility is under way,

and peacekeeping when the parties are attempting to destroy one another (Keashly and Fisher, 1996, 244–9). Webb argues that the case of Yugoslavia demonstrates that the type of sequencing and coordination Fisher and Keashly urge is unattainable in international conflicts, and that their model is too formulaic and schematic, but he accepts the case for the complementarity of a variety of third party methods (Webb et al., 1996).

8 Such as the African Centre for the Constructive Resolution of Disputes (ACCORD), the Berghof Research Centre for Constructive Conflict Management in Berlin, the Carter Center in the USA, the Comunità di Sant'Egidio in Italy, the Conflict Analysis Centre at the University of Kent in Canterbury, the Harvard Center of Negotiation, the Institute for Multi-track Diplomacy in Washington, DC, International Alert in London and Search for Common Ground, based in Washington, DC, and with a European office in Brussels.

9 Although, arguably, responsibility for the failures lies mainly with the major states (Parsons, 1995).

10 For reviews of the UN's post-Cold War role as a conflict manager, see Berridge, 1991; Parsons, 1995. For an account of its recent work, see Findlay, 1996.

11 The UN has not been able to impose settlements (Parsons, 1995). Boutros Boutros-Ghali retracted his advocacy of coercive peacemaking one year after making it (Boutros-Ghali, 1992; 1993).

12 The South Tyrol settlement is a good example of such a process. The initial agreement of 1946, that South Tyrol should be Italian but autonomous, was interpreted to the disfavour of the German speakers by including a large Italian-speaking province in the area defined as having autonomy. This led to a period of tension crowned by bomb explosions in the 1960s, but then a series of de-escalatory steps led towards an interim settlement in 1969. A joint study commission was set up and after lengthy negotiations agreement was reached on a sequence of steps which would provide full autonomy and cultural and linguistic rights to the German speakers. It was not until 1992 that both sides agreed that the implementation of measures was complete (Alcock, 1970, 1994).

13 There is an increasing process of learning between peace processes. For example, parties from Northern Ireland visited South Africa in June 1997 and returned with ideas that helped to overcome the hurdle of decommissioning as a precondition to negotiations.

14 The account here rests heavily on Zartman's account of the negotiations (ed., 1996).

15 In 1984 Hendrik van der Merwe, a conflict researcher and director of the Centre for Intergroup Studies in Cape Town, had pioneered contacts with the ANC leadership in Lusaka, with the help of the newspaper editor Piet Muller. Others were also active, for example the Foundation for International Conciliation, which engaged in a facilitated mediation over features of a constitution that might be widely acceptable in 1985–6 (Miall, 1992, 78–80).

16 They did not, however, do much to affect the strength of the pro-Israeli lobby in the United States; and the massive influx of Soviet Jews into Israel made possible by the end of the Cold War was to strengthen support for the Likud Party and for the policy of maintaining and even expanding Israeli settlements in occupied territories.

17 The Irish government made most of the running in the intergovernmental

negotiations, as did the SDLP in the peace process generally (Coogan, 1995; Drower, 1995).

18 For a review of changes in Unionist analysis and discourse, see Cash, 1996. For a thoughtful Unionist reconceptualization, see Porter, 1996. For an analysis of political developments among the Unionists since the Anglo-Irish Agreement, see Cochrane, 1997.

Chapter 7   Post-Settlement Peacebuilding

1 UN interventions in pre-Dayton Bosnia (UNPROFOR) and Somalia (UNO-SOM) did much to discredit such enterprises, but these were interventions in active war zones where there had been no prior formal peace agreements. Interventions in Rwanda (UNAMIR) and in Liberia to the end of 1996 (UNOMIL) were also abortive, the former blamed by some for precipitating the 1994 genocide, the latter a relatively small operation in support of the regional ECOWAS states. To set against these is the contribution made by ONUCA to the peace process in Honduras and Nicaragua, not included here because it was originally deployed to verify an interstate non-intervention agreement, even though ONUCA's mandate was subsequently expanded to take on something of a peacebuilding role in those two countries. The UN Mission in Haiti (UNMIH) did not constitute an intervention after a war.

2 'It is, of course, well known that the only source of war is politics – the intercourse of governments and peoples; but it is apt to be assumed that war suspends that intercourse and replaces it with a wholly different condition, ruled by no law but its own.

We maintain, on the contrary, that war is simply a continuation of political intercourse, with the addition of other means. We deliberately use the phrase "with the addition of other means" because we also want to make it clear that war in itself does not suspend political intercourse or change it into something entirely different. In essentials, that intercourse continues, irrespective of the means it employs' (K. M. von Clausewitz, 1976 [1832], 75).

3 See also Mitchell, 1991, 23–38.

4 'The simultaneous occurrence of contradictory forms of *Vergesellschaftung* [roughly, socialization] is thus the basic fact that characterizes developing countries at war, for whereas the traditional patterns are dissolved by the advancement of the market economy, new "modern" forms cannot yet be developed sufficiently to resolve emerging social conflicts' (Jung et al., 1996, 55).

5 This can be seen in the eleven annexes to the 14 December 1995 General Framework Agreement, *Unfinished Peace: Report of the International Commission on the Balkans* (Washington, DC: Carnegie Endowment for International Peace, 1996). Specific UN missions surviving in former Yugoslavia after the demise of UNPROFOR in December 1995 included: the UN Confidence Restoration Operation in Croatia (UNCRO); the United Nations Preventive Deployment Force in Macedonia (UNPREDEP); the United Nations Mission in Bosnia and Herzegovina (UNMIBH); the United Nations Transitional Administration for Eastern Slavonia, Baranja and Western Sirmium (UNTAES) and the United Nations Mission of Observers in Prevlaka (UNMOP).

6 By spring 1998 the UN Security Council was considering establishing a

peacekeeping operation in the Central African Republic on the recommendation of the Secretary-General in support of the Inter-African Mission to Monitor the Implementation of the Bangui Agreements (MISAB). The possibility of a UN military presence in Sierra Leone to support ECOWAS forces in implementing the Conakry Agreement was also being contemplated.

7 On peacebuilding in Cambodia, see United Nations Security Council, 1992; Evans, 1994; Heininger, 1994; Doyle, 1995; Findlay, 1995; Prasso, 1995; United Nations Blue Book Series, vol. II, 1996; Hampson, 1996b, 171–204; United Nations, 1996, 447–84.

On peacebuilding in Namibia, see Jabri, ed., 1990; Jaster, 1990; Fortna, 1993, 353–75; Fetherston, 1994, 59–70; Madden, 1994; Hampson, 1996b, 53–86; United Nations, 1996, 203–29.

On peacebuilding in Angola, see Anstee, 1993; Holt, 1994; Hampson, 1996b, 87–128; Malaquias, 1996; Prendergast and Smock, 1996; Saferworld, 1996; United Nations, 1996, 231–66; United Nations Document S/1996/503, 1996; Krska, 1997.

On peacebuilding in Mozambique, see Hume, 1994; Vives, 1995; Alden, 1995; United Nations Blue Books Series, vol. V, 1996; Malaquias, 1996; United Nations, 1996, 319–38.

On peacebuilding in El Salvador, see Pearce, 1988; Karl, 1992; United Nations, 1992; 1993; 1994; 1995; 1996, 423–46; Holliday and Stanley, 1993; de Soto and del Castello, 1994; Stuart, 1994; Sullivan, 1994; Grenier and Daudelin, 1995; Montgomery, 1995; Hampson, 1996b, 129–70.

On peacebuilding in Bosnia, see Shear, 1996; Sharp, J., 1997.

8 For example, Lake, ed., 1990; de Soto and del Castillo, 1994; Bertram, 1995; Ball and Halevy, 1996; Crocker and Hampson, eds, 1996 (Part IV: *Consolidating Peace: New Challenges and Dilemmas*, pp. 533–622); Hampson, 1996b; Ginifer, ed., 1997 (includes chapters on conceptual issues by Stedman, Rothchild and Shaw); Kumar, ed., 1997; Paris, 1997.

9 For example, *The Blue Helmets: A Review of United Nations Peacekeeping* (1996), and the UN Blue Books Series.

10 For example, Hampson, 1996, which, based on a study of peace settlements in Cyprus, Namibia, Angola, El Salvador and Cambodia, concludes that there were successes (El Salvador, Namibia), partial successes (Cambodia) and failures (Cyprus, Angola) and assesses reasons for this. Hampson is more concerned with task (a) – preventing a relapse into war – than with the wider ambitions of task (b) – constructing a self-sustaining peace.

11 For example, Paris, 1997.

12 For example, Lizee, 1994, 135–48.

13 For the psychological aspects of conflict, see Larsen, ed., 1993. On its application to peacebuilding, see Charters, ed., 1994; Maynard, 1997.

14 On the role of third parties in conflict intervention, see Encarnacion et al., 1990; Laue, 1990. For criticism of the actions and impact of particular UN missions, see references in note 7.

15 On the culture question in general, see Augsburger, 1991; Avruch and Black, 1991; Avruch et al., eds, 1991; Cohen, 1991; Duffey, 1993; Salem, 1993; Fry and Björkquist, 1997.

16 For example, Fetherston (1995). Behind this lie sociological, anthropological and feminist critiques of militarized 'cultures' and 'discourses' of violence seen

to be as much a part of the UN's SOP as of the conflicts it is intended to address (Nordstrom, 1994; Jabri, 1996).

17 Kumar lists five tasks in political rehabilitation in peacebuilding: improving the institutional capacity for governance; providing support for elections; human rights monitoring and promotion; disarmament and demobilization; reforming the security sector (1997, 4–14).

18 Ball lists ten ways in which donors can help to meet postwar social and economic needs: assessing damage and planning reconstruction; rehabilitating basic infrastructure; resettling displaced groups; revitalizing communities; reactivating the smallholder agricultural sector; rehabilitating export agriculture, key industries and housing; generating employment; settling disputes over land and other assets; demining; and implementing environmental awareness and protection programmes (1996, 616).

19 Maynard gives five phases in psycho/social recovery: establishing safety; communalization and bereavement; rebuilding trust and the capacity to trust; re-establishing personal and social morality; reintegrating and restoring democratic discourse (1997, 210).

20 We cannot enter here into the elaborate discussion on the nature of various conceptions of democracy (see Held, 1993).

21 '[T]he data supports the argument that separation of groups is the key to ending ethnic civil wars ... There is not a single case where non-ethnic civil politics were created or restored by reconstruction of ethnic identities, power-sharing coalitions, or state-building' (Kaufmann, 1996, 161). In other words, Kaufmann rejects the 'contact hypothesis' that the more the contact between potential or erstwhile enemies the more the likelihood of accommodation (Hewstone and Brown, eds, 1986).

22 Conflict managers have: an inclusive approach; a goal of reconciliation; a pragmatic focus; an emphasis on process; a recognition of particular norms and cultures of the societies in conflict; an assumption of moral equivalence; the idea that conflict resolution is negotiable; and that outside actors should be politically neutral. Democratizers have: an exclusive approach; a goal of justice; a principled focus; an emphasis on outcomes; an insistence on universal norms endorsed by the international community; an insistence on moral accountability; the conviction that justice is not negotiable; and that outside actors cannot be morally neutral (Baker, 1996, 567).

23 On the debate about war crimes tribunals compare Meron, 1993 and Mak, 1995. On justice, see the three-volume Kritz, ed., 1995, although none of our six cases is included in the case studies of 'transitional justice' in vol. 2.

24 We may contrast deontological views of justice, in which past crimes must be punished, with other conceptions and approaches, although the subject is too complex to be entered into properly here.

References

Aall, P. 1996: Nongovernmental organisations and peacemaking. In Crocker and Hampson (eds), 433–42.

Adelman, H. and Suhrke, A. 1996: Early warning and conflict management. In B. Jones: *Study of the Project on International Response to Conflict and Genocide: Lessons from the Rwanda Experience*. York University: Centre for Refugee Studies.

Adeyemi, A. 1997: Post-armistice violence: the upsurge of crime after armed conflicts – African examples. Paper presented ISPAC International Conference on 'Violent Crime and Conflicts', Courmayeur, Italy, October.

Agger, I. 1995: *Theory and Practice of Psycho-Social Projects Under War Conditions in Bosnia–Herzegovina and Croatia*. Zagreb: ECHO/ECTF.

Agger, I. and Mimica, J. 1996: *Psycho-Social Assistance to Victims of War in Bosnia–Herzegovina and Croatia*. Zagreb: ECHO/ECTF.

Akashi, Y. 1994: The challenge of peacekeeping in Cambodia. *International Peacekeeping*, 1(2), 204–15.

Albin, C. 1997: Negotiating intractable conflicts: on the future of Jerusalem. *Cooperation and Conflict*, 32(1), 29–77.

Alcock, A. E. 1970: *A History of the South Tyrol Question*. London: Michael Joseph.

Alcock, A. E. 1994: South Tyrol. In Miall (ed.), 46–55.

Alden, C. 1995: Swords into ploughshares? The United Nations and demilitarization in Mozambique. *International Peacekeeping*, 2(2), 175–193.

Anderson, B. 1983: *Imagined Communities*. London: Verso.

Anderson, M. 1996: *Do No Harm: Supporting Local Capacities for Peace Through Aid*. Cambridge, MA: Development for Collaborative Action.

Anderson, M. 1996b: Humanitarian NGOs in conflict intervention. In Crocker and Hampson (eds), 343–54.

Anderson, M. and Woodrow, P. 1989: *Rising from the Ashes: Development Strategies in Times of Disaster*. Boulder, CO: Westview and UNESCO Presses.

Annan, K. 1997: *Renewal Amid Transition: Annual Report on the Work of the Organization*. New York: United Nations.

Annan, K. 1997b: Peace operations and the UN. *Conflict Resolution Monitor*, 1,

Bradford: Centre for Conflict Resolution, Department of Peace Studies, 25–32.

Annan, K. 1997c: UN Secretary-General's reform announcement: Part II measures and proposals, 16 July. *Conflict Resolution Monitor*, 2, Bradford: Centre for Conflict Resolution, Department of Peace Studies, 34–6.

Anstee, M. 1993: Angola: the forgotten tragedy, a test case for UN peacekeeping. *International Relations*, 11(6).

Anstee, M. 1996: *Orphan of the Cold War: The Inside Story of the Collapse of the Angolan Peace Process 1992–93*. Basingstoke: Macmillan.

Ashford, O. 1985: *Prophet – or Professor? The Life and Work of Lewis Fry Richardson*. Bristol: Adam Hilger.

Askandar, K. 1997: ASEAN as a conflict management organization. Ph.D. thesis, Bradford University.

Asmal, K., Asmal, L., and Roberts, R. 1996: *Reconciliation Through Truth: A Reckoning of Apartheid's Criminal Governance*. Capetown: Mayibuye Books.

Aspen Institute 1997: *Conflict Prevention: Strategies to Sustain Peace in the Post-Cold War World*. Aspen, CO: The Aspen Institute.

Augsburger, D. 1991: *Intercultural Mediation*. Philadelphia: Westminster Press.

Avruch, K. and Black, P. 1987: A generic theory of conflict resolution: a critique. *Negotiation Journal*, 3(1), 87–96; 99–100.

Avruch, K. and Black, P. 1991: The culture question and conflict resolution. *Peace and Change*, 16(1), 22–45.

Avruch, K., Black, P. and Scimecca, J. 1991: *Conflict Resolution: Cross Cultural Perspectives*. Westport, CT: Greenwood Press.

Axelrod, R. 1984: *The Evolution of Cooperation*. New York: Basic Books.

Axelrod, R. and Keohane, R. 1986: Achieving co-operation under anarchy. In K. Oye (ed.), *Co-operation under Anarchy*. Princeton, NJ: Princeton University Press, 226–54.

Ayoob, M. 1996: State making, state breaking, and state failure. In Crocker and Hampson (eds), 37–52.

Azar, E. 1979: Peace amidst development. *International Interactions*, 6(2), 203–40.

Azar, E. 1986: Protracted international conflicts: ten propositions. In Azar and Burton, 28–39.

Azar, E. 1990: *The Management of Protracted Social Conflict: Theory and Cases*. Aldershot: Dartmouth.

Azar, E. 1991: The analysis and management of protracted social conflict. In Volkan, Montville and Julius (eds), 93–120.

Azar, E. and Burton, J. 1986: *International Conflict Resolution: Theory and Practice*. Sussex: Wheatsheaf.

Azar, E. and Cohen, S. 1981: The transition from war to peace between Israel and Egypt. *Journal of Conflict Resolution*, 7(4), 317–36.

Azar, E., Jureidini, P. and McLaurin, R. 1978: Protracted social conflict: theory and practice in the Middle East. *Journal of Palestine Studies* 8(1), 41–60.

Bailey, S. 1982: *How Wars End: The United Nations and the Termination of Armed Conflict 1946–64*. 2 vols. Oxford: Clarendon Press.

Bailey, S. 1985: Non-official mediation in disputes: reflections on Quaker experience. *International Affairs*, 61(2), 205–22.

Baker, P. 1996: Conflict resolution versus democratic governance: divergent paths to peace? In Crocker and Hampson (eds), 563–72.

Bakwesegha, C. 1997: The role of the Organisation of African Unity in conflict prevention, management, and resolution in the context of the political evolution of Africa. *African Journal on Conflict Prevention, Management and Resolution*, 1(1), 4–22.

Ball, N. 1996: The challenge of rebuilding war-torn societies. In Crocker and Hampson (eds), 607–22.

Ball, N. and Halevy, T. 1996: *Making Peace Work: The Role of the International Development Community*. Baltimore: The Johns Hopkins University Press.

Banks, M. (ed.) 1984: *Conflict in World Society*. Brighton: Harvester.

Bauwens, W. and Reychler, L. (eds) 1994: *The Art of Conflict Prevention*. London: Brassey's.

Bendahmane, D. (ed.) 1987: *Conflict Resolution: Track Two Diplomacy*. Washington, DC: Foreign Services Institute, US Department of State.

Bennett, C. 1995: *Yugoslavia's Bloody Collapse: Causes, Course and Consequences*. London: Hurst.

Bercovitch, J. (ed.) 1991: International Mediation. *Journal of Peace Research*, 28(1) (Special Issue on International Mediation).

Bercovitch, J. (ed.) 1996: *Resolving International Conflicts: The Theory and Practice of Mediation*. Boulder, CO: Lynne Rienner.

Bercovitch, J., Anagnoson, J. T. and Wille, D. L. 1991: Some conceptual issues and empirical trends in the study of successful mediation in international relations. *Journal of Peace Research*, 28(1), 7–17.

Bercovitch, J. and Rubin, J. (eds) 1992: *Mediation in International Relations: Multiple Approaches to Conflict Management*. London: Macmillan.

Berdal, M. 1996: Disarmament and demobilisation after civil wars. Adelphi Paper 303. Oxford: Oxford University Press, for International Institute of Strategic Studies.

Berdal, M. and Keen D. 1998: Violence and economic agendas in civil wars: some policy implications. *Millennium*, 26(3), 795–818.

Berhane-Selassie, T. 1994: African women in conflict resolution. *Counter Focus*, 120, 1–3.

Berman, M. and Johnson, J. (eds) 1977: *Unofficial Diplomats*. New York: Columbia University Press.

Berridge, G. 1991: *Return to the UN*. London: Macmillan.

Bertram, E. 1995: Reinventing governments: the promise and perils of United Nations peacebuilding. *Journal of Conflict Resolution*, 39(3), 387–418.

Betts, R. 1994: The delusions of impartial intervention. *Foreign Affairs*, 73(6), 20–33.

Bew, P. and Gillespie, G. 1996: *The Northern Ireland Peace Process, 1993–96: A Chronology*. London: Serif.

Bhaskar, R. 1989: *The Possibility of Naturalism*. Hemel Hempstead: Harvester.

Blake, P., Shephard, H. and Mouton, J. 1963: *Managing Intergroup Conflict in Industry*. Houston: Gulf Publishing.

Bloed, A. 1993: *The Conference on Security and Cooperation in Europe: Analysis and Basic Documents, 1972–1993*. Boston: Dordrecht.

Bloomfield, D. 1997: *Peacemaking Strategies in Northern Ireland: Building Complementarity in Conflict Management Theory*. London: Macmillan.

Bloomfield, L. and Leiss, A. 1969: *Controlling Small Wars: A Strategy for the 1970s*. New York: Knopf.

Bloomfield, L. and Moulton, A. 1997: *Managing International Conflict: From Theory to Policy*. New York: St Martin's Press.

Boraine, A., Levy, J. and Scheffer, R. (eds) 1997: *Dealing with the Past: Truth and Reconciliation in South Africa*. Cape Town: IDASA.

Boulding, E. 1976: *The Underside of History: A View of Women through Time*. Boulder, CO: Westview.

Boulding, E. 1990: *Building a Global Civic Culture: Education for an Interdependent World*. Syracuse: Syracuse University Press.

Boulding, K. 1961: *Perspectives on the Economics of Peace*. New York: Institute for International Orders.

Boulding, K. 1962: *Conflict and Defense*. New York: Harper and Row.

Boulding, K. 1977: Twelve friendly quarrels with Johan Galtung. *Journal of Peace Research*, 14(1), 75–86.

Boulding, K. 1978: Future directions in conflict and peace studies. *Journal of Conflict Resolution*, 22(2), 342–54.

Boulding, K. 1989: *Three Faces of Power*. Newbury Park, CA: Sage.

Boutros-Ghali, B. 1992: *An Agenda for Peace*. New York: United Nations.

Boutros-Ghali, B. 1993: An agenda for peace: one year later. *Orbis*, 37(3), 323–32.

Boutros-Ghali, B. 1994: *General Assembly Report of the Secretary-General on the Work of the Organization*. New York: United Nations.

Boutros-Ghali, B. 1995: *Supplement to An Agenda for Peace: Position Paper of the Secretary-General on the Occasion of the Fiftieth Anniversary of the United Nations*. New York: United Nations.

Boutros-Ghali, B. 1995b: *An Agenda for Development: Report of the Secretary-General*. New York: United Nations.

Boutwell, J., Klare, M. and Reed, L. (eds) 1995: *Lethal Commerce: The Global Trade in Small Arms and Light Weapons*. Cambridge, MA: American Academy of Arts and Sciences.

Brauwens, W. and Reychler, L. 1994: *The Art of Conflict Prevention*. London: Brassey's.

Bringe, T. 1993: We are all neighbours. Film. *Disappearing World*. London: Granada TV.

Brinton, C. 1938: *The Anatomy of Revolution*. New York: W.W. Norton.

Broome, B. 1993: Managing differences in conflict resolution: the role of relational empathy. In Sandole and van der Merwe (eds), 97–111.

Brown, M. (ed.) 1993: *Ethnic Conflict and International Security*. Princeton: Princeton University Press.

Brown, M. (ed.) 1996: *The International Dimensions of Internal Conflict*. Cambridge, MA: MIT Press.

Brundtland, H. 1987: *Our Common Future*. Oxford: Oxford University Press for the World Commission on Environment and Development.

Bull, H. and Watson, A. 1984: *The Expansion of International Society*. Oxford: Clarendon Press.

Burton, J. 1968: *Systems, States, Diplomacy and Rules*. London: Macmillan.

Burton, J. 1969: *Conflict and Communication: The Use of Controlled Communication in International Relations*. London: Macmillan.

Burton, J. W. 1972: *World Society*. London: Macmillan.

Burton, J. 1984: *Global Conflict: The Domestic Sources of International Crisis*. Brighton: Wheatsheaf.

Burton, J. 1987: *Resolving Deep-Rooted Conflict: A Handbook*. Lanham, MD: University Press of America.

Burton, J. 1990: *Conflict: Resolution and Provention* (vol. 1 of the Conflict Series). London: Macmillan.

Burton, J. (ed.) 1990: *Conflict: Human Needs Theory* (vol. 2 of the Conflict Series). London: Macmillan.

Burton, J. and Dukes, F. (eds) 1990: *Conflict: Readings in Management and Resolution* (vol. 3 of the Conflict Series). London: Macmillan.

Burton, J. and Dukes, F. 1990: *Conflict: Practices in Management, Settlement and Resolution* (vol. 4 of the Conflict Series). London: Macmillan.

Bush, K. 1995: Towards a balanced approach to rebuilding war-torn societies. *Canadian Foreign Policy*, 3(3), 49–69.

Buzan, B. 1991: *People, States and Fear: An Agenda for International Security Studies in the Post-Cold War Era* (2nd edn) Boulder, CO: Lynne Rienner.

Buzan, B., Waever, O. and de Wilde, J. 1997: *Security: A New Framework for Analysis*. Boulder, CO: Lynne Rienner.

Byrne, B. 1996: Towards a gendered understanding of conflict. *IDS Bulletin*, 27(3), 31–40.

Cairns, E. 1997: *A Safer Future: Reducing the Human Costs of War*. Oxford: Oxfam Publications.

Carnegie Commission on Preventing Deadly Conflict 1997: *Preventing Deadly Conflict*. Washington, DC: Carnegie Corporation of New York.

Carnegie Endowment for International Peace 1996: *Unfinished Peace: Report of the International Commission on the Balkans*. Washington, DC: Carnegie Institute.

Carter, J. 1992: The real cost of war. *Security Dialogue*, 23(4), 21–4.

Carter Center 1995: *State of World Conflict Report*. Atlanta, GA: International Negotiation Network.

Cash, J. 1996: *Identity, Ideology and Conflict*. Cambridge: Cambridge University Press.

Charters, D. (ed.) 1994: *Peacekeeping and the Challenge of Civil Conflict Resolution*. New Brunswick: Centre for Conflict Studies, University of New Brunswick.

Chayes, A. and Raach, G. 1995: *Peace Operations: Developing the American Strategy*. Washington, DC: National Defense University Press, Institute for National Strategic Studies.

Chazan, N., Mortimer, R., Ravenhill, J. and Rothchild, D. 1992: *Politics and Society in Contemporary Africa*. Boulder, CO: Lynne Rienner.

Choukri, N. and North, R. 1975: *Nations in Conflict: National Growth and International Violence*. San Francisco: Freeman.

Chubin, S. 1993: The South and the New World Order. *Washington Quarterly*, 16(4), 87–107.

Cioffi-Revilla, C. 1990: *The Scientific Measurement of International Conflict: Handbook of Datasets on Crises and Wars 1495–1988*. Boulder, CO: Lynne Rienner.

Clapham, C. 1996: Rwanda: the perils of peace-making. *Journal of Peace Research*, 35(2), 193–210.

Clark, I. 1997: *Globalization and Fragmentation: International Relations in the Twentieth Century*. Oxford: Oxford University Press.

Clausewitz, K. von 1976 [1832]: *On War*, translated and edited by M. Howard and P. Paret. Princeton, NJ: Princeton University Press.

Clements, K. and Ward, W. 1994: *Building International Community: Cooperating for Peace Case Studies*. St Leonards, NSW: Allen and Unwin Australia.

CMI 1997: See Sorbo, Macrae and Wohlgemuth.

Cochrane, F. 1997: *Unionist Politics and the Politics of Unionism Since the Anglo-Irish Agreement*. Cork: Cork University Press.

Cohen, R. 1990: *Culture and Conflict in Egyptian-Israeli Negotiations: A Dialogue of the Deaf*. Bloomington: University of Indiana Press.

Cohen, R. 1991: *Negotiation Across Cultures*. Washington: United States Institute of Peace.

Cohen, R. 1994: Pacific Unions: A reappraisal of the theory that democracies do not go to war with each other. *Review of International Studies*, 20(3), 207–23.

Cohen, R. 1996: Cultural aspects of international mediation. In Bercovitch (ed.), 107–28.

Coleman, J. 1957: *Community Conflict*. New York: Free Press.

Conflict Management Group 1993: *Methods and Strategies in Conflict Prevention: Report of an Expert Consultation in Connection with the Activities of the CSCE High Commissioner on National Minorities*. Cambridge, MA: Conflict Management Group.

Coogan, T. 1995: *The Troubles: Ireland's Ordeal 1966–1995 and the Search for Peace*. London: Hutchinson.

Corbin, J. 1994: *Gaza First: The Secret Norway Channel to Peace Between Israel and the PLO*. London: Bloomsbury.

Coser, L. 1956: *The Functions of Social Conflict*. New York: Free Press.

Cox, M. 1997: The IRA ceasefire and the end of the Cold War. *International Affairs*, 73(4), 671–93.

Cox, R. 1981: Social forces, states and world order: beyond international relations. *Millennium*, 10(2), 126–55.

Cox, R. 1996: *Approaches to World Order*. Cambridge: Cambridge University Press.

Cranna, M. (ed.) 1994: *The True Cost of Conflict*. London: Earthscan, for Saferworld.

Creative Associates 1997: *Preventing and Mitigating Violent Conflicts*. Washington, DC: Creative Associates International Inc.

Crocker, C. and Hampson, F. (eds) 1996: *Managing Global Chaos: Sources of and Responses to International Conflict*. Washington, DC: United States Institute of Peace.

Crocker, C. and Hampson, F. 1996b: Making peace settlements work, *Foreign Policy*, 104 (Fall), 54–71.

Curle, A. 1971: *Making Peace*. London: Tavistock.

Curle, A. 1981: *True Justice: Quaker Peacemakers and Peacemaking*. London: Swarthmore.

Curle, A. 1986: *In the Middle: Non-Official Mediation in Violent Situations*. Oxford: Berg.

Curle, A. 1990: *Tools for Transformation*. Stroud: Hawthorn Press.

Curle, A. 1994: New challenges for citizen peacemaking. *Medicine and War*, 10(2), 96–105.

Curle, A. 1996: *Another Way: Positive Response to Contemporary Conflict*. Oxford: John Carpenter.

Dahrendorf, R. 1957: Towards a theory of social conflict. *Journal of Conflict Resolution*, 2(2), 170–83.

Dallaire, R. 1996: The changing role of United Nations peacekeeping forces: the relationship between UN peacekeepers and NGOs in Rwanda. In Whitman and Pocock (eds), 205–18.

Darby, J. 1998: *Scorpions in a Bottle: Conflicting Cultures in Northern Ireland.* London: Minority Rights Publications.

Davies, J. and Gurr, T. (eds) 1998: *Crisis Early Warning Systems.* Boulder, CO: Rowman and Littlefield.

Davies, J., Harff, B. and Speca, A. 1997: *Dynamic Data for Conflict Early Warning: Synergy in Early Warning.* Toronto: Prevention/Early Warning Unit, Centre for International and Security Studies.

Davies, N. 1996: *Europe: A History.* Oxford: Oxford University Press.

Dawkins, R. 1989: *The Selfish Gene.* Oxford: Oxford University Press.

Dedring, J. 1994: Early warning and the United Nations. *Journal of Ethno-Political Development,* 4(1), 98–104.

De Nevers, R. 1993: Democratization and ethnic conflict. In Brown (ed.), 61–78.

de Reuck, A. 1984: The logic of conflict: its origin, development and resolution. In Banks (ed.), 96–111.

de Reuck, A. and Knight, J. (eds) 1966: *Conflict in Society.* London: CIBA Foundation.

des Forges, A. 1996: Making noise effectively: lessons from the Rwanda catastrophe. In Rotberg (ed.), 213–32.

de Soto, A. and del Castillo, G. 1994: Obstacles to peacebuilding. *Foreign Policy* (Spring), 69–83.

de Wilde, J. 1991: *Saved From Oblivion: Interdependence Theory in the First Half of the Twentieth Century.* Aldershot: Dartmouth.

Deutsch, K. 1954: *Political Community at the International Level: Problems of Definition and Measurement.* Garden City, NY: Doubleday.

Deutsch, K. 1957: *Political Community and the North Atlantic Area.* Princeton, NJ: Princeton University Press.

Deutsch, M. 1949: A theory of cooperation and conflict. *Human Relations,* 2, 129–52.

Deutsch, M. 1973: *The Resolution of Conflict: Constructive and Destructive Processes.* New Haven: Yale University Press.

Deutsch, M. 1990: Sixty years of conflict. *International Journal of Conflict Management* 1(3), 237–63.

Diamond, L. and McDonald, J. 1996: *Multi-Track Diplomacy: A Systems Approach to Peace.* Washington, DC: Kumarian Press.

Dmitrichev, T. 1992: Early warning and conflict resolution. Paper presented at IPRA Conference, Kyoto, July 1992.

Dollard, J., Doob, L., Miller, N., Mowrer, O. and Sears, R. 1939: *Frustration and Aggression.* New Haven: Yale University Press.

Doob, L. (ed.) 1970: *Resolving Conflict in Africa: The Fermeda Workshop.* New Haven: Yale University Press.

Dougherty, J. and Pfalzgraff, R. 1990: *Contending Theories of International Relations.* New York: Harper and Row.

Doyle, M. 1986: Liberalism and world politics. *The American Political Science Review,* 80, 1151–69.

Doyle, M. 1995: *UN Peacekeeping in Cambodia: UNTAC's Civil Mandate.* Boulder, CO: Lynne Rienner.

Drakulic, S. 1994: *Balkan Express.* London: Harper.

Drower, G. 1995: *John Hume: Man of Peace.* London: Vista.

Druckman, D. 1986: Four cases of conflict management: lessons learned. In D. Bendahmane and J. McDonald (eds), *Perspectives on Negotiation: Four Case Studies and Interpretations*. Washington, DC: Centre for the Study of Foreign Affairs, Foreign Service Institute, US Department of State, 263–88.

Druckman, D. (ed.) 1977: *Negotiations: Social-Psychological Perspectives*. Beverly Hills, CA: Sage.

Druckman, D. and Green, J. 1995: Playing two games: internal negotiations in the Philippines. In Zartman (ed.), 299–331.

Duffey, T. 1993: The Role of Culture in Conflict Research. MA thesis, University of Bradford, UK.

Duffey, T. 1998: Culture, Conflict Resolution and Peacekeeping. Ph.D. thesis, Department of Peace Studies, University of Bradford.

Duffield, M. 1994: The political economy of internal war. In Macrae and Zwi (eds), 50–69.

Duffield, M. 1997: Evaluating conflict resolution. In Sorbo, Macrae and Wohlgemuth, 79–112.

Dugan, M. 1996: A nested theory of conflict. *Women in Leadership*, 1(1), 9–20.

Dukes, F. 1993: Public conflict resolution: a transformative approach. *Negotiation Journal*, 9(1), 45–57.

Dunn, D. 1995: Articulating an alternative: the contribution of John Burton. *Review of International Studies*, 21, 197–208.

Durch, W. (ed.) 1993: *The Evolution of UN Peacekeeping*. Basingstoke: Macmillan.

Encarnacion, T., McCartney, C. and Rosas, C. 1990: The impact of concerned parties on the resolution of disputes. In Lindgren, Wallensteen and Nordquist (eds), 42–96.

Eriksson 1996: *The International Response to Conflict and Genocide: Lessons from the Rwanda Experience*. Copenhagen: Steering Committee of Joint Evaluation of Emergency Assistance to Rwanda.

Esty, D. et al. 1995: *State Failure Task Force, Final Report*. Vol. 1: Science Applications International Corporation Inc.

Esty, D. et. al. 1998: The state failure project: early warning research for US foreign policy planning. In Davies and Gurr (eds).

European Platform for Conflict Prevention and Transformation 1998: *Prevention and Management of Violent Conflicts: An International Directory*. Utrecht: ECCP.

Evans, G. 1993: *Cooperating for Peace: The Global Agenda for the 1990s and Beyond*. Victoria: Allen and Unwin.

Evans, G. 1994: Peacekeeping in Cambodia: lessons learned. *NATO Review*, 42(4), 24–7.

Falk, R. 1985: A new paradigm for international legal studies: prospects and proposals. In R. Falk et al. (eds), *International Law: A Contemporary Perspective*. Boulder, CO: Westview, 651–702.

Falkenmark, M. 1990: Global water issues confronting humanity. *Journal of Peace Research*, 27(2), 177–90.

Farah, A. 1993: *The Roots of Reconciliation*. London: ActionAid.

Fein, H. 1990: Explanations of genocide. *Current Sociology*, 38(1), 32–50.

Fetherston, B. 1994: *Towards a Theory of United Nations Peacekeeping*. London: Macmillan/St Martin's Press.

Fetherston, B. 1995: UN peacekeepers and cultures of violence. *Cultural Survival Quarterly* (Spring), 19–23.

Fetherston, B. 1998: Transformative peacebuilding: peace studies in Croatia. Paper presented at the International Studies Association Annual Convention, Minneapolis, March.

Fetherston, B., Ramsbotham, O. and Woodhouse, T. 1994: UNPROFOR: some observations from a conflict resolution perspective. *International Peacekeeping*, 1(2), 179–203.

Findlay, T. 1995: *Cambodia: The Legacy and Lessons of UNTAC*. Oxford: Oxford University Press for SIPRI.

Findlay, T. 1996: Armed conflict prevention, management and resolution. In *SIPRI Yearbook 1996: Armaments, Disarmament and International Security*. Stockholm: Stockholm International Peace Research Institute.

Fisher, G. 1980: *International Negotiation: A Cross Cultural Perspective*. Chicago: Intercultural Press.

Fisher, R. 1990: *The Social Psychology of Intergroup and International Conflict*. New York: Springer-Verlag.

Fisher, R. and Keashly, L. 1991: The potential complementarity of mediation and consultation within a contingency model of third party intervention. *Journal of Peace Research*, 28(1), 29–42.

Fisher, R. and Ury, W. 1981: *Getting to Yes*. Boston: Houghton Mifflin.

Fitzduff, M. 1989: *A Typology of Community Relations Work and Contextual Necessities*. Belfast: Community Relations Council.

Follet, M. 1942: *Dynamic Administration: The Collected Papers of Mary Parker Follett*, edited by H. Metcalf and L. Urwick. New York: Harper.

Fortna, V. 1993: United Nations Transition Assistance Group. In Durch (ed.), 59–70.

Foundation on Inter-Ethnic Relations 1996: *Bibliography of Works on the OSCE High Commissioner on National Minorities*. The Hague: Foundation on Inter-Ethnic Relations.

Francis, D. 1994: Power and conflict resolution. In International Alert, *Conflict Resolution Training in the North Caucasus, Georgia and the South of Russia*. London: International Alert, 11–20 April 1994.

Freeman, H. (ed.) 1969: *Progress in Mental Health*. London: Churchill.

Fry, D. and Bjorkqvist, K. 1997: *Cultural Variation in Conflict Resolution: Alternatives to Violence*. Mahwah, New Jersey: Lawrence Earlbaum Associates.

Furley, O. (ed.) 1995: *Conflict in Africa*. London: I. B. Tauris.

Gadamer, H. 1975: *Truth and Method*. New York: Seabury Press.

Galtung, J. 1959: Pacifism from a sociological point of view. *Journal of Conflict Resolution*, 3(1), 67–84.

Galtung, J. 1969: Conflict as a way of life. In Freeman (ed.).

Galtung, J. 1975: Three approaches to peace: peacekeeping, peacemaking and peacebuilding. In Galtung, *Peace, War and Defence – Essays in Peace Research*, vol. 2. Copenhagen: Christian Ejlers, 282–304.

Galtung, J. 1975–88: *Essays in Peace Research* (6 vols), Copenhagen: Christian Ejlers.

Galtung, J. 1980: *Papers in English* (7 vols), Oslo: PRIO.

Galtung, J. 1984: *There Are Alternatives! Four Roads to Peace and Security*. Nottingham: Spokesman.

Galtung, J. 1985: Twenty-five years of peace research: ten challenges and some responses. *Journal of Peace Research*, 22(2), 141–58.

Galtung, J. 1987: Only one friendly quarrel with Kenneth Boulding. *Journal of Peace Research*, 24(2), 199–203.

Galtung, J. 1989: *Solving Conflicts: A Peace Research Perspective*. Honolulu: University of Hawaii Press.

Galtung, J. 1990: Cultural violence. *Journal of Peace Research*, 27(3), 291–305.

Galtung, J. 1996: *Peace by Peaceful Means: Peace and Conflict, Development and Civilization*. London: Sage.

Gastrow, P. 1995: *Bargaining for Peace: South Africa and the National Peace Accord*. Washington, DC: United States Institute of Peace.

Geller, D. and Singer, D. 1998: *Nations at War: A Scientific Study of International Conflict*. Cambridge: Cambridge University Press.

Giddens, A. 1979: *Central Problems in Social Theory: Action, Structure and Contradiction in Social Analysis*. London: Macmillan.

Giddens, A. 1987: *The Nation State and Violence*. Berkeley: University of California Press.

Ginifer, J. (ed.) 1997: *Beyond the Emergency: Development Within UN Peace Missions*. London: Frank Cass.

Glazer, N. 1983: *Ethnic Dilemmas 1964–1982*. Cambridge, MA: Harvard University Press.

Gleditsch, N. and Hegre, H. 1997: Democracy and peace, three levels of analysis. *Journal of Conflict Resolution*, 41, 283–310.

Gleick, P. 1995: Water and conflict: fresh water resources and international security. In Lynn-Jones and Miller (eds), 84–117.

Goldstone, R. 1997: War crimes: a question of will. *The World Today*, 53(4), 106–8.

Grant, J. 1992: *The State of the World's Children*. New York: UNICEF.

Graybill, L. 1998: South Africa's Truth and Reconciliation Commission: ethical and theological perspectives. *Ethics and International Affairs*, 12, 43–62.

Grenier, Y. and Daudelin, J. 1995: Foreign assistance and the market-place of peacemaking: lessons from El Salvador. *International Peacekeeping*, 2(3), 350–64.

Gulliver, P. 1979: *Disputes and Negotiations: A Cross-Cultural Perspective*. New York: Academic Press.

Gurr, T. 1970: *Why Men Rebel*. Princeton, NJ: Princeton University Press.

Gurr, T. 1993: *Minorities at Risk: A Global View of Ethnopolitical Conflict*. Washington, DC: United States Institute of Peace.

Gurr, T. 1995: Transforming ethnopolitical conflicts: exit, autonomy or access? In Rupesinghe (ed.), 1–30.

Gurr, T. 1996: Minorities, nationalists and ethnopolitical conflict. In Crocker and Hampson (eds), 53–78.

Gurr, T. 1998: Strategies of accommodation in plural societies. Paper given at the International Studies Association Conference, Minneapolis, USA, March 1998.

Gurr, T. 1998b: Assessing risks of future ethnorebellions. In Gurr (ed.), *Peoples Versus States*, Washington: United States Institute of Peace.

Gurr, T. and Harff, B. 1994: *Ethnic Conflict in World Politics*. Boulder, CO: Westview Press.

Gurr, T. and Harff, B. 1996: *Early Warning of Communal Conflicts and Genocide: Linking Empirical Research to International Responses*. Tokyo: United Nations University.

Haass, R. 1990: *Conflicts Unending: The United States and Regional Disputes.* New Haven: Yale University Press.

Hall, L. (ed.) 1993: *Negotiation: Strategies for Mutual Gain.* London: Sage.

Hampson, F. 1996: *Nurturing Peace: Why Peace Settlements Succeed or Fail.* Washington, DC: United States Institute of Peace.

Hampson, F. 1996b: Why orphaned peace settlements are more prone to failure. In Crocker and Hampson (eds), 533–50.

Hampson, F. 1997: Third-party roles in the termination of intercommunal conflict. *Millennium*, 26(3), 727–50.

Hannum, H. 1990: *Autonomy, Sovereignty and Self-Determination: The Accommodation of Conflicting Rights.* Philadelphia: University of Pennsylvania Press.

Hansen, A. 1997: Political legitimacy, confidence-building and the Dayton Peace Agreement. *International Peacekeeping*, 4(2), 74–90.

Harding, J. 1994: *Small Wars, Small Mercies: Journeys in Africa's Disputed Nations.* London: Penguin.

Heininger, J. 1994: *Peacekeeping in Transition: The United Nations in Cambodia.* New York: Twentieth Century Press.

Held, D. (ed.) 1993: *Prospects for Democracy.* Cambridge: Polity Press.

Heldt, B. (ed.) 1992: *States in Armed Conflict 1990–91.* Uppsala: Uppsala University.

Helman, G. and Ratner, S. 1992–3: Saving failed states. *Foreign Policy*, 89 (Winter), 3–30.

Heraclides, A. 1998: The ending of unending conflicts: separatist wars. *Millennium*, 26(3), 679–708.

Hewstone, N. and Brown, R. (eds) 1986: *Contact and Conflict in Intergroup Encounters.* Oxford: Basil Blackwell.

Hill, S. and Rothchild, D. 1996: The contagion of political conflict in Africa and the world. *Journal of Conflict Resolution*, 30(4), 716–35.

Hinsley, F. 1963: *Power and the Pursuit of Peace.* Cambridge: Cambridge University Press.

Hinsley, F. 1987: Peace and war in modern times. In R. Vayrynen (ed.), *The Quest for Peace: Transcending Collective Violence and War Among Societies, Cultures and States.* London: Sage.

Holliday, D. and Stanley, W. 1993: Building the peace: preliminary lessons from El Salvador. *Journal of International Affairs*, 46(2), 415–38.

Holsti, K. 1991: *Peace and War: Armed Conflicts and International Order 1648–1989.* Cambridge: Cambridge University Press.

Holsti, K. 1992: Governance without government: polyarchy in nineteenth century European international politics. In J. Rosenau and E. Czempiel (eds), *Governance Without Government: Order and Change in World Politics.* Cambridge: Cambridge University Press.

Holsti, K. 1996: *The State, War, and the State of War.* Cambridge: Cambridge University Press.

Holt, D. 1994: United Nations Angola Verification Mission II. In Clements and Ward (eds), 302–10.

Homer-Dixon, T. 1995: On the threshold: environmental changes as causes of acute conflict. In Lynn-Jones and Miller (eds), 43–83.

Horowitz, D. 1985: *Ethnic Groups in Conflict.* Berkeley, CA: University of California Press.

Horowitz, D. 1991: Making moderation pay: the comparative politics of ethnic conflict management. In Montville (ed.), 451–75.

Horowitz, D. 1993: Democracy in divided societies. *Journal of Democracy*, 4(4), 18–38.

Howard, M. 1976: *War in European History*. London: Oxford University Press.

Howard, M. 1983: *The Causes of War and Other Essays*. Cambridge, MA: Harvard University Press.

Human Rights Watch 1995: *Slaughter Among Neighbours: The Political Origins of Communal Violence*. New Haven: Yale University Press.

Hume, C. 1994: *Ending Mozambique's War: The Role of Mediation and Good Offices*. Washington, DC: United States Institute of Peace.

Huntington, S. 1991: *The Third Wave: Democratization in the Late Twentieth Century*. Oklahoma: Oklahoma University Press.

Huntington, S. 1997: *The Clash of Civilizations and the Remaking of World Order*. New York: Simon and Schuster.

Ikle, F. 1971: *Every War Must End*. New York: University of Columbia Press.

International Alert 1996: *Resource Pack for Conflict Transformation*. London: International Alert.

International Commission on the Balkans 1996: *Unfinished Peace: Report of the International Commission on the Balkans*. Washington, DC: Brookings Institution.

International Federation of Red Cross and Red Crescent Societies (IFRCRCS) 1996: *World Disasters Report 1996*. Oxford: Oxford University Press.

Jabri, V. 1996: *Discourses on Violence: Conflict Analysis Reconsidered*. Manchester: Manchester University Press.

Jabri, V. (ed.) 1990: *Mediating Conflict: Decision-Making and Western Intervention in Namibia*. Manchester: Manchester University Press.

Jackson, R. 1990: *Quasi-states, Sovereignty, International Relations and the Third World*. Cambridge: Cambridge University Press.

Janning, J. and Brusis, M. 1997: *Exploring Futures for Kosovo: Kosovo Albanians and Serbs in Dialogue*. Munich: Research Group on European Affairs.

Jaster, R. 1990: The 1988 Peace Accords and the future of South-Western Africa. Adelphi Paper 253. London: International Institute of Strategic Studies.

Jean, F. (ed.) 1993: *Life, Death and Aid: The Médecins Sans Frontières Report on World Crisis Intervention*. London: Routledge.

Jentleson, B. 1996: Preventive diplomacy and ethnic conflict: possible, difficult, necessary. In Jentleson (ed.).

Jentleson, B. (ed.) 1996: *Preventive Diplomacy in the Post-Cold War World: Opportunities Missed, Opportunities Seized and Lessons to be Learned*. Carnegie Commission on Preventing Deadly Conflict. New York: Rowman and Littlefield.

Jervis, R. 1976: *Perception and Misperception in International Politics*. Princeton: Princeton University Press.

Jervis, R. 1982: Security regimes. *International Organization*, 36(2), 357–78.

Jongman, A. and Schmid, A. 1996: Contemporary armed conflicts – a brief survey. In van Tongeren (ed.), 25–9.

Jongman, A. and Schmid, A. 1998: *World Conflict and Human Rights Map*. Leiden: Leiden University.

Jung, D., Schlichte, K. and Siegelberg, J. 1996: Ongoing wars and their explanation. In van de Goor, Rupesinghe and Sciarone (eds), 50–66.

Kacowicz, A. 1995: Explaining zones of peace: democracies as satisfied powers? *Journal of Conflict Resolution*, 32(3), 265–76.

Kagan, D. 1995: *On the Origins of War*. New York: Doubleday.

Kaldor, M. 1991: *The Imaginary War: Understanding the East–West Conflict*. London: Blackwell.

Kaldor, M. and Vashee, B. (eds) 1997: *New Wars: Restructuring the Global Military Sector*. London: Pinter.

Kaplan 1994: The coming anarchy. *Atlantic Monthly*, 273 (Feb), 44–76.

Karl, T. 1992: El Salvador's negotiated revolution. *Foreign Affairs* (Spring), 147–64.

Karp, A. 1994: The arms trade revolution: the major impact of small arms. *Washington Quarterly*, 17(4), 65–77.

Kaufmann, C. 1996: Possible and impossible solutions to ethnic civil wars. *International Security*, 20(4), 136–75.

Keashly, L. and Fisher, R. 1996: A contingency perspective on conflict interventions: theoretical and practical considerations. In Bercovitch (ed.), 235–61.

Keegan, J. 1993: *A History of Warfare*. New York: Alfred A. Knopf.

Keen, D. 1998: *The Economic Function of Violence in Civil Wars*, Adelphi Paper 320, London: International Institute for Strategic Studies.

Kelly, G. 1955: *A Theory of Personality: The Psychology of Personal Constructs*. New York: W. W. Norton.

Kelman, H. 1992: Informal mediation by the scholar/practitioner. In Bercovitch and Rubin (eds), 191–237.

Kelman, H. 1996: The interactive problem-solving approach. In Crocker and Hampson (eds), 500–20.

Kelman, H. 1997: Social-psychological dimensions of international conflict. In Zartman and Rasmussen (eds), 191–237.

Kelman, H. and Cohen, S. 1976: The problem-solving workshop: a social-psychological contribution to the resolution of international conflicts. *Journal of Peace Research*, 13(2), 79–90.

Kennedy, P. 1993: *Preparing for the Twenty First Century*. London: Harper Collins.

Keohane, R. and Nye, J. 1986: *Power and Interdependence*. Harvard: Harper Collins.

Kerman, C. 1974: *Creative Tension: The Life and Thought of Kenneth Boulding*. Ann Arbor: Michigan.

Keukeleire, S. 1994: The European Community and Conflict Management. In Bauwens and Reychler (eds), 137–79.

Kim, S. and Russett, B. 1996: The new politics of voting alignments in the United Nations General Assembly. *International Organization*, 50, 629–52.

King, C. 1997: *Ending Civil Wars*, Adelphi Paper 308, Oxford: Oxford University Press, for International Institute of Strategic Studies.

Krause, K. 1996: Armaments and conflict: the causes and consequences of 'military development'. In van de Goor, Rupesinghe and Sciarone (eds), 173–96.

Kressel, K. and Pruitt, D. (eds) 1989: *Mediation Research*. San Francisco: Jossey-Bass.

Kriesberg, L. 1973: *The Sociology of Social Conflicts*. Englewood Cliffs, NJ: Prentice-Hall.

Kriesberg, L. 1982: *Social Conflicts*. Englewood Cliffs, NJ: Prentice-Hall.

Kriesberg, L. 1991: Conflict resolution applications to peace studies. *Peace and Change* 16(4), 400–17.

Kriesberg, L. 1997: The development of the conflict resolution field. In Zartman and Rasmussen (eds), 51–77.

Kriesberg, L. 1998: *Reconciliation: Conceptual and Empirical Issues.* Paper given at the International Studies Association Annual Convention, Minneapolis, March.

Kriesberg, L., Northrup, A. and Thorson, S. (eds) 1989: *Intractable Conflicts and Their Transformation.* Syracuse, NY: Syracuse University Press.

Kritz, N. 1996: The rule of law in the postconflict phase: building a stable peace. In Crocker and Hampson (eds), 587–606.

Kritz, N. (ed.) 1995: *Transitional Justice: How Emerging Democracies Reckon with Former Regimes.* Washington, DC: United Nations Institute of Peace.

Krska, V. 1997: Peacekeeping in Angola (UNAVEM I and II). *International Peacekeeping,* 4(1), 75–97.

Kumar, K. (ed.) 1997: *Rebuilding Societies After Civil War: Critical Roles for International Assistance.* Boulder, CO: Lynne Rienner.

Kymlicka, W. 1995: *The Rights of Minority Cultures.* Oxford: Oxford University Press.

Lake, A. (ed.) 1990: *After the Wars: Reconstruction in Afghanistan, Indochina, Central America, South Africa and the Horn of Africa.* New Brunswick, NJ: Transaction Publishers.

Lake, D. and Rothchild, D. 1997: *The International Spread and Management of Ethnic Conflict.* Princeton: Princeton University Press.

Large, J. 1997: *The War Next Door: A Study of Second Track Intervention During the War in ex-Yugoslavia.* Stroud: Hawthorn Press.

Larsen, K. (ed.) 1993: *Conflict and Social Psychology.* London: Sage (PRIO).

Last, D. 1997: *Theory, Doctrine, and Practice of Conflict De-Escalation in Peacekeeping Operations.* Nova Scotia: Lester B. Pearson Canadian International Peacekeeping Training Centre.

Laue, J. 1990: The emergence and institutionalisation of third-party roles in conflict. In Burton and Dukes (eds), 256–72.

Lawler, P. 1995: *A Question of Values: Johan Galtung's Peace Research.* Boulder CO: Lynne Rienner.

Lederach, J. 1994: *Building Peace – Sustainable Reconciliation in Divided Societies.* Tokyo: United Nations University Press.

Lederach, J. 1995: *Preparing for Peace: Conflict Transformation Across Cultures.* New York: Syracuse University Press.

Lederach, J. 1995b: Conflict transformation in protracted internal conflicts: the case for a comprehensive framework. In Rupesinghe (ed.), 201–22.

Lederach, J. 1997: *Building Peace: Sustainable Reconciliation in Divided Societies.* Washington, DC: United States Institute of Peace.

Lederach, J. and Wehr, P. 1991: Mediating conflict in Central America. *Journal of Peace Research,* 28(1), 85–98.

Lentz, T. 1955: *Towards a Science of Peace.* New York: Bookman Associates.

LeVine, R. 1961: Anthropology and the study of conflict: an introduction. *Journal of Conflict Resolution,* 5(1), 5–15.

Levy, J. 1989: The causes of war: a review of theories and evidence. In Tetlock, Husbands, Jervis, Stern and Tilly (eds), 209–333.

Levy, J. 1996: Contending theories of international conflict: a levels-of-analysis approach. In Crocker and Hampson (eds), 3–24.

Lewer, N. and Schofield, S. 1997: *Non-Lethal Weapons: A Fatal Attraction?: Military Strategies and Technologies for 21st Century Conflict*. London: Zed Books.

Lewin, K. 1948: *Resolving Social Conflicts*. New York: Harper and Brothers.

Lichbach, M. 1989: An evaluation of 'does economic inequality breed conflict?' studies. *World Politics*, 41(4), 431–71.

Licklider, R. (ed.) 1993: *Stopping the Killing: How Civil Wars End*. New York: New York University Press.

Licklider, R. 1995: The consequences of negotiated settlements in civil wars 1945–1993. *American Political Science Review*, 89(3), 681–90.

Lijphart, A. 1968: *The Politics of Accommodation: Pluralism and Democracy in the Netherlands*. Berkeley: University of California Press.

Lijphart, A. 1977: *Democracy in Plural Societies*. New Haven, CT: Yale University Press.

Lijphart, A. 1995: Self-determination versus pre-determination of ethnic minorities in power-sharing systems. In Kymlicka (ed.), 275–87.

Lindgren, G., Wallensteen, G. and Nordquist, K. (eds) 1990: *Issues in Third World Conflict Resolution*. Uppsala: Department of Peace and Conflict Research.

Lizee, P. 1994: Peacekeeping, peacebuilding and the challenge of conflict resolution in Cambodia. In Charters (ed.), 135–48.

Londregan, J. and Poole, K. 1990: Poverty, the coup trap and the seizure of executive power. *World Politics*, 42(2), 151–83.

Luard, E. 1986: *War in International Society: A Study in International Sociology*. London: I. B. Tauris.

Lund, M. 1995: Underrating Preventive Diplomacy. *Foreign Affairs*, July/August, 160–3.

Lund, M. 1996: *Preventing Violent Conflicts*. Washington, DC: United States Institute of Peace.

Lund, M. 1996b: Preventive Diplomacy for Macedonia, 1992–1996: Containment Becomes Nation-Building. In Jentleson (ed.).

Lynn-Jones, S. and Miller, S. (eds) 1995: *Global Dangers*. Cambridge, MA: MIT Press.

Mack, A. 1985: *Peace Research in the 1980s*. Canberra: Australian National University.

Mackinlay, J. (ed.) 1996: *A Guide to Peace Support Operations*. Providence, RI: Brown University, Thomas J. Watson Jr. Institute for International Studies.

Macrae, J. and Zwi, A. (eds) 1994: *War and Hunger: Rethinking International Responses to Complex Emergencies*. London: Zed Books for Save the Children Fund (UK).

Madden, J. 1994: *Namibia: A Lesson for Success*. In Clements and Ward (eds), 255–60.

Magas, B. 1993: *The Destruction of Yugoslavia: Tracing the Break-Up 1980–92*. London: Verso.

Mak, T. 1995: The case against an International War Crimes Tribunal for former Yugoslavia. *International Peacekeeping*, 2(4), 536–63.

Malaquias, A. 1996: The UN in Mozambique and Angola: lessons learned. *International Peacekeeping*, 3(2), 87–103.

Mani, R. 1997: Conflict resolution, justice and the law: rebuilding the rule of law in the aftermath of complex political emergencies. Paper presented at the BISA

(British International Studies Association) Annual Conference, University of Leeds, December 1997.

Mansbach, R. and Vasquez, J. 1981: *In Search of Theory: A New Paradigm for Global Politics*. New York: Columbia University Press.

Mansfield, E. and Snyder, J. 1995: Democratization and the danger of war. *International Security*, 20(1), 5–38.

Martin, M. 1994: *Cambodia: A Shattered Society*. Los Angeles: University of California Press.

Maslow, H. 1954: *Motivation and Personality*. New York: Harper Bros.

Maxwell, J. and Maxwell, D. 1989: Male and female mediation styles and their effectiveness. Paper presented at the National Conference on Peacemaking and Conflict Resolution, Montreal, 28 Feb–5 March.

Mayall, J. (ed.) 1996: *The New Interventionism 1991–94: United Nations Experience in Cambodia, former Yugoslavia and Somalia*. Cambridge: Cambridge University Press.

Maynard, K. 1997: Rebuilding community: psychosocial healing, reintegration and reconciliation at grassroots level. In Kumar (ed.), 203–26.

McConnell, J. 1995: *Mindful Mediation: A Handbook for Buddhist Peacemakers*. Bangkok: Buddhist Research Institute.

McCoubrey, H. and White, N. 1995: *International Organizations and Civil Wars*. Aldershot: Dartmouth.

McDonald, J. and Bendahmane, D. 1987: *Conflict Resolution: Track Two Diplomacy*. Washington, DC: Institute for Multitrack Diplomacy.

McGarry, J. and O'Leary, B. (eds) 1993: *The Politics of Ethnic Conflict Regulation*. London: Routledge.

McGarry, J. and O'Leary, B. 1995: *Explaining Northern Ireland: Broken Images*. Oxford: Blackwell.

Medlicott, W. 1956: *Bismarck, Gladstone and the Concert of Europe*. London: Athlone Press.

Meron, T. 1993: The case for war crimes trials in Yugoslavia. *Foreign Affairs*, 72(3), 122–35.

Miall, H. 1991: *New Conflicts in Europe: Prevention and Resolution*, vol. 10. Oxford: Oxford Research Group Current Decisions Report.

Miall, H. 1992: *The Peacemakers: Peaceful Settlement of Disputes Since 1945*. London: Macmillan.

Miall, H. 1995: *Albania: Development and Conflict*. London: International Alert.

Miall, H. 1997: The OSCE role in Albania: a success for conflict prevention? *Helsinki Monitor*, December.

Miall, H. (ed.), 1994: *Minority Rights in Europe*. London: Pinter/Royal Institute of International Affairs.

Mickey, R. and Albion, A. 1993: Ethnic relations in the Republic of Macedonia. In I. Cuthbertson and J. Liebowitz (eds), *Minorities: The New Europe's Old Issue*. Prague: Institute for East–West Studies.

Midlarsky, M. (ed.) 1989: *Handbook of War Studies*. Boston: Unwin Hyman.

Mitchell, C. 1981: *The Structure of International Conflict*. London: Macmillan.

Mitchell, C. 1991: Classifying conflicts: asymmetry and resolution. *The Annals of the American Academy of Political and Social Science*, 518, 23–38.

Mitchell, C. 1993: Problem-solving exercises and theories of conflict resolution. In Sandole and van der Merwe (eds), 78–94.

Mitchell, C. 1995: Cutting losses: reflections on appropriate timing. Paper given at George Mason University.

Mitchell, C. and Banks, M. 1996: *Handbook of Conflict Resolution: The Analytical Problem-Solving Approach*. London: Pinter/Cassell.

Mitchell, C. and Webb, K. (eds) 1988: *New Approaches to International Mediation*. Westport, Conn: Greenwood Press.

Mitchell, P. 1995: Party competition in an ethnic dual party system. *Ethnic and Racial Studies*, 18(4), 773–93.

Mitrany, D. 1943: *A Working Peace System: An Argument for the Functional Development of International Organization*. New York: Oxford University Press.

Montgomery, T. 1995: *Revolution in El Salvador: From Civil Strife to Civil Peace*. Boulder, CO: Westview Press.

Montville, J. 1993: The healing function in political conflict resolution. In Sandole and van der Merwe (eds), 112–28.

Montville, J. (ed.) 1991: *Conflict and Peacemaking in Multiethnic Societies*. New York: Lexington Books.

Moore, J. 1972: *Law and the Indo-China War*. Princeton: Princeton University Press.

Moore, J. 1974: Towards an applied theory for the regulation of intervention. In Moore (ed.), 3–37.

Moore, J. (ed.) 1974: *Law and Civil War in the Modern World*. Baltimore: Johns Hopkins University Press.

Msabaha, I. 1995: Mozambique's murderous rebellion. In Zartman (ed.), 204–30.

Mueller, J. 1989: *Retreat from Doomsday: The Obsolescence of Major War*. New York: Basic Books.

Munck, R. 1986: *The Difficult Dialogue: Marxism and Nationalism*. London: Zed Books.

Muravchik, J. 1996: Promoting peace through democracy. In Crocker and Hampson (eds), pp. 573–86.

Newman, S. 1991: Does modernization breed ethnic conflict? *World Politics*, 43(3), 451–78.

Nordstrom, C. 1992: The backyard front. In Nordstrom and Martin (eds), 260–74.

Nordstrom, C. 1994: *Warzones: Cultures of Violence, Militarisation and Peace*. Canberra: Australian National University, Peace Research Center.

Nordstrom, C. 1995: Contested identities, essentially contested powers. In Rupesinghe (ed.), 93–111.

Nordstrom, C. and Martin, J. (eds) 1992: *The Paths to Domination, Resistance and Terror*. Berkeley: University of California Press.

Northrup, T. 1989: The dynamic of identity in personal and social conflict. In Kriesberg, Northrup and Thorson (eds), 35–82.

Nye, J. 1993: *Understanding International Conflicts: An Introduction to Theory and History*. New York: Harper Collins.

Ogata, S. 1993: *The State of the World's Refugees: The Challenge of Protection*. New York: Penguin.

Ogata, S. and Volcker, P. 1993: *Financing an Effective United Nations*. New York: Ford Foundation.

O'Leary, B. and McGarry, J. 1996: *The Politics of Antagonism: Understanding Northern Ireland*. London: Athlone.

Organski, A. 1958: *World Politics*. New York: Knopf.

Osgood, C. 1962: *An Alternative to War or Surrender*. Urbana: Urbana University Press.

Ottoway, M. 1995: Eritrea and Ethiopia: negotiations in a transitional conflict. In Zartman (ed.), 103–19.

Outram, Q. 1997: 'It's terminal either way': an analysis of armed conflict in Liberia 1989–1996. *Review of African Political Economy*, 73, 355–71.

Pankhurst, D. 1998: *Issues of Justice and Reconciliation in Complex Political Emergencies*. Paper given at the British International Studies Association Annual Conference, Leeds, December.

Paris, R. 1997: Peacebuilding and the limits of liberal internationalism. *International Security*, 22(2), 54–89.

Parker, M. 1996: The mental health of war-damaged populations. *War and Rural Development in Africa*, 27(3), 77–85.

Parsons, A. 1995: *From Cold War to Hot Peace: UN Interventions 1947–1995*. London: Penguin.

Peang-Meth, A. 1991: Understanding the Khmer: sociological-cultural observations. *Asian Survey*, 30(5), 442–55.

Pearce, J. 1986: *Promised Land: Peasant Rebellion in Chalatenango El Salvador*. London: Latin American Bureau.

Peck, C. 1993: *Preventive Diplomacy: A Perspective for the 1990s*. New York: Ralph Bunche Institute on the United Nations.

Peck, C. 1998: *Sustainable Peace: The Role of the UN and Regional Organizations in Preventing Conflict*. Lanham, NJ: Rowman and Littlefield.

Peirce, C. 1958: *Collected Papers*, vol. VII. Cambridge, MA: Harvard University Press, 89–164.

Pettifer, J. 1992: The new Macedonian question. *International Affairs*, 68(3), 475–85.

Petty, C. and Campbell, S. 1996: *Re-Thinking the Trauma of War*. London: Save the Children conference report.

Pillar, P. R. 1983: *Negotiating Peace: War Termination as a Bargaining Process*. Princeton: Princeton University Press.

PIOOM 1997: see Jongman and Schmid.

Ploughshares, Project 1995: *Armed Conflicts Report 1995*. Waterloo, Ont: Institute of Peace and Conflict Studies.

Porter, N. 1996: *Rethinking Unionism: An Alternative Vision for Northern Ireland*. Belfast: Blackstaff.

Posen, B. P. 1993: The security dilemma and ethnic conflict. In Brown (ed.), 103–24.

Poulton, H. 1995: *Who are the Macedonians?* London: Hurst and Co.

Prasso, S. 1995: Cambodia a three billion dollar boondoggle. *Bulletin of the Atomic Scientists*, 51(2), 36–40.

Prendergast, J. and Smock, D. 1996: *NGOs and the Peace Process in Angola*. Washington, DC: United States Institute of Peace.

Pruitt, D. and Rubin, J. 1986: *Social Conflict: Escalation, Stalemate and Settlement*. New York: Random House.

Prunier, G. 1995: *The Rwanda Crisis: History of a Genocide 1959–1994*. London: Hurst and Company.

Pugh, M. 1995: Peacebuilding as developmentalism: concepts from disaster research. *Contemporary Security Policy*, 16(3), 320–46.

Raiffa, H. 1982: *The Art and Science of Negotiation*. Cambridge, MA: Harvard University Press.

Raknerund, A. and Herge, H. 1997: The hazard of war: re-assessing the evidence for the democratic peace. *Journal of Peace Research*, 34, 385–404.

Ramsbotham, O. 1997: Humanitarian intervention 1990–5: a need to reconceptualize? *Review of International Studies*, 23, 445–67.

Ramsbotham, O. 1998: Islam, Christianity and forcible humanitarian intervention. *Ethics and International Affairs*, 12, 81–102.

Ramsbotham, O. and Woodhouse, T. 1996: *Humanitarian Intervention in Contemporary Conflict*. Cambridge: Polity.

Rapoport, A. 1967: *Fights, Games and Debates*. Ann Arbor, MI: University of Michigan Press.

Rapoport, A. 1971: Various conceptions of peace research. *Peace Research Society (International) Papers* XIX, 91–106.

Rapoport, A. 1989: *The Origins of Violence*. New York: Paragon House.

Rapoport, A. 1992: *Peace: An Idea Whose Time Has Come*. Ann Arbor, MI: University of Michigan Press.

Rapoport, A. and Chammah, A. 1965: *The Prisoner's Dilemma: A Study in Conflict and Cooperation*. Ann Arbor, MI: University of Michigan Press.

Rice, E. 1988: *Wars of the Third Kind: Conflict in Underdeveloped Countries*. Berkeley: University of California Press.

Richardson, L. 1960: *Arms and Insecurity*. Pittsburg, PA: Boxwood Press.

Richardson, L. 1960b: *Statistics of Deadly Quarrels*. Pittsburg, PA: Boxwood Press.

Rogers, P. and Dando, M. 1992: *A Violent Peace: Global Security after the Cold War*. London: Brassey's.

Rogers, P. and Ramsbotham, O. 1999: Peace research – past and future. *Political Studies* (forthcoming).

Rosecrance, R. 1986: *The Rise of the Trading State: Commerce and Conquest in the Modern World*. New York: Basic Books.

Ross, M. 1993: *The Culture of Conflict: Interpretations and Interests in Comparative Perspective*. New Haven: Yale University Press.

Rotberg, R. (ed.) 1996: *Vigilance and Vengeance: NGOs Preventing Ethnic Conflict in Divided Societies*. Washington, DC: Brookings Institution.

Rothman, J. 1992: *From Confrontation to Cooperation: Resolving Ethnic and Regional Conflict*. Newbury Park, CA: Sage.

Ruane, J. and Todd, J. 1996: *The Dynamics of Conflict in Northern Ireland*. Cambridge: Cambridge University Press.

Rubin, B. 1994: *Revolution Until Victory? The Politics and History of the PLO*. Cambridge, MA and London: Harvard University Press.

Rubin, B. 1996: *Towards Comprehensive Peace in Southeast Europe: Conflict Prevention in the Southern Balkans*. New York: Twentieth Century Fund. Report of the South Balkans Working Group of the Council on Foreign Relations Center for Preventive Action.

Rufin, J. 1993: The paradoxes of armed protection. In Jean (ed.), 11–23.

Rule, J. 1988: *Theories of Civil Violence*. Berkeley: University of California Press.

Rummel, R. 1970: *Applied Factor Analysis*. Evanston, IL: Northwestern University Press.

Rummell, R. 1996: *Common Foreign and Security Policy and Conflict Prevention*. London: Saferworld and International Alert.

Rupesinghe, K. 1996: *General Principles of Multi-Track Diplomacy*. London: International Alert.

Rupesinghe, K. 1996b: Teaching the elephant to dance: developing a new agenda at the UN. In Y. Sakomoto (ed.), *Global Transformation: Challenges to the State System*. Tokyo: United Nations University.

Rupesinghe, K. (ed.) 1995: *Conflict Transformation*. London: Macmillan.

Russett, B. 1993: *Grasping the Democratic Peace: Principles for a Post-Cold War World*. Princeton, NJ: Princeton University Press.

Ryan, S. 1990: *Ethnic Conflict and International Relations*. Brookfield, VT: Dartmouth.

Saferworld 1996: *Angola: Conflict Resolution and Peace-Building*. London: Saferworld.

Sahnoun, M. 1994: *Somalia: The Missed Opportunities*. Washington, DC: United States Institute of Peace.

Salem, P. 1993: In theory: a critique of western conflict resolution from a non-western perspective. *Negotiation Journal*, 9(4), 361–9.

Salem, P. (ed.) 1997: *Conflict Resolution in the Arab World: Selected Essays*. New York: American University of Beirut.

Sandole, D. and Sandole-Saroste, I. 1987: *Conflict Management and Problem Solving: Interpersonal to International Applications*. Manchester: Manchester University Press.

Sandole, D. and van der Merwe, H. (eds) 1993: *Conflict Resolution Theory and Practice: Integration and Application*. Manchester: Manchester University Press.

Schelling. T. 1960: *The Strategy of Conflict*. Cambridge, MA: Harvard University Press.

Schmeidl, S. and Adelman, H. (eds) 1997: *Synergy in Early Warning: Conference Proceedings*, Toronto: Centre for International and Security Studies, York University.

Schmid, A. 1997: Early Warning of Violent Conflicts. In P. Schmid (ed.), *Violent Crime and Conflicts*, Milan: ISPAC (International Scientific and Professional Advisory Council of the United Nations Crime Prevention and Criminal Justice Programme).

Schmid, H. 1968: Peace research and politics. *Journal of Peace Research*, 5(3), 217–32.

Schöpflin, G. 1994: *Politics in Eastern Europe*. London: Blackwell.

Schuett, O. 1997: The International War Crimes Tribunal for the Former Yugoslavia and the Dayton Peace Agreement: peace versus justice? *International Peacekeeping*, 4(2), 91–114.

Serbe, G., Macrae, J. and Wohlgemuth, L. 1997: *NGOs in Conflict – An Evaluation of International Alert*. Fantoft-Bergen, Norway: Christian Michelsen Institute.

Sharp, G. 1973: *The Politics of Nonviolent Action*. Boston: Porter Sargent.

Sharp, J. 1997/8: Dayton report card. *International Security*, 22(3), 101–37.

Shear, J. 1996: Bosnia's post-Dayton traumas. *Foreign Policy*, 104 (Fall), 87–101.

Sherif, M. 1966: *In Common Predicament: Social Psychology, Intergroup Conflict and Cooperation*. Boston: Houghton Mifflin.

Sherman, F. 1987: *Pathway to Peace: The United Nations and the Road to Nowhere*. Pennsylvania: Pennsylvania State University.

Shlaim, A. 1995: *War and Peace in the Middle East: A Concise History*. London: Penguin.

Shue, H. 1980: *Basic Rights: Subsistence, Affluence and US Foreign Policy*. Princeton: Princeton University Press.

Siccama, J. G. 1996: *Conflict Prevention and Early Warning in the Political Practice of International Organizations*. The Hague: Netherlands Institute of International Relations 'Clingendael'.

Simmel, G. 1902: The number of members as determining the sociological form of the group. *American Journal of Sociology*, 8, 158–96.

Singer, D. 1996: Armed conflict in the former colonial regions: from classification to explanation. In van de Goor, Rupesinghe and Sciarone (eds), 35–49.

Singer, D. and Small, M. 1968: Alliance aggregation and the onset of war 1815–1945. In Singer (ed.), *Quantitative International Politics: Insights and Evidence*. New York: Free Press, 247–86.

Singer, D. and Small, M. 1972: *The Wages of War, 1816–1965: A Statistical Handbook*. New York: Wiley.

SIPRI Yearbook: 1997. Oxford: Oxford University Press (Stockholm International Peace Research Institute).

Sisk, T. 1996: *Power Sharing and International Mediation in Ethnic Conflicts*. Washington, DC: United States Institute of Peace.

Sites, P. 1990: Needs as analogues of emotions. In Burton (ed.), 7–33.

Skjelsbaek, K. 1991: The UN Secretary General and the mediation of international disputes. *Journal of Peace Research*, 28(1), 99–115.

Slim, H. 1997: *Doing the Right Thing: Relief Agencies, Moral Dilemmas and Moral Responsibility in Political Emergencies and War*. Uppsala: Nordiska Afrikainstitutet, Studies on Emergencies and Disaster Relief, No. 6.

Smith, A. 1986: *The Ethnic Origins of Nations*. Oxford: Blackwell.

Smith, A. 1995: *Nations and Nationalism in a Global Era*. Cambridge: Polity Press.

Smith, C. 1996: *Palestine and the Arab–Israeli Conflict*. New York: St Martin's Press.

Smith, J. 1995: *Stopping Wars: Defining the Obstacles to Cease-fire*. Boulder, CO: Westview.

Smock, D. and Crocker, C. 1995: *African Conflict Resolution: The US Role in Peacemaking*. Washington, DC: United States Institute of Peace.

Snow, D. 1996: *Uncivil Wars: International Security and the New Internal Conflicts*. Boulder, CO: Lynne Rienner.

Sollom, R. and Kew, D. 1996: *Humanitarian Assistance and Conflict Prevention in Burundi*. In Rotberg (ed.), 235–59.

Solomon, R. 1997: The global information revolution and international conflict management. Overview presentation to the conference on 'Virtual Diplomacy', Washington, DC, United States Institute of Peace, April.

Sorokin, P. 1937: *Social and Cultural Dynamics*. New York: American Books.

South Commission 1990: *The Challenge to the South*. Oxford: Oxford University Press.

Stamato, L. 1992: Voice, place and process: research on gender, negotiation and conflict resolution. *Mediation Quarterly*, 9(4), 375–86.

Stavenhagen, R. 1996: *Ethnic Conflicts and the Nation-State*. Houndmills: Macmillan.

Stedman, S. 1991: *Peacemaking in Civil War: International Mediation in Zimbabwe, 1974–1980*. Boulder, CO: Lynne Rienner.

Stedman, S. 1995: Alchemy for a New World Order: overselling 'preventive diplomacy'. *Foreign Affairs*, 74 (May/June), 14–20.

Stedman, S. 1997: Spoiler problems in peace processes. *International Security*, 22(2), 5–53.

Stewart, R. 1993: *Broken Lives: A Personal View of the Bosnian Conflict*. London: Harper Collins.

Stiehm, J. 1995: Men and women in peacekeeping: a research note. *International Peacekeeping*, 2(4), 564–9.

Stuart, D. 1994: United Nations involvement in the peace process in El Salvador. In Clements and Ward (eds), 261–72.

Suganami, H. 1996: *On the Causes of War*. Oxford: Clarendon Press.

Sullivan, J. 1994: How peace came to El Salvador. *Orbis*, 38(1), 83–98.

Summerfield, D. 1996: *The Impact of War and Atrocity on Civilian Populations: Basic Principles for NGO Interventions and a Critique of Psychosocial Trauma Projects*. London: Overseas Development Institute.

Sumner, W. 1906: *Folkways*. New York: Ginn.

Susskind, L. 1987: *Breaking the Impasse: Consensual Approaches to Resolving Public Disputes*. New York: Basic Books.

Taylor, A. and Miller, J. (eds) 1994: *Conflict and Gender*. Cresskill, NJ: Hampton Press.

Tajfel, H. (ed.) 1978: *Differentiation Between Social Groups: Studies in the Social Psychology of Intergroup Relations*. London: Academic Press. European Monographs in Social Psychology, No. 14.

Tetlock, P., Husbands, J., Jervis, R., Stern, P. and Tilly, C. (eds) 1989: *Behaviour, Society and Nuclear War*. Oxford: Oxford University Press.

Tilly, C. 1978: *From Mobilization to Revolution*. Reading, MA: Addison-Wesley.

Touval, S. 1985: *The Peace Brokers; Mediators in the Arab–Israeli Conflict, 1948–1979*. Princeton: Princeton University Press.

Touval, S. 1992: The study of conflict resolution: is there unity in diversity? *Negotiation Journal*, 8(2), 147–52.

Touval, S. 1994: Why the UN fails. *Foreign Affairs*, 73(5), 44–57.

Touval, S. and Zartman, W. (eds) 1985: *International Mediation: Theory and Practice*. Boulder, CO: Westview Press.

Trachtenberg, M. 1993: Intervention in historical perspective. In L. Reed and C. Kaysen (eds), *Emerging Norms of Justified Intervention*. Cambridge, MA: American Academy of Arts and Sciences, 15–36.

Travers, D. 1993: The use of Article 99 of the Charter by the Secretary-General. In House of Commons Foreign Affairs Committee, *Third Report*, Session 1992–3, vol. II, HC235-II, 336–57.

Troebst, S. 1998. *Conflict in Kosovo: Failure of Prevention? An Analytical Documentation, 1992–1998*. European Centre for Minority Issues, Flensburg, 1998.

Ugglas, M. 1994: Conditions for successful preventive diplomacy. In S. Carlsson (ed.), *The Challenge of Preventive Diplomacy: The Experience of the CSCE*. Stockholm: Ministry of Foreign Affairs, Norstedts Tryckeri AB, 11–32.

UNDP 1996: *Human Development Index 1996*. New York: United Nations Development Programme.

UNHCR 1995: *The State of the World's Refugees*. Oxford: Oxford University Press.

UNIDIR 1996: *Managing Arms in Peace Processes: The Issues.* Geneva: United Nations Publications.

United Nations 1992: *Report of the Secretary-General on the United Nations Observer Mission in El Salvador,* New York: UN Department of Public Information.

United Nations 1993: *The Truth Commission Report: From Madness to Hope, The 12-Year War in El Salvador.* New York: UN Department of Public Information.

United Nations 1994: *Report of the Secretary-General on the UN Observer Mission in El Salvador.* New York: UN Department of Public Information.

United Nations 1995: *The United Nations and El Salvador, 1990–1995.* New York: UN Department of Public Information.

United Nations 1996: *The Blue Helmets: A Review of United Nations Peace-Keeping.* New York: UN Department of Public Information.

United Nations 1996b: *Report of the Secretary-General on the United Nations Angola Verification Mission (UNAVEM III), 27 June 1996.* New York: UN Department of Information.

United Nations 1996c: *The United Nations and Rwanda, 1993–1996.* New York: UN Department of Information.

United Nations Blue Book Series 1996: Vol II: *The United Nations and Cambodia.* Vol. V: *The United Nations and Mozambique.* New York: UN.

United Nations Security Council 1992: *Second Special Report of the Secretary-General on the United Nations Transitional Authority in Cambodia.* New York: UN Department of Information.

Utting, P. 1994: *Between Hope and Insecurity: The Social Consequences of the Cambodian Peace Process.* Geneva: UNRISD.

van Creveld, M. 1991: *The Transformation of War.* New York: The Free Press.

van de Goor, L., Rupesinghe, K. and Sciarone, P. (eds) 1996: *Between Development and Destruction: An Enquiry into the Causes of Conflict in Post-Colonial States.* New York: St Martin's Press.

van den Dungen, P. 1996: Initiatives for the pursuit and institutionalisation of peace research. In L. Broadhead (ed.), *Issues in Peace Research.* Bradford: Department of Peace Studies, University of Bradford, 5–32.

van der Merwe, H. 1989: *Pursuing Justice and Peace in South Africa.* London: Routledge.

van der Stoel, M. 1994: The role of the CSCE High Commissioner on National Minorities in CSCE preventive diplomacy. In S. Carlson (ed.), *The Challenge of Preventive Diplomacy.* Stockholm: Ministry for Foreign Affairs, 33–54.

van Evera, S. 1994: Hypotheses on nationalism and war. *International Security,* 18(4), 5–39.

van Tongeren, P. (ed.) 1996: *Prevention and Management of Conflicts: An International Directory.* The Hague: Dutch Centre for Conflict Prevention.

Vasquez, J. 1993: *The War Puzzle.* Cambridge: Cambridge University Press.

Vasquez, J. 1995: Why global conflict resolution is possible: meeting the challenge of the new world order. In Vasquez, Johnson, Jaffe and Stamato (eds), 131–53.

Vasquez, J. 1987: The steps to war: toward a scientific explanation of correlates of war findings. *World Politics* 40 (October), 108–45.

Vasquez, J., Johnson, J., Jaffe, S. and Stamato, L. (eds) 1995: *Beyond Confrontation: Learning Conflict Resolution in the Post-Cold War Era.* Ann Arbor: University of Michigan Press.

Vassall Adams, G. 1994: *Rwanda: An Agenda for International Action*. Oxford: Oxfam.

Vayrynen, R. 1984: Regional conflict formations: an intractable problem of international relations. *Journal of Peace Research*, 21(4), 337–59.

Vayrynen, R. (ed.) 1991: *New Directions in Conflict Theory: Conflict Resolution and Conflict Transformation*. London: Sage.

Vickers, M. 1995: *The Albanians, A Modern History*. London: I. B. Tauris.

Vickers, M. 1998: *Between Serb and Albanian: A History of Kosovo*. London: Hurst.

Vickers, M. and Pettifer, J. 1997: *From Anarchy to a Balkan Identity*. London: Hurst and Co.

Vives, A. 1994: *No Democracy Without Money: The Road to Peace in Mozambique*. London: Catholic Institute for International Relations.

Volkan, J., Montville, J. and Julius, D. (eds) 1991: *The Psychodynamics of International Relationships*, vol. II. Lexington, MA: D. C. Heath.

Wallace, M. 1977: Arms races and escalation: some new evidence. *Journal of Conflict Resolution*, 23, 3–16.

Wallensteen, P. 1984: Universalism vs. particularism: on the limits of major power order. *Journal of Peace Research*, 21(3), 243–57.

Wallensteen, P. (ed.) 1988: *Peace Research: Achievements and Challenges*. Boulder/London: Westview Press.

Wallensteen, P. and Axell, K. 1995: Armed conflict at the end of the Cold War, 1989–93. *Journal of Peace Research*, 30(3), 331–46.

Wallensteen, P. and Sollenberg, M. 1996: After the Cold War: emerging patterns of armed conflicts. *Journal of Peace Research*, 32(3), 345–60.

Wallensteen, P. and Sollenberg, M. 1997: Armed conflicts, conflict termination and peace agreements 1989–96. *Journal of Peace Research*, 34(3), 339–58.

Wallerstein, I. 1979: *The Capitalist World Economy*. Cambridge: Cambridge University Press.

Walton, R. and McKersie, R. 1965: *A Behavioral Theory of Labor Negotiations: An Analysis of a Social Interaction System*. New York: McGraw-Hill.

Waltz, K. 1959: *Man, the State and War*. New York: Columbia University Press.

Waltz, K. 1979: *Theory of International Politics*. Reading, MA: Addison-Wesley.

Webb, K., Koutrakou, V. and Walters, M. 1996: The Yugoslavian conflict, European mediation and the contingency model: a critical perspective. In Bercovitch (ed.), 171–89.

Wehr, P. 1979: *Conflict Regulation*. Boulder, CO: Westview Press.

Wehr, P. and Lederach, J. 1996: Mediating conflict in Central America. In Bercovitch (ed.), 55–74.

Weiss, T. and Collins, C. 1996: *Humanitarian Challenges and Intervention: World Politics and the Dilemmas of Help*. Boulder, CO: Westview Press.

White, N. 1993: *Keeping the Peace: The United Nations and the Maintenance of International Peace and Security*. Manchester: Manchester University Press, Melland Schill Monographs in International Law.

Whitman, J. and Pocock, D. (eds) 1996: *After Rwanda: The Co-ordination of United Nations Humanitarian Assistance*. London: Macmillan.

Whyte, J. 1990: *Interpreting Northern Ireland*. Oxford: Clarendon Press.

Wider Peacekeeping 1995. British Army Field Manual, Vol. 5. London: HMSO.

Wilkinson, P. 1996: *Peace Support Operations*. London: Joint Warfare Publication 3.01.

Williams, D. and Young, T. 1994: Governance, the World Bank and liberal theory. *Policy Studies*, 42.

Williams, S. and Williams, S. 1994: *Being in the Middle by Being at the Edge: Quaker Experience of Non-Official Political Mediation*. London: Quaker Peace and Service.

Woodhouse, T. 1991: *Peacemaking in a Troubled World*. Oxford: Berg.

Woodhouse, T. 1996: Commentary, negotiating a new millennium? Prospects for African conflict resolution. *Review of African Political Economy* 68, 129–37.

Woodhouse, T. and Ramsbotham, O. 1996: *Peacekeeping: Terra Incognita – Here be Dragons – Peacekeeping and Conflict Resolution in Contemporary Conflict: Some Relationships Considered*. University of Ulster: INCORE/ United Nations University.

Woodward, S. 1995: *Balkan Tragedy: Chaos and Dissolution After the Cold War*. Washington, DC: Brookings Institution.

Wright, Q. 1942: *A Study of War*. Chicago: University of Chicago Press.

Yarrow, C. H. 1978: *Quaker Experiences in International Conciliation*. New Haven, CT: Yale University Press.

Young, O. 1967: *The Intermediaries: Third Parties in International Crises*. Princeton: Princeton University Press.

Zaagman, R. and Thorburn, J. 1997: *The Role of the High Commissioner on National Minorities in OSCE Conflict Prevention*. The Hague: Foundation on Inter-Ethnic Relations.

Zartman, W. 1985: *Ripe for Resolution: Conflict and Intervention in Africa*. New York: Oxford University Press.

Zartman, W. 1997: Toward the resolution of international conflicts. In Zartman and Rasmussen (eds), 3–22.

Zartman, W. (ed.) 1978: *The Negotiation Process: Theories and Applications*. Beverly Hills, CA: Sage.

Zartman, W. (ed.) 1996: *Elusive Peace: Negotiating an End to Civil Wars*. Washington, DC: Brookings Institution.

Zartman, W. and Rasmussen, J. (eds) 1997: *Peacemaking in International Conflict: Methods and Techniques*. Washington, DC: United States Institute of Peace.

Zartman, W. and Rubin, J. 1996: *Power and Asymmetry in International Negotiations*. Laxenburg, Austria: International Institute of Applied Systems Analysis.

Index

13; international pressure on 164;
and mediation 160, settlement by
negotiation 155; statistics 27
sovereignty 47; breakdown in fixed
structures of 4; human rights
violations 208–9; reconciliation
210; and the state 84
South Tyrol 234
Soviet Union, former: responses to
break-up of communist rule 120
spoilers 3, 166, 204, 219, 222; Israel–
Palestine 176; Northern Ireland
180, 181–2; South Africa 172–3
Spratly Islands 117
Stability Pact (EU) 117
stand-off, bipolar 68, 70, 103–4
state, the 74, 78; disarticulation with
society 73, 85–6; Latin America
82–3; and PSC 84–8
Stedman, Stephen 114
Stoel, Max van der 99, 109–11
structural relationships 14–15, 73,
108, 222–3
structurationist theory 58
symmetric/asymmetric conflict,
principle of 12–14, 15–17; and
culture question 63

Taylor, Charles 131
third party involvement 9–13, 33–8,
198–200, 214; and autonomy 223;
controversy 3, 140; and mediation
158–62; objectives 147; and peace
processes 201; regional 82, 109; see
also coercive/non-coercive
intervention
'threat power' (K. Boulding) 10, 12,
221
'Tit-for-Tat' strategy (Rapaport) 8,
225
Transnational Foundation for Peace
and Future Research 211, 213
Tudjman, Franjo 90
'200-year present' (E. Boulding) 55–6

United Nations 34, 35–7; and
Albania 123; and Angola 197,
200–1; and Cambodia 193, 197,
200–4, 213; and Central America
235; conflict management 161; and
conflict prevention 117;

departments 36, 197–8; and El
Salvador 142, 196–7, 200, 207–9;
and end of Cold War 2;
humanitarian concerns 144–5; and
Liberia 235; and Mozambique 200;
and Namibia 195–6, 198, 200;
peacebuilding 185–6, 194–214;
peacekeeping 141–2; Register of
Conventional Arms 137;
resolutions 140; and Rwanda
133–8, 214, 232, 235; Security
Council 35, 36, 135, 136, 195; and
Somalia 214, 235: and South Africa
208–9; and Yugoslavia (former)
114, 121,141, 142, 211–13, 214,
235
United States: and Bosnia 161; and
Central America 161; as conflict
manager 140–1; and Israel 173;
and Northern Ireland 179
'universalist/particularist' periods
(international relations) 103–4

Vergesellschaftung 235
'vertical/horizontal legitimacy' (Azar)
85
violence: 'cultures of' 132–3, 203–4;
direct/structural/cultural 15, 43, 44,
187; 'economies of' 131–2, 155
violent conflict 23, 32–3, 44, 58–9,
87, 233; definition 21; ending of
153–5; prevention 95–6, 109–27
Vranitzky, Franz 124

Wales 231
war: causes 97–100; endings 152–83;
preventors 96–108
war zones 129–33
win–lose/lose–lose/win–win outcomes
5–8, 12, 109
women 60–1; see also *names of
individual women in conflict
resolution*
World Bank 117, 198
Wright, Philip Quincy 40, 95, 228

Yugoslavia, former 96: EU and 117,
118–19; failures of strategy 88–9;
peacemaking in war zone 133, 234;

Introduction to Environmental Impact Assessment

4th edition

Introduction to Environmental Impact Assessment provides students and practitioners with a clearly structured overview of the subject, as well as critical analysis and support for further studies. Written by three authors with extensive research, training and practical experience in EIA, the book covers the latest EIA legislation, guidance and good practice.

This edition updates essential information on:

- the evolving nature of EIA;
- experience of the implementation of the changing EU and UK EIA procedures;
- best practice in the EIA process;
- other key issues in the process, explored in an extended case studies section;
- comparative EIA systems worldwide;
- development of SEA/SA legislation and practice;
- prospects for the future of EIA.

Although the book's focus is on the UK and the EU, the principles and techniques it describes are applicable internationally. With colour images and a new modern design, the book provides an essential introduction to EIA for undergraduate and postgraduate students on planning courses, as well as those studying environmental management and policy, environmental sciences, geography and the built environment. Planners, developers, community groups and decision-makers in government and business will also welcome the book as an effective way to get to grips with this important and evolving subject that affects a wide range of development projects.

John Glasson is Emeritus Professor of Environmental Planning, Founding Director of the Impacts Assessment Unit (IAU) and of the Oxford Institute for Sustainable Development (OISD), at Oxford Brookes University. He is also Visiting Professor at Curtin University in Western Australia.

Riki Therivel is Visiting Professor at Oxford Brookes University, a Senior Research Associate in the IAU and partner in Levett-Therivel sustainability consultants. Both Riki Therivel and John Glasson were appointed Commissioners of the UK Infrastructure Planning Commission (IPC).

Andrew Chadwick is Senior Research Associate in the IAU.

The Natural and Built Environment Series

Editor: Professor John Glasson
Oxford Brookes University

http://www.routledge.com/cw/nbe/

Introduction to Environmental Impact Assessment

4th edition

John Glasson, Riki Therivel
and Andrew Chadwick

Routledge
Taylor & Francis Group

LONDON AND NEW YORK

First edition published 1994
by UCL Press

Second edition published 1999
by UCL Press

Third edition published 2005
by Routledge

This edition first published 2012
by Routledge
2 Park Square, Milton Park, Abingdon, Oxon OX14 4RN

Simultaneously published in the USA and Canada
by Routledge
711 Third Avenue, New York, NY 10017

Routledge is an imprint of the Taylor & Francis Group, an informa business

© 2005, 2012 John Glasson, Riki Therivel and Andrew Chadwick

British Library Cataloguing in Publication Data
A catalogue record for this book is available from the British Library

Library of Congress Cataloging in Publication Data
Glasson, John
   Introduction to environmental impact assessment / John Glasson,
   Riki Therivel and Andrew Chadwick. — 4th ed.
   p. cm. — (The natural and built environment series)
   Includes bibliographical references and index.
   1. Environmental impact assessment—Great Britain. 2. Environmental
   impact assessment. I. Therivel, Riki II. Chadwick, Andrew III. Title.
   TD194.68.G7G58 2012
   333.71′4—dc23   2011026482

ISBN: 978–0–415–66468–4 (hbk)
ISBN: 978–0–415–66470–7 (pbk)

Typeset in Stone Serif and Akzidenz Grotesk
by Florence Production Ltd, Stoodleigh, Devon
Printed by Ashford Colour Press Ltd., Gosport, Hampshire

In memory of Clive Briffett and Joe Weston,
two very good friends and colleagues

Contents

Preface to the first edition

There has been a remarkable and refreshing interest in environmental issues over the past few years. A major impetus was provided by the 1987 Report of the World Commission on the Environment and Development (the Brundtland Report); the Rio Summit in 1992 sought to accelerate the impetus. Much of the discussion on environmental issues and on sustainable development is about the better management of current activity in harmony with the environment. However, there will always be pressure for new development. How much better it would be to avoid or mitigate the potential harmful effects of future development on the environment at the planning stage. Environmental impact assessment (EIA) assesses the impacts of planned activity on the environment in advance, thereby allowing avoidance measures to be taken: prevention is better than cure.

Environmental impact assessment was first formally established in the USA in 1969. It has spread worldwide and received a significant boost in Europe with the introduction of an EC Directive on EIA in 1985. This was implemented in the UK in 1988. Subsequently there has been a rapid growth in EIA activity, and over 300 environmental impact statements (EISs) are now produced in the UK each year. EIA is an approach in good currency. It is also an area where many of the practitioners have limited experience. This text provides a comprehensive introduction to the various dimensions of EIA. It has been written with the requirements of both undergraduate and postgraduate students in mind. It should also be of considerable value to those in practice – planners, developers and various interest groups. EIA is on a rapid 'learning curve'; this text is offered as a point on the curve.

The book is structured into four parts. The first provides an introduction to the principles of EIA and an overview of its development and agency and legislative context. Part 2 provides a step-by-step discussion and critique of the EIA process. Part 3 examines current practice, broadly in the UK and in several other countries, and in more detail through selected UK case studies. Part 4 considers possible future developments. It is likely that much more of the EIA iceberg will become visible in the 1990s and beyond. An outline of important and associated developments in environmental auditing and in strategic environmental assessment concludes the text.

Although the book has a clear UK orientation, it does draw extensively on EIA experience worldwide, and it should be of interest to readers from many countries. The book seeks to highlight best practice and to offer enough insight to methods, and to supporting references, to provide valuable guidance to the practitioner. For information on detailed methods for assessment of impacts in particular topic areas (e.g. landscape, air quality, traffic impacts), the reader is referred to the complementary volume, *Methods of environmental impact assessment* (Morris and Therivel, 1995, London, UCL Press).

John Glasson
Riki Therivel
Andrew Chadwick
Oxford Brookes University

Preface to the fourth edition

The aims and scope of this fourth edition are unchanged from those of the first edition. However, as noted in the preface to the first edition, EIA continues to evolve and adapt, and any commentary on the subject must be seen as part of a continuing discussion. The worldwide spread of EIA is becoming even more comprehensive. In the European Union there is now over 25 years' experience of the implementation of the pioneering EIA Directive, including 10 years' experience of the important 1999 amendments. There has been considerable interest in the development of the EIA process, in strengthening perceived areas of weakness, in extending the scope of activity and also in assessing effectiveness. Reflecting such changes, this fully revised edition updates the commentary by introducing and developing a number of issues that are seen as of growing importance to both the student and the practitioner of EIA.

The structure of the first edition has been retained, plus much of the material from the third edition, but considerable variations and additions have been made to specific sections. In Part 1 (on principles and procedures), the importance of an adaptive EIA, plus the burgeoning range of EA activity, are addressed further. In the EU context, the implementation of the amended EIA Directive is discussed more fully, including the divergent practice across the widening range of Member States. The specific new 2011 regulations and procedures operational in the UK are set out in Chapter 3. In Part 2 (discussion of the EIA process), most elements have been updated, including screening and scoping, alternatives, impact identification, prediction, participation and presentation, mitigation and enhancement, and monitoring and auditing.

We have made major changes to Part 3 (overview of practice), drawing on the findings of important reviews of EIA effectiveness and operation in practice. For example, Chapter 8 includes much new material on the implication of legal challenges in EIA. Chapter 9 includes some new practice case studies. Most of the case studies are UK-based and involve EIA at the individual project level, although two examples of SEA are also discussed, plus new topics such as health impact assessment. While it is not claimed that the selected case studies all represent best examples of EIA practice, they do include some novel and innovative approaches towards particular issues in EIA, such as new methods of public participation and the treatment of cumulative effects. They also draw attention to some of the limitations of the process in practice. Chapter 10 (Comparative practice) has also had a major revision, reflecting, for example, growing experience in African countries, China and countries in transition, and major reviews for some well-established EIA systems in, for example, Canada and Australia.

Part 4 of the book (Prospects) has also been substantially revised to reflect some of the changing prospects for EIA. Chapter 11 discusses the need for strategic environmental assessment (SEA) and some of its limitations. It reviews the status of SEA in the USA, European Union and UNECE, and China. It then discusses in more detail how the European SEA Directive is being implemented in the UK. It concludes with the results of recent research into the effectiveness of the SEA Directive. Chapter 12 has been extensively revised and extended. It includes, for example, more consideration of cumulative impacts, socio-economic impacts, health impact assessment, equalities impact assessment, appropriate assessment, the new area of resilience thinking, and the vitally important topic of planning for climate change in EIA, plus possible shifts towards more integrated assessment. The chapter concludes with a discussion of the parallel and complementary development of environmental management systems and audits. Together, these topics act as a kind of action list for future improvements to EIA. This chapter in particular, but also much else in the book, draws on some of the findings of recent reviews of EIA practice undertaken by, among others, the EC, the IAIA (International Association for Impact Assessment) and the IEMA (the Institute of Environmental Management and Assessment).

The Appendices include the full versions of the amended EIA Directive and the SEA Directive, a revised IAU EIS review package, and a guide to key EIA journals and websites worldwide.

John Glasson
Riki Therivel
Andrew Chadwick
Oxford 2011

Acknowledgements

• •

Our grateful thanks are due to many people without whose help this book would not have been produced. We are particularly grateful for the tolerance and moral support of our families. Our thanks also go to Rob Woodward for his production of many of the illustrations. In addition, Louise Fox of Taylor and Francis, and copy-editor Rosalind Davies, and editorial assistant Aimee Miles have provided vital contributions in turning the manuscript into the innovative published document. We are very grateful to our consultancy clients and research sponsors, who have underpinned the work of the Impacts Assessment Unit in the School of Planning at Oxford Brookes University (formerly Oxford Polytechnic). In particular we wish to record the support of UK government departments (variously DoE, DETR, ODPM and DCLG), the EC Environment Directorate, the Economic and Social Research Council (ESRC), the Royal Society for the Protection of Birds (RSPB), many local and regional authorities, and especially the various branches of the UK energy industry that provided the original impetus to and continuing positive support for much of our EIA research and consultancy.

Our students at Oxford Brookes University on both undergraduate and postgraduate programmes have critically tested many of our ideas. In this respect we would like to acknowledge, in particular, the students on the MSc course in Environmental Assessment and Management. The editorial and presentation support for the fourth edition by the staff at Taylor and Francis is very gratefully acknowledged. We have benefited from the support of colleagues in the Schools of Planning and Biological and Molecular Sciences, and from the wider community of EIA academics, researchers and consultants, who have helped to keep us on our toes. We are grateful to Angus Morrison-Saunders for some very useful pointers in his most constructive review of our third edition, and to Shanshan Yang for advice on the evolving approach to EIA in China. We owe particular thanks in this edition for the willingness of Josh Fothergill at IEMA, and Kim Chowns at DCLG, to provide advance copies of the IEMA 2011 Report on UK EIA practice, and the new 2011 DCLG EIA Regulations and Guidance. We are also grateful for permission to use material from the following sources:

British Association of Nature Conservationists (cartoons: Parts 2 and 3)
RPS, Symonds/EDAW and Magnox Electric (Plate 1.1)
EIA Review (Figure 1.9)
ENDS (Tables 3.1 and 3.2)
Scottish government (Figures 4.1 and 4.2)
Pattersons Quarries (Figure 4.3)
South Yorkshire Integrated Transport Authority (Figure 4.6)
Scottish Power Systems (Figure 4.8)
IEMA (Figure 5.1 and 12.6, Tables 8.5, 12.4, 12.6 and 12.7)
EDF Energy, Southampton Daily Echo, Guardian Newspaper (Figure 6.1)
Metropolitan Council (Minneapolis/St Paul), AREVA Resources Canada , Griff Wigley, Evelop (Figure 6.2)
University of Manchester, EIA Centre (Appendix 4)
Olympic Delivery Authority (Figure 7.7)
Highlands and Islands Enterprise (Figure 9.3)
John Wiley & Sons (Table 6.2)
Baseline Environmental Consulting, West Berkeley, California (Figure 7.2)
UK Department of Environment (Table 6.3)
UK Department of Communities and Local Government (Tables 3.5, 3.6 and 3.7; Appendix 2)

Planning newspaper (cartoon: Part 4)

Beech Tree Publishing (Figure 7.8)

European Commission (Table 4.3, Box 11.1, Table 12.5)

West Australian Environmental Protection Agency (Table 10.2, Figure 10.5)

West Australian Department of Health (Figure 12.2)

Scott Wilson (Table 12.3)

Dover District Council (Figure 11.3)

Office of the Deputy Prime Minister (Box 11.2)

Abbreviations and acronyms

●●●

AA	Appropriate assessment	CEAA	Canadian Environmental Assessment Agency
ABI	UK Annual Business Inquiry		
ADB	African Development Bank	CEAM	Cumulative effects assessment and management
ADB	Asian Development Bank		
AEE	Assessment of environmental effects	CEARC	Canadian Environmental Assessment Research Council
AEP	Association of Environmental Professionals		
		CEC	Commission of the European Communities
ANZECC	Australia and New Zealand Environment and Conservation Council		
		CEGB	Central Electricity Generating Board
		CEMP	Construction environmental management plan
AONB	Area of Outstanding Natural Beauty		
APC	Air pollution control	CEPA	Commonwealth Environmental Protection Agency (Australia)
API	Assessment on Proponent Information (WA)		
		CEQ	US Council on Environmental Quality
AQMA	Air quality management area		
BAA	BAA Airports Limited (previously British Airports Authority)	CEQA	California Environmental Quality Act
BANANA	Build absolutely nothing anywhere near anything	CHP	Combined heat and power
		CIA	Cultural impact assessment
BG	Bulgaria	CIE	Community impact evaluation
BIO	Bio Intelligence Service S.A.S.	CISDL	Centre for International Sustainable Development Law
BME	Black and minority ethnic		
BP	BP (previously British Petroleum)	CITES	Convention on Trade in Endangered Species
BPEO	Best practicable environmental option		
		CO_2	Carbon dioxide
BS	British Standard	COWI	COWI A/S
BWEA	British Wind Energy Association	CPO	Compulsory purchase order
CAREC	Regional Environmental Centre for Central Asia	CPRE	Campaign to Protect Rural England
		CRM	Contingent ranking method
CBA	Cost benefit analysis	CRS	US Congressional Research Service
CC	County Council	CRTN	Calculation of road traffic noise
CCGT	Combined-cycle gas turbine	CSR	Corporate social responsibility
CCHP	Combined cooling heat and power	CVM	Contingent valuation method
CCS	Carbon capture and storage	CY	Cyprus
CCW	Countryside Council for Wales	CZ	Czech Republic
CE	Categorical exclusion	dB	Decibels
CEA	Cumulative effects assessment	dBA	A-weighted decibels

DA	Devolved administration (in the UK)	EPA	West Australian Environmental Protection Authority
DBIS	UK Department for Business, Innovation and Skills	EPB	Environmental Protection Bureau (China)
DC	District Council	EPBCA	Environmental Protection and Bio-diversity Conservation Act (Australia)
DCLG	UK Department for Communities and Local Government	EPD	Hong Kong Environmental Protection Department
DECC	UK Department of Energy and Climate Change	EqIA	Equality impact assessment
DEFRA	UK Department for Environment, Food and Rural Affairs	ERM	Environmental Resources Management Limited
DETR	UK Department of Environment, Transport and the Regions	ES	Environmental statement
DFID	UK Department for International Development	ESRC	Economic and Social Research Council
		ETSU	Energy Technology Support Unit
DfT	UK Department for Transport	EU	European Union
DG	Directorate General (CEC)	FEARO	Federal Environmental Assessment Review Office
DMRB	Design manual for roads and bridges		
DoE	UK Department of the Environment	FEIS	Final environmental impact statement
DOEn	UK Department of Energy	FHWA	US Federal Highway Administration
DoT	UK Department of Transport	FoE	Friends of the Earth
DTI	UK Department for Trade and Industry	FONSI	Finding of no significant impact
		G1; G2	Generation 1; Generation 2
EA	Environmental assessment	GAM	Goals achievement matrix
EA	UK Environment Agency	GHG	Greenhouse gases
EAGGF	European Agricultural Guidance and Guarantee Fund	GHK	GHK Consulting Limited
		GIS	Geographical information systems
EAP	Environmental action plan	GNP	Gross national product
EBRD	European Bank for Reconstruction and Development	GP	General practitioner
		GPDO	General Permitted Development Order
EC	European Commission		
EcIA	Ecological impact assessment	GW	Gigawatt
ECJ	European Court of Justice	ha	Hectare
EDF	Électricité de France	HEP	Hydro-electric power
EE	Estonia	HGV	Heavy goods vehicle
EEA	European Environment Agency	HIA	Health impact assessment
EIA	Environmental impact assessment	HMG	Her Majesty's Government
EIB	European Investment Bank	HMIP	Her Majesty's Inspectorate of Pollution
EID	Environmental impact design	HMSO	Her Majesty's Stationery Office
EIR	Environmental impact report	HPF	Household production function
EIR	Environmental impact review	HPM	Hedonic price methods
EIS	Environmental impact statement	HRA	Habitats regulation assessment
EM&A	Environmental monitoring and audit	HSE	Health and Safety Executive
EMAS	Eco-Management and Audit Scheme	HU	Hungary
EMP	Environmental management plan	HWS	Hampshire Waste Services
EMS	Environmental management system	IA	Impact assessment
EN	English Nature	IAIA	International Association for Impact Assessment
ENDS	Environmental Data Services		
EPA	UK Environmental Protection Act	IAU	Impacts Assessment Unit (Oxford Brookes)
EPA	US Environmental Protection Act		
EPA	US Environmental Protection Agency	IEA	Institute of Environmental Assessment

IEMA	Institute of Environmental Management and Assessment	NEPA	US National Environmental Policy Act
IFI	International Funding Institution	NGC	National Grid Company
IIA	Integrated impact assessment	NGO	Non-governmental organization
IMD	Index of Multiple Deprivation	NHS	National Health Service
INEM	International Network for Environmental Management	NIMBY	Not in my back yard
		NO_x	Nitrogen oxide
IOCGP	Inter-organizational Committee on Guidelines and Principles for Social Impact Assessment	NPDV	Net present day value
		NPS	National Policy Statement
		NSIP	Nationally significant infrastructure project
IPC	Infrastructure Planning Commission	NTS	Non-technical summary
IPC	Integrated pollution control	ODA	Olympic Delivery Authority
IPCC	Intergovernmental Panel on Climate Change	ODPM	UK Office of the Deputy Prime Minister
IPHI	Institute of Public Health in Ireland	OECD	Organisation for Economic Co-operation and Development
ISO	International Organization for Standardization	OISD	Oxford Institute for Sustainable Development
IWM	Institute of Waste Management	OJ	Official Journal of the European Communities
JEAPM	Journal of Environmental Assessment Policy and Management		
		OTP	Operational Transport Programme
JNCC	Joint Nature Conservancy Council	PADC	Project Appraisal for Development Control
KSEIA	Korean Society of Environmental Impact Assessment		
		PAS	Planning Advisory Service
kV	Kilovolt	PBS	Planning balance sheet
L_{10}	Noise level exceeded for no more than 10 per cent of a monitoring period	PEIR	Programme environmental impact report
LB	London Borough	PEIS	Programmatic environmental impact statement
LCA	Life cycle assessment		
LNG	Liquified natural gas	PER	Public Environmental Review (WA)
LPA	Local planning authority	PIC	Partnerships in Care
LT	Lithuania	PL	Poland
LTP	Local transport plan	PM_{10}	Particulate matter of less than 10 microns in diameter
LTP3	Third local transport plan		
LULU	Locally unacceptable land uses	PPG	Planning Policy Guidance
LV	Latvia	PPPs	Policies, plans and programmes
MAFF	UK Ministry of Agriculture, Forestry and Fisheries	PPPP	Policy, plan, programme or project
		PPS	Planning policy statement
MAUT	Multi-attribute utility theory	PWR	Pressurized water reactor
MBC	Metropolitan Borough Council	QBL	Quadruple bottom line
MCA	Multi-criteria assessment	QOLA	Quality of life assessment
MCDA	Multi-criteria decision analysis	RA	Resilience Alliance
MEA	Manual of Environmental Appraisal	RA	Risk assessment
MMO	Marine Management Organization (UK)	RMA	Resource Management Act (NZ)
		RO	Romania
MoD	UK Ministry of Defence	ROD	Record of decision
MOEP	Ministry of Environmental Protection (China)	RSPB	Royal Society for the Protection of Birds
MT	Malta		
MW	Megawatt	RTPI	Royal Town Planning Institute
NE	Natural England	S106	Section 106

SA	Sustainability appraisal	TBL	Triple bottom line
SAC	Special Area of Conservation	T&CP	Town and country planning
SAIEA	Southern African Institute for Environmental Assessment	TIA	Transport impact assessment
		TRL	Transport Research Laboratory
SAVE	SAVE Britain's Heritage	UKNEA	UK National Ecosystem Assessment
SD	Sustainable development	UN	United Nations
SDD	Scottish Development Department	UNCED	United Nations Conference on Environment and Development
SEA	Strategic environmental assessment		
SEERA	South East England Regional Assembly	UNECE	United Nations Economic Commission for Europe
S&EIA	Socio-economic and environmental impact assessment	UNEP	United Nations Environment Programme
SEPA	Scottish Environment Protection Agency	US	United States
		USAID	United States Agency for International Development
SI	Slovenia		
SIA	Social impact assessment	VEC	Valued ecosystem component
SK	Slovakia	VMP	Visitor management plan
SNH	Scottish Natural Heritage	VROM	Netherlands Ministry of Housing, Spatial Planning and the Environment
SNIFFER	Scotland and Northern Ireland Forum for Environmental Research		
		WA	Western Australia
SO_2	Sulphur dioxide	WBCSD	World Business Council for Sustainable Development
SOER	State of the Environment Report		
SoS	Secretary of State	WHO	World Health Organization
SPA	Special Protection Area	WID	USAID Women in Development
SSE	Stop Stansted Expansion	WTA	Willingness to accept
SSSI	Site of Special Scientific Interest	WTP	Willingness to pay

Part 1

Principles and procedures

1 Introduction and principles

1.1 Introduction

Over the last four decades there has been a remarkable growth of interest in environmental issues – in sustainability and the better management of development in harmony with the environment. Associated with this growth of interest has been the introduction of new legislation, emanating from national and international sources such as the European Commission, that seeks to influence the relationship between development and the environment. Environmental impact assessment (EIA) is an important example. EIA legislation was introduced in the USA over 40 years ago. A European Community (EC) directive in 1985 accelerated its application in EU Member States and it has spread worldwide. Since its introduction in the UK in 1988, it has been a major growth area for planning practice; the originally anticipated 20 environmental impact statements (EIS) per year in the UK has escalated to several hundreds, and this is only the tip of the iceberg. The scope of EIA continues to widen and grow.

It is therefore perhaps surprising that the introduction of EIA met with strong resistance from many quarters, particularly in the UK. Planners argued, with partial justification, that they were already making such assessments. Many developers saw it as yet another costly and time-consuming constraint on development, and central government was also unenthusiastic. Interestingly, initial UK legislation referred to environmental assessment (EA), leaving out the apparently politically sensitive, negative-sounding reference to impacts. The scope of the subject continues to evolve. This chapter therefore introduces EIA as a process, the purposes of this process, types of development, environment and impacts, and current issues in EIA.

1.2 The nature of EIA

1.2.1 Definitions

Definitions of EIA abound. They range from the oft-quoted and broad definition of Munn (1979), which refers to the need 'to identify and predict the impact on the environment and on man's health and well-being of legislative proposals, policies, programmes, projects and operational procedures, and to interpret and communicate information about the impacts', to the narrow and early UK DoE (1989) operational definition:

> The term 'environmental assessment' describes a technique and a process by which information about the environmental effects of a project is collected, both by the

developer and from other sources, and taken into account by the planning authority in forming their judgements on whether the development should go ahead.

UNECE (1991) had an altogether more succinct and pithy definition: 'an assessment of the impact of a planned activity on the environment'. The EU EIA Directive requires an assessment of the effects of certain public and private projects, which are likely to have significant effects on the environment, before development consent is granted; it is procedurally based (see

Appendix 1). The EIA definition adopted by the International Association for Impact Assessment (IAIA 2009) is 'the process of identifying, predicting, evaluating and mitigating the biophysical, social and other relevant effects of proposed development proposals prior to major decisions being taken and commitments made'. This process emphasis is now explored further.

1.2.2 EIA: a process

In essence, EIA is *a process*, a systematic process that examines the environmental consequences of

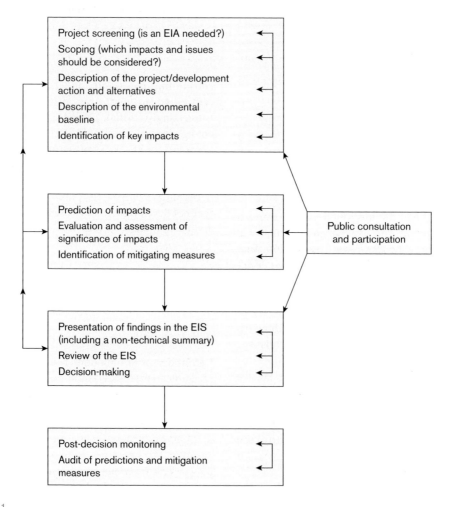

Figure 1.1

Important steps in the EIA process

Note that EIA should be a cyclical process, with considerable interaction between the various steps. For example, public participation can be useful at most stages of the process; monitoring systems should relate to parameters established in the initial project and baseline descriptions.

development actions, in advance. The emphasis, compared with many other mechanisms for environmental protection, is on prevention. Of course, planners have traditionally assessed the impacts of developments on the environment, but invariably not in the systematic, holistic and multidisciplinary way required by EIA. The process involves a number of steps, as outlined in Figure 1.1.

The steps are briefly described below, pending a much fuller discussion in Chapters 4–7. It should be noted at this stage that, although the steps are outlined in a linear fashion, EIA should be a cyclical activity, with feedback and interaction between the various steps. It should also be noted that practice can and does vary considerably from the process illustrated in Figure 1.1. For example, UK EIA legislation still does not require post-decision monitoring. The order of the steps in the process may also vary.

- *Project screening* narrows the application of EIA to those projects that may have significant environmental impacts. Screening may be partly determined by the EIA regulations operating in a country at the time of assessment.
- *Scoping* seeks to identify at an early stage, from all of a project's possible impacts and from all the alternatives that could be addressed, those that are the crucial, significant issues.
- *The consideration of alternatives* seeks to ensure that the proponent has considered other feasible approaches, including alternative project locations, scales, processes, layouts, operating conditions and the 'no action' option.
- *The description of the project/development action* includes a clarification of the purpose and rationale of the project, and an understanding of its various characteristics – including stages of development, location and processes.
- *The description of the environmental baseline* includes the establishment of both the present and future state of the environment, in the absence of the project, taking into account changes resulting from natural events and from other human activities.
- *The identification of the main impacts* brings together the previous steps with the aim of ensuring that all potentially significant environmental impacts (adverse and beneficial) are identified and taken into account in the process.
- *The prediction of impacts* aims to identify the magnitude and other dimensions of identified change in the environment with a project/action, by comparison with the situation without that project/action.
- *The evaluation and assessment of significance* assesses the relative significance of the predicted impacts to allow a focus on the main adverse impacts.
- *Mitigation* involves the introduction of measures to avoid, reduce, remedy or compensate for any significant adverse impacts. In addition *enhancement* involves the development of beneficial impacts where possible.
- *Public consultation and participation* aim to ensure the quality, comprehensiveness and effectiveness of the EIA, and that the public's views are adequately taken into consideration in the decision-making process.
- *EIS presentation* is a vital step in the process. If done badly, much good work in the EIA may be negated.
- *Review* involves a systematic appraisal of the quality of the EIS, as a contribution to the decision-making process.
- *Decision-making* on the project involves a consideration by the relevant authority of the EIS (including consultation responses) together with other material considerations.
- *Post-decision monitoring* involves the recording of outcomes associated with development impacts, after a decision to proceed. It can contribute to effective project management.
- *Auditing* follows from monitoring. It can involve comparing actual outcomes with predicted outcomes, and can be used to assess the quality of predictions and the effectiveness of mitigation. It provides a vital step in the EIA learning process.

1.2.3 Environmental impact statements: the documentation

The EIS documents the information about and estimates of impacts derived from the various steps in the process.[1] Prevention is better than cure; an EIS revealing many significant unavoidable adverse impacts would provide valuable information that could contribute to the abandonment or substantial modification of a proposed development action. Where adverse impacts can be successfully reduced through mitigation measures, there may be a different decision. Table 1.1 provides an example of the content of an EIS for a project.

Table 1.1 An EIS for a project – example of contents

Non-technical summary

Part 1: Introduction, methods and key issues
Introduction
Methodology
Summary of key issues

Part 2: Background to the proposed development
Preliminary studies: need, planning, alternatives and site
   selection
Site description, baseline conditions
Description of proposed development
Development programme, including site preparation,
   construction, operation, decommissioning and restoration
   (as appropriate)

Part 3: Environmental impact assessment – topic areas
Land use
Geology, topography and soils
Hydrology and water quality
Air quality
Climate change
Ecology: terrestrial and aquatic
Noise and vibration
Socio-economics
Transport
Landscape, visual quality
Historic environment
Recreation and amenity
Interrelationships between effects
Cumulative impacts
Summary of residual impacts

Part 4: Follow-up and management
Monitoring of impacts
Management of impacts

The *non-technical summary* is an important element in the documentation; EIA can be complex, and the summary can help to improve communication with the various parties involved. Reflecting the potential complexity of the process, an *introduction* should clarify, for example, who the developer is, who has produced the EIS, and the relevant legal framework. Also at the beginning, a *methodology section*, provides an opportunity to clarify some basic information (e.g. what methods have been used, how the key issues were identified, who was consulted and how, what difficulties have been encountered, and what are the limitations of the EIA). The *background to the proposed development* covers the early steps in the EIA process, including clear descriptions of a project, and baseline conditions (including relevant planning policies and plans).

Within each of the *topic areas* of an EIS there would normally be a discussion of existing conditions, predicted impacts, scope for mitigation and enhancement, and residual impacts. The list here is generic, and there are some topics that are still poorly covered, for example climate change and cumulative impacts (as appropriate). A concluding section, although often omitted from EISs, should cover key *follow-up issues*, including monitoring and management.

Environmental impact assessment and EIS practices vary from study to study, from country to country, and best practice is constantly evolving. An early UN study of EIA practice in several countries advocated changes in the process and documentation (UNECE 1991). These included giving a greater emphasis to the socio-economic dimension, to public participation and to 'after the decision' activity, such as monitoring. More recent reviews of the operation of the amended EC Directive (CEC 2003a, 2009) raised similar issues, and other emerging issues, a decade later (see Chapter 2). Sadler (1996) provided a wider agenda for change based on a major international study of the effectiveness of EIA, being updated in 2010–11 (see Chapters 8 and 12).

1.3 The purposes of EIA

1.3.1 An aid to decision-making

EIA is an aid to decision-making. For the decision-maker, for example a local authority, it provides a systematic examination of the environmental implications of a proposed action, and sometimes alternatives, before a decision is taken. The EIS can be considered by the decision-maker along with other documentation related to the planned activity. EIA is normally wider in scope and less quantitative than other techniques, such as cost–benefit analysis (CBA). It is not a substitute for decision-making, but it does help to clarify some of the trade-offs associated with a proposed development action, which should lead to more informed and structured decision-making. The EIA process has the potential, not always taken up, to be a basis for negotiation between the developer, public interest groups and the planning regulator. This can lead to an outcome that balances well the interests of the development action and the environment.

1.3.2 An aid to the formulation of development actions

Developers may see the EIA process as another set of hurdles to jump before they can proceed with their various activities; the process can be seen as yet another costly and time-consuming activity in the development consent process. However, EIA can be of great benefit to them, since it can provide a framework for considering location and design issues and environmental issues in parallel. It can be an aid to the formulation of development actions, indicating areas where a project can be modified to minimize or eliminate altogether its adverse impacts on the environment. The consideration of environmental impacts early in the planning life of a development can lead to more environmentally sensitive development; to improved relations between the developer, the planning authority and the local communities; to a smoother development consent process; and sometimes to a worthwhile financial return on the extra expenditure incurred. O'Riordan (1990) links

such concepts of negotiation and redesign to the important environmental themes of 'green consumerism' and 'green capitalism'. The growing demand by consumers for goods that do no environmental damage, plus a growing market for clean technologies, is generating a response from developers. EIA can be the signal to the developer of potential conflict; wise developers may use the process to negotiate 'environmental gain' solutions, which may eliminate or offset negative environmental impacts, reduce local opposition and avoid costly public inquiries. This can be seen in the wider and contemporary context of corporate social responsibility (CSR) being increasingly practised by major businesses (Crane *et al.* 2008).

1.3.3 A vehicle for stakeholder consultation and participation

Development actions may have wide-ranging impacts on the environment, affecting many different groups in society. There is increasing emphasis by government at many levels on the importance of consultation and participation by key stakeholders in the planning and development of projects; see for example the 'Aarhus Convention' (UNECE 2000) and the EC Public Participation Directive (CEC 2003b). EIA can be a very useful vehicle for engaging with communities and stakeholders, helping those potentially affected by a proposed development to be much better informed and to be more fully involved in the planning and development process.

1.3.4 An instrument for sustainable development

Existing environmentally harmful developments have to be managed as best as they can. In extreme cases, they may be closed down, but they can still leave residual environmental problems for decades to come. It would be much better to mitigate the harmful effects in advance, at the planning stage, or in some cases avoid the particular development altogether. Prevention is better than cure. This is the theme of the pioneering US and EC legislation on EIA. For example, the preamble to the 1985 EC EIA Directive includes 'the best environmental policy consists in preventing the creation of pollution or nuisances at source, rather than subsequently trying to counteract their effects' (CEC 1985). This of course leads on to the fundamental role of EIA as an instrument for sustainable development – a role some writers have drawn attention to as one often more hidden than it should be when EIA effectiveness is being assessed (Jay *et al.* 2007).

The nature of sustainable development

Economic development and social development must be placed in their environmental contexts. The classical work by Boulding (1966) vividly portrays the dichotomy between the 'throughput economy' and the 'spaceship economy' (Figure 1.2). The economic goal of increased *gross national product* (GNP), using more inputs to produce more goods and services, contains the seeds of its own destruction. Increased output brings with it not only goods and services, but also more waste products. Increased inputs demand more resources. The natural environment is the 'sink' for the wastes and the 'source' for the resources. Environmental pollution and the depletion of resources are invariably the ancillaries to economic development.

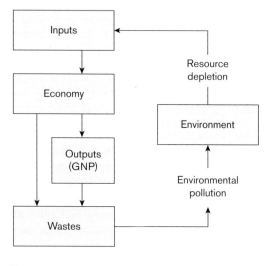

Figure 1.2

The economic development process in its environmental context (adapted from Boulding 1966)

The interaction of economic and social development with the natural environment and the reciprocal impacts between human actions and the biophysical world have been recognized by governments from local to international levels, and attempts have been made to manage the interaction better. However towards the end of the first decade of the twentieth-first century, the European Environment Agency report, *European Environment – State and Outlook 2010* (EEA 2010), still showed some good progress mixed with remaining fundamental challenges, with potentially very serious consequences for the quality of the environment. For example, while greenhouse gas emissions have been cut and the EU is on track to reach a reduction target of 20 per cent by 2020, the Member States still produced close to 5 billion tonnes of CO_2 equivalent emissions in 2008. Similarly while Europe's waste management has shifted steadily from landfill to recycling and prevention, still half of the 3 billion tonnes of total waste generated in the EU-27 in 2006 was landfilled. In nature and biodiversity, Europe has expanded its Natura 2000 network of protected areas to cover 18 per cent of EU land, but missed its 2010 target to halt biodiversity loss. Europe's freshwaters are affected by water scarcity, droughts, floods, physical modifications and the continuing presence of a range of pollutants. Both ambient air and water quality remain inadequate and health impacts are widespread. We also live in an interconnected world. European policy-makers aren't only contending with complex systematic interactions within Europe. There are also unfolding global drivers of change that are likely to affect Europe's environment, and many are beyond Europe's control. Some environmental trends are likely to be even more pronounced in developing countries, where, because population growth is greater and current living standards lower, there will be more pressure on environmental resources.

The 1987 Report of the UN World Commission on Environment and Development (usually referred to as the Brundtland Report, after its chairwoman) defined sustainable development as 'development which meets the needs of the present generation without compromising the ability of future generations to meet their own needs' (UN World Commission on Environment and Development 1987). Sustainable development means handing down to future generations not only 'man-made capital' (such as roads, schools and historic buildings) and 'human capital' (such as knowledge and skills), but also 'natural/environmental capital' (such as clean air, fresh water, rainforests, the ozone layer and biological diversity). The Brundtland Report identified the following chief characteristics of sustainable development: it maintains the quality of life, it maintains continuing access to natural resources and it avoids lasting environmental damage. It means living on the earth's income rather than eroding its capital (DoE *et al.* 1990). In addition to a concern for the environment and the future, Brundtland also emphasizes participation and equity, thus highlighting both inter- and intra-generational equity. This definition is much wider than ecology and the natural environment; it entails social organization of intra- and inter-generational equity. Importance is also assigned to economic and cultural aspects, such as preventing poverty and social exclusion, concern about the quality of life, attention to ethical aspects of human well being, and systematic organization of participation by all concerned stakeholders.

There is, however, a danger that 'sustainable development' becomes a weak catch-all phrase; there are already many alternative definitions. Holmberg and Sandbrook (1992) found over 70 definitions of sustainable development. Redclift (1987) saw it as 'moral convictions as a substitute for thought'; to O'Riordan (1988) it was 'a good idea which cannot sensibly be put into practice'. But to Skolimowski (1995), sustainable development

> ... struck a middle ground between more radical approaches which denounced all development, and the idea of development conceived as business as usual. The idea of sustainable development, although broad, loose and tinged with ambiguity around its edges, turned out to be palatable to everybody. This may have been its greatest virtue. It is radical and yet not offensive.

Readers are referred to Reid (1995), Kirkby *et al.* (1995) and Faber *et al.* (2005) for an overview of the concept, responses and ongoing debate.

Over time, 'sustainability' has evolved as a partial successor to the term 'sustainable development' (although they can be seen as synonymous), partly because the latter has become somewhat ill used (for example, governments seeking to equate sustainable development with sustained growth, firms seeking to equate it with sustained profits).[2] However, despite the global acceptance of the 'sustainability/sustainable development' concept, its scope and nature are a somewhat contested and confused territory (Faber *et al.* 2005). There are numerous definitions, but a much-used one is that of the triple bottom line (TBL), reflecting the importance of environmental, social and economic factors in decision-making, although it is important to go beyond that to emphasize the importance of integration and synergies between factors (Figure 1.3); however the assessment of such synergies presents particular challenges. Figure 1.4 emphasizes that within this three-element definition of sustainability, there is an important hierarchy. The environment and its natural systems are the foundation to any concept of sustainability. We cannot survive without the 'goods and services' provided by Earth's natural and physical systems – breathable air, drinkable water and food. Living on Earth, we need social systems to provide social justice, security, cultural identity and a sense of place. Without a well-functioning social system, an economic system cannot be productive.

Institutional responses to sustainable development

Institutional responses to meet the goal of sustainable development are required at several levels. A *global response* is needed for issues of global concern, such as ozone-layer depletion, climate change, deforestation and biodiversity loss. The United Nations Conference on Environment and Development (UNCED) held in Rio de Janeiro in 1992 was an example not only of international concern, but also of the problems of securing concerted action to deal with such issues. Agenda 21, an 800-page action plan for the international community into the twenty-first century, set out what nations should do to achieve sustainable development. It included topics such as biodiversity, desertification, deforestation, toxic

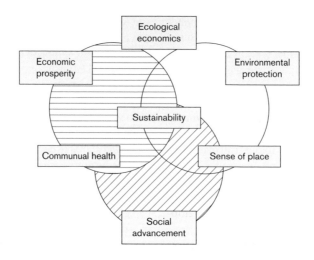

Figure 1.3

Integrating environmental, social and economic dimensions of sustainability

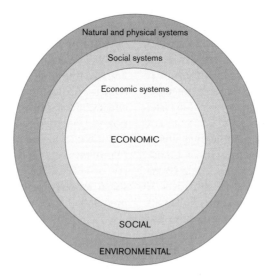

Figure 1.4

An alternative (hierarchical) perspective on the dimensions of sustainability

wastes, sewage, oceans and the atmosphere. For each of its 115 programmes, the need for action, the objectives and targets to be achieved, the activities to be undertaken, and the means of implementation are all outlined. Agenda 21 offered policies and programmes to achieve a sustainable balance between consumption, population and Earth's life-supporting capacity. Unfortunately it was not legally binding, being dependent on national governments, local governments and others to implement most of the programmes.

The Johannesburg Earth Summit of 2002 re-emphasized the difficulties of achieving international commitment on environmental issues. While there were some positive outcomes – for example, on water and sanitation (with a target to halve the number without basic sanitation – about 1.2 billion – by 2015), on poverty, health, sustainable consumption and on trade and globalization – many other outcomes were much less positive. Delivering the Kyoto Protocol on legally enforceable reductions of greenhouse gases continued to be difficult; the results of the 2009 Copenhagen climate conference fell short of the EU's goal of progress towards the finalization of an ambitious and legally binding global climate treaty to succeed the Kyoto Protocol in 2013 (Wilson and Piper 2010). Similarly, we hear regularly of the continuing loss of global biodiversity and of natural resources, and on the challenges of delivering human rights in many countries. All, of course, is now complicated further by the severe challenges and uncertainties of the serious global economic situation. Together, such problems severely hamper progress on sustainable development.

Within the EU, four Community Action Programmes on the Environment were implemented between 1972 and 1992. These gave rise to specific legislation on a wide range of topics, including waste management, the pollution of the atmosphere, the protection of nature and EIA. The Fifth Programme, 'Towards sustainability' (1993–2000), was set in the context of the completion of the Single European Market (CEC 1992). The latter, with its emphasis on major changes in economic development resulting from the removal of all remaining fiscal, material and technological barriers between Member States, could pose additional threats to the environment. The Fifth Programme recognized the need for the clear integration of performance targets – in relation to environmental protection – for several sectors, including manufacturing, energy, transport and tourism. EU policy on the environment would be based on the 'precautionary principle' that preventive action should be taken, that environmental damage should be rectified at source and that the polluter should pay. Whereas previous EU programmes relied almost exclusively on legislative instruments, the Fifth Programme advocated a broader mixture, including 'market-based instruments', such as the internalization of environmental costs through the application of fiscal measures, and 'horizontal, supporting instruments', such as improved baseline and statistical data and improved spatial and sectoral planning.

The Sixth Programme, *Our future, our choice (2001–12)*, built on the broader approach introduced in the previous decade. It recognized that sustainable development has social and economic as well as physical environmental dimensions, although the focus is on four main priority issues: tackling climate change, protecting nature and biodiversity, reducing human health impacts from environmental pollution, and ensuring the sustainable management of natural resources and waste. It also recognized the importance of empowering citizens and changing behaviour, and of 'greening land-use planning and management decisions'.

> The Community directive on EIA and (the then) proposal on SEA, which aim to ensure that the environmental implications of planned infrastructure projects and planning are properly addressed, will also help ensure that the environmental considerations are better integrated into planning decisions. (CEC 2001)

The EC has not yet decided on the nature of a possible Seventh Programme, including the key role of climate change – either as within the EU environmental policy or as having a more overarching role in the Commission's organization.

In the UK, the publication of *This common inheritance: Britain's environmental strategy* (DoE *et al*. 1990) provided the country's first comprehensive White Paper on the environment. The report included a discussion of the greenhouse effect, town and country, pollution control, and awareness and organization with regard to environmental issues. Throughout it emphasized that responsibility for our environment should be shared between the government, business and the public. The range of policy instruments advocated included legislation, standards, planning and economic measures. The last, building on work by Pearce *et al*. (1989), included charges, subsidies, market creation and enforcement incentives. The report also noted, cautiously, the recent addition of EIA to the 'toolbox' of instruments. Subsequent UK government reports, such as *Sustainable development: the UK strategy* (HMG 1994), recognized the role of EIA in contributing to sustainable development and raised the EIA profile among key user groups. The UK government reports also reflect the extension of the scope of sustainable development to include social, economic and environmental factors. This is reflected in the UK Strategy for Sustainable Development, *A better quality of life* (DETR 1999a), with its four objectives of:

- social progress which recognizes the needs of everyone;
- effective protection of the environment;
- prudent use of natural resources; and
- maintenance of high and stable levels of economic growth and employment.

To measure progress, the UK government published a set of sustainable development indicators, including a set of 15 key headline indicators (DETR 1999b). It also required a high-level sustainable development framework to be produced for each English region (see, for example, *A better quality of life in the South East*, SEERA, 2001).

Planning Policy Statement 1 (PPS1, DCLG 2005) reinforced the commitment to sustainable development. 'Sustainable development is the core principle underpinning planning. At the heart of sustainable development is the simple idea of ensuring a better quality of life for everyone, now and for future generations.' This was further reinforced and developed in an update of the national strategy, *Securing the future: delivering the UK sustainable development strategy* (DEFRA 2005), in which the UK government introduced a revised set of guiding principles, priorities for action and 20 key headline indicators, with a focus on delivery. The guiding principles are:

- living within environmental limits;
- ensuring a strong, healthy and just society;
- achieving a sustainable economy;
- promoting good governance; and
- using sound science responsibly.

The good governance principle adds an important fourth pillar to the other three pillars (environmental, social and economic) of sustainable development, shifting from a triple to a quadruple bottom line (QBL) approach. Good governance, at all levels from central government to the individual, is needed to foster the integration of the three other pillars. Again, EIA can be a useful vehicle for such integration.

1.4 Projects, environment and impacts

1.4.1 The nature of major projects

As noted in Section l.2, EIA is relevant to a broad spectrum of development actions, including policies, plans, programmes and projects. The focus here is on projects, reflecting the dominant role of project EIA in practice. The strategic environmental assessment (SEA) and sustainability appraisal (SA) of the 'upper tiers' of development actions are considered further in Chapter 11. The scope of projects covered by EIA is widening, and is discussed further in Chapters 3 and 4. Traditionally, project EIA has applied to major projects; but what are major projects, and what criteria can be used to identify them? One could take Lord Morley's approach to defining an elephant: it is difficult, but you easily recognize one when you see it. In a similar vein, the acronym LULU (locally unacceptable land uses) has been applied in the USA to many major projects, such as in energy, transport and manufacturing, clearly reflecting the public perception of the potential negative impacts associated with such developments. There is no easy definition, but it is possible to highlight some important characteristics (see Plate 1.1 and Table 1.2).

Most large projects involve considerable investment. In the UK context, 'megaprojects' such as the Channel Tunnel and the associated Rail Link, London Heathrow Terminal 5, the Olympic 2012 project, motorways (and their widening), nuclear power stations, gas-fired power stations and renewable energy projects (such as major offshore wind farms and the proposed Severn Barrage) constitute one end of the spectrum. At the other end may be industrial estate developments, small stretches of road, and various waste-disposal facilities, with considerably smaller, but still substantial, price tags. Such projects often cover large areas and employ many workers, usually in construction, but also in operation for some projects. They also invariably generate a complex array of inter- and intra-organizational activity during the various stages of their lives. The developments may have wide-ranging, long-term and

1 Kings Cross, London – urban redevelopment

2 Construction at London 2012 Olympics site

3 Olkiluoto nuclear power plant, Finland

4 The Oresund Bridge connecting Sweden and Denmark

5 Danish offshore wind farm

Hinkley Point A Nuclear Power Station

Environmental Statement
(In support of the Application to decommission Hinkley Point A Nuclear Power Station as required by Statutory Instrument 1999 No. 2892: Nuclear Reactors (Environmental Impact Assessment for Decommissioning) Regulations 1999).

6 ES for decommissioning Hinkley Point A, UK

Plate 1.1

Some examples of major projects

Source: Magnox Electric (2002); RPS (2004); Symonds/EDAW (2004); Wikimedia.

Table 1.2 Characteristics of major projects

Substantial capital investment

Cover large areas; employ large numbers (construction and/or operation)

Complex array of organizational links

Wide-ranging impacts (geographical and by type)

Significant environmental impacts

Require special procedures

Infrastructure and utilities, extractive and primary (including agriculture); services

Band, point

often very significant impacts on the environment. The definition of significance with regard to environmental effects is an important issue in EIA. It may relate, *inter alia*, to scale of development, to sensitivity of location and to the nature of adverse and beneficial effects; it will be discussed further in later chapters. Like a large stone thrown into a pond, a major project can create significant ripples, with impacts spreading far and wide. In many respects such projects tend to be regarded as exceptional, requiring special procedures. In the UK, these procedures have included public inquiries, hybrid bills that have to be passed through parliament (for example, for the Channel Tunnel) and EIA procedures. Under the 2008 Planning Act (HMG 2008), a special subset of nationally significant infrastructure projects (NSIPs) has been identified, with impacts to be examined by new procedures led by the Infrastructure Planning Commission (IPC) (to become the National Infrastructure Unit of the UK Planning Inspectorate in 2012). NSIPs include major energy projects, transport projects (road, rail and port), water and waste facilities.

Major projects can also be defined according to type of activity. In addition to the infrastructure and utilities, they also include manufacturing and extractive projects, such as petrochemical plants, steelworks, mines and quarries, and services projects, such as leisure developments, out-of-town shopping centres, new settlements and education and health facilities. An EC study adopted a further distinction between band and point infrastructures. Point infrastructure would include, for example, power stations, bridges and harbours; band or linear infrastructure would include electricity transmission lines, roads and canals (CEC 1982).

A major project also has a planning and development life cycle, including a variety of stages. It is important to recognize such stages because impacts can vary considerably between them. The main stages in a project's life cycle are outlined in Figure 1.5. There may be variations in timing between stages, and internal variations within each stage, but there is a broadly common sequence of events. In EIA, an important distinction is between 'before the decision' (stages A and B) and 'after the decision' (stages C, D and E). As noted in Section 1.2, the monitoring and auditing of the implementation of a project following approval are often absent from the EIA process.

Projects are initiated in several ways. Many are responses to market opportunities (e.g. a holiday village, a sub-regional shopping centre, a gas-fired power station; a wind farm); others may be seen as necessities (e.g. the Thames Barrier); others may have an explicit prestige role (e.g. the programme of Grands Travaux in Paris including the Bastille Opera, Musée d'Orsay and Great Arch). Some major projects are public-sector initiatives, but with the move towards privatization in many countries, there has been a move towards private sector funding, exemplified in the UK by such projects as the North Midlands Toll Road, the Channel Tunnel, and now most major utility energy, water and waste projects. The initial planning stage A may take several years, and lead to a specific proposal for a particular site. It is at stage B that the various control and regulatory procedures, including EIA, normally come into play. The construction stage can be particularly disruptive, and may last up to 10 years for some projects. Major projects invariably have long operational lives, although extractive projects can be short compared with infrastructure projects. The environmental impact of the eventual closedown/decommissioning of a facility should not be forgotten; for nuclear power facilities it is a major undertaking. Figure 1.6 shows how the stages in the life cycles of different kinds of project may vary.

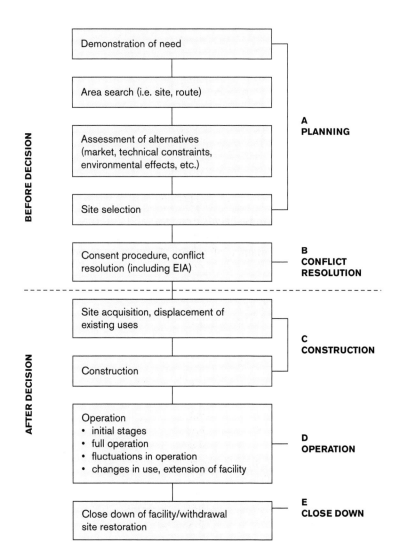

Figure 1.5

Generalized planning and development life cycle for major projects (with particular reference to impact assessment on host area)

Source: Adapted from Breese *et al.* 1965

BEFORE DECISION

Demonstration of need

Area search (i.e. site, route)

Assessment of alternatives (market, technical constraints, environmental effects, etc.)

Site selection

A PLANNING

Consent procedure, conflict resolution (including EIA)

B CONFLICT RESOLUTION

AFTER DECISION

Site acquisition, displacement of existing uses

Construction

C CONSTRUCTION

Operation
• initial stages
• full operation
• fluctuations in operation
• changes in use, extension of facility

D OPERATION

Close down of facility/withdrawal site restoration

E CLOSE DOWN

1.4.2 Dimensions of the environment

The environment can be structured in several ways, including components, scale/space and time. A narrow definition of environmental components would focus primarily on the biophysical environment. For example, the UK Department of the Environment (DoE) used the term to include all media susceptible to pollution, including: air, water and soil; flora, fauna and human beings; landscape, urban and rural conservation; and the built heritage (DoE 1991). The DoE checklist of environmental components is outlined in Table 1.3. However, as already noted in Section 1.2, the environment has important economic and socio-cultural dimensions. These include economic structure, labour markets, demography, housing, services (education, health, police, fire, etc.), lifestyles and values; and these are added to the checklist in Table 1.3. This wider definition is more in line with international definitions, as noted by the IAIA definition of EIA in 1.2.1. Similarly, an Australian definition notes, 'For the purposes of EIA, the meaning of environment incorporates physical, biological, cultural, economic and social factors' (ANZECC 1991).

The environment can also be analysed at various scales (Figure 1.7). Many of the spatial impacts of projects affect the local environment, although the nature of 'local' may vary according to the

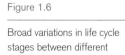

Figure 1.6

Broad variations in life cycle stages between different types of project

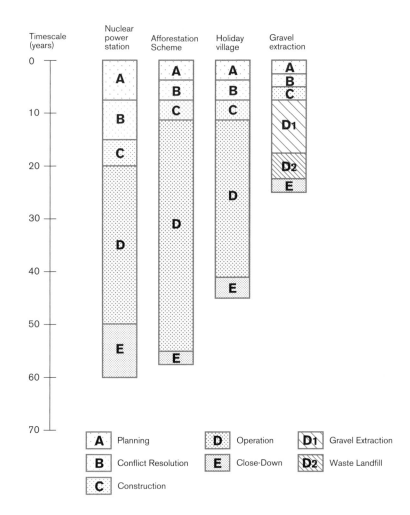

Table 1.3 Environmental components

Physical environment	
Air and atmosphere	Air quality
Water resources and water bodies	Water quality and quantity
Soil and geology	Classification, risks (e.g. erosion, contamination)
Flora and fauna	Birds, mammals, fish, etc.; aquatic and terrestrial vegetation
Human beings	Physical and mental health and well-being
Landscape	Characteristics and quality of landscape
Cultural heritage	Conservation areas; built heritage; historic and archaeological sites; other material assets
Climate	Temperature, rainfall, wind, etc.
Energy	Light, noise, vibration, etc.
Socio-economic environment	
Demography	Population structure and trends
Economic base – direct	Direct employment; labour market characteristics; local and non-local trends
Economic base – indirect	Non-basic and services employment; labour supply and demand
Housing; transport; recreation	Supply and demand
Other local services	Supply and demand of services: health, education, police, etc.
Socio-cultural	Lifestyles, quality of life; social problems; community stress and conflict

Source: adapted from DoE 1991; DETR 2000; CEC 2003a

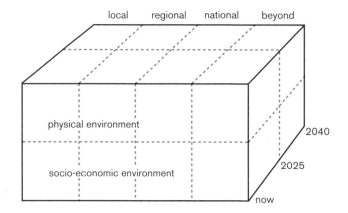

Figure 1.7

local   regional   national   beyond

physical environment

socio-economic environment

2040

2025

now

aspect of environment under consideration and to the stage in a project's life. However, some impacts are more than local. Traffic noise, for example, may be a local issue, but changes in traffic flows caused by a project may have a regional impact, and the associated CO_2 pollution contributes to the global greenhouse problem. The environment also has a time dimension. Baseline data on the state of the environment are needed at the time a project is being considered. There has been a vast increase in data available on the Internet, from the local to the national level (e.g. in the UK via local authority development plans and national statistical sources, such as the e-Digest of Environment Statistics produced by the Department of Environment, Food and Rural Affairs). For some areas such data may be packaged in tailor-made state-of-the-environment reports and audits. See Chapters 5 and 12, and Appendix 6 for further

guides to data sources. For all data it is important to have a time-series highlighting trends in environmental quality, as the environmental baseline is constantly changing, irrespective of any development under consideration, and requires a dynamic rather than a static analysis

1.4.3 The nature of impacts

The environmental impacts of a project are those resultant changes in environmental parameters, in space and time, compared with what would have happened had the project not been undertaken. The parameters may be any of the type of environmental receptors noted previously: air quality, water quality, noise, levels of local unemployment and crime, for example. Figure 1.8 provides a simple illustration of the concept.

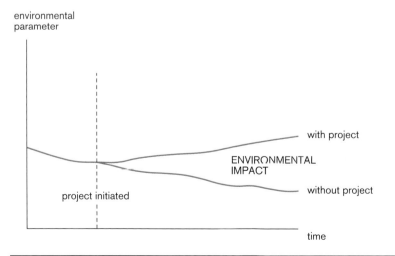

environmental parameter

with project

ENVIRONMENTAL IMPACT

without project

project initiated

time

Figure 1.8

The nature of an environmental impact

Table 1.4 Types of impact

Physical and socio-economic
Direct and indirect
Short-run and long-run
Local and strategic (including regional, national and beyond)
Adverse and beneficial
Reversible and irreversible
Quantitative and qualitative
Distribution by group and/or area
Actual and perceived
Relative to other developments; cumulative

Table l.4 provides a summary of some of the types of impact that may be encountered in EIA. The biophysical and socio-economic impacts have already been noted. These are sometimes seen as synonymous with adverse and beneficial, respectively. Thus, new developments may produce harmful wastes but also produce much needed jobs in areas of high unemployment. However, the correlation does not always apply. A project may bring physical benefits when, for example, previously polluted and derelict land is brought back into productive use; similarly, the socio-economic impacts of a major project on a community could include pressure on local health services and on the local housing market, and increases in community conflict and crime. Projects may also have immediate and direct impacts that give rise to secondary and indirect impacts later. A reservoir based on a river system not only takes land for the immediate body of water but also may have severe downstream implications for flora and fauna and for human activities such as fishing and sailing. The direct and indirect impacts may sometimes correlate with short-run and long-run impacts. For some impacts the distinction between short-run and long-run may also relate to the distinction between a project's construction and its operational stage; however, other construction-stage impacts, such as change in land use, are much more permanent. Impacts also have a spatial dimension. One distinction is between local and strategic, the latter covering impacts on areas beyond the immediate locality. These are often regional, but may sometimes be of national or even international significance.

Environmental resources cannot always be replaced; once destroyed, some may be lost forever.

The distinction between reversible and irreversible impacts is a very important one, and the irreversible impacts, not susceptible to mitigation, can constitute particularly significant impacts in an EIA. It may be possible to replace, compensate for or reconstruct a lost resource in some cases, but substitutions are rarely ideal. The loss of a resource may become more serious later, and valuations need to allow for this. Some impacts can be quantified, others are less tangible. The latter should not be ignored. Nor should the distributional impacts of a proposed development be ignored. Impacts do not fall evenly on affected parties and areas. Although a particular project may be assessed as bringing a general benefit, some groups and/or geographical areas may be receiving most of any adverse effects, the main benefits going to others elsewhere. There is also a distinction between actual and perceived impacts. Subjective perceptions of impacts may significantly influence the responses and decisions of people towards a proposed development. They constitute an important source of information, to be considered alongside more objective predictions of impacts.

> Social constructions are not mere perceptions or emotions, to be distinguished from reality; rather, how we view a social situation determines how we behave. Furthermore, social constructions of reality are characteristic of all social groups, including the agencies that are attempting to implement change as well as the communities that are affected. (IOCGP 2003)

Finally, all impacts should be compared with the 'do-nothing' situation, and the state of the environment predicted without the project. This can be widened to include comparisons with anticipated impacts from alternative development scenarios for an area. Some projects may also have cumulative impacts in combination with other development actions, current and future; for example, the impacts of several wind farms in an area, or the build-up of several major, but different, developments (e.g. port; power station; steel works; waste water facility) around an estuary. The important area of cumulative impacts is discussed further in Chapters 9 and 12.

We conclude on a semantic point: the words 'impact' and 'effect' are widely used in the literature and legislation on EIA, but it is not always clear whether they are interchangeable or should be used only for specifically different meanings. In the United States, the regulations for implementing the National Environmental Policy Act (NEPA) expressly state that 'effects and impacts as used in these regulations are synonymous'. This interpretation is widespread, and is adopted in this text. But there are other interpretations relating to timing and to value judgements. Catlow and Thirlwall (1976) make a distinction between effects that are 'the physical and natural changes resulting, directly or indirectly, from development' and impacts that are 'the consequences or end products of those effects represented by attributes of the environment on which we can place an objective or subjective value'. In contrast, an Australian study (CEPA 1994) reverses the arguments, claiming that 'there does seem to be greater logic in thinking of an impact resulting in an effect, rather than the other way round'. Other commentators have introduced the concept of value judgement into the differentiation. Preston and Bedford (1988) state that 'the use of the term "impacts" connotes a value judgement'. This view is supported by Stakhiv (1988), who sees a distinction between 'scientific assessment of facts (effects), and the evaluation of the relative importance of these effects by the analyst and the public (impacts)'. The debate continues!

1.5 Changing perspectives on EIA

1.5.1 The importance of adaptive EIA

The arguments for EIA vary in time, in space and according to the perspective of those involved. From a minimalist defensive perspective, some developers, and still possibly some parts of some governments, might see EIA as a necessary evil, an administrative exercise, something to be gone through that might result in some minor, often cosmetic, changes to a development that would probably have happened anyway. In contrast, for the 'deep ecologists' or 'deep greens', EIA cannot

provide total certainty about the environmental consequences of development proposals; they feel that any projects carried out under uncertain or risky circumstances should be abandoned. EIA and its methods must straddle such perspectives on weak and strong sustainability. EIA can be, and now often is, seen as a positive process that seeks a harmonious relationship between development and the environment. The nature and use of EIA will change as relative values and perspectives also change. EIA must adapt, and as O'Riordan (1990) very positively noted over 20 years ago:

> One can see that EIA is moving away from being a defensive tool of the kind that dominated the 1970s to a potentially exciting environmental and social betterment technique that may well come to take over the 1990s . . . If one sees EIA not so much as a technique, rather as a process that is constantly changing in the face of shifting environmental politics and managerial capabilities, one can visualize it as a sensitive barometer of environmental values in a complex environmental society. Long may EIA thrive.

EIA must continue to adapt in our rapidly changing world, a world where there are serious challenges to all the pillars of sustainability. Climate change is now recognized by many governments as the most important challenge of the twenty-first century, necessitating major initiatives – yet progress is sporadic. In recent years the world has also been on the edge of financial meltdown, and has endured serious economic recession, leading to stimulus investment, often through infrastructure projects, but also to drastic measures for deficit reduction. Poverty and social inequalities persist and are deep-seated. But before addressing the changing nature of the impact assessment family, we first consider EIA in its theoretical context.

1.5.2 EIA in its theoretical context

EIA must also be reassessed in its *theoretical context*, and in particular in the context of decision-making theory (see Lawrence 1997, 2000; Bartlett and Kurian, 1999; Weston 2000, 2003). EIA had its origins in a climate of a rational approach to decision-making in the USA in the 1960s (Caldwell 1988). The focus was on the systematic process, objectivity, a holistic approach, a consideration of alternatives and an approach often seen as primarily linear. This rational approach is assumed to rely on a scientific process in which facts and logic are pre-eminent. In the UK this rational approach was reflected in planning in the writings of, *inter alia*, Faludi (1973), McLoughlin (1969), and Friend and Jessop (1977).

However, other writings on the theoretical context of EIA have recognized the importance of the subjective nature of the EIA process. Kennedy (1988) identified EIA as both a 'science' and an 'art', combining political input and scientific process. More colourfully, Beattie (1995), in an article entitled 'Everything you already know about EIA, but don't often admit', reinforces the point that EIAs are not science; they are often produced under tight deadlines and data gaps, and simplifying assumptions are the norm under such conditions. They always contain unexamined and unexplained value judgements, and they will always be political. They invariably deal with controversial projects, and they have distributional effects – there are winners and losers. EIA professionals should therefore not be surprised, or dismayed, when their work is selectively used by various parties in the process. Leknes (2001) notes that it is particularly in the later stage of decision-making that the findings of EIA are likely to give way to political considerations. Weston (2003) notes the weakening of deference to science, experts and the rational approach. Confidence in decision-making for major projects is eroded by events such as nuclear accidents, chemical spills, numerous environmental disasters, and massive financial and time overruns of projects (Flyberg 2003). The public increasingly fear the consequences of change over which they have little control, and there is more emphasis on risk (see Beck 1992, 2008).

However, in the context of decision-making theory, this recognition of the political, the subjective and value judgement is reflected in a variety of behavioural/participative theories, and is not new. For example, in the 1960s Braybrooke and Lindblom (1963) saw decisions as incremental adjustments, with a process that is not comprehensive, linear and orderly, and is best characterized as 'muddling through'. Lindblom (1980) further developed his ideas through the concept of 'disjointed incrementalism', with a focus on meeting the needs and objectives of society, often politically defined. The importance of identifying and confronting trade-offs, a major issue in EIA, is clearly recognized. The participatory approach includes processes for open communication among all affected parties. The recognition of multiple parties and the perceived gap between government and citizens has stimulated other theoretical approaches, including communicative and collaborative planning (Healey 1996, 1997). This approach draws upon the work of Habermas (1984), Forester (1989) and others. Much attention is devoted to consensus-building, co-ordination and communication, and the role of government in promoting such actions as a means of dealing with conflicting stakeholder interests and achieving collaborative action. Critics of such an approach highlight in particular the lack of regard for power relationships within society, and especially the role of private sector developers – invariably the proponents in EIA.

It is probably now realistic to place the current evolution of EIA somewhere between the rational and behavioural approaches – reflecting elements of both. It does include important strands of rationalism, but there are many participants, and many decision points – and politics, power relationships and professional judgement are often to the fore. In EIA there are many decisions; for example, on whether EIA is needed at all (screening), the scope of the EIA, the alternatives under consideration, project design and redesign, the range of mitigation and enhancement measures, and implementation and monitoring during the 'post-key-decision' stages of the project life cycle (Glasson 1999). This tends to fit well with the classic concept of 'mixed scanning' advocated by Etzioni (1967), utilizing rational techniques of assessment, in combination with more intuitive value judgements, based upon experience and values. The rational–adaptive approach of Kaiser *et al.* (1995) also stresses the importance of a series of steps in decision-making, with both (scientific-based) rationality and (community-informed) participation, moderating the selection of policy options and desired outcomes.

1.5.3 EIA in a rapidly growing Impact Assessment (IA) family

Over the last 40 years, EIA has been joined by a growing family of assessment tools. The IAIA uses the generic term of impact assessment (IA) to encompass the semantic explosion; whereas Sadler (1996) suggested that we should view environmental assessment (EA) as 'the generic process that includes EIA of specific projects, SEA of PPPs, and their relationships to a larger set of impact assessment and planning-related tools'. Whatever the family name, there is little doubt that membership is increasing apace, with a focus on widening the *scope, scale and integration of assessment*. Impact assessment now includes, for example, SIA, HIA, EqIA, TIA, SEA, SA, S&EIA, HRA/AA, EcIA, CIA, plus a range of associated techniques such as RA, LCA, MCA, CBA – and many more. Some of the tools have been led by legislation; others have been more driven by practitioners from various disciplines that have endeavoured to separate out and highlight the theme(s) of importance to their discipline, resulting in thematically focused forms of assessment. Dalal-Clayton and Sadler (2004) rightly observe that 'the alphabet soup of acronyms [and terms] currently makes for a confusing picture'. The various assessment tools are now briefly outlined in terms of scope, scale and integration; most are discussed much further in subsequent chapters.

Scope

Development actions may have impacts not only on the physical environment but also on the social and economic environment. Typically, employment opportunities, services (e.g. health, education), community structures, lifestyles and values may be affected. *Socio-economic impact assessment* or *social impact assessment* (SIA) is regarded in this book as an integral part of EIA. However, in some countries it is (or has been) regarded as a separate process, sometimes parallel to EIA, and the reader should be aware of its separate existence (Carley and Bustelo 1984; Finsterbusch 1985; IAIA 1994; Vanclay 2003). Some domains explicitly use *S&EIA* to denote *Socio-economic and environmental impact assessment*. *Health impact assessment* (*HIA*) has been a particularly important area of growth in recent years, evolving out of the socio-economic strand; its focus is on the effects that a development action may have on the health of its host population (IPHI 2009). A more recent area still is *equality impact assessment* (*EqIA*), which seeks to identify the important distributional impacts of development actions on various groups in society (e.g. by gender, race, age, disability, sexual orientation etc., Downey 2005). Vanclay and Bronstein (1995) and others note several other relevant definitions, based largely on particular foci of specialization and including, for example, transport impact assessment, demographic impact assessment, climate impact assessment, gender impact assessment, psychological impact assessment, noise impact assessment, economic impact assessment, and cumulative impacts assessment (Canter and Ross 2010).

Scale

Strategic environmental assessment (SEA) expands the scale of operation from the EIA of projects to a more strategic level of assessment of programmes, plans and policies (PPPs). Development actions may be for a project (e.g. a nuclear power station), for a programme (e.g. a number of pressurized water reactor (PWR) nuclear power stations), for a plan (e.g. in the town and country planning (T&CP) system in England) or for a policy (e.g. the development of renewable energy). EIA to date has generally been used for individual projects, and that role is the primary focus of this book. But EIA for programmes, plans and policies, otherwise known as SEA, has been introduced in the European Union (EU) since 2004 and is also used in many other countries worldwide (Therivel 2010; Therivel and Partidario 1996; Therivel et al. 1992). SEA informs a higher, earlier, more strategic tier of decision-making. In theory, EIA should be carried out in a tiered fashion first for policies, then for plans and programmes, and finally for projects. The focus of SEA has been primarily biophysical, and there are close links with another relatively new area of assessment, *habitats regulation assessment/appropriate assessment (HRA/AA)*, which is required in the EU for projects and plans that may have significant impacts on key Natura 2000 sites of biodiversity. In contrast, a wider approach to strategic assessment, seeking to include bio-physical and socio-economic impacts, is provided by *SA*. In England this is required for the assessment of the impacts of plans under the T&CP system. In some domains, where there is not a strategic level of assessment or planning, project-level assessment may adopt, to varying degrees, a strategic perspective, with features of either SEA or SA; good examples are provided by mega-projects, such as the major mineral development projects in the remote areas of Australia.

Integration

Hacking and Guthrie (2008) have sought to provide a relational framework (Figure 1.9) to clarify the position of various assessment tools, in the context of planning and decision-making for sustainable development. In addition to scope (referred to as comprehensiveness of coverage) and scale (strategicness of the focus and scope), they also

include integratedness of techniques and themes. The latter includes a package of techniques that seek to achieve integration in the assessment process (e.g. between biophysical and socio-economic impacts; Scrase and Sheate 2002); this was termed 'horizontal integration' by Lee (2002). Petts (1999) provides a good overview of some of the techniques that include, for example, *life cycle assessment* (LCA), *cost-benefit analysis* (CBA), *environmental auditing, multi-criteria assessment* (MCA) *and risk assessment* (RA). LCA differs from EIA in its focus not on a particular site or facility, but on a product or system and the cradle-to-grave environmental effects of that product or system (see White *et al.* 1995). In contrast, CBA focuses on the economic impacts of a development, but taking a wide and long view of those impacts. It involves as far as possible the monetization of all the costs and benefits of a proposal. It came to the fore in the UK in relation to major transport projects in the 1960s, but has subsequently enjoyed

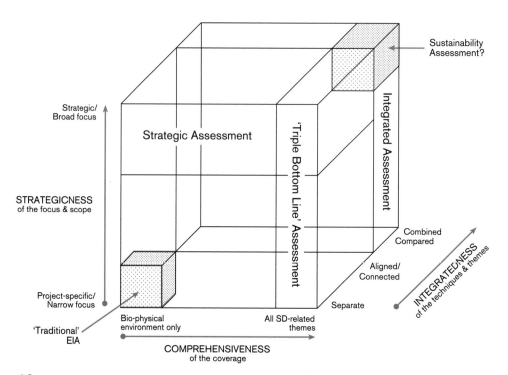

Figure 1.9

A relational framework of SD-focused assessment tools

Source: Hacking and Guthrie 2008

a new lease of life (see Hanley and Splash 1993; Lichfield 1996). Environmental auditing is the systematic, periodic and documented evaluation of the environmental performance of facility operations and practices, and this area has seen the development of procedures, such as the international standard ISO 14001.

Multi-criteria decision assessment (MCDA) covers a collection of approaches, often quantitative, that can be used to help key stakeholders to explore alternative approaches to important decisions by explicitly taking account of multiple criteria (Belton and Stewart 2002); it is quite widely used. *Risk assessment* is another term sometimes found associated with EIA. Partly in response to events such as the chemicals factory explosion at Flixborough (UK), and nuclear power station accidents at Three Mile Island (USA) and Chernobyl (Ukraine), RA developed as an approach to the analysis of risks associated with various types of development. Calow (1997) gives an overview of the growing area of environmental RA and management, and Flyberg (2003) provides a critique of risk assessment in practice. While these tools tend to be more technocentric, they can be seen as complementary to EIA, seeking to achieve a more integrated approach. Thus Chapter 5 explores the potential role of CBA and MCA approaches in EIA evaluation; Chapter 12 develops further the concept of integrated assessment, and explores the role of environmental auditing and LCA in relation to environmental management systems (EMSs).

This brief discussion on changing perspectives, on the theoretical context, associated tools and processes, emphasizes the need to continually reassess the role and operation of EIA and the importance of an adaptive EIA. This will be developed further in several chapters – especially in Part 4.

• •

1.6 Current issues in EIA

Although EIA now has over 40 years of history in the USA, elsewhere the development of concepts and practice is more recent. Development is moving apace in many other countries, including the UK and the other EU Member States. There is

much to welcome; Gibson (2002) noted some worldwide trends in EIA, such as that it is earlier in the process, more open and participative, more comprehensive (not just biophysical environment), more mandatory, more closely monitored, more widely applied (e.g. at various levels), more integrative, more ambitious (regarding sustainability objectives) and more humble (recognizing uncertainties, applying precaution). Yet such progress is variable, and has not been without its problems. A number of the current issues in EIA are highlighted here and will be discussed more fully in later chapters.

1.6.1 The nature of methods of assessment

As noted in Section 1.2, some of the main steps in the EIA process (e.g. auditing and monitoring) may be missing from many studies. There may also be problems with the steps that are included. The prediction of impacts raises various conceptual and technical problems. The problem of establishing the environmental baseline position has already been noted. It may also be difficult to establish the dimensions and development stages of a project clearly, particularly for new technology projects. Further conceptual problems include establishing what would have happened in the relevant environment without a project, clarifying the complexity of interactions of phenomena, and especially making trade-offs in an integrated way (i.e. assessing the trade-offs between economic apples, social oranges and physical bananas). Other technical problems relate to data availability and the tendency to focus on the quantitative, and often single, indicators in some areas. There may also be delays and gaps between cause and effect, and projects and policies may discontinue. The lack of auditing of predictive techniques limits the feedback on the effectiveness of methods. Nevertheless, innovative methods are being developed to predict and evaluate impacts, ranging from simple checklists and matrices to complex mathematical models and multi-criteria approaches. It should be noted however that these methods may not be neutral, in the sense that the more complex they are, the more difficult it becomes for the general public to participate in the EIA process.

1.6.2 The quality and efficiency of the EIA process

One assessment of quality is that of the immediate output of the process, the EIS. Many EISs may fail to meet even minimum standards. For example, an early survey by Jones *et al.* (1991) of the EISs published under UK EIA regulations highlighted some shortcomings. They found

> . . . that one-third of the EISs did not appear to contain the required non-technical summary, that, in a quarter of the cases, they were judged not to contain the data needed to assess the likely environmental effects of the development, and that in the great majority of cases, the more complex, inter-active impacts were neglected.

The DoE (1996) later suggested that although there had been some learning from experience, many EISs in the UK were still unsatisfactory (see Chapter 8 for further and updated discussion). Quality may vary between types of project. It may also vary between countries supposedly operating under the same legislative framework.

EISs can run the risk of being voluminous, un-integrated, documents that can be difficult for most of the participants in the EIA process. Such outcomes raise various questions about the efficiency of the EIA process. For example, are 'safety first' policies resulting in too many projects being screened for EIA and the EIA scoping stage being too all embracing of potential impacts? Is there too much focus on over-descriptive baseline work and not enough focus on the key impacts that matter? Is the EIS still a set of segregated specialist chapters rather than a well-integrated document? Are the key steps of monitoring and auditing well enough built into the process? Considerations of efficiency, however, can also run counter to considerations of fairness in the process.

1.6.3 The relative roles of participants in the process

The various 'actors' in the EIA process – the developer, the affected parties, the general public and the regulators at various levels of government – have differential access to the process, and their influence on the outcome varies. Some would argue that in countries such as the UK the process is too developer-orientated. The developer or the developer's consultant carries out the EIA and prepares the EIS, and is unlikely to predict that the project will be an environmental disaster. Notwithstanding this, developers themselves are concerned about the potential delays associated with the requirement to submit an EIS. They are also concerned about cost. Details about costs are difficult to obtain. Early estimates (Clark 1984; Hart 1984; Wathern 1988) were of EIA costs of 0.5–2.0 per cent of a project's value. The UK DETR (1997) suggested £35,000 as an appropriate median figure for the cost of undertaking an EIA under the EC regulations, but for major projects the monetary figure can be much higher than this. A more recent EU commissioned study evaluating the EIA Directive indicated that, as a share of the project costs, EIAs tend to range from an upper limit of 1 per cent for small projects to 0.1 per cent for larger projects (CEC 2006).

Procedures for and the practice of public participation in the EIA process vary between, and sometimes within, countries, from the very comprehensive to the very partial and largely cosmetic. An important issue is the stages in the EIA process to which the public have access. Government roles in the EIA process may be conditioned by caution at extending systems, by resource considerations and by limited experience and expertise for what in some domains is still a relatively new and developing area. A central government may offer only limited guidance on best practice, and make inconsistent decisions. A local government may find it difficult to handle the scope and complexity of the content of EISs, especially for major projects.

1.6.4 The effectiveness of the EIA process

While EIA systems are now well established in many countries of the world, there is considerable soul-searching about how effective it all is, whether EIA is achieving its purposes – as set out in Section 1.3? There is also considerable debate about *how we assess EIA effectiveness*. There can be various (inter-related) dimensions to this. For example, a procedural/narrow approach would focus on how well EIA is being carried out according to its own procedural requirements in the country of concern; a procedural/wider approach might consider the extent to which EIA is contributing to increased environmental awareness and learning among the array of key stakeholders. These dimensions are partly covered in the preceding sections (1.6.1–1.6.3). However, more fundamental, in relation to EIA core purposes, are substantive approaches. For example, a substantive/narrow approach would concentrate on whether EIA is having a direct impact on the quality of planning decisions and the nature of developments. A substantive/wider approach would focus on the fundamental question of whether EIA is maintaining, restoring, and enhancing environmental quality; is it contributing towards more sustainable development? These issues of EIA effectiveness are examined in various sections, and particularly in Chapter 8.

1.6.5 Beyond the decision

Many EISs are for one-off projects, and there may be little incentive for developers to audit the quality of the assessment predictions and to monitor impacts as an input to a better assessment for the next project. Yet EIA up to and no further than the decision on a project is a very partial exercise. It is important to ensure that the required mitigation and enhancement measures are implemented in practice. In some areas of the world (e.g. California, Western Australia, the Netherlands, and Hong Kong to mention just a few), the monitoring of impacts is mandatory, and monitoring procedures must be included in an EIS. It is also important to take the opportunity for a cyclical learning process, auditing predicted outcomes as fully as possible – to check the accuracy of predictions. The relationship with environmental management processes is another vital area of concern; EISs can effectively lead to environmental management plans for project implementation – but, again, good practice is patchy. The extension of such approaches constitutes another significant current issue in the project-based EIA process.

1.6.6 Managing the widening scope and complexity of IA activity

As noted in Section 1.5, the IA family has grown apace, especially in recent years. How can this complexity be managed? For example, what should be the norm for the content of a contemporary EIS? There is a strong case for widening the dimensions of the environment under consideration to include socio-economic impacts more fully. The trade-off between the often adverse biophysical impacts of a development and the often beneficial socio-economic impacts can constitute the crucial dilemma for decision-makers. Coverage can also be widened to include other types of impacts only very partially covered to date. Should the EIS include social, health and equality elements as standard, or should these be separate activities, and documents? In a similar vein, which projects should have EIAs? For example, project EIA may be mandatory only for a limited set of major projects, but in practice many others may be included. Case law is now building up in many countries, but the criteria for the inclusion or exclusion of a project for EIA may not always be clear.

As also noted in Section 1.5, the SEA/SA of PPPs represents a logical extension of project assessment. SEA/SA can cope better with cumulative impacts, alternatives and mitigation measures than project assessment. But what is the nature of the relationship between the different scales of impact assessment? Strategic levels of assessment of plans and programmes should provide useful frameworks for the more site-specific project assessments, hopefully reducing workload and leading to more concise and effective EIAs. But the anticipated tiered relationship may be more in theory than practice, leading to unnecessary and wasteful duplication of activity.

1.7 An outline of subsequent parts and chapters

This book is in four parts. The first establishes the context of EIA in the growth of concern about environmental issues and in relevant legislation, with particular reference to the UK and the EU.

Following from this first chapter, which provides an introduction to EIA and an overview of principles, Chapter 2 focuses on the origins of EIA under the US NEPA of 1969, on interim developments in the UK, and on the subsequent introduction of EC Directive 85/337 and subsequent amendments and developments. The details of the UK legislative framework for EIA, under T&CP and other legislation are discussed in Chapter 3.

Part 2 provides a rigorous step-by-step approach to the EIA process. This is the core of the text. Chapter 4 covers the early start-up stages, establishing a management framework, clarifying the type of developments for EIA, and outlining approaches to scoping, the consideration of alternatives, project description, establishing the baseline and identifying impacts. Chapter 5 explores the central issues of prediction, the assessment of significance and impact mitigation and enhancement. The approach draws out broad principles affecting prediction exercises, exemplified with reference to particular cases. Chapter 6 provides coverage of an important issue identified above: participation in the EIA process. Communication in the EIA process, EIS presentation and EIA review are also covered in this chapter. Chapter 7 takes the process beyond the decision on a project and examines the importance of, and approaches to, monitoring and auditing in the EIA process.

Part 3 exemplifies the process in practice. Chapter 8 provides an overview of UK practice to date, including quantitative and qualitative analyses of the EISs prepared. Chapter 9 provides a review of EIA practice in several key sectors, including energy, transport, waste management and tourism. A feature of the chapter is the provision of a set of case studies of recent and topical EIA studies from the UK and overseas, illustrating particular features of and issues in the EIA process. Chapter 10 draws on comparative experience from developed countries (e.g. Canada and Australia) and from a number of countries from the developing and emerging economies (Peru, China, Benin and Poland) – presented to highlight some of the strengths and weaknesses of other systems in practice. The important role of international agencies in EIA practice – such as the European Bank for Reconstruction and Development and the World Bank – is also discussed in this chapter.

Part 4 looks to the future; it illuminates many of the issues noted in Section 1.6. The penultimate chapter discusses the need for SEA and some of its limitations. It reviews the status of SEA in the USA, European Union and UNECE, and China. It then discusses in more detail how the European SEA Directive is being implemented in the UK. Chapter 12, the final chapter, focuses on improving the effectiveness of, and the prospects for, project-based EIA. It considers the array of perspectives on change from the various participants in the EIA process, followed by a consideration of possible developments in some important areas of the EIA process and in the nature of EISs. The chapter concludes with a discussion of the parallel and complementary development of environmental management systems and audits. Together, these topics act as a kind of action list for future improvements to EIA. A set of appendices provide details of legislation and practice, and websites and journals not considered appropriate to the main text.

SOME QUESTIONS

The following questions are intended to help the reader focus on the important issues of this chapter, and to start building some understanding of the principles of EIA.

1 Revisit the definitions of EIA given in this chapter. Which one do you prefer and why?
2 Some steps in the EIA process have proved to be more difficult to implement than others. From your initial reading, identify which these might be and consider why they might have proved to be problematic.
3 Taking a few recent examples of environmental impact statements for projects in your country, review their structure and content against the outline information in this chapter. Do they raise any issues on structure and content?
4 What are the differences between (i) project screening and project scoping, and (ii) impact mitigation and impact enhancement?
5 Review the purposes for EIA, and assess their importance from your own perspective.
6 Apply the characteristics of major projects set out in Table 1.2 to two major projects with which you are familiar. Are there any important variations between the applications? If so, can you explain why?
7 Similarly, for one of the projects identified in Q6, plot the likely stages in its life cycle – applying approximate timings as far as possible.
8 What do you understand by a multi-dimensional approach to the environment, in EIA?
9 What is an impact in EIA? Do you see any difference between impacts and effects?
10 What do you understand by (i) irreversible impacts, (ii) cumulative impacts and (iii) distributional impacts, in EIA?
11 Why should it be important to adopt an adaptive approach to EIA?
12 This question may be a little deep at this stage of your reading, but we will ask it all the same: do you think it is reasonable to consider the EIA process as a rational, linear scientific process?
13 What are the main differences between EIA and SEA?
14 What might be some of the reasons for the widening scope of EIA?
15 What do you understand by 'beyond the decision' in EIA?
16 How might we measure (i) the efficiency, and (ii) the effectiveness of EIA?

Notes

1 In some domains the EIS is referred to more simply as an ES; these terms are used interchangeably in this book.
2 Turner and Pearce (1992) and Pearce (1992) have drawn attention to alternative interpretations of maintaining the capital stock. A policy of conserving the whole capital stock (man-made, human and natural) is consistent with running down any part of it as long as there is substitutability between capital degradation in one area and investment in another. This can be interpreted as a 'weak sustainability' position. In contrast, a 'strong sustainability' position would argue that it is not acceptable to run down environmental assets, for several reasons: uncertainty (we do not know the full consequences for human beings), irreversibility (lost species cannot be replaced), life support (some ecological assets serve life-support functions) and loss aversion (people are highly averse to environmental losses). The 'strong sustainability' position has much to commend it, but institutional responses have varied.

References

ANZECC (Australia and New Zealand Environment and Conservation Council) 1991. *A national approach to EIA in Australia*. Canberra: ANZECC.

Bartlett, R.V. and Kurian, P.A. 1999. The theory of environmental impact assessment: implicit models of policy making. *Policy and Politics* 27 (4), 415–33.

Beattie, R. 1995. Everything you already know about EIA, but don't often admit. *Environmental Impact Assessment Review* 15.

Beck, U. 1992. *Risk society: towards a new modernity*. London: Sage.

Beck, U. 2008. *World at risk*. Cambridge: Polity Press.

Belton,V. and Stewart ,T.J. 2002. *Multiple criteria decision analysis*. Boston/London: Kluwer Academic.

Boulding, K. 1966. The economics of the coming Spaceship Earth. In *Environmental quality to a growing economy*, H. Jarrett (ed), 3–14. Baltimore: Johns Hopkins University Press.

Braybooke, C., and Lindblom, D. 1963. *A strategy of decision*. New York: Free Press of Glencoe.

Breese, G. *et al*. 1965. *The impact of large installations on nearby urban areas*. Los Angeles: Sage.

Caldwell, L. 1988. Environmental impact analysis: origins, evolution and future directions. *Review of Policy Research*, 8 (1), 75–83.

Calow, P. (ed) 1997. *Handbook of environmental risk assessment and management*. Oxford: Blackwell Science.

Canter, L. and Ross, W. 2010. State of practice of cumulative effects assessment and management: the good, the bad and the ugly. *Impact Assessment and Project Appraisal* 28 (4), 261–8.

Carley, M.J. and Bustelo, E.S. 1984. *Social impact assessment and monitoring: a guide to the literature*. Boulder: Westview Press.

Catlow, J. and Thirlwall, C.G. 1976. *Environmental impact analysis*. London: DoE.

CEC (Commission of the European Communities) 1982. *The contribution of infrastructure to regional development*. Brussels: CEC.

CEC 1985. On the assessment of the effects of certain public and private projects on the environment. *Official Journal* L175, 5 July.

CEC 1992. *Towards sustainability: a European Community programme of policy and action in relation to the environment and sustainable development*, vol. 2, Brussels: CEC.

CEC 2001. *Our future, our choice. The sixth EU environment action programme 2001–10*. Brussels: CEC.

CEC 2003a. (Impacts Assessment Unit, Oxford Brookes University) Five years' report to the European Parliament and the Council on the application and effectiveness of the EIA Directive. Available on website of EC DG Environment: www.europa.eu. int/comm/environment/eia/home.htm.

CEC 2003b. *Directive 2003/35/EC of the European Parliament and of the Council of 26 May 2003 providing for public participation in respect of the drawing up of certain plans and programmes relating to the environment and amending with regard to public participation and access to justice Council Directives 85/337/EEC and 96/61/EC – statement by the Commission*. Brussels: CEC.

CEC 2006. Evaluation *of EU legislation – Directive 85/337EEC and associated amendments*. Carried out by GHK-Technopolis. Brussels: DG Enterprise and Industry.

CEC 2009. *Report to the Council, European Parliament, European Economic and Social Committee and the Committee of the Regions on the application and effectiveness of the EIA Directive*. Brussels: CEC.

CEPA (Commonwealth Environmental Protection Agency) 1994. *Assessment of cumulative impacts and strategic assessment in EIA*. Canberra: CEPA.

Clark, B.D. 1984. Environmental impact assessment (EIA): scope and objectives. In *Perspectives on environmental impact assessment*, B.D. Clark *et al*. (eds). Dordrecht: Reidel.

Crane, A., McWilliams, A., Matten, D., Moon, J. and Siegel, D.S (eds). 2008. *The Oxford handbook of corporate social responsibility*. Oxford: Oxford University Press.

Dalal-Clayton, B. and Sadler, B. 2004. *Sustainability appraisal: a review of international experience and practice, first draft of work in progress*. International Institute for Environment and Development. Available at: www.iied.org/Gov/spa/docs.html#pilot.

DCLG (Department for Communities and Local Government) 2005. Planning Policy Statement 1(PPS1). London: DCLG.

DEFRA (Department for Environment, Food and Rural Affairs) 2005. *Securing the future: delivering the UK sustainable development strategy*. London: HM Government.

DETR (Department of Environment, Transport and the Regions) 1997. *Consultation paper: implementation of the EC Directive (97/11/EC) – determining the need for environmental assessment*. London: DETR.

DETR 1999a. *UK strategy for sustainable development: A better quality of life*. London: Stationery Office.

DETR 1999b. *Quality of life counts – Indicators for a strategy for sustainable development for the United Kingdom: a baseline assessment*. London: Stationery Office.

DETR 2000. *Environmental impact assessment: a guide to the procedures*. Tonbridge: Thomas Telford Publishing.

DoE (Department of the Environment) 1989. *Environmental assessment: a guide to the procedures.* London: HMSO.

DoE et al. 1990. *This common inheritance: Britain's environmental strategy* (Cmnd 1200). London: HMSO.

DoE 1991. *Policy appraisal and the environment.* London: HMSO.

DoE 1996. *Changes in the quality of environmental impact statements.* London: HMSO.

Downey, L. 2005. Assessing environmental inequality: how the conclusions we draw vary according to the definitions we employ. *Sociological Spectrum*, 25, 349–69.

EEA (European Environment Agency) 2010. *European environment: state and outlook 2010.* EEA: Copenhagen.

Etzioni, A. 1967. Mixed scanning: a 'third' approach to decision making. *Public Administration Review* 27(5), 385–92.

Faber, N., Jorna, R. and van Engelen, J. 2005. A Study into the conceptual foundations of the notion of 'sustainability'. *Journal of Environmental Assessment Policy and Management*, 7 (1).

Faludi, A. (ed) 1973. *A reader in planning theory.* Oxford: Pergamon.

Finsterbusch, K. 1985. State of the art in social impact assessment. *Environment and Behaviour* 17, 192–221.

Flyberg, B. 2003. *Megaprojects and risk: on anatomy of risk.* Cambridge: Cambridge University Press.

Forester, J. 1989. *Planning in the face of power.* Berkeley, CA: University of California Press.

Friend, J. and Jessop, N. 1977. *Local government and strategic choice*, 2nd edn, Toronto: Pergamon Press.

Gibson, R. 2002. From Wreck Cove to Voisey's Bay: the evolution of federal environmental assessment in Canada. *Impact Assessment and Project Appraisal* 20 (3), 151–60.

Glasson, J. 1999. EIA – impact on decisions, Chapter 7 in *Handbook of environmental impact assessment*, J. Pettes (ed), vol. 1. Oxford: Blackwell Science.

Habermas, J. 1984. *The theory of communicative action*, vol. 1: *Reason and the rationalisation of society*. London: Polity Press.

Hacking, T. and Guthrie, P. 2008. A framework for clarifying the meaning of triple bottom line, integrated and sustainability assessment. *Environmental Impact Assessment Review 28*, 73–89.

Hanley, N.D. and Splash, C. 1993. *Cost–benefit analysis and the environment.* Aldershot: Edward Elgar.

Hart, S.L. 1984. The costs of environmental review. In *Improving impact assessment*, S.L. Hart et al. (eds). Boulder, CO: Westview Press.

Healey, P. 1996. The communicative turn in planning theory and its implication for spatial strategy making. *Environment and Planning B: Planning and Design* 23, 217–34.

Healey, P. 1997. *Collaborative planning: shaping places in fragmented societies.* Basingstoke: Macmillan.

HMG, Secretary of State for the Environment 1994. *Sustainable development: the UK strategy.* London: HMSO.

HMG 2008. *Planning Act 2008.* London: Stationery Office.

Holmberg, J. and Sandbrook, R. 1992. Sustainable development: what is to be done? In *Policies for a small planet*, J. Holmberg (ed), 19–38. London: Earthscan.

IAIA (International Association for Impact Assessment) 1994. Guidelines and principles for social impact assessment. *Impact Assessment* 12 (2).

IAIA 2009. *What is impact assessment?* Fargo, ND: IAIA.

IOCGP (Inter-organizational Committee on Guidelines and Principles for Social Impact Assessment) 1994. *Guidelines and Principles for Social Impact Assessment*, 12 (Summer), 107–52.

IOCGP 2003. Principles and guidelines for social impact assessment in the USA, *Impact Assessment and Project Appraisal* 21 (3), 231–50.

IPHI (Institute of Public Health in Ireland) 2009. *Health impact assessment guidance.* Dublin and Belfast: IPHI.

Jay, S., Jones, C., Slinn, P. and Wood, C. 2007. Environmental impact assessment: retrospect and prospect. *Environmental Impact Assessment Review* 27, 287–300.

Jones, C., Lee, N., Wood, C.M. 1991. *UK environmental statements 1988–1990: an analysis.* Occasional Paper 29, Department of Planning and Landscape, University of Manchester.

Kaiser, E., Godshalk, D. and Chapin, S. 1995. *Urban land use planning*, 4th edn. Chicago: University of Illinois Press.

Kennedy, W. V. 1988. Environmental impact assessment in North America, Western Europe: what has worked where, how and why? *International Environmental Reporter* 11 (4), 257–62.

Kirkby, J., O'Keefe, P. and Timberlake, L. 1995. *The earthscan reader in sustainable development.* London: Earthscan.

Lawrence, D. 1997. The need for EIA theory building. *Environmental Impact Assessment Review* 17, 79–107.

Lawrence, D. 2000. Planning theories and environmental impact assessment. *Environmental Impact Assessment Review* 20, 607–25.

Lee, N. 2002. Integrated approaches to impact assessment: substance or make-believe? *Environmental Assessment Yearbook*. Lincoln: IEMA, 14–20.

Leknes, E. 2001. The role of EIA in the decision-making process. *Environmental Impact Assessment Review* 21, 309–03.

Lichfield, N. 1996. *Community impact evaluation*. London: UCL Press.

Lindblom, E.C.E. 1980. *The policy making process*, 2nd edn. Englewood Cliffs: Prentice Hall.

Magnox Electric 2002. *ES for Decommissioning of Hinkley Point A Nuclear Power Station*. Berkeley, UK: Magnox Electric.

McLoughlin, J.B. 1969. *Urban and regional planning – a systems approach*. London: Faber & Faber.

Munn, R.E. 1979. *Environmental impact assessment: principles and procedures*, 2nd edn, New York: Wiley.

O'Riordan, T. 1988. The politics of sustainability. In *Sustainable environmental management: principles and practice*, R.K. Turner (ed). London: Belhaven.

O'Riordan, T. 1990. EIA from the environmentalist's perspective. VIA 4, March, 13.

Pearce, D.W. 1992. *Towards sustainable development through environment assessment*. Working Paper PA92–11, Centre for Social and Economic Research in the Global Environment, University College London.

Pearce, D., Markandya, A. and Barbier, E. 1989. *Blueprint for a green economy*. London: Earthscan.

Petts, J. 1999. Environmental impact assessment versus other environmental management decision tools. In *Handbook of environmental impact assessment*, J. Petts (ed), vol. 1, Oxford: Blackwell Science.

Preston, D. and Bedford, B. 1988. Evaluating cumulative effects on wetland functions: a conceptual overview and generic framework. *Environmental Management* 12 (5).

Redclift, M. 1987. *Sustainable development: exploring the contradictions*. London: Methuen.

Reid, D. 1995. *Sustainable development: an introductory guide*. London: Earthscan.

RPS, 2004. *ES for Kings Cross Central*. RPS for Argent St George, London and Continental Railways & Excel.

Sadler, B. 1996. *Environmental assessment in a changing world: evaluating practice to improve performance*. International study on the effectiveness of environmental assessment. Ottawa: Canadian Environmental Assessment Agency.

Scrase, J and Sheate, W. 2002. Integration and integrated approaches to assessment: what do they mean for the environment? *Journal of Environmental Policy and Planning* 4 (4), 276–94.

SEERA 2001. *A better quality of life in the south east*. Guildford: South East England Regional Assembly.

Skolimowski, P. 1995. Sustainable development – how meaningful? *Environmental Values* 4.

Stakhiv, E. 1988. An evaluation paradigm for cumulative impact analysis. *Environmental Management* 12 (5).

Symonds/EDAW 2004. *ES for Lower Lea Valley: Olympics and legacy planning application*. Symonds/EDAW for London Development Agency.

Therivel, R. 2010. *Strategic environmental assessment in action*, 2nd edn. London: Earthscan.

Therivel, R. and Partidario, M.R. 1996. *The practice of strategic environmental assessment*. London: Earthscan.

Therivel, R., Wilson, E., Thompson, S., Heaney, D. and Pritchard, D. 1992. *Strategic environmental assessment*. London: RSPB/Earthscan.

Turner, R.K. and Pearce, D.W. 1992. *Sustainable development: ethics and economics*. Working Paper PA92–09, Centre for Social and Economic Research in the Global Environment, University College London.

UNECE (United Nations Economic Commission for Europe) 1991. *Policies and systems of environmental impact assessment*. Geneva: United Nations.

UNECE 2000. Access to information, public participation and access to justice in environmental matters Geneva: United Nations.

UN World Commission on Environment and Development 1987. *Our common future*. Oxford: Oxford University Press.

Vanclay, F. 2003. International principles for social impact assessment. International Assessment and Project Appraisal 21 (1), 5–12.

Vanclay, F. and Bronstein, D. (eds) 1995. *Environment and social impact assessments*. London: Wiley.

Wathern, P. (ed) 1988. *Environmental impact assessment: theory and practice*. London: Unwin Hyman.

Weston, J. 2000. EIA, Decision-making theory and screening and scoping in UK practice. *Journal of Environmental Planning and Management* 43 (2), 185–203.

Weston, J. 2003. Is there a future for EIA? Response to Benson. *Impact Assessment and Project Appraisal* 21 (4), 278–80.

White, P.R., Franke, M. and Hindle, P. 1995. *Integrated solid waste management: a lifecycle inventory*. London: Chapman Hall.

Wilson, E. and Piper, J. 2010. *Spatial planning and climate change*. Abingdon: Routledge.

2 Origins and development

2.1 Introduction

Environmental impact assessment was first formally established in the USA in 1969 and has since spread, in various forms, to most other countries. In the UK, EIA was initially an ad hoc procedure carried out by local planning authorities and developers, primarily for oil- and gas-related developments. A 1985 European Community directive on EIA (Directive 85/337) introduced broadly uniform requirements for EIA to all EU Member States and significantly affected the development of EIA in the UK. However, 10 years after the Directive was agreed, Member States were still carrying out widely diverse forms of EIA, contradicting the Directive's aim of 'levelling the playing field'. Amendments of 1997, 2003 and 2009 aimed to improve this situation. The nature of EIA systems (e.g. mandatory or discretionary, level of public participation, types of action requiring EIA) and their implementation in practice vary widely from country to country. However, the rapid spread of the concept of EIA and its central role in many countries' programmes of environmental protection attest to its universal validity as a proactive planning tool.

This chapter first discusses how the system of EIA evolved in the USA. The present status of EIA worldwide is then briefly reviewed (Chapter 10 will consider a number of countries' systems of EIA in greater depth). EIA in the UK and the EU are then discussed. Finally, we review the various systems of EIA in the EU Member States.

2.2 The National Environmental Policy Act and subsequent US systems

The US National Environmental Policy Act of 1969, also known as NEPA, grew out of increasing concern in the USA about widespread examples of environmental damage, vividly highlighted in the 1960s by the books *Silent Spring* (Carson 1962) and *The Population Bomb* (Ehrlich 1968). NEPA was the first legislation to require EIAs. Consequently it has become an important model for other EIA systems, both because it was a radically new form of environmental policy and because of the successes and failures of its subsequent development. Since its enactment, NEPA has resulted in the preparation of well over 25,000 full and partial EISs, which have influenced countless decisions and represent a powerful base of environmental information. On the other hand, NEPA is unique. Other countries have shied away from the form it takes and the procedures it sets out, not least because they are unwilling to face a situation like that in the USA, where there has been extensive litigation over the interpretation and workings of the EIA system.

This section covers NEPA's legislative history (i.e. the early development before it became law), the interpretation of NEPA by the courts and the Council on Environmental Quality (CEQ), the main EIA procedures arising from NEPA, and likely future developments. The reader is referred to Anderson *et al.* (1984), Bear (1990), Canter (1996), CEQ (1997a), CRS (2006), Greenberg (2012), Mandelker (2000), Orloff (1980) and the annual reports of the CEQ for further information.

2.2.1 Legislative history

The National Environmental Policy Act is in many ways a fluke, strengthened by amendments that should have weakened it, and interpreted by the courts to have powers that were not originally intended. The legislative history of NEPA is interesting not only in itself but also because it explains many of the anomalies of its operation and touches on some of the major issues involved in designing an EIA system. Several proposals to establish a national environmental policy were discussed in the US Senate and House of Representatives in the early 1960s. All these proposals included some form of unified environmental policy and the establishment of a high-level committee to foster it. In February 1969, Bill S1075 was introduced in the Senate; it proposed a programme of federally funded ecological research and the establishment of a CEQ. A similar bill, HR6750, introduced in the House of Representatives, proposed the formation of a CEQ and a brief statement on national environmental policy. Subsequent discussions in both chambers of Congress focused on several points:

- The need for a declaration of national environmental policy (now Title I of NEPA).
- A proposed statement that 'each person has a fundamental and inalienable right to a healthful environment' (which would put environmental health on a par with, say, free speech). This was later weakened to the statement in §101(c) that 'each person should enjoy a healthful environment'.
- Action-forcing provisions similar to those then being proposed for the Water Quality

Improvement Act, which would require federal officials to prepare a detailed statement concerning the probable environmental impacts of any major action; this was to evolve into NEPA's §102(2)(C), which requires EIA. The initial wording of the Bill had required a 'finding', which would have been subject to review by those responsible for environmental protection, rather than a 'detailed statement' subject to inter-agency review. The Senate had intended to weaken the Bill by requiring only a detailed statement. Instead, the 'detailed assessment' became the subject of external review and challenge; the public availability of the detailed statements became a major force shaping the law's implementation in its early years. NEPA became operational on 1 January 1970. Table 2.1 summarizes its main points.

2.2.2 An interpretation of NEPA

The National Environmental Policy Act is a generally worded law that required substantial early interpretation. The CEQ, which was set up by NEPA, prepared guidelines to assist in the Act's interpretation. However, much of the strength of NEPA came from early court rulings. NEPA was immediately seen by environmental activists as a significant vehicle for preventing environmental harm, and the early 1970s saw a series of influential lawsuits and court decisions based on it. These lawsuits were of three broad types, as described by Orloff (1980):

1   Challenging an agency's decision not to prepare an EIA. This generally raised issues such as whether a project was major, federal, an 'action', or had significant environmental impacts (see NEPA §102(2)(C)). For instance, the issue of whether an action is federal came into question in some lawsuits concerning the federal funding of local government projects.[1]

2   Challenging the adequacy of an agency's EIS. This raised issues such as whether an EIS adequately addressed alternatives, and whether it covered the full range of significant environmental impacts. A famous early court case concerned the Chesapeake Environmental Protection Association's claim that

Table 2.1 Main points of NEPA

NEPA consists of two titles. Title I establishes a national policy on the protection and restoration of environmental quality. Title II set up a three-member CEQ to review environmental programmes and progress, and to advise the president on these matters. It also requires the president to submit an annual 'Environmental Quality Report' to Congress. The provisions of Title I are the main determinants of EIA in the USA, and they are summarized here.

Section 101 contains requirements of a substantive nature. It states that the federal government has a continuing responsibility to 'create and maintain conditions under which man and nature can exist in productive harmony, and fulfil the social, economic and other requirements of present and future generations of Americans'. As such the government is to use all practicable means, 'consistent with other essential considerations of national policy', to minimize adverse environmental impact and to preserve and enhance the environment through federal plans and programmes. Finally, 'each person should enjoy a healthful environment', and citizens have a responsibility to preserve the environment.

Section 102 requirements are of a procedural nature. Federal agencies are required to make full analyses of all the environmental effects of implementing their programmes or actions. Section 102(1) directs agencies to interpret and administer policies, regulations and laws in accordance with the policies of NEPA. Section 102(2) requires federal agencies

- To use 'a systematic and interdisciplinary approach' to ensure that social, natural and environmental sciences are used in planning and decision-making.
- To identify and develop procedures and methods so that 'presently unquantified environmental amenities and values may be given appropriate consideration in decision-making along with traditional economic and technical considerations'.
- To 'include in every recommendation or report on proposals for legislation and other *major Federal actions significantly affecting the quality of the human environment, a detailed statement* by the responsible official' on:
    - the environmental impact of the proposed action;
    - any adverse environmental effects that cannot be avoided should the proposal be implemented;
    - alternatives to the proposed action;
    - the relationship between local short-term uses of man's environment and the maintenance and enhancement of long-term productivity;
    - any irreversible and irretrievable commitments of resources that would be involved in the proposed action should it be implemented. [Emphasis added]

Section 103 requires federal agencies to review their regulations and procedures for adherence to NEPA, and to suggest any necessary remedial measures.

---

the Atomic Energy Commission did not adequately consider the water quality impacts of its proposed nuclear power plants, particularly in the EIA for the Calvert Cliffs power plant.[2] The Commission argued that NEPA merely required the consideration of water quality standards; opponents argued that it required an assessment beyond mere compliance with standards. The courts sided with the opponents.

3   Challenging an agency's substantive decision, namely its decision to allow or not to allow a project to proceed in the light of the contents of its EIS. Another influential early court ruling laid down guidelines for the judicial review of agency decisions, noting that the court's only function was to ensure that the agency had taken a 'hard look' at environmental consequences, not to substitute its judgement for that of the agency.[3]

The early proactive role of the courts greatly strengthened the power of environmental movements and caused many projects to be stopped or substantially amended. In many cases the lawsuits delayed construction for long enough to make them economically unfeasible or to allow the areas where projects would have been sited to be designated as national parks or wildlife areas (Turner 1988). More recent decisions have been less clearly pro-environment than the earliest decisions. The flood of early lawsuits, with the delays and costs involved, was a lesson to other countries in how *not* to set up an EIA system. As will be shown later, many countries carefully distanced their EIA systems from the possibility of lawsuits.

The CEQ was also instrumental in establishing guidelines to interpret NEPA, producing interim guidelines in 1970, and guidelines in 1971 and 1973. Generally the courts adhered closely to these guidelines when making their rulings. However, the guidelines were problematic: they were not detailed enough, and were interpreted by the federal agencies as being discretionary rather than binding. To combat these limitations, President Carter issued Executive Order 11992 in 1977, giving the CEQ authority to set enforceable regulations for implementing NEPA. These were issued in 1978 (CEQ 1978) and sought to make the NEPA process more useful for decision-makers and the public, to reduce paperwork and delay and to emphasize real environmental issues and alternatives.

2.2.3 A summary of NEPA procedures

The process of EIA established by NEPA, and developed further in the CEQ regulations, is summarized in Figure 2.1. The following citations are from the CEQ regulations (CEQ 1978).

> [The EIA process begins] as close as possible to the time the agency is developing or is presented with a proposal . . . The statement shall be prepared early enough so that it can serve practically as an important contribution to the decision-making process and will not be used to rationalize or justify decisions already made. (§1502.5)

A 'lead agency' is designated that co-ordinates the EIA process. The lead agency first determines whether the proposal requires the preparation of a full EIS, no EIS at all, or a 'finding of no significant impact' (FONSI). This is done through a series of tests. A first test is whether a federal action is likely to individually or cumulatively have a significant environmental impact. All federal agencies have compiled lists of 'categorical exclusions' that are felt not to have such impacts. If an action is on such a list, then no further EIA action is generally needed. If an action is not categorically excluded, an 'environmental assessment' is carried out to determine whether a full EIS or a FONSI is needed. A FONSI is a public document that explains why the action is not expected to have a significant environmental impact.

If a FONSI is prepared, then a permit would usually be granted following public discussion. If a full EIS is found to be needed, the lead agency publishes a 'Notice of intent', and the *process of scoping begins*. The aim of the scoping exercise is to determine the issues to be addressed in the EIA: to eliminate insignificant issues, focus on those that are significant and identify alternatives to be addressed. The lead agency invites the participation of the proponent of the action, affected parties and other interested persons.

> [The alternatives] section is the heart of the environmental impact statement . . . [It] should present the environmental impacts of the proposal and the alternatives in comparative form, thus sharply defining the issues and providing a clear basis for choice . . . (§1502.14)

The agency must analyse the full range of direct, indirect and cumulative effects of the preferred alternative, if any, and of the reasonable alternatives identified in the process. For the purpose of NEPA, 'effects' and 'impacts' mean the same thing, and include ecological, aesthetic, historic, cultural, economic, social or health impacts, whether adverse or beneficial.

A draft EIS is then prepared, and is reviewed and commented on by the relevant agencies and the public. These comments are taken into account in the subsequent preparation of a final EIS. An EIS is normally presented in the format shown in Table 2.2. In an attempt to be comprehensive, early EISs tended to be so bulky as to be virtually unreadable. The CEQ guidelines consequently emphasize the need to concentrate only on important issues and to prepare readable documents: 'The text of final environmental impact statements shall normally be less than 150 pages . . . Environmental impact statements shall be written in plain language . . . ' (§1502.7–8)

The public is involved in this process, both at the scoping stage and after publication of the draft and final EISs:

> Agencies shall: (a) Make diligent efforts to involve the public in preparing and implementing NEPA procedures . . . (b) Provide public notice of NEPA-related hearings, public

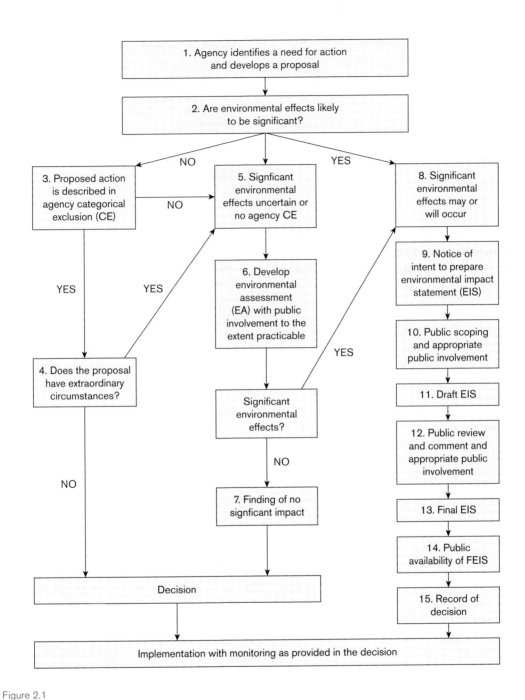

Figure 2.1

Process of EIA under NEPA

Source: CEQ 2007

Table 2.2 Typical format for an EIS under NEPA

(a) Cover sheet

- list of responsible agencies
- title of proposed action
- contact persons at agencies
- designation of EIS as draft, final or supplement
- abstract of EIS
- date by which comments must be received

(b) Summary (usually 15 pages or less)

- major conclusions
- areas of controversy
- issues to be resolved

(c) Table of contents

(d) Purpose of and need for action

(e) Alternatives, including proposed action

(f) Affected environment

(g) Environmental consequences

- environmental impacts of alternatives, including proposed action
- adverse environmental effects that cannot be avoided if proposal is implemented
- mitigation measures to be used and residual effects of mitigation
- relation between short-term uses of the environment and maintenance and enhancement of long-term productivity
- irreversible or irretrievable commitments of resources if proposal is implemented discussion of:
  - direct, indirect and cumulative effects and their significance
  - possible conflicts between proposed action and objectives of relevant land-use plans, policies and controls
  - effects of alternatives, including proposed action
  - energy requirements and conservation potential of various alternatives and mitigation measures
  - natural or depletable resource requirements and conservation of various alternatives and mitigation measures
  - effects on urban quality, historic and cultural resources, and built environment
  - means to mitigate adverse impacts

(h) Monitoring arrangements, and environmental management system

(i) List of preparers

(j) List of agencies, etc. to which copies of EIS are sent

(k) Index

(l) Appendices, including supporting data

meetings and the availability of environmental documents ... (c) Hold or sponsor public hearings ... whenever appropriate ... (d) Solicit appropriate information from the public. (e) Explain in its procedures where interested persons can get information or status reports ... (f) Make environmental impact statements, the comments received, and any underlying documents available to the public pursuant to the provisions of the Freedom of Information Act ... (§1506.6)

Finally, a decision is made about whether the proposed action should be permitted:

Agencies shall adopt procedures to ensure that decisions are made in accordance with the policies and purposes of the Act. Such procedures shall include but not be limited to: (a) Implementing procedures under section 102(2) to achieve the requirements of sections 101 and 102(1) ... (e) Requiring that ... the decision-maker consider the alternatives described in the environmental impact statement. (§1505.1)

Where all relevant agencies agree that the action should not go ahead, permission is denied, and a judicial resolution may be attempted. Where agencies agree that the action can proceed, permission is given, possibly subject to specified conditions (e.g. monitoring, mitigation). Where the relevant agencies disagree, the CEQ acts as arbiter (§1504). Until a decision is made, 'no action concerning the proposals shall be taken which could: (1) have an adverse environmental impact; or (2) limit the choice of reasonable alternatives ... ' (§1506.1).

The Record of Decision (ROD) is the final step for agencies in the process. It states what the decision is; identifies the alternatives considered, including the environmentally preferred alternative; and discusses mitigation plans, including any enforcement and monitoring commitments. It also discusses if all practical means to avoid or minimize environmental harm have been adopted and, if not, why they were not. It is a publicly available document published in the Federal Register or on the website of the relevant agency.

2.2.4 Recent trends

EIS activity

During the first 10 years of NEPA's implementation, about 1,500 EISs were prepared annually. Subsequently, negotiated improvements to the environmental impacts of proposed actions have become increasingly common during the preparation of 'environmental assessments' (EA). This has led to many 'mitigated findings of no significant impact' (no perfect acronym exists for this), reducing the number of EISs prepared: whereas 1,273 EISs were prepared in 1979, only 456 were prepared in 1991 and the annual number has been approximately 500–550 in recent years (NEPA website). This trend can be viewed positively, since it means that environmental impacts are considered earlier in the decision-making process, and hence it reduces the costs of preparing EISs. However, the fact that this abbreviated process allows less public participation causes some concern. Table 2.3 summarizes activity for 2008, indicating the predominance of EISs filed by the Department of Agriculture (primarily for forestry projects) and the Department of Transportation (primarily for road construction). Between 1979 and 2008, the number of EISs filed by the Department of Housing and Urban Development fell from 170 to 0! The number of legal cases filed against federal departments and agencies on the basis of NEPA has been on average 100–150 per annum. Plaintiffs are mainly public interest groups and individual citizens; common complaints are 'no EIS when one should have been prepared' and 'inadequate EIS'.

It is important to set this EIS activity in context. Important though they are, including some of the projects with the greatest impacts and highest stakeholder interest, the EISs represent only the tip of the iceberg of the wider EA activity. By comparison, in 1997 CEQ reported that federal agencies in total estimated that approximately 50,000 EAs were produced annually (CEQ 1997a). Determining the total number of federal actions subject to NEPA is difficult, but one agency, the Federal Highway Administration (FHWA), has tracked all projects. In 2001, FHWA estimated that 3 per cent of projects required an EIS, 7 per cent required an EA, and 90 per cent of all highway projects were classified as categorical exclusions.

Table 2.3 EISs filed under NEPA in 2008

Department	Number of EISs filed	Of which
Agriculture	128	Forest Service: 124
Commerce	36	National Oceanic and Atmospheric Admin: 36
Defense	79	Corp of Engineers: 42; Navy: 24
Energy	36	Federal Energy Regulatory Commission: 19
Health and human services	1	
Homeland security	8	US Coast Guard: 6
Housing and urban development	0	
Interior	128	Bureau of Land Management: 48; National Parks Service: 25
Justice	2	
Labor	0	
State	3	
Transportation	104	Federal Highway Admin: 64
Treasury	0	
Veteran affairs	0	
Independent agency	25	Nuclear Regulatory Commission: 14
TOTAL	550	

Source: NEPA website

The National Environmental Policy Act's twentieth year of operation, 1990, was marked by a series of conferences on the Act and the presentation to Congress of a bill of NEPA amendments. Under the Bill (HR1113), which was not passed, federal actions that take place outside the USA (e.g. projects built in other countries with US federal assistance) would have been subject to EIA, and all EISs would have been required to consider global climatic change, the depletion of the ozone layer, the loss of biological diversity and transboundary pollution. This latter amendment was controversial: although the need to consider the global impacts of programmes was undisputed, it was felt to be infeasible at the level of project EIA.

The context of EIA has also become a matter of concern. EIA is only one part of a broader environmental policy (NEPA), but the procedural provisions set out in NEPA's §102(2)(C) have overshadowed the rest of the Act. It has been argued that mere compliance with these procedures is not enough, and that greater emphasis should be given to the environmental goals and policies stated in §101. EIA must also be seen in the light of other environmental legislation. In the USA, many laws dealing with specific aspects of the environment were enacted or strengthened in the 1970s, including the Clean Water Act and the Clean Air Act. These laws have in many ways superseded NEPA's substantive requirements and have complemented and buttressed its procedural requirements. Compliance with these laws does not necessarily imply compliance with NEPA. However, the permit process associated with these other laws has become a primary method for evaluating project impacts, reducing NEPA's importance except for its occasional role as a focus of debate on major projects (Bear 1990).

The scope of EIA, and in particular the recognition of the social dimension of the environment, has been another matter of concern. After long campaigning by black and ethnic groups, particularly about inequalities in the distribution of hazardous waste landfills and incinerators, a working group was set up within the Environmental Protection Act (EPA) to make recommendations for dealing with environmental injustice (Hall 1994). The outcome was the Clinton 'Executive Order on Federal Actions to Address Environmental Justice in Minority Populations and Low-Income Populations' (White House 1994). Under this Order, each federal agency must analyse the environmental effects, including human health, economic and social effects, of federal actions, including effects on minority and low-income communities, when such analysis is required under NEPA. Mitigation measures, wherever feasible, should also address the significant and adverse environmental effects of federal actions on the same communities. In addition, each federal agency must provide opportunities for communities to contribute to the NEPA process, identifying potential effects and mitigation measures in consultation with affected communities and improving the accessibility of meetings and crucial documents.

Discussion of issues, NEPA effectiveness, and amendments to the EA process, has continued to date. Canter (1996) highlighted four areas for which NEPA requirements needed further elaboration:

1 how much an agency should identify and plan mitigation before issuing an EIS;
2 ways to assess the cumulative impacts of proposed developments;
3 ways to conduct 'reasonable foreseeability' (or worst-case) analyses; and
4 monitoring and auditing of impact predictions.

In 1997 CEQ carried out a review of the effectiveness of NEPA after 25 years. Overall the view was that NEPA had been a success:

> . . . it had made agencies take a hard look at the environmental consequences of their actions, and it had brought the public into the agency decision-making process like no other statute. In a piece of legislation barely three pages long, NEPA gave a voice to the new national consensus to protect and improve the environment, and substance to the determination articulated by many to work together to achieve that goal. (CEQ 1997a)

But there was concern about several features: a focus on the documentation, rather than on the enhancement of decision making; an associated focus on litigation-proof documentation; consultation that was too late in the process; and an overlong process. Some recommendations for the future included better interagency co-ordination; and better monitoring and adaptive management. There was also a concern for a more integrated interdisciplinary place-based approach bringing together expertise and information from many fields, as illustrated in the example in Box 2.1.

There has been progress in a number of areas, including the consideration of: cumulative impacts, the relationship between the EIS and environmental management systems (EMS), and approaches to the 'streamlining' of the overall system. Although the original NEPA does define the nature of cumulative impacts, agencies have been left very much to their own devices to develop relevant procedures and methods. However, in 1997 (non-legally binding) guidance for the consideration of cumulative effects assessment under the NEPA was provided by the Council for Environmental Quality. The CEQ handbook presents practical methods for addressing coincident effects (adverse or beneficial) on specific resources, ecosystems, and human communities of all related activities, not just the proposed project or alternatives that initiate the assessment process (CEQ

1997b). Although NEPA affirms a 'predict–mitigate–implement' model, there can be major weaknesses in the implementation stage. The issuance of an Executive Order (Exec. Order 13423, January 2007), which directs all Federal agencies to implement EMSs at all organizational levels, helps to address this issue, providing a means to enhance EIS compliance. CEQ has again issued relevant guidance, on *Aligning NEPA Processes with Environmental Management Systems* (CEQ 2007). There is also a general and ongoing concern about the time consumed by the NEPA processes, accompanied by calls for more 'streamlining'. A Congressional Research Service report identified two main categories of delay attributed to the NEPA process: those related to the time needed to complete the required documentation (primarily the EISs), and delays resulting from NEPA-related litigation (CRS 2006). The report discusses a range of responses, including limits on the length of EISs, establishing limits on judicial review, updating lists of Categorically Excluded and Exempt projects, and many others, some of which have been implemented while others are still subject to debate!

2.2.5 Little NEPAs and the particular case of California

Many state-level EIA systems have been established in the USA in addition to NEPA. Fifteen of the

---

Branson, Missouri is one of the hottest entertainment centers in the country, receiving more than 3.7 million visitors during the six month tourist season in 1991. At peak times, 30,000 cars are jammed onto Country Music Boulevard each day, resulting in average speeds of 10 mph for much of the day and intolerable delays. In early June, 1992, the governor of Missouri declared the traffic congestion in the Branson area an "economic emergency" and announced a plan to fast-track the planning and design process of a proposed four-lane $160 million Ozark Mountain Highroad. The challenge to the Missouri Highway and Transportation Department was to plan a totally new highway in six months without compromising safety or the integrity of the environmental process. With the fast track in mind and the NEPA process in hand, an interdisciplinary team of agencies met on a regular and frequent basis. This resulted in the preparation of a quality project that integrated the needs of the environmentally sensitive Ozark Mountain Ecosystem with the need for increased recreational traffic in the area. With all the players and disciplines involved, every reasonable design alternative and associated impact was on the table for discussion.

There were those on the team who, in the past, had seen NEPA as a burden, a hindrance, and something to be overcome. But as a result of the Highroad experience, these same people came to realize that NEPA could help to shape projects in a way that met the project purpose and need while serving to protect the environment and preserve other community values. Most important, the new attitudes forged during the NEPA planning process have carried over into other projects that involve the same local, state, and federal agencies, and consulting firms.

Box 2.1 Example of an integrated and accelerated approach – the Ozark Mountain Highroad

Source: CEQ 1997a

USA's states, plus the District of Columbia and Puerto Rico,[4] have their own EIA systems that, because they are largely modelled on the Federal NEPA, are collectively referred to as the 'little NEPAs'. They require EIA for state actions (actions that require state funding or permission) and/or projects in sensitive areas. Other states have no specific EIA regulations, but have EIA requirements in addition to those of NEPA. [5]

Of particular interest is the Californian system, established under the California Environmental Quality Act (CEQA) of 1973, and subsequent amendments. This is widely recognized as one of the most advanced EIA systems in the world. The legislation applies not only to government actions but also to the activities of private parties that require the approval of a government agency. It is not merely a procedural approach but one that requires state and local agencies to protect the environment by adopting feasible mitigation measures and alternatives in environmental impact reviews (EIRs). The legislation extends beyond projects to higher levels of actions, and an amendment in 1989 also added mandatory mitigation, monitoring and reporting requirements to CEQA. Guidance on the California system is provided in invaluable annual publications by the State of California, which sets out the CEQA Statutes and Guidelines in considerable detail. For the latest 2009 update of the Statute and Guidelines see the Association of Environmental Professionals, California website. A further amendment in 2010 added GHG emissions to the list of environmental impacts that must be analysed under CEQA.

. . . .

2.3 The worldwide spread of EIA

Since the enactment of NEPA, EIA systems have been established in various forms throughout the world, beginning with more developed countries (e.g. Canada in 1973, Australia in 1974, West Germany in 1975, France in 1976) and later also in the less developed countries. The approval of a European Directive on EIA in 1985 stimulated the enactment of EIA legislation in many European countries in the late 1980s. The formation of new countries after the break-up of the Soviet Union in 1991 led to the enactment of EIA legislation in many of these countries in the early to mid-1990s. The early 1990s also saw a large growth in the number of EIA regulations and guidelines established in Africa and South America. By 1996, more than 100 countries had EIA systems (Sadler 1996). Now, at least 140 countries have EIA systems; Figure 2.2 summarizes the present state of EIA systems worldwide, to the best of the authors' knowledge.

These EIA systems vary greatly. Some are in the form of *mandatory regulations, acts* or *statutes*; these are generally enforced by the authorities requiring the preparation of an adequate EIS before permission is given for a project to proceed. In other cases, EIA *guidelines* have been established. These are not enforceable but generally impose obligations on the administering agency. Other legislation allows government officials to require EIAs to be prepared at their *discretion*. Elsewhere, EIAs are prepared in an ad hoc manner, often because they are required by funding bodies (e.g. the World Bank, USAID) as part of a funding approval process. However, these classifications are not necessarily indicative of how thoroughly EIA is carried out. For instance, the EIA regulations of Brazil and the Philippines are not well carried out or enforced in practice (Glasson and Salvador 2000; Moreira 1988), whereas Japan's guidelines are thoroughly implemented.

Another important distinction between types of EIA system is that sometimes the actions that require EIA are given as *a definition* (e.g. the USA's definition of 'major federal actions significantly affecting the quality of the human environment'), sometimes as *a list of projects* (e.g. roads of more than 10 km in length). Most countries use a list of projects, in part to avoid legal wrangling such as that surrounding NEPA's definition. Another distinction asks whether EIA is required for *government projects only* (as in NEPA), for *private projects only* or for both. Finally, some international development and funding agencies have set up EIA guidelines, including the European Bank for Reconstruction and Development (1992, 2010), UK Overseas Development Administration (1996), DFID (2003), UNEP (1997, 2002) and World Bank (1991, 1995, 1997, 1999, 2002, 2006).

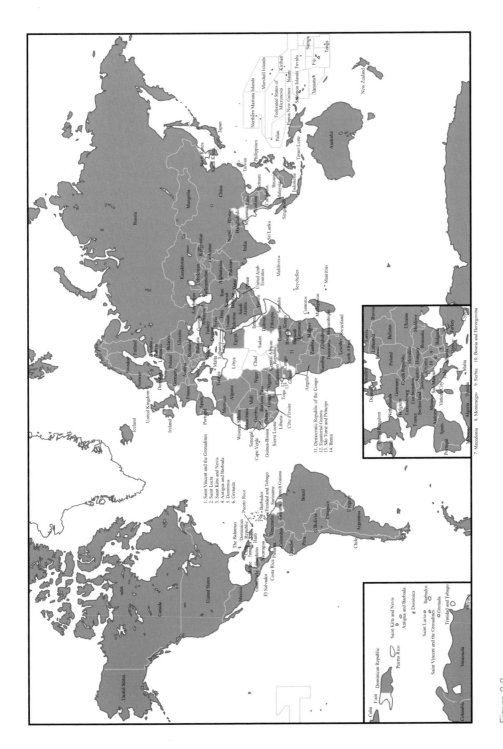

Figure 2.2

EIA systems worldwide. The countries marked in green represent, to the best of our knowledge, those with EIA legislation (either framework or detailed). The figure makes no judgement about the breadth and quality of the legislation, or whether it is adequately implemented. The authors apologize for any omissions or inaccuracies.

2.4 Development in the UK

The UK has had formal legislation for EIA since 1988, in the form of several laws that implement European Community Directive 85/337/EEC (CEC 1985) and subsequent amendments. It is quite possible that without pressure from the European Commission such legislation would have been enacted much more slowly, since the UK government felt that its existing planning system more than adequately controlled environmentally unsuitable developments. However, this does not mean that the UK had no EIA system at all before 1988; many EIAs were prepared voluntarily or at the request of local authorities, and guidelines for EIA preparation were drawn up.

2.4.1 Limitations of the land-use planning system

The UK's statutory land-use planning system has since 1947 required local planning authorities (LPAs) to anticipate likely development pressures, assess their significance, and allocate land, as appropriate, to accommodate them. Environmental factors are a fundamental consideration in this assessment. Most developments require planning consent, so environmentally harmful developments can be prevented by its denial. This system resulted in the accumulation of considerable planning expertise concerning the likely consequences of development proposals.

After the mid-1960s, however, the planning system began to seem less effective at controlling the impacts of large developments. The increasing scale and complexity of developments, the consequent greater social and physical environmental impacts and the growing internationalization of developers (e.g. oil, gas and chemicals companies) all outstripped the capability of the development control system to predict and control the impacts of developments. In the late 1960s, public concern about environmental protection also grew considerably, and the relation between statutory planning controls and the development of large projects came under increasing scrutiny. This became particularly obvious in the case of the proposed third London Airport. The Roskill Commission was established to select the most suitable site for

an airport in south-east England, with the mandate to prepare a cost-benefit analysis (CBA) of alternative sites. The resulting analysis (HMSO 1971) focused on socio-economic rather than physical environmental impacts; it led to an understanding of the difficulties of expanding CBA to impacts not easily measured in monetary terms, and to the realization that other assessment methods were needed to achieve a balance between socio-economic and physical environmental objectives.

2.4.2 North Sea oil- and gas-related EIA initiatives

The main impetus towards the further development of EIA, however, was the discovery of oil and gas in the North Sea. The extraction of these resources necessitated the construction of large developments in remote areas renowned for their scenic beauty and distinctive ways of life (e.g. the Shetlands, the Orkneys and the Highlands region). Planning authorities in these areas lacked the experience and resources needed to assess the impacts of such large developments. In response, the Scottish Development Department (SDD) issued a technical advice note to LPAs (SDD 1974). *Appraisal of the impact of oil-related development* noted that these developments and other large and unusual projects need 'rigorous appraisal', and suggested that LPAs should commission an impact study of the developments if needed. This was the first government recognition that major developments needed special appraisal. Some EIAs were carried out in the early 1970s, mostly for oil and gas developments. Many of these were sponsored by the SDD and LPAs, and were prepared by environmental consultants, but some (e.g. for the Flotta Oil Terminal and Beatrice Oilfield) were commissioned by the developers. Other early EIAs concerned a coal mine in the Vale of Belvoir, a pumped-storage electricity scheme at Loch Lomond, and various motorway and trunk road proposals (Clark and Turnbull 1984).

In 1973, the Scottish Office and DoE commissioned the University of Aberdeen's Project Appraisal for Development Control (PADC) team to develop a systematic procedure for planning authorities to make a balanced appraisal of the environmental, economic and social impacts of large industrial developments. PADC produced an interim report, *The assessment of major industrial applications – a manual* (Clark *et al.* 1976), which was issued free of charge to all LPAs in the UK and 'commended by central government for use by planning authorities, government agencies and developers'. The PADC procedure was designed to fit into the existing planning framework, and was used to assess a variety of (primarily private sector) projects. An extended and updated version of the manual was issued in 1981 (Clark *et al.* 1981).

In 1974, the Secretaries of State for the Environment, Scotland and Wales commissioned consultants to investigate the 'desirability of introducing a system of impact analysis in Great Britain, the circumstances in which a system should apply, the projects it should cover and the way in which it might be incorporated into the development control system' (Catlow and Thirwall 1976). The resulting report made recommendations about who should be responsible for preparing and paying for EIAs, what legislative changes would be needed to institute an EIA system, and similar issues. The report concluded that about 25–50 EIAs per year would be needed, for both public and private sector projects. EIA was given further support by the Dobry Report on the development control system (Dobry 1975), which advocated that LPAs should require developers to submit impact studies for particularly significant development proposals. The report outlined the main topics such a study should address, and the information that should be required from developers. Government reactions to the Dobry Report were mixed, although the influential Royal Commission on Environmental Pollution endorsed the report.

2.4.3 Department of the Environment scepticism

However, overall the DoE remained sceptical about the need, practicality and cost of EIA. In fact, the government's approach to EIA was described as being 'from the outset grudging and minimalist' (CPRE 1991). In response to the Catlow and Thirwall report, the DoE stated: 'Consideration of the report by local authorities should not be allowed to delay normal planning procedures and any new procedures involving additional calls on central or local government finance and manpower

are unacceptable during the present period of economic restraint' (DoE 1977). A year later, after much deliberation, the DoE was slightly more positive:

> We fully endorse the desirability . . . of ensuring careful evaluation of the possible effects of large developments on the environment . . . The approach suggested by Thirwall/Catlow is already being adopted with many [projects] . . . The sensible use of this approach [should] improve the practice in handling these relatively few large and significant proposals. (DoE 1978)

The government's foreword to the PADC manual of 1981 also emphasized the need to minimize the costs of EIA procedures: 'It is important that the approach suggested in the report should be used selectively to fit the circumstances of the proposed development and with due economy' (Clark *et al.* 1981). As will be seen in later chapters, the government remained sceptical for some time about the value of EIA, and about extending its remit, as suggested by the EC. But by the early 1980s, more than 200 studies on the environmental impacts of projects in the UK had been prepared on an ad hoc basis (Petts and Hills 1982). Many of these studies were not full EIAs, but focused on only a few impacts. However, large developers such as British Petroleum, British Gas, the Central Electricity Generating Board and the National Coal Board were preparing a series of increasingly comprehensive statements. In the case of British Gas, these were shown to be a good investment, saving the company £30 million in 10 years (House of Lords 1981a).

2.5 EC Directive 85/337

The development and implementation of Directive 85/337 greatly influenced the EIA systems of the UK and other EU Member States. In the UK, central government research on a UK system of EIA virtually stopped after the mid-1970s, and attention focused instead on ensuring that any future Europe-wide system of EIA would fully incorporate the needs of the UK for flexibility and discretion. Other Member States were eager to ensure that the Directive reflected the requirements of their own more rigorous systems of EIA. Since the Directive's implementation, EIA activity in all the EU Member States has increased dramatically.

2.5.1 Legislative history

The EC had two main reasons for wanting to establish a uniform system of EIA in all its Member States. First, it was concerned about the state of the physical environment and eager to prevent further environmental deterioration. The EC's First Action Programme on the Environment of 1973 (CEC 1973) advocated the prevention of environmental harm: 'the best environmental policy consists of preventing the creation of pollution or nuisances at source, rather than subsequently trying to counteract their effects', and, to that end, 'effects on the environment should be taken into account at the earliest possible stage in all technical planning and decision-making processes'. Further Action Programmes of 1977, 1983, 1987, 1992 and 2001 have reinforced this emphasis. Land-use planning was seen as an important way of putting these principles into practice, and EIA was viewed as a crucial technique for incorporating environmental considerations into the planning process.

Second, the EC was concerned to ensure that no distortion of competition should arise through which one Member State could gain unfair advantage by permitting developments that, for environmental reasons, might be refused by another. In other words, it considered environmental policies necessary for the maintenance of a level economic playing field. Further motivation for EC action included a desire to encourage best practice across Member States. In addition, pollution problems transcend territorial boundaries (witness acid rain and river pollution in Europe), and the EC can contribute at least a sub-continental response framework.

The EC began to commission research on EIA in 1975. Five years later and after more than 20 drafts, the EC presented a draft directive to the Council of Ministers (CEC 1980); it was circulated throughout the Member States. The 1980 draft attempted to reconcile several conflicting needs. It sought to benefit from the US experience with NEPA, but to develop policies appropriate to

European need. It also sought to make EIA applicable to all actions likely to have a significant environmental impact, but to ensure that procedures would be practicable. Finally, and perhaps most challenging, it sought to make EIA requirements flexible enough to adapt to the needs and institutional arrangements of the various Member States, but uniform enough to prevent problems arising from widely varying interpretations of the procedures. The harmonization of the types of project to be subject to EIA, the main obligations of the developers and the contents of the EIAs were considered particularly important (Lee and Wood 1984; Tomlinson 1986).

As a result, the draft directive incorporated a number of important features. First, planning permission for projects was to be granted only after an adequate EIA had been completed. Second, LPAs and developers were to co-operate in providing information on the environmental impacts of proposed developments. Third, statutory bodies responsible for environmental issues, and other Member States in cases of trans-frontier effects, were to be consulted. Finally, the public was to be informed and allowed to comment on issues related to project development.

In the UK the draft directive was examined by the House of Lords Select Committee on the European Commission, where it received widespread support:

> The present draft Directive strikes the right kind of balance: it provides a framework of common administrative practices which will allow Member States with effective planning controls to continue with their system ... while containing enough detail to ensure that the intention of the draft cannot be evaded ... The Directive could be implemented in the United Kingdom in a way which would not lead to undue additions delay and costs in planning procedures and which need not therefore result in economic and other disadvantages. (House of Lords 1981a)

However, the Parliamentary Undersecretary of State at the DoE dissented. Although accepting the general need for EIA, he was concerned about the bureaucratic hurdles, delaying objections and litigation that would be associated with the proposed directive (House of Lords 1981b). The UK Royal Town Planning Institute (RTPI) also commented on several drafts of the directive. Generally the RTPI favoured it, but was concerned that it might cause the planning system to become too rigid:

> The Institute welcomes the initiative taken by the European Commission to secure more widespread use of EIA as it believes that the appropriate use of EIA could both speed up and improve the quality of decisions on certain types of development proposals. However, it is seriously concerned that the proposed Directive, as presently drafted, would excessively codify and formalize procedures of which there is limited experience and therefore their benefits are not yet proven. Accordingly the Institute recommends the deletion of Article 4 and annexes of the draft. (House of Lords 1981a)

More generally, slow progress in the implementation of EC legislation was symptomatic of the wide range of interest groups involved, of the lack of public support for increasing the scope of town planning and environmental protection procedures, and of the unwillingness of Member States to adapt their widely varying planning systems and environmental protection legislation to those of other countries (Williams 1988). In March 1982, after considering the many views expressed by the Member States, the Commission published proposed amendments to the draft directive (CEC 1982). Approval was further delayed by the Danish government, which was concerned about projects authorized by Acts of Parliament. On 7 March 1985, the Council of Ministers agreed on the proposal; it was formally adopted as a directive on 27 June 1985 (CEC 1985) and became operational on 3 July 1988.

Subsequently, the EC's Fifth Action Programme, *Towards sustainability* (CEC 1992), stressed the importance of EIA, particularly in helping to achieve sustainable development, and the need to expand the remit of EIA:

> Given the goal of achieving sustainable development it seems only logical, if not essential, to apply an assessment of the environmental implications of all relevant policies, plans and programmes. The integration of environmental assessment within the macro-planning process would not only enhance the protection of the environment and encourage optimization of resource management but would also help to reduce those disparities in the international and inter-regional competition for new development projects which at present arise from disparities in assessment practices in the Member States . . .

The EIA Directive can be seen as a work in progress. It has undergone regular reviews to improve procedures and to seek consistency of application. In response to a five-year review of the Directive (CEC 1993), amendments to the Directive were agreed in 1997. Further minor amendments followed in 2003 and 2009. Appendix 1 gives the complete consolidated version of the amended Directive as at June 2011. The rest of Section 2.5 now summarizes the original Directive. Section 2.6 discusses the important amendments in Directive 97/11. Section 2.7 considers in particular the findings of a major review of the implementation of the implementation of the amended Directive 97/11. This is followed in Section 2.8 with a summary of the more minor reviews and amendments in 2003, and in 2009; but importantly now set in the context of the enlarged EU-27.

2.5.2 Summary of EC Directive 85/337 procedures

The Directive differs in important respects from NEPA. It requires EIAs to be prepared by both public agencies and private developers, whereas NEPA applies only to federal agencies. It requires EIA for a specified list of projects, whereas NEPA uses the definition 'major federal actions'. It specifically lists the impacts that are to be addressed in an EIA, whereas NEPA does not. Finally, it includes fewer requirements for public consultation than does NEPA. Under the provisions of the European Communities Act of 1972, Directive 85/337 is the controlling document, laying down rules for EIA in Member States. Individual states enact their own regulations to implement the

Directive and have considerable discretion. According to the Directive, EIA is required for two classes of project, one mandatory (Annex I) and one discretionary (Annex II):

> projects of the classes listed in Annex I shall be made subject to an assessment . . . for projects listed in Annex II, the Member States shall determine through: (a) a case-by-case examination; or (b) thresholds or criteria set by the Member State whether the project shall be made subject to an assessment . . . When [doing so], the relevant selection criteria set out in Annex III shall be taken into account. (Article 4)

Table 2.4 summarizes the projects listed in Annexes I and II. The EC (CEC 1995) also published guidelines to help Member States determine whether a project requires EIA.

Similarly, the information required in an EIA is listed in Annex III of the Directive, but must only be provided

> inasmuch as: (a) The Member States consider that the information is relevant to a given stage of the consent procedure and to the specific characteristics of a particular project . . . and of the environmental features likely to be affected; (b) The Member States consider that a developer may reasonably be required to compile this information having regard *inter alia* to current knowledge and methods of assessment. (Article 5.1)

Table 2.5 summarizes the information required by Annex III (Annex IV, post-amendments). A developer is thus required to prepare an EIS that includes the information specified by the relevant Member State's interpretation of Annex III (Annex IV, post-amendments) and to submit it to the 'competent authority'. This EIS is then circulated to other relevant public authorities and made publicly available: 'Member States shall take the measures necessary to ensure that the authorities likely to be concerned by the project . . . are given an opportunity to express their opinion' (Article 6.1).

Member States are also to ensure that:

- any request for development consent and any information gathered pursuant to [the

Table 2.4 Projects requiring EIA under EC Directive 85/337 (*as amended*)*

Annex I (mandatory)

1   Crude oil refineries, coal/shale gasification and liquefaction
2   Thermal power stations and other combustion installations; nuclear power stations and other nuclear reactors
3   Radioactive waste processing and/or storage installations
4   Cast-iron and steel smelting works
5   Asbestos extraction, processing or transformation
6   Integrated chemical installations
7   Construction of motorways, express roads, other large roads, railways, airports
8   Trading ports and inland waterways
9   Installations for incinerating, treating or disposing of toxic and dangerous wastes
10 *Large-scale installation for incinerating or treating non-hazardous waste*
11 *Large-scale groundwater abstraction or recharge schemes*
12 *Large-scale transfer of water resources*
13 *Large-scale waste water treatment plants*
14 *Large-scale extraction of petroleum and natural gas*
15 *Large dams and reservoirs*
16 *Long pipelines for gas, oil or chemicals*
17 *Large-scale poultry or pig-rearing installations*
18 *Pulp, timber or board manufacture*
19 *Large-scale quarries or open-cast mines*
20 *Long overhead electrical power lines*
21 *Large-scale installations for petroleum, petrochemical or chemical products*
22 *Any change or extension to an Annex I project that meets the thresholds***
23 *Carbon storage sites***
24 *Carbon capture installations***

Annex II (discretionary)

1   Agriculture, silviculture and aquaculture
2   Extractive industry
3   Energy industry
4   Production and processing of metals
5   *Minerals industry* (projects not included in Annex I)
6   Chemical industry
7   Food industry
8   Textile, leather, wood and paper industries
9   Rubber industry
10 *Infrastructure projects*
11 *Other projects*
12 *Tourism and leisure*
13 Modification, extension or temporary testing of Annex I projects

* 1997 amendments are shown in italic; ** are from later amendments in 2003 and 2009.

Table 2.5 Information required in an EIA under EC Directive 85/337 *(as amended)**

Annex III (*IV*)

1 Description of the project
2 Where appropriate (*an outline of main alternatives studied and an indication of the main reasons for the final choice*)
3 Aspects of the environment likely to be significantly affected by the proposed project, including population, fauna, flora, soil, water, air climatic factors, material assets, architectural and archaeological heritage, landscape, and the interrelationship between them
4 Likely significant effects of the proposed project on the environment
5 Measures to prevent, reduce and where possible offset any significant adverse environmental effects
6 Non-technical summary
7 Any difficulties encountered in compiling the required information

* Amendment is shown in italics.

Directive's provisions] are made available to the public;

- the public concerned is given the opportunity to express an opinion before the project is initiated.

The detailed arrangements for such information and consultation shall be determined by the Member States (Articles 6.2 and 6.3) (see Section 6.2 also). The competent authority must consider the information presented in an EIS, the comments of relevant authorities and the public, and the comments of other Member States (where applicable) in its consent procedure (Article 8). The CEC (1994) published a checklist to help competent authorities to review environmental information. It must then inform the public of the decision and any conditions attached to it (Article 9).

2.6 EC Directive 85/337, as amended by Directive 97/11/EC

Directive 85/337 included a requirement for a five-year review, and a report was published in 1993 (CEC 1993). While there was general satisfaction that the 'basics of the EIA are mostly in place', there was concern about the incomplete coverage of certain projects, insufficient consultation and public participation, the lack of information about alternatives, weak monitoring and the lack of consistency in Member States' implementation. The review process, as with the original Directive, generated considerable debate between the Commission and the Member States, and the amended Directive went through several versions, with some weakening of the proposed changes. The outcome, finalized in March 1997, and to be implemented within two years, included the following amendments:

- Annex I (mandatory): the addition of 12 new classes of project (e.g. dams and reservoirs, pipelines, quarries and open-cast mining) (Table 2.4).
- Annex II (discretionary): the addition of 8 new sub-classes of project (plus extension to 10 others), including shopping and car parks, and particularly tourism and leisure (e.g. caravan sites and theme parks) (Table 2.4).
- New Annex III lists matters that must be considered in EIA, including:
  - Characteristics of projects: size, cumulative impacts, the use of natural resources, the production of waste, pollution and nuisance, the risk of accidents.
  - Location of projects: designated areas and their characteristics, existing and previous land uses.
  - Characteristics of the potential impacts: geographical extent, trans-frontier effects, the magnitude and complexity of impacts, the probability of impact, the duration, frequency and reversibility of impacts.
- Change of previous Annex III to Annex IV: small changes in content.
- Other changes:
  - Article 2.3: There is no exemption from consultation with other Member States on transboundary effects.
  - Article 4: When deciding which Annex II projects will require EIA, Member States can use thresholds, case by case or a combination of the two.

- Article 5.2: A developer may request an opinion about the information to be supplied in an environmental statement (ES), and a competent authority must provide that information. Member States may require authorities to give an opinion irrespective of the request from the developer.
- Article 5.3: The minimum information provided by the developer *must include* an outline of the main alternatives studied and an indication of the main reasons for the final choice between alternatives.
- Article 7: This requires consultation with affected Member States, and other countries, about transboundary effects.[6]
- Article 9: A competent authority must make public the *main* reasons and considerations on which decisions are based, together with a description of the *main* mitigation measures (CEC 1997a).

A consolidated version of the full Directive, as amended by these changes, is included in Appendix 1. There are more projects subject to mandatory EIA (Annex I) and discretionary EIA (Annex II). Alternatives also became mandatory, and there is more emphasis on consultation and participation. The likely implication is more EIA activity in the EU Member States, which also have to face up to some challenging issues when dealing with topics such as alternatives, risk assessment (RA) and cumulative impacts.

· ·

2.7 An overview of EIA systems in the EU: divergent practice in a converging system?

The EU has been active in the field of environmental policy, and the EIA Directive is widely regarded as one of its more significant environmental achievements (see CEC 2001). However, there has been, and continues to be, concern about the inconsistency of application across the (increasing number of) Member States (see CEC 1993, CEC 2003, Glasson and Bellanger 2003). This partly reflects the nature of EC/EU directives,

which seek to establish a mandatory framework for European policies while leaving the 'scope and method' of implementation to each Member State. In addition, whatever the degree of 'legal harmonization' of Member State EIA policies, there is also the issue of 'practical harmonization'. Implementation depends on practitioners from public and private sectors, who invariably have their own national cultures and approaches.

An early inconsistency was in the timing of implementation of the original Directive. Some countries, including France, the Netherlands and the UK, implemented the Directive relatively on time; others (e.g. Belgium, Portugal) did not. Other differences, understandably, reflected variations in legal systems, governance and culture between the Member States, and several of these differences are outlined below.

• The legal implementation of the Directive by the Member States differed considerably. For some, the regulations come under the broad remit of nature conservation (e.g. France, Greece, the Netherlands, Portugal); for some they come under the planning system (e.g. Denmark, Ireland, Sweden, the UK); in others specific EIA legislation was enacted (e.g. Belgium, Italy). In addition, in Belgium, and to an extent in Germany and Spain, the responsibility for EIA was devolved to the regional level.

• In most Member States, EIAs are carried out and paid for by the developers or consultants commissioned by them. However, in Flanders (Belgium) EIAs are carried out by experts approved by the authority responsible for environmental matters, and in Spain the competent authority carries out an EIA based on studies carried out by the developer.

• In a few countries, or national regions, EIA commissions have been established. In the Netherlands the commission assists in the scoping process, reviews the adequacy of an EIS and receives monitoring information from the competent authority. In Flanders, it reviews the qualifications of the people carrying out an EIA, determines its scope and reviews an EIS for compliance with legal requirements. Italy also has an EIA commission.

- The decision to proceed with a project is, in the simplest case, the responsibility of the competent authority (e.g. in Flanders, Germany, the UK). However, in some cases the minister responsible for the environment must first decide whether a project is environmentally compatible (e.g. in Denmark, Italy, Portugal).

2.7.1 Reviews of the original Directive 85/337/EC

The first five-year review of the original Directive (CEC 1993) expressed concern about a range of inconsistencies in the operational procedures across the Member States (project coverage, alternatives, public participation, etc.). As a result, several Member States strengthened their regulations to achieve a fuller implementation. A second five-year review in 1997 (CEC 1997b) had the following key findings:

- EIA is a regular feature of project licensing/ authorization systems, yet wide variation exists in relation to those procedures (e.g. different procedural steps, relationships with other relevant procedures);
- While all Member States had made provision for the EIA of the projects listed in Annex I, there were different interpretations and procedures for Annex II projects;
- quality control over the EIA process is deficient;
- Member States did not give enough attention to the consideration of alternatives;
- improvements had been made on public participation and consultation; and
- Member States, themselves, complained about the ambiguity and lack of definitions of several key terms in the Directive.

The amendments of 1997 sought to reduce further several of the remaining differences. In addition to the substantial extensions and modification to the list of projects in Annex I and Annex II, the amended Directive (CEC 1997a) also strengthened the procedural base of the EIA Directive. This included a provision for new screening arrangements, including new screening criteria (in Annex III) for Annex II projects. It also introduced EIS content changes, including an obligation on developers to include an outline of the main alternatives studied, and an indication of the main reasons for their choices, taking into account environmental effects. The amended Directive also enables a developer, if it so wishes, to ask a competent authority for formal advice on the scope of the information that should be included in a particular EIS. Member States, if they so wish, can require competent authorities to give an opinion on the scope of any new proposed EIS, whether the developer has requested one or not. The amended Directive also strengthens consultation and publicity, obliging competent authorities to take into account the results of consultations with the public and the reasons and considerations on which the decision on a project proposal has been based.

2.7.2 Review of the amended Directive 97/11/EC

A third review of the original Directive, as amended by Directive 97/11/EC (CEC 1997a), undertaken for the EC by the Impacts Assessment Unit at Oxford Brookes University (UK), provided a detailed overview of the implementation of the Directive (as amended) by Member States, and recommendations for further enhancement of application and effectiveness (CEC 2003). Some of the key implementation issues identified included:

- Further delays in the transposition of the Directive. Many Member States missed the 1999 deadline, and by the end of 2002 transposition was still incomplete for Austria, France, and Walloon and Flanders regions of Belgium. There was a complete lack of transposition for Luxembourg.
- Variations in thresholds used to specify EIA for Annex II projects. In all Member States, EIA is mandatory for Annex I projects, and some countries have added in additional Annex I categories. Until the amendments to the Directive, Member States differed considerably in their interpretation of which Annex II projects required EIA. In some (e.g. the Netherlands), a compiled list specified projects requiring EIA. Subsequent to the amendments, most of the Member States appeared to make use of a combination of both thresholds and a case-by-case approach

for Annex II projects. However, the 2003 review revealed that there were still major variations in the nature of the thresholds used. For example, with afforestation projects the area of planting that triggered mandatory EIA ranged from 30 ha in Denmark to 350 ha in Portugal. Similarly, three turbines would trigger mandatory EIA for a wind farm in Sweden, compared with 50 in Spain. Considerable variations also continue to exist in the detailed specification of which projects were covered by some Annex II categories, with 10(b) (urban development) being particularly problematic.

- Considerable variation in the number of EIAs being carried out in Member States. Documentation is complicated by inadequate data in some countries, but Table 2.6 shows the continuing great variation in annual output from over 7,000 (in France, where a relatively low financial criterion is a key trigger) to fewer than 20 (in Austria). While some of the variation may be explained by the relative economic conditions within countries, it also relates to the variations in levels at which thresholds have been set. The amendments to the Directive do seem to be bringing more projects into the EIA process in some Member States.

- Some improvement, but still issues in relation to the scoping stage, and consideration of alternatives. Until the amendments made it a more formal stage of the EIA process, scoping was carried out as a discrete and mandatory step in only a few countries. The amended Directive allows Member States to make this a mandatory procedure if they so wish; seven of the Member States have such procedures in place. Commitment to scoping in the other Member States is more variable. Similarly, the consideration of alternatives to a proposed project was mandatory in only a very few countries, including the Netherlands, which also required an analysis of the most environmentally acceptable alternatives in each case. The amended Directive required developers to include an outline of the main alternatives studied. The 2003 review showed that in some Member States the consideration of alternatives is a central focus of the EIA process; elsewhere the coverage is less adequate – although the majority of countries do now require assessment of the zero ('do minimum') alternative.

Table 2.6 Change in the amount of EIA activity in EU-15 Member States

Country	Pre-1999 (average p.a.)	Post-1999 (average p.a.)
Austria	4	10–20
Belgium – Brussels	20	20
Belgium – Flanders	No data	20% increase
Belgium – Walloon	No data	est. increase
Denmark	28	100
Finland	22	25
France	6,000–7,000	7,000+
Germany	1,000	est. increase
Greece	1,600	1,600
Ireland	140	178
Italy	37	No data
Luxembourg	20	20
Netherlands	70	70
Portugal	87	92
Spain	120	290
Sweden	1,000	1,000
UK	300	500

Source: CEC 2003

- Variations in nature of public consultation required in the EIA process. The Directive requires an EIS to be made available after it is handed to the competent authority, and throughout the EU the public is given an opportunity to comment on the projects that are subject to EIA. However, the extent of public involvement and the interpretation of 'the public concerned' varied from quite narrow to wide. In Denmark, the Netherlands and Wallonia, the public is consulted during the scoping process. In the Netherlands and Flanders, a public hearing must be held after the EIS is submitted. In Spain, the public must be consulted before the EIS is submitted. In Austria, the public can participate at several stages of an EIA, and citizens' groups and the Ombudsman for the Environment have special status. The transposition of the Aarhus Convention into EIA legislation provided an opportunity for further improvements in public participation in EIA (CEC 2001).
- Variations in some key elements of EIA/EIS content, relating in particular to biodiversity, human health, risk and cumulative impacts. While the EIA Directive does not make explicit reference to biodiversity and to health impacts, both can be seen as of increasing importance for EIA. There are some examples of good practice in the Netherlands and Finland for biodiversity, and in the Netherlands again for health impact assessment. On the other hand, the amended Directive (Annex III) includes risk and cumulative impacts. The 2003 review showed that although RAs appear in many EISs, for most Member States risk was seen as separate from the EIA process and handled by other control regimes. The review also showed a growing awareness of cumulative impacts, with measures put in place in many Member States (e.g. France, Portugal, Finland, Germany, Sweden and Denmark) to address them. However, it would seem that Member States are still grappling with the nature and dimensions of cumulative impacts.
- Lack of systematic monitoring of a project's actual impacts by the competent authority. Despite widespread concern about this Achilles' heel in the EIA Directive, there was considerable resistance to the inclusion of a requirement for mandatory monitoring. As such, there are very few good examples (e.g. the Netherlands) of a mandatory and systematic approach. Dutch legislation requires the competent authority to draw up an evaluation programme, which compares actual outcomes with those predicted in the EIS. If the evaluation shows effects worse than predicted, the competent authority may order extra environmental measures. In Greece, legislation provides for a review of the EIA outcome as part of the renewal procedure for an environmental permit.

Overall, the 2003 review showed that there were both strengths and weaknesses in the operation of the Directive, as amended. There are many examples of good practice, and the amendments have provided a significant strengthening of the procedural base of EIA, and have brought more harmonization in some areas – for example on the projects subject to EIA. Yet, as noted here, there is still a wide disparity in both the approach and the application of EIA in the Member States, and significant weaknesses remain to be addressed. The review concluded with a number of recommendations. These included advice to Member States to, *inter alia*, better record on an annual basis the nature of EIA activity; check national legislation with regard to aspects such as thresholds, quality control, cumulative impacts; make more use of EC guidance (e.g. on screening, scoping and review); and improve training provision for EIA. Section 2.8 continues the ongoing story of review and refinement of the Directive in the enlarged EU.

• •

2.8 Continuing issues, review and refinement of the EIA Directive in EU-27

There have been further reviews of the application and effectiveness of the EIA Directive, and as a result some limited changes were made to the Directive in 2003 and in 2009. Appendix 1 provides a consolidated version of the Directive (as at June 2011), but there may be further changes following another round of consultation (in late 2010) on implementation. A particular interesting feature of recent reviews, especially on the operation of the 2003 amended Directive, is the nature of implementation by the new Member States that joined the EU in 2004 and 2007 (CEC 2009a).

The 2009 review had a wide brief, examining: the application of the amended Directive as a whole, including the additional 2003 EIA procedures (which focused particularly on the integration of the requirements of the Aarhus Convention on public participation into the Directive), general trends in the performance of the Directive, the status of national systems, developments in EIA systems in the old Member States and the new Member States, and the relationships with other Directives. The main changes introduced by Directive 2003/35/EC were:

- definition of the 'public' and 'the public concerned' (new Article 1.2);
- option to include provisions in law exempting national defence projects from EIA now only allowed on a case-by-case basis (new Article 1.4);
- strengthened public consultation provision: early in the decision-making procedure, detailed list of information to be provided, reasonable time frames (new Articles 6.2 and 6.3);
- information on the public participation process within the information provided on the final decision (Article 9.1);
- new provisions on public access to a review procedure (Article 10(a)); and
- changes or extensions of Annex I projects and other modifications of Annex I projects and modifications of Annex II projects.

The 2009 changes were much more limited and focused on the addition of new projects – for example carbon capture and storage installations. Overall, the European Commission was very positive about the benefits of the Directive:

Two major benefits have been identified. Firstly, the EIA ensures that environmental considerations are taken into account as early as possible in the decision-making process. Secondly, by involving the public, the EIA procedure ensures more transparency in

environmental decision-making and, consequently, social acceptance. Even if most benefits of the EIA cannot be expressed in monetary terms, there is widespread agreement, confirmed by the studies available, that the benefits of carrying out an EIA outweigh the costs of preparing an EIA. (CEC 2009b)

The experience and performance of the 12 new Member States (Bulgaria, Cyprus, Czech Republic, Estonia, Hungary, Latvia, Lithuania, Malta, Poland, Romania, Slovakia and Slovenia) is of particular interest. In these countries, the EIA Directive had been transposed as part of the accession requirements to ensure harmonization of the national legislation with the EU *Acquis*, and these Member States were ready to incorporate the requirements of the Aarhus Convention. In many respects, the new Member States have the advantage of learning from the evolving EIA procedures and practice of the EU and its old Member States, and can provide some examples of innovative practice (see example of Poland in Chapter 10). But they have also encountered some of the issues raised by the other states in earlier reviews. The number of EIAs is increasing in many of the new Member States, but there is considerable variation between the states (although the data in Table 2.7 are distorted by the inclusion of total screening decisions in some cases). Scoping is mandatory in all the states, with the exception of Cyprus and Slovenia. Quality review of the EIA documentation, either by the competent authority, or an expert committee, is a legal requirement in all the states, and several make good use of EU guidance on topics such as review and screening. But there are concerns about carrying out EIA in a transboundary context, consideration of human health protection in EIA, the 'salami slicing' of projects to fit under EIA thresholds, and the need for updated EU guidance on several issues, including how to address the thorny issue of the cumulative impacts of projects.

Notwithstanding good progress over 20 years of implementation, the EU has ongoing concerns about some stubborn issues, including those already mentioned – such as variations in screening, transboundary problems, and concerns about quality control. Another serious and longstanding

Table 2.7 Number of EIAs carried out in the new EU Member States

Member State	Annex I		Annex II		Tendencies in EIAs carried out
	2005	2006	2005	2006	
Bulgaria	77	88	2,212	2,457 (incl. screening decisions)	Increase
Cyprus		30		45	Increase
Czech Republic		72		125	Increase
Estonia		57		20	Decrease
Hungary		70–90		370–400 (incl. screening procedures)	Static
Latvia		40		5 (the number indicates finished EIAs)	Increase
Lithuania		12		838	Static
Malta	4		6		Increase
Poland	n/a	n/a	n/a	n/a	n/a
Romania		179		643	Increase
Slovakia	90	135	429	363	Static
Slovenia	n/a	n/a	n/a	n/a	n/a

Source: CEC 2009a

issue is the lack of a mandatory monitoring requirement; a more recent issue includes the relationship between the EIA and SEA Directives, and the very limited hierarchical tiering in practice. There is also recognition of the urgent need to improve requirements and guidance on covering climate change issues in EIA, especially for energy and transport infrastructure projects, and those for which energy efficiency is a key issue. Further changes to EIA legislation are likely following the 2010 round of consultation on implementation of the Directive.

2.9 Summary

This chapter has reviewed the development of EIA worldwide, from its unexpectedly successful beginnings in the USA to recent developments in the EU. In practice, EIA ranges from the production of very simple ad hoc reports to the production of extremely bulky and complex documents, from wide-ranging to non-existent consultation with the public, from detailed quantitative predictions to broad statements about likely future trends. In the EU, reviews of EIA experience show that 'overall, although practice is divergent, it may not be diverging, and recent actions such as the amended Directive appear to be "hardening up" the regulatory framework and may encourage more convergence' (Glasson and Bellanger 2003). All these systems worldwide have the broad aim of improving decision-making by raising decision-makers' awareness of a proposed action's environmental consequences. Over the past 40 years, EIA has become an important tool in project planning, and its applications are likely to expand further. Chapter 10 provides further discussion of EIA systems internationally and Chapter 11 discusses the widening of scope to strategic environmental assessment of policies, plans and programmes. The next chapter focuses on EIA in the UK context.

SOME QUESTIONS

The following questions are intended to help the reader focus on the important issues of this chapter, and to start building some understanding of the origins and development of EIA.

1   Why do you think EIA had its origins, in NEPA, in the USA in the late 1960s?
2   What are the key differences, under NEPA, of the processes for a FONSI and for a full EIS?
3   How do you explain the recent trends in EISs filed under NEPA over the last 10–15 years?
4   As for all EIA systems, there are concerns about procedural issues. Note some of the recent concerns about the operation of EIA under NEPA.
5   Is there any clear pattern to the spread of EIA across countries and continents?
6   Why was there strong initial resistance to the introduction of EIA in the UK?
7   What were the key drivers behind the introduction of the EC EIA Directive 85/337?
8   What is the difference between Annex I and Annex II projects under the EC EIA Directive?
9   What were the main changes introduced to the EIA Directive under the 97/11/EC amendments?
10 Identify several examples of (i) good practice and (ii) significant weaknesses highlighted by the 2003 review of the implementation of the amended EIA Directive.
11 What factors might explain the variations in Member States' EIA activity illustrated in Tables 2.6 and 2.7?
12 What is the Aarhus Convention, and what are its implications for the EIA Directive?
13 What do you see as some of the stubborn issues still to be resolved in the EC EIA Directive?
14 From what you have covered in Chapter 2, are there now grounds for saying that there is clear evidence of a more consistent system of EIA across the 27 EU Member States?

Notes

1   For example, *Ely v. Velds*, 451 F.2d 1130, 4th Cir. 1971; *Carolina Action v. Simon*, 522 F.2d 295, 4th Cir. 1975.
2   *Calvert Cliff's Coordinating Committee, Inc. v. United States Atomic Energy Commission* 449 F.2d 1109, DC Cir. 1971.
3   *Natural Resources Defense Council, Inc. v. Morton*, 458 F.2d 827, DC Cir. 1972.
4   California, Connecticut, Georgia, Hawaii, Indiana, Maryland, Massachusetts, Minnesota, Montana, New York, North Carolina, South Dakota, Virginia, Washington and Wisconsin, plus the District of Columbia and Puerto Rica.
5   Arizona, Arkansas, Delaware, Florida, Louisiana, Michigan, New Jersey, North Dakota, Oregon, Pennsylvania, Rhode Island and Utah.
6   Amendments to Articles 7 and 9 were influenced by the requirements of the Espoo Convention on EIA in a Transboundary Context, signed by 29 countries and the EU in 1991. This widened and strengthened the requirements for consultation with Member States where a significant transboundary impact is identified. The Convention deals with both projects and impacts that cross boundaries and is not limited to a consideration of projects that are in close proximity to a boundary.

References

Anderson, F.R., Mandelker, D.R. and Tarlock, A.D. 1984. *Environmental protection: law and policy*. Boston: Little, Brown.

Association of Environmental Professionals (AEP) 2009. *California Environmental Quality Act: statute and guidelines*. Palm Desert, CA: AEP.

Bear, D. 1990. EIA in the USA after twenty years of NEPA. *EIA Newsletter* 4, EIA Centre, University of Manchester.

Canter, L.W. 1996. *Environmental impact assessment*, 2nd edn. London: McGraw-Hill.

Carson, R. 1962. *Silent Spring*. Boston: Houston Mifflin Company.

Catlow, J. and Thirwall, C.G. 1976. *Environmental impact analysis* (DoE Research Report 11). London: HMSO.

CEC (Commission of the European Communities) 1973. First action programme on the environment. *Official Journal* C112, 20 December.

CEC 1980. Draft directive concerning the assessment of the environmental effects of certain public and private projects. COM (80), 313 final. *Official Journal* C169, 9 July.

CEC 1982. Proposal to amend the proposal for a Council directive concerning the environmental effects of certain public and private projects. COM (82), 158 final. *Official Journal* C110, 1 May.

CEC 1985. On the assessment of the effects of certain public and private projects on the environment. *Official Journal* L175, 5 July.

CEC 1992. *Towards sustainability*. Brussels: CEC.

CEC 1993. *Report from the Commission of the Implementation of Directive 85/337/EEC on the assessment of the effects of certain public and private projects on the environment*. COM (93), 28 final. Brussels: CEC.

CEC 1994. *Environmental impact assessment review checklist*. Brussels: EC Directorate-General XI.

CEC 1995. *Environmental impact assessment: guidance on screening DG XI*. Brussels: CEC.

CEC 1997a. Council Directive 97/11/EC of 3 March 1997 amending Directive 85/337/EEC on the assessment of certain public and private projects on the environment. *Official Journal* L73/5, 3 March.

CEC 1997b. *Report from the Commission of the Implementation of Directive 85/337/EEC on the assessment of the effects of certain public and private projects on the environment*. Brussels: CEC.

CEC 2001. *Proposal for a directive of the European Parliament and of the Council providing for public participation in respect of the drawing up of certain plans and programmes relating to the environment and amending council directives 85/337/EEC and 96/61/EC*. COM (2000), 839 final, 18 January 2001. Brussels: DG Environment, EC.

CEC 2003. (Impacts Assessment Unit, Oxford Brookes University). *Five years' report to the European Parliament and the Council on the application and effectiveness of the EIA Directive*. Available on the website of DG Environment, EC: www.europa.eu.int/comm/environment/eia/home.htm.

CEC 2009a. *Study concerning the report on the application and effectiveness of the EIA Directive: Final Report*. Brussels: DG Env

CEC 2009b. *Report from the Commission to the Council, the European Parliament, the European Economic and Social Committee and the Committee of the Regions on the application and effectiveness of the EIA Directive (Directive 85/337/EEC, as amended by Directives 97/11/EC and 2003/35/EC)*. Brussels: CEC.

CEQ (Council on Environmental Quality) 1978. National Environmental Policy Act. Implementation of procedural provisions: final regulations. *Federal Register* 43(230), 55977–6007, 29 November.

CEQ 1997a. *The National Environmental Policy Act: a study of its effectiveness after 25 years*. Washington, DC: US Government Printing Office.

CEQ 1997b. *Considering cumulative effects – under the NEPA*. Washington, DC: US Government Printing Office.

CEQ 2007. *A citizens' guide to the NEPA*. Washington, DC: US Government Printing Office.

CEQ 2007. *Aligning NEPA processes with environmental management systems*. Washington, DC: US Government Printing Office.

Clark, B.D. and Turnbull, R.G.H. 1984. Proposals for environmental impact assessment procedures in the UK. In *Planning and ecology*, R.D. Roberts and T.M. Roberts (eds), l35–44. London: Chapman & Hall.

Clark, B.D., Chapman, K., Bisset, R. and Wathern, P. 1976. *Assessment of major industrial applications: a manual* (DoE Research Report 13). London: HMSO.

Clark, B.D., Chapman, K., Bisset, R., Wathern, P. and Barrett, M. 1981. *A manual for the assessment of major industrial proposals*. London: HMSO.

CPRE 1991. *The environmental assessment directive: five years on*. London: Council for the Protection of Rural England.

CRS (Congressional Research Services) 2006. *The National Environmental Policy Act – streamlining NEPA*. Washington, DC: Library of Congress.

DFID (Department for International Development) 2003. *Environment guide*. London: DFID. Available at: www.eldis.org/vfile/upload/1/document/0708/DOC12943.pdf.

Dobry, G. 1975. *Review of the development control system: final report*. London: HMSO.

DoE (Department of the Environment) 1977. Press Notice 68. London: Department of the Environment.

DoE 1978. Press Notice 488. London: Department of the Environment.

Ehrlich, P. 1968. *The population bomb*. New York: Ballantine.

European Bank for Reconstruction and Development 1992. *Environmental procedures*. London: European Bank for Reconstruction and Development.

European Bank for Reconstruction and Development 2010. *Environmental and social procedures*. Available at: www.ebrd.com/downloads/about/sustainability/esprocs10.pdf.

Glasson, J. and Bellanger, C. 2003. Divergent practice in a converging system? The case of EIA in France and the UK. *Environmental Impact Assessment Review* 23, 605–24.

Glasson, J. and Salvador, N.N.B. 2000. EIA in Brazil: a procedures-practice gap. A comparative study with reference to the EU, and especially the UK. *Environmental Impact Assessment Review* 20, 191–225.

Greenberg, M. 2012. *The environmental impact statement after two generations*. Abingdon: Routledge.

Hall, E. 1994. *The environment versus people? A study of the treatment of social effects in EIA* (MSc dissertation). Oxford: Oxford Brookes University.

HMSO (Her Majesty's Stationery Office) 1971. *Report of the Roskill Commission on the Third London Airport*. London: HMSO.

House of Lords 1981a. *Environmental assessment of projects*. Select Committee on the European Communities, 11th Report, Session 1980–81. London: HMSO.

House of Lords 1981b. *Parliamentary debates (Hansard) official report, session 1980–81*, 30 April, 1311–47. London: HMSO.

Lee, N. and Wood, C.M. 1984. Environmental impact assessment procedures within the European Economic Community. In *Planning and ecology*, R.D. Roberts and T.M. Roberts (eds), 128–34. London: Chapman & Hall.

Mandelker, D.R. 2000. *NEPA law and litigation*, 2nd edn. St Paul, MN: West Publishing.

Moreira, I.V. 1988. EIA in Latin America. In *Environmental impact assessment: theory and practice*, P. Wathern (ed), 239–53. London: Unwin Hyman.

NEPA (National Environmental Policy Act) 1970. 42 USC 4321–4347, 1 January, as amended.

O'Riordan, T. and Sewell, W.R.D. (eds) 1981. *Project appraisal and policy review*. Chichester: Wiley.

Orloff, N. 1980. *The National Environmental Policy Act: cases and materials*. Washington, DC: Bureau of National Affairs.

Overseas Development Administration 1996. *Manual of environmental appraisal: revised and updated*. London: ODA.

Petts, J. and Hills, P. 1982. *Environmental assessment in the UK*. Nottingham: Institute of Planning Studies, University of Nottingham.

Sadler, B. 1996. *Environmental assessment in a changing world: evaluating practice to improve performance*, International study on the effectiveness of environmental assessment. Ottawa: Canadian Environmental Assessment Agency.

SDD (Scottish Development Department) 1974. *Appraisal of the impact of oil-related development, DP/TAN/16*. Edinburgh: SDA.

Tomlinson, P. 1986. Environmental assessment in the UK: implementation of the EEC Directive. *Town Planning Review* 57 (4), 458–86.

Turner, T. 1988. The legal eagles. *Amicus Journal* (winter), 25–37.

UNEP (United Nations Environment Programme) 1997. *Environmental impact assessment training resource manual*. Stevenage: SMI Distribution.

UNEP 2002. *UNEP Environmental Impact Assessment Training Resource Manual*, 2nd edn. Available at www.unep.ch/etu/publications/EIAMan_2edition_toc.htm.

White House 1994. *Memorandum from President Clinton to all heads of all departments and agencies on an executive order on federal actions to address environmental injustice in minority populations and low income populations*. Washington, DC: White House.

Williams, R.H. 1988. The environmental assessment directive of the European Community. In *The role of environmental assessment in the planning process*, M. Clark and J. Herington (eds), 74–87. London: Mansell.

World Bank 1991. *Environmental assessment sourcebook*. Washington, DC: World Bank, www.worldbank.org

World Bank 1995. *Environmental assessment: challenges and good practice*. Washington, DC: World Bank.

World Bank 1997. *The impact of environmental assessment: A Review of World Bank Experience*. World Bank Technical Paper no. 363. Washington, DC: World Bank.

World Bank 1999. *Environmental assessment*, BP 4.01. Washington, DC: World Bank.

World Bank 2002. Environmental impact assessment systems in Europe and Central Asia Countries. Available at: www.worldbank.org/eca/environment.

World Bank 2006. Environmental impact assessment regulations and strategic environmental assessment requirements: practices and lessons learned in East and Southeast Asia. Environment and social development safeguard dissemination note no. 2. Available at: www.vle.worldbank.org/bnpp/files/TF055249EnvironmentalImpact.pdf.

3 UK agency and legislative context

●●

3.1 Introduction

This chapter discusses the legislative framework within which EIA is carried out in the UK. It begins with an outline of the principal actors involved in EIA and in the associated planning and development process. It follows with an overview first of relevant regulations and the types of project to which they apply, and then of the EIA procedures required by the recently revised Town and Country Planning (T&CP) regulations 2011.These can be considered the 'generic' EIA regulations that apply to most projects and provide a model for the other EIA regulations. The latter are then summarized. Readers should refer to Chapter 8 for a discussion of the main effects and limitations of the application of these regulations.

3.2 The principal actors

3.2.1 An overview

Any proposed major development has an underlying configuration of interests, strategies and perspectives. But whatever the development, be it a motorway, a power station, a reservoir or a forest, it is possible to divide those involved in the planning and development process broadly into four main groups. These are:

- the developers;
- those directly or indirectly affected by or having an interest in the development;
- the government and regulatory agencies; and
- various intermediaries (consultants, advocates, advisers) with an interest in the interaction between the developer, the affected parties and the regulators (Figure 3.1).

An introduction to the range of 'actors' involved is an important first step in understanding the UK legislative framework for EIA.

3.2.2 Developers

In the UK, EIA applies to projects in both the public and private sectors, although there are notable exemptions, including Ministry of Defence developments and those of the Crown Commission. Public sector developments are sponsored by central government departments such as the Department for Transport (DfT), by local authorities and by statutory bodies, such as the Environment Agency and the Highways Agency. Some were also sponsored by nationalized industries (such as the former British Rail and the nuclear industry), but the rapid privatization programme since the 1980s has transferred most former nationalized industries to the private sector. Some, such as the major energy companies (British Gas, National Grid and EDF) and the regional water authorities, have major and continuing programmes of projects, where it may be possible to develop and refine EIA procedures, learning from experience. Many other private-sector companies, often of multinational form, may also produce a stream of projects. However, for many developers, a major project may be a one-off or 'once in a lifetime' activity. For them, the EIA process, and the associated planning and development process, may be much less familiar, requiring quick learning and, it is to be hoped, the provision of some good advice.

3.2.3 Affected parties

Those parties directly or indirectly affected by such developments are many. In Figure 3.1 they have been broadly categorized, according to their role or degree of power (e.g. statutory, advisory), level of operation (e.g. international, national, local) or emphasis (e.g. environmental, economic). The growth in environmental groups, such as Greenpeace, Friends of the Earth, the Campaign to Protect Rural England (CPRE) and the Royal Society for the Protection of Birds (RSPB), is of particular note and is partly associated with the growing public interest in environmental issues. For instance, membership of the RSPB grew from

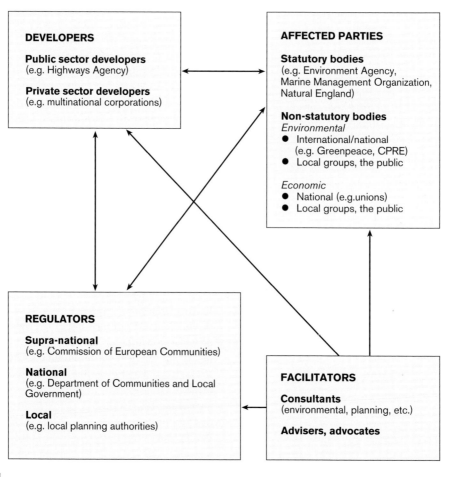

Figure 3.1

Principal actors in the EIA and planning and development processes

100,000 in 1970 to over a million in 1997, and has maintained this high level since. Membership of Sustrans, a charity that promotes car-free cycle routes, rose from 4,000 in 1993 to 20,000 in 1996; CPRE has over 60,000 members. Such groups, although often limited in resources, may have considerable 'moral weight'. The accommodation of their interests by a developer is often viewed as an important step in the 'legitimization' of a project. Like the developers, some environmental groups, especially at the national level, may have a long-term, continuing role. Some local amenity groups also may have a continuing role and an accumulation of valuable knowledge about the local environment. Others, usually at the local level, may have a short life, being associated with one particular project. In this latter category we can place local pressure groups, which can spring up quickly to oppose developments. Such groups have sometimes been referred to as NIMBY ('not in my back yard'), and their aims often include the maintenance of property values and existing lifestyles, and the diversion of any necessary development elsewhere. Another colourful relation of this group is BANANA ('build absolutely nothing anywhere near anything').

Statutory consultees are an important group in the EIA process. The planning authority must consult such bodies before making a decision on a major project requiring an EIA. Statutory consultees in England include Natural England (NE), the Marine Management Organization (MMO), the Environment Agency (for certain developments), and the principal local council for the area in which the project is proposed. Other consultees often involved include the local highway authority and the county archaeologist. As noted above, non-statutory bodies, such as the RSPB and the general public, may provide additional valuable information on environmental issues.

3.2.4 Regulators

The government, at various levels, will normally have a significant role in regulating and managing the relationship between the groups previously outlined. As discussed in Chapter 2, the European Commission has adopted a Directive on EIA procedures (CEC 1985 and amendments). The UK government has subsequently implemented these through an array of regulations and guidance (see Section 3.3). The principal department involved currently is (2012) the Department for Communities and Local Government (DCLG; formerly ODPM, DTLR, DETR and DoE!) through its London headquarters. Of particular importance in the EIA process is the local authority, and especially the relevant local planning authority (LPA). This may involve district, county and unitary authorities. Such authorities act as filters through which schemes proposed by developers usually have to pass. In addition, the LPA often opens the door for other agencies to become involved in the development process.

3.2.5 Facilitators

A final group, but one of particular significance in the EIA process, includes the various consultants, advocates and advisers who participate in the EIA and the planning and development processes. Such agents are often employed by developers; occasionally they may be employed by local groups, environmental groups and others to help to mount opposition to a proposal. They may also be employed by regulatory bodies to help them in their examination process.

Environmental and planning consultancies carry out most of the EIA work, supported by smaller consultancies specializing in such issues as archaeology, noise, health and socio-economic impacts. There has been a massive growth in the number of environmental consultancies in the UK (Figure 3.2). The numbers have increased by over 400 per cent since the mid-1980s, and it has been estimated that clients in the year 2008 were spending approximately £1.5 billion on their services (ENDS 2009). Major factors underpinning the consultancy growth included the advent of the UK Environmental Protection Act (EPA) in 1990, EIA regulations, the growing UK business interest in environmental management systems (e.g. BS 7750, ISO 14001), and a whole raft of EC regulations including on SEA, eco-auditing, and the Water Framework Directive. Tables 3.1 and 3.2 provide a summary of skills in demand and the main work areas of work for UK environmental consultancies. EIA and planning is a specialism in considerable demand, and the area was also

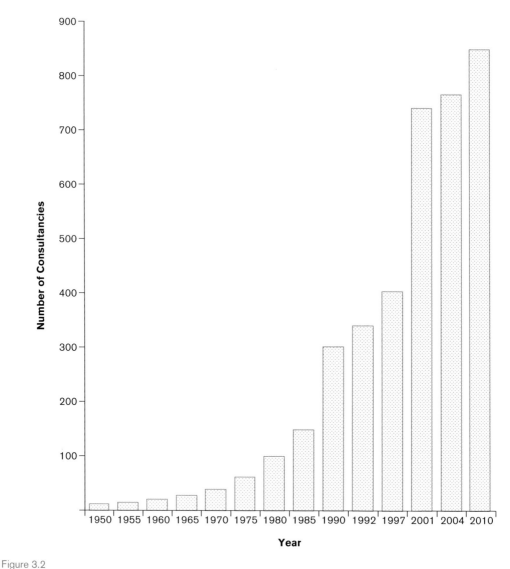

Figure 3.2

Increase in the number of environmental consultancies in the UK (1950–2010)

Source: Based on ENDS 1993, 1997, 2001 and website

mentioned by about a quarter of all respondents to the Environmental Data Services (ENDS) survey as a major area of activity. Further characteristics of recent consultancy activity are discussed in Chapter 8.

3.2.6 Agency interaction

The various agencies outlined here represent a complex array of interests and aims, any combination of which may come into play for a particular development. This array has several dimensions, and within each there may be a range of often conflicting views. For example, there may be conflict between local and national views, between the interests of profit maximization and those of environmental conservation, between short-term and long-term perspectives and between corporate bodies and individuals. The agencies are also linked in various ways. Some links are

Table 3.1 Skills in demand by UK environmental consultancies (2008)

Specialism	%
Waste management	62
Energy management	53
Sustainable development	52
EIA and planning	50
Environmental management and auditing	49
Water and waste management	46
GHG and carbon management	44
Pollution prevention and control (IPPC)	44
Health, safety and environmental management	42
Contaminated land and remediation	40
Renewable energy and clean energy	40
Air pollution and control	38
Corporate policy, CSR and communications	37
Ecology and nature conservation	35
Hydrology and hydrogeology	30
Public affairs and stakeholder communication	29
Hazard risk management	28
Acoustics	22
Process engineering	20

Source: ENDS 2009

Table 3.2 Environmental consultants' main professional activities (2009)

Activity	%
Environmental management	44
Waste management/recycling	35
Environmental protection/regulation	29
Health, safety and environmental management	26
Sustainable development	24
Auditing/verification	23
Environmental education/training	23
Environmental impact assessment (inc. EIA, SEA and SA) and planning	23
Carbon management	19
Energy	19
Climate change and GHG management	18
Pollution control	18
Risk assessment	18
Corporate policy, CSR and communications	16

Source: ENDS 2010

statutory, others advisory. Some are contractual, others regulatory. The EIA regulations and guidance provide a set of procedures linking the various actors discussed, and these are now outlined.

3.3 EIA regulations: an overview

In the UK, EC Directive 85/337 was implemented through over 40 different secondary regulations under Section 2.2 of the European Communities Act 1972. The large number of regulations was symptomatic of how EIA has been implemented in the UK. Different regulations apply to projects covered by the planning system, projects covered by other authorization systems and projects not covered by any authorization system but still requiring EIA. Different regulations apply to England, and the Devolved Administrations (DA) of Wales, Scotland and Northern Ireland. The introduction of various revisions to the regulations from 1999 onwards (the most recent being those of 2011), to implement the amended EC Directive,

provided opportunities for some tidying up of the list, but as Table 3.3 shows, there are still many regulations to ensure that all of the Directive's requirements are met. The regulations are supplemented by an array of EIA guidance from government and other bodies (Table 3.4). In addition, the Planning and Compensation Act 1991 allows the government to require EIA for other projects that fall outside the Directive.

In contrast to the US system of EIA, the EC EIA Directive applies to both public and private sector development. The developer carries out the EIA, and the resulting EIS must be handed in with the application for authorization. In England, most of the developments listed in Annexes I and II of the Directive fall under the remit of the planning system, and are thus covered by the Town and Country Planning (EIA) Regulations 2011 (the T&CP Regulations), previously the Town and Country Planning (Assessment of Environmental Effects (AEE)) Regulations 1988 and 1999. Over time various incremental additions and amendments have been made to the T&CP Regulations to plug loopholes and extend the remit of the regulations, for instance:

Table 3.3 Key UK EIA regulations and dates of implementation

UK regulations for projects subject to the Town and Country Planning system

England
Town and Country Planning (EIA) Regulations 2011
Town and Country Planning (General Permitted Development) Order 1995

Wales
Under review

Scotland
Town and Country Planning (EIA) (Scotland) Regulations 2011

Northern Ireland
Under review

UK EIA regulations for projects subject to alternative consent systems

Agriculture
Environmental Impact Assessment (Agriculture) (England) (no. 2) Regulations 2006

Afforestation
Environmental Impact Assessment (Forestry) (England and Wales) Regulations 1999
Environmental Impact Assessment (Forestry) Regulations (Northern Ireland) 1999
Environmental Impact Assessment (Forestry) Regulations (Scotland) 1999

Infrastructure/major projects
Infrastructure Planning (EIA) Regulations 2009

Land drainage improvements
Environmental Impact Assessment (Land Drainage Improvement Works) Regulations 1999
Land Drainage (EIA) (Scotland) Regulations 1999
Drainage (EA) Regulations (Northern Ireland) 2001

Fish farming
Environmental Impact Assessment (Fish Farming in Marine Waters) Regulations 1999
Environmental Impact Assessment (Fish Farming in Marine Waters) Regulations (Northern Ireland) 2006

Trunk roads and motorways
Highways (AEE) Regulations 1999
Roads (EIA) Regulations (Northern Ireland) 1999

Railways, tramways, inland waterways and works interfering with navigation rights
Transport and Works (AEEs) 2000

Ports and harbours, and marine dredging
Environmental impact assessment and Natural Habitats (Extraction of Minerals by Marine Dredging) (England and Northern Ireland)
    Regulations 2007
Harbour Works (EIA) Regulations 1999
Harbour Works (AEE) Regulations (Northern Ireland) 1990

Power stations, overhead power lines and long-distance oil and gas pipeline
Electricity Works (AEE) (England and Wales) Regulations 2000
Electricity Works (EIA) (Scotland) Regulations 2000
Pipeline Works (EIA) Regulations 2000
The Nuclear Reactors (EIA for Decommissioning) Regulations 1999
The Gas Transporter Pipeline Works (EIA) Regulations 1999
Offshore Petroleum Production and Pipelines (AEE) Regulations 1999

Water Resources
The Water Resources (EIA) (England and Wales) Regulations 2003

Table 3.4 UK government EIA procedural guidance

DoE 1991. Monitoring environmental assessment and planning. London: HMSO

DoE 1994. Evaluation of environmental information for planning projects: a good practice guide. London: HMSO

DoE 1995. Preparation of environmental statements for planning projects that require environmental assessment. London: HMSO

DoE 1996. Changes in the quality of environmental statements for planning projects. London: HMSO

Environment Agency 1996. A scoping handbook for projects. London: HMSO

DETR 1997. Mitigation measures in environmental statements. London: HMSO

Scottish Executive Development Department 1999b. Planning advice note 58. Edinburgh: SEDD

National Assembly for Wales 1999. Circular 11/99 Environmental impact assessment. Cardiff: National Assembly

Planning Service (Northern Ireland) *Development control advice note 10* 1999. Belfast: NI Planning Service.

DETR 2000. Environmental impact assessment: a guide to the procedures. London: DCLG

DCLG 2006. Circular and guide to good practice. London: DCLG

DfT 2007b. Guidance on transport assessment (GTA). London: DfT

DfT 2011. Design manual for roads and bridges. London: DfT

Scottish Government 2011a. Circular 3/2011: The Town and Country Planning Environmental Impact Assessment (Scotland) Regulations 2011. Edinburgh: Scottish government. (Also available as EasyRead Guide).

DCLG 2011. Guidance on the Environmental Impact Assessment (EIA) Regulations 2011 for England. London: DCLG

- to expand and clarify the original list of projects for which EIA is required (e.g. to include motorway service areas and wind farms, and more recently to add carbon capture and storage projects);
- to require EIA for projects that would otherwise be permitted (e.g. land reclamation, waste water treatment works, projects in Simplified Planning Zones);
- to require EIA for projects resulting from a successful appeal against a planning enforcement notice;
- to allow the relevant Secretary of State (SoS) to direct that a particular development should be subject to EIA even if it is not listed in the regulations; and

- to be consistent with various EC and UK legal rulings, for instance about screening processes and documentation.

Other types of projects listed in the EC Directive require separate legislation, since they are not governed by the planning system. Of the various *transport* projects, local highway developments and airports are dealt with under the T&CP Regulations by the local planning (highways) authority, but motorways and trunk roads proposed and regulated by the Department for Transport (DfT) fall under the Highways (Assessment of environmental effects) Regulations 1999. Applications for harbours are regulated by the DfT under the various Harbour Works (EIA) Regulations. New railways and tramways require EIA under the Transport and Works (AEE) procedure 2000.

Energy projects producing less than 50 MW are regulated by the local authority under the T&CP Regulations. Those of 50 MW or over, most electricity power lines, and pipelines (in Scotland as well as in England and Wales) are controlled by the Department of Energy and Climate Change (DECC) under the various Electricity and Pipeline Works (EIA) Regulations 2000.

New *land drainage* works, including flood defence and coastal defence works, require planning permission and are thus covered by the T&CP Regulations. Improvements to drainage works carried out by the Environment Agency and other drainage bodies require EIA through the EIA (Land Drainage Improvement Works) Regulations, which are regulated by the Department for Environment, Food and Rural Affairs (DEFRA). *Forestry* projects require EIA under the EIA (Forestry) Regulations 1999. *Marine fish farming* within 2 km of the coast of England, Wales or Scotland requires a lease from the Crown Estates Commission, but not planning permission. For these developments, EIA is required under the EA (Fish Farming in Marine Waters) Regulations 1999.

Many other developments in Scotland, Wales and Northern Ireland are increasingly being covered by country-specific legislation. For example the T&CP (EIA) (Scotland) Regulations 2011 have also been revised recently, and provide an interesting parallel system with the regulations for England. They also include a very useful *User Guide/EasyRead* short version for the busy reader (see Table 3.4). Wales is also developing its own separate T&CP (EIA) Regulations.

As will be discussed in Chapter 8, about 60–70 per cent of all the EIAs prepared in the UK fall under the T&CP Regulations, about 10 per cent fall under each of the EIA (Scotland) Regulations and the Highways (EIA) Regulations; almost all the rest involve land drainage, electricity and pipeline works, forestry projects in England and Wales and planning-related developments in Northern Ireland.

The enactment of this wide range of EIA regulations has made many of the early concerns regarding procedural loopholes (e.g. CPRE 1991, Fortlage 1990) obsolete. However, several issues still remain – not least the sheer complexity of this array of regulation. First is the ambiguity inherent in the term project. An example of this is the EIA procedures for electricity generation and transmission, in which a power station and the transmission lines to and from it are seen as separate projects for the purposes of EIA, despite the fact that they are inextricably linked (Sheate 1995; see also Section 9.2). Another example is the division of road construction into several separate projects for planning and EIA purposes even though none of them would be independently viable.

● ●

3.4 The Town and Country Planning (EIA) Regulations 2011 (previously the Town and Country Planning (EIA) Regulations 1999 and the Town and Country Planning (AEE) Regulations 1988)

The T&CP Regulations implement the EC Directive for those projects that require planning permission in England (Wales now has separate regulations). They are the central form in which the Directive is implemented in the UK; the other UK EIA regulations were established to cover projects that are not covered by the T&CP Regulations. As a result, the T&CP Regulations are the main focus of discussions on EIA procedures and effectiveness. This section presents the procedures of the T&CP

Regulations. **Figure 3.3** summarizes these procedures; the letters in the figure correspond to the letters in bold preceding the explanatory paragraphs below. Section 3.5 considers other main EIA regulations as variations of the T&CP Regulations and Section 3.6 comments on the changes following from the amended EC Directive.

The original T&CP Regulations were issued in July 1988. Guidance on the Regulations followed soon after; DoE Circular 15/88 (Welsh Office Circular 23/88) was aimed primarily at local planning authorities; a guidebook entitled *Environmental assessment: a guide to the procedures* (DoE 1989), was aimed more at developers and their advisers. Further DoE guidance on good practice in carrying out and reviewing EIAS was published in 1994 and 1995 (DoE 1994a, b, 1995) and in 1997 (DETR). The revised 1999 T&CP Regulations were accompanied by new circulars on EIA (DETR 1999; Scottish Executive Development Department 1999, NAFW 1999), which give comprehensive guidance on the Regulations. A valuable guidebook, *Environmental impact assessment: a guide to the procedures* (DETR 2000) was also issued. *Guidance on the Environmental Impact Assessment (EIA) Regulations 2011 for England* (DCLG 2011b), and the parallel document for Scotland, now provide the latest versions in this stream of very useful documents. The circulars and other government guidance are strongly recommended reading. However, only the regulations are mandatory: the guidance interprets and advises, but cannot be enforced.

3.4.1 Which projects require EIA?

The T&CP Regulations require EIAs to be carried out for two broad categories of project, given in Schedules 1 and 2. These schedules correspond very closely to Annexes I and II in the amended EC Directive, as outlined in Table 2.4 and detailed in Appendix 1.[1] Schedule 1 has very minor wording changes from Annex I, plus the switch of Annex I, 1.20, long overhead electrical power lines, to the Electricity Works (AEE) Regulations 2000 (S1 1927). The decommissioning of nuclear power stations and reactors is also covered by separate EIA regulations in the UK. Schedule 2 has only very minor modifications from Annex II; primarily in 2.10 where (b) also includes sports stadiums, leisure centres and multiplex cinemas. Also, there is a

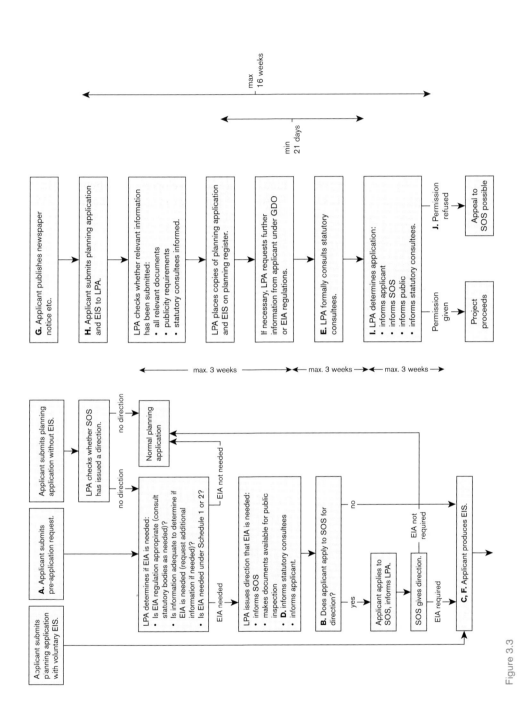

Figure 3.3 Summary of T&CP Regulations in EIA procedure

Source: Based on DETR 2000

separate category (p) for motorway service areas, and a few other categories are split or relocated. Schedule 2.12 also includes an additional category (f) for golf courses and associated developments. For Schedule 1 projects, EIA is required in every case. A Schedule 2 project requires EIA if it is deemed 'likely to give rise to significant environmental effects'.

The 'significance' of a project's environmental effects is determined on the basis of a set of applicable thresholds and criteria for Schedule 2 development (see Appendix 2), and the selection criteria in Schedule 3 of the Regulations (see Table 3.5). Three categories of criteria are listed in Schedule 3 (DETR 2000; DCLG 2011a):

- whether it is a development of more than local importance [for example, in terms of physical scale];
- whether the development is proposed for a particularly environmentally sensitive or vulnerable location [for example, a national park or a site of special scientific interest]; and
- whether the development is likely to have unusually complex and potentially hazardous environmental effects [for example, in terms of the discharge of pollutants].

The third category is designed to help in determining whether the interactions between the first two categories (i.e. between a development and its environment) are likely to be significant. A project constitutes Schedule 2 development for EIA when: (a) it meets criteria or exceeds thresholds listed in the second column of the Schedule 2 table (see Appendix 2); or (b) is located in, or partly in, a 'sensitive area', as defined in the regulations (see Table 3.5). The more environmentally sensitive the location, the more likely it is that the effects will be significant and require EIA.

Screening criteria have raised many issues over the life of the UK EIA regulations, including giving rise to several celebrated legal cases – many of which are covered in Section 8.6, Chapter 8. These include, for instance, cases about dealing with extensions to projects, multi-stage consents, and the extent to which proposed project mitigation measures can be taken into account in screening decisions.

The 2011 Regulations have responded on many of the legal issues raised.

Table 3.5 Selection criteria for screening Schedule 2 development

1 Characteristics of development

The characteristics of development must be considered having regard, in particular, to:

(a) the size of the development;
(b) the cumulation with other development;
(c) the use of natural resources;
(d) the production of waste;
(e) pollution and nuisances;
(f) the risk of accidents, having regard in particular to substances or technologies used.

2 Location of development

The environmental sensitivity of geographical areas likely to be affected by development must be considered, having regard, in particular, to:

(a) the existing land use;
(b) the relative abundance, quality and regenerative capacity of natural resources in the area;
(c) the absorption capacity of the natural environment, paying particular attention to the following areas
    (i)   wetlands;
    (ii)   coastal zones;
    (iii) mountain and forest areas;
    (iv)   nature reserves and parks;
    (v)   areas designated by Member States pursuant to Council Directive 2009/147/EC on the conservation of wild birds[1] and Council Directive 92/43/EEC on the conservation of natural habitats and of wild fauna and flora[2];
    (vi)   areas in which the environmental quality standards laid down in EU legislation have already been exceeded;
    (vii) densely populated areas;
    (viii) landscapes of historical, cultural or archaeological significance

3 Characteristics of the potential impact

The potential significant effects of development must be considered in relation to criteria set out under paragraphs 1 and 2 above, and having regard, in particular, to:

(a) the extent of the impact (geographical area and size of the affected population);
(b) the transfrontier nature of the impact;
(c) the magnitude and complexity of the impact;
(d) the probability of the impact;
(e) the duration, frequency and reversibility of the impact.

Source: DCLG 2011a

Notes: (1) O.J. no. L 20, 26.1.2010, p. 7.   (2) O.J. no. L 206, 22.7.1992, p. 7.

- Schedule 2.13 has been amended so that the thresholds in Schedule 2 apply to the development as a whole once changed or extended, and not just to the change or extension. For example, the construction of a 0.2 ha extension to an industrial estate may not have previously qualified for EIA by virtue of falling below the relevant 0.5 ha threshold. Now, this extension must be considered with the original development. If the latter was 0.4 ha, this would take the combined development over the EIA threshold size of 0.6ha.
- The 2011 Regulations also include amendments in relation to a European Court of Justice (ECJ) preliminary ruling on screening decisions, known as the Mellor case, which now requires reasons for a negative EIA screening decision to be made available on request.
- Further to another ECJ ruling on multi-stage consents, the 2011 Regulations provide for the limitation to the requirement for subsequent applications to be subject to screening in those cases where the development is likely to have significant effects on the environment, which were not identified at the time the initial planning permission was granted.
- New categories for carbon capture and storage (CCS) have been included in both Schedules.

The 2011 Regulations also include the simplification of the thresholds from the more comprehensive applicable *and* indicative thresholds and criteria introduced under the 1999 Regulations, to applicable thresholds and criteria only. As can be seen in Appendix 2, these are largely spatially based ('the area of the development exceeds 0.5 ha'; 'the area of new floorspace exceeds 1000 square metres'). A current interesting issue (at the time of going to press) concerns a widening of screening actions to more cases of project demolition/ decommissioning. The European Court ruled in 2011 that demolition work comes within the scope of the EIA Directive; the effect is that where demolition works are likely to have significant environmental effects (for instance demolition of a listed building), the LPA must issue a screening opinion on whether EIA is required. Similarly, applicants who intend to demolish a structure must consider whether this may have significant environmental effects and require EIA. If this is the case the applicant must ask for a screening opinion. Finally, reflecting the continuing momentum in the evolving nature of developments, and EU and domestic legislation, there is a commitment to a further review of the 2011 Regulations within five years of their introduction!

A. A developer may decide that a project requires EIA under the T&CP Regulations, or may want to carry out an EIA even if it is not required. If the developer is uncertain, the LPA can be asked for an opinion ('screening opinion') on whether an EIA is needed. To do this the developer must provide the LPA with a plan showing the development site, a description of the proposed development and an indication of its possible environmental impacts. The LPA must then make a decision within three weeks. The LPA can ask for more information from the developer, but this does not extend the three week decision-making period.

If the LPA decides that no EIA is needed, the application is processed as a normal planning application. If instead the LPA decides that an EIA is needed, it must explain why, and make both the developer's information and the decision publicly available. In all cases the LPA must explain clearly and precisely the full reasons for its conclusion whether EIA is required or not. If the LPA receives a planning application without an EIA when it feels that it is needed, the LPA must notify the developer within three weeks, explaining why an EIA is needed. The developer then has three weeks in which to notify the LPA of the intention either to prepare an EIS or to appeal to the Secretary of State (SoS); if the developer does not do so, the planning application is refused.

B. If the LPA decides that an EIA is needed but the developer disagrees, the developer can refer the matter to the SoS for a ruling.[2] The SoS must give a decision within three weeks. If the SoS decides that an EIA is needed, an explanation is needed; it is published in the *Journal of Planning and Environment Law*. No explanation is needed if no EIA is required. The SoS may make a decision if a developer has not requested an opinion, and may rule, usually as a result of information made available by other bodies, that an EIA is needed where the LPA has decided that it is not needed.

3.4.2 The contents of the EIA

Schedule 4 of the T&CP Regulations, which is shown in Table 3.6, lists the information that should be included in an EIA. Schedule 4 interprets the requirements of the EIA Directive Annex IV according to the criteria set out in Article 5 of the Directive, namely:

> Member States shall adopt the necessary measures to ensure that the developer supplies in an appropriate form the information specified in Annex IV inasmuch as:

(a) the Member States consider that the information is relevant to a given stage of the consent procedure and to the specific characteristics of a particular project or type of project and of the environmental features likely to be affected;

(b) the Member States consider that a developer may reasonably be required to compile this information having regard *inter alia* to current knowledge and methods of assessment.

Table 3.6 Content of EIS required by the T&CP Regulations (2011) – Schedule 4

Under the definition in Regulation 2.1, 'environmental statement' means a statement:

(a) that includes such of the information referred to in Part 1 of Schedule 4 as is reasonably required to assess the environmental effects of the development and which the applicant can, having regard in particular to current knowledge and methods of assessment, reasonably be required to compile, but

(b) that includes at least the information referred to in Part 2 of Schedule 4.

Part 1

1   Description of the development, including, in particular:
   (a) a description of the physical characteristics of the whole development and the land-use requirements during the construction and operational phases;
   (b) a description of the main characteristics of the production processes, for instance, nature and quantity of the materials used;
   (c) an estimate, by type and quantity, of expected residues and emissions (water, air and soil pollution, noise, vibration, light, heat, radiation, etc.) resulting from the operation of the proposed development.

2   An outline of the main alternatives studied by the applicant or appellant and an indication of the main reasons for the choice made, taking into account the environmental effects.

3   A description of the aspects of the environment likely to be significantly affected by the development, including, in particular, population, fauna, flora, soil, water, air, climatic factors, material assets, including the architectural and archaeological heritage, landscape and the inter-relationship between the above factors.

4   A description of the likely significant effects of the development on the environment, which should cover the direct effects and any indirect, secondary, cumulative, short, medium and long-term, permanent and temporary, positive and negative effects of the development, resulting from:
   (a) the existence of the development;
   (b) the use of natural resources;
   (c) the emission of pollutants, the creation of nuisances and the elimination of waste, and the description by the applicant of the forecasting methods used to assess the effects on the environment.

5   A description of the measures envisaged to prevent, reduce and, where possible, offset any significant adverse effects on the environment.

6   A non-technical summary of the information provided under paragraphs 1 to 5 of this Part.

7   An indication of any difficulties (technical deficiencies or lack of know-how) encountered by the applicant in compiling the required information.

Part 2

1   A description of the development comprising information on the site, design and size of the development.

2   A description of the measures envisaged in order to avoid, reduce and, if possible, remedy significant adverse effects.

3   The data required to identify and assess the main effects which the development is likely to have on the environment.

4   An outline of the main alternatives studied by the applicant or appellant and an indication of the main reasons for his choice, taking into account the environmental effects.

5   A non-technical summary of the information provided under paragraphs 1 to 4 of this Part.

Source: DCLG 2011a

In Schedule 4, the information required in Annex IV has been interpreted to fall into two parts. The EIS must contain the information specified in Part 2, and such relevant information in Part 1 'as is reasonably required to assess the effects of the project and which the developer can reasonably be required to compile'. This distinction is important: as will be seen in Chapter 8, the EISs prepared to date have generally been weaker on Part 1 information, although this includes such important matters as the alternatives that were considered and the expected wastes or emissions from the development. In addition, in Appendix 5 of the guidebook (DETR 2000), there is a longer checklist of matters that may be considered for inclusion in an EIA: this list is for guidance only, but it helps to ensure that all the possible significant effects of the development are considered (Table 3.7).

C. Until the implementation of the amended Directive in 1999, there was no mandatory requirement in the UK for a formal 'scoping' stage at which the LPA, the developer and other interested parties could agree on what would be included in the EIA. Indeed, there was no requirement for any kind of consultation between the developer and other bodies before the submission of the formal EIA and planning application, although guidance (DoE 1989) did stress the benefits of early consultation and early agreement on the scope of the EIA. The 1999 and subsequent Regulations enable a developer to ask the LPA for a formal 'scoping opinion' on the information to be included in an EIS – in advance of the actual planning application. This allows a developer to be clear on LPA views on the anticipated key significant effects. The request must be accompanied by the same information provided for a screening opinion, and may be made at the same time as for the screening opinion. The LPA must consult certain bodies (see **D**), and must produce the scoping opinion within five weeks. The time period may be extended if the developer agrees. There is no provision for appeal to the SoS if the LPA and developer disagree on the content of an EIS. But if the LPA fails to produce a scoping opinion within the required timescale, the developer may apply to the SoS (or Assembly) for a scoping direction, also to be produced within five weeks, and also to be subject to consultation

with certain bodies. The checklist (DETR 2000) provides a useful aid to developer–LPA discussions (see Table 3.7).

3.4.3 Statutory and other consultees

Under the T&CP Regulations, a number of statutory consultees are involved in the EIA process, as noted in Section 3.2. These bodies are involved at two stages of an EIA, in addition to possible involvement in the scoping stage.

D. First, when an LPA determines that an EIA is required, it must inform the statutory consultees of this. Current consultation bodies in England include the relevant planning authority, Natural England, the Environment Agency and more recently the Marine Management Organization (primarily in relation to projects with potential marine impacts). The consultees in turn must make available to the developer, if so requested and at a reasonable charge, any relevant environmental information in their possession. For example, Natural England might provide information about the ecology of the area. This does not include any confidential information or information that the consultees do not already have in their possession.

E. Second, once the EIS has been submitted, the LPA or developer must send a free copy to each of the statutory consultees. The consultees may make representations about the EIS to the LPA for at least two weeks after they receive the EIS. The LPA must take account of these representations when deciding whether to grant planning permission. The developer may also contact other consultees and the general public while preparing the EIS. The government guidance explains that these bodies may have particular expertise in the subject or may highlight important environmental issues that could affect the project. Although the developer is under no obligation to contact any of these groups, again the government guidance stresses the benefits of early and thorough consultation.

3.4.4 Carrying out the EIA: preparing the EIS

F. The government gives no formal guidance about what techniques and methodologies should be used in EIA, noting only that they will vary depending on the proposed development, the

Table 3.7 Checklist of matters to be considered for inclusion in an environmental statement

This checklist is intended as a guide to the subjects that need to be considered in the course of preparing an environmental statement. It is unlikely that all the items will be relevant to any one project.

The environmental effects of a development during its construction and commissioning phases should be considered separately from the effects arising while it is operational. Where the operational life of a development is expected to be limited, the effects of decommissioning or reinstating the land should also be considered separately.

Section 1: *Information describing the project*

1.1 Purpose and physical characteristics of the project, including details of proposed access and transport arrangements, and of numbers to be employed and where they will come from.

1.2 Land-use requirements and other physical features of the project:
   - during construction;
   - when operational;
   - after use has ceased (where appropriate).

1.3 Production processes and operational features of the project:
   - type and quantities of raw materials, energy and other resources consumed;
   - residues and emissions by type, quantity, composition and strength including:
     discharges to water; emissions to air; noise; vibration; light; heat; radiation; deposits/residues to land and soil; others.

1.4 Main alternative sites and processes considered, where appropriate, and reasons for final choice.

Section 2: *Information describing the site and its environment*

Physical features

2.1 Population – proximity and numbers.

2.2 Flora and fauna (including both habitats and species) – in particular, protected species and their habitats.

2.3 Soil: agricultural quality, geology and geomorphology.

2.4 Water: aquifers, watercourses, shoreline, including the type, quantity, composition and strength of any existing discharges.

2.5 Air: climatic factors, air quality, etc.

2.6 Architectural and historic heritage, archaeological sites and features, and other material assets.

2.7 Landscape and topography.

2.8 Recreational uses.

2.9 Any other relevant environmental features.

The policy framework

2.10 Where applicable, the information considered under this section should include all relevant statutory designations such as national nature reserves, sites of special scientific interest, national parks, areas of outstanding natural beauty, heritage coasts, regional parks, country parks and designated green belt, local nature reserves, areas affected by tree preservation orders, water protection zones, conservation areas, listed buildings, scheduled ancient monuments and designated areas of archaeological importance. It should also include references to relevant national policies (including Planning Policy Guidance (PPG) notes) and to regional and local plans and policies (including approved or emerging development plans).

2.11 Reference should also be made to international designations, e.g. those under the EC 'Wild Birds' or 'Habitats' Directives, the Biodiversity Convention and the Ramsar Convention.

Section 3: *Assessment of effects*

Including direct and indirect, secondary, cumulative, short-, medium- and long-term, permanent and temporary, positive and negative effects of the project.

Effects on human beings, buildings and man-made features

3.1 Change in population arising from the development, and consequential environment effects.

3.2 Visual effects of the development on the surrounding area and landscape.

3.3 Levels and effects of emissions from the development during normal operation.

3.4 Levels and effects of noise from the development.

3.5 Effects of the development on local roads and transport.

3.6 Effects of the development on buildings, the architectural and historic heritage, archaeological features and other human artefacts, e.g. through pollutants, visual intrusion, vibration.

Effects on flora, fauna and geology

3.7 Loss of, and damage to, habitats and plant and animal species.

3.8 Loss of, and damage to, geological, palaeontological and physiographic features.

3.9 Other ecological consequences.

Effects on land

3.10 Physical effects of the development, e.g. change in local topography, effect of earth-moving on stability, soil erosion, etc.

3.11 Effects of chemical emissions and deposits on soil of site and surrounding land.

3.12 Land-use/resource effects:
- quality and quantity of agricultural land to be taken;
- sterilization of mineral resources;
- other alternative uses of the site, including the 'do nothing' option;
- effect on surrounding land uses including agriculture;
- waste disposal.

Effects on water

3.13 Effects of development on drainage pattern in the area.

3.14 Changes to other hydrographic characteristics, e.g. groundwater level, watercourses, flow of underground water.

3.15 Effects on coastal or estuarine hydrology.

3.16 Effects of pollutants, waste, etc. on water quality.

Effects on air and climate

3.17 Level and concentration of chemical emissions and their environmental effects.

3.18 Particulate matter.

3.19 Offensive odours.

3.20 Any other climatic effects.

Other indirect and secondary effects associated with the project

3.21 Effects from traffic (road, rail, air, water) related to the development.

3.22 Effects arising from the extraction and consumption of materials, water, energy or other resources by the development.

3.23 Effects of other development associated with the project, e.g. new roads, sewers, housing, power lines, pipelines, telecommunications, etc.

3.24 Effects of association of the development with other existing or proposed development.

3.25 Secondary effects resulting from the interaction of separate direct effects listed above.

Section 4: *Mitigating measures*

4.1 Where significant adverse effects are identified, a description of the measures to be taken to avoid, reduce or remedy those effects, e.g.:
 (a) site planning;
 (b) technical measures, e.g.:
- process selection;
- recycling;
- pollution control and treatment;
- containment (e.g. bunding of storage vessels).
 (c) aesthetic and ecological measures, e.g.:
- mounding;
- design, colour, etc.;
- landscaping;
- tree plantings;
- measures to preserve particular habitats or create alternative habitats;
- recording of archaeological sites;
- measures to safeguard historic buildings or sites.

4.2 Assessment of the likely effectiveness of mitigating measures.

Section 5: *Risk of accidents and hazardous development*

5.1 Risk of accidents as such is not covered in the EIA Directive or, consequently, in the implementing Regulations. However, when the proposed development involves materials that could be harmful to the environment (including people) in the event of an accident, the environmental statement should include an indication of the preventive measures that will be adopted so that such an occurrence is not likely to have a significant effect. This could, where appropriate, include reference to compliance with Health and Safety legislation.

5.2 There are separate arrangements in force relating to the keeping or use of hazardous substances and the HSE provides local planning authorities with expert advice about risk assessment on any planning application involving a hazardous installation.

5.3 Nevertheless, it is desirable that, wherever possible, the risk of accidents and the general environmental effects of developments should be considered together, and developers and planning authorities should bear this in mind.

Source: DETR 2000

receiving environment and the information available, and that predictions of effects will often have some uncertainty attached to them.

3.4.5 Submitting the EIS and planning application: public consultation

G. When the EIS has been completed, the developer must publish a notice in a local newspaper and post notices at the site. These notices must fulfil the requirements of Article 8 of the Town and Country Planning Act (General Permitted Development) Order 1995 (GPDO), state that a copy of the EIS is available for public inspection, give a local address where copies may be obtained and state the cost of the EIS, if any. The public can make written representations to the LPA for at least 20 days after the publication of the notice, but within 21 days of the LPA's receipt of the planning application.

H. After the EIS has been publicly available for at least 21 days, the developer submits to the LPA the planning application, copies of the EIS,[3] and certification that the required public notices have been published and posted. The LPA must then send copies of the EIS to the statutory consultees, inviting written comments within a specified time (at least two weeks from receipt of the EIS), forward another copy to the SoS and place the EIS on the planning register. It must also decide whether any additional information about the project is needed before a decision can be made, and, if so, obtain it from the developer. The clock does not stop in this case: a decision must still be taken within the appropriate time.

3.4.6 Planning decision

I. Before making a decision about the planning application, the LPA must collect written representations from the public within three weeks of the receipt of the planning application, and from the statutory consultees at least two weeks from their receipt of the EIS. It must wait at least 14 days after receiving the planning application before making a decision. In contrast to normal planning applications, which must be decided within eight weeks, those accompanied by an EIS must be decided within 16 weeks. If the LPA has not made a decision after 16 weeks, the applicant can appeal

to the SoS for a decision. The LPA cannot consider a planning application invalid because the accompanying EIS is felt to be inadequate: it can only ask for further information within the 16-week period.

In making its decision, the LPA must consider the EIS and any comments from the public and statutory consultees, as well as other material considerations. The environmental information is only part of the information that the LPA considers, along with other material considerations. The decision is essentially still a political one, but it comes with the assurance that the project's environmental implications are understood. The LPA may grant or refuse permission, with or without conditions. It is important for LPAs to consider how mitigation measures proposed in an ES are likely to be secured; they may be included in conditions attached to a planning permission; they can also be secured through enforceable planning obligations. Further to the changes resulting from the EC Directive the LPA must, in addition to the normal requirements to notify the applicant, notify the SoS and publish a notice in the local press, giving the decision, the main reasons on which the decision was based, together with a description of the main mitigation measures.

J. If an LPA refuses planning permission, the developer may appeal to the SoS, as for a normal planning application. The SoS may request further information before making a decision.

· ·

3.5 Other EIA regulations

This section summarizes the procedures of the other EIA regulations under which a large number of EISs have been prepared to date. We discuss the regulations in approximate descending order of frequency of application to date, although category 7 is likely to rise quickly up the order soon.

1 The Town and Country Planning Environmental Impact Assessment (Scotland) Regulations 2011.
2 Highways (AEE) Regulations 1999.
3 Environmental Impact Assessment (Land Drainage Improvement Works) Regulations 1999.

4   Electricity Works (AEE) Regulations 2000.

5   Pipeline Works (Environmental Impact Assessment) Regulations 2000.

6   Environmental Assessment (Forestry) Regulations 1999.

7   Infrastructure Planning (Environmental Impact Assessment) Regulations 2009.

3.5.1 EIA (Scotland) Regulations: including The Town and Country Planning (EIA) (Scotland) Regulations 2011

The EIA (Scotland) Regulations are broadly similar to those for England. They implement the Directive for projects that are subject to planning permission, but also cover some land drainage and trunk road projects. There is separate guidance on the Scottish Regulations (see Table 3.2). For some projects (for example, for the decommissioning of nuclear power stations), Scotland is included in regulations that also apply to other parts of the UK. In Northern Ireland, the Directive is implemented for projects subject to planning permission by the Planning (EIA) Regulations (Northern Ireland) 1999 (currently being revised).

The T&CP (EIA) (Scotland) Regulations were amended roughly in line with the English Regulations and for similar reasons. The commentary on the 2011 Regulations notes that:

> The existing 1999 Regulations had been repeatedly amended (12 times in 11 years) to take into account case law from domestic and European Courts, and changes to the Directive and/or domestic legislation. This made the 1999 Regulations increasingly complex and difficult to follow. The Scottish Parliament's subordinate legislation committee called for the Regulations to be consolidated in order to make them more accessible. (Scottish Government 2011b)

Under the Scottish Regulations, screening for Schedule 2 projects is on a case by case taking into account the key selection criteria: characteristics of the development, location of the development, and characteristics of the potential impacts. LPAs are encouraged to use checklists, including the one on the Scottish government's (Planning) EIA web page.

3.5.2 Highways (AEE) Regulations 1999

The Highways (AEE) Regulations apply to motorways and trunk roads proposed by the Department of Transport (DoT). The regulations are approved under procedures set out in the Highways Act 1980, which require the SoS for Transport to publish an EIS for the proposed route when draft orders for certain new highways, or major improvements to existing highways, are published. The SoS determines whether the proposed project comes under Annex I or Annex II of the Directive, and whether an EIA is needed. EIA is mandatory for projects to construct new motorways and certain other roads, including those with four or more lanes, and for certain road improvements. The regulations require an EIS to contain:

- a description of the published scheme and its site;
- a description of measures proposed to mitigate adverse environmental effects;
- sufficient data to identify and assess the main effects that the scheme is likely to have on the environment; and
- a non-technical summary.

Before 1993, the requirements of the Highways (AEE) Regulations were further elaborated in DoT standard AD 18/88 (DoT 1989) and the *Manual of Environmental Appraisal* (DoT 1983). In response to strong criticism,[4] particularly by the SACTRA (1992), these were superseded in 1993 by the *Design manual for roads and bridges* (DMRB), vol. II: *Environmental assessment* (DoT 1993). The manual proposed a three-stage EIA process and gave extensive, detailed advice on how these EIAs should be carried out. DMRB (DfT 2011) provides the latest evolution of the guidance for road projects. Other very useful transport assessment documentation can be found on the DfT WebTAG Transport Analysis Guidance website, including Guidance on Transport Assessment (GTA) (DfT 2007a).

3.5.3 Environmental Impact Assessment (Land Drainage Improvement Works) Regulations 1999

The EIA (Land Drainage Improvement Works) Regulations apply to almost all watercourses in

England and Wales except public-health sewers. If a drainage body (including a local authority acting as a drainage body) determines that its proposed improvement actions are likely to have a significant environmental effect, it must publish a description of the proposed actions in two local newspapers and indicate whether it intends to prepare an EIS. If it does not intend to prepare one, the public can make representations within 28 days concerning any possible environmental impacts of the proposal; if no representations are made, the drainage body can proceed without an EIS. If representations are made, but the drainage body still wants to proceed without an EIS, DEFRA (National Assembly in Wales) gives a decision on the issue at ministerial level.

The contents required of the EIS under these regulations are virtually identical to those under the T&CP Regulations. When the EIS is complete, the drainage body must publish a notice in two local newspapers, send copies to NE, the Environment Agency (EA), the MMO and any other relevant bodies and make copies of the EIS available at a reasonable charge. Representations must be made within 28 days and are considered by the drainage body in making its decision. If all objections are then withdrawn, the works can proceed; otherwise the minister gives a decision. Overall, these regulations are considerably weaker than the T&CP Regulations because of their weighting in favour of consent, unless objections are raised, and their minimal requirements for consultation with environmental organizations.

3.5.4 Electricity Works (AEE) Regulations 2000; Nuclear Reactors (EIA for Decommissioning) Regulations 1999

The construction or extension of power stations exceeding 50 MW, and the installation of overhead power lines, requires consent from the relevant SoS (currently Department of Energy and Climate Change) under Sections 36 and 37 of the Electricity Act 1989. The Electricity Works (EIA) Regulations 2000 is part of the procedure for applications under these provisions. EIA is required for:

- all thermal and nuclear power stations that fall under Annex 1 of the Directive (i.e. thermal

power stations of 300 MW or more, and nuclear power stations of at least 50 MW); and
- construction of overhead power lines of 220 KV or more and over 15 km in length.

The regulations also require proposed power stations not covered by Annex I, and all overhead power lines of at least 132 KV, to be screened for EIA. Power stations of less than 50 MW are approved under the planning legislation, through the T&CP (EIA) Regulations. The Electricity Works Regulations allow a developer to make a written request to the SoS to decide whether an EIA is needed. The SoS must consult with the LPA before making a decision. When a developer gives notice that an EIS is being prepared, the SoS must notify the LPA or the principal council for the relevant area, NE, the EA and the MMO, in the case of a power station, so that they can provide relevant information to the applicant. The contents required of the EIS are almost identical to those listed in the T&CP Regulations.

The regulations on decommissioning of nuclear power stations were added in 1999. Dismantling and decommissioning require the consent of the Health and Safety Executive (HSE). A licensee who applies for consent must provide the HSE with an EIS. The regulations apply also to changes to existing dismantling or decommissioning projects that may have significant effects on the environment.

3.5.5 The Pipeline Works (EIA) Regulations 2000; The Gas Transporter Pipeline Works (EIA) Regulations 1999; Offshore Petroleum Production and Pipelines (AEE) Regulations

The evolving array of regulations relating to pipelines reflects not only the growing importance of such development, but also the continuation of the fragmented UK approach to EIA legislation. The on-shore Pipeline Works, and the Gas Transporter Pipeline Works, Regulations apply to England, Wales and Scotland; the Offshore Petroleum Production and Pipelines Regulations apply to the whole of the UK. Oil and gas pipelines with a diameter of more than 800 mm and longer than 40 km come within Annex I of the Directive; those that fall below either of these thresholds are in Annex II. For the latter, pipelines 10 miles long or less are approved under the planning legislation. The rest fall under the above pipeline regulations, normally with determination by the relevant SoS in relation to associated consent and authorization procedures and to various criteria and thresholds. For example, on-shore gas pipeline works in Annex II of the Directive may be subject to EIA if they have a design operating pressure exceeding 7 bar gauge or they either wholly or in part cross a sensitive area (e.g. national park).

3.5.6 Environmental Impact Assessment (Forestry) (England and Wales) Regulations 1999)

Under the original EIA Directive and associated UK regulations, forestry EIAs were limited to those projects where applicants wished to apply for a grant or loan, for afforestation purposes, from the Forestry Agency. The lack of EIA requirements for other forestry projects, the perceived vested interest of the then Forestry Agency as a promoter of forestry and the lack of EIA requirements for the Agency's own projects have all been criticized (e.g. by the CPRE; see CPRE 1991). The amended Directive and associated UK legislation have subsequently brought about some changes.

Afforestation and deforestation come under Annex II of the Directive. Under the above Regulations, anyone who proposes to carry out a forestry project that is likely to have significant effects on the environment must apply for consent from the Forestry Commission before starting work. Those who apply for consent will be required to produce an EIS. The Regulations include: afforestation (creating new woodlands); deforestation (conversion of woodland to another use) and constructing forest roads and quarrying material to construct forest roads. Where projects are below 5 ha (afforestation) and 1 ha (others), they may be deemed unlikely to have significant effects on the environment, unless they are in sensitive areas. Given the variability of sites and projects, the Forestry Commission considers applications on a case-by-case basis. An applicant who disagrees with the Forestry Commission's opinion may apply to the relevant SoS for a direction. The contents required of an EIA under the Forestry Regulations

are almost identical to those required under the T&CP Regulations.

3.5.7 Infrastructure Planning (EIA) Regulations 2009

Context

As noted in Section 1.4.1, under the 2008 Planning Act (HMG 2008), a special subset of nationally significant infrastructure projects (NSIPs) has been identified, with impacts to be examined by new procedures led by the Infrastructure Planning Commission (IPC) (to be merged with the UK Planning Inspectorate in 2012). NSIPs include major energy projects, transport projects (road, rail and port), water and waste facilities – many of which were formally covered by some of the previously discussed regulations (especially highways, electricity, and pipelines). The IPC examination involves the consideration of environmental impacts, as relevant, under the Infrastructure Planning (EIA) Regulations 2009. The EIA Regulations impose procedural requirements for carrying out EIA on certain NSIP proposals. For example, EIA is always required for NSIPs such as nuclear power stations, but others, such as wind farms, only require EIA if they are likely to have significant effects on the environment by virtue of their nature, size or location. The role of the IPC under the EIA regulations includes:

*   'screening' proposals to determine whether they are EIA developments;
*   'scoping' proposals to advise the applicant what information should be provided within the environmental statement – involving seeking views from consultation bodies;
*   facilitating the preparation of ESs by notifying consultation bodies about their duty to provide information and informing the applicant;
*   evaluating environmental information in the ES and any representations made about the environmental effects before making a decision;
*   publicizing the IPC's screening and scoping opinions; and
*   publicizing any decision in relation to an application that has been accompanied by an ES (IPC 2010).

The IPC may not grant development consent unless it has first taken account of the 'environmental information' (ES and/or any further information about the environmental effects of the development). It will not accept an application if the supporting ES is considered inadequate, or it is deemed to be an EIA development but is not accompanied by an ES.

Screening

A proposal will be an EIA development if: the applicant notifies the IPC that it intends to submit an ES; the IPC adopts a screening opinion to the effect that the proposal is an EIA development; the SoS directs that it is an EIA development; or the proposal falls within Schedule 1 of the EIA Regulations. Many NSIPs are likely to fall within Schedule 1, for which EIA is mandatory. Others that fall within Schedule 2 must be considered for EIA against 'selection criteria' specified in Schedule 3 of the EIA Regulations; this differs from proposals under the T&CP (EIA) Regulations 2011, which are considered for EIA against applicable thresholds and criteria. For others, and where the applicant has not notified an intention to submit an ES, they must request that the IPC adopts a screening opinion in respect of the proposed development. Ideally the applicant should provide information on the characteristics of the development, the location of the development and characteristics of the potential impacts. Following the submission of a screening request, the IPC must issue its screening opinion within 21 days.

Scoping

Before making an application for a development consent order, the applicant has the opportunity to ask the IPC for a formal 'scoping opinion' on the information to be included in the ES. When making the request, the applicant must provide as a minimum: a plan sufficient to identify the land involved; a brief description of the nature and purpose of the development and of its possible effects on the environment; and such other information or representations as the applicant may wish to provide. However it is common practice for applicants to provide a scoping report as part of their formal request for a scoping opinion. Ideally this should include:

- a description of the scheme or proposal;
- interpretation of the site settings and surroundings;
- outline of alternatives and methods used in reaching a preferred opinion;
- results of desktop and baseline studies where available;
- methods to predict impacts and the significance criteria framework;
- mitigation and residual impacts to be considered;
- key topics covered as part of the scoping exercise; and
- an outline of the structure of the proposed ES.

Before adopting a scoping opinion the IPC has a duty to consult the 'consultation bodies', as defined in the EIA Regulation. These bodies have 28 days to respond. The IPC must adopt a scoping opinion within 42 days of receiving a scoping request; to date, these scoping opinions have tended to be long and detailed. Finally, all IPC project EIAs are made available on the IPC website.[5]

....

3.6 Summary and conclusions on changing legislation

The original (and amended) EC EIA Directive has been implemented in the UK through an array of regulations that link those involved – developers, affected parties, regulators and facilitators – in a variety of ways. The T&CP (EIA) Regulations are central. Other regulations cover projects that do not fall under the English and Welsh planning systems, such as motorways and trunk roads, power stations, pipelines, land drainage works, forestry projects, and development projects in Scotland and Northern Ireland.

The original UK Regulations had a number of weaknesses, relating to the range of projects included in the ambit of the EIA procedures, approaches to screening, scoping, consideration of alternatives, mandatory and discretionary EIS content, public consultation and others. Directive 97/11/EC, and subsequent amendments, has sought to address some of these issues that had arisen in the UK and other Member States.

UK regulations have been amended many times, partly in response to changes to the EC Directive and to domestic legislation, and partly also to case law from domestic and European Courts. The evolving UK Regulations replicate closely the four annexes of the amended EC Directive. This has brought a wider array of projects into the UK EIA system, has increased the number of mandatory categories and has led to some growth in EIA activity and EIS output. Screening procedures have been developed, and the consideration of scoping and alternatives now has a higher profile. There has been considerable rationalization of legislation, most recently in the 2011 consolidation of the T&CP (EIA) Regulations, but the array is still wide and complex. EIA guidance is a particular strength of the UK system, and government publications, especially the relevant circulars and guide to the procedures, help to navigate the legislative array.

SOME QUESTIONS

The following questions are intended to help the reader focus on the important issues of this chapter, and to start building some understanding of the UK agency and legislative context of EIA.

1   For a project with which you are familiar, identify the various sets of principal actors, and outline the potential areas of conflict between their interests with regard to the project.

2   How does EIA legislation, and the relevant key regulators, vary in England between (a) a Schedule 2 golf course project; (b) a motorway development; and (c) the decommissioning of a nuclear power station?

3   What is the role of statutory consultees in the EIA process?

4   Under the T&CP (EIA) Regulations, a Schedule 2 project requires EIA if it is deemed 'likely to give rise to significant environmental effects'. What criteria and thresholds are used to determine that significance?

5   Outline some of the changes introduced in the T&CP (EIA) Regulations for England (2011). What were the key drivers behind the changes?

6   Over time the projects covered by EIA have grown in response to both new technology and changes in social and economic infrastructure. What new additions might you anticipate for inclusion in the next review of legislation by 2016?

7   Currently a separate EIA for decommissioning or dismantling of a project only applies to nuclear power stations and reactors in the UK. Examine the case for extending this requirement to other projects.

8   What is a 'screening opinion', and who provides it?

9   Identify any particularly innovative features associated with the Infrastructure Planning (EIA) Regulations 2009.

Notes

1 There are some discrepancies. For instance, power stations of 300 MW or more are included in Schedule 1, although they actually fall under the Electricity Works (AEE) Regulations, and all 'special roads' are included, although the regulations should apply to special roads under local authority jurisdiction.

2 Decisions were actually made by the relevant government office in the region concerned (or the Assembly) – subsequently disbanded in 2011. As will be discussed in Chapter 8, this led to some discrepancies where two or more offices made different decisions on very similar projects.

3 This includes enough copies for all the statutory consultees to whom the developer has not already sent copies, one copy for the LPA and several for the Secretary of State.

4 The criticism was well deserved. The circular's assertion that '. . . individual highway schemes do not have a significant effect on climatic factors and, in most cases, are unlikely to have significant effects on soil or water' is particularly interesting in view of the cumulative impact of private transport on air quality.

5 IPC practice is developing fast and includes much more focus on pre-application activities, including the EIA process. There is also an important role for a Statement of Common Ground (SOCG) between the developer and the LPAs, and the production of separate Local Impact Reports (LIRs) by the relevant LPAs.

References

CEC (Commission of the European Communities) 1985. On the assessment of the effects of certain public and private projects on the environment. *Official Journal* L175, 5 July.

CPRE (Council for the Protection of Rural England) 1991. *The environmental assessment directive: five years on.* London: CPRE.

DCLG 2011a Town and Country (T&CP) (Environmental impact assessment (EIA)) regulations 2011. London: DCLG.

DCLG 2011b *Guidance on the Environmental Impact Assessment (EIA) Regulations 2011 for England.* London: DCLG.

DETR 1997. *Mitigation measures in environmental assessment.* London: HMSO.

DETR 1999. *Circular 02/99. Environmental impact assessment.* London: HMSO.

DETR 2000. *Environmental impact assessment: a guide to the procedures.* Tonbridge, UK: Thomas Telford Publishing.

DfT (Department for Transport) 2007a. *WebTAG: Transport Analysis Guidance.* (www.webtag.org.uk). London: DfT.

DfT 2007b. *Guidance on transport assessment* (GTA). London: DfT.

DfT 2011. *Design manual for roads and bridges* (DMRB). London: DfT.

DoE (Department of the Environment) 1989. *Environmental assessment: a guide to the procedures.* London: HMSO.

DoE 1991. *Monitoring environmental assessment and planning.* London: HMSO.

DoE 1994a. *Evaluation of environmental information for planning projects: a good practice guide.* London: HMSO.

DoE 1994b. *Good practice on the evaluation of environmental information for planning projects: research report.* London: HMSO.

DoE 1995. *Preparation of environmental statements for planning projects that require environmental assessment: a good practice guide.* London: HMSO.

DoE 1996. *Changes in the quality of environmental statements for planning projects.* London: HMSO.

DoT (Department of Transport) 1983. *Manual of environmental appraisal.* London: HMSO.

DoT 1989. *Departmental standard HD 18/88: environmental assessment under the EC Directive 85/337.* London: Department of Transport.

DoT 1993. *Design manual for roads and bridges, vol. 11: Environmental assessment.* London: HMSO.

ENDS 1993. *Directory of environmental consultants 1993/94.* London: Environmental Data Services.

ENDS 1997. *Directory of environmental consultants 1997/98.* London: Environmental Data Services.

ENDS 2001. *Environmental consultancy directory,* 8th edn. London: Environmental Data Services.

ENDS 2003. *Directory of environmental consultants 2003/2004.* London: Environmental Data Services.

ENDS 2009. *Salary and careers survey.* London: Environmental Data Services.

ENDS 2010. *Survey of environmental professionals.* London: Environmental Data Services.

Environment Agency 1996. *A scoping handbook for projects.* London: HMSO.

Fortlage, C. 1990. *Environmental assessment: a practical guide*. Aldershot: Gower.

HMG (Her Majesty's Government) 2008. *Planning Act 2008*. London: The Stationery Office.

IPC 2010. *Identifying the right environmental impacts: advice note 7-EIA, screening and scoping*. Bristol: IPC.

NAFW (National Assembly for Wales) 1999. *Circular 11/99 Environmental impact assessment*. Cardiff: National Assembly.

Planning Service (Northern Ireland) *Development control advice note 10* 1999. Belfast: NI Planning Service.

SACTRA (Standing Advisory Committee on Trunk Road Assessment) 1992. *Assessing the environmental impact of road schemes*. London: HMSO.

Scottish Executive Development Department 1999a. *Circular 1999 15/99. The environmental impact assessment regulations 1999*. Edinburgh: SEDD.

Scottish Executive Development Department 1999b. *Planning Advice Note 58*. Edinburgh: SEDD.

Scottish Government 2011a. Town and Country Planning (Environmental impact assessment) (Scotland) Regulations 2011 Edinburgh: Scottish Government.

Scottish Government 2011b. EasyRead version – Town and Country Planning (Environmental impact assessment) (Scotland) Regulations 2011 Edinburgh: Scottish Government.

Sheate, W.R. 1995. Electricity generation and transmission: a case study of problematic EIA implementation in the UK. *Environmental Policy and Practice* 5 (1), 17–25.

Part 2

Process

This illustration and the illustration opening Part 3 are by Neil Bennett, reproduced from Bowers, J. (1990), *Economics of the environment: the conservationist's response to the Pearce Report*, British Association of Nature Conservationists, 69 Regent Street, Wellington, Telford, Shropshire TE1 1PE.

4 Starting up: early stages

4.1 Introduction

This is the first of four chapters that discuss how an EIA is carried out. The focus throughout is on both the procedures required by UK legislation and the ideal of best practice. Although Chapters 4–7 seek to provide a logical step-by-step approach through the EIA process, there is no one exclusive approach. Every EIA process is set within an institutional context, and the context will vary from country to country (see Chapter 10). As already noted, even in one country, the UK, there may be a variety of regulations for different projects (see also Chapter 9). The various steps in the process can be taken in different sequences. Some may be completely missing in certain cases. The process should also not just be linear but build in cycles, with feedback from later stages to the earlier ones.

Chapter 4 covers the early stages of the EIA process. These include setting up a management process for the EIA activity, clarifying whether an EIA is required at all ('screening') and an outline of the extent of the EIA ('scoping'), which may involve consultation between several of the key actors outlined in Chapter 3. Early stages of EIA should also include an exploration of possible alternative approaches for a project. Baseline studies, setting out the parameters of the develop-

ment action (including associated policy positions) and the present and future state of the environment involved, are also included in Chapter 4. However, the main section in the chapter is devoted to impact identification. This is important in the early stages of the process, but, reflecting the cyclical, interactive nature of the process, some of the impact identification methods discussed here may also be used in the later stages. Conversely, some of the prediction, evaluation, communication and mitigation approaches discussed in Chapter 5 can be used in the early stages, as can the participation approaches outlined in Chapter 6. The discussion in this chapter starts, however, with a brief introduction to the management of the EIA process.

4.2 Managing the EIA process

Environmental impact assessment is a management-intensive process. EIAs often deal with major (and sometimes poorly defined) projects, with many wide-ranging and often controversial impacts. It is important that the EIA process is well managed. This section discusses some of the inter-related aspects of such management: the EIA team, the style of the EIA process, and costs and resourcing.

4.2.1 The EIA team

The EIA process invariably involves an *interdisciplinary team* approach. Early US legislation strongly advocated such an approach:

> Environmental impact statements shall be prepared using an interdisciplinary approach which will ensure the integrated use of the natural and social sciences and the environmental design arts. The disciplines of the preparers shall be appropriate to the scope and issues identified in the scoping approach. (CEQ 1978, par. 1502.6)

Such an interdisciplinary approach not only reflects the normal scope of EIA studies, from the biophysical to the socio-economic, but also brings to the process the advantages of multiple viewpoints and perspectives on the complex issues involved.

The team producing the EIS may be one, or a combination, of proponent in-house, lead external consultant, external sub-consultants and individual specialists. The team size can range from just a few people to more than a dozen members for larger projects. The team's skills should be complementary: technically for the skills needed to complete the task, and personally for those in the core management team. A small team of three, for instance, could cover the areas of physical/chemical, biological/ecological and cultural/socio-economic, with a membership that might include, for example, an environmental engineer, an ecologist and a planner, at least one member having training or experience in EIA and management. Additional input could be required from experts in ecology, archaeology, air quality, traffic and other specialist fields. However, the finalization of a team's membership may be possible only after an initial scoping exercise has been undertaken.

Many EIA teams make a clear distinction between a 'core/focal' management team and associated specialists, often reflecting the fact that no one organization can cover all the inputs needed in the production of an EIS for a major project. Some commentators (see Weaver *et al.* 1996) promote the virtues of this approach. On a study for a major open-cast mining project in South Africa, Weaver *et al.* had a core project team

of five people: a project manager, two senior authors, an editorial consultant and a word processor. This team managed the inputs into the EIA process, co-ordinated over 60 scientific and non-scientific contributors, and organized various public participation and liaison programmes.

The *team project manager* has a pivotal role. In addition to personnel and team management skills, the manager should have a broad appreciation of the project type under consideration, knowledge of the relevant processes and impacts subject to EIA, the ability to identify important issues and preferably a substantial area of expertise. The project manager must:

- select an appropriate project team, and deal with typical personnel issues including staff turn-over;
- manage specialist inputs;
- liaise with the project proponent, various stakeholders and the public, including choosing the participation techniques to use, and subsequent follow-through;
- keep the EIA team on schedule, make sure that the EIA is carried out efficiently, and adapt the team's work to unanticipated events;
- ensure that the EIA process focuses on key issues, and is fit for purpose, internally coherent and robust; and
- co-ordinate the contributions of the team in the various documentary outputs. (IEMA 2011; Lawrence 2003; Morrison-Saunders and Bailey 2009; Petts & Eduljee 1994)

4.2.2 The style of the EIA process

EIAs can involve many participants with very different perspectives on the relative merits and impacts of projects. In interdisciplinary team work, co-ordination is particularly important: findings and data should be co-ordinated (e.g. they should work to agreed map scales, spatial and temporal boundaries, mitigation measures, and EIS chapter formats) and should be fed into a central source.

This is one of the weakest aspects of most assessment teams; all consultants must be aware, and stay aware, of others' work, in order to avoid lacunae, anomalies and contradictions that will be the delight of opposing counsel and the media (Fortlage 1990).

Beyond this, different projects – and their EIAs – will require different scientific techniques, methods of participation, focuses and ways of responding to unanticipated events. A large, controversial project proposed near a population centre will require a different style of EIA process than a less controversial project, or one in an uninhabited area. An EIA carried out where much detailed data already exist will be different from one in a remote and unstudied location. An EIA for a project that affects groups of people that have traditionally been deprived, or environmental components already subject to cumulative impacts, will be different from one for a homogeneous, wealthy population or a robust environment.

Lawrence (2003) suggests that:

- A *rigorous* EIA process is more appropriate where scientific analysis can contribute significantly to decision-making: for instance, where the environment can be scientifically analysed, and where the resources for such an analysis exist.
- A *rational* EIA process is appropriate for situations where stakeholders can engage in the process in a free and 'reasonable' manner, where views are not overly polarised, and where well-defined options and proposals can be put forward.
- A *streamlined* EIA process is appropriate in a polarised situation where resources are limited, relatively little data exists, and changes are likely to take the form of incremental adjustments to the status quo.
- A *democratic* EIA process works best when proponents are willing to delegate their decision-making authority to representatives, who in turn have the time, energy and resources to participate in planning and decision-making processes with other parties.
- A *collaborative* EIA process is like a democratic process, but with stakeholders being directly engaged in the process, and having the resources to do so.
- An *ethical* EIA process is required when issues of fairness, equity and justice predominate, and when the stakeholders are willing to identify and reconcile these ethical conflicts.
- An *adaptive* EIA process is appropriate for turbulent and complex situations where risk,

uncertainty and health predominate, and where the EIA needs to take into account knowledge limits and uncertainty-related concerns.

4.2.3 EIA costs and resources

The EIA team and the style of the EIA process will affect, and be affected by, resources. Most of the cost of EIA is incurred in carrying out environmental studies and writing the EIS, and is borne by the developer. However, the planning authority, statutory consultees and the public will also incur costs in reviewing the EIA and commenting on it.

European Commission research showed that, for countries with several years of EIA experience, the costs of carrying out EIAs tend to range from 0.1 per cent to 1 per cent of the capital cost of the project. Although the actual cost of an EIA tended to rise with the capital cost of the project, it fell as a percentage of the total cost of the project. For smaller projects, EIA costs were typically closer to 1 per cent of the project cost, whereas for larger projects they were typically closer to 0.1 per cent (EC 2006; COWI 2009; Oosterhuis 2007). This is broadly consistent with EIA costs in the UK, which are discussed at Chapter 8. The World Bank (1999) *Environmental assessment sourcebook* also states that EIA costs typically range from a few thousand to over a million dollars, and that they rarely exceed 1 per cent of the total capital cost of the project.

A French study (BIO 2006) suggested that EIAs are generally more expensive for linear projects such as roads and electricity lines, nuclear and industrial activities, projects where health impact assessments are required, projects related to the marine environment, and large companies or administrations. The World Bank (1999) notes that EIA costs can be reduced if local personnel are used to do most of the work.

The sources above suggest that a typical EIA will take 6–18 months to carry out. However, the time required for the full EIA process can be significantly extended, for instance if the developer proposes modifications to the project, or if there are changes in government. Good scoping can reduce the time needed for EIA by ensuring that the EIA process focuses on key issues and is carried out efficiently. In contrast, a main cause of delay is where the EIA does not provide adequate or relevant data, leading to the need for supplementary information (EC 2006).

···

4.3 Project screening: is an EIA needed?

The number of projects that could be subject to EIA is potentially very large. Yet many projects have no substantial or significant environmental impact. The screening stage seeks to focus on those projects with potentially significant adverse environmental impacts or whose impacts are not fully known. Those with few or no impacts are 'screened out' and allowed to proceed to the normal planning permission and administrative processes without any additional assessment or additional loss of time and expense.

Screening can be partly determined by the EIA regulations operating in a country at the time of an assessment. Chapter 3 indicated that in the EC, including the UK, there are some projects (Annex/Schedule 1) that will always be 'screened in' for full assessment, by virtue of their scale and potential environmental impacts (for example a crude oil refinery, a sizeable thermal power station, a special road). There are many other projects (Annex/Schedule 2) for which the screening decision is less clear. Here two examples of a particular project may be screened in different ways (one 'in' for full assessment, one 'out') by virtue of the project scale, the sensitivity of the proposed location and/or the expectation of adverse environmental impacts. In such cases it is important to have guidelines, indicative criteria or thresholds on conditions considered likely to give rise to significant environmental impacts (see Section 3.4).

In California, a draft environmental impact report is required 'if there is substantial evidence, in light of the whole record before a lead agency, that a project may have a significant effect on the environment'. A full environmental impact report is required where there is substantial evidence, in light of the whole record, that the project would cause significant impacts on environmental quality, habitats and species, or historical artefacts;

negatively affect long-term environmental goals; have 'cumulatively considerable' effects; or would cause substantial adverse effects on human beings (State of California 2010). These constitute 'inclusion list' approaches. In addition, there may be an 'exclusion list', as used in California and Canada, which identifies those categories of project for which an EIA is not required because experience has shown that their adverse effects are not significant.

Some EIA procedures require an initial outline EIA study to check on likely environmental impacts and their significance. Under the California Environmental Quality Act a 'negative declaration' can be produced by the project proponent, claiming that the project has minimal significant effects and does not require a full EIA. The declaration must be substantiated by an initial study, which is usually a simple checklist against which environmental impacts must be ticked as *yes, maybe* or *no*. If the responses are primarily *no*, and most of the *yes* and *maybe* responses can be mitigated, then the project may be screened out from a full EIA.

In general there are two main approaches to screening. The use of *thresholds* involves placing projects in categories and setting thresholds for each project type. These may relate, for example, to project characteristics (e.g. 20 hectares and over), anticipated project impacts (e.g. 50,000 tonnes or more of waste per annum to be taken from a site) or project location (e.g. a designated landscape area). Appendix 2 shows the applicable thresholds used in the UK.

A *case-by-case* approach involves the appraisal of the characteristics of projects, as they are submitted for screening, against a checklist of guidelines and criteria. Some of the advantages and disadvantages of these two approaches are summarized in Table 4.1. The EC (2001a) has published guidance to help in such case-by-case screening processes. There are also many hybrid approaches with, for example, indicative thresholds used in combination with a flexible case-by-case approach.

The DCLG (2011) EIA guidance gives detailed guidance on how screening should be carried out for English development projects, with extensive reference to case law (see Sections 3.4 and 8.6).

Neither the threshold nor the case-by-case approach gives wholly consistent results, and the

ttTable 4.1 Thresholds versus case-by-case approach to screening: advantages and disadvantages

Advantages	Disadvantages
Thresholds	
Simple to use	Place arbitrary, inflexible rules on a variable environment (unless tiered)
Quick to use; more certainty	Less room for common sense or good judgement
Consistent between locations	May be or become inconsistent, depending on neighbouring receivers and developments
Consistent between decisions within locations	Difficult to set and, once set, difficult to change
Consistent between project types	Lead to a proliferation of projects lying just below the thresholds
Case by case	
Allows common sense and good judgement	Likely to be complex and ambiguous
Flexible – can incorporate variety in project and environment	Likely to be slow and costly
	Open to abuse by decision-makers because of political or financial interests
	Open to poor judgement of decision-makers
	Likely to be swayed by precedent and therefore lose flexibility

Table 4.2 Number of EIAs carried out in European Union Member States, 2006–08

Member State	Average number of EIAs/yr (2006–08)	Average number of EIAs/yr per million population (2006–08)	Member State	Average number of EIAs/yr (2006–08)	Average number of EIAs/yr per million population (2006–08)
Austria	23	3	Latvia	11	5
Belgium	183	17	Lithuania	142	42
Bulgaria	249	33	Luxembourg	70	149
Cyprus	117	136	Malta	10	24
Czech Rep.	96	9	Netherlands	123	7
Denmark	125	22	Poland	4,000	105
Estonia	80	61	Portugal	323	29
Finland	38	7	Romania	596	27
France	3,867	59	Slovak Rep.	670	124
Germany	1,000	12	Slovenia	108	54
Greece	425	38	Spain	1,054	23
Hungary	152	15	Sweden	288	31
Ireland	197	44	United Kingdom	334	5
Italy	1,548	26			

Source: Adapted from GHK 2010

thresholds used by different countries can vary widely. Table 4.2 takes another view of EIAs carried out in European Union Member States (here for the period 2006–08). It shows that the number of EIAs prepared per head of population varies by a factor of 50+ between countries with a consistent legislative basis, namely the EIA Directive; this further reinforces the earlier (Chapter 2) theme of divergent practice in a converging system. These differences can be attributed to factors such as different consenting regimes, levels of development, environmental sensitivity and cultural values. As such, lower (or indeed higher) levels of EIA activity do not necessarily indicate a problem (IEMA 2011).

A series of European Court of Justice rulings have provided further guidance on how EIA screening should be carried out (EU 2010). They have clarified that, whatever method is used by a Member State to determine whether a project requires EIA or not, the method must not undermine the objective of the EIA Directive, which is that no project likely to have significant environmental effects should be exempt from assessment. In particular:

- The EIA Directive should be interpreted as having a 'wide scope and broad purpose' with respect to screening. A project should not be screened out simply because that type of project is not directly referred to in the EIA Directive or implementing regulations (Kraaijeveld ('Dutch Dykes') case C-72/95).
- Even small-scale projects can have significant effects on the environment if they are in a sensitive location (C-392/96).
- EIA is required for refurbishment, improvement and demolition projects that are likely to have significant effects on the environment (C-142/07, C-2/07, C-50/09).
- The purpose of the EIA Directive cannot be circumvented by splitting larger projects that would require EIA into smaller projects that would not. Similarly, EIAs must consider the cumulative effects of several projects where, individually, these might not have significant environmental effects (C-392/96, C-142/07, C-205/08).
- Although the EIA Directive allows Member States to exempt 'exceptional case' projects from EIA, the interpretation of 'exceptional cases' should be narrow. Possible rules for qualifying as an 'exceptional case' are that there is an urgent and substantial need for the project; inability to undertake the project earlier; and/or inability to meet the full requirements of the EIA Directive (C-435/97, C-287/98).
- Although a decision to screen a project out of EIA does not require a formal statement explaining the reasons for doing so, planning authorities have a duty to provide further information on the reasons for the decision if an interested person subsequently requests (C87/02, C121/03, C-75/08).

UK court cases regarding screening are discussed at Section 8.6.

4.4 Scoping: which impacts and issues to consider?

The scope of an EIA is the impacts, issues and alternatives it addresses. The process of scoping is that of deciding, from all of a project's possible impacts and from all the alternatives that could be addressed, which are the significant ones. Effective scoping can help to save time and money, shorten the length of EISs, and reduce the need for developers to provide further environmental information after a planning application has been submitted (IEMA 2011).

An initial scoping of possible impacts may identify those impacts thought to be potentially significant, those thought to be not significant and those whose significance is unclear. Further study should examine impacts in the various categories in more depth. Those confirmed by such a study to be not significant are eliminated; those in the uncertain category are added to the initial category of other potentially significant impacts. This refining of focus onto the most significant impacts continues throughout the EIA process.

Scoping is generally carried out in discussions between the developer, the LPA, other relevant agencies and, ideally, the public. It is often the first stage of negotiations and consultation between a developer and other interested parties. It is an important step in EIA because it enables the limited resources of the EIA team to be allocated to best effect, and prevents misunderstanding between the parties concerned about the information required in an EIS. Scoping can also identify issues that should later be monitored.

Scoping should begin with the identification of individuals, communities, local authorities and statutory consultees likely to be affected by the project; good practice would be to bring them together in a working group and/or meetings with the developer. One or more of the impact identification techniques discussed in Section 4.8 can be used to structure a discussion and suggest important issues to consider. Other issues could include:

- environmental attributes that are particularly valued;

- impacts considered to be of particular concern to the affected parties;
- the methodology that should be used to predict and evaluate different impacts;
- the scale at which those impacts should be considered;[1] and
- broad alternatives that might be considered.

The result of this process of information collection and negotiation should be the identification of the chief issues, impacts and alternatives, an explanation of why other issues are not considered significant, and, for each key impact, a defined temporal and spatial boundary within which it will be measured.

Box 4.1 shows excerpts from an admirably brief scoping report prepared by a local planning authority in response to a developer's request for such a report. It illustrates how many of the above points are dealt with in practice.

The European Court of Justice has ruled that an EIA should consider the overall effects of a project, not just its direct effects. In the case of Liege Airport (C-2/07), it ruled that the EIA should consider not only the proposed modifications to the airport's infrastructure but also the increased airport activity that these modifications would permit. Similarly, transboundary impacts are within the scope of EIA (C-205/08).

Although scoping is an important step in the EIA process, it is not legally required in the UK. Some developers produce a scoping report as a matter of good practice, and since 1999 LPAs must provide a formal 'scoping opinion' on the information to be included in an EIS when a developer requests one. A study on UK scoping practice showed that developers formally requested scoping opinions from LPAs for half of the EIA projects examined, with less formal scoping discussions occurring in a further 18 per cent of cases.

Socio economic impact: This subject area should include a consideration of access and public amenity issues in relation to the loss of land open to public access, as well as a consideration of the impact of the security/safety of the site. It should include a consideration of the impact of the development on the grazing rights of commoners. Although perhaps outside the statutory scope of the EIA the applicant may like to consider whether a basic assessment of the role of Yennadon Quarry in the local employment/product market may support any accompanying planning application.

Archaeology: Existing records do not provide a lot of evidence of in terms of archaeological features already identified in this area. As such this section of the EIA should include a walkover survey and a test pit to provide an assessment by a qualified archaeologist of the nature of below ground conditions (e.g. presence of peat, depth of subsoil). Any further survey work identified as necessary should then also be undertaken as part of the EIA.

Geology and hydrogeology: The site is identified as being on an Aquifer of Intermediate Vulnerability; it is approximately 450m from the inner water Source Protection Zone 1 and approximately 200m from the Devonport Leat. The EIA should consider the impact of the development on these features. Further advice from the Environment Agency is available in their publication *Scoping guidelines on the EIA of projects* (2002) (part D2 – opencast mining and quarrying operations).

Ecological impacts and biodiversity: This Authority would require assessment to comprise a Phase 1 habitat survey, as well as any specialist surveys then identified as necessary. The assessment should include a consideration of avoidance, mitigation and compensation measures as necessary.

Cumulative impacts and an assessment of alternatives: Further to the above topic areas it is essential that the EIA includes a consideration of cumulative impacts and demonstrates a consideration of alternatives. The Authority would advise that the assessment should refer each subject to its potential impact upon the special qualities of the National Park and the purposes of National Park designation.

The adoption of this scoping opinion does not preclude the Mineral Planning Authority from requesting additional information following submission by the applicant, under Regulation 19 of the Town and Country Planning (EIA) (England and Wales) Regulations 1999.

Source: Dartmoor National Park Authority 2010

Box 4.1 Extracts from a scoping opinion for extension of a quarry in a National Park

In almost two-thirds of cases, developers provided scoping reports to accompany their requests for a scoping opinion. Most of the scoping opinions were prepared in-house by the LPA, and they consulted with other statutory bodies in nearly three-quarters of cases. Two-thirds of the respondents felt that scoping improved the quality of the EIS subsequently submitted, by improving the report's focus, bringing a wider range of concerns to the discussion, and reducing the need to request further information at later stages (DCLG 2006). In contrast, IEMA (2011) suggests that many scoping opinions are overly exigent, do not help to scope out issues, and do not prevent local authorities or statutory consultees from requesting further information after an EIS is prepared.

Other countries (e.g. Canada and The Netherlands) have a formal scoping stage, in which the developer agrees with the competent authority or an independent EIA commission, sometimes after public consultation, on the subjects the EIA will cover. The EC (2001b) has published a detailed scoping checklist; Carroll and Turpin (2009) provide lists of potential issues associated with a range of development projects; and the Environment Agency (2002) and Government of New South Wales (1996) are examples of organizations that have developed EIA guidance for particular types of projects.

4.5 The consideration of alternatives

4.5.1 Regulatory requirements

The US Council on Environmental Quality (CEQ 1978) calls the discussion of alternatives 'the heart of the environmental impact statement': how an EIA addresses alternatives will determine its relation to the subsequent decision-making process. A discussion of alternatives ensures that the developer has considered both other approaches to the project and the means of preventing environmental damage. It encourages analysts to focus on the *differences* between real choices. It can allow people who were not directly involved in the decision-making process to evaluate various aspects of a proposed project and understand how

decisions were arrived at. It also provides a framework for the competent authority's decision, rather than merely a justification for a particular action. Finally, if unforeseen difficulties arise during the construction or operation of a project, a re-examination of these alternatives may help to provide rapid and cost-effective solutions.

The US NEPA requires federal agencies to analyse 'alternatives to the proposed action'. The implementation of this requirement has been the subject of a range of legal challenges, mostly on the basis that federal agencies had not considered a full range of reasonable alternatives, or that they had improperly constructed the purpose and need for their projects so that the resulting alternatives were too narrow. Generally the courts have ruled in favour of the federal agencies, accepting their reasons for eliminating seemingly 'reasonable' alternatives from analysis in the EIA (Smith 2007).

The original EC Directive 85/337 stated that alternative proposals should be considered in an EIA if the information was relevant and if the developer could reasonably be required to compile this information. Annex III required 'where appropriate, an outline of the main alternatives studied by the developer and an indication of the main reasons for this choice, taking into account the environmental effects'. In the UK, this requirement was interpreted as being discretionary, and in the 1990s the consideration of alternatives was one of the weakest aspects of EIS quality (Barker and Wood 1999; Eastman 1997; Jones *et al.* 1991). One of the main changes resulting from the 1997 amendments to the EIA Directive (CEC 1997) was a strengthening of the requirements on alternatives: EISs are now required to include 'an outline of the main alternatives studied by the developer and an indication of the main reasons for the developer's choice, taking into account the environmental effects'. Government guidance (DCLG 2011) is that:

> Where alternative approaches to development have been considered, including alternative choices of process or design, or phasing of construction, the ES should include an outline of the main ones, and the main reasons for the choice made. Although the Directive and the Regulations do not expressly require the applicant to study

alternatives, and do not define 'alternatives', the nature of certain developments and their location may make the consideration of alternative sites a material consideration . . . In such cases, the ES must record this consideration of alternative sites.

4.5.2 Types of alternative

During the course of project planning, many decisions are made concerning the type and scale of the project proposed, its location and the processes involved. Most of the possible alternatives that arise will be rejected by the developer on economic, technical or regulatory grounds. The role of EIA is to ensure that environmental criteria are also considered at these early stages, and to document the results of this decision-making stage. A thorough consideration of alternatives begins early in the planning process, before the type and scale of development and its location have been agreed on. A number of broad types of alternative can be considered: the 'no action' option, alternative locations, alternative scales of the project, alternative processes or equipment, alternative site layouts, alternative operating conditions and alternative ways of dealing with environmental impacts. We shall discuss the last of these in Section 5.4.

The *'no action'* or *'business as usual'* option refers to environmental conditions if a project were not to go ahead. In essence, consideration of the 'no action' option is equivalent to a discussion of the need for the project: do the benefits of the project outweigh its costs? This option must be considered in some countries (e.g. the USA), but is rarely discussed in UK EISs.[2]

The consideration of alternative *locations* is an essential component of the project planning process. In some cases, a project's location is constrained in varying degrees: for instance, gravel extraction can take place only in areas with sufficient gravel deposits, and wind farms require locations with sufficient wind speed. In other cases, the best location can be chosen to maximize, for example, economic, planning or environmental considerations. For industrial projects, for instance, economic criteria such as land values, the availability of infrastructure, the distance from sources and markets, and the labour supply are likely to

be important. For road projects, engineering criteria strongly influence the alignment (e.g. Figure 4.1). In all these cases, however, siting the project in 'environmentally robust' areas, or away from designated or environmentally sensitive areas, should be considered.

The consideration of different *scales* of development is also integral to project planning. In some cases, a project's scale will be flexible. For instance, the size of a waste disposal site can be changed, depending, for example, on the demand for landfill space, the availability of other sites and the presence of nearby residences or environmentally sensitive sites. The number of turbines on a wind farm could vary widely. In other cases, the developer will need to decide whether an entire unit should be built or not. For instance, the reactor building of a nuclear power station is a large discrete structure that cannot easily be scaled down. Pipelines or bridges, to be functional, cannot be broken down into smaller sections.

Alternative *processes and equipment* involve the possibility of achieving the same objective by a different method. For instance, 1500 MW of electricity can be generated by one combined-cycle gas turbine power station, by a tidal barrage, by several waste-burning power stations or by hundreds of wind turbines. Gravel can be directly extracted or recycled, using wet or dry processes. Waste may be recycled, incinerated or put in a landfill.

Once the location, scale and processes of a development have been decided upon, different *project/site layouts and designs* can still have different impacts. For instance, noisy plants can be sited near or away from residences. Power station cooling towers can be few and tall (using less land) or many and short (causing less visual impact). Buildings can be sited either prominently or to minimize their visual impact. Figure 4.2 shows different bridge designs. Similarly, *operating conditions* can be changed to minimize impacts. For instance, a level of noise at night is usually more annoying than the same level during the day, so night-time work could be avoided. Establishing designated routes for project-related traffic can help to minimize disturbance to local residents. Construction can take place at times of the year that minimize environmental impacts on, for example, migratory and nesting birds. These kinds of 'alternatives' act like mitigation measures.

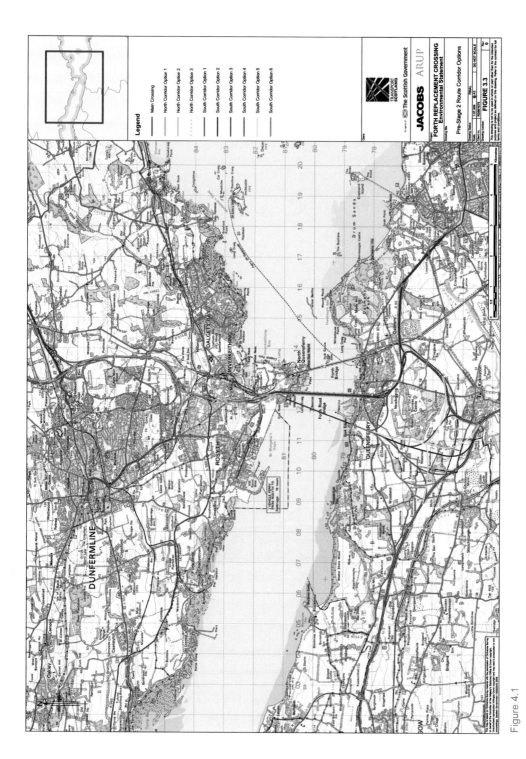

Figure 4.1

Example of locational alternatives: some of the routes considered for the Forth Replacement Crossing

Source: Scottish Government, Jacobs, and Arup 2009

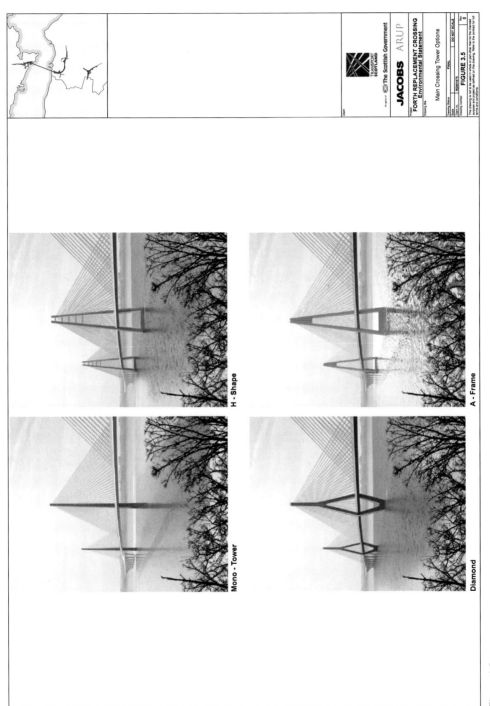

Mono - Tower

H - Shape

Diamond

A - Frame

Figure 4.2

Example of alternative designs: designs considered for the Forth Replacement Crossing

Source: Scottish Government, Jacobs, and Arup 2009

As can be seen from Figures 4.1 and 4.2, alternatives can be tiered, with decisions made at an earlier stage (or higher tier) acting as the basis for the consideration of lower-tier decisions. In the case of the Forth Bridge Replacement, the bridge route was chosen first, and then various bridge designs for that route were considered. Another example of tiering is the choice of a location for a new wind farm, then the choice of the preferred turbine design, and then the detailed siting of individual turbines.

Alternatives must be reasonable: they should not include ideas that are not technically possible, or illegal. The type of alternatives that can realistically be considered by a given developer will also vary. A mineral extraction company that has put a deposit on a parcel of land in the hope of extracting sand and gravel from it will not consider the option of using it for wind power generation: 'reasonable' in such a case would be other sites for sand and gravel extraction, or other scales or processes. Essentially, alternatives should allow the competent authority to understand why this project, and not some other, is being proposed in this location and not some other.

On the other hand, from a US context (where EISs are prepared by government agencies) Steinemann (2001) argues that alternatives that do not meet a narrow definition of project objectives tend to be too easily rejected, and that alternatives should reflect social, not just agency, goals. She also suggests that

> the current sequence – propose action, define purpose and need, develop alternatives, then analyze alternatives – needs to be revised. Otherwise the proposed action can bias the set of alternatives for the analysis. Agencies should explore more environmentally sound approaches before proposing an action. Then, agencies should construct a purpose and need statement that would not summarily exclude less damaging alternatives, nor unduly favour the proposed action. Agencies should also be careful not to adhere to a single 'problem' and 'solution' early on.

Smith (2007) concludes, in a US context, that:

- project proponents should explain the reasons for the choices they make, particularly in terms of how they selected the range of alternatives that is studied in detail in the EIA;
- if someone proposes an alternative that they feel is 'reasonable', the project proponent should carefully consider this, and the EIA should provide a well-reasoned explanation for why it is dismissed;
- where a proposed action is unlikely to have significant impacts, then developing additional alternatives to the 'do minimum' alternative does not make sense.

These very reasonable rules of thumb also make sense in other contexts.

4.5.3 The presentation and comparison of alternatives

The impacts and costs of alternatives vary for different groups of people and for different environmental components. Discussions with local residents, statutory consultees and special interest groups may rapidly eliminate some alternatives from consideration and suggest others. However, it is unlikely that one alternative will emerge as being most acceptable to all the parties concerned. The EIS should distil information about a reasonable number of realistic alternatives into a format that will facilitate public discussion and, finally, decision-making. Methods for comparing and presenting alternatives span the range from simple, non-quantitative descriptions to quite detailed, quantitative modelling.

Many of the impact identification methods discussed later in this chapter can also help to compare alternatives. Overlay maps compare the impacts of various locations in a non-quantitative manner. Checklists or less complex matrices can be applied to various alternatives and compared; this may be the most effective way to present the impacts of alternatives visually. Weighted or multi-criteria matrices assign quantitative importance weightings to environmental components, rating each alternative (quantitatively) according to its impact on each environmental component, multiplying the ratings by their weightings to obtain a weighted impact, and aggregating these weighted impacts to obtain a total score for each alternative. These scores can be compared with each other to identify preferable alternatives.

4.6 Understanding the project/development action

4.6.1 Understanding the dimensions of the project

At first glance, the description of a proposed development would appear to be one of the more straightforward steps in the EIA process. However, projects have many dimensions, and relevant information may be limited. As a consequence, this early step may pose challenges. Crucial dimensions to be clarified include the purpose of the project, its life cycle, physical presence, process(es), policy context and associated policies.

The 2011 EIA Regulations require an environmental statement to include

- a description of the development, including in particular a description of the physical characteristics of the whole development and the land-use requirements during the construction and operational phases;
- a description of the main characteristics of the production processes, for instance, nature and quantity of the materials used; and
- an estimate, by type and quantity, of expected residues and emissions (water, air and soil pollution, noise, vibration, light, heat, radiation, etc.) resulting from the operation of the proposed development.

Such information must be given where it 'is reasonably required to assess the environmental effects of the development and which the applicant can, having regard in particular to current knowledge and methods of assessment, reasonably be required to compile' (DCLG 2011).

An outline of *the purpose and rationale* of a project provides a useful introduction to the project description. This may, for example, set the project in a wider context – the missing section of road, a power station in a programme of developments, a new housing project in an area of regeneration or major population growth. A discussion of purpose may include the rationale for the particular type of project, for the choice of the project's location and for the timing of the development.

It may also provide background information on planning and design activities to date.

As we noted in Section 1.4, all projects have a *life cycle of activities*, and a project description should clarify the various stages in the project's life cycle, and their relative duration. A minimum description would usually involve the identification of construction and operational stages and associated activities. Further refinement might include planning and design (including consultation), project commissioning, expansion, close-down and site rehabilitation stages. The size of the development at various stages in its life cycle should also be specified. This can include reference to physical size, inputs, outputs, and the number of people to be employed.

The *location and physical presence* of a project should also be clarified at an early stage. This should include its general location on a base map in relation to other activities (e.g. housing, employment sites and recreational areas) and to administrative boundaries. A more detailed site layout of the proposed development, again on a large-scale base map, should illustrate the land area and the main disposition of the elements of the project (e.g. storage areas, main processing plant, waste-collection areas, transport connections to the site). Where the site layout may change substantially between different stages in the life cycle, it is valuable to have a sequence of anticipated layouts or phases of working (see Figure 4.3 for an example). Any associated projects and activities (e.g. transport connections to the site; pipes and transmission lines from the site) should also be identified and described, as should elements of a project that, although integral, may be detached from the main site (e.g. the construction of a barrage in one area may involve opening up a major quarry development in another area). A description of the physical presence of a project is invariably improved by a three-dimensional visual image, which may include a photo-montage of what the site layout may look like at, for example, full operation. A clear presentation of location and physical presence is important for an assessment of change in land uses, any physical disruption to other infrastructures, severance of activities (e.g. agricultural holdings, villages) and visual intrusion and landscape changes.

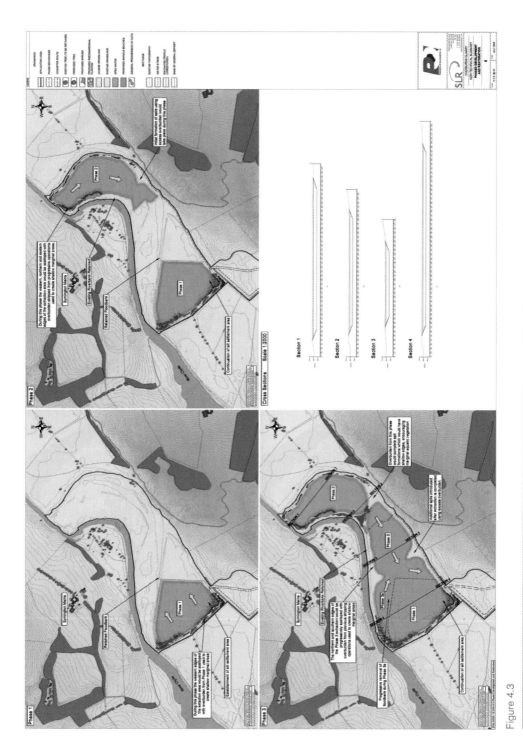

Figure 4.3

Three extraction phases for a sand and gravel quarry

Source: Pattersons Quarries/SLR 2009

Understanding a project also involves an understanding of the *processes* integral to it. The nature of processes varies between industrial, service and infrastructure projects, but many can be described as a flow of inputs through a process and their transformation into outputs. Where relevant, a process diagram for the different activities associated with a project should accompany the location and site-layout maps. This could identify the nature, origins and destinations of the inputs and outputs, and the timescale over which they are expected. This may be presented in the form of a simplified pictorial diagram or in a block flow chart. Figure 4.4 shows an example of a materials flow chart for a waste management facility comprising waste sorting and energy from waste production; it outlines the types of inputs and outputs, their expected quantities, and where the outputs will end up. A comprehensive flow chart of a production process should include the types, quantities and locations of resource inputs, intermediate and final product outputs, and wastes generated by the total process.

Physical characteristics of the project may include:

- the land take and physical transformation of a site (e.g. clearing, grading), which may vary between different stages of a project's life cycle;
- the total operation of the process involved (usually illustrated with a process-flow diagram);

- the types and quantities of resources used (e.g. water abstraction, minerals, energy);
- transport requirements (of inputs and outputs);
- the generation of wastes, including estimates of types, quantity and strength of aqueous wastes, gaseous and particulate emissions, solid wastes, noise and vibration, heat and light, radiation, etc.;
- the potential for accidents, hazards and emergencies; and
- processes for the containment, treatment and disposal of wastes and for the containment and handling of accidents; monitoring and surveillance systems.

Socio-economic characteristics may include:

- the labour requirements of a project – including size, duration, sources, particular skills categories and training;
- the provision or otherwise of housing, transport, health and other services for the workforce;
- the direct services required from local businesses or other commercial organizations;
- the flow of expenditure from the project into the wider community (from the employees and subcontracting); and
- the flow of social activities (service demands, community participation, community conflict).

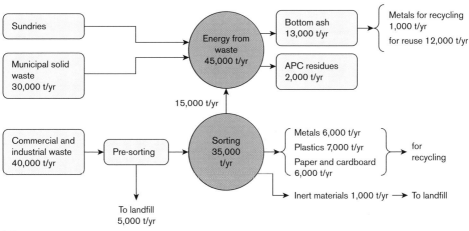

Figure 4.4

Materials flow chart for a hypothetical waste management facility

Clearly the physical/ecological and socio-economic dimensions of projects interact with each other. Research on ecosystem services (e.g. UKNEA 2011) is clarifying the value to society of ecosystems in the form of products (e.g. food, fibre, fuel) and services (e.g. pollination, carbon fixing). In turn, social interventions such as training or people's travel behaviour can improve or reduce the delivery of ecosystem services.

The projects may also have *associated policies*, not obvious from site layouts and process-flow diagrams, but which are nevertheless significant for subsequent impacts. For example, shift-working will have implications for transport and noise that may be very significant for nearby residents. The use of a construction site hostel, camp or village can significantly internalize impacts on the local housing market and on the local community. The provision of on- or off-site training can greatly affect the mixture of local and non-local labour and the balance of socio-economic effects.

Projects should be seen in their *planning policy context*. In the UK, the main local policy context is outlined and detailed in Local Development Frameworks. The description of location must pay regard to land-use designations and development constraints that may be implicit in some of the designations. Of particular importance is a project's location in relation to various environmental designations (e.g. areas of outstanding natural beauty, Special Areas of Conservation and Special Protection Areas, heritage designations such as listed buildings). Attention should also be given to national planning guidance, provided in the UK by Planning Policy Guidance and Statements and National Policy Statements (NPSs).

4.6.2 Sources and presentation of data

The initial brief from the developer provides the starting point. Ideally, the developer would have detailed knowledge of the proposed project's characteristics, likely layout and production processes, and be able to draw on previous experience. An analyst can supplement information with reference to other EISs for similar projects; although these are normally not monitored so the correctness of their predictions is untested (see Chapters 7 and 8). The analyst may also draw on EIA literature (books and journals), guidelines, manuals

and statistical sources, including NPSs, CEC (1993), Morris and Therivel (2009), Rodriguez-Bachiller with Glasson (2004), and United Nations University (2007). Site visits can be made to comparable projects, and advice can be gained from consultants with experience of the type of project under consideration.

As the project design and assessment process develop – in part in response to early EIA findings – so the developer will have to provide more detailed information on the characteristics specific to the project. The identification of sources of potential significant impacts may lead to changes in layout and process.

Data about the project can be presented in different ways. The life cycle of a project can be illustrated on a linear bar chart. Particular stages may be identified in more detail where the impacts are considered of particular significance; this is often the case for the construction stage of major projects. Location and physical presence are best illustrated on a map base, with varying scales to move from the broad location to the specific site layout. This may be supplemented by aerial photographs, photo-montages and visual mock-ups according to the resources and issues involved.

The various information and illustrations should clearly identify the main variations between a project's stages. Figure 4.5 illustrates a labour-requirements diagram that identifies the widely differing requirements, in absolute numbers and in skill categories, of the construction and operational stages. More sophisticated flow diagrams could indicate the type, frequency (normal, batch, intermittent or emergency) and duration (minutes or hours per day or week) of each operation. Seasonal and material variations, including time periods of peak pollution loads, can also be documented.

Unfortunately, in some cases the situation may be far from ideal, with inadequate information provided by the developer – especially in the case of new types of projects. Site layout diagrams and process-flow charts may be only in outline, provisional form at the initial design stage, and the project may change significantly during the planning stage (Frost 1994). The planning application may be an outline application only. A series of European Court of Justice rulings has concluded that, where a consent procedure involves a principal decision and a subsequent implementing decision that cannot go beyond the parameters set by the principal decision, then the EIS must assess the project's environmental effects in time to inform for the principal decision. Only those effects that are not identifiable until the implementing decision should be assessed to inform the later decision (C-201/02, C-508/03, C-290/03; and C2/07).

Further information on these cases is provided in COWI (2009). Even where the project's parameters are well understood early on, and the planning application is a detailed application, there will still need to be considerable interaction between the EIS analyst and the developer to refine the project's characteristics.

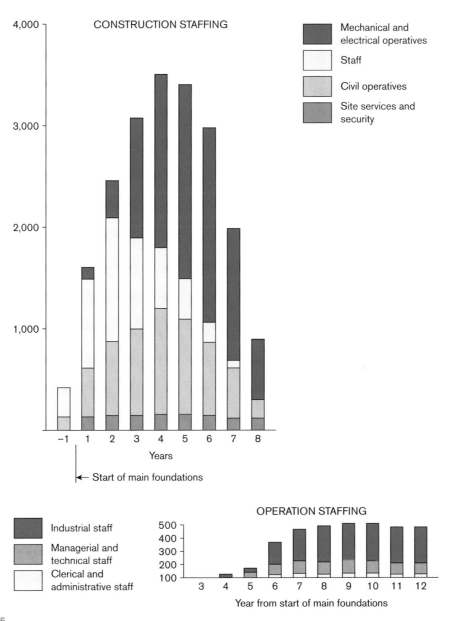

Figure 4.5

Labour requirements (in numbers of workers) for a project during construction and operation

4.7 Establishing the environmental baseline

4.7.1 General considerations

The establishment of an environmental baseline includes both the present and likely future state of the environment, assuming that a proposed project is not undertaken, taking into account changes resulting from natural events and from other human activities. For example, the population of a species of fish in a lake may already be declining before the proposed introduction of an industrial project on the lake shore. Figure 1.7 illustrated the various time, component and scale dimensions of the environment, and all these dimensions need to be considered in the establishment of the environmental baseline. The period for the prediction of the future state of the environment should be comparable with the life of the proposed development; this may mean predicting for several decades. Components include both the biophysical and socio-economic environment. Spatial coverage may focus on the local, but refer to the wider region and beyond for some environmental elements.

Initial baseline studies may cover a wide range of environmental, social and economic variables, but comprehensive overviews can be wasteful of resources. The studies should focus as quickly as possible on those aspects of the environment that may be significantly affected by the project, either directly or indirectly:

> While every environmental statement (ES) should provide a full factual description of the development, the emphasis of Schedule 4 is on the 'main' or 'significant' environmental effects to which a development is likely to give rise. The ES should not be any longer than is necessary to properly assess those effects. Impacts that have little or no significance for the particular development in question will need only very brief treatment to indicate that their possible relevance has been considered (DCLG 2011).

The rationale for the choice of focus should be explained as part of the documentation of the scoping process. Although the studies would normally consider the various environmental elements separately, it is also important to understand the interaction between them and the functional relationships involved; for instance, flora will be affected by air and water quality, and fauna will be affected by flora. This will facilitate prediction. As with most aspects of the EIA process, establishing the baseline is not a 'one-off' activity. Studies will move from broad-brush to more detailed and focused approaches. The identification of new potential impacts may open up new elements of the environment for investigation; the identification of effective measures for mitigating impacts may curtail certain areas of investigation.

4.7.2 Sources and presentation of data

The quality and reliability of environmental data vary a great deal, and this can influence the use of such data in the assessment of impacts. Fortlage (1990) clarifies this in the following useful classification:

- 'hard' data from reliable sources which can be verified and which are not subject to short-term change, such as geological records and physical surveys of topography and infrastructure;
- 'intermediate' data which are reliable but not capable of absolute proof, such as water quality, land values, vegetation condition and traffic counts, which have variable values;
- 'soft' data which are a matter of opinion or social values, such as opinion surveys, visual enjoyment of landscape and numbers of people using amenities, where the responses depend on human attitudes and the climate of public feeling.

Important UK data sources are the *Census of Population, Measuring Progress, Environmental Accounts, Transport Statistics,* public health observatories and other national and regional Internet data sources, many of which are compiled for the local and ward level in *Neighbourhood statistics.* Local authority monitoring units can also provide very useful data on the physical, social and economic environment. Additional data is unpublished or 'semi-published' and internal to various organizations. In the UK, consultation bodies (e.g. Natural England, Environment Agency and Marine

Management Organization) must make environmental information available to any person who requests it, particularly applicants preparing EISs. However, they do not have to undertake research or obtain information that they do not already have (DCLG 2011). See also Chapter 5 (Section 5.3), and Appendix 6, for other UK and international data sources.

There are of course many other organizations, at local and other levels, which may be able to provide valuable information. Local history, conservation and naturalist societies may have a wealth of information on, for example, local flora and fauna, rights of way and archaeological sites. National bodies such as the RSPB and the Forestry Commission may have particular knowledge and expertise to offer. Consultation with local amenity groups at an early stage in the EIA process can help not only with data but also with the identification of those key environmental issues for which data should be collected.

Even where every use has been made of data from existing sources, there will invariably be gaps in the required environmental baseline data for the project under consideration. Environmental monitoring and surveys may be necessary. Surveys and monitoring raise a number of issues; they are inevitably constrained by budgets and time, and must be selective. However, such selectivity must ensure that the length of time over which monitoring and surveys are undertaken is appropriate to the task in hand. For example, for certain environmental features (e.g. many types of flora and fauna) a survey period of 12 months or more may be needed to take account of seasonal variations or migratory patterns. Sampling procedures will often be used for surveys; the extent and implications of the sampling error involved should be clearly established.

Baseline studies can be presented in the EIS in a variety of ways. A brief overview of the biophysical and socio-economic environments for the area of study may be followed by the project description, with the detailed focused studies in subsequent impact chapters (e.g. air quality, geology, employment), or a more comprehensive set of detailed studies at an early stage providing a point of reference for future and often briefer impact chapters. Maps are typically – but not necessarily – prepared using geographical information systems (GIS). GIS

can also be used for more complex analytical functions, for instance map overlays and intersections, buffering around given features, multi-factor map algebra, and visibility analysis derived from terrain modelling (Rodriguez-Bachiller 2000).

The analyst should also be wary of the seductive attraction of quantitative data at the expense of qualitative data; each type has a valuable role in establishing baseline conditions. Finally, it should be remembered that all data sources suffer from some uncertainty, and this needs to be explicitly recognized in the prediction of environmental effects (see Chapter 5).

•••

4.8 Impact identification

4.8.1 Aims and methods

Impact identification brings together project characteristics and baseline environmental characteristics with the aim of ensuring that all potentially significant environmental impacts (adverse or favourable) are identified and taken into account in the EIA process. When choosing among the existing wide range of impact identification methods, the analyst needs to consider more specific aims, some of which conflict:

- to ensure compliance with regulations;
- to provide a comprehensive coverage of a full range of impacts, including social, economic and physical;
- to distinguish between positive and negative, large and small, long-term and short-term, reversible and irreversible impacts;
- to identify secondary, indirect and cumulative impacts, as well as direct impacts;
- to distinguish between significant and insignificant impacts;
- to allow a comparison of alternative development proposals;
- to consider impacts within the constraints of an area's carrying capacity;
- to incorporate qualitative as well as quantitative information;
- to be easy and economical to use;
- to be unbiased and to give consistent results; and
- to be of use in summarizing and presenting impacts in the EIS.

The simplest impact identification methods involve the use of lists of impacts to ensure that none has been forgotten. The most complex include the use of interactive computer programmes, networks, or the use of weightings to denote impact significance. This section presents a range of these methods, from the simplest checklists needed for compliance with regulations to more complex approaches that developers, consultants and academics who aim to further 'best practice' may wish to investigate further. The methods are divided into the following categories:

- checklists;
- matrices;
- quantitative methods;
- networks; and
- overlay maps.

In the UK, simple checklists and consultation with the local planning authority and statutory consultees are the most widely used impact identification methods. This focus on simple approaches may be attributable to the high degree of flexibility and discretion in the UK's implementation of the EIA Directive, a general unwillingness to make the EIA process over-complex, or disillusionment with some of the early complex approaches. For this reason, although earlier editions of this book covered the more complex

impact identification methods (e.g. Sorensen and Moss 1973), this edition does not.

The discussion of the methods here relates primarily to impact identification, but most of the approaches can also be useful in other stages of the EIA process – in impact prediction, evaluation, communication, mitigation and enhancement, presentation, monitoring and auditing. As such, there is considerable interaction between Chapters 4–7, paralleling the interaction in practice between these various stages.

Checklists

Most checklists are based on a list of special bio-physical, social and economic factors which may be affected by a development. The simple checklist can help only to identify impacts and ensure that impacts are not overlooked. Checklists do not usually include direct cause–effect links to project activities. Nevertheless, they have the advantage of being easy to use. Table 3.7 (DETR 2000) is an example of a simple checklist.

Questionnaire checklists are based on a set of questions to be answered. Some of the questions may concern indirect impacts and possible mitigation measures. They may also provide a scale for classifying estimated impacts, from highly adverse to highly beneficial. Table 4.3 shows part of the EC's (2001b) questionnaire checklist.

Table 4.3 Part of a questionnaire checklist

No.	Questions to be considered in scoping	Yes/ No/?	Which characteristics of the project environment could be affected and how?	Is the effect likely to be significant? Why?
7	Will the project lead to risks of contamination of land or water from releases of pollutants onto the ground or into sewers, surface waters, ground water, coastal waters or the sea?			
7.1	From handling, storage, use or spillage of hazardous or toxic materials?			
7.2	From discharge of sewage or other effluents (whether treated or untreated) to water or the land?			
7.3	By deposition of pollutants emitted to air, onto the land or into water?			
7.4	From any other sources?			
7.5	Is there a risk of long-term build-up of pollutants in the environment from these sources?			

Source: EC 2001b

Matrices

Simple matrices are merely two-dimensional charts showing environmental components on one axis and development actions on the other. They are, essentially, expansions of checklists that acknowledge the fact that various components of a development project (e.g. construction, operation, decommissioning, buildings, and access road) have different impacts. The action likely to have an impact on an environmental component is identified by placing a tick or cross in the appropriate cell. Table 4.4 shows an example of a *simple matrix*.

Magnitude matrices go beyond the mere identification of impacts by describing them according to their magnitude, importance and/or time frame (e.g. short, medium or longterm). Table 4.5 is an example of a magnitude matrix that represents whether the impact is positive or negative with either a red or green circle (red/green/amber 'traffic light' type colours are often used in EIA), and the magnitude of the impact by the depth of colour.

Distributional impact matrices aim to broadly identify who might lose and who might gain from the potential impacts of a development. This is useful information, which is rarely included in the matrix approach, and indeed is often missing from EISs. Impacts can have varying spatial impacts – varying, for example, between urban and rural areas. Spatial variations may be particularly marked for a linear project, such as a road or rail line. A project can also have different impacts on different groups in society (for example the impacts of a proposed new settlement on old people, retired with their own houses, and young people, perhaps with children, seeking affordable housing and a way into the housing market; see Figure 5.8).

Where matrices use numerical values to describe impacts, people may attempt to add these values to produce a composite value for the development's impacts and compare this with that for other developments; this should not be done unless each of the impacts is broadly as important as the others, otherwise these differences in impact importance will not be reflected in the outcome. *Weighted matrices* try to deal with this issue by assigning weightings to different impacts – and sometimes to different project components – to reflect their relative importance. The impact of the project (component) on the environmental component is then assessed and multiplied by the appropriate weighting(s), to obtain a total for the project. Weightings could reflect environmental

Table 4.4 Example of a simple matrix

	Project action				
	Construction		Operation		
	Utilities	Residential and commercial buildings	Residential buildings	Commercial buildings	Parks and open spaces
Soil and geology	✓	✓			
Flora	✓	✓			✓
Fauna	✓	✓			✓
Air quality				✓	
Water quality	✓	✓	✓		
Population density			✓	✓	
Employment		✓		✓	
Traffic	✓	✓	✓	✓	
Housing			✓		
Community structure		✓	✓		✓

Table 4.5 Example of a magnitude matrix

	Project action				
	Construction		Operation		
	Utilities	Residential and commercial buildings	Residential buildings	Commercial buildings	Parks and open spaces
Soil and geology	small negative	small negative	neutral	neutral	neutral
Flora	small negative	large negative	neutral	neutral	small negative
Fauna	small negative	small negative	neutral	neutral	small negative
Air quality	neutral	neutral	neutral	small negative	neutral
Water quality	small negative	neutral	neutral	small negative	neutral
Population density	neutral	neutral	small positive	small positive	neutral
Employment	neutral	small negative	neutral	small negative	neutral
Traffic	small negative	neutral	small negative	large negative	neutral
Housing	neutral	neutral	neutral	neutral	neutral
Community structure	neutral	small negative	small negative	neutral	small positive

large positive impact · small positive impact · neutral impact · small negative impact · large negative impact

components that are close to legal standards or thresholds; project components that will have long-term and irreversible impacts (Odum *et al.* 1975); or future long-term impacts that could be given more weight than short-term impacts (Stover 1972).

Table 4.6 shows a small weighted matrix that compares three alternative project sites. Each environmental component is assigned an importance weighting (a), relative to other environmental components: in the example, air quality is weighted 21 per cent of the total environmental components. The magnitude (c) of the impact of each project on each environmental component is then assessed on a scale 0–10, and multiplied by (a) to obtain a weighted impact (a × c): for instance, site A has an impact of 3 out of 10 on air quality, which is multiplied by 21 to give the weighted impact, 63. For each site, the weighted impacts can then be added up to give a project total. The site with the lowest total, in this case site B, is the least environmentally harmful.

The attraction of weighted matrices (or, more generally, multi-criteria analysis) lies in their ability to 'substantiate' numerically that a particular course of action is better than others. This may save decision-makers considerable work, and it ensures consistency in assessment and results. However, these approaches, and the 'answers' they lead to, depend heavily on the weightings and impact scales. They effectively take decisions away from decision-makers; they are difficult for lay people to understand; and their acceptability depends on the assumptions (especially the weighting schemes, built into them). People carrying out assessments may manipulate – or be perceived to manipulate – results by changing assumptions. The main problems implicit in such weighting approaches are considered further in Chapter 5.

More generally, checklists and matrices treat the environment as if it consisted of discrete units: impacts are related only to particular parameters, and the complex relationship between environmental components is not described. Much information is lost when impacts are reduced to symbols or numbers. Checklists and matrices do not specify the probability of an impact occurring, their scoring systems are inherently subjective and open

Table 4.6 A weighted matrix: alternative project sites

Environmental component		Alternative sites						
		Site A			Site B		Site C	
	(a)	(c)	(a x c)	(c)	(a x c)	(c)	(a x c)	
Air quality	21	3	63	5	105	3	63	
Water quality	42	6	252	2	84	5	210	
Noise	9	5	45	7	63	9	81	
Ecosystem	28	5	140	4	112	3	84	
Total	100		500		364		438	

(a) = relative weighting of environmental component (total 100)

(c) = impact of project at particular site on environmental component (0–10)

to bias, and they cannot reveal indirect effects of developments. However, they are (relatively) quick and simple, and they can be used to present scoping findings as well as identifying possible impacts.

Networks or causal chain analyses

Network methods explicitly recognize that environmental systems consist of a complex web of relationships, and try to reproduce that web. Impact identification using networks involves following the effects of development through changes in the environmental parameters in the model.

A simple network method is used in the development of many UK Local Transport Plans. Network diagrams are drawn by planners to identify how one action – say, changes to carriageways, junctions or public transport provision (Figure 4.6) – leads to changes in social, economic and environmental conditions. They also identify what preconditions are needed to achieve a positive outcome, and problems to avoid. Network methods do not establish the magnitude or significance of interrelationships between environmental components, or the extent of change. They can require considerable knowledge of the environment. Their main advantage is their ability to trace the higher-order impacts of proposed developments.

Overlay (or constraints) maps

Overlay maps have been used in environmental planning since the 1960s (McHarg 1968) before the NEPA was enacted. A series of overlays – originally in the form of transparencies, now more typically in the form of GIS layers – is used to identify, predict, assign relative significance to and communicate impacts. A base map is prepared, showing the general area within which the project may be located. Successive overlay maps are then prepared for the environmental components that are likely to be affected by the project (e.g. agriculture, woodland, noise). The composite impact of the project is found by superimposing the overlay maps and noting the relative intensity of the total shading. Areas with little or no shading are those where a development project would not have a significant impact. Figure 4.7 shows the principle of overlay maps and Figure 4.8 provides a particularly attractive example.

GIS can be used to assign different importance weightings to the impacts: this enables a sensitivity analysis to be carried out, to see whether changing assumptions about impact importance would alter the decision.

Overlay maps are easy to use and understand and are popular. They are an excellent way of showing the spatial distribution of impacts. They also lead intrinsically to a low-impact decision. The overlay maps method is particularly useful for identifying optimum corridors for developments such as electricity lines (Figure 4.8) and roads, for comparisons between alternatives, and for assessing large regional developments. However, the method does not consider factors such as the likelihood of an impact, indirect impacts or the difference between reversible and irreversible impacts. It

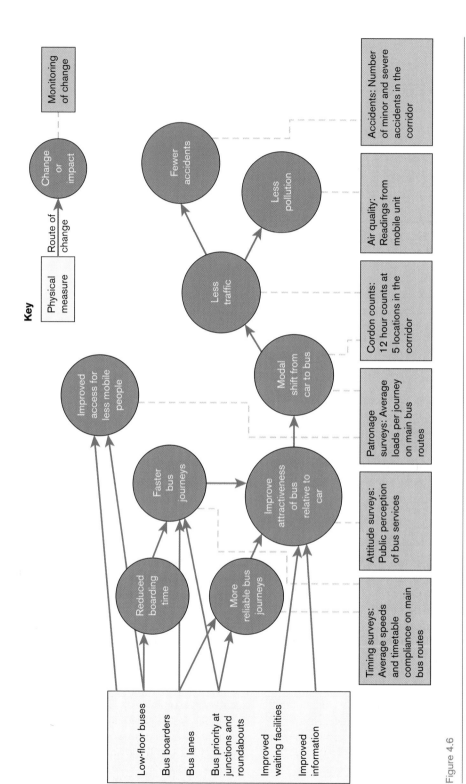

Figure 4.6

Causal chain analysis for bus corridor improvements

Source: Adapted from South Yorkshire Integrated Transport Authority 2001

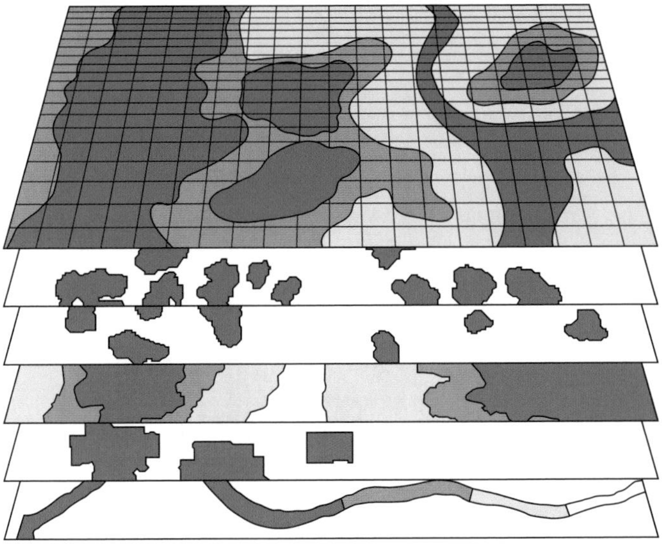

Figure 4.7

Overlay map: general principle

Composite

Ecological sites

Historic sites

Visual

Settlements

Water

requires the clear classification of often indeterminate boundaries (such as between forest and field), and so may not be a true representation of conditions on the ground. It relies on the user to identify likely impacts before it can be used.

Maps can also be used to show distributional impacts – who wins, who loses, and whether groups that are traditionally disadvantaged will lose out disproportionately. Figure 4.9 shows a US airport development's noise impacts on 'environmental justice populations' – areas with a high proportion of low-income or minority populations.

4.8.2 Quality of life assessment

The quality of life assessment (QOLA) (or quality of life capital) approach was developed jointly by the Countryside Agency et al. (2001) as a way of integrating the different agencies' approaches to environmental management. QOLA focuses not on the things but on the benefits that would be affected by a development proposal. It starts with the assumption that things (e.g. woodlands, historical buildings) are important because of the benefits that they provide to people (e.g. visual amenity, recreation, CO_2 fixing), and conversely that management of those things should aim to optimize the benefits that they provide. This emphasis on benefits has subsequently been incorporated in the ecosystem services approach (e.g. DEFRA 2007).

Quality of life assessment involves six steps (a–f). Having identified the purpose of the assessment (a) and described the proposed development site (b), the benefits/disbenefits that the site offers to sustainability (i.e. to present and future generations) are identified (c). The technique then asks the following questions (d):

- How important is each of these benefits or disbenefits, to whom, and why?
- On current trends, will there be enough of each of them?
- What (if anything) could substitute for the benefits?

The answers to these questions lead to a series of management implications (e), which allow a 'shopping list' to be devised of things that any development/management on that site should achieve, how they could be achieved, and their relative importance. Finally, monitoring of these benefits is proposed (f). Thus the process concludes by clearly stipulating the benefits that the development would have to provide before it was considered acceptable and, as a corollary, indicates where development would not be appropriate. It can be used to set a management framework (e.g. for planning conditions or mitigation measures) for any development on a given site (and also for management of larger areas). The QOLA approach can be used as a vehicle for public participation

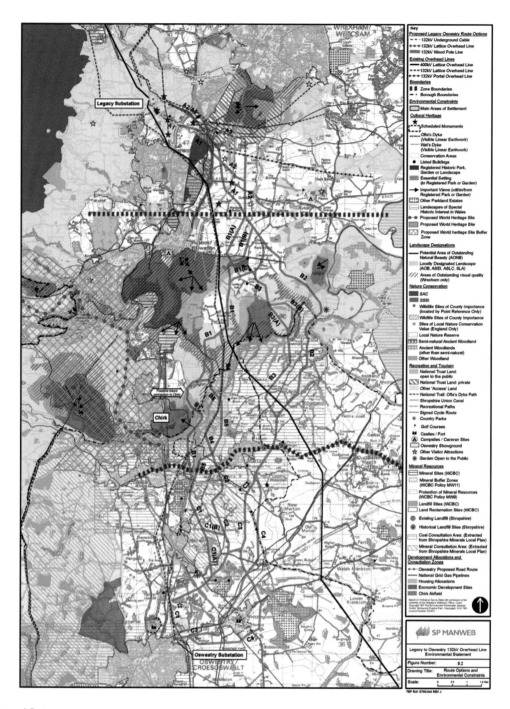

Figure 4.8

Overlay map showing constraints associated with siting an electricity transmission line (NB: possible routes for the transmission line are shown in red)

Source: Scottish Power 2009

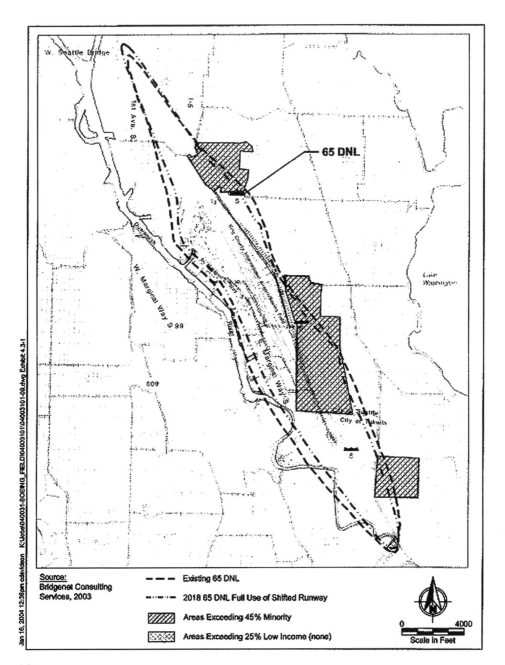

Figure 4.9

Impact on 'environmental justice' populations: areas exceeding 45 per cent minority and areas exceeding 25 per cent low income

Source: King County International Airport 2004

Table 4.7 Comparison of impact identification methods

Criterion
1 Compliance with regulations
2 Comprehensive coverage (social, economic and physical impacts)
3 Positive vs. negative, reversible vs. irreversible impacts, etc.
4 Secondary, indirect, cumulative impacts
5 Significant vs. insignificant impacts
6 Compare alternative options
7 Compare against carrying capacity
8 Uses qualitative and quantitative information
9 Easy to use
10 Unbiased, consistent
11 Summarizes impacts for use in EIS

	1	2	3	4	5	6	7	8	9	10	11
Checklists	✓	✓						✓	✓	✓	✓
Matrices											
• simple	✓	✓						✓	✓	✓	✓
• magnitude	✓	✓	✓					✓	✓	✓	✓
• weighted	✓	✓			✓	✓		✓	✓		✓
Network	✓			✓		✓		✓		✓	
Overlay maps		✓	✓		✓	✓		✓	✓	✓	✓

and/or the integration of different experts' analyses of a site.

4.8.3 Summary

Table 4.7 summarizes the respective advantages of the main impact identification methods discussed in this section. Impact identification methods need to be chosen with care: they are not politically neutral, and the more sophisticated the method becomes, often the more difficult becomes clear communication and effective participation (see Chapter 6 for more discussion). The simpler methods are generally easier to use, more consistent and more effective in presenting information in the EIS, but their coverage of impact significance, indirect impacts or alternatives is either very limited or non-existent. The more complex models incorporate these aspects, but at the cost of immediacy.

··

4.9 Summary

The early stages of the EIA process are typified by several interacting steps. These include deciding whether an EIA is needed at all (screening), consulting with the various parties involved to help focus on the chief impacts (scoping), and an outline of possible alternative approaches to the project, including alternative locations, scales and processes. Scoping and the consideration of alternatives can greatly improve the quality of the process. Early in the process an analyst will also wish to understand the nature of the project concerned, and the environmental baseline conditions in the likely affected area. Projects have several dimensions (e.g. physical presence, processes and policies) over several stages in their life cycles; a consideration of the environmental baseline also involves several dimensions. For both projects and the affected environment, obtaining relevant data may present challenges.

Impact identification includes most of the activities already discussed. It usually involves the use of impact identification methods, ranging from simple checklists and matrices to more complex networks and maps. The methods discussed here have relevance also to the prediction, assessment, communication and mitigation of environmental impacts, which are discussed in the following chapters.

SOME QUESTIONS

The following questions are intended to help the reader focus on the key issues of this chapter.

1   Assume that a developer is proposing to build a wind farm (or another project of your choice) in an area that you know well, and for which you have been asked to manage the EIS for the project.
    * What kind of experts would you want on your team?
    * What information about the project would you need to know before you could carry out the EIA scoping stage?
    * What types of project alternatives might be relevant? Would there be tiers of alternatives?
    * What technique would you use to identify the impacts of the project, and why?

2   Table 4.2 shows that the number of EISs prepared in different European Union Member States varies widely. What issues associated with the screening process might account for these differences?

3   Should all EISs consider the 'no action' alternative? Different locations? Different scales? Different processes? Different designs? Why or why not?

4   What minimum level of information about the project should be presented in the EIS? What additional information could be useful?

5   Of the different figures and tables presented in this chapter, which two or three would you find most helpful when trying to understand a project and its impacts?

6   Section 4.8.1 suggests that quite complex impact identification methods have been devised in the past but not used much in practice. What might be the reason for this?

....

Notes

1   This refers both to the spatial extent that will be covered and to the scale at which it is covered. João (2002) suggests that the latter – which has been broadly ignored as an issue to date – could be crucial enough to lead to different decisions depending on the scale chosen.

2   In the US, 'agencies should: consider the option of doing nothing; consider alternatives outside the remit of the agency; and consider achieving only a part of their objectives in order to reduce impact'.

....

References

Barker, A. and Wood, C. 1999. An evaluation of EIA system performance in eight EU countries. *Environmental Impact Assessment Review* 19, 387–404.

BIO 2006. Cost and benefits of the implementation of the EIA Directive in France, Unpublished document.

Carroll, B. and Turpin, T. 2009. *Environmental impact assessment handbook.* London: Thomas Telford.

CEC (Commission of the European Communities) 1993. *Environmental manual: user's guide; sectoral environment assessment sourcebook.* Brussels: CEC DG VIII.

CEC 1997. Council Directive 97/11/EC amending Directive 85/337/EEC on the assessment of certain public and private projects on the environment. *Official Journal* L73/5, 3 March.

CEQ (Council on Environmental Quality) 1978. National Environmental Policy Act. Implementation of procedural provision: final regulations. *Federal Register* 43 (230), 5977–6007, 29 November.

Countryside Agency, English Nature, Environment Agency, English Heritage 2001. *Quality of Life Capital: What matters and why.* Available at: www.qualityoflifecapital.org.uk.

COWI 2009. Study concerning the report on the application and effectiveness of the EIA Directive. Final report to the European Commission, DG ENV. Kongens Lyngby, Denmark.

Dartmoor National Park Authority 2010. Town and Country (Environmental Impact Assessment (England and Wales), Regulations 1999 (Part IV) Scoping Opinion (12 August 2010). Available at: www.dartmoor-npa.gov.uk/pl-2010–06–10_yennadon_eia_scoping_opinion.pdf.

DCLG (Department for Communities and Local Government) 2006. *Evidence review of scoping in environmental impact assessment*. London: DCLG.

DCLG (Department for Communities and Local Government) 2011. *Guidance on the environmental impact assessment (EIA) regulations 2011 for England*. London: DCLG.

DEFRA (Department for Environment, Food and Rural Affairs) 2007. *An introductory guide to valuing ecosystem services*. Available at: www.defra.gov.uk/environment/policy/natural-environ/documents/eco-valuing.pdf.

DETR (Department of the Environment, Transport and the Regions) 2000. *Environmental impact assessment: a guide to the procedure*. Available at: www.communities.gov.uk/publications/planningandbuilding/environmentalimpactassessment.

Eastman, C. 1997. *The treatment of alternatives in the environmental assessment process* (MSc dissertation). Oxford: Oxford Brookes University.

EC (European Commission) 2001a. *Screening checklist*. Brussels: EC.

EC 2001b. *Scoping checklist*. Brussels: EC.

EC 2006. Evaluation of EU legislation – Directive 85/337/EEC (Environmental Impact Assessment, EIA) and associated amendments. Brussels: DG Enterprise and Industry.

Environment Agency 2002. *Environmental impact assessment: scoping guidelines for the environmental impact assessment of projects*. Reading: Environment Agency.

EU (European Union) 2010. *Environmental Impact Assessment of Projects: Rulings of the Court of Justice*. Brussels: EU.

Fortlage, C. 1990. *Environmental assessment: a practical guide*. Aldershot: Gower.

Frost, R. 1994. *Planning beyond environmental statements* (MSc dissertation). Oxford: Oxford Brookes University, School of Planning.

GHK 2010. *Collection of information and data to support the impact assessment study of the review of the EIA Directive*. London: GHK.

Government of New South Wales 1996. *EIS guidelines*. Sydney: Department of Urban Affairs and Planning.

IEMA (Institute of Environmental Management and Assessment) 2011. *The State of Environmental Impact Assessment Practice in the UK*. Grantham: IEMA.

João, E. 2002. How scale affects environmental impact assessment. *Environmental Impact Assessment Review* 22, 289–310.

Jones, C.E., Lee, N. and Wood, C. 1991. *UK environmental statements 1988–1990: an analysis*. Occasional Paper 29, Department of Town and Country Planning, University of Manchester.

King County International Airport 2004. NEPA environmental assessment, SEPA Environmental impact statement for proposed master plan improvements at King County Inernational Airport (Boeing Field), Seattle. Available at: www.your.kingcounty.gov/airport/plan/EIS-EA_2–23–04.pdf.

Lawrence, D.P. 2003. *Environmental Impact Assessment: practical solutions to recurrent problems*. Hoboken: Wiley-Interscience.

McHarg, I. 1968. A *comprehensive route selection method*. Highway Research Record 246. Washington, DC: Highway Research Board.

Morris, P. and Therivel, R. (eds) 2009. *Methods of environmental impact assessment*, 3rd edn. London: Routledge.

Morrison-Saunders, A. and Bailey, M. 2009. Appraising the role of relationships between regulators and consultants for effective EIA. *Environmental Impact Assessment Review* 29, 284–94.

Odum, E.P., Zieman, J.C., Shugart, H.H., Ike, A. and Champlin, J.R. 1975. In *Environmental impact assessment*, M. Blisset (ed). Austin: University of Texas Press.

Oosterhuis, F. 2007. Costs and benefits of the EIA Directive: Final report for DB Environment under specific agreement no. 07010401/2006/447175/FRA/G1. Available at: www.ec.europa.eu/environment/eia/pdf/Costs%20and%20benefits%20of%20the%20EIA%20Directive.pdf.

Pattersons Quarries/SLR 2009. Planning application for proposed sand and gravel quarry at Overburns Farm, Lamington, Non-technical summary. Available at: www.patersonsquarries.co.uk/images/downloads/Overburns_Quarry_NTS-SM.pdf.

Petts, J. and Eduljee, G. 1994. Integration of monitoring, auditing and environmental assessment: waste facility issues. *Project Appraisal* 9 (4), 231–41.

Rodriguez-Bachiller, A. 2000. Geographical information systems and expert systems for impact assessment, Parts I and II. *Journal of Environmental Assessment Policy and Management* 2 (3), 369–448.

Rodriguez-Bachiller, A. with J. Glasson 2004. *Expert systems and geographical information systems for impact assessment*. London: Taylor and Francis.

Scottish Government, Jacobs, and Arup 2009, Forth Replacement Crossing environmental statement. Edinburgh: Scottish Government.

Smith, M.D. 2007. A review of recent NEPA alternatives analysis case law, *Environmental Impact Assessment Review* 27, 126–40.

Sorensen, J. C. and Moss, M.L. 1973. *Procedures and programmes to assist in the environmental impact statement process*. Berkeley, CA: Institute of Urban and Regional Development, University of California.

South Yorkshire Integrated Transport Authority 2001. South Yorkshire Local Transport Plan 2001–06. Available at: www.southyorks.gov.uk/index.asp?id=3086.

State of California 2010. Title 14 California Code of Regulations section 15000 *et seq*. Sacramento, CA: State of California.

Steinemann, A. 2001. Improving alternatives for environmental impact assessment. *Environmental Impact Assessment Review* 21, 3–21.

Stover, L.V. 1972. *Environmental impact assessment: a procedure*. Pottstown, PA: Sanders & Thomas.

UKNEA (National Ecosystem Assessment) 2011. Understanding nature's value to society. Available at: www.uknea.unep-wcmc.org.

United Nations University (2007). Environmental Impact Assessment Open Educational Resource. Available at: www.eia.unu.edu.

Weaver, A.B., Greyling, T., Van Wilyer, B.W. and Kruger, F.J. 1996. Managing the ETA process. Logistics and team management of a large environmental impact assessment – proposed dune mine at St. Lucia, South Africa. *Environmental Impact Assessment Review* 16, 103–13.

World Bank (1999) Environmental Assessment Sourcebook 1999. Available at: www.siteresources.worldbank.org/INTSAFEPOL/1142947–1116495579739/20507372/Chapter1TheEnvironmentalReviewProcess.pdf.

5 Impact prediction, evaluation, mitigation and enhancement

● ●

5.1 Introduction

The focus of this chapter is the central steps of impact prediction, evaluation, mitigation and enhancement. This is the heart of the EIA process, although, as we have already noted, the process is not linear. Indeed the whole EIA exercise is about prediction. It is needed at the earliest stages, when a project, including its alternatives, is being planned and designed, and it continues through to mitigation and enhancement, monitoring and auditing. Yet, despite the centrality of prediction in EIA, there is a tendency for many studies to underemphasize it at the expense of more descriptive studies. Prediction is often not treated as an explicit stage in the process; clearly defined models are often missing from studies. Even when used, models are not detailed, and there is little discussion of limitations. Section 5.2 examines the dimensions of prediction (what to predict), the methods and models used in prediction (how to predict) and the limitations implicit in such exercises (living with uncertainty). It also includes a brief summary of some useful international and UK forecasting sources.

Evaluation follows from prediction and involves an assessment of the relative significance of the impacts. Methods range from the simple to the complex, from the intuitive to the analytical, from qualitative to quantitative, from formal to informal. CBA, monetary valuation techniques and multi-criteria/multi-attribute methods, with their scoring and weighting systems, provide a number of ways into the evaluation issue. The chapter concludes with a discussion of approaches to the mitigation of significant adverse effects. This may involve measures to avoid, reduce, remedy or compensate for the various impacts associated with projects. There is also a discussion of the increasingly considered aspect of impact enhancement – that is, where possible, developing the significant beneficial impacts of projects.

● ●

5.2 Prediction

5.2.1 Dimensions of prediction (what to predict)

The object of prediction is to identify the magnitude and other dimensions of identified change in the environment *with* a project or action, in comparison with the situation *without* that project or action. Predictions also provide the basis for the assessment of significance, which is discussed in Section 5.3.

One starting point to identify the dimensions of prediction in the UK is the *legislative requirements* (see Table 3.6, Parts 1 and 2). These basic specifications are amplified in guidance given in *Environmental assessment: a guide to the procedures* (DETR 2000) as outlined in Table 5.1. As already noted, this listing is limited on the assessment of socio-economic impacts. Table 1.3 provides a broader

Table 5.1 Assessment of effects, as outlined in UK guidance

Assessment of effects (including direct and indirect, secondary, cumulative, short-, medium- and long-term, permanent and temporary, and positive and negative effects of project)

Effects on human beings, buildings and man-made features

1   Change in population arising from the development, and consequential environmental effects.
2   Visual effects of the development on the surrounding area and landscape.
3   Levels and effects of emissions from the development during normal operation.
4   Levels and effects of noise from the development.
5   Effects of the development on local roads and transport.
6   Effects of the development on buildings, the architectural and historic heritage, archaeological features, and other human artefacts, e.g. through pollutants, visual intrusion, vibration.

Effects on flora, fauna and geology

7   Loss of, and damage to, habitats and plant and animal species.
8   Loss of, and damage to, geological, palaeotological and physiographic features.
9   Other ecological consequences.

Effects on land

10   Physical effects of the development, e.g. change in local topography, effect of earth-moving on stability, soil erosion, etc.
11   Effects of chemical emissions and deposits on soil of site and surrounding land.
12   Land-use/resource effects:
    (a)   quality and quantity of agricultural land to be taken;
    (b)   sterilization of mineral *resources*;
    (c)   other alternative uses of the site, including the 'do nothing' option;
    (d)   effect on surrounding land uses including agriculture;
    (e)   waste disposal.

Effects on water

13   Effects of development on drainage pattern in the area.
14   Changes to other hydrographic characteristics, e.g. groundwater level, watercourses, flow of underground water.
15   Effects on coastal or estuarine hydrology.
16   Effects of pollutants, waste, etc. on water quality.

Effects on air and climate

17   Level and concentration of chemical emissions and their environmental effects.
18   Particulate matter.
19   Offensive odours.
20   Any other climatic effects.

Other indirect and secondary effects associated with the project

21   Effects from traffic (road, rail, air, water) related to the development.
22   Effects arising from the extraction and consumption of material, water, energy or other, resources by the development.
23   Effects of other development associated with the project, e.g. new roads, sewers, housing power lines, pipelines, telecommunications, etc.
24   Effects of association of the development with other existing or proposed development.
25   Secondary effects resulting from the interaction of separate direct effects listed above.

Source: DETR 2000

view of the scope of the environment, and of the environmental receptors that may be affected by a project.

Prediction involves the identification of potential change in indicators of such environment receptors. Scoping will have identified the broad categories of impact in relation to the project under consideration. If a particular environmental indicator (e.g. SO_2 levels in the air) revealed an increasing problem in an area, irrespective of the project or action (e.g. a power station), this should be predicted forwards as the baseline for this particular indicator. These indicators need to be disaggregated and specified to provide variables that are measurable and relevant. For example, an economic impact could be progressively specified as

direct employment →
local employment →
local skilled employment

In this way, a list of significant impact indicators of policy relevance can be developed.

An important distinction is often made between the prediction of the likely *magnitude* (i.e. size) and the *significance* (i.e. the importance for decision-making) of the impacts. Magnitude does not always equate with significance. For example, a large increase in one pollutant may still result in an outcome within generally accepted standards in a 'robust environment', whereas a small increase in another may take it above the applicable standards in a 'sensitive environment' (Figure 5.1). This also highlights the distinction between *objective* and *subjective* approaches. The prediction of the magnitude of an impact should be an objective exercise, although it is not always easy. The determination of significance is often a more subjective exercise, as it normally involves value judgements.

As Table 1.4 showed, prediction should also identify *direct* and *indirect* impacts (simple cause–effect diagrams can be useful here), the *geographical extent* of impacts (e.g. local, regional, national), whether the impacts are *beneficial* or *adverse*, and the *duration* of the impacts. In addition to prediction over the life of a project (including, for example, its construction, operational and other stages), the analyst should also be alert to the *rate of change* of impacts. A slow build-up in an impact

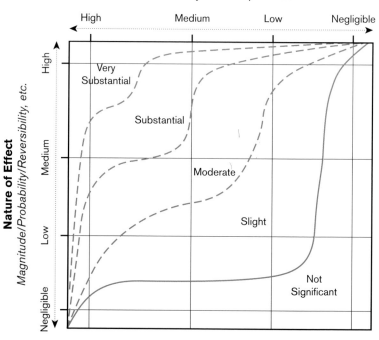

Figure 5.1

Example of generic significance matrix (e.g. 'impact magnitude' vs. 'environmental sensitivity')

Source: IEMA 2011

may be more acceptable than a rapid change; the development of tourism projects in formerly remote or undeveloped areas provides an example of the damaging impacts of rapid change. Projects may be characterized by non-linear processes, by delays between cause and effect, and the intermittent nature of some impacts should be anticipated. The *reversibility* or otherwise of impacts, their permanency, and their *cumulative* and synergistic impacts should also be predicted. Cumulative (or additive) impacts are the collective effects of impacts that may be individually minor but in combination, often over time, can be major. Such cumulative impacts are difficult to predict, and are often poorly covered or are missing altogether from EIA studies (see Chapter 12).

Another dimension is the unit of measurement, and the distinction between *quantitative* and *qualitative* impacts. Some indicators are more readily quantifiable than others (e.g. a change in the quality of drinking water, in comparison, for example, with changes in community stress associated with a project). Where possible, predictions should present impacts in explicit units, which can provide a basis for evaluation and trade-off. Quantification can allow predicted impacts to be assessed against various local, national and international standards. Predictions should also include estimates of the *probability* that an impact will occur, which raises the important issue of uncertainty.

5.2.2 *Methods and models for prediction (how to predict)*

There are many possible methods to predict impacts; a study undertaken by Environmental Resources Ltd for the Dutch government in the early 1980s identified 150 different prediction methods used in just 140 EIA studies from The Netherlands and North America (VROM 1984). None provides a magic solution to the prediction problem.

All predictions are based on conceptual models of how the universe functions; they range in complexity from those that are totally intuitive to those based on explicit assumptions concerning the nature of environmental processes . . . the environment is

never as well behaved as assumed in models, and the assessor is to be discouraged from accepting off-the-shelf formulae. (Munn 1979)

Predictive methods can be classified in many ways; they are not mutually exclusive. In terms of *scope*, all methods are *partial* in their coverage of impacts, but some seek to be more *holistic* than others. Partial methods may be classified according to type of project (e.g. retail impact assessment) and type of impact (e.g. wider economic impacts). Some may be *extrapolative*, others may be more *normative*. For extrapolative methods, predictions are made that are consistent with past and present data. Extrapolative methods include, for example, trend analysis (extrapolating present trends, modified to take account of changes caused by the project), scenarios (common-sense forecasts of future state based on a variety of assumptions), analogies (transferring experience from elsewhere to the study in hand) and intuitive forecasting (e.g. the use of the Delphi technique to achieve group consensus on the impacts of a project) (Green *et al.* 1989; Briedenhann and Butts 2006). Normative approaches work backwards from desired outcomes to assess whether a project, in its environmental context, is adequate to achieve them. For example, a desired socio-economic outcome from the construction stage of a major project may be 50 per cent local employment. The achievement of this outcome may necessitate modifications to the project and/or to associated employment policies (e.g. on training). Various scenarios may be tested to determine the one most likely to achieve the desired outcomes. Methods can also be classified according to their *form*, as the following types of model illustrate.

Mathematical and computer-based models

Mathematical models seek to represent the behaviour of aspects of the environment through the use of mathematical functions. They are usually based upon scientific laws, statistical analysis or some combination of the two, and are often computer based. The underpinning functions can range from simple direct input–output relationships to more complex dynamic mathematical models with a wide array of interrelationships.

Mathematical models can be spatially aggregated (e.g. a model to predict the survival rate of a cohort population, or an economic multiplier for a particular area), or more locationally based, predicting net changes in detailed locations throughout a study area. Of the latter, retail impact models, which predict the distribution of retail expenditure using gravity model principles, provide a simple example; the comprehensive land-use locational models of Harris, Lowry, Cripps and others provide more holistic examples (Bracken, 2008). Mathematical models can also be divided into deterministic and stochastic models. Deterministic models, like the gravity model, depend on fixed relationships. In contrast, a stochastic model is probabilistic, and indicates 'the degree of probability of the occurrence of a certain event by specifying the statistical probability that a certain number of events will take place in a given area and/or time interval' (Loewenstein 1966).

There are many mathematical models available for particular impacts. Reference to various EISs (especially from the USA), and to the literature (e.g. Bregman and Mackenthun 1992; Hansen and Jorgensen 1991; Rau and Wooten 1980; Suter 1993; US Environmental Protection Agency 1993; Westman 1985) reveals the availability of a rich array. For instance, Kristensen et al. (1990) list 21 mathematical models for phosphorus retention in lakes alone. An example of a deterministic mathematical model, often used in socio-economic impact predictions, is the multiplier (Lewis 1988), an example of which is shown in Figure 5.2. The injection of money into an economy – local, regional or national – will increase income in the economy by some multiple of the original injection. Modification of the basic model allows

it to be used to predict income and employment impacts for various groups over the stages of the life of a project (Glasson et al. 1988). The more disaggregated (by industry type) input–output member of the multiplier family provides a particularly sophisticated method for predicting economic impacts, but with major data requirements, and limitations.

Statistical models use statistical techniques such as regression or principal components analysis to describe the relationship between data, to test hypotheses or to extrapolate data. For instance, they can be used in a pollution-monitoring study to describe the concentration of a pollutant as a function of the stream-flow rates and the distance downstream. They can compare conditions at a contaminated site and a control site to determine the significance of any differences in monitoring data. They can extrapolate a model to conditions outside the data range used to derive the model (e.g. from toxicity at high doses of a pollutant to toxicity at low doses) or from data that are available to data that are unavailable (e.g. from toxicity in rats to toxicity in humans).

Physical/architectural models and experimental methods

Physical, image or architectural models are illustrative or scale models that replicate some element of the project–environment interaction. For example, a scale model (or computer graphics) could be used to predict the impacts of a development on the landscape or built environment. Photo-montages can be used to show the views of the project site from the 'receptor' areas, with images of the project superimposed to give an

$$Y_r = \frac{1}{1-(1-s)(1-t-u)(1-m)} \, J$$

where

Y_r = change in level of income (Y) in region (r), in £
J = initial income injection (or multiplicand)
t = proportion of additional income paid in direction taxation and National Insurance contributions
s = proportion of income saved (and therefore not spent locally)
u = decline in transfer payments (e.g. unemployment benefits) which result from the rise in local income and employment
m = proportion of additional income spent on imported consumer goods

Figure 5.2

A simple multiplier model for the prediction of local economic impacts

impression of visual impact. The image could be a photograph of a model of the project, or a simple 'wire-line' profile of the project as it will appear to the viewer, showing just its skyline or a more sophisticated 3D impression. More sophisticated representations, where resources permit, can include 'fly-through' computer graphics, showing a proposed project in its proposed setting from a variety of perspectives.

Field and laboratory experimental methods use existing data inventories, often supplemented by special surveys, to predict impacts on receptors. Field tests are carried out in unconfined conditions, usually at approximately the same scale as the predicted impact; an example would be the testing of a pesticide in an outdoor pond. Laboratory tests, such as the testing of a pollutant on seedlings raised in a hydroponic solution, are usually cheaper to run but may not extrapolate well to conditions in natural systems.

Expert judgements and analogue models

All predictive methods in EIA make some use of expert judgement. Such judgement can make use of some of the other predictive methods, such as mathematical models and cause–effect networks or flow charts, discussed below. Expert judgement can also draw on analogue models – making predictions based on analogous situations. They include comparing the impacts of a proposed development with a similar existing development; comparing the environmental conditions at one site with those at similar sites elsewhere; comparing an unknown environmental impact (e.g. of wind turbines on radio reception) with a known environmental impact (e.g. of other forms of development on radio reception). Analogue models can be developed from site visits, literature searches or the monitoring of similar projects. The Internet now provides a wealth of information on potential comparative projects.

Other methods for prediction

The various impact identification methods discussed in Chapter 4 may also be of value in impact prediction. For example, overlays can also be used to predict spatial impacts.

Choice of prediction methods

The nature and choice of prediction methods do vary according to the impacts under consideration, and Rodriguez-Bachiller with Glasson (2004) have identified the following types:

- *Hard-modelled impacts*: areas of impact prediction where mathematical simulation models play a central role. These include, for example, air and noise impacts. Air pollution impact prediction has been dominated by approaches based on the so-called 'Gaussian dispersion model' which simulates the shape of the pollution plume from the development under concern (Elsom 2009).
- *Soft-modelled impacts*: areas of impact prediction where the use of mathematical simulation modelling is virtually non-existent. Examples here include terrestrial ecology and landscape. Terrestrial ecology depends very much on field sample survey for plant and animal species, where the expert's perception of what requires sampling plays an important role (Morris and Thurling 2001). Perception is also important in landscape assessment, but simple photomontages, and the use of GIS, can help in the prediction of impacts (Knight 2009; Wood 2000). Figure 5.3 provides an outline of key steps in landscape assessment.
- *Mixed-modelled impacts*: areas of impact prediction where simulation modelling is complemented (and sometimes replaced) by more technically lower-level approaches. Traffic impacts make considerable use of modelling, but often with some sample survey input. Socio-economic impacts may use simple flow diagrams, and mathematical models (as in Figures 5.2 and 5.3) particularly for economic impacts, but they tend to build a great deal on survey methods and expert judgement. This is particularly so with regard to social impacts.

When choosing prediction methods, an assessor should be concerned about their appropriateness for the task involved, in the context of the resources available. Will the methods produce what is wanted (e.g. a range of impacts, for the appropriate geographical area, over various stages), from

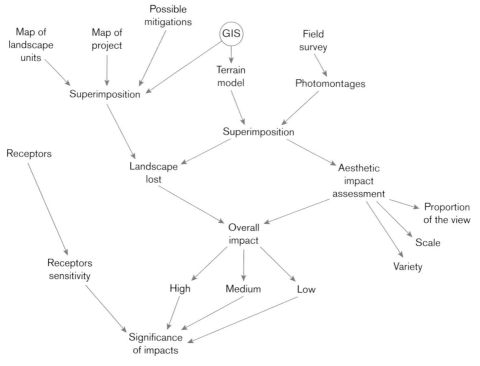

Figure 5.3

Key steps in landscape impact assessment

Source: Rodriguez-Bachiller with Glasson 2004

the resources available (including time, data, range of expertise)? In addition, the criteria of replicability (method is free from analyst bias), consistency (method can be applied to different projects to allow predictions to be compared) and adaptability should also be considered in the choice of methods. In many cases, more than one method may be appropriate. For instance, the range of methods available for predicting impacts on air quality is apparent from the 165 closely typed pages on the subject by Rau and Wooten (1980). Table 5.2 provides an overview of some of the methods of predicting the initial emissions of pollutants, which, with atmospheric interaction, may degrade air quality, which may then have adverse effects, for example on humans.

In practice, there has been a tendency to use the less formal predictive methods, and especially expert opinion (VROM 1984). Even where more formal methods have been used, they have tended to be simple, for example the use of photo-

montages for visual impacts, or of simple dilution and steady-state dispersion models for water quality. However, simple methods need not be inappropriate, especially for early stages in the EIA process, nor need they be applied uncritically or in a simplistic way. Lee (1987) provides the following illustration:

(a) a single expert may be asked for a brief, qualitative opinion; or

(b) the expert may also be asked to justify that opinion (i) by verbal or mathematical description of the relationships he has taken into account and/or (ii) by indicating the empirical evidence which supports that opinion; or

(c) as in (b), except that opinions are also sought from other experts; or

(d) as in (c), except that the experts are also required to reach a common opinion, with supporting reasons, qualifications, etc.; or

Table 5.2 Examples of methods used in predicting air quality impacts

Sources	• Original project design data on activity and emissions
↓	
POLLUTANT EMISSIONS	• Published emission data for similar projects
↓	• Emission factor models
↓	• Emission standards
Atmospheric interactions	• Gaussian dispersion models (interactive programmes)
↓	
DEGRADED AIR QUALITY	• Wind tunnel models
↓	• Water analogue simulation models
↓	• Expert opinion
↓	• Mathematical deposition models
EFFECTS ON RECEPTORS	• Laboratory or field experimental methods
e.g. humans	• Inventories/surveys
	• Dose–response factors

Sources: VROM 1984; Rau and Wooten 1980

(e) as in (d), except that the experts are expected to reach a common opinion using an agreed process of consensus building (e.g. based on 'Delphi' techniques; Golden *et al.* 1979).

The development of more complex methods can be very time-consuming and expensive, especially since many of these models are limited to specific environmental components and physical processes, and may only be justified when a number of relatively similar projects are proposed. However, notwithstanding the emphasis on the simple informal methods, there is scope for mathematical simulation models in the prediction stage, especially where the assessment requires the handling of large numbers of simple calculations, some processes are time-dependent, and some assessment relationships can only be defined in terms of statistical probabilities.

Causal networks in EIA prediction

An important element in prediction, as noted in some of the previous methods, is the cause and effects relationship. But such relationships are often poorly expressed, if at all, in the EIA process. Yet there would seem to be a good case for the use of causal networks – diagrams that demonstrate causal relationships between their elements – as vehicles that can easily relate and transparently demonstrate cause and effects (Perdicoulis and Glasson 2006, 2009). The special identifiers of causal

networks are a diagrammatic representation of relationships among elements and the attribution of causality to those relationships; the networks are abstract diagrams with nodes and links. Both the network logic and the causality logic of causal networks seem to tie in well with the EIA process. They do presuppose that (a) there are links between individual elements of the environment and projects (network logic) and (b) when one element is specifically affected this will have an effect on those elements that interact with it (causality logic) (CEC 1999). A key strength of causal networks is their capability to follow impacts to several levels through sequences of interactions – a fact that also gives them the alternative name of 'sequence diagrams' (Canter 1996). Two drawbacks are their difficulty in dealing with time and space, and the potential risk for increased complexity (CEC 1999). When they become too complex, they tend to be simplified in ad hoc ways or ignored altogether (Goldvarg and Johnson–Laird 2001).

Two examples of causal networks are illustrated here. The digraph, or directed graph (Figure 5.4), is perhaps the simplest form of causal network. The elements are nodes and directional links (uni-directional arrows), with optional additional information marked directly on those elements. The + and – symbols are used in the sense of accompanying change (+) or reacting to change (–).

Cause and effect flow diagrams are directed graphs, but their elements are stated textually in various shapes – mostly rectangles. Causal

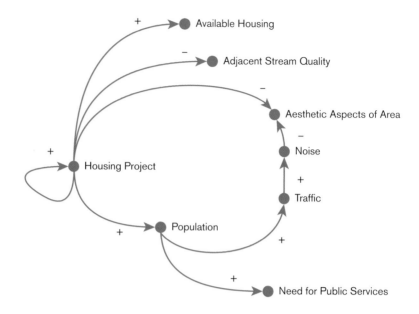

Figure 5.4

Example of a digraph, or
directed graph

Source: Adapted from Canter
1996

relationships are marked by uni-directional arrows, usually carrying no quantitative information. In general, they are more elaborated graphically, but can be less rich in information than the simple digraphs. Cause and effect flow diagrams are mainly used in EIA for the identification and prediction of impacts related to development projects (CEC 1999; Glasson 2009). Figure 5.5 provides a simple flow diagram for the prediction of the local socio-economic impacts of a power station development. Key determinants in the model are the details of the labour requirements for the project, the conditions in the local economy, and the policies of the relevant local authority and developer on topics such as training, local recruitment and travel allowances. The local recruitment ratio is a crucial factor in the determination of subsequent impacts.

5.2.3 Living with uncertainty

Environmental impact statements often appear more certain in their predictions than they should. This may reflect a concern not to undermine credibility and/or unwillingness to attempt to allow for uncertainty. Yet all predictions have an element of uncertainty, and this should be acknowledged in the EIA process (Beattie 1995; De Jongh 1988). The amended EIA Directive (CEC 1997) and subsequent UK guidance (DETR 2000) include 'the

probability of the impact' in the characteristics of the potential impact of a project that must be considered. There are many sources of uncertainty relevant to the EIA process as a whole. In their classic works on strategic choice, Friend and Jessop (1977) and Friend and Hickling (1987) identified three broad classes of uncertainty: uncertainties about the physical, social and economic working environment (UE), uncertainties about guiding values (UV) and uncertainties about related decisions (UR) (Figure 5.6). All three classes of uncertainty may affect the accuracy of predictions, but the focus in an EIA study is usually on uncertainty about the environment. This may include the use of inaccurate and/or partial information on the project and on baseline-environmental conditions, unanticipated changes in the project during one or more of the stages of the life cycle, and oversimplification and errors in the application of methods and models. Socio-economic conditions may be particularly difficult to predict, as underlying societal values may change quite dramatically over the life, say 30–40 years, of a project.

Uncertainty in EIA predictive exercises can be handled in several ways. The assumptions underpinning predictions should be clearly stated; issues of probability and confidence in predictions should be addressed, and *ranges* may be attached to predictions within which the analyst is *n* per cent confident that the actual outcome will lie.

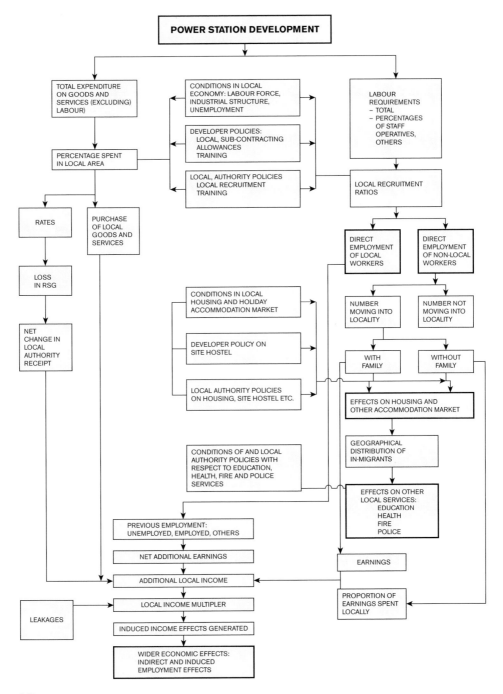

Figure 5.5

A cause–effect flow diagram for the local socio-economic impacts of a power station proposal

Source: Glasson *et al.* 1987

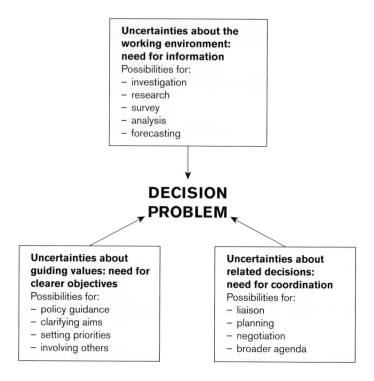

For example, scientific research may conclude that the 95 per cent confidence interval for the noise associated with a new industrial project is 65–70 dBA, which means that only 5 times out of 100 would the dBA be expected to be outside this range. Tomlinson (1989) draws attention to the twin issues of probability and confidence involved in predictions. These twin factors are generally expressed through the same word. For example, in the prediction 'a major oil spill would have major ecological consequences', a high degree of both probability and confidence exists. Situations may arise, however, where a low probability event based upon a low level of confidence is predicted. This is potentially more serious than a higher probability event with high confidence, since low levels of confidence may preclude expenditure on mitigating measures, ignoring issues of significance. Monitoring measures may be an appropriate response in such situations. It may also be useful to show impacts under 'peak' as well as 'average' conditions for a particular stage of a project; this may be very relevant in the construction stage of major projects.

Sensitivity analysis may be used to assess the consistency of relationships between variables. If the relationship between input A and output B is such that whatever the changes in A there is little change in B, then no further information may be needed. However, where the effect is much more variable, there may be a need for further information. Of course, the best check on the accuracy of predictions is to check on the outcomes of the implementation of a project after the decision. This is too late for the project under consideration, but could be useful for future projects. Conversely, the monitoring of outcomes of similar projects may provide useful information for the project in hand. Holling (1978), who believes that the 'core issue of EIA is how to cope with decision-making under uncertainty', recommends a policy of *adaptive EIA*, with periodic reviews of the EIA through a project's life cycle. Such adaptive assessment, using a 'predict, monitor and manage' approach is a valuable and sensible response to dealing with the inherent problem of uncertainty in prediction in impact assessment. Another procedural approach would be to require an *uncertainty report* as one step in the process; such a report would bring together the various sources of uncertainty associated with a project and the means by which they might be reduced (uncertainties are rarely eliminated).

Table 5.3 Some forecasting data sources: international and UK

Source (international)	Brief summary of content
United Nations Environment Programme (UNEP)	The UNEP *Global environment outlook 3* (GEO) project (2002: past, present and future perspectives) reviews trends over the period 1972 to 2002, and then uses scenarios to explore possible futures to 2030. The scenarios are: market first, policy first, security first, and sustainability first. Key topics covered include land use, population, biodiversity, climate change and water resources.
Organisation for Economic Co-operation and Development (OECD)	In *Environmental outlook to 2030* (OECD 2008), the organization reviews economic and social developments that will influence environmental changes. Key environmental impacts considered include climate change, biodiversity loss, water scarcity and the health impacts of pollution. The research can help in recommending policies to reduce detrimental environmental impacts.
World Business Council for Sustainable Development (WBCSD)	In *Pathways to 2050: energy and climate change* (WBCSD 2005), the Council identifies megatrends in socio-economic variables and uses them to project to 2050, with 2025 as an intermediate checkpoint. Regional trends are examined in the USA and Canada, China, Japan and the EU. Identified megatrends include: power generation, industry and manufacturing, mobility, buildings and consumer choices.
Intergovernmental Panel on Climate Change (IPCC)	The IPCC undertakes scenario analysis for climate change, socio-economics and the environment, assessing the interactions between socio-economic parameters and greenhouse gas emissions up to 2100. The IPCC Data Distribution Centre (DDC) holds data on population and human development, economic conditions, land use, water, agriculture, energy and biodiversity.
European Environment Agency (EEA)	The *European outlook state and outlook 2010* report (EEA 2010) includes a set of assessments of the current state of Europe's environment, likely future state, effects of global megatrends, and actions needed to reduce detrimental environmental effects. The report primarily focuses on 2020, but scenarios to 2100 are included for climate change and flooding. Another report, *EEA research foresight for environment and sustainability* (EEA 2007), reviews previous forecasting reports and techniques, including: brainstorming, scenarios, emerging issues analysis, forecasts and modelling. It also identifies some key trends, and associated uncertainties.

Source (UK)	Brief summary of content
Department for Food and Rural Affairs (DEFRA)	A DEFRA-commissioned *Baseline scanning project* (Fast Futures 2005) identified trends and emerging issues that could affect the DEFRA work area. Longest term projections were made to 2051 onwards; trends were also prioritised. Key categories and sub categories were: • Social: demographics, values, lifestyles and culture. • Economic: production, labour and trade. • Political: governance, policies, laws and regulations. • Environmental: biosphere, geosphere, atmosphere and hydrosphere. • Science: basic research, technology and health.
Department of Energy and Climate Change (DECC)	A *2050 pathways analysis* (DECC 2010) seeks to illustrate how an 80% reduction in greenhouse gas emissions by 2050 can be achieved. It considers different economic sectors, possible future energy choices and subsequent emissions. It also includes a calculator tool to show impacts of different levels of energy use – with scenarios ranging from' little effort' to 'extremely ambitious'.
Department for Business Innovation and Skills (DBIS)	DBIS and its predecessors have been undertaking foresight projects, since 2002, 'forecasting' for periods of up to 80 years into the future. The projects use expert advice to outline a range of possible outcomes, to assist decision makers. Two recent examples of reports include: • *Land use futures*, February 2010. • *Powering our lives: sustainable energy management and the built environment*, November 2008.
Natural England (NE)	*The state of the natural environment* (NE 2008) highlights existing trends and likely future changes, primarily in terms of biodiversity and landscapes. *Global drivers of change to 2060* (NE 2009) and *England's natural environment in 2060* (NE 2009) include the development of four scenarios of how the world might look in 2060. Topics covered in the scenarios are wide ranging, including: growth and prosperity, global relations, settlements, population and demographics, social structure and cohesion, governance, resource availability, response to climate change, mobility and transport, food and farming, employment skills, pace and direction of innovation, environmental values, and leisure and tourism.
Environment Agency (EA)	The EA website includes an array of environmental information. It also includes information on horizon scanning the future for emerging issues. The EA sees such horizon scanning as different from routine forecasting in that it is predicated on less certain potential changes and risks. For example, whereas 'traditional' climate change forecasting is based largely upon extrapolation of trends, as modified by certain variable, horizon scanning involves methods of divining and examining less predictable effects.

5.2.4 Some current data forecasting sources

Published government and agency documents, plus of course the Internet, provide access to a wide range of sources. Some examples of key international and UK sources are briefly noted in Table 5.3.

5.3 Evaluation

5.3.1 Evaluation in the EIA process

Once impacts have been predicted, there is a need to assess their relative significance to inform decision-makers whether the impacts may be considered acceptable. Criteria for significance include the magnitude and likelihood of the impact and its spatial and temporal extent, the likely degree of the affected environment's recovery, the value of the affected environment, the level of public concern, and political repercussions. As with prediction, the choice of evaluation method should be related to the task in hand and to the resources available. Evaluation should feed into most stages of the EIA process, but the nature of the methods used may vary, for example, according to the number of alternatives under consideration, according to the level of aggregation of information and according to the number and type of stakeholder involved (e.g. 'in-house' and/or 'external' consultation).

Evaluation methods can be of various types, including simple or complex, formal or informal, quantitative or qualitative, aggregated or disaggregated (see Maclaren and Whitney 1985; Voogd 1983). Much, if not most, current evaluation of significance in EIA is simple and often pragmatic, drawing on experience and expert opinion rather than on complex and sophisticated analysis. Table 5.4 provides an example of key factors used in Western Australia, where there is a particularly well-developed EIA system (see Chapter 10 also). To the factors in Table 5.4 could also be added scope for reversibility. The factor of public interest or perception ((h) in Table 5.4) is an important consideration, and past and current perceptions of the significance of particular issues and impacts can raise their profile in the evaluation.

Table 5.4 Determinants of environmental significance

A decision by the (West Australian) EPA (Environmental Protection Authority) as to whether a proposal is likely to have a significant effect on the environment is made using professional judgement, which is gained through knowledge and experience in the application of EIA. In determining whether a proposal is likely to have a significant effect on the environment, the EPA may have regard to the following:

(a) the values, sensitivity and quality of the environment which is likely to be impacted;

(b) the extent (intensity, duration, magnitude and geographic footprint) of the likely impacts;

(c) the consequence of the likely impacts (or change);

(d) resilience of the environment to cope with change;

(e) the cumulative impact with other projects;

(f) level of confidence of the impacts predicted;

(g) objects of the Act, policies, guidelines, procedures and standards against which a proposal can be assessed;

(h) the public concern;

(i) presence of strategic planning policy framework; or

(j) the extent to which other statutory decision-making processes meet the EPA's objectives and principles for EIA.

Source: West Australian Environmental Protection Authority 2010

The most formal evaluation method is the *comparison of likely impacts against legal requirements and standards* (e.g. air quality standards, building regulations). Table 5.5 illustrates some of the standards that may be used to evaluate the traffic noise impacts of projects in Britain. Table 5.6 provides an example of more general guidance on standards and on environmental priorities and preferences, from the European Commission, for tourism developments. Of course, for some type of impacts, including socio-economic, there are no clear-cut standards. Socio-economic impacts provide a good example of 'fuzziness' in assessment, where the line between being significant or not significant extends over a range of values that build on perceptions as much as facts.

Socio-economic impacts do not have recognized standards. There are no easily applicable 'state of local society' standards against which the predicted impacts of a development can be assessed. While a reduction in local unemployment may be regarded as positive, and an increase in local crime as negative, there are no absolute standards. Views on the significance of economic impacts, such as the proportion and types of local employment on

Table 5.5 Examples of standards in relation to impacts of projects on traffic noise in Britain

- BS 7445 is the standard for description and measurement of environmental noise. It is in three parts: Part 1: Guide to quantities and procedures; Part 2: Guide to acquisition of data; and Part 3: Guide to application of noise limits.
- Noise is measured in decibels (dB) at a given frequency. This is an objective measure of sound pressure. Measurements are made using a calibrated sound meter. Human hearing is approximately in the range 0–140 dBA.

  dB Example of noise

  <40 quiet bedroom
  60 busy office
  72 car at 60 km/h at a distance of 7 m
  85 Heavy goods vehicle (HGV) at 40 km/h at a distance of 7 m
  90 hazardous to hearing from continuous exposure
  105 jet flying overhead at 250 m
  120 threshold of pain

- Traffic noise is perceived as a nuisance even at low dB levels. Noise comes from tyres on the road, engines, exhausts, brakes and HGV bodies. Poor maintenance of roads and vehicles and poor driving also increase road noise. Higher volumes of traffic and higher proportions of HGVs increase the noise levels. In general, annoyance is proportional to traffic flow for noise levels above 55 dB(A). People are sensitive to a change in noise levels of 1 dB (about 25% change in flow).
- Assessment of traffic noise is assessed in terms of impacts within 300 m of the road. The EIA will estimate the number of properties and relevant locations (e.g. footpaths and sports fields) in bands of distance from the route: 0–50 m, 50–100 m, 100–200 m, 200–300 m, and then classify each group according to the baseline ambient noise levels (in bands of <50, 50–60, 60–70, >70 dB(A)) and the increase in noise (1–3, 3–5, 5–10, 10–15 and >15 dB(A)).
- Façade noise levels are measured at 1.7 m above ground, 1 m from façade or 10 m from kerb, and are usually predicted using the Department of Transport's Calculation of road traffic noise (CRTN), which measures dB(A) $L_{A10,18h}$. This is the noise level exceeded 10% of the time between 6:00 and 24:00. Noise levels at the façade are approximately 2 dB higher than 10 m from the building. PPG 13 uses dB(A) $L_{Aeq,16h}$. This is between 7:00 and 23:00. Most traffic noise meters use dB(A) L_{A10}, and an approximate conversion is:

  $$L_{Aeq,16h} = L_{A10,18h} - 2dB.$$

- The DTP recommends an absolute upper limit for noise of 72 dB(A) $L_{eq,18h}$ (= 70 dB(A) $L_{A10,18h}$) for residential properties. Compensation is payable to properties within 300 m of a road development for increases greater than 1 dB(A) which result in $L_{A10,18h}$ above 67.5.
- The DTP considers a change of 30% slight, 60% moderate and 90% substantial. PPG 13 considers 5% to be significant.
- There are four categories of noise in residential areas:

Day (16 h)	*Night* (8 h) A <55 L_{Aeq} <42 L_{Aeq}	Not determining the application
B 55–63 L_{Aeq}	<42–57 L_{Aeq}	Noise control measures are required
C 63–72 L_{Aeq}	57–66 L_{Aeq}	Strong presumption against developer
D >72 L_{Aeq}	>66 L_{Aeq}	Normally refuse the application

  For night-time noise, unless the noise is already in category D, a single event occurring regularly (e.g. HGV movements) where L_{Aeq} >82dB puts the noise in category C.

Source: Bourdillon 1996

a project, are often political and arbitrary. Nevertheless it is sometimes possible to identify what might be termed *threshold or step changes* in the socio-economic profile of an area. For example, it may be possible to identify predicted impacts that threaten to swamp the local labour market, and that may produce a 'boom–bust' scenario. It may also be possible to identify likely high levels of leakage of anticipated benefits out of a locality, which may be equally unacceptable. It is valuable if the practitioner can identify possible criteria used in the analysis for a range of levels of impacts, which at least provides the basis for informed debate. Table 5.7 provides an example assessing impact magnitude from nuclear power station projects.

Table 5.6 Example of EC guidance on assessing significance of impacts for tourism projects for Asian, Caribbean and Pacific countries

The significance of certain environmental impacts can be assessed by contrasting the predicted magnitude of impact against a relevant environmental standard or value. For tourism projects in particular, impact significance should also be assessed by taking due regard of those environmental priorities and preferences held by society but for which there are no quantifiable objectives. Particular attention needs to be focused upon the environmental preferences and concerns of those likely to be directly affected by the project.

Environmental Standards

- Water quality standards
  - potable water supplies (*apply country standards; see also Section 1.3.2, WHO (1982) Guidelines for Drinking Water Quality Directives 80/778/EEC and 75/440/EEC*)
  - wastewater discharge (apply country standards for wastewaters and fisheries; see also 76/160/EEC and 78/659/EEC)
- National and local planning regulations
  - legislation concerning change in land use
  - regional/local land-use plans (particularly management plans for protected areas and coastal zones)
- National legislation to protect certain areas
  - national parks
  - forest reserves
  - nature reserves
  - natural, historical or cultural sites of importance
- International agreements to protect certain areas
  - World Heritage Convention
  - Ramsar Convention on wetlands
- Conservation/preservation of species likely to be sold to tourists or harmed by their activities
  - national legislation
  - international conventions
  - CITES (Convention on International Trade in Endangered Species).

Environmental Priorities and Preferences

- Participation of affected people in project planning to determine priorities for environmental protection, including:
  - public health
  - revered areas, flora and fauna (e.g. cultural/medicinal value, visual landscape)
  - skills training to undertake local environmental mitigation measures
  - protection of potable water supply
  - conservation of wetland/tropical forest services and products, e.g. hunted wildlife, fish stocks
  - issues of sustainable income generation and employment (including significance of gender – *see WID manual*)
- Government policies for environmental protection (including, where appropriate, incorporation of objectives from country environmental studies/environmental action plans, etc.)
- Environmental priorities of tourism boards and trade associations representing tour operators

Source: CEC 1993

Socio-economic impacts can raise in particular the distributional dimension to evaluation, 'who wins and who loses' (Glasson 2009; Vanclay 1999). Beyond the use of standards and legal requirements, all assessments of significance either implicitly or explicitly apply weights to the various impacts (i.e. some are assessed as more important than others). This involves interpretation and the application of judgement. Such judgement can be rationalized in various ways and a range of methods are available, but all involve values and all are subjective. Parkin (1992) sees judgements as being on a continuum between an analytical mode and an intuitive mode. In practice, many are at the intuitive end of the continuum, but such judgements, made without the benefit of analysis, are likely to be flawed, inconsistent and biased. The 'social effects of resource allocation decisions are too extensive to allow the decision to "emerge" from some opaque procedure free of overt political

Table 5.7 Example of an approach to assessing the local impact magnitude of a major energy project: socio-economic impacts dimension

Type of impact	Local context	Negligible impact	Minor impact	Moderate impact	Major impact
Demographic impacts					
Change in local population level	Population growth (2001 to 2009):	Change in local population of less than ± 0.25%	Change in local population of ± 0.25–1%	Change in local population of ± 1–2%	Change in local population of more than ± 2%
Direct and indirect employment impacts					
Change in employment level in local economy	Employment growth (ABI estimates 2001to 2007):	Change of less than ± 0.25% on baseline employment levels in the local economy	Change of ± 0.25–1% on baseline employment levels in the local economy	Change of ± 1–2% on baseline employment levels in the local economy	Change of more than ± 2% on baseline employment levels in local economy
Change in unemployment level in local economy	Claimant % unemployment rates (June 2010):	Change of less than ± 2% in claimant unemployment level	Change of ± 2–5% in claimant unemployment level	Change of ± 5–10% in claimant unemployment level	Change of more than ± 10% in claimant unemployment level
Accommodation pressures and development					
Change in stock of local housing	Housing stock growth (2001 to 2008)	Change of less than ± 0.25% on baseline housing stock	Change of ± 0.25–1% on baseline housing stock	Change of ± 1–2% on baseline housing stock	Change of more than ± 2% on baseline housing stock

Source: Authors, drawing on various consultancy studies

scrutiny' (Parkin 1992). Analytical methods seek to introduce a rational approach to evaluation.

Two sets of methods are distinguished: those that assume a common utilitarian ethic with a single evaluation criterion (money), and those based on the measurement of personal utilities, including multiple criteria. The CBA approach, which seeks to express impacts in monetary units, falls into the former category. A variety of methods, including *multi-criteria analysis, decision analysis,* and *goals achievement,* fall into the latter category. The very growth of EIA is partly a response to the limitations of CBA and to the problems of the monetary valuation of environmental impacts. Yet, after several decades of limited concern, there is renewed interest in the monetizing of environmental costs and benefits (DoE 1991; HM Treasury 2003). The multi-criteria/multi-attribute methods involve scoring and weighting systems that are also not problem-free. The various approaches are now outlined. In practice, there are many hybrid variations between these two main categories, and these are referred to in both categories.

5.3.2 Cost–benefit analysis and monetary valuation techniques

Cost–benefit analysis (CBA) itself lies in a range of project and plan appraisal methods that seek to apply monetary values to costs and benefits (Lichfield *et al.* 1975). At one extreme are *partial* approaches, such as financial-appraisal, cost-minimization and cost-effectiveness methods, which consider only a subsection of the relevant population or only a subsection of the full range of consequences of a plan or project. *Financial appraisal* is limited to a narrow concern, usually of the developer, with the stream of financial costs and returns associated with an investment. *Cost effectiveness* involves selecting an option that achieves a goal at least cost (for example, devising a least cost approach to produce coastal bathing waters that meet the CEC Blue Flag criteria). The cost-effectiveness approach is more problematic where there are a number of goals and where some actions achieve certain goals more fully than others (Winpenny 1991).

Cost–benefit analysis is more *comprehensive* in scope. It takes a long view of projects (farther as well as nearer future) and a wide view (in the sense of allowing for side effects). It is based in welfare economics and seeks to include all the relevant costs and benefits to evaluate the net social benefit of a project. It was used extensively in the UK in the 1960s and early 1970s for public sector projects, the most famous being the third London Airport (HMSO 1971). The methodology of CBA has several stages: project definition, the identification and enumeration of costs and benefits, the evaluation of costs and benefits, and the discounting and presentation of results. Several of the stages are similar to those in EIA. The basic evaluation principle is to measure in monetary terms where possible – as money is the common measure of value and monetary values are best understood by the community and decision-makers – and then reduce all costs and benefits to the same capital or annual basis. Future annual flows of costs and benefits are usually discounted to a net present value (Table 5.8). A range of interest rates may be used to show the sensitivity of the analysis to changes. If the net social benefit minus cost is positive, then there may be a presumption in favour of a project. However, the final outcome may not always be that clear. The presentation of results should distinguish between tangible and intangible costs and benefits, as relevant, allowing the decision-maker to consider the trade-offs involved in the choice of an option.

Cost–benefit analysis has excited both advocates (e.g. Dasgupta and Pearce 1978; Pearce 1989; Pearce *et al.* 1989) and opponents (e.g. Bowers 1990). Hanley and Splash (2003) provide an interesting review of CBA and the environment. CBA does have many problems, including identifying, enumerating and monetizing intangibles. Many environmental impacts fall into the intangible category, for example the loss of a rare species, the urbanization of a rural landscape and the saving of a human life. The incompatibility of monetary and non-monetary units makes decision-making

Table 5.8 Cost-benefit analysis: presentation of results – tangibles and intangibles

Category	Alternative 1	Alternative 2
Tangibles		
Annual benefits	£B1	£b1
	£B2	£b2
	£B3	£b3
Total annual benefits	£B1 + B2 + B3	£b1 + b2 + b3
Annual costs	£C1	£c1
	£C2	£c2
	£C3	£c3
Total annual costs	£C1 + C2 + C3	£c1 + c2 + c3
Net discounted present value (NDPV) of benefits and costs over '*m*' years at X%*	£D	£E
Intangibles		
Intangibles are likely to include costs and benefits	I1	i1
	I2	i2
	I3	i3
	I4	i4
Intangibles summation (undiscounted)	I1 + I2 + I3 + I4	i1 + i2 + i3 + i4

*e.g NPDV (Alt 1)

$$D = \sum \left[\frac{B1}{(1+X)^1} + \frac{B1}{(1+X)^2} + \ldots + \frac{B1}{(1+X)^n} + \frac{B2}{(1+X)^1} + \ldots + \frac{B2}{(1+X)^n} + \frac{B3}{(1+X)^1} + \ldots + \frac{B3}{(1+X)^n} \right]$$

$$- \sum \left[\frac{C1}{(1+X)^1} + \frac{C1}{(1+X)^2} + \ldots + \frac{C1}{(1+X)^n} + \frac{C2}{(1+X)^1} + \ldots + \frac{C2}{(1+X)^n} + \frac{C3}{(1+X)^1} + \ldots + \frac{C3}{(1+X)^n} \right]$$

problematic (Bateman 1991). Another problem is the choice of discount rate: for example, should a very low rate be used to prevent the rapid erosion of future costs and benefits in the analysis? This choice of rate has profound implications for the evaluation of resources for future generations. There is also the underlying and fundamental problem of the use of the single evaluation criterion of money, and the assumption that £1 is worth the same to any person, whether a tramp or a millionaire, a resident of a rich commuter belt or of a poor and remote rural community. CBA also ignores distribution effects and aggregates costs and benefits to estimate the change in the welfare of society as a whole.

The *planning balance sheet* (PBS) is a variation on the theme of CBA, and it goes beyond CBA in its attempts to identify, enumerate and evaluate the distribution of costs and benefits between the affected parties. It also acknowledges the difficulty of attempts to monetize the more intangible impacts. It was developed by Lichfield *et al.* (1975) to compare alternative town plans. PBS is basically a set of social accounts structured into sets of 'producers' and 'consumers' engaged in various transactions. The transaction could, for example, be an adverse impact, such as noise from an airport (the producer) on the local community (the consumers), or a beneficial impact, such as the time savings resulting from a new motorway development (the producer) for users of the motorway (the consumers). For each producer and consumer group, costs and benefits are quantified per transaction, in monetary terms or otherwise, and weighted according to the numbers involved. The findings are presented in tabular form, leaving the decision-maker to consider the trade-offs, but this time with some guidance on the distributional impacts of the options under consideration (Figure 5.7). Subsequently, Lichfield (1996) sought to integrate EIA and PBS further in an approach he called *community impact evaluation* (CIE).

Partly in response to the 'intangibles' problem in CBA, there has also been considerable interest in the development of *monetary valuation techniques* to improve the economic measurement of the more intangible environmental impacts (Barde and Pearce 1991; DoE 1991; Winpenny 1991, Hanley and Splash 2003). The techniques can be broadly classified into direct and indirect, and they are concerned with the measurement of preferences about the environment rather than with the intrinsic values of the environment. The direct approaches seek to measure directly the monetary value of environmental gains – for example, better air quality or an improved scenic view. Indirect approaches measure preferences for a particular effect via the establishment of a 'dose–response'-type relationship. The various techniques found under the direct and indirect categories are summarized in Table 5.9. Such techniques can contribute to the assessment of the total economic value of an action or project, which should not only include user values (preferences people have for using an environmental asset, such as a river for fishing) but also non-user values (where people value an asset but do not use it, although some may wish to do so some day). Of course, such techniques have their problems, for example the potential bias in people's replies in the contingent valuation method (CVM) approach (for a fascinating example of this, see Willis and Powe 1998).

	Plan A				Plan A			
	Benefits		Costs		Benefits		Costs	
	Capital	Annual	Capital	Annual	Capital	Annual	Capital	Annual
Producers								
X	£a	£b	–	£d	–	–	£b	£c
Y	i_1	i_2	–	–	i_3	i_4	–	–
Z	M_1	–	M_2	–	M_3	–	M_4	–
Consumers								
X′	–	£e	–	£f	–	£g	–	£h
Y′	i_5	i_6	–	–	i_7	i_8	–	–
Z′	M_1	–	M_3	–	M_2	–	M_4	–

£ = benefits and costs that can be monetized
M = where only a ranking of monetary values can be estimated
i = intangibles

Figure 5.7

Example of structure of a planning balance sheet (PBS)

Table 5.9 Summary of environmental monetary valuation techniques

Direct household production function (HPF)

HPF methods seek to determine expenditure on commodities that are substitutes or complements for an environmental characteristic to value changes in that characteristic. Subtypes include the following:

1 Avertive expenditures: expenditure on various substitutes for environmental change (e.g. noise insulation as an estimate of the value of peace and quiet).
2 Travel cost method: expenditure, in terms of cost and time, incurred in travelling to a particular location (e.g. a recreation site) is taken as an estimate of the value placed on the environmental good at that location (e.g. benefit arising from use of the site).

Direct hedonic price methods (HPM)

HPM methods seek to estimate the implicit price for environmental attributes by examining the real markets in which those attributes are traded. Again, there are two main subtypes:

1 Hedonic house land prices: these prices are used to value characteristics such as 'clean air' and 'peace and quiet', through cross-sectional data analysis (e.g. on house price sales in different locations).
2 Wage risk premia: the extra payments associated with certain higher risk occupations are used to value changes in morbidity and mortality (and implicitly human life) associated with such occupations.

Direct experimental markets

Survey methods are used to elicit individual values for non-market goods. Experimental markets are created to discover how people would value certain environmental changes. Two kinds of questioning, of a sample of the population, may be used:

1 Contingent valuation method (CVM): people are asked what they are willing to pay (WTP) for keeping X (e.g. a good view, a historic building) or preventing Y, or what they are willing to accept (WTA) for losing A, or tolerating B.
2 Contingent ranking method (CRM or stated preference): people are asked to rank their preferences for various environmental goods, which may then be valued by linking the preferences to the real price of something traded in the market (e.g. house prices).

Indirect methods

Indirect methods seek to establish preferences through the estimation of relationships between a 'dose' (e.g. reduction in air pollution) and a response (e.g. health improvement). Approaches include the following:

1 Indirect market price approach: the dose–response approach seeks to measure the effect (e.g. value of loss of fish stock) resulting from an environmental change (e.g. oil pollution of a fish farm), by using the market value of the output involved. The replacement-cost approach uses the cost of replacing or restoring a damaged asset as a measure of the benefit of restoration (e.g. of an old stone bridge eroded by pollution and wear and tear).
2 Effect on production approach: where a market exists for the goods and services involved, the environmental impact can be represented by the value of the change in output that it causes. It is widely used in developing countries, and is a continuation of the dose–response approach.

Sources: Adapted from DoE 1991; Winpenny 1991; Pearce and Markandya 1990; Barde and Pearce 1991; Nijkamp 2004

However, simply through the act of seeking a value for various environmental features, such techniques help to reinforce the understanding that such features are not 'free' goods and should not be treated as such.

5.3.3 Scoring and weighting and multi-criteria methods

Multi-criteria and multi-attribute methods seek to overcome some of the deficiencies of CBA; in particular they seek to allow for a pluralist view of society, composed of diverse 'stakeholders' with diverse goals and with differing values concerning environmental changes. Most of the methods use – and sometimes misuse – some kind of simple scoring and weighting system; such systems generate considerable debate. Here we discuss some key elements of good practice, and then offer a brief overview of the range of multi-criteria/multi-attribute methods available to the analyst.

Scoring may use quantitative or qualitative scales, according to the availability of information on the impact under consideration. Lee (1987)

provides an example (Table 5.10) of how different levels of impact (in this example noise, whose measurement is in units of $L_{10}dB_A$) can be scored in different systems. These systems seek to standardize the impact scores for purposes of comparison. Where quantitative data are not available, ranking of alternatives may use other approaches, for example using letters (A, B, C, etc.) or words (not significant, significant, and very significant).

Weighting seeks to identify the relative importance of the various impact types for which scores of some sort may be available (for example, the relative importance of a water pollution impact, the impact on a rare flower). Different impacts may be allocated weights (normally numbers) out of a total budget (e.g. 10 points to be allocated between 3 impacts) – but by whom?

Multi-criteria/multi-attribute methods seek to recognize the plurality of views and weights in their methods; the Delphi approach also uses individuals' weights, from which group weights are then derived. In many studies, however, the weights are those produced by the technical team. Indeed the various stakeholders may be unwilling to reveal all their personal preferences, for fear of undermining their negotiating positions. This internalization of the weighting exercise does not destroy the use of weights, but it does emphasize the need for clarification of scoring and weighting systems and, in particular, for the identification of the origin of the weightings used in an EIA. Wherever possible, scoring and weighting should be used to reveal the trade-offs in impacts involved in particular projects or in alternatives. For example,

Table 5.11 shows that the main issue is the trade-off between the impact on flora of one scheme and the impact on noise of the other scheme.

Several approaches to the scoring and weighting of impacts have already been introduced in the outline of impact identification methods in Chapter 4. The matrix approach can also be usefully modified to identify the distribution of impacts among geographical areas and/or among various affected parties (Figure 5.8). Weightings can also be built into overlay maps to identify areas with the most development potential according to various combinations of weightings. Some of the limitations of such approaches have already been noted in Chapter 4.

Other methods in the multi-criteria/multi-attribute category include decision analysis, the goals achievement matrix (GAM), multi-attribute utility theory (MAUT) and judgement analysis. *Multi-criteria decision analysis* (MCDA) techniques have emerged as a major approach for resolving natural resource management problems (Herath and Prato 2006; DCLG 2009), and are becoming increasingly used in EIA, especially for major projects. MCDA is a tool that is particularly applicable to cases where a single criterion approach is inappropriate. It allows decision makers to integrate the environmental, social and economic values and preferences of stakeholders, while overcoming the difficulties in monetizing the more intangible non-monetary attributes. Typically the approach defines objectives, chooses the criteria to measure the objectives, specifies alternatives, transforms the criterion scales into units, weights

Table 5.10 A comparison of different scoring systems

Method	Alternatives				Basis of score
	A (no action)	B	C	D	
Ratio	65		62	71	75	Absolute $L_{10}dB_A$ measure
Interval	0		−3	+6	+10	Difference in $L_{10}dB_A$ using alternative A as base
Ordinal	B		A	C	D	Ranking according to ascending value of $L_{10}dB_A$
Binary	0		0	1	1	0 = less than $70L_{10}dB_A$ 1 = $70L_{10}dB_A$ or more

Source: Based on Lee 1987

Table 5.11 Weighting, scoring and trade-offs

Impact	Weight (w)	Scheme A		Scheme B	
		Score (a)	(aw)	Score (b)	(bw)
Noise	2	5	10	1	2
Loss of flora	5	1	5	4	20
Air pollution	3	2	6	2	6
Total			21		28

Figure 5.8

Simple matrix
identification of
distribution of impacts

Group environmental component	Project Action							
	Construction stage actions				Operational stage actions			
	A	B	C	D	a	b	c	d
Group 1 (e.g. indigenous population ≥ 45 years old) various • Social • Physical • Economic components								
Group 2 (e.g. indigenous population < 45 years old) various • Social • Physical • Economic components								

the criteria to reflect relative importance, selects and applies a mathematical algorithm for ranking alternatives, and chooses alternatives. The evaluation can use a variety of quantitative/semi-quantitative and qualitative assessment, and survey methods (Figueira *et al.* 2005). The former applies metrics to the selected criteria, which allows the calculation of outcomes as noted above. The latter, qualitative approach, uses subjective judgements and rating methods; there are no numbers used, and hence no calculations. In summary, both have their strengths. Quantitative/semi-quantitative tools are systematic, repeatable and inputs and outputs can be verified. Qualitative tools are effective at capturing diverse information, particularly intangible information and insights; while they are less repeatable, they provide narratives to explain results.

While MCDA can be quite complex, it can also be presented in very simple summary fashion, which can be very appealing to decision makers – but such presentations can also oversimplify the issues and trade-offs involved. A familiar approach is the use of a traffic lights colour approach (green – positive; amber – neutral; red – negative), indicating the extent to which the specified alternatives satisfy the various environmental, social and economic objectives. Figure 5.9 provides a schematic example of a summary matrix for a qualitative MCDA (with 5 shadings from deep red to deep green), for alternative locations for a major project. Some of the key elements, and

issues, are set out in the figure. The red shadings indicate a more disadvantageous option performance against the relevant criterion/objective; the green shadings indicate more advantageous option performance. In this example, project option 3 is the preferred option by virtue of the spread of good overall performance against the QBL criteria.

The GAM was developed as a planning tool by Hill (1968) to overcome the perceived weaknesses of the PBS approach. GAM makes the goals and objectives of a project/plan explicit, and the evaluation of alternatives is accomplished by measuring the extent to which they achieve the stated goals. The existence of many diverse goals leads to a system of weights. Since all interested parties are not politically equal, the identified groups should also be weighted. The end result is a matrix of weighted objectives and weighted interests/agencies (Figure 5.10). The use of goals and value weights to evaluate plans in the interests of the community, and not just for economic efficiency, has much to commend it. The approach also provides an opportunity for public participation. Unfortunately, the complexity of the approach has limited its use, and the weights and goals used may often reflect the views of the analyst more than those of the interests and agencies involved.

Finally, brief reference is made to the *Delphi method*, which provides another way of incorporating the views of various stakeholders into the

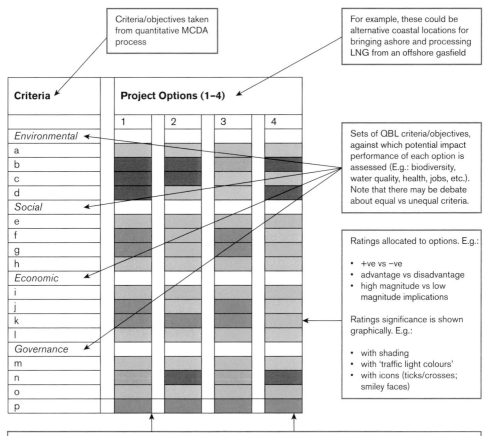

Figure 5.9

Schematic example of a summary matrix for a qualitative MCDA

Text within the figure:

Criteria/objectives taken from quantitative MCDA process

For example, these could be alternative coastal locations for bringing ashore and processing LNG from an offshore gasfield

Criteria

Project Options (1–4)

| | 1 | 2 | 3 | 4 |

Environmental
a
b
c
d
Social
e
f
g
h
Economic
i
j
k
l
Governance
m
n
o
p

Sets of QBL criteria/objectives, against which potential impact performance of each option is assessed (E.g.: biodiversity, water quality, health, jobs, etc.). Note that there may be debate about equal vs unequal criteria.

Ratings allocated to options. E.g.:

- +ve vs −ve
- advantage vs disadvantage
- high magnitude vs low magnitude implications

Ratings significance is shown graphically. E.g.:

- with shading
- with 'traffic light colours'
- with icons (ticks/crosses; smiley faces)

- The ratings are undertaken in turn with explanations provided by the technical team to help inform participants, who will not have technical knowledge in all areas of the MCDA process
- A more sophisticated approach would rate impact performance for each option, for each stage in the project life-cycle, especially for construction, operation and decommissioning (with each of the above project option columns having construction/operation/decommissioning subsections).
- The degree to which a criterion is considered advantageous or disadvantageous for a given location is entirely subjective, based on best technical and non-technical judgement as appropriate.
- The process is repeated for each location. It is acceptable to scan the judgements made for other locations; this can provide a 'reality check' and can help keep a consistent relative level of judgement.
- The final comparison of the relative merits of all locations is made and explained in narrative form, rather than a quantification of matrix results, although limited notional summing of the overall mix of judgements awarded may be used to assist the narrative with supporting logic.

evaluation process. The method is an established means of collecting expert opinion and of gaining consensus among experts on various issues under consideration. It has the advantage of obtaining expert opinion from the individual, with guaranteed anonymity, avoiding the potential distortion caused by peer pressure in group situations. Compared with other evaluation methods it can also be quicker and cheaper.

There have been a number of interesting applications of the Delphi method in EIA (Green et al. 1989, 1990; Richey et al. 1985). Green et al. used the approach to assess the environmental impacts of the redevelopment and reorientation of Bradford's famous Salt Mill. The method involved drawing up a Delphi panel; in the Salt Mill case, the initial panel of 40 included experts with a working knowledge of the project (e.g. planners,

Figure 5.10

Goals achievement
matrix (GAM)

Source: Adapted from
Hill 1968

Goal description: Relative weight:			α 2			β 3
Incidence	Relative weight	Costs	Benefits	Relative weight	Costs	Benefits
Group a	1	A	D	5	E	1
Group b	3	H	J	4	M	2
Group c	1	L	J	3	M	3
Group d	2	–	J	2	V	4
Group e	1	–	K	1	T	5
		Σ	Σ	Σ	Σ	

tourism officers), councillors, employees, academics, local residents and traders. This was designed to provide a balanced view of interests and expertise. The Delphi exercise usually has a three-stage approach: (1) a general questionnaire asking panel members to identify important impacts (positive and negative); (2) a first-round questionnaire asking panel members to rate the importance of a list of impacts identified from the first stage; and (3) a second-round questionnaire asking panel members to re-evaluate the importance of each impact in the light of the panel's response to the first round. However, the method is not without its limitations. The potential user should be aware that it is difficult to draw up a 'balanced' panel in the first place, and to avoid distorting the assessment by the varying drop-out rates of panel members between stages of the exercise, and by an overzealous structuring of the exercise by the organizers. For other application and critique, see Breidenhann and Butts (2006), and Landeta (2006).

• •

5.4 Mitigation and enhancement

5.4.1 Types of mitigation measures

Mitigation is defined in EC Directive 97/11 as 'measures envisaged in order to avoid, reduce and, if possible, remedy significant adverse effects' (CEC 1997). In similar vein, the US CEQ, in its regulations implementing the NEPA, defines mitigation as including:

> not taking certain actions; limiting the proposed action and its implementation;

repairing, rehabilitating, or restoring the affected environment; presentation and maintenance actions during the life of the action; and replacing or providing substitute resources or environments. (CEQ 1978)

The guidance on mitigation measures provided by the UK government is set out in Table 5.12. It is not possible to specify here all the types of mitigation measures that could be used. Instead, the following text provides a few examples, relating to biophysical and socio-economic impacts. The reader is also referred to Morris and Therivel (2009) and Rodriguez-Bachiller with Glasson (2004) for useful coverage of mitigation measures for particular impact types. A review of EISs for developments similar to the development under consideration may also suggest useful mitigation measures.

At one extreme, the prediction and evaluation of impacts may reveal an array of impacts with such significant adverse effects that the only effective mitigation measure may be to abandon the proposal altogether. A less draconian (and more normal) situation would be to modify aspects of the development action to avoid various impacts. Examples of methods to *avoid* impacts include:

• The control of solid and liquid wastes by recycling on site or by removing them from the site for environmentally sensitive treatment elsewhere.
• The use of a designated lorry route, and daytime working only, to avoid disturbance to village communities from construction lorry traffic and from night construction work.

Table 5.12 Mitigation measures, as outlined in *UK guide to procedures*

Where significant adverse effects are identified, [describe] the measures to be taken to avoid, reduce or remedy those effects, e.g:

(a) site planning;
(b) technical measures, e.g.:
  (i)   process selection;
  (ii)   recycling;
  (iii) pollution control and treatment;
  (iv)   containment (e.g. bunding of storage vessels).
(c) aesthetic and ecological measures, e.g.:
  (i)   mounding;
  (ii)   design, colour, etc.;
  (iii) landscaping;
  (iv)   tree plantings;
  (v)   measure to preserve particular habitats or create alternative habitats;
  (vi)   recording of archaeological sites;
  (vii) measures to safeguard historic buildings or sites.

[Assess] the likely effectiveness of mitigating measures.

Source: DETR 2000

- The establishment of buffer zones and the minimal use of toxic substances, to avoid impacts on local ecosystems.

Some adverse effects may be less easily avoided; there may also be less need to avoid them completely. Examples of methods to *reduce* adverse effects include:

- The sensitive design of structures, using simple profiles, local materials and muted colours, to reduce the visual impact of a development, and landscaping to hide it or blend it into the local environment.
- The use of construction-site hostels, and coaches for journeys to work to reduce the impact on the local housing market, and on the roads, of a project employing many workers during its construction stage.
- The use of silting basins or traps, the planting of temporary cover crops and the scheduling of activities during the dry months, to reduce erosion and sedimentation.

During one or more stages of the life of a project, certain environmental components may be temporarily lost or damaged. It may be possible to *repair*, *rehabilitate* or *restore* the affected component to varying degrees. For example:

- Agricultural land used for the storage of materials during construction may be fully rehabilitated; land used for gravel extraction may be restored to agricultural use, but over a much longer period and with associated impacts according to the nature of the landfill material used.
- A river or stream diverted by a road project can be unconverted and re-established with similar flow patterns as far as is possible.
- A local community astride a route to a new tourism facility could be relieved of much of the adverse traffic effects by the construction of a bypass (which, of course, introduces a new flow of impacts).

There will invariably be some adverse effects that cannot be reduced. In such cases, it may be necessary to *compensate* people for adverse effects. For example:

- For the loss of public recreational space or a wildlife habitat, the provision of land with recreation facilities or the creation of a nature reserve elsewhere.
- For the loss of privacy, quietness and safety in houses next to a new road, the provision of sound insulation and/or the purchase by the developer of badly affected properties.

Mitigation measures can become linked with discussions between a developer and the local planning authority (LPA) on what is known in the UK as 'planning gain'. Fortlage (1990) talks of some of the potential complications associated with such discussions, and of the need to distinguish between mitigation measures and planning gain:

Before any mitigating measures are put forward, the developer and the local planning authority must agrcc as to which effects are to be regarded as adverse, or sufficiently adverse to warrant the expense of remedial work, otherwise the whole exercise becomes a bargaining game which is likely to be unprofitable to both parties . . .

Planning permission often includes conditions requiring the provision of planning gains by the developer to offset some deterioration of the area caused by the development, but it is essential to distinguish very clearly between those benefits offered by way of compensation for adverse environmental effects and those which are a formal part of planning consent. The local planning authority may decide to formulate the compensation proposals as a planning condition in order to ensure that they are carried out, so the developer should beware of putting forward proposals that he does not really intend to implement.

Mitigation measures must be planned in an integrated and coherent fashion to ensure that they are effective, that they do not conflict with each other and that they do not merely shift a problem from one medium to another. The results of a research project on the treatment of mitigation within EIA (DETR 1997) found that UK practice varied considerably. For example, there was too much emphasis on physical measures, rather than on operational or management controls, and a lack of attention to the impacts of construction and to residual impacts after mitigation.

Table 5.13 provides a wider classification of mitigation, adopted in the project, by levels of mitigation, mitigation hierarchy and project phase. The levels relate to broad decisions that are made during the design of a project, with the last two reflecting the fact that effective mitigation can be achieved through measures other than physical ones. The *mitigation hierarchy* focuses on the principle of prevention rather than cure where, in principle at least, the options higher in the list

should be tried before those lower down the list. The project phases relate to the life cycle of the project first discussed in Chapter 1. Any particular mitigation measure can be classified in a combination of the three ways – for example, physical design measures can be used to minimize an impact at source, during the construction phase (DETR 1997).

5.4.2 Mitigation in the EIA process

Like many elements in the EIA process, and as noted in Table 5.13, mitigation is not limited to one point in the assessment. Although it may follow logically from the prediction and assessment of the relative significance of impacts, it is in fact inherent in all aspects of the process. An original project design may already have been modified, possibly in the light of mitigation changes made to earlier comparable projects or perhaps as a result of early consultation with the LPA or with the local community. The consideration of alternatives, initial scoping activities, baseline studies and impact identification studies may suggest further mitigation measures. Although more in-depth studies may identify new impacts, mitigation measures may alleviate others. The prediction and evaluation exercise can thus focus on a limited range of potential impacts.

Mitigation measures are normally discussed and documented in each topic section of the EIS (e.g. air quality, visual quality, transport, employment). Those discussions should clarify the extent to which the significance of each adverse impact has been offset by the mitigation measures proposed. A summary chart (Table 5.14) can provide a clear and very useful overview of the envisaged outcomes, and may be a useful basis for agreement

Table 5.13 A wider classification of mitigation

Levels of mitigation	Mitigation hierarchy	Project phase
• Alternatives (strategic, alternative locations and processes) • Physical design measures • Project management measures • Deferred mitigation	• Avoidance at source • Minimize at source • Abatement on site • Abatement at receptor • Repair • Compensation in kind • Other compensation and enhancement	• Construction • Commissioning • Operation • Decommissioning • Restoration, afteruse/aftercare

Source: DETR 1997

Table 5.14 Example of a section of a summary table for impacts and mitigation measures

Impact	Mitigation measure(s)	Level of significance after mitigation
1. 400 acres of prime agricultural land would be lost from the county to accommodate the petrochemical plant.	The only full mitigating measure for this impact would be to abandon the project.	Significant unavoidable impact
2. Additional lorry and car traffic on the adjacent hilly section of the motorway will increase traffic volumes by 10–20 per cent above those predicted on the basis of current trends.	A lorry crawler lane on the motorway, funded by the developer, will help to spread the volume, but effects may be partial and short-lived.	Significant unavoidable impact
3. The project would block the movement of most terrestrial species from the hilly areas to the east of the site to the wetlands to the west of the site.	A wildlife corridor should be developed and maintained along the entire length of the existing stream which runs through the site. The width of the corridor should be a minimum of 75 ft. The stream bed should be cleaned of silt and enhanced through the construction of occasional pools. The buffer zone should be planted with native riparian vegetation, including sycamore and willow.	Less than significant impact

on planning consents. Residual unmitigated or only partially mitigated impacts should be identified. These could be divided according to the degree of severity: for example, into 'less than significant impacts' and 'significant unavoidable impacts'.

Mitigation measures are of little or no value unless they are implemented. Commitment to mitigation can be demonstrated through implementation or management plans. These may take the form of an all-encompassing Environmental Management Plan (EMP) or Environmental Action Plan (EAP) (see Chapter 12); they may also include more specific sub-plans for particular impact types – see for example the following section for workforce and procurement plans to deliver socio-economic benefits. There is also a clear link between mitigation and the monitoring of outcomes, when a project is approved and moves to the construction and operational stages. Indeed, the incorporation of a clear monitoring programme can be one of the most important mitigation measures. Monitoring, which is discussed in Chapter 7, must include the effectiveness or otherwise of mitigation and enhancement measures. The measures must therefore be devised with monitoring in mind; they must be clear enough to allow for the checking of effectiveness. The use

of particular mitigation measures may also draw on previous experience of relative effectiveness, from previous monitoring activity in other relevant and comparable cases.

5.4.3 Enhancement of potential benefits

UK guidance (DETR 1997) also notes the importance of including measures in EIA to create environmental benefits. Benefit enhancement is becoming an increasingly important element in EIA, especially for major projects. Such enhancements can include biophysical actions – for example creating a nature reserve from an abandoned quarry that lies adjacent to a project site and which has been acquired by the developer. However they tend to be more often socio-economic actions related to socio-economic issues. A project may bring considerable benefit to an area, often socio-economically; where such benefits are identified, as a minimum there should be a concern to ensure that they do occur and do not become diluted, and that they may be enhanced. For example:

- The potential local employment benefits of a project can be encouraged and enhanced by the offer of appropriate skills training programmes, apprenticeships, plus a 'one-stop-shop' local recruitment facility. For the construction stage of a project, this might be brought together in a Construction Workforce Management Plan, developed between the developer and key local stakeholders. The implementation of such a plan, with clear indicators and targets, can provide an important means of internalising employment benefits to the project host area, reducing employment benefit leakage often associated with major projects.

- Similarly, a procurement management plan could help to enhance opportunities for local contractors to benefit from a project. It could include supplier events to provide information on local contact opportunities with the project, improved local supply information for the developer such as an online database of local suppliers, and the employment of a supply chain officer to improve interactions with the local business sector.
- In the housing domain, various tenure arrangements, construction site hostels/campuses might have *legacy use* for the local area. A high quality construction site campus might have legacy use as an educational, recreational or even hotel facility. Vacated construction worker housing might provide valuable affordable housing for local people in need.
- Similar legacy use might flow from transport activities associated with the construction, and possibly also the operation, of a major project. For example, to minimize car travel to a project construction site, there might be agreement with LPAs to build a park and ride facility, with connecting buses to the site. The buses might be used for other local needs between work start and end times – for example as local school buses. Further, if conveniently located near to a town/city, the park and ride facility could be left in place for the use of the community after the end of project use.
- For some large projects there are always likely to be some indirect disturbance effects and

changes in lifestyle which are less easy to address directly. In an attempt to offer some compensation for such impacts with regard to Sizewell B nuclear power station, the CEGB as long ago as 1987 issued a Social Policy Statement (CEGB 1987) which included the provision for grants to be made available for various charitable, social and recreational projects of benefit to the local community, as part of a package of 'ameliorative measures'. Such measures were very well received by the local community. Elsewhere, and much more recently, there has been increasing focus on the development of Community Benefits Agreements/ Community Impacts Agreements to bring together packages of measures for locally impacted communities (Baxamusa 2008).

As for mitigation, the consideration of enhancement of impacts in EIA should be built in at an early stage of the process, building on wide stakeholder consultation. Enhancement measures should be clearly specified, and identified in management plans for subsequent monitoring of performance.

5.5 Summary

Impact prediction and the evaluation of the significance of impacts often constitute a 'black box' in EIA studies. Intuition, often wrapped up as expert opinion, cannot provide a firm and defensible foundation for this important stage of the process. Various methods, ranging from simple to complex, are available to the analyst, and these can help to underpin analysis. Mitigation and enhancement measures come into play particularly at this stage. However, the sophistication of some methods does run the risk of cutting out key actors, and especially the public, from the EIA process. Chapter 6 discusses the important, but currently weak, role of public participation, the value of good presentation, and approaches to EIS review and decision-making.

SOME QUESTIONS

The following questions are intended to help the reader focus on the key issues of this chapter.

1 Magnitude of impact is not always synonymous with significance of impact. Provide examples from your experience to illustrate this point.
2 Assess the case for using expert judgement as a key prediction method in EIA.
3 Similarly, examine the case for using causal network analysis in EIA.
4 How can uncertainty in the prediction of impacts be handled in EIA? Consider the merits of different approaches.
5 Consider the value of the qualitative multi-criteria decision analysis (MCDA) exemplified in Figure 5.9, for various stakeholder groups, for assessing the trade-offs between different types of impacts.
6 Examine the application of the mitigation hierarchy to the impacts of a major project with which you are familiar. What constraints might there be in following the logical steps in that hierarchy in practice?
7 The enhancement of beneficial impacts has had a low profile in EIA until recently. Why do you think this has been so, and why is the situation now changing?
8 Consider what might be included in a Community Benefits Agreement for
   (a) a major wind farm development in a remote rural location; and
   (b) the redevelopment of a major football (soccer) stadium in a heavily populated urban area.

References

Barde, J.P. and Pearce, D.W. 1991. *Valuing the environment: six case studies.* London: Earthscan.

Bateman, I. 1991. Social discounting, monetary evaluation and practical sustainability. *Town and Country Planning* 60 (6), 174–6.

Baxamusa, M. 2008. Empowering communities through deliberation: the model of community. *Journal of Planning Education and Research* 27, 61–276.

Beattie, R. 1995. Everything you already know about EIA, but don't often admit. *Environmental Impact Assessment Review* 15.

Bourdillon, N. 1996. *Limits and standards in EIA.* Oxford: Oxford Brookes University, Impacts Assessment Unit, School of Planning.

Bowers, J. 1990. *Economics of the environment: the conservationists' response to the Pearce Report.* British Association of Nature Conservationists.

Bracken, I. 2008, *Urban Planning Methods: Research and Policy Analysis.* London: Routledge.

Bregman, J.I. and Mackenthun, K.M. 1992. *Environmental impact statements.* Boca Raton, FL: Lewis.

Briedenhann, J. and Butts, S. 2006. Application of the Delphi technique to rural tourism project evaluation, *Current Issues in Tourism,* 9 (2), 171–90.

Canter, L. 1996. *Environmental impact assessment.* McGraw-Hill International Editions.

CEC 1993. *Environmental manual: sectoral environmental assessment sourcebook.* Brussels: CEC, DG VIII.

CEC 1997. Council Directive 97/11/EC of 3 March 1997 amending Directive 85/337 EEC on the assessment of certain public and private projects on the environment. *Official Journal.* L73/5, 3 March.

CEC 1999. *Guidelines for the assessment of indirect and cumulative impacts as well as impact interactions.* Luxembourg: Office for Official Publications of the CEC.

CEQ (Council on Environmental Quality) 1978. *National Environmental Policy Act,* Code of Federal Regulations, Title 40, Section 1508.20.

Dasgupta, A.K. and Pearce, D.W. 1978. *Cost–benefit analysis: theory and practice.* London: Macmillan.

DCLG 2009. *Multi-criteria analysis: a manual.* London: DCLG.

De Jongh, P. 1988. Uncertainty in EIA. In *Environmental impact assessment: theory and practice.* P. Wathern (ed), 62–83. London: Unwin Hyman.

DETR (Department of the Environment, Transport and the Regions) 1997. *Mitigation measures in environmental statements*. London: DETR.

DETR 2000. *Environmental impact assessment: guide to the procedures*. Tonbridge, UK: Thomas Telford.

DoE 1991. *Policy appraisal and the environment*. London: HMSO.

Elsom, D. 2009. Air quality and climate. In *Methods of environmental impact assessment*, P. Morris and R. Therivel (eds), 3rd edn (Ch. 8). London: Routledge.

Figueira, J., Greco, S. and Ehrgott, M. 2005. *Multi-criteria decision analysis: state of the art surveys*. New York: Springer.

Friend, J.K. and Hickling, A. 1987. *Planning under pressure: the strategic choice approach*. Oxford: Pergamon.

Friend, J.K. and Jessop, W.N. 1977. *Local government and strategic choice: an operational research approach to the processes of public planning*, 2nd edn. Oxford: Pergamon.

Glasson, J. 2009. Socio-economic impacts 1: overview and economic impacts. In *Methods of Environmental Impact Assessment*, P. Morris and R. Therivel (eds), 3rd edn (Ch. 2). London: Routledge.

Glasson, J., Elson, M.J., Van der Wee, M. and Barrett, B. 1987. *Socio-economic impact assessment of the proposed Hinkley Point C power station*. Oxford: Oxford Polytechnic, Impacts Assessment Unit.

Glasson, J., Van der Wee, M. and Barrett, B. 1988. A local income and employment multiplier analysis of a proposed nuclear power station development at Hinkley Point in Somerset. *Urban Studies* 25, 248–61.

Golden, J., Duellette, R.P., Saari, S. and Cheremisinoff, P.N. 1979. *Environmental impact data book*. Ann Arbor, MI: Ann Arbor Science Publishers.

Goldvarg, E., and Johnson-Laird, P.N. 2001. Naïve causality: A mental model theory of causal meaning and reasoning. *Cognitive Science*, 25, 565–610.

Green, H., Hunter, C. and Moore, B. 1989. Assessing the environmental impact of tourism development – the use of the Delphi technique. *International Journal of Environmental Studies* 35, 51–62.

Green, H., Hunter, C. and Moore, B. 1990. Assessing the environmental impact of tourism development. *Tourism Management*, June, 11–20.

Hanley, N. and Splash, C. 2003. Cost–benefit analysis and the environment. Cheltenham: Edward Elgar.

Hansen, P.E. and Jorgensen, S.E. (eds) 1991. *Introduction to environmental management*. New York: Elsevier.

Herath, G and Prato, T. 2006 *Using multi-criteria decision analysis in natural resource management*. Aldershot: Ashgate.

Hill, M. 1968. A goals-achievement matrix for evaluating alternative plans. *Journal of the American Institute of Planners* 34, 19.

HMSO 1971. *Report of the Roskill Commission on the third London Airport*. London: HMSO.

HM Treasury 2003. 'Green Book' *Appraisal and evaluation in central government*. Available at: www.greenbook.treasury.gov.uk.

Holling, C.S. (ed) 1978. *Adaptive environmental assessment and management*. New York: Wiley.

IEMA (Institute of Environmental Management and Assessment) 2011. *The state of environmental impact assessment practice in the UK*. Lincoln: IEMA.

Knight, R. 2009. Landscape and visual. In *Methods of environmental impact assessment*, P. Morris and R. Therivel (eds), 3rd edn, London: Routledge.

Kristensen, P., Jensen, J.P. and Jeppesen, E. 1990. *Eutrophication models for lakes*. Research Report C9. Copenhagen: National Agency of Environmental Protection.

Landeta, J. 2006. Current validity of the Delphi method in social sciences, *Technological forecasting and social change*, 73, 467–82.

Lee, N. 1987. *Environmental impact assessment: a training guide*. Occasional Paper 18, Department of Town and Country Planning, University of Manchester.

Lewis, J.A. 1988. Economic impact analysis: a UK literature survey and bibliography. *Progress in Planning* 30 (3), 161–209.

Lichfield, N. 1996. *Community impact evaluation*. London: UCL Press.

Lichfield, N., Kettle, P. and Whitbread, M. 1975. *Evaluation in the planning process*. Oxford: Pergamon.

Loewenstein, L.K. 1966. On the nature of analytical models. *Urban Studies* 3.

Maclaren, V.W. and Whitney, J.B. (eds) 1985. *New directions in environmental impact assessment in Canada*. London: Methuen.

Morris, P. and Therivel, R. (eds) 2009. *Methods of environmental impact assessment*, 3rd edn, London: Routledge.

Morris, P. and Thurling, D. 2001. Phase 2–3 ecological sampling methods. In *Methods of environmental impact assessment*, P. Morris and R. Therivel (eds), 2nd edn, (Appendix G). London: Spon Press.

Munn, R.E. 1979. *Environmental impact assessment: principles and procedures*. New York: Wiley.

Nijkamp, P. 2004. *Environmental Economics and Evaluation* . Cheltenham: Edward Elgar.

Parkin, J. 1992. *Judging plans and projects*. Aldershot: Avebury.

Pearce, D. 1989. Keynote speech at the 10th International Seminar on Environmental Impact Assessment and Management, University of Aberdeen, 9–22 July.

Pearce, D. and Markandya, A. 1990. *Environmental policy benefits: monetary valuation.* Paris: OECD.

Pearce, D., Markandya, A. and Barbier, E.B. 1989. *Blueprint for a green economy.* London: Earthscan.

Perdicoulis, A and Glasson, J. 2006. Causal Networks in EIA, *Environmental Impact Assessment Review* 26, 553–69.

Perdicoulis, A. and Glasson, J. 2009. The causality premise of EIA in practice. *Impact Assessment and Project Appraisal*, 27 (3), 247–50.

Rau, J.G. and Wooten, D.C. 1980. *Environmental impact analysis handbook.* New York: McGraw-Hill.

Richey, J.S., Mar, B.W. and Homer, R. 1985. The Delphi technique in environmental assessment. *Journal of Environmental Management* 21 (1), 135–46.

Rodriguez-Bachiller, A. with J. Glasson 2004. *Expert Systems and Geographical Information Systems.* London: Taylor and Francis.

Suter II, G.W. 1993. *Ecological risk assessment.* Chelsea, MI: Lewis.

Tomlinson, P. 1989. Environmental statements: guidance for review and audit. *The Planner* 75 (28), 12–15.

US Environmental Protection Agency 1993. *Sourcebook for the environmental assessment (EA) process.* Washington, DC: EPA.

Vanclay, F. 1999. Social impact assessment. In *Handbook of environmental impact assessment*, J. Petts (ed). Oxford: Blackwell Science (vol. 1, Ch. 14).

Voogd, J.H. 1983. *Multicriteria evaluation for urban and regional planning.* London: Pion.

VROM 1984. *Prediction in environmental impact assessment.* The Hague: The Netherlands Ministry of Public Housing, Physical Planning and Environmental Affairs.

West Australian Environmental Protection Authority 2010. *Environmental Impact Assessment: Administrative Procedures 2010.* Perth: EPA.

Westman, W.E. 1985. *Ecology, impact assessment and environmental planning.* New York: Wiley.

Willis, K.G. and Powe, N.A. 1998. Contingent valuation and real economic commitments: a private good experiment. *Journal of Environmental Planning and Management* 41 (5), 611–19.

Winpenny, J.T. 1991. *Values for the environment: a guide to economic appraisal.* Overseas Development Institute. London: HMSO.

Wood, G. 2000. Is what you see what you get? Post development auditing of methods used for predicting the zone of visual influence in EIA. *Environmental Impact Assessment Review* 20 (5), 537–56.

6 Participation, presentation and review

●●

6.1 Introduction

One of the key aims of the EIA process is to provide information about a proposal's likely environmental impacts to the developer, public, statutory consultees and decision-makers, so that a better decision may be made. Consultation with the public and statutory consultees in the EIA process can help to improve the quality, comprehensiveness and effectiveness of the EIA, as well as ensuring that the various groups' views are adequately taken into consideration in the decision-making process. Consultation and participation can be useful at most stages of the EIA process:

- in determining the scope of an EIA;
- in providing specialist knowledge about the site;
- in suggesting alternatives;
- in evaluating the relative significance of the likely impacts;
- in proposing mitigation measures;
- in ensuring that the EIS is objective, truthful and complete; and
- in monitoring any conditions of the development agreement.

As such, how the information is presented, how the various interested parties use that information, and how the final decision incorporates the results of the EIA and the views of the various parties, are essential components in the EIA process.

Traditionally, the British system of decision-making has been characterized by administrative discretion and secrecy, with limited public input (McCormick 1991). However, there have been moves towards greater public participation in decision-making, and especially towards greater public access to information. In the environmental arena, the UK Environmental Protection Act of 1990 requires the Environment Agency and local authorities to establish public registers of information on potentially polluting processes; *Neighbourhood statistics, data.gov.uk* and other government data sources provide environmental data in a publicly available form; the public participation requirements of the Aarhus Convention, 2003 amendments to the EIA and SEA Directives, and Planning Act 2008 allow greater public access to information previously not compiled, or considered confidential; and Directive 2003/4/EC, which requires Member States to make provisions for freedom of access to information on the environment, has been implemented in the UK through the Environmental Information

Regulations 2004. The 2009 review on the operation of the 2003 amended EIA Directive (CEC 2009) provided some positive feedback on public participation, especially from the new Member States, which, overall, see the EIA directive as contributing directly to the consolidation of democratic development by securing fundamental rights based on improvements in public participation rights and adding transparency in decision making.

However, despite the positive trends towards greater consultation and participation in the EIA process and the improved communication of EIA findings, both are still relatively underdeveloped in the UK. Few developers make a real effort to gain a sense of the public's views before presenting their applications for authorization and EISs. Few competent authorities have the time or resources to gauge public opinion adequately before making their decisions. Few EISs are presented in a manner that encourages public participation.

This chapter discusses how consultation and participation of both the public (Section 6.2) and statutory consultees (Section 6.3) can be fostered, and how the results can be used to improve a proposed project and speed up its authorization process. The effective presentation of the EIS is then discussed in Section 6.4. The review of EISs and assessment of their accuracy and comprehensiveness are considered in Section 6.5. The chapter concludes with a discussion about decision-making and post-decision legal challenges.

6.2 Public consultation and participation

This section discusses how 'best practice' public participation can be encouraged.[1] It begins by considering the advantages and disadvantages of public participation. It then discusses dimensions of effective public participation and reviews methods for such participation. Finally, it discusses the UK approach to public participation, including the changes brought about by the Planning Act 2008. The reader is also referred to the Audit Commission (2000) and IEMA (2002) for further information on public participation; and to the NGO Forum on ADB (2006) for a good example of a guide to EIA participation written with the public in mind.

6.2.1 Advantages and disadvantages of public participation

Developers do not usually favour public participation. It may upset a good relationship with the LPA. It carries the risk of giving a project a high profile, with attendant costs in time and money. It may not lead to a conclusive decision on a project, as diverse interest groups have different concerns and priorities; the decision may also represent the views of the most vocal interest groups rather than of the general public. Most developers' contact with the public comes only at the stage of planning appeals and inquiries; by this time, participation has often evolved into a systematic attempt to stop their projects. Thus, many developers never see the positive side of public participation.

Historically, public participation has also had connotations of extremism, confrontation, delays and blocked development. In the USA, NEPA-related lawsuits have stopped major development projects, including oil and gas developments in Wyoming, a ski resort in California and a clear-cut logging project in Alaska (Turner 1988). In Japan in the late 1960s and early 1970s, riots so violent that six people died delayed the construction of the Narita Airport near Tokyo by five years. In the UK, perhaps the most visible forms of public 'participation' have been protesters wearing gas masks at nuclear power station sites, being forcibly evicted from tunnels and tree houses on the Newbury bypass route (which cost more than £6 million for policing before construction even began), and setting up a protest camp at Simpson where a third Heathrow runway would have been built. More typically, all planners are familiar with acrimonious public meetings and 'ban the project' campaigns. Public participation may provide the legal means for intentionally obstructing development; the protracted delay of a project can be an effective method of defeating it.

On the other hand, from a developer's point of view, public participation can be used positively to convey information about a development, clear up misunderstandings, allow a better understanding of relevant issues and how they will be dealt with, and identify and deal with areas of controversy while a project is still in its early planning phases. The process of considering and responding to the unique contributions of local people or special interest groups may suggest measures the developer could take to avoid local opposition and environmental problems. These measures are likely to be more innovative, viable and publicly acceptable than those proposed solely by the developer. Project modifications made early in the planning process, before plans have been fully developed, are more easily and cheaply accommodated than those made later. Projects that do not have to go to inquiry are considerably cheaper than those that do. Early public participation also prevents an escalation of frustration and anger, so it helps to avoid the possibility of more forceful 'participation'; Figure 6.1 shows three quite different examples of participation in EIA. The implementation of a project generally proceeds more cheaply and smoothly if local residents agree with the proposal, with fewer protests, a more willing labour force, and fewer complaints about impacts such as noise and traffic.

For instance, the conservation manager of Europe's (then) largest zinc/lead mine noted that:

> properly defined and widely used, [EIA is] an advantage rather than a deterrent. It is a mechanism for ensuring the early and orderly consideration of all relevant issues and for the involvement of affected communities. It is in this last area that its true benefit lies. We have entered an era when the people decide. It is

(a)

(b)

(c)

Figure 6.1

Different forms of public 'participation': (a) public meeting about the proposed Hinkley 'C' nuclear power station; (b) protest against the proposed Southampton biomass plant; (c) some Newbury bypass route protest methods

Sources: (a) EDF Energy 2009; (b) Daily Echo 2011; (c) Guardian 1996

therefore in the interests of developers to ensure that they, the people, are equipped to do so with the confidence that their concern is recognized and their future life-style protected. (Dallas 1984)

Similarly, the developers of a motor-racing circuit noted:

The [EIS] was the single most significant factor in convincing local members, residents and interested parties that measures designed to reduce existing environmental impacts of motor racing had been uppermost in the formulation of the new proposals. The extensive environmental studies which formed the basis of the statement proved to be a robust defence against the claims from objectors and provided reassurance to independent bodies such as the Countryside Commission and the Department of the Environment. Had this not been the case, the project would undoubtedly have needed to be considered at a public inquiry. (Hancock 1992)

From the public's point of view, participation in an EIA process can increase people's say in decision-making, thus improving governance and making decision-making more democratic. For instance, O'Faircheallaigh (2010) cites cases where indigenous people would not release information unless they were fully informed about the proposed project and given the opportunity to negotiate

with the development and government on management of their cultural heritage. This, in turn, can change the power balance in favour of groups that have traditionally been marginalized. Table 6.1 summarizes the main aims of public participation in EIA.

6.2.2 Requirements and methods for effective participation

The United Nations Environment Programme lists five interrelated components of effective public participation:

- identification of the groups/individuals interested in or affected by the proposed development;
- provision of accurate, understandable, pertinent and timely information;
- dialogue between those responsible for the decisions and those affected by them;
- assimilation of what the public say in the decision; and
- feedback about actions taken and how the public influenced the decision. (Clark 1994)

These points will be discussed in turn.

Although the *identification of relevant interest groups* seems superficially simple, it can be fraught with difficulty. The simple term 'the public' actually refers to a complex amalgam of interest groups, which changes over time and from project to project. The public can be broadly classified

Table 6.1 Purposes for public participation in EIA

Broad purpose		Specific purposes and activities
Obtain public input into decisions taken elsewhere	1	Provide information to public
	2	Fill information gaps
	3	Information contestability/testing information provided by the developer
	4	Problem-solving and social learning
Share decision making with public	5	Reflect democratic principles/EIA used to obtain the consent of those affected
	6	Democracy in practice/participation as an educative function
	7	Pluralist representation
Alter distribution of power and structures of decision making	8	Involve marginalised groups (or, alternatively, entrench marginalization)
	9	Shift the locus of decision making, e.g. to agreements between developers and local people

Source: Adapted from O'Faircheallaigh 2010

into two main groups. The first consists of the voluntary groups, quasi-statutory bodies or issues-based pressure groups that are concerned with a specific aspect of the environment or with the environment as a whole. The second group consists of the people living near a proposed development who may be directly affected by it. These two groups can have very different interests and resources. The organized groups may have extensive financial and professional resources at their disposal, may concentrate on specific aspects of the development, and may see their participation as a way to gain political points or national publicity. People living locally may lack the technical, educational or financial resources, and familiarity with relevant procedures to put their points across effectively, yet they are the ones who will be the most directly affected by the development (Mollison 1992). The people in the two groups, in turn, come from a wide range of backgrounds and have a wide variety of opinions. A multiplicity of 'publics' thus exits, each of which has specific views, which may well conflict with those of other groups and those of EIA 'experts'.

It is debatable whether all these publics should be involved in all decisions; for instance, whether 'highly articulate members of the NGO, Green-peace International, sitting in their office in Holland, also have a right to express their views on, and attempt to influence, a decision on a project that may be on the other side of the world' (Clark 1994). Participation may be rightly controlled by regulations specifying the groups and organizations that are eligible to participate or by criteria identifying those considered to be directly affected by a development (e.g. living within a certain distance of it). For instance, under the Planning Act 2008, 'affected persons' who own or manage the land proposed for development are treated differently from more generally 'interested parties'.

The EIA Directive distinguishes between (1) 'the public', who must be informed of the request for development consent, the availability of accompanying environmental information, the nature of the possible decision, and details of arrangements for public consultation (Article 6.2); and (2) 'the public concerned', to whom the environmental statement, main advice and reports issued to the competent authority, and other relevant information must be made available, and who must be given an early and effective opportunity to participate in the environmental decision-making procedures (Articles 6.3 and 6.4). Although all Members States seem to use a broad definition for the former, many are more restrictive for the latter. Different Member States permit NGOs to participate in the EIA process depending on how long they have existed, their regional coverage, whether environmental protection is one of their objectives, or whether they are legal entities (COWI 2009).

Lack of information, or misinformation, about the nature of a proposed development prevents adequate public participation and causes resentment and criticism of the project. One objective of public participation is thus *to provide information* about the development and its likely impacts. Before an EIS is prepared, information may be provided at public meetings, exhibitions or telephone hotlines. This information should be as candid and truthful as possible: people will be on their guard against evasions or biased information, and will look for confirmation of their fears. A careful balance needs to be struck between consultation that is early enough to influence decisions and consultation that is so early that there is no real information on which to base any discussions. For instance, after several experiences of problematic pre-EIS consultation, one UK developer decided to conduct quite elaborate consultation exercises, but only after the EISs were published (McNab 1997). The Infrastructure Planning Commission publishes all of its communications from and with any parties on its website, to avoid any accusations of bias and behind-the-scenes dealings.

The way information is conveyed can influence public participation. Highly technical information can be understood by only a small proportion of the public. Information in different media (e.g. newspapers, radio) will reach different sectors of the public. Ensuring the participation of groups that generally do not take part in decision-making – notably minority and low-income groups – may be a special concern, especially in the light of the Brundtland Commission's emphasis on intra-generational equity and participation. Ross (2000) gives a compelling example of the difficulties of communicating technical information across a language barrier in Canada:

> At one of the hearings in an aboriginal community, there was a discussion of chlorinated organic emissions involving one of the elders, who was speaking in Cree through a translator. The translator needed to convey the discussions to the Elder. The difficult question was how to translate the phrase 'chlorinated organic compounds' into Cree. Fellow panel member Jim Boucher . . . who spoke Cree, listened to the translator, who had solved the problem by using the translation 'bad medicine'.

Williams and Hill (1996) identified a number of disparities between traditional ways of communicating environmental information and the needs of minority and low-income groups in the US. For instance agencies:

- focus on desk studies rather than working actively with these groups;
- often do not understand existing power structures, and so do not involve community leaders such as preachers for low-income churches, or union leaders;
- hold meetings where the target groups are not represented, for instance in city centres away from where the project will be located;
- hold meetings in large 'fancy' places which disenfranchised groups feel are 'off-limits', rather than in local churches, schools or community centres;
- use newspaper notices, publication in official journals and mass mailings instead of telephone trees or leaflets handed out in schools;
- prepare thick reports which confuse and overwhelm; and
- use formal presentation techniques such as raised platforms and slide projections.

These points suggest that a wide variety of methods for conveying information should be used, with an emphasis on techniques that would be useful for traditionally less participative groups: EIS summaries with pictures and maps as well as technical reports, meetings in less formal venues, and contact through established community networks, as well as through leaflets and newspaper notices.

Public participation in EIA also aims to *establish a dialogue* between the public and the decision-makers (both the project proponent and the authorizing body) and to ensure that decision-makers *assimilate the public's views* into their decisions. It can help to challenge the underlying assumptions behind an EIS, its balance and veracity, and the alternatives it considers (O'Faircheallaigh 2010). Public participation can help to identify issues that concern local residents. These issues are often not the same as those of concern to the developer or outside experts. Public participation exercises should thus achieve a two-way flow of information to allow residents to voice their views. The exercises may well identify conflicts between the needs of the developer and those of various sectors of the community; but this should ideally lead to solutions of these conflicts, and to agreement on future courses of action that reflect the joint objectives of all parties (Petts 1999, 2003).

Effective public participation methods could include deliberative techniques, such as focus groups, Delphi panels and consultative committees, plus appropriate resourcing, perhaps through intervenor funding. Petts (2003) highlights some of the possibilities and problems of deliberative participation, or communication through dialogue; she also stresses the need for such participation to be integral to the EIA process rather than an 'add-on'. Balram *et al.* (2003) provide an interesting development of the Delphi approach, Collaborative Spatial Delphi, using a GIS-based approach, and there may be considerable potential for using spatial technology in participation in EIA. There is then of course the great potential of the continuously and rapidly evolving Internet and social networking systems. As discussed in the Hong Kong case study in Section 7.3, the Internet can be used to facilitate participation at several stages in the EIA process.

Arnstein (1971) identified 'eight rungs on a ladder of citizen participation', ranging from non-participation (manipulation, therapy), through tokenism (informing, consultation, placation), to citizen power (partnership, delegated power, citizen control). Assimilation of what the public say in the decision is likely to be higher the further up

Table 6.2 Advantages and disadvantages of levels of increasing public influence

Approaches	Extent of public power in decision-making	Advantages	Disadvantages
Information feedback Film or Powerpoint presentation, television, information kit, newspaper account or advertisement, news conference, press release, print materials, technical report, website, notice, etc.	Nil	Informative, quick presentation subject to bias	No feedback
Consultation Public hearing, briefing, ombudsperson or representative, survey, interview, response sheets, etc.	Low	Allows two-way information transfer; allows limited discussion	Does not permit ongoing communication; somewhat time-consuming
Joint planning Advisory committee, workshop, informal meeting, role playing, panels, interactive polling, future search conference, etc.	Moderate	Permits continuing input and feedback; increases education and involvement of citizens	Very time-consuming; dependent on what information is provided by planners
Delegated authority Citizens' review board, Citizens' planning commission etc	High	Permits better access to relevant information; permits greater control over options and timing of decision.	Long-term time commitment; difficult to include wide representation on small board.

Source: Adapted from: Westman 1985; International Association for Public Participation 2001

the ladder one goes. Similarly, Westman (1985) has identified four levels of increasing public power in participation methods: information-feedback approaches, consultation, joint planning and delegated authority. Table 6.2 lists advantages and disadvantages of these levels.

There are many different forms of public participation. A few are listed in Table 6.3, along with an indication of how well they provide information, cater for special interests, encourage dialogue and affect decision-making.

However, different stakeholders may have very different views on how effective a given EIA process is in influencing a planning decision. Hartley and Wood (2005) interviewed 22 stakeholders – planning officers, a developer, local action group members, and members of the public – involved in the EIAs for four waste disposal sites. Although the different types of stakeholders had broadly similar views on many aspects of the EIA public participation process (e.g. timing, information provision), they differed significantly in their views of its influence on decision-making:

The planning officers in all the case studies indicated that public representations are carefully considered in the decision-making process and that suggestions from the public are often used when formulating planning conditions . . . However, members of action groups believed that their influence on the final decision was limited, that the planning process was too political and that decisions had largely been made before they were informed . . .

Finally, an essential part of effective public participation is *feedback about any decisions* and actions taken, and how the public's views affected those decisions. In the US, for instance, comments on a draft EIS are incorporated into the final EIS along with the agency's response to those comments. For example:

- *Comment*: I am strongly opposed to the use of herbicides in the forest. I believe in a poison-free forest!

Table 6.3 Methods of public participation and their effectiveness

	Provide information	Cater for special interests	Two-way communication	Impact decision-making
Explanatory meeting, slide/film presentation	✓	½	½	–
Presentation to small groups	✓	✓	✓	½
Public display, exhibit, models	✓	–	–	–
Press release, legal notice	½	–	–	–
Written comment	–	½	½	½
Poll	½	–	✓	
Field office	✓	✓	½	–
Site visit	✓	✓	–	–
Advisory committee, task force, community representatives	½	½	✓	✓
Working groups of key actors	✓	½	✓	✓
Citizen review board	½	½	✓	✓
Public inquiry	✓	½	½	✓/–
Litigation	½	–	½	✓/–
Demonstration, protest, riot	–	–	½	✓/–

Source: Adapted from Westman 1985

- *Response*: Your opposition to use of herbicides was included in the content analysis of all comments received. However, evidence in the EIS indicates that low-risk use of selected herbicides is assured when properly controlled – the evaluated herbicides pose minimal risk as long as mitigation measures are enforced.

Without such feedback, people are likely to question the use to which their input was put, and whether their participation had any effect at all; this could affect their approach to subsequent projects as well as their view of the one under consideration.

6.2.3 UK procedures

Articles 6 and 10(a) of EC Directive 85/337 (as amended by Directives 97/11 and 2003/35/EC) requires Member States to ensure that:

- The public is notified early in the environmental decision-making procedures about the request for development consent, the fact that the project is subject to EIA, and information about how they can participate in the EIA process.
- Copies of the environmental information and other information relevant to the decision are made available to the public.

- The public concerned is given the opportunity to express an opinion before development consent is granted. The detailed arrangements for such information and consultation are determined by the Member States which may, depending on the particular characteristics of the projects or sites concerned:
  - determine the public concerned;
  - specify the places where the information can be consulted;
  - specify the ways in which the public may be informed, for example, by bill posting within a certain radius, publication in local newspapers, organization of exhibitions with plans, drawings, tables, graphs and models;
  - determine the manner in which the public is to be consulted, for example by written submissions or by public enquiry; and
  - fix reasonable time limits for the various stages of the procedure in order to ensure that a decision is taken within a reasonable period.

- Members of the public who have a sufficient interest or whose rights are impaired have access to a decision review procedure before a court of law.

In the UK, this has been translated by the various EIA regulations (with minor differences) into the following general requirements. Notices must be published in a local newspaper and posted at a proposed site at least seven days before the submission of the development application and EIS. These notices must describe the proposed development, state that a copy of the EIS is available for public inspection with other documents relating to the development application, give an address where copies of the EIS may be obtained and the charge for the EIS, and state that written representations on the application may be made to the competent authority for at least 21 days after the notice is published. When a charge is made for an EIS, it must be reasonable, taking into account printing and distribution costs.

Environmental impact assessment: guide to the procedures (DETR 2000), the government manual to developers, notes:

> Developers should also consider whether to consult the general public, and non-statutory bodies concerned with environmental issues, during the preparation of the environmental statement. Bodies of this kind may have particular knowledge and expertise to offer . . . While developers are under no obligation to publicise their proposals before submitting a planning application, consultation with local amenity groups and with the general public can be useful in identifying key environmental issues, and may put the developer in a better position to modify the project in ways which would mitigate adverse effects and recognize local environmental concerns. It will also give the developer an early indication of the issues which are likely to be important at the formal application stage if, for instance, the proposal goes to public inquiry.

This suggests that, although the UK has broadly implemented the EIA Directive's minimal requirements for public participation, this has been done half-heartedly at best, with no extension ('gold plating') of these requirements. The European Commission (EC 2010a) has also formally warned the UK about the prohibitive expense for members of the public who wish to challenge the legality

of decisions on the environment, and this may still result in a judicial review. However the UK is not unusual in this respect: a recent review of the application and effectiveness of the EIA Directive (CEC 2009) concluded that public participation practice varies widely across European Member States, with most Member States adhering only to the Directive's minimum requirements.

The situation for nationally significant infrastructure projects is different from that described above. The Planning Act 2008 requires that decisions about such projects are made by a new Infrastructure Planning Commission in accordance with new National Policy Statements, with more 'front loaded' and exigent public participation requirements.[2] Developers for such projects need to demonstrate that they have undertaken public consultation and acted on public feedback before they submit an application to the IPC. The IPC then has 28 days to accept or reject the proposal, and inadequate consultation is one of the criteria for rejecting proposals. If an application is accepted, the public can register to provide their views in writing to the IPC, and to participate in open-floor and special topic hearings. All of the EIA-related documents are put on the IPC website.

· ·

6.3 Consultation with statutory consultees and other countries

Statutory consultees have accumulated a wide range of knowledge about environmental conditions in various parts of the country, and they can give valuable feedback on the appropriateness of a project and its likely impacts (Wende 2002; Wood and Jones 1997). However, the consultees may have their own priorities, which may prejudice their response to the EIS.

Article 6(1) of Directive 85/337 (as amended) states:

> Member States shall take the measures necessary to ensure that the authorities likely to be concerned by the project by reasons of their specific environmental responsibilities

are given an opportunity to express their opinion on the information supplied by the developer and other requests for development consent. To this end, Member States shall designate the authorities to be consulted . . . The information gathered . . . shall be forwarded to those authorities. Detailed arrangements for consultation shall be laid down by Member States.

In the UK, different statutory consultees have been designated for different devolved administrations (England, Wales, Scotland and Northern Ireland) and different types of development. For planning projects in England, for instance, the statutory consultees are any principal council to the area in which the land is situated (if not the LPA), Natural England, and the MMO and the Environment Agency where relevant.

The EIA Directive also requires consultation of other European Member States. Where one Member State is aware that a project is likely to have significant environmental impacts in another Member State – or if requested by a Member State that is likely to be significantly affected – the first Member State must send to the affected Member State information on the project, its likely impacts and the decision that will be taken. If the affected Member State subsequently indicates that it wants to participate in the EIA process, then it subsequently must be treated essentially as though it was a statutory consultee. The UK has had a limited number of these transboundary consultations – 12 by 2009, compared to the Republic of Ireland, which had the most at 43 (COWI 2009).

Ideally, consultees should already be consulted at the scoping stage. In addition, it is a legal requirement that the consultees should be consulted before a decision is made. Once the EIS is completed, copies can be sent to the consultees directly by the developer or by the competent authority. In practice, many competent authorities only send particular EIS chapters to the consultees (e.g. the chapter on archaeology to the archaeologist). However, this may limit the consultee's understanding of the project context and wider impacts; generally consultees should be sent a copy of the entire EIS.

6.4 EIA presentation

Although EIA legislation specifies the minimum contents required in an EIS, it does not give any standard for the presentation of this information. Past EISs have ranged from a three-page typed and stapled report to glossy brochures with computer graphics and multi-volume documents in purpose-designed binders. This section discusses the contents, organization, and clarity of communication and presentation of an EIS.

6.4.1 Contents and organization

An EIS should be *comprehensive*, and it must at least fulfil the requirements of the relevant EIA legislation. As we shall discuss in Chapter 8, past EISs have not all fulfilled these requirements; however, most EISs nowadays are adequate, in part because LPAs are increasingly likely to require information on topics they feel have not been adequately discussed in an EIS. A good EIS will also go further than the minimum requirements if other significant impacts are identified. Most EISs are broadly organized into four sections: a non-technical summary; a description of the project, alternatives considered, and a brief outline of the environmental context; a discussion of methodology, including scoping and public participation; and then a series of chapters that discuss, for individual topics such as air and water, baseline conditions, likely environmental impacts, proposed mitigation measures and residual impacts. Ideally, an EIS should also include the proposals for planning conditions or environmental management systems, and monitoring. It could include much or all of the information given in Appendix 5 of *Environmental impact assessment: guide to the procedures* (DETR 2000): see Table 3.7. Table 1.1 provides an example of a good EIS outline.

An EIS should *explain why some impacts are not dealt with*. It should include a scoping section to explain why some impacts may be considered insignificant. If, for instance, the development is unlikely to affect the climate, a reason should be given explaining this conclusion. An EIS should *emphasize key points*. These should have been identified during the scoping exercise, but additional issues may arise during the course of the

EIA. The EIS should set the context of the issues. The names of the developer, relevant consultants, relevant LPAs and consultees should be listed, along with a contact person for further information. The main relevant planning issues and legislation should be explained. The EIS should also indicate any references used, and give a bibliography at the end.

The *non-technical summary* is a particularly important component of the EIS, as this is often the only part of the document that the public and decision-makers will read. It should thus summarize the main findings of the EIS, including the project description, alternatives and proposed mitigation measures. Chapter 4 gave examples of techniques for identifying and summarizing impacts, and Table 6.4 shows how the impacts of a project can be summarized.

An EIS should ideally be one *unified document*, with perhaps a second volume for appendices. The courts have stated that an EIS should not be a 'paper chase' (Berkeley vs. Sos and Fulham Football Club, 2001):

the point about the environmental statement contemplated by the Directive is that it constitutes a single and accessible compilation, produced by the applicant at the very start of the application process, of the relevant environmental information and the summary in non-technical language.

A common problem with the organization of EISs stems from how environmental impacts are assessed. The developer (or the consultants co-ordinating the EIA) often subcontracts parts of the EIA to consultancies that specialize in those fields (e.g. ecological specialists, landscape consultants). These in turn prepare reports of varying lengths and styles, making a number of (possibly different) assumptions about the project and likely future environmental conditions, and proposing different and possibly conflicting mitigation measures. One way developers have attempted to circumvent this problem has been to summarize the impact predictions in a main text, and add the full reports as appendices to the main body of the EIS. Another

Table 6.4 Extract from an EIS summary table showing relative weights given to significance of impacts

Topic area	Description of impact	Geographical scale of importance of issue					Impact	Nature	Significance
		I	N	R	D	L			
Human beings	Disturbance to existing properties from traffic and noise				*		Adverse	St, R	Major
	Coalescence of existing settlements			*			Adverse	Lt, IR	Major
Flora and fauna	Loss of grassland of local nature conservation value					*	Adverse	Lt, IR	Minor
	Creation of new habitats					*	Beneficial	Lt, R	Minor
	Increased recreational pressure on SSSI		*				Adverse	Lt, R	Minor
Soil and geology	Loss of 120 hectares agricultural soil (grade 3B)		*				Adverse	Lt, IR	Minor
Water	Increased rates of surface water run-off					*	Adverse	Lt, IR	Minor
	Reduction in groundwater recharge		*				Adverse	Lt, R	Minor

Key: I International   St Short term
       N National   Lt Long term
       R Regional   R Reversible
       D District   IR Irreversible
       L Local

Source: DoE 1995

Note: only a selection of key issues are given here

has been to put a 'company cover' on each report and present the EIS as a multi-volume document, each volume discussing a single type of impact. Both of these methods are problematic: the appendix method in essence discounts the great majority of findings, and the multi-volume method is cumbersome to read and carry. Neither method attempts to present findings in a cohesive manner, emphasizes crucial impacts or proposes a coherent package of mitigation and monitoring measures. A good EIS would incorporate the information from the subcontractors' reports into one coherent document, which uses consistent assumptions and proposes consistent mitigation measures.

The EIS should be kept as *brief* as possible while still *presenting the necessary information*. The main text should include all the relevant discussion about impacts, and appendices should present only additional data and documentation. In the US, the length of an EIS is generally expected to be less than 150 pages.

6.4.2 Clarity of communication

Weiss (1989) suggests that an unreadable EIS is an environmental hazard:

> The issue is the quality of the document, its usefulness in support of the goals of envir-onmental legislation, and, by implication, the quality of the environmental steward-ship entrusted to the scientific community ... An unreadable EIS not only hurts the environmental protection laws and, thus, the environment. It also turns the sincere environmental engineer into a kind of 'polluter'.

An EIS has to communicate information to many audiences, from the decision-maker to the environmental expert to the lay person. Although it cannot fulfil all the expectations of all its readers, it can go a long way towards being a useful document for a wide audience. It should at least be *well written*, with good spelling and punctuation. It should have a clear structure, with easily visible titles and a logical flow of information. A table of contents, with page numbers marked, should be included before the main text, allowing easy access to information. Principal points should be clearly

indicated, perhaps in a table at the front or back.

An EIS should *avoid technical jargon*. Any jargon it does include should be explained in the text or in footnotes. All the following examples are from actual EISs:

- *Wrong*: It is believed that the aquiclude properties of the Brithdir seams have been reduced and there is a degree of groundwater communication between the Brithdir and the underlying Rhondda beds, although ... numerous seepages do occur on the valley flanks with the retention regime dependent upon the nature of the superficial deposits.
- *Right*: The accepted method for evaluating the importance of a site for waterfowl (i.e. waders and wildfowl) is the '1 per cent criterion'. A site is considered to be of National Importance if it regularly holds at least 1 per cent of the estimated British population of a species of waterfowl. 'Regularly' in this context means counts (usually expressed as annual peak figures), averaged over the last five years.

The EIS should clearly *state any assumptions* on which impact predictions are based:

- *Wrong*: As the proposed development will extend below any potential [archaeological] remains, it should be possible to establish a method of working which could allow ade-quate archaeological examinations to take place.
- *Right*: For each operation an assumption has been made of the type and number of plant involved. These are: demolition: 2 pneumatic breakers, tracked loader; excavation: backacter excavator, tracked shovel ...

The EIS should be *specific*. Although it is easier and more defensible to claim that an impact is significant or likely, the resulting EIS will be little more than a vague collection of possible future trends.

- *Wrong*: The landscape will be protected by the flexibility of the proposed [monorail] to be positioned and designed to merge in both location and scale into and with the existing environment.

- *Right*: From these [specified] sections of road, large numbers of proposed wind turbines would be visible on the skyline, where the towers would appear as either small or indistinct objects and the movement of rotors would attract the attention of road users. The change in the scenery caused by the proposals would constitute a major visual impact, mainly due to the density of visible wind turbine rotors.

Predicted impacts should be *quantified* if possible, perhaps with a range, and the use of non-quantified descriptions, such as severe or minimal, should be explained:

- *Wrong*: The effect on residential properties will be minimal with the nearest properties . . . at least 200 m from the closest area of filling.
- *Right*: Without the bypass, traffic in the town centre can be expected to increase by about 50–75 per cent by the year 2008. With the bypass, however, the overall reduction to 65–75 per cent of the 1986 level can be achieved.

Even better, predictions should give an *indication of the probability* that an impact will occur, and the degree of confidence with which the prediction can be made. In cases of uncertainty, the EIS should propose worst-case scenarios:

- *Right*. In terms of traffic generation, the 'worst case' scenario would be for 100 per cent usage of the car park . . . For a more realistic analysis, a redistribution of 50 per cent has been assumed.

Finally, an EIS should be *honest and unbiased*. A 1991 review of local authorities noted that '[a] number of respondents felt that the environmental statement concentrated too much on supporting the proposal rather than focusing on its impacts and was therefore not sufficiently objective' (Kenyan 1991). O'Faircheallaigh (2010) suggests that lack of objectivity is still a problem, with EISs being used to justify, not assess, decisions. Developers cannot be expected to conclude that their projects have such major environmental impacts that they should be stopped (otherwise one would hope that they would already have been stopped). However, it is unlikely that all major environmental issues will have been resolved by the time the statement is written.

- *Wrong*: The proposed site lies adjacent to lagoons, mud and sands which form four regional Special Sites of Scientific Interest [*sic*]. The loss of habitat for birds is unlikely to be significant, owing to the availability of similar habitats in the vicinity.

6.4.3 Presentation

Although it would be good to report that EISs are read only for their contents and clarity, in reality, presentation can have a great influence on how they are received. EIAs are, indirectly, public relations exercises, and an EIS can be seen as a publicity document for the developer. Good presentation can convey a concern for the environment, a rigorous approach to the impact analysis and a positive attitude to the public. Bad presentation, in turn, suggests a lack of care, and perhaps a lack of financial backing. Similarly, good presentation can help to convey information clearly, whereas bad presentation can negatively affect even a well-organized EIS.

The presentation of an EIS will say much about the developer. The type of paper used – recycled or not, glossy or not, heavy or light weight – will affect the image projected, as will the choice of coloured or black-and-white diagrams and the use of dividers between chapters. The ultra-green company will opt for double-sided printing on recycled paper, while the luxury developer will use glossy, heavyweight paper with a distinctive binder. Generally, a strong binder that stands up well under heavy handling is most suitable for EISs. Unless the document is very thin, a spiral binder is likely to snap or bend open with continued handling; similarly, stapled documents are likely to tear. Multi-volume documents are difficult to keep together unless a box is provided. EISs can also be made public on the Internet or through CDs (see Figure 6.2).

The use of maps, graphs, photo-montages, diagrams and other forms of visual communication can greatly help the EIS presentation. As we noted

Figure 6.2

Different types of EIS presentation

Sources: (a) Metropolitan Council (Minneapolis/St Paul); (b) AREVA
Resources Canada Inc.; (c) Griff Wigley; (d) Evelop

in Chapter 4, a location map, a site layout of the project and a process diagram are essential to a proper description of the development. Maps showing, for example, the extent of visual impacts, the location of designated areas or classes of agricultural land are a succinct and clear way of presenting such information. Graphs are often much more effective than tables or figures in conveying numerical information. Forms of visual communication break up the page, and add interest to an EIS. Increasingly some developers are also producing the EIS as a CD, and putting it on the Internet.

6.5 Review of EISs

A range of stakeholders will want to check the accuracy and comprehensiveness of an EIS. The developer will want to ensure that they are not vulnerable to legal challenge. Opponents of the scheme will want to see whether it is. Statutory consultees will want to ensure that it covers all the relevant information on their topics of interest in a fair manner. The local planning authority will want to confirm that it is 'fit for purpose' for informing its decision.

The DCLG (2011) guidance notes that the competent authority must satisfy itself of the adequacy of the EIS, but gives no information on how it should do this:

LPAs should satisfy themselves that submitted ES contains the information specified in Part II of Schedule 4 to the Regulations and the relevant information set out in Part I of that Schedule that the applicant can reasonably be required to compile. To avoid delays in determining EIA applications, the need for any further information should be considered and, if necessary, requested as early as possible. It is important to ensure that all the information needed to enable the likely significant environmental effects to be properly assessed is gathered as part of the EIA process. If tests or surveys are needed to establish the likelihood or extent of significant environmental effects, the results of these should form part of the ES ... Whether there is a breach of the regulations through failing to include the outcomes of surveys in an ES depends on the level of information already at the LPA's disposal, and whether this is sufficient to enable the authority to make an informed judgment as to the likely significant effects.

As will be shown in Chapter 8, many EISs do not meet even the minimum regulatory requirements, much less provide comprehensive information on which to base decisions. In some countries, for example the Netherlands, Canada, Malaysia and Indonesia, EIA Commissions or panels have been established to review EISs and act as a quality assurance process. However, in the UK there are no mandatory requirements regarding the pre-decision review of EISs to ensure that they are comprehensive and accurate. A planning application cannot be judged invalid simply because it is accompanied by an inadequate or incomplete EIS: a competent authority may only request further information, or refuse permission and risk an appeal.[3]

Many competent authorities do not have the full range of technical expertise needed to assess the adequacy and comprehensiveness of an EIS. Some authorities, especially those that receive few EISs, have consequently had difficulties in dealing with the technical complexities of EISs. In some cases, consultants are brought in to review the EISs. Other authorities have joined the Institute of Environmental Management and Assessment (IEMA), which reviews EISs. Others have been reluctant to buy outside expertise, especially at a time of restrictions on local spending. A technique advocated by the International Association for Impact Assessment (IAIA), although not seen often in practice, is to involve parties other than just the competent authority in EIS review, especially the public (Partidario 1996).

In an attempt to fill the void left by the national government, several organizations have devised non-mandatory review criteria that aim to ensure that EISs analyse and present all relevant information and (to a lesser extent) that this information is accurate. Such a review also allows the reader to become familiar with the proposed project, assess the significance of its effects, and determine whether mitigation of its impacts is needed. Indirectly, it also makes the reviewer more familiar with the EIA process. The review process can be used by any of the stakeholders in the process.

Lee and Colley (1990) developed a hierarchical review framework. At the top of the hierarchy is a comprehensive mark (A = well-performed and complete, through to F = very unsatisfactory) for the entire report. This mark is based on marks given to four broad sub-headings: description of the development, local environment and baseline conditions; identification and evaluation of key impacts; alternatives and mitigation of impacts; and communication of results. Each of these, in turn, is based on two further layers of increasingly specific topics or questions. Lee and Colley's criteria have been used either directly or in a modified form (e.g. by the IEMA) to review a range of EISs in the UK. Appendix 4 gives the Lee and Colley framework.

The European Commission has also published review criteria (CEC 2001). These are similar to Lee and Colley's, but use seven sub-headings instead of four, include a longer list of specific questions, and judge the information based on relevance to the project context and importance for decision-making as well as presence/absence in the EIS. The review criteria given in Appendix 4 are an

Table 6.5 Examples of possible uses for EIS review criteria

(a) Test of minimum legal requirements

Criterion	Presence/absence (page number)	Information	Key information absent
Describes the proposed development, including its design, and size or scale	✓ (p. 5)	Location (in plans), existing operations, access	Working method, vehicle movements, restoration plans
Indicates the physical presence of the development	X		Site buildings (location, size), restoration

(b) Simple grading for each criterion

Criterion	Presence/ absence (page number)	Comments	Grade
Explains the purposes and objectives of the development	✓ (p. 11)	Briefly in introduction, more details in Sec. 2	A
Gives the estimated duration of construction etc. phases	✓ (p. 12)	Not decommissioning	B

(c) Test of relevance and then completeness

Criterion	Relevant? (Y/N)	Judgement (C/A/I)*	Comment
Considers the 'no action' alternative, alternative processes, etc.	Y	A	Alternative sites discussed, but not alternative processes
If unexpectedly severe adverse impacts are identified, alternatives are reappraised	N		Impacts of sand/gravel working well understood

C = complete; A = adequate; I = inadequate

amalgamation and extension of Lee and Colley's and the EC's criteria, developed by the Impacts Assessment Unit at Oxford Brookes University. Rodriguez-Bachiller with Glasson (2004) have also devised an expert system approach to EIS review.

It is unlikely that any EIS will fulfil all the criteria. Similarly, some criteria may not apply to all projects. However, they should act as a checklist of good practice for both those preparing and those reviewing EISs. Table 6.5 shows a number of possible ways of using these criteria. Example (a), which relates to minimum requirements, amplifies the presence or otherwise of key information. Example (b) includes a simple grading, which could be on the A–F scale used by Lee and Colley, for each criterion (only one of which is shown here). Example (c) takes the format of the EC criteria, which appraise the relevance of the information and then judge whether it is complete, adequate (not complete but need not prevent decision-

making from proceeding) or inadequate for decision-making.

Where a local planning authority believes that an EIS does not provide the information they require to allow them to give full consideration of the proposed development's likely environmental effects, it must require the developer to provide further information. Any further information must be publicized and consulted on again.[4]

6.6 Decisions on projects

6.6.1 EIA and project authorization

Decisions to authorize or reject projects are made at several levels:

At the top of the tree are the relevant Secretaries of State . . . ; below them are a host of Inspectors, sometimes called Reporters (Scotland); further down the list come Councillors, the elected members of district, county, unitary or metropolitan borough councils; and at the very bottom are chief or senior planning officers who deal with 'delegated decisions' . . . [as] a rough guide, the larger the project the higher up the pyramid of decision makers the decision is made. (Weston 1997)

Different decision-making rules apply for different UK jurisdictions. For instance, the Town and Country Planning Act 1990 (and parallel legislation in Scotland) requires planning decisions to be made with 'regard to the provisions of the development plan, so far as material to the application, and to any other material considerations'. There is no definitive list of material planning considerations, but they commonly include visual amenity, noise, traffic generation, nature conservation and other topics covered by EIA. This is expected to change under the proposed National Planning Policy Framework that would, instead, introduce a 'presumption in favour of sustainable development', namely that:

> individuals and businesses have the right to build homes and other local buildings provided that they conform to national environmental, architectural, economic and social standards, conform with the local plan, and pay a tariff that compensates the community for loss of amenity and costs of additional infrastructure. (Parliament 2011)

When determining an application for a nationally significant infrastructure project, the Infrastructure Planning Commission must have regard to any local impact report, other prescribed matters, and other matters that the IPC thinks are important and relevant to the decision; and it must decide the application in accordance with any relevant national policy statements unless, *inter alia*, the adverse impacts of the proposed development would outweigh its benefits (Planning Act 2008). However, in all cases, where a project requires EIA, the decision-maker must take into account the 'environmental information' in the decision. This is the information contained in the EIS and other documents, and any comment made by the statutory consultees and representations from members of the public.

The decision on an application with an EIS must be made within a specified period (e.g. 16 weeks for a local authority planning application), unless the developer agrees to a longer period. By any standards, making decisions on development projects is a complex undertaking. Decisions for projects requiring EIAs tend to be even more complex, because by definition they deal with larger, more complex projects, and probably a greater range of interest groups:

> The competition of interests is not simply between the developer and the consultees. It can also be a conflict between consultees, with the developer stuck in the middle hardly able to satisfy all parties and the 'competent authority' left to establish a planning balance where no such balance can be struck. (Weston 1997)

Whereas the decision-making process for projects with EIA was initially accepted as being basically a black box, attempts have subsequently been made to make the process more rigorous and transparent. Research by the University of Manchester (Wood and Jones 1997) and Oxford Brookes University (Weston *et al.* 1997) have focused on how environmental information is used in UK decision-making; this is discussed further in Chapter 8. A government good practice guide on the evaluation of environmental information for planning projects (DoE 1994) begins with a definition of evaluation:

> . . . in the context of environmental assessment, there are a number of different stages or levels of evaluation. These are concerned with:
>
> - checking the adequacy of the information supplied as part of the ES, or contributed from other sources;
> - examining the magnitude, importance and significance of individual environmental impacts and their effects on specific areas of concern . . . ;
> - preparing an overall 'weighing' of environmental and other material considerations in order to arrive at a basis for the planning decision.

The guide suggests that, after vetting the application and EIS, advertising the proposals and EIS, and relevant consultation, the planning authority should carry out two stages of decision-making: an evaluation of the individual environmental impacts and their effects, and weighing the information to reach a decision. The evaluation of impacts and effects first involves verifying any factual statements in the EIS, perhaps by highlighting any statements of concern and discussing these with the developer. The nature and character of particular impacts can then be examined; either the EIS will already have provided such an analysis (e.g. in the form of Table 6.4) or the case-work officer could prepare such a table. Finally, the significance and importance of the impacts can be weighed up, taking into consideration such issues as the extent of the area affected, the scale and probability of the effects, the scope for mitigation and the importance of the issue.

The range of decision options are as for any application for project authorization: the competent authority can grant permission for the project (with or without conditions) or refuse permission. It can also suggest further mitigation measures following consultations, and may seek to negotiate these with the developer. If the development is refused, the developer can appeal against the decision. If the development is permitted, individuals or organizations can challenge the permission. The relevant Secretary of State may also be able to 'call in' an application, for a variety of reasons. A public inquiry may result.

But decision-making is not a clinical exercise. Decision letters have been described as 'a letter to the loser' (Des Rosiers 2000), suggesting a type of personal relationship between decision-maker and decision-receiver. In a Canadian context, Ross (2000) explains how he and fellow panel member Mike Fanchuk wrote the report that explained their decision about whether to permit a pulp mill:

> Mike Fanchuk [is] a farmer from just north of the pulp mill site ... During my work with Mike, we discussed when we would be satisfied with the report, and thus when we would be willing to sign it ... I believe Mike's approach is the best I have ever encountered. He would only be willing to sign the report when he felt that, in future years, he would

be pleased to tell his eight-year old granddaughter that he had served on the panel and authored the report. In academic terms, this intergenerational equity illustrates very well the principles of sustainable development ... More importantly, however, it illustrates the basic human need to be proud of work one has done.

An initial decision may need to be ratified by others, and may be overturned at that stage. In the case of a planning application, the planning officer's recommendations will go to the planning committee, which makes the final decision. In the UK, the IPC's decision will be passed to the relevant Secretary of State. Other procedures will apply to other jurisdictions.

6.6.2 EIA and public inquiries

A Secretary of State may 'call in' a planning application if a developer challenges a refusal of planning permission, a planning decision is not reached within a given time limit, or if the Secretary of State wants to consider the application for other reasons. A public inquiry must then be held if the developer or local planning authority requests one. At the inquiry, various parties can provide evidence and may be able to cross-question other parties. Public inquiries are expensive to all parties, and can be very drawn out. For instance, the public inquiry for Heathrow Terminal 5 lasted nearly four years. Weston (1997) compellingly discusses why all parties involved in EIA try to avoid public inquiries:

> By the time a project becomes the subject of a public inquiry the sides are drawn and the hearing becomes a focus for adversarial debate between opposing, expensive, experts directed and spurred on by advocates schooled in the art of cajoling witnesses into submission and contradictions. Such debates are seldom rational or in any other way related to the systematic, iterative and cooperative characteristics of good practice EIA. By the time the inquiry comes around, and all the investment has been made in expert witnesses and smooth talking barristers, it is far too late for all that.

Nevertheless, hundreds of projects involving EIA have gone to inquiry.

The environmental impact of proposals, especially traffic, landscape and amenity issues, will certainly be examined in detail during any inquiry. The EIA regulations allow inquiry inspectors and the Secretary of State to require (a) the submission of an EIS before a public inquiry, if they regard this as appropriate, and (b) further information from the developer, if they consider the EIS is inadequate as it stands. In practice, before public inquiries involving EIAs the inspector generally receives a case file, including the EIS, which is examined to determine whether any further information is required. Pre-inquiry meetings may be held where the inspector may seek further information. These meetings may also assist the developer and competent authority to arrive at a list of agreed matters before the start of the inquiry; this can avoid unnecessary delays during it. At the inquiry, inspectors often ask for further information, and they may adjourn the inquiry if the information cannot be produced within the available time. The information contained in the EIS will be among the material considerations taken into account. However, an inadequate EIS is not a valid reason for preventing authorization, or even for delaying an inquiry.[5]

An analysis of ten public inquiries involving projects for which EISs had been prepared (Jones and Wood 1995) suggested that in their recommendations most inspectors give 'moderate' or 'considerable' weight to the EIS and consultations on the EIS, and that environmental information is of 'reasonable' importance to the decision whether to grant consent. However, a subsequent study of 54 decision letters from inspectors (Weston 1997) suggested that EIA has had little influence on the inquiry process: in about two-thirds of the cases, national or local land-use policies were the determining issues identified by the inspectors and the Secretary of State, and in the remaining cases other traditional planning matters predominated:

> The headings which dominate the decision letters of the Inspectors and Secretaries of State are the traditional planning material considerations such as amenity, various forms of risk, traffic and need, although some

factors such as flora and fauna, noise and landscape do tend to be discussed separately. (Weston 1997)

6.6.3 Challenging a decision: judicial review

The UK planning system has no official provisions for an appeal against development consent. However, if permission is granted, a third party may challenge that decision through judicial review proceedings in the UK courts, or through the European Commission.

In the UK, an application for judicial review of a decision should be made promptly, typically within 6 weeks or 3 months of the decision (depending on the type of decision). Judicial review proceedings first require that the third party shows it has 'standing' to bring in the application, namely sufficient interest in the project by virtue of attributes specific to it or circumstances, which differentiate it from all other parties (e.g. a financial or health interest). Establishing standing is one of the main difficulties in applying for judicial review.[6] If standing is established, the third party must then convince the court that the competent authority did not act according to the relevant EIA procedures. The court does not make its own decision about the merits of the case, but only reviews the way in which the competent authority arrived at its decision:

> The court will only quash a decision of the [competent authority] where it acted without jurisdiction or exceeded its jurisdiction or failed to comply with the rules of natural justice in a case where those rules apply or where there is an error of law on the face of the record or the decision is so unreasonable that no [competent authority] could have made it. (Atkinson and Ainsworth 1992)

Various possible scenarios emerge. A competent authority may fail to require an EIA for project that should have had one; a planning officer without formal delegated authority may make a planning decision; a planning authority may make a planning decision without having access to, or having adequately considered, all relevant environmental information. In such a case, its decision would be void. Several court cases have also revolved around the level of detail needed in EISs of outline planning applications. Section 8.6 discusses these in more detail. Although recent UK court cases have interpreted the requirements of the EIA Directive as having a 'wide scope and broad purpose', it is very unlikely that the UK courts will ever play as active a role as those in the US did in relation to the NEPA.

6.6.4 Challenging a decision: the European Commission

Another avenue by which third parties can challenge a competent authority's decision to permit development, or not to require EIA, is the European Commission. Such cases need to show that the UK failed to fulfil its obligations as a Member State under the Treaty of Rome by not properly implementing EC legislation, in this case Directive 85/337. In such a case, Article 169 of the Treaty allows a declaration of non-compliance to be sought from the European Court of Justice. The issue of standing is not a problem here, since the European Commission can begin proceedings either on its own initiative or based on the written complaint of any person. To use this mechanism, the Commission must first state its case to the Member State and seek its observations. The Commission may then issue a 'reasoned opinion'. If the Member State fails to comply within the specified time, the case proceeds to the European Court of Justice.

Under Article 171 of the Treaty of Rome, if the European Court of Justice finds that a Member State has failed to fulfil an obligation under the Treaty, it may require the Member State to take the necessary measures to comply with the Court's judgement. Under Article 186, the EC may take interim measures to require a Member State to desist from certain actions until a decision is taken on the main action. However, to do so the Commission must show the need for urgent relief, and that irreparable damage to community interests would result if these measures were not taken. Readers are referred to Atkinson and Ainsworth (1992), Buxton (1992) and Salter (1992a, b, c) for further information on procedures.

Of the environmental infringement cases handled by the European Commission, about 10 per cent relate to environmental impact assessment. The largest number of environmental infringements in 2008 and 2009 were against Italy, Spain, Ireland, France and the UK (EC 2010b).

••

6.7 Summary

Active public participation, thorough consultation with relevant consultees and good presentation are important aspects of a successful EIA process. All have been undervalued to date, despite the transposition of the Aarhus Convention. The presentation of environmental information has improved, and statutory consultees are becoming increasingly familiar with the EIA process, but public participation is likely to remain a weak aspect of EIA until developers and competent authorities see the benefits exceeding the costs.

Formal reviews of EIAs are also rarely carried out, despite the availability of several non-mandatory review guidelines and government advice on the use of environmental information in decision-making. Such reviews can help to ensure that the EIS is fully taken into consideration in the decision-making stage. The links between the quality of an EIS and that of the planning decision are discussed in Chapter 8.

Several appeals against development consents or against competent authorities' failure to require EIA have been brought to the UK courts or the EC. The UK courts have historically taken a relatively narrow interpretation of the requirements of the EIA regulations, but this has recently been changing. The EC, by contrast, has challenged the UK government on its implementation of Directive 85/337 and on a number of specific decisions resulting from this implementation.

More positively, the next step in a good EIA procedure is the monitoring of the development's actual impacts and the comparison of actual and predicted impacts. This is discussed in the next chapter.

SOME QUESTIONS

The following questions are intended to help the reader focus on the key issues of this chapter.

1   Public participation and public consultation are often used synonymously. What is the difference between them?
2   Different stakeholders require different techniques to learn about a project's environmental impacts and provide optimum input to the project planning process. Assume that you are devising a public participation programme for a wind farm EIS (or a different kind of project with which you are familiar). Using Table 6.3 as a basis, which three techniques would you use for local residents? Which three would you use for a national-level non-governmental organization opposed to wind power on landscape grounds? Which three would you use for the government agency responsible for biodiversity? (NB: some of them might be the same from group to group).
3   The introductory section to the EIA Directive refers to public participation in the following way: 'Whereas development consent for public and private projects ... should be granted only after prior assessment ... ; whereas this assessment must be conducted on the basis of the appropriate information supplied by the developer, which may be supplemented by the authorities and by the people who may be concerned by the project in question.' How might it be rephrased to promote a higher level of public participation in EIA?
4   Section 6.2.3 lists the UK procedural requirements for public participation. Do they match the level of participation set out in the introductory section to the EIA Directive (see question 3 above)?
5   For a country and type of plan of your choice, identify the statutory consultees.
6   In one page, explain the EIA process in a non-technical way.
7   Explain what is wrong with the 'wrong' quotes in Section 6.4.2. Try to rephrase them in a 'right' way.
8   Figure 6.2 shows different ways of presenting an EIS. Which do you think would work best for: (i) technically minded consultees; (ii) people with access to the Internet, and those without access; (iii) people who have problems reading small print (or at all); (iv) people who might struggle to pay for the 'reasonable cost' of printing and distributing the EIS?
9   Under what circumstances might each of the grading approaches (a–c) in Table 6.5 be used?

....

Notes

1   Although this section refers to public consultation and participation together as 'public participation', the two are in fact separate. Consultation is in essence an exercise concerning a passive audience: views are solicited, but respondents have little active influence over any resulting decisions. In contrast, public participation involves an active role for the public, with some influence over any modifications to the project and over the ultimate decision.
2   The coalition government of 2010 will change this, although details are not yet available at the time of writing (spring 2011). The IPC and the Planning Inspectorate will be merged, and the IPC will make recommendations to the relevant secretary of state, who will make the final decision.
3   Weston (1997) notes that LPAs need to be aware that they have the power to ask for further information, and that failure to use it could later be seen as tacit acceptance of the information provided. For instance, when deciding on an appeal for a Scottish quarry extension, the Reporter noted that it was significant that the LPA had not requested further information when they were processing the application, and had not objected to the EIS until the development came to appeal.

4   Where the project has already been built without authorization, the competent authority considers the environmental information when determining whether the project will be demolished or not.

5   For instance, in the case of a Scottish appeal regarding a proposed quarry extension (Scottish Office, P/PPA/SQ/336, 6 January 1992), the Reporter noted that: 'The ES has been strongly criticised . . . [it] does not demonstrate that a proper analysis of environmental impacts has been made . . . Despite its shortcomings, the ES appears to me to comply broadly with the statutory requirements of the EA regulations.'

6   An EC court case, for instance, ruled that Greenpeace had insufficient individual concerns to contest a decision to use regional funds to help build power stations in the Canary Islands (Greenpeace vs. Commission of the European Communities, *Journal of Environmental Law*, 8 (1996), 139). Similar judgements have been made in the UK context. COWI (2009) provides further information on standing in different Member States.

••

References

ADB (NGO Forum on ADB) 2006. *The Advocacy Guide to ADB EIA Requirement, Philippines*. Available at: www.forum-adb.org/BACKUP/pdf/guidebooks/EIA%20Guidebook.pdf.

Arnstein, S.R. 1971. A ladder of public participation in the USA. *Journal of the Royal Town Planning Institute*, April, 216–24.

Atkinson, N. and Ainsworth, R. 1992. Environmental assessment and the local authority: facing the European imperative. *Environmental Policy and Practice* 2 (2), 111–28.

Audit Commission 2000. *Listen Up! Effective Community Consultation*. Available at: www.audit-commission.gov.uk/SiteCollectionDocuments/AuditCommission Reports/NationalStudies/listenup.pdf.

Balram, S., Dragicevic, S. and Meredith, T. 2003. Achieving effectiveness in stakeholder participation using the GIS-based Collaborative Spatial Delphi methodology. *Journal of Environmental Assessment Policy and Management* 5 (3), 365–94.

Buxton, R. 1992. Scope for legal challenge. In *Environmental assessment and audit: a user's guide*, Ambit (ed), 43–4. Gloucester: Ambit.

CEC (European Commission of Communities) 2001. *Guidance on EIA: EIS review. DG XI*. Brussels: CEC.

CEC 2009. On the application and effectiveness of the EIA Directive (Directive 85/337/EEC, as amended by Directives 97/11/EC and 2003/35/EC). Available at: www.eur-lex.europa.eu/LexUriServ/LexUriServ.do?uri=COM:2009:0378:FIN:EN:PDF.

Clark, B. 1994. Improving public participation in environmental impact assessment. *Built Environment* 20 (4), 294–308.

COWI 2009. *Study concerning the report on the application and effectiveness of the EIA Directive*, Final report to European Commission DG ENV. Kongens Lyngby, Denmark: COWI.

Daily Echo 2011. Southampton biomass plant plans 'beyond belief' says New Forest District Council. 14 April. Available at: www.dailyecho.co.uk/news/8974234.Biomass_plans__beyond_belief_.

Dallas, W.G. 1984. Experiences of environmental impact assessment procedures in Ireland. In *Planning and Ecology*, R.D. Roberts and T.M. Roberts (eds), 389–95. London: Chapman & Hall.

DCLG (Department for Communities and Local Government) 2009. *Publicity for planning applications: consultation*. London: DCLG.

DCLG (Department for Communities and Local Government) 2011. *Guidance on the Environmental Impact Assessment (EIA) Regulations 2011 for England*. London: DCLG.

Des Rosiers 2000. From telling to listening: a therapeutic analysis of the role of courts in miniority-majority conflicts. *Court Review*, Spring.

DETR 2000. *Environmental impact assessment: a guide to the procedures*. London: HMSO.

DoE (Department of the Environment) 1994. *Evaluation of environmental information for planning projects: a good practice guide*. London: HMSO.

DoE 1995. *Preparation of environmental statements for planning projects that require environmental assessment*. London: HMSO.

EC (European Commission) 2010a. Environment: Commission warns UK about unfair cost of challenging decisions. Available at: www.europa.eu/rapid/pressReleasesAction.do?reference=IP/10/312&type=HTML.

EC 2010b. Statistics on environmental infringements. Available at: www.ec.europa.eu/environment/legal/law/statistics.htm.

EDF Energy 2009. *Hinkley Point C: Consultation on initial proposals and options*. Available at: www.hinkley point.edfenergyconsultation.info/websitefiles/PPS_SW_XXXX_EDF_HINK_POINT_BDS_12.09_1_pps.pdf.

Hancock, T. 1992. Statement as an aid to consent. In *Environmental assessment and audit: a user's guide*, Ambit (ed), 34–35. Gloucester: Ambit.

Hartley, N. and Wood, C. 2005. Public participation in environmental impact assessment – implementing the Aarhus Convention. *Environmental Impact Assessment Review* 25, 319–40.

IEMA (Institute of Environmental Management and Assessment) 2002. *Perspectives: participation in environmental decision-making.* Lincoln: IEMA.

International Association for Public Participation 2001. IAP2's Public Participation Toolbox. Available at: www.iap2.affiniscape.com/associations/4748/ files/06Dec_Toolbox.pdf.

Jones, C.E. and Wood, C. 1995. The impact of environmental assessment in public inquiry decisions. *Journal of Planning and Environment Law*, October, 890–904.

Kenyan, R.C. 1991. Environmental assessment: an overview on behalf of the R.I.C.S. *Journal of Planning and Environment Law*, 419–22.

Lee, N. and Colley, R. 1990. *Reviewing the quality of environmental statements.* Occasional Paper no. 24. Manchester: University of Manchester, EIA Centre.

McCormick, J. 1991. *British politics and the environment.* London: Earthscan.

McNab, A. 1997. Scoping and public participation. In *Planning and EIA in practice*, J. Weston (ed), 60–77. Harlow: Longman.

Mollison, K. 1992. A discussion of public consultation in the EIA process with reference to Holland and Ireland (written for MSc Diploma course in Environmental Assessment and Management). Oxford: Oxford Polytechnic.

O'Faircheallaigh, C. 2010. Public participation and environmental impact assessment: purposes, implications and lessons for public policy making. *Environmental Impact Assessment Review* 30, 19–27.

Parliament (2011) The Localism Bill. Available at: www.publications.parliament.uk/pa/cm201011/ cmselect/cmenvaud/799/79903.htm.

Partidario, M.R. 1996. *16th Annual Meeting, International Association for Impact Assessment: Synthesis of Workshop Conclusions.* Estoril: IAIA.

Petts, J. 1999. Public participation and EIA. In *Handbook of environmental impact assessment*, J. Petts (ed), vol. 1. Oxford: Blackwell Science.

Petts, J. 2003. Barriers to deliberative participation in EIA: learning from waste policies, plans and projects. *Journal of Environmental Assessment Policy and Management* 5 (3), 269–94.

Rodriguez-Bachiller, A. with J. Glasson 2004. *Expert Systems and Geographical Information Systems for Impact Assessment.* London: Taylor and Francis.

Ross, W.A. 2000. Reflections of an environmental assessment panel member. *Impact Assessment and Project Appraisal* 18 (2), 91–8.

Salter, J.R. 1992a. Environmental assessment: the challenge from Brussels. *Journal of Planning and Environment Law*, January, 14–20.

Salter, J.R. 1992b. Environmental assessment – the need for transparency. *Journal of Planning and Environment Law*, March, 214–21.

Salter, J.R. 1992c. Environmental assessment – the question of implementation. *Journal of Planning and Environment Law*, April, 313–18.

Turner, T. 1988. The legal eagles. *Amicus Journal*, winter, 25–37.

Weiss, E.H. 1989. An unreadable EIS is an environmental hazard. *Environmental Professional* 11, 236–40.

Wende, W. 2002. Evaluation of the effectiveness and quality of environmental impact assessment in the Federal Republic of Germany. *Impact Assessment and Project Appraisal* 20 (2), 93–99.

Westman, W.E. 1985. *Ecology, impact assessment and environmental planning.* New York: Wiley.

Weston, J. (ed) 1997. *Planning and EIA in practice.* Harlow: Longman.

Weston, J., Glasson, J., Therivel, R., Weston, E., Frost, R. 1997. *Environmental information and planning projects*, Working Paper no. 170. Oxford: Oxford Brookes University, School of Planning.

Williams, G. and Hill, A. 1996. Are we failing at environment justice? How minority and low income populations are kept out of the public involvement process. *Proceedings of the 16th Annual Meeting of the International Association for Impact Assessment.* Estoril: IAIA.

Wood, C.M. and Jones, C. 1997. The effect of environmental assessment on UK local authority planning decisions. *Urban Studies* 34 (8), 1237–57.

7 Monitoring and auditing: after the decision

●●

7.1 Introduction

Major projects, such as roads, airports, power stations, waste processing plants, mineral developments and holiday villages, have a life cycle with a number of key stages (see Figure 1.5). The life cycle may cover a very long period (e.g. 50–60 years for the planning, construction, operation and decommissioning of a fossil-fuelled power station). EIA, as it is currently practised in the UK and in many other countries, relates primarily to the period *before* the decision. At its worst, it is a partial linear exercise related to one site, produced in-house by a developer, without any public participation. There has been a danger of a short-sighted 'build it and forget it' approach (Culhane 1993). However, EIA should not stop at the decision. It should be more than an auxiliary to the procedures to obtain a planning permission; rather it should be a means to obtain good environmental management *over the life* of the project. This means including monitoring and auditing fully into the EIA process. There is a continuing danger that emphasis on pre-decision analysis will keep EIA away from its key goal of environmental protection. EIA should seek to maximize the potential for continuous improvement. Resources spent on baseline studies and predictions may be rendered of little value unless there is some way of testing the predictions and determining whether mitigation and enhancement measures are appropriately applied (Ahammed and Nixon 2006). It is good to record that there is now more learning from experience and some good progress to note; see for example Morrison-Saunders and Arts (2004) and the special edition of the *Impact Assessment and Project Appraisal* journal (IAPAY 2005) on EIA Follow-Up.

Section 7.2 clarifies some relevant definitions, for example between monitoring and auditing, and outlines their important roles in EIA. An approach to the better integration of monitoring into the process, drawing in particular on international practice, is then outlined in Section 7.3. We then discuss approaches to environmental impact auditing, including a review of attempts to audit a range of EISs in a number of countries. The final section draws on detailed monitoring and auditing studies of the local socio-economic impacts of the construction of the Sizewell B pressurized water reactor (PWR) nuclear power station in the UK, and also briefly notes monitoring of the more recent London 2012 Olympics project.

7.2 The importance of monitoring and auditing in the EIA process

In many aspects of EIA there has been considerable semantic development and a widening of relevant terms. In earlier editions of this chapter we have focused primarily on *monitoring* and *auditing* as key elements in the after the decision process, or the follow- up process as it is known in some countries such as Canada and Australia. These elements are still crucial and the main focus of Chapter 7, but note should also be taken of a widening of those key elements to also include *management* and *communications* (Arts *et al.* 2001; Marshall *et al.* 2005). In total such elements can facilitate learning from experience, preventing EIA from becoming just a pro-forma exercise with little clout after the project decision has been taken.

Monitoring involves the measuring and recording of physical, social and economic variables associated with development impacts (e.g. traffic flows, air quality, noise, employment levels). The activity seeks to provide information on the characteristics and functioning of variables in time and space, and in particular on the occurrence and magnitude of impacts. Monitoring can improve project management. It can be used, for example, as an early warning system, to identify harmful trends in a locality before it is too late to take remedial action. It can help to identify and correct unanticipated impacts. Monitoring can also provide an accepted database, which can be useful in mediation between interested parties. Thus, monitoring of the origins, pathways and destinations of, for example, dust in an industrial area may clarify where the responsibilities lie. Monitoring is also essential for successful environmental impact auditing, and can be one of the most effective guarantees of commitment to undertakings and to mitigation and enhancement measures.

Environmental impact auditing, which is covered in this chapter, involves comparing the impacts predicted in an EIS with those that actually occur after implementation, in order to assess whether the impact prediction performs satisfactorily (Buckley 1991). In some of the literature this step is sometimes referred to as evaluation. The audit can be of both impact predictions (how good were the predictions?) and of mitigation and enhancement measures and conditions attached to the development (are the mitigation and enhancement measures effective; are the conditions being honoured?). This approach to auditing contrasts with *environmental management auditing*, which focuses on public and private corporate structures and programmes for environmental management and the associated risks and liabilities. We discuss this latter approach further in Chapter 12.

Management is an important element in terms of making decisions and taking appropriate action in response to issues raised from the monitoring and auditing activities (Marshall *et al.* 2005). For example, monitoring may show lower levels of local recruitment than predicted for the construction stage of a major project. A management response may be to redouble efforts on local training programmes. *Communication* is to inform stakeholders about the results of EIA monitoring, auditing and management activities. Such communication may emanate from both proponents and regulators; hopefully there may be a partnership approach between the two. Ideally the community stakeholder's role is more than that of passive recipient of follow-up activities, and rather more one of partner in the process, being involved directly in the follow-up activities.

In total, such activities can make important contributions to the better planning and EIA of future projects (Figure 7.1). There is a vital need to introduce feedback in order to learn from experience; we must avoid the constant 'reinventing of the wheel' in EIA (Sadler 1988). Monitoring and auditing of outcomes, and the resultant management responses and associated communication, can contribute to an improvement in all aspects of the EIA process, from understanding baseline conditions to the framing of effective mitigating and enhancement measures. In addition, Greene *et al.* (1985) noted that monitoring and auditing should reduce time and resource commitments to EIA by allowing all participants to learn from past experience; they should also contribute to a general enhancing of the credibility of proponents, regulatory agencies and EIA processes. We are learning, and there is a considerable growth of interest in examining the effectiveness of the EIA process in practice. However, there are still a number of significant issues that have limited the

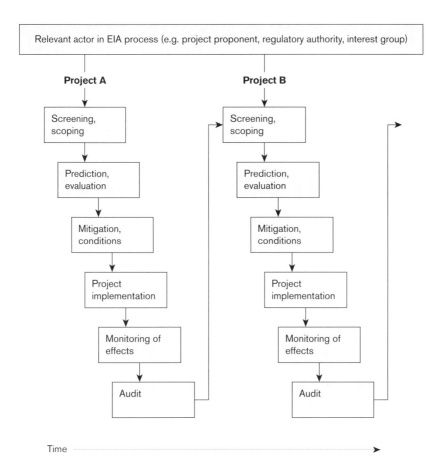

Figure 7.1

Monitoring, auditing and learning from experience in the EIA process

Source: Adapted from Bisset and Tomlinson 1988; Sadler 1988

use of monitoring and auditing to date. These issues and possible ways forward for monitoring and auditing in practice are now discussed.

••••••••••••••••••••••••••••••••••••••

7.3 Monitoring in practice

7.3.1 Key elements

Monitoring implies the systematic collection of a potentially large quantity of information over a long period of time. Such information should include not only the traditional *indicators* (e.g. ambient air quality, noise levels, the size of a work-force) but also *causal underlying factors* (e.g. the *decisions* and *policies* of the local authority and developer). The causal factors determine the

impacts and may have to be changed if there is a wish to modify impacts. *Opinions* about impacts are also important. Individual and group 'social constructions of reality' (IOCGP 2003) are often sidelined as 'mere perceptions, or emotions', not to be weighted as heavily as facts. But such opinions can be very influential in determining the response to a project. To ignore or undervalue them may not be methodologically defensible and is likely to raise hostility. Monitoring should also analyse impact equity. The distribution of impacts will vary between groups and locations; some groups may be more vulnerable than others, as a result of factors such as age, race, gender and income. So a systematic attempt to identify opinions can be an important input into a monitoring study.

The information collected needs to be stored, analysed and communicated to relevant participants in the EIA process. A primary requirement, therefore, is to focus monitoring activity only on 'those environmental parameters expected to experience a significant impact, together with those parameters for which the assessment methodology or basic data were not so well established as desired' (Lee and Wood 1980).

Monitoring is an integral part of EIA; baseline data, project descriptions, impact predictions and mitigation and enhancement measures should be developed with monitoring implications in mind. An EIS should include a *monitoring programme* that has clear objectives, temporal and spatial controls, an adequate duration (e.g. covering the main stages of the project's implementation), practical methodologies, sufficient funding, clear responsibilities and open and regular reporting. Ideally, the monitoring activity should include a partnership between the parties involved; for example, the collection of information could involve the developer, local authority and local community. Monitoring programmes should also be adapted to the dynamic nature of the environment (Holling 1978).

7.3.2 Mandatory or discretionary?

Unfortunately, monitoring is not a mandatory step in many EIA procedures, including those current in the UK. In contrast to the more recent SEA regulations, European Commission EIA regulations do not specifically require monitoring. This omission was recognized in the review of Directive 85/337 (CEC 1993). The Commission is a strong advocate for the inclusion of a formal monitoring programme in an EIS, but EU Member States are normally more defensive and reactive. In consequence, the amended Directive does not include a mandatory monitoring requirement.[1] However, this has not deterred some Member States. For example, in The Netherlands the competent authority is required to monitor project implementation, based on information provided by the developer, and to make the monitoring information publicly available. If actual impacts exceed those predicted, the competent authority must take measures to reduce or mitigate these impacts.

However, despite such legal provisions, practice has been limited and little post-EIA monitoring and evaluation has been carried out. See Arts (1998) for a comprehensive coverage of EIA follow-up in The Netherlands.

In other Member States, as noted in Chapter 2 and CEC (2009), the lack of a mandatory monitoring requirement is a continuing, serious and long-standing issue. In the absence of mandatory procedures, it is usually difficult to persuade developers that it is in their interest to have a continuing approach to EIA. This is particularly the case where the proponent has a one-off project, and has less interest in learning from experience for application to future projects. Fortunately, we can turn to some examples of good practice in a few other countries. A brief summary of monitoring procedures in Canada is included in Chapter 10. In Western Australia (also see Chapter 10), the environmental consequences of developments are commonly monitored and reported. If it is shown that conditions are not being met, the government may take appropriate action. Interestingly, there is provision in Western Australian procedures for an 'environmental review and management programme' (Morrison-Saunders 1996).

7.3.3 The case of California

The monitoring procedures used in California, for projects subject to the CEQA, are of particular interest (California Resources Agency 1988). Since January 1989, state and local agencies in California have been required to adopt a monitoring and/or reporting programme for mitigation measures and project changes that have been imposed as conditions to address significant environmental impacts. The aim is to provide a mechanism that will help to ensure that mitigation measures will be implemented in a timely manner in accordance with the terms of the project's approval. Monitoring refers to the observation and oversight of mitigation activities at a project site, whereas reporting refers to the communication of the monitoring results to the agency and public. If the implementation of a project is to be phased, the mitigation and subsequent reporting and monitoring may also have to be phased. If monitoring reveals that mitigation measures are ignored or are not completed, sanctions could be imposed;

these can include, for example, 'stop work' orders, fines and restitution. The components of a monitoring programme would normally include the following:

- a summary of the significant impacts identified in the environmental impact report (EIR);
- the mitigation measures recommended for each significant impact;
- the monitoring requirements, and responsible agency(ies), for each mitigation measure;

- the person or agency responsible for the monitoring of the mitigation measure;
- the timing and/or frequency of the monitoring;
- the agency responsible for ensuring compliance with the monitoring programme; and
- the reporting requirements.

Figure 7.2 provides an extract from a monitoring programme for a woodwaste conversion facility at West Berkeley in California.

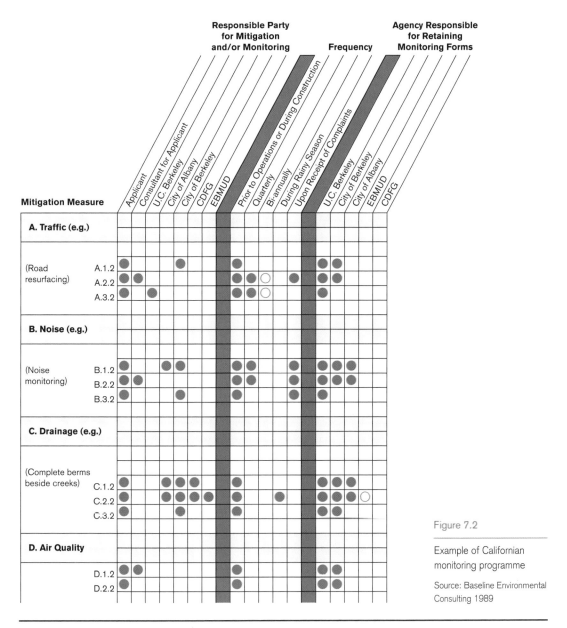

Figure 7.2

Example of Californian monitoring programme

Source: Baseline Environmental Consulting 1989

7.3.4 The case of Hong Kong

In Hong Kong, a systematic, comprehensive environmental monitoring and auditing system was introduced in 1990 for major projects. A major impetus for action was the construction of the new $20 billion airport at Chap Lap Kok, which included the construction of not only the airport island, but also a railway, highways and crossings and a major Kowloon reclamation project. The Environmental Monitoring and Audit (EM&A) manual includes three stages of an event action plan: (1) trigger level, to provide an early warning; (2) action level, at which action is to be taken before an upper limit of impacts is reached; and (3) target level, beyond which a predetermined plan response is initiated to avoid or rectify any problems. The approach does build monitoring much more into project decision-making, requiring proponents to agree monitoring and audit protocols and event action plans in advance; however, enforcement has been problematic (Au and Sanvícens 1996). The EM&A is intended to be a dynamic document to be reviewed regularly and updated (as necessary) during the implementation of the project.

Since April 1998 there have been EIA regulations in force that stipulate in detail when and how environmental monitoring and auditing should be done (EPD 1997, 1998). The regulations normally result in permit conditions relating to project approval. This has provided a statutory basis for follow-up work, and offences carry stiff penalties (up to $250,000 and six months imprisonment). A recent and fascinating innovation in the Hong Kong system is the use of the Internet for monitoring the effects of large projects and of compliance with the permit conditions. Under procedures introduced since 2000 major projects must set up a monitoring website (see www.info.gov.hk/epd/eia). Some sites include webcams focused on parts of the project. There is public access to the websites, and concerned members of the public can report their views on project performance back to both the government and the developer (Hui and Ho 2002). Is this the shape of things to come? Table 7.1 provides an extract from an EM&A report for a Hong Kong helipad development.

7.3.5 UK experience

Although monitoring is still not a mandatory requirement under UK EIA regulations, there is monitoring activity. An early research study at Oxford Brookes University (see Frost 1997; Glasson 1994) sought to provide an estimate of the extent of such activity using a 'contents analysis' and a 'practice analysis'. The contents analysis of references to monitoring intentions used a representative sample of almost 700 EISs and summaries of EISs (taken from the Institute of Environmental Assessment's *Digest of environmental statements*) (IEA 1993). For some EISs there was a clearly indicated monitoring section; for others, monitoring was covered in sections related to mitigation. In several cases there were generic monitoring proposals with, for example, a proposal to check that contractors are in compliance with contract specifications. Overall, approximately 30 per cent of the cases included at least one reference to impact monitoring. The maximum number of monitoring types was six, suggesting that impact monitoring was unlikely to be approaching comprehensiveness in even a select few cases. Table 7.2 shows the types of monitoring in EISs. Water quality monitoring was more frequently cited than air quality monitoring. Point of origin monitoring of air and aqueous emissions was also frequently cited. There was only very limited reference to the monitoring of non-biophysical (i.e. socio-economic) impacts. The type of monitoring varied between project types. For combined-cycle gas turbine (CCGT) power stations, proposals were often made for monitoring air emissions, air quality and construction noise; for landfill projects, the proposals were skewed towards the monitoring of leachate, landfill gas and water quality.

The practice analysis used a small representative sample of 17 projects, with EIS monitoring proposals, which had started. The LPAs were contacted to clarify monitoring arrangements including, for example, whether monitoring arrangements had been made operational under the terms of various consents (e.g. planning conditions, S106 agreements, integrated pollution control (IPC) conditions, site licence conditions) or whether monitoring was being carried out voluntarily. The findings revealed that overall EISs tended to

Table 7.1 Extract from an EM&A report for a helipad project in Hong Kong: implementation schedule of recommended mitigation measures for construction of Yung Shue Wan Helipad (air quality mitigation measures)

EIA Ref.	EM&A Ref.	Recommended environmental protection/mitigation measures	Objectives of the recommended measures and main concerns to address	Who to implement the measure?	Location/timing of implementation measures	What requirements or standards for the measure to achieve?
S3.5.1	S2.5	All dust control measures as recommended in the Air Pollution Control Regulation, where applicable, should be implemented	Air quality during construction	Contractors	At all construction works sites through duration of construction works	EIAO-TM, Air Pollution Control (Construction Dust) Regulations
S3.5.1	S2.4	Typical dust control measures include: • restricting heights from which materials are dropped, as far as practicable, to minimize the fugitive dust arising from loading/unloading	Air quality during construction	Contractors	At all construction works sites through duration of construction works	EIAO-TM, Air Pollution Control (Construction Dust) Regulations
S3.5.1	S2.4	• all stockpiles of excavated materials or spoil of more than 50m³ should be enclosed, covered or dampened during dry or windy conditions	Air quality during construction	Contractors	At all construction works sites through duration of construction works	EIAO-TM, Air Pollution Control (Construction Dust) Regulations
S3.5.1	S2.4	• effective water sprays should be used to control potential dust emission sources such as unpaved haul roads and active construction areas	Air quality during construction	Contractors	At all construction works sites through duration of construction works	EIAO-TM, Air Pollution Control (Construction Dust) Regulations

Source: CWE-ZHEC Joint Venture 2007

understate, on average by about 30 per cent, the amount of monitoring actually undertaken. This may be a response to planning conditions and agreements resulting from the decision-making process; it may also relate to other relevant licensing procedures, such as IPC. Whatever the case, the findings do suggest that some monitoring proposals in EISs are carried out and are often more extensive than the, admittedly often limited, coverage in EIAs. The findings do not, of course, provide any information on the quality of the monitoring or about the accuracy of the predictions.

7.4 Auditing in practice

Auditing has developed a considerable variety of types. Tomlinson and Atkinson (1987a, b) attempted to standardize *definitions* with a set of terms for seven different points of audit in the 'standard' EIA process, as follows:

• Decision point audit (draft EIS): by regulatory authority in the planning approval process.

Table 7.2 Types of impact monitoring in UK EISs

Type	% of total monitoring proposals
Water quality	16
Air emissions	15
Aqueous emissions	13
Noise	12
General	9
Others	7
Ecological	7
Archaeological	6
Air quality	5
Structural survey	4
Liaison group	3
Water levels	3
	100

Source: Glasson 1994

- Decision point audit (final EIS): also by regulatory authority in the planning approval process.
- Implementation audit: to cover start-up; it could include scrutiny by the government and the public and focus on the proponent's compliance with mitigation and other imposed conditions.
- Performance audit: to cover full operation; it could also include government and public scrutiny.
- Predictive techniques audit: to compare actual with predicted impacts as a means of comparing the value of different predictive techniques.
- Project impact audits: also to compare actual with predicted impacts and to provide feedback for improving project management and for future projects.
- Procedures audit: external review (e.g. by the public) of the procedures used by the government and industry during the EIA processes.

These terms can and do overlap. The focus here is on project, performance and implementation audits. Whatever the focus, auditing faces a number of major *problems* as outlined in Table 7.3.

Such problems may partly explain the dismal record of the early set of Canadian EISs examined, from an ecological perspective, by Beanlands and Duinker (1983), for which accurate predictions appeared to be the exception rather than the rule.

Table 7.3 Problems associated with post-auditing studies

Nature of impact predictions

Many EISs contain few testable predictions; instead, they simply identify issues of potential concern.

Many EIS predictions are vague, imprecise and qualitative.

Testable predictions often relate to relatively minor impacts, with major impacts being referred to only in qualitative terms.

Project modifications

Post-EIS project modifications invalidate many predictions.

Monitoring data

Monitoring data and techniques often prove inadequate for auditing purposes.

Pre-development baseline monitoring is often insufficient, if undertaken at all.

Most monitoring data are collected and provided by the project proponent, which may give rise to fears of possible bias in the provision of information.

Comprehensiveness

Many auditing studies are concerned only with certain types of impacts (e.g. biophysical but not socio-economic; operational but not construction-stage impacts) and are therefore not full-project EIA audits.

Clarity

Few published auditing studies are explicit about the criteria used to establish prediction accuracy; this lack of clarity hampers comparisons between different studies.

Interpretation

Most auditing studies pay little attention to examining the underlying causes of predictive errors: this needs to be addressed if monitoring and auditing work is to provide an effective feedback in the EIA process.

Source: Chadwick and Glasson 1999

There are several examples, also from Canada, of situations where an EIA has failed to predict significant impacts. Berkes (1988) indicated how an EIA on the James Bay mega-HEP (1971–85) failed to pick up a sequence of interlinked impacts, which resulted in a significant increase in the mercury contamination of fish and in the mercury poisoning of native people. Dickman (1991) identified the failings of an EIA to pick up the impacts of increased lead and zinc mine tailings on the fish population in Garrow Lake, Canada's most northerly hypersaline lake. Such outcomes are not unique to Canada, which is a leader in monitoring; hopefully the incidence of such

research is leading to improved and better predictions.

Findings from the early limited auditing activity in the UK were also not too encouraging . A study of four major developments – the Sullom Voe (Shetlands) and Flotta (Orkneys) oil terminals, the Cow Green reservoir and the Redcar steelworks – suggested that 88 per cent of the predictions were not auditable. Of those that were auditable, fewer than half were accurate (Bisset 1984). Mills's (1992) monitoring study of the visual impacts of five 1990s UK major project developments (a trunk road, two wind farms, a power station and an opencast coal mine) revealed that there were often significant differences between what was stated in an EIS and what actually happened. Project descriptions changed fundamentally in some cases, landscape descriptions were restricted to land immediately surrounding the site and aesthetic considerations were often omitted. However, mitigation measures were generally carried out well.

Other early examples of auditing included the Toyota plant study (Ecotech Research and Consulting Ltd 1994), and various wind farm studies (Blandford, C. Associates 1994; ETSU 1994). The Toyota study took a wide perspective on environmental impacts; auditing revealed some underestimation of the impacts of employment and emissions, some overestimation of housing impacts and a reasonable identification of the impacts of construction traffic. The study by Blandford, C. Associates of the construction stage of three wind farms in Wales confirmed the predictions of low ecological impacts, but suggested that the visual impacts were greater than predicted,

with visibility distance greater than the predicted 15 km. However, the latter finding related to a winter audit; visibility may be less in the haze of summer.

One of the most comprehensive nationwide auditing studies of the precision and accuracy of environmental impact predictions was carried out by Buckley (1991) in Australia. At the time of his study, he found that adequate monitoring data to test predictions were available for only 3 per cent of the up to 1,000 EISs produced between 1974 and 1982. In general, he found that testable predictions and monitoring data were available only for large, complex projects, which had often been the subject of public controversy, and whose monitoring was aimed primarily at testing compliance with standards rather than with impact predictions. Some examples of over 300 major and subsidiary predictions tested are illustrated in Table 7.4. Overall, Buckley found the average accuracy of quantified, critical, testable predictions was 44 ± 5 per cent standard error. The more severe the impact, the lower the accuracy. Inaccuracy was highest for predictions of groundwater seepage. Accuracy assessments are of course influenced by the degree of precision applied to a prediction in the first place. In this respect, the use of ranges, reflecting the probabilistic nature of many impact predictions, may be a sensible way forward and would certainly make compliance monitoring more straightforward and less subject to dispute. Buckley's national survey, showing less than 50 per cent accuracy, provided no grounds for complacency. Indeed, as it was based on monitoring data provided by the operating corporations concerned, it may present a better result than would be

Table 7.4 Examples of auditing of environmental impact predictions

Component/parameter	Type of development	Predicted impact	Actual impact	Accuracy/ precision
Surface water quality: salts, pH	Bauxite mine	No detectable increase in stream salinity	None detected	Correct
Noise	Bauxite mine	Blast noise <115dBA	Only 90 per cent <115 dBA	Incorrect: 90 per cent accurate, worse
Workforce	Aluminium smelter	1,500 during construction	Up to 2,500	Incorrect: 60 per cent accurate, worse

Source: Buckley 1991

generated from a wider trawl of EISs. On the other hand, we are learning from experience, and more recent EISs may contain better and more accurate predictions. Marshall (2001) reviewed a set of 1,118 mitigation proposals from 41 EISs in the UK. He found that in 38 per cent of the cases (418 in total), the mitigation proposals were expressed in such a way that the proponent could not be held to be committed to their implementation. In such cases mitigation is of little value, and there may be major compliance issues.

There has not, until recently, been much emphasis on auditing studies on the important area of predictive techniques audit, and on the value of particular predictive techniques. Where there have been studies, they have tended to focus on identifying errors associated with predictive methods rather than on explaining the errors. There is a need to develop appropriate audit methodologies, and as more projects are implemented there should be more scope for such studies. The pioneering study by Wood on visibility, noise and air quality impacts, using GIS to audit and model EIA errors, provides an example of a way forward for such work (Wood 1999a, b, 2000).

••

7.5 A UK case study: monitoring and auditing the local socio-economic impacts of the Sizewell B PWR construction project

7.5.1 Background to the case study

Although monitoring and auditing impacts are not mandatory in EIA procedures in the UK, the physical and socio-economic effects of developments are not completely ignored. For example, a number of public agencies monitor particular pollutants. LPAs monitor some of the conditions attached to development permissions. However, there is no systematic approach to the monitoring and auditing of impact predictions and mitigation measures. This case study reports on one early and still very topical attempt (in the context of a raft of proposals for many new energy projects in the

UK over the period to 2025) to introduce a more systematic, although still partial, approach to the subject.

In the 1970s and early 1980s, Britain had an active programme of nuclear power station construction. This included a commitment, revised in the 1990s (but now very much alive), to build a family of new nuclear plants (at the time they were PWR stations). The first such station to be approved was Sizewell B in East Anglia. The approval was controversial, and followed the longest public inquiry in UK history. Construction started in 1987, and the project was completed in 1995. The IAU in the School of Planning at Oxford Brookes University had studied the impacts of a number of power stations and made contributions to EISs, with a focus on the socio-economic impacts. A proposal was made to the relevant public utility, the Central Electricity Generating Board (CEGB), that the construction of Sizewell B provided an invaluable opportunity to monitor in detail the project construction stage, and to check on the predictions made at the public inquiry and on the mitigating conditions attached to the project's approval. Although the predictions were not formally packaged in an EIS, but rather as a series of reports based on the inquiry, the research was extensive and comprehensive (DOEn 1986). The CEGB supported a monitoring study, which began in 1988. To the credit of the utility, which became Nuclear Electric/British Energy, and latterly EDF (Électicité de France) following privatization, there was a continuing commitment to the monitoring study – despite the uncertainty about further nuclear power station developments in Britain. Monitoring reports for the whole construction period and on the project's operation were completed (Glasson *et al.* 1989–97; see also Glasson 2005 for further reflection on the project).

7.5.2 Operational characteristics of the monitoring study

It is important to clarify the *objectives of the monitoring study*, otherwise irrelevant information may be collected and resources wasted. Figure 7.3 outlines the scope of the study. The development under consideration was the construction stage of the Sizewell B PWR 1,200 MW nuclear power station. The focus was on the socio-economic impacts of the development, although with some limited consideration of physical impacts. The socio-economic element of EIA involves 'the systematic advanced appraisal of the impacts on the day to day quality of life of people and communities when the environment is affected by development or policy change' (Bowles 1981). This involves a consideration of the impacts on employment, social structure, expenditure, services, etc. Although socio-economic studies have often been the poor relation in impact assessment studies to date, meriting no more than a chapter or two in EISs, they are important, not least because they consider the impacts of developments on people, who can answer back and object to developments.

The highest priority in the study was to identify the impacts of the development on local employment; this emphasis reflected the pivotal role of employment impacts in the generation of other local impacts, particularly accommodation and local services. In addition to providing an updated

and improved database to inform future assessments, assisting project management of the Sizewell B project in the local community and auditing impact predictions, the study also monitored and audited some of the conditions and undertakings associated with permission to proceed with the construction of the power station. These included undertakings on the use of rail and the routeing of road construction traffic, as well as conditions on the use of local labour and local firms, local liaison arrangements and (traffic) noise (DOEn 1986).

The monitoring study included the collection of a range of information, including statistical data (e.g. the mixture of local and non-local construction-stage workers, the housing tenure status and expenditure patterns of workers), decisions, opinions and perceptions of impacts. The spatial scope of the study extended to the commuting zone for construction workers (Figure 7.4). The study included information from the

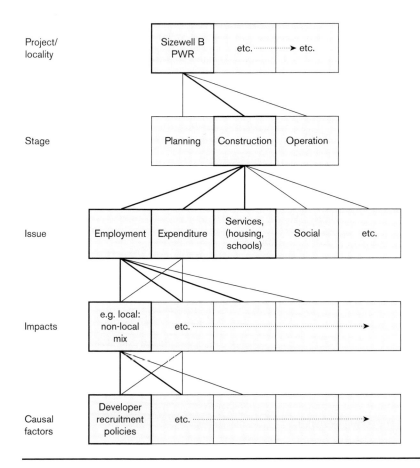

Figure 7.3

Scope of study and database organization: Sizewell B monitoring study

Source: Glasson *et al.* 1989–97

developer and the main contractors on site, from the relevant local authorities and other public agencies, from the local community and from the construction workers. The local upper-school geography A-level students helped to collect data on the local perceptions of impacts via biennial questionnaire surveys in the town of Leiston, which is adjacent to the project site. A major survey of the socio-economic characteristics and activities of a 20 per cent sample of the project workforce was also carried out every two years. The IAU team operated as the catalyst to bring the data together. There was a high level of support for the study, and the results were made openly available in published annual monitoring reports and in summary broadsheets, which were available free to the local community (Glasson *et al.* 1989–97).

The study highlighted a number of *methodo-logical difficulties with monitoring and auditing*. The first relates to the disaggregation of project-related impacts from baseline trends. Data are available that indicate local trends in a number of variables, such as unemployment levels, traffic volumes and crime levels. But problems are encountered when we attempt to explain these local trends. To what extent are they due to (a) the construction project itself, (b) national and regional factors, or (c) other local changes independent of the construction project? It is straightforward to isolate the role of national and regional factors, but the relative roles of the construction project and other local changes are very difficult to determine. 'Controls' are used where possible to isolate the project-related impacts.

A second problem related to the identification of the indirect, knock-on effects of a construction project. Indirect impacts – particularly on employ-ment – may well be significant, but they are not easily observed or measured. For example, indirect employment effects may result from the replace-ment of employees leaving local employment to take up work on site. Are these local recruits replaced by their previous employers? If so, do these replacements come from other local employ-ees, the local unemployed or in-migrant workers? It was not possible to obtain this sort of informa-tion. Further indirect employment impacts may stem from local businesses gaining work as suppliers or contractors at Sizewell B. They may need to take on additional labour to meet their extra workload. The extent to which this has occurred is again difficult to estimate, although surveys of local companies have provided some useful information on these issues (Glasson and Heaney 1993).

7.5.3 Some findings from the studies

A very brief summary of a number of the findings is outlined below and in Figure 7.5.

Employment

An important prediction and condition was that at least 50 per cent of construction employment should go to local people (within daily commuting distance of the site). This was the case, although, predictably in a rural area, local people have the largely semi-skilled or unskilled jobs. As the employment on site increased, with a shift from civil engineering to mechanical and electrical engineering trades, the pressure on maintaining the 50 per cent proportion increased. In 1989, a training centre was opened in the nearest local town, Leiston, to supply between 80 and 120 trainees from the local unemployed.

Local economy

A major project has an economic multiplier effect on a local economy. By the end of 1991, Sizewell B workers were spending about £500,000 per week in Suffolk and Norfolk, Nuclear Electric had placed orders worth over £40 million with local com-panies and a 'good neighbour' policy was funding a range of community projects (including £1.9 million for a swimming pool in Leiston).

Housing

A major project, with a large in-migrant workforce, can also distort the local housing market, and tourism accommodation in tourist industry locations. One mitigating measure at Sizewell B was the requirement of the developer to provide a large site hostel. A 600-bed hostel (subsequently increased to 900) was provided. It was very well used, accommodating in 1991 over 40 per cent of the in-migrants to the development, at an average occupancy rate of over 85 per cent, and it helped to reduce demand for accommodation in the locality.

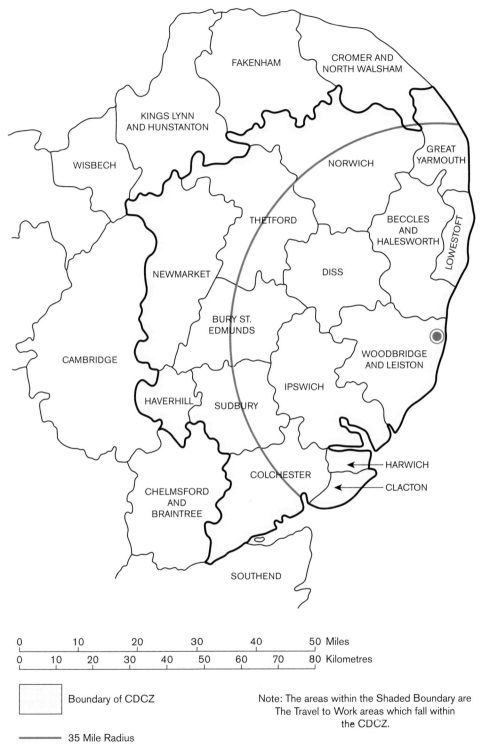

FAKENHAM

CROMER AND
NORTH WALSHAM

KINGS LYNN
AND HUNSTANTON

WISBECH

NORWICH

GREAT
YARMOUTH

THETFORD

BECCLES
AND
HALESWORTH

LOWESTOFT

NEWMARKET

DISS

BURY ST.
EDMUNDS

CAMBRIDGE

WOODBRIDGE
AND LEISTON

IPSWICH

HAVERHILL

SUDBURY

HARWICH

COLCHESTER

CLACTON

CHELMSFORD
AND
BRAINTREE

SOUTHEND

0	10	20	30	40	50 Miles
0	10 20	30 40	50	60 70	80 Kilometres

Boundary of CDCZ

Note: The areas within the Shaded Boundary are
The Travel to Work areas which fall within
the CDCZ.

35 Mile Radius

Figure 7.4

Sizewell B commuting zone: monitoring study area

Source: Glasson *et al.* 1989–97

Figure 7.5

Brief summary of
some findings from
the Sizewell B PWR
construction project
monitoring and
auditing study

Source: Glasson *et al.*
1989–97

Employment impacts

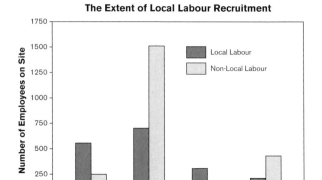

The Extent of Local Labour Recruitment

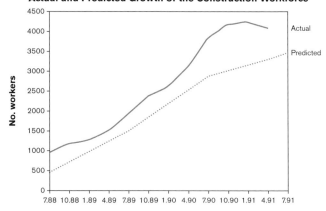

Actual and Predicted Growth of the Construction Workforce

Social impacts

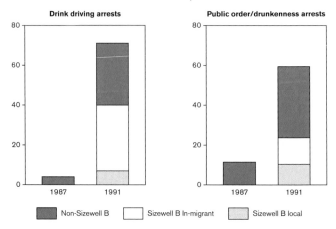

Number of Local Arrests, 1987 and 1991

Traffic Impacts

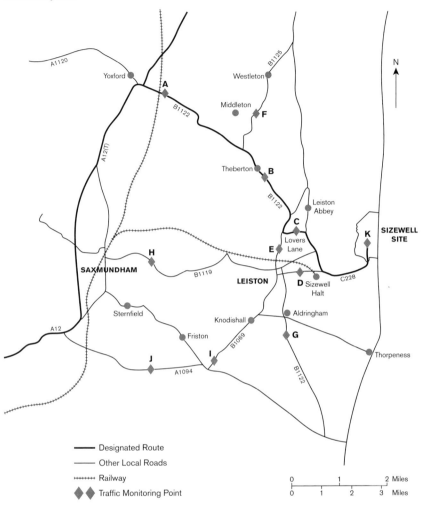

Designated Route
Other Local Roads
Railway
◆◆ Traffic Monitoring Point

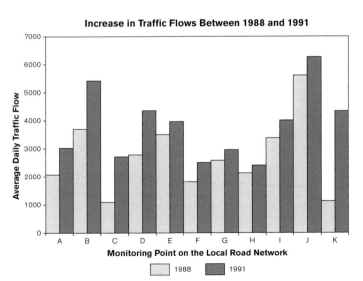

Increase in Traffic Flows Between 1988 and 1991

1988   1991

Traffic and noise

The traffic generated by a large construction project can badly affect local towns and villages. To mitigate such impacts, there was a designated construction traffic route to Sizewell B. The monitoring of traffic flows on designated and non-designated (control) routes indicated that this mitigation measure was working. Between 1988 and 1991, the amount of traffic rose substantially at the four monitoring points on the designated route, but much less so at most of the seven points not on that route. Construction noise on site was a local issue. Monitoring led to modifications in some construction methods, notably improvements to the railway sidings and changes in the piling methods used.

Crime

An increase in local crime is normally associated with the construction stage of major projects. The Leiston police division did see a significant increase in the number of arrests in certain offence categories after the start of the project. However, local people not employed on the project were involved in most of the arrests, and in the increase in arrests, with the exception of drink-driving, for which Sizewell B employees (mainly in-migrants) accounted for most arrests and for most of the increase. However, the early diagnosis of the problems facilitated swift remedial action, including the introduction of a shuttle minibus service for workers, the provision of a large bar in the site hostel, the stressing of the problems of drink-driving at site-workers' induction courses, and the exclusion from the site (effectively the exclusion from Sizewell B jobs) of workers found guilty of serious misconduct or crime. After the early stages of the project, worker-related crime fell substantially, and the police considered the project workforce to be relatively trouble-free, with fewer serious offences than anticipated.

Residents' perceptions

Surveys of local residents in 1989 and 1991 revealed more negative than positive perceived impacts, increased traffic and disturbance by workers being seen as the main negative impacts. The main positive impacts of the project were seen to be the employment, additional trade and ameliorative measures associated with the project. The monitoring of complaints about the development revealed substantially fewer complaints over time, despite the rapid build-up of the project.

7.5.4 Learning from monitoring: Sizewell B and Sizewell C

Table 7.5 shows the nature and auditability of the Sizewell B socio-economic predictions. In contrast to the findings from previous post-auditing studies (see Dipper *et al.* 1998), a vast majority of the Sizewell B predictions were expressed in quantitative terms. The monitoring of impacts and the auditing of the predictions and mitigation measures revealed (Table 7.6) that many of the predictions used in the Sizewell B public inquiry were reasonably accurate – although there was an underestimate of the build-up of construction employment and an overestimate of the secondary effects on the local economy. Predictions of traffic impacts, and on the local proportion of the construction workforce, were very close to the actual outcomes. Mitigation measures also appeared to have some effect. Overall, approximately 60 per cent of the predictions had errors of less than 20 per cent. Explanations of variations from the predictions included the inevitable project modification (particularly associated with new-technology projects, with few or no comparators at the time of prediction), and the very lengthy project authorization process (with a gap of almost 10 years between the predictions and peak construction). Other local issues were revealed by the monitoring, allowing some modifications to manage the project better in the community (Glasson 2005). Unfortunately, such systematic monitoring is still discretionary in the UK and very much dependent on the goodwill of developers.

Information gained from monitoring can also provide vital intelligence for the planning and assessment of future projects. This is particularly so when the subsequent project is of the same type, and in the same location, as that which has been monitored. Nuclear Electric applied for consent to build and operate a replica of Sizewell B, to be known as Sizewell C. A full EIS was produced for the project (Nuclear Electric 1993). Its prediction

Table 7.5 Nature and auditability of the Sizewell B predictions

	No. of predictions	% of total
Nature of prediction		
Quantitative		
Expressed in absolute terms	35	51
Expressed in % terms	21	30
Qualitative	11	16
Incorporates quantitative and qualitative elements	2	3
Total: all predictions	69	100
Auditability of predictions		
Auditable: monitoring data subject to no or little potential error	30	43
Auditable: but monitoring data subject to greater potential error	28	41
Not auditable	11	16
Total: all predictions	69	100

Source: Chadwick and Glasson 1999

Table 7.6 Accuracy of auditable Sizewell B predictions

% error in prediction	No. of predictions	% of total
None: prediction correct or within predicted range	15	26
Less than 10%	9	16
10–20%	11	19
20–30%	5	9
30–40%	5	9
40–50%	2	3
Over 50%	8	14
Prediction incorrect, but % error cannot be calculated	3	5
Prediction cannot be audited	11	–
Total: all predictions	69	100

Source: Chadwick and Glasson 1999

Note: For quantified predictions, the predicted value was used as the denominator in the calculation of the % errors in the table. For non-quantified predictions, the % error could not be calculated and predictions were classified as either 'correct' or 'incorrect', based on assessment by the research team.

of the socio-economic impacts drew directly on the findings from the Sizewell B monitoring study, but this proposed follow-on project fell victim to the abandonment in the early 1990s of the UK nuclear power station programme. However, since about 2007 there has been much activity, and increasingly advanced planning, for a new generation of UK nuclear power stations, including a new Sizewell C. In this context the monitoring data from the construction of Sizewell B is proving of considerable value.

7.6 A UK case study: monitoring the local impacts of the London 2012 Olympics project

7.6.1 Nature of the project and its impacts life cycle

The London Olympics 2012 project has been one of the largest projects in Europe, with a peak construction work force of almost 12,000 in 2011. The site of about 250 ha is located in the east of London, approximately 5 km from the centre of the city. The Olympic, Paralympic and Legacy Facilities have been designed to create not only an exceptional venue for the games, but also a lasting legacy to bring about the regeneration of the formerly rundown Lower Lea Valley – creating a new urban quarter for London. The life cycle of the project is reflected in the chronology of impacts highlighted in the environmental statement (Symonds/EDAW 2004), and summarized in Figure 7.6. This also provides a framework for the monitoring of the biophysical and socio-economic impacts of the project.

7.6.2 Construction stage monitoring

The project has a detailed monitoring programme, co-ordinated by the Olympics Delivery Authority (ODA). Two examples of the detailed nature of the monitoring are illustrated below. Figure 7.7 provides an extract from the monthly construction noise monitoring across the site, showing a generally good performance. Table 7.7 provides some extracts from the monthly socio-economics

Impacts	Pre-Olympic Construction Phase	Olympic Games Phase	Post-Olympic Legacy Construction Phase	Post-Olympic Legacy Phase
Premature loss of existing housing, industry, jobs and waste management infrastructure				
Potential loss of archaeological baseline				
Damage to built heritage from demolition and contextual changes				
Loss of district character of historic areas				
Improved quality of townscape and views				
Undergrounding of power cables				
Consequences of remediation				
Energy efficiency gains from CCHP and other sustainable/renewable energy features incorporated into buildings/structures				
Creation of Olympic jobs				
'Feel good' factor, social cohesiveness and community pride				
Encouragement to participate in sporting/healthy activities				
Impacts on local transport infrastructure				
Wind impacts on queues/crowd near large buildings (including Olympic Village)				
Potential flood risk due to Security Perimeter Fence at river crossings				
Potential impacts from existing contamination in newly public areas				
Additional parkland, open ground and allotments				
Additional /replacement habitat creation				
Improved accessibility/permeability				
Creation of Legacy jobs, with associated skills and training				
Improved community facilities (schools, nurseries, crèches, medical etc.)				
Improved buildings (e.g. 'access for all' standards)				
Impact on household waste management infrastructure of LB Newham				

Notes: Green = Significant beneficial, Red = Significant adverse. Hatched = Significant with or without mitigation, Plain colour = Significant without mitigation

Figure 7.6

Life cycle of impacts for the London 2012 Olympics project

Source: Symonds/EDAW 2004

Noise* monitoring information at the Olympic Park for August 2010

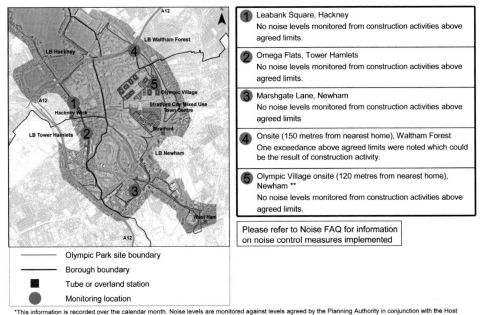

Figure 7.7

Construction noise monitoring across the London 2012 Olympics site (August 2010)

Source: Olympics Delivery Authority 2010

monitoring, with a focus on the characteristics of the construction workforce. For January 2011, it shows a workforce of almost 12,000 across the two main projects (park and athletes' village). A high proportion of the workforce is locally sourced from within the London boroughs, and much is very local to the site. Recruitment from the unemployed and from black, Asian and ethnic minority groups is also monitored as good against benchmark targets; this contrasts with poorer performance against benchmarks for female recruitment and for recruitment from those with disabilities. The project has used a range of construction work-force development activities to enhance beneficial local recruitment impacts, including: a job broker-age scheme that has placed over 1,250 people (primarily local borough residents) into employ-ment on the project, and a training programme that has exceeded targets by training (up to 2011) 3,250

people (against a target of 2,250), including 400 apprentices (against a target of 350).

7.7 Summary

A mediation of the relationship between a project and its environment is needed throughout the life of a project. Environmental impact assessment is meant to establish the terms and conditions for project implementation; yet there is often little follow-through to this stage, and even less follow-up after it. Arts (1998) concluded, after a thorough examination of 'ex-post evaluation of EIA', that in practice it is lagging behind the practice of EIA itself. Few countries have made arrangements for some form of follow-up. In those that have, experience has not been too encouraging –

Table 7.7 Workforce/employment monitoring for the London 2012 Olympics site (December 2010)

Workforce on site	Olympic Park		Athletes' Village	
	6500	(benchmark)	5400	(benchmark)
% resident in host boroughs	21	—	27	—
% resident elsewhere in London	34	—	40	—
% resident elsewhere in UK	42	—	30	—
% residing outside UK/or no information	3	—	3	—
% previously unemployed	12	7	10	7
% women	4	11	3	11
% disabled	1	3	0.5	3
% black, Asian or ethnic minority	19	15	13	15

Source: Adapted from *Employment and Skills Update*, Olympics Delivery Authority (January 2011)

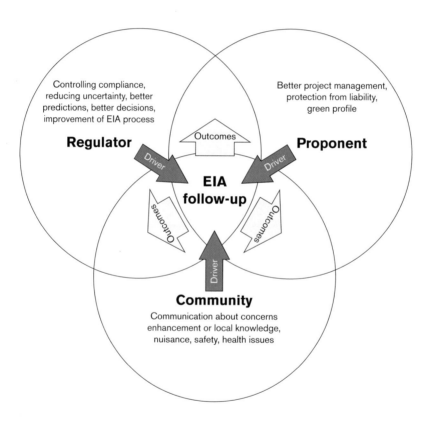

Figure 7.8

Outcome of EIA follow-up for different stakeholders

Source: Morrison-Saunders *et al.* 2001

reflecting deficiencies in often over-descriptive EISs, inadequate techniques for follow-up, organizational and resource limitations, and limited support from authorities and project proponents alike. Yet many projects have very long lives, and their impacts need to be monitored on a regular basis. Morrison-Saunders *et al.* (2001) show how this could bring positive outcomes for different stakeholders.

Figure 7.8 shows the benefits not only to the proponent and the community (as exemplified by the Sizewell B case study), but also to the regulator – in the form of a better decision and improvement of the EIA process. Such monitoring can improve project management and contribute to the auditing of both impact predictions and mitigating measures. Monitoring and auditing can provide essential feedback to improve the EIA process, yet this is still probably the weakest step of the process in many countries. Discretionary measures are not enough; monitoring and auditing need to be more fully integrated into EIA procedures on a mandatory basis.

SOME QUESTIONS

The following questions are intended to help the reader focus on the key issues of this chapter, and to start building some understanding of the importance and nature of monitoring and auditing in EIA.

1 What do you understand by the distinction between 'before the decision' and 'after the decision' in EIA?
2 Why is it important to continue the EIA process beyond the decision for those projects which proceed to implementation?
3 What do you understand by the distinction between monitoring and auditing in EIA?
4 Consider the sort of monitoring information which would be useful to collect for a major project with which you are familiar. Include indicators and underlying factors, and quantitative and qualitative information.
5 Why do you think that there has been such resistance in many countries to more mandatory monitoring and auditing systems for EIA?
6 Compare and contrast some of the key features of the monitoring systems in California and Hong Kong.
7 Review the problems that can be associated with post-auditing studies, as set out in Table 7.3, and consider how some of these problems might be overcome.
8 As exemplified by the Sizewell B project, consider ways of overcoming the two highlighted methodological issues, often encountered in monitoring, of (i) disaggregating project-related impacts from baseline trends, and (ii) identifying the indirect impacts of projects.
9 Review the relative accuracy of auditable Sizewell B predictions, as displayed in Table 7.6. What factors might contribute to the findings set out there?
10 Figure 7.6 illustrates the importance of monitoring over the life cycle of a project. Some of the impacts noted in the figure are likely to be easier to monitor than others. Briefly run through the impact list and identify, as far as possible, relevant impact indicators that could be used in the monitoring process for the London 2012 Olympics project.
11 Drawing on the two UK monitoring case studies, plus any others with which you might be familiar, outline the potential benefits of EIA monitoring/follow-up to the relevant sets of stakeholders identified in Figure 7.8.

Note

1   Early drafts of the EC Directive did include a requirement for an ex-post evaluation of EIA projects. Section 11 of the 1980 draft (CEC 1980) stated that the competent authority should check at set intervals whether the provisions attached to the planning permission are observed or adequate, or other provisions for environmental protection are observed, and whether additional measures are required to protect the environment against the project's impacts.

References

Ahammed, A.K.M.Rafique, and Nixon, B.M. 2006, Environmental impact monitoring in the EIA process of South Australia, *Environmental Impact Assessment and Review*, 26, 426–47.

Arts, J. 1998. *EIA follow-up: on the role of ex-post evaluation in environmental impact assessment.* Groningen: Geo Press.

Arts, J., Caldwell, P and Morrison-Saunders, A. 2001. Environmental impact assessment follow-up: good practice and future directions – findings from a workshop at the IAIA 2000 Conference. *Impact Assessment and Project Appraisal*, 19 (3), 175–185.

Au, E. and Sanvícens, G. 1996. EIA follow-up monitoring and management. *EIA Process Strengthening.* Canberra: Environmental Protection Agency.

Baseline Environmental Consulting 1989. *Mitigation monitoring and reporting plan for a woodwaste conversion facility, West Berkeley, California.* Emeryville, CA: Baseline Environmental Consulting.

Beanlands, G.E. and Duinker, P. 1983. *An ecological framework for environmental impact assessment.* Halifax, Nova Scotia: Dalhousie University, Institute for Resource and Environmental Studies.

Berkes, F. 1988. The intrinsic difficulty of predicting impacts: lessons from the James Bay hydro project. *Environmental Impact Assessment Review* 8, 201–20.

Bisset, R. 1984. Post development audits to investigate the accuracy of environmental impact predictions. *Zeitschift für Umweltpolitik* 7, 463–84.

Bisset, R. and Tomlinson, P. 1988. Monitoring and auditing of impacts. In *Environmental impact assessment*, P. Wathern (ed). London: Unwin Hyman.

Blandford, C. Associates 1994. *Wind turbine power station construction monitoring study.* Gwynedd: Countryside for Wales.

Bowles, R.T. 1981. *Social impact assessment in small communities.* London: Butterworth.

Buckley, R. 1991. Auditing the precision and accuracy of environmental impact predictions in Australia. *Environmental Monitoring Assessment* 18, 1–23.

California Resources Agency 1988. *California eia monitor.* State of California.

CEC (Commission of the European Communities) 1980. Proposal for a council directive concerning the assessment of the environmental effects of certain public and private projects on the environment, 9 July 1980. *Official Journal of the EC*, L175, 40–49. Brussels: EC.

CEC 1993. *Report from the Commission of the implementation of Directive 85/337/EEC on the assessment of the effects of certain public and private projects on the environment*, vol. 13, *Annexes for all Member States*, COM (93), 28 final. Brussels: EC, Directorate-General XI.

CEC 2009. *Study concerning the report on the application and effectiveness of the EIA Directive: Final Report.* Brussels: DG Env.

Chadwick, A. and Glasson, J. 1999. Auditing the socio-economic impacts of a major construction project: the case of Sizewell B Nuclear Power Station. *Journal of Environmental Planning and Management* 42 (6), 811–36.

Culhane, P.J. 1993. Post-EIS environmental auditing: a first step to making rational environmental assessment a reality. *Environmental Professional* 5.

CWE-ZHEC Joint Venture, 2007, *Construction of Yung Shue Wan Helipad:EM&A Manual,* Hong Kong: Environmental Protection Department EIA Ordinance website (at 2011).

Dickman, M. 1991. Failure of environmental impact assessment to predict the impact of mine tailings on Canada's most northerly hypersaline lake. *Environmental Impact Assessment Review* 11, 171–80.

Dipper, B., Jones, C. and Wood, C. 1998. Monitoring and post-auditing in environmental impact assessment: a review. *Journal of Environmental Planning and Management* 41 (6), 731–47.

DOEn (Department of Energy) 1986. *Sizewell B public inquiry: report by Sir Frank Layfield.* London: HMSO.

Ecotech Research and Consulting 1994. *Toyota impact study summary*, unpublished.

EPD (Environmental Protection Department) 1997. *Environmental impact assessment ordinance and technical memorandum on environmental impact* assessment. Hong Kong: EPD Hong Kong Government.

EPD 1998. *Guidelines for development projects in Hong Kong – environmental monitoring and audit*. Hong Kong: EPDHK.

ETSU (Energy Technology Support Unit) 1994. *Cemmaes Wind Farm: sociological impact study*. Market Research Associates and Dulas Engineering, ETSU.

Frost, R. 1997. EIA monitoring and audit. In *Planning and eia in practice*, J. Weston (ed), 141–64. Harlow: Longman.

Glasson, J. 1994. Life after the decision: the importance of monitoring in EIA. *Built Environment* 20 (4), 309–20.

Glasson, J. 2005. Better monitoring for better impact management: the local socio-economic impacts of constructing Sizewell B nuclear power station. *Impact Assessment and Project Appraisal,* July .

Glasson, J. and Heaney, D. 1993. Socio-economic impacts: the poor relations in British environmental impact statements. *Journal of Environmental Planning and Management* 36 (3), 335–43.

Glasson, J., Chadwick, A. and Therivel, R. 1989–97. *Local socio-economic impacts of the Sizewell B PWR Construction Project*. Oxford: Oxford Polytechnic/Oxford Brookes University, Impacts Assessment Unit.

Greene, G., MacLaren, J.W. and Sadler, B. 1985. Workshop summary. In *Audit and evaluation in environmental assessment and management: Canadian and international experience*, 301–21. Banff: The Banff Centre.

Holling, C.S. (ed) 1978. *Adaptive environmental assessment and management*. Chichester: Wiley.

Hui, S.Y.M. and Ho, M.W. 2002. EIA follow-up: Internet-based reporting. In *Conference Proceedings of 22nd Annual Meeting IAIA June 15–21, The Hague*. IAIA.

IAPA 2005, Special issue on EIA Follow-up, *Impact Assessment and Project Appraisal*, 23 (3).

IEA 1993. *Digest of environmental statements*. London: Sweet & Maxwell.

IOCGP (Inter-Organisational Committee on Principles and Guidelines) 2003. Principles and guidelines for social impact assessment in the USA. *Impact Assessment and Project Appraisal*, 21 (3), 231–50.

Lee, N. and Wood, C. 1980. *Methods of environmental impact assessment for use in project appraisal and physical planning*. Occasional Paper no. 7. University of Manchester, Department of Town and Country Planning.

Marshall, R. 2001. Mitigation linkage: EIA follow-up through the application of EMPS in transmission construction projects. In *Conference Proceedings of 21st Annual Meeting IAIA*, 26 May–1 June, Cartagena, Colombia, IAIA.

Marshall, R., Arts, J. and Morrison-Saunders, A. 2005. International principles for best practice EIA follow-up. *Impact Assessment and Project Appraisal* 23 (3), 175–81.

Mills, J. 1992. *Monitoring the visual impacts of major projects*. MSc dissertation in Environmental Assessment and Management, School of Planning, Oxford Brookes University.

Morrison-Saunders, A. 1996. Auditing the effectiveness of EA with respect to ongoing environmental management performance. In *Conference Proceedings 16th Annual Meeting IAIA June 17–23 1996*, M. Rosario Partidario (ed), vol 1, IAIA, Lisbon 317–22.

Morrison–Saunders, A. and Arts, J. (2004) (eds), *Assessing impact: handbook of EIA and SEA follow-up*. London: Earthscan.

Morrison-Saunders, A., Arts, J., Baker, J. and Caldwell, P. 2001. Roles and stakes in EIA follow-up. *Impact Assessment and Project Appraisal* 19 (4), 289–96.

Olympics Delivery Authority 2010. *Dust and Noise Monitoring*. London: Olympics Delivery Authority.

Olympics Delivery Authority 2011. *Employment and Skills Update: January 2011*. London: Olympics Delivery Authority.

Sadler, B. 1988. The evaluation of assessment: post-EIS research and process. In *Environmental Impact Assessment*, E. Wathern (ed). London: Unwin Hyman.

Symonds/EDAW 2004. *ES for Lower Lea Valley: Olympics and Legacy Planning Application*. Symonds/EDAW for London Development Agency.

Tomlinson, E. and Atkinson, S.F. 1987a. Environmental audits: proposed terminology. *Environmental Monitoring and Assessment* 8, 187–98.

Tomlinson, E. and Atkinson, S.F. 1987b. Environmental audits: a literature review. *Environmental Monitoring and Assessment* 8, 239.

Wood, G. 1999a. Assessing techniques of assessment: post-development auditing of noise predictive schemes in environmental impact assessment. *Impact Assessment and Project Appraisal* 17 (3), 217–26.

Wood, G. 1999b. Post-development auditing of EIA predictive techniques: a spatial analysis approach. *Journal of Environmental Planning and Management* 42 (5), 671–89.

Wood, G. 2000. Is what you see what you get? Post-development auditing of methods used for predicting the zone of visual influence in EIA. *Environmental Impact Assessment Review* 20 (5), 537–56.

Part 3

• •

Practice

LET'S MAKE SURE I'VE GOT THIS RIGHT. WE GET TO
KEEP SOME LIZARDS AND BLUE BUTTERFLIES ON OUR
HEATHLAND, AND IN RETURN YOU GET TO BUILD 3,200
NEW HOUSES ON OUR GREEN BELT . . . .

8 An overview of UK practice to date

•••

8.1 Introduction

Part 3 considers EIA practice: what is done rather than what should be done. This chapter provides an overview of the first 20 years or so of UK practice since EC Directive 85/337 became operational. We develop this further with reference to particular case studies in Chapter 9. The case studies seek to develop particular themes and aspects of the EIA process raised in this and in earlier chapters (for example, on the treatment of alternatives, of public participation and on widening environmental assessment to also consider social and economic issues). The case studies are largely UK-based, and project-focused, although two cases of SEA are also included. Chapter 10 discusses international practice in terms of 'best practice' systems, emerging EIA systems and the role of international funding agencies in EIA, such as the World Bank.

These chapters can be set in the context of international studies on EIA effectiveness, whose results have been written up by Sadler (1996, 2012). In the 2011 study, Sadler sets three effectiveness tests, setting out an effectiveness 'triage' (three clearance bars): (1) enabling conditions (what must or should be done; legal and institutional framework and methodological realities); (2) state of practice (what is done; macro and micro level cases of good practice – what is the art of the possible); and (3) effectiveness and performance (what is the outcome; contribution to decision-making and

environmental benefits). Sadler notes that these questions and the attendant techniques for investigating them must be seen in the context of the decision-making framework in which the relevant EIA system operates.

Chapter 8 broadly addresses Sadler's first two points in sequence. Section 8.2 considers the number, type and location of projects for which EIAs have been carried out in the UK, as well as where the resulting EISs can be found. Section 8.3 discusses the stages of EIA before the submission of the EIS and application for authorization. Section 8.4 addresses what has, to date, been the most heavily studied aspect of EIA practice, the quality of EISs. Section 8.5 considers the post-submission stages of EIA, and how environmental information is used in decision-making by LPAs and inspectors. Section 8.6 considers legal challenges to EIA, many of which have informed the recent changes to UK legislation and guidance discussed at Chapter 3. Finally, section 8.7 discusses the costs and benefits of EIA as seen from various perspectives. Sadler's third point is partially addressed by government-published good-practice guides on EIA preparation and review (e.g. DETR 1999a, 2000; DCLG 2011a), which over time have introduced some policy changes in response to research findings regarding EIS and EIA effectiveness.

The information in this chapter was correct at the time of writing in mid-2011; it will obviously change as more EISs are carried out.

8.2 Number and type of EISs and projects

This section considers how many, and for what types of projects, EISs have been produced. It concludes with a brief review of where collections of EISs are kept. UK EIS collections, and databases on EISs, are fragmented (see Section 8.2.3). Analysis is further complicated by several problems. First, some projects fall under more than one schedule classification; for example mineral extraction schemes (Schedule 2.2) that are later filled in with waste (Schedule 2.11), or industrial/residential developments (Schedule 2.10) that also have a leisure component (Schedule 2.12). Second, the mere description of a project is often not enough to identify the regulations under which its EIA was carried out. For instance, power stations may fall under Schedule 1.2 or 2.3(a), depending on size. Roads may come under highways or planning regulations, depending on whether they are trunk roads or local highways. Third, many EISs do not mention when, by whom or for whom they were prepared. Fourth, locational analysis after 1995 is complicated by local government reorganization and many changes in the nature and boundaries

of authorities in England, Scotland and Wales. All these factors affect the analysis. This chapter is based primarily on information from DCLG (2011b), IEMA (2011), supplemented by older information from Wood and Bellanger (1998) and Wood (1996, 2003).

8.2.1 Number and broad location of EISs

Between the mid-1970s and the mid-1980s, approximately 20 EISs were prepared annually in the UK (Petts and Hills 1982). After the implementation of Directive 85/337, this number rose dramatically and, despite the recession, about 350 EISs per year were produced in the early 1990s; but, as can be seen from Figure 8.1, this number began to drop in the mid-1990s partly as a result of a fall in major development activity under the planning regulations. However, the numbers quickly recovered in the late 1990s and, as noted in Chapter 3, there were over 600 per year for several years after the implementation of the 1997 amendments to the Directive. This probably reflected many factors – more projects, included in the amended Directive, a stronger UK economy and concern by developers and LPAs about certain court judgements involving the EIA Directive.

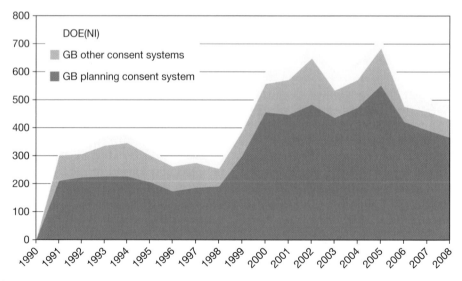

Figure 8.1

EISs prepared in the UK (1991–2008)

Source: DCLG (2011b)

By the end of 2008, over 9,000 EISs had been prepared, with approximately 70 per cent produced under the Planning Regulations for England, Wales and Scotland. The remainder are for projects in Northern Ireland and, more significantly, for projects under the other consent procedures (e.g. highways, forestry) discussed in Chapter 3. However the fall in numbers since 2005 illustrates that EIS activity can perhaps be seen as an interesting measure of the economic fortunes of a country.

In parallel with the increase in the number of EISs, the participants in EIA have become increasingly familiar with the process. Surveys of UK local authorities carried out by Oxford Brookes University in the mid-1990s showed that over 80 per cent of LPAs even then had received at least one EIS. On average, strategic-level authorities (county and regional councils and national park authorities) had received 12 EISs and local-level authorities (district, borough, metropolitan boroughs and development corporations) had received four. Surveys of environmental consultants (e.g. Radcliff and Edward-Jones 1995; Weston 1995) found that about one-third of the consultancies surveyed had prepared 10 or more EISs. As noted, the total number of EISs is now over 9,000, compared with approximately 2,500 by the

end of 1995, and LPA and consultancy activity and experience with the process has continued to grow accordingly. Figure 8.2 shows the distribution of EISs by national authority. With only about 10 per cent of the UK population, the EIS activity in Scotland is often much higher than the UK average; recent activity includes many Scottish wind farm developments.

Types of projects

Figure 8.3(a) shows the types of projects for which EISs were prepared in the early years of EIA in the UK. The largest numbers were for project types in waste (largely landfill/raise projects, wastewater or sewage treatment schemes and incinerators), urban/retail developments, roads, extraction schemes and energy projects (Wood and Bellanger 1998). In contrast, data for 2004–2010 (for England only) highlights the predominance of urban/retail development projects. Figure 8.3(b) (also for England) illustrates some regional variations – for example between project types in the NE and SE of the country.

Table 8.1 shows the distribution of EISs produced under other consent systems. There are basically three groups of projects relating to transport, agriculture and fisheries, and energy. The highway

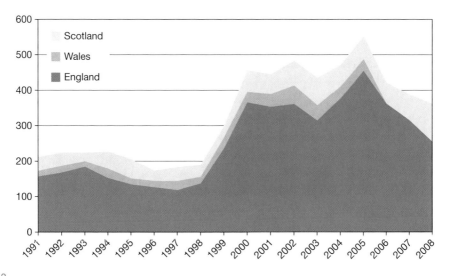

Figure 8.2

Country distribution of EISs produced under the GB planning consent systems (including England, Wales and Scotland)

Source: DCLG (2011b)

group is a large group, although numbers fell away around the turn of the century, but have increased again since. In contrast, forestry, land drainage and fish farming projects have recently fallen back from much higher numbers at the turn of the century. Electricity and pipeline works is a major category, boosted by the more recent addition of gas pipelines and offshore wind farms to the category; there have been about 600 EISs in total in this category. In contrast, and as expected, there have been only a handful of EISs for the decommissioning of nuclear reactors, following the introduction of legislation in 1999; but more will follow as the UK's ageing reactors reach the end of their operational life.

In the first few years following the implementation of Directive 85/337, 40 per cent of EISs were produced for the public sector and 60 per cent for the private sector (Wood 1991). The percentage of private sector projects has since increased considerably owing to privatization, but much of this was offset in the 1990s and early 2000s by the heavy government investment in – and consequently EISs for – new roads. A particularly

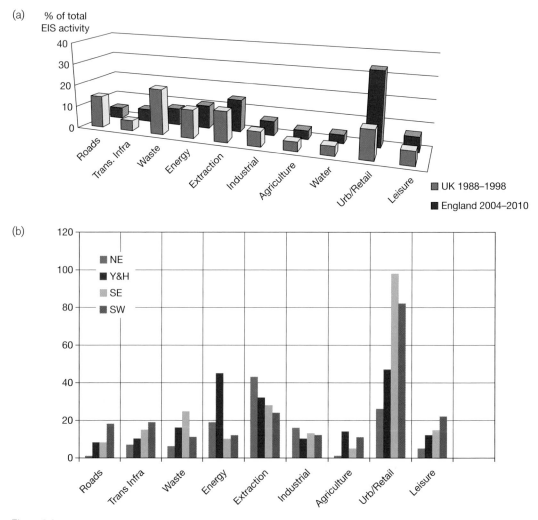

Figure 8.3

Trends in EISs for particular project types. (a) By project type % of total EIS activity – comparing UK (1988–1998) and England (2004–2010); (b) By project type – comparing numbers of EISs produced for particular English regions (2004–2010)

Source: (a) Wood and Bellanger 1998; (a and b) adapted from DCLG Library database 2011

Table 8.1 EISs produced under other consent systems (highways, forestry, electricity, etc.)

Year	EISs received							
	Highways	Harbour works	Transport and works	Forestry	Land drainage	Fish farming	Nuclear reactor decommissioning	Electricity and pipelines works (including gas pipelines and offshore wind farms)
1991	43	0		8	10	0		29
1992	38	2		9	11	0		23
1993	52	3	3	30	14	0		12
1994	61	5	3	18	9			23
1995	27	7	1	15	22	0		19
1996	19	8	3	12	29	0		17
1997	17	9	4	13	22	1		25
1998	6	1	10	13	20	2		12
1999	5	6	9	11	27	10	0	21
2000	3	12	8	7	17	13	0	42
2001	8	7	2	10	31	20	0	48
2002	21	4	7	8	37	32	2	54
2003	12	1	8	10	8	17	0	42
2004	17	2	6	3	3	11	2	53
2005	28	3	2	5	17	12	2	64
2006	24		1	1	0	0	1	27
2007	30		3	2	0	0	1	25
2008	11		3	2	0	0	2	42
Total	412	70	73	177	273	118	10	578

Source: DCLG 2011b

interesting subset is that of those EIAs for which one agency acts as both the project proponent and the competent authority (e.g. the Highway Agency for roads).

8.2.3 Sources of EISs

Copies of EISs received by English LPAs are forwarded to the Environmental Assessment Division of the Department of Communities and Local Government (DCLG) library in London once the application has been dealt with. However, this process can be a long one. The DCLG library is open to the public by appointment; photocopies can be made on the premises. In Wales, planning EISs are forwarded to the Welsh Assembly. In Scotland, all EISs are sent to the Scottish Assembly, while in Northern Ireland they are sent to the

Northern Ireland DoE. Other government agencies, such as the Highways Agency, also hold collections and lists of the EISs that fall under their jurisdiction. These collections are, however, generally not publicly available, although limited access for research purposes may be allowed.

In addition to government collections, EIS collections can also be found in several universities (e.g. at Oxford Brookes University, Manchester University and University of East Anglia), and at the Institute of Environmental Assessment and Management (IEMA). Some EISs can also be found on the Internet, although this access may be fleeting and only as long as there is an active planning application. The Institute of Environmental Management and Assessment (IEMA), based in Lincoln, has a substantial collection of EISs, which are available by pre-arrangement with institute staff, but primarily for corporate bodies. The EIA Centre at the University of Manchester keeps a database of EISs and EIA-related literature: its collection of EISs is, like its database, open to the public, by appointment. Oxford Brookes University's collection of approximately 1,000 EISs is open to the public, by appointment, and photocopies can be made on the premises. Other organizations, such as the Royal Society for the Protection of Birds, the Institute of Terrestrial Ecology, Natural England and the Campaign to Protect Rural England, as well as many environmental consultancies, also have limited collections of EISs, but these are generally kept by individuals within the organization for in-house use only, and are not available to the public. EISs are also increasingly being made available on the websites of local authorities and/or developers.

The difficulty of finding out which EISs exist, and their often prohibitive cost, can make the acquisition and analysis of EISs arduous. Various organizations (e.g. IEMA, the University of Manchester and Oxford Brookes University), have called for one central repository for all EISs in the UK. One positive new development was the launch in Spring 2011 of the IEMA's Quality Mark system. To acquire the Quality Mark, organizations will have to sign up to seven EIA commitments (relating to EIA team capabilities, EIA content, EIA presentation etc.). One of the indirect benefits of the scheme is that it will gather a substantial proportion of the UK's annual EIS output and make their non-technical summaries (NTSs) available to search on line, which will provide a valuable resource for research and practice.

8.3 The pre-submission EIA process

This is the first of three sections that discuss how EIAs are carried out in practice in the UK. It focuses on some of the pre-EIS submission stages of EIA, namely screening, scoping and pre-submission consultation.

8.3.1 Screening

Underpinning any analysis of the implementation of EIA in the UK are the requirements of the EC and UK government legislation. Under the original legislation, competent authorities in the UK were given wide discretion to determine which Schedule 2 projects require EIA within a framework of varying criteria and thresholds established by the 40-plus regulations and additional guidance. Generally, this screening process worked quite well (CEC 1993). However, some specific problems did arise regarding screening in the UK. For example, because of the largely discretionary system for screening, LPAs often – about half of the time – required an EIS to be submitted only after they had received a planning application (DoE 1996). For the same reason, screening requirements varied considerably between competent authorities. In the early days of EIA, the decision not to require an EIA had often been taken by junior members of staff who had never considered the need for an EIA, or who thought (incorrectly) that no EIA was required if the land was designated for the type of use specified in the development plan, or if the site was being extended or redeveloped rather than newly developed. Similarly, different government regional offices gave different decisions on appeals for what were essentially very similar developments (Gosling 1990).

The screening criteria established by the amendments to the Directive sought to reduce these problems post-1999 (see Sections 3.4 and 4.3). A government-sponsored study, undertaken by the Oxford Brookes University's IAU (IAU 2003), provided some research evidence on the nature and characteristics of LPA screening decision-making under the T&CP (EIA) Regulations 1999. The research, based on survey responses from over 100 LPAs in England and Wales in 2002, sought information on frequency of screening activity, on main considerations in the LPA decision whether or not an EIA should be undertaken and on the importance of different screening criteria. For screening activity in general, and for LPAs in total, the indicative thresholds were identified as the main consideration in screening decision-making (44 per cent of LPAs). The criteria of Schedule 3 and associated guidance (project is a major development of more than local importance, is in a sensitive location or will have complex/hazardous environmental effects), which require a greater degree of professional judgement, were noted second most frequently (35 per cent of LPAs).

Tables 8.2 and 8.3 relate to views on the LPAs' (then) most recent single screening decision. Using regulations and thresholds is seen as the most effective approach overall, but professional judgement is an equally important approach among the more experienced LPAs.

The most important factors in the screening decision are the size and scale of the project with 87 per cent of LPAs indicating that these are 'important' or 'very important'. Proximity to sensitive environmental receptors (87 per cent) and the nature of the project (74 per cent) are the next most important factors. At the other extreme, only 15 per cent indicated that risk of accidents was important or very important. The main constraints on screening decision-making were identified as lack of resources (45 per cent), time-frame constraints (44 per cent), lack of clarity of the regulations (33 per cent) and uncertainty over baseline data, project characteristics, etc. (32 per cent). Overall, the findings show that while thresholds are clearly important in the screening decision, they are often conditioned by professional judgement. In other words, in themselves, they do not provide sufficient justification for a screening decision (Weston 2000). This is supported by the 2011 guidance on EIA, which notes that

the basic question to be asked is: 'Would this particular development be likely to have significant effects on the environment?' For the majority of development proposals, it will be necessary to consider the characteristics of the development in combination with its proposed location, in order to determine whether there are likely to be significant environmental effects. (DCLG, 2011a)

Table 8.3 Importance of issues in most recent screening decision

Issue (n = 97)	Very important (%)	Important (%)
Size/scale of project	47	40
Proximity to receptor	44	43
Nature of project	42	32
Traffic/access impacts	33	32
Ecological impacts	32	31
Emissions	31	31
Landscape impacts	26	35
Cumulative impacts	20	26
Economic impacts	6	24
Social impacts	5	22
Controversy/concern	9	16
Risk of accidents	5	10
Other	3	1

Source: IAU 2003

Table 8.2 Most effective approach in most recent screening decision

Screening approach considered most effective	LPA (%) n = 56	< 5 EIAs 56 (n = 26)	>5 EIAs (n = 30)
Consultation with own organization	3.6	7.7	0.0
Community consultation	12.5	11.5	13.3
Asked for screening direction from Secretary of State	0.0	0.0	0.0
Followed screening guidance in local development plan	1.8	3.8	0.0
Followed guidance in other plans/policies	7.1	11.5	3.3
Used regulations and thresholds as guide	35.7	38.5	33.3
Consulted examples of other similar projects	1.8	0.0	3.3
Used professional judgement/experience	26.8	19.2	33.3
Used checklist to identify possible impacts	1.8	0.0	3.3
Used other formal technique	1.8	3.8	0.0
Own standard approach	0.0	0.0	0.0
Likely controversy of project	0.0	0.0	0.0
Other	7.1	3.8	10.0

Source: IAU 2003

As noted in Chapter 3, screening is still considered a problematic area in several EU Member States, including the UK. A survey of UK practitioners reported in a recent IEMA study (2011) found that while most practitioners agreed that the UK's screening process was an effective tool to ensure that only projects likely to have significant environmental effects are subject to an EIA, there was still serious concern that EIA had not been required for some Schedule 2 projects with what they considered to be likely significant environmental effects. Over time, this has led to a number of important legal challenges, some of which are discussed in Section 8.6. This might partly explain the lower level than might be expected of EIA activity for a country of England and Wales population size, and in comparison with other EU Member States with similarly large populations.

Progress has been made over the last decade, through a combination of some or all of the following: simplified procedures for small-scale development applications, adoption of thresholds, regulatory initiatives against the 'salami slicing' of projects (into sub-projects that then fall below threshold levels), and improved guidance on the application of screening procedures. The Scottish Government has introduced an example methodology for undertaking case by case screening (Scottish government 2007), although DCLG (2011a) guidance still refers to screening thresholds. There has also been progress on the automation of screening procedures. For example, in Denmark, an electronic model has been developed for intensive animal farming projects in which the developer simply, by inserting the required data in a calculation sheet, may get a clear picture of whether the proposed project will result in an EIA procedure or not. For the UK, see Rodriguez-Bachiller and Glasson (2004), for the Screen Expert System, and also for a Scope Expert System, developed at Oxford Brookes University.

8.3.2 Scoping and pre-submission consultation

Competent authorities also have much discretion to determine the scope of EIAs. As discussed in Chapter 3, the original Directive 85/337's Annex III was interpreted in UK legislation as being in part mandatory and in part discretionary. A survey of

early EIS output (Jones et al. 1991) showed that although the mandatory requirements of the legislation were generally carried out, the discretionary elements (e.g. the consideration of alternatives, forecasting methods, secondary and indirect impacts, and scoping) were, understandably, carried out less often. Subsequent studies showed that although early scoping discussions between the developer, the consultants carrying out the EIA work, the competent authority and relevant consultees were advised in government guidance and were considered increasingly vital for effective EIA (Jones 1995; Sadler 1996), in practice, pre-submission consultation was carried out only sporadically. For instance, a survey of environmental consultants (Weston 1995) showed that only 3 per cent had been asked to prepare their EISs before site identification, and 28 per cent before detailed design. LPAs were consulted by the developer before EIS submission in between 30 and 70 per cent of cases, although this subsequently increased (DoE 1996; Lee et al. 1994; Leu et al. 1993; Radcliff and Edward-Jones 1995; Weston 1995).

As noted in Chapters 2 and 3, the amended EC 1997 Directive and subsequent UK regulations have raised the profile of scoping in the EIA process. The ODPM study noted earlier (IAU 2003; Wood 2003) also carried out research on the nature and characteristics of scoping activities by LPAs, consultants and statutory consultees. Nearly 75 per cent of the LPAs had been involved in producing scoping opinions. All three sets of stakeholders ranked very high the preliminary assessment of characteristics of the site, consideration of mitigation and consideration of impact magnitude in formulating the scoping opinion/report. Similarly, all ranked professional judgement and consultation within their own organization as key approaches to impact identification; use of legal regulations and thresholds were also very important for LPAs and consultancies, but much less so for statutory consultees. Table 8.4 shows the issues of most concern in the most recent scoping project (at the time of the survey) for each group of participants in the process. There is considerable similarity in emphasis between the LPAs and consultancies, with traffic/transport, landscape/visual and flora/fauna issues ranking particularly high. For statutory consultees, there are some

Table 8.4 Ranking of issues of major concern in most recent project scoping opinion/report (% ranking of major concern)

	LPAs (n = 78)	Consultancies (n = 98)	Statutory consultees (n = 28)
Social issues	10	20	11
Culture/heritage	19	29	18
Economic	21	22	4
Flora/fauna	46	50	68
Soil	18	20	21
Air quality	35	21	14
Noise and vibration	42	45	11
Other emissions	26	31	39
Climatic factors	6	5	7
Waste disposal	13	19	32
Water resources	37	31	43
Geo-technical issues	18	21	29
Landscape/visual	58	57	32
Traffic/transportation	47	55	11
Risk of accidents	5	9	7
Inter-relationships of above	18	17	43
Others	3	9	4

Source: IAU 2003

Table 8.5 The frequency of inclusion of environmental topic chapters in a sample of 100 UK environmental statements from 2010

Environmental topic (bold text denotes that the topic is included in either Article 3 or Annex IV of the EIA Directive)	Occurrence rate in 100 UK Environmental Statements from 2010
Ecology (**flora and fauna**)	92%
Noise (and vibration)	92%
Water	90%
Landscape/townscape/visual analysis	88%
Transport	88%
Cultural/built **heritage** (inc. archaeology)	82%
Soil and land quality/ground conditions	81%
Air	79%
Socio-economic	64%
Cumulative effects (**interactions/inter-relationships**)	46%
Waste	28%
Climate change	17%
EMP, summary - residual effects and mitigation	17%
Population/human beings	13%
Amenity, access, recreation, rights of way	12%
Daylight/sunlight	11%
Material assets	10%
Micro-**climate**/wind	9%
Electronic interference (radio and TV)	7%
Sustainability	7%
Public health	6%
Lighting	5%
Aviation	5%
Geomorphology and coastal processes	4%
Energy	3%
Shadow flicker	3%

Source: IEMA 2011

similarities, but other environmental issues (e.g. other emissions, waste disposal) come more into play. Climatic factors and risk of accidents (health and safety) ranked surprisingly low, reflecting perhaps uncertainty about what were then seen as more long-term and less predictable issues.

Considerable experience has been gained with screening and scoping. After initial hiccups, the screening process now seems to be relatively well accepted and has been refined after the 1999 amendments. Scoping is generally considered to be a very valuable and cost-effective part of EIA by all those concerned, and again following the 1999 amendments, has increased in significance in the UK EIA process although, in comparison with 10 of the 12 new EU Member States, for example, it is still not mandatory in the UK – but it is clearly encouraged by good practice guidance. The good practice guidance on screening and scoping by the IPC for NSIPs has already been set out in Section 3.5.7. However, there is still a real concern that a combination of factors, including risk aversion, poor planning and commercial reality, may be leading to over-broad and insufficiently focused scoping activity – with 'everything plus the kitchen sink' included to be on the safe side. Table 8.5

shows the frequency of inclusion of environmental topic chapters in a sample of 100 UK environmental statements, submitted in the UK in 2010, which were reviewed by the IEMA (2011).

The review found that over 90 per cent included chapters assessing ecology, noise and water effects (Table 8.5), with a further five environmental issues being found to have their own chapter in nearly 80 per cent of all the ES reviewed. Overall this research found that the average UK environmental statement in 2010 had 9.63 environmental topic chapters. While IEMA's analysis did not extend to assessing whether the inclusion of each chapter was appropriate it is clear that current practice in scoping rarely leads to an assessment focused on a handful of key environmental issues (IEMA 2011).

··

8.4 EIS quality

As we mentioned in Section 8.1, the preparation of high-quality EISs is one component of an effective translation of EIA policy into practice. Submission of EISs of the highest standard from the outset reduces the need for costly interaction between developer and competent authority (Ferrary 1994), provides a better basis for public participation (Sheate 1994), places the onus appropriately on the developer and increases the chance of effective EIA overall. That said, the entirety of environmental information is also important, and the advice of statutory consultees, the comments of the general public and the expertise of the competent authority can help to overcome the limitations of a poor EIS (Braun 1993). This theme is considered further in Section 8.6 on judicial review.

8.4.1 Academic studies of EIS quality

Environmental impact statement quality in the UK is affected by the limited legal requirements for EIA and by the fact that planning applications cannot be rejected if the EIS is inadequate, that some crucial steps of the EIA process (e.g. public participation and monitoring) are not mandatory, and that developers undertake EIAs for their own projects. This section first considers the quality of EISs produced in the UK, based on several academic studies. It continues with a brief discussion of other perceptions of EIS quality, since competent authorities, statutory consultees and developers require different things from EIA and may thus have different views of EIA quality. It concludes with a discussion of factors that may influence EIS quality.

A range of academic studies of EIS quality were carried out in the first 10 years of the EIA Directive's implementation, typically using the criteria of Lee and Colley (1990) (see Appendix 4). Based on these criteria, EISs were divided into 'satisfactory' (i.e. marks of A, B or C) and 'unsatisfactory' (D or below). Table 8.6, which summarizes some of the findings, shows that EIS quality increased over time, but only after dismal beginnings. Generally, the description of the project, and communication and presentation of results, tended to be done better than the identification of key impacts, alternatives and mitigation.

Some studies focused on specific project types: for instance Kobus and Lee (1993) and Pritchard *et al.* (1995) reviewed EISs for extractive industry projects, Prenton-Jones for pig and poultry developments (Weston 1996), Radcliff and Edward-Jones (1995) for clinical waste incinerators, Davison (1992) and Zambellas (1995) for roads, and Gray and Edward-Jones (1999) for forestry projects.

Table 8.6 Examples of aggregated EIS quality (percentage satisfactory*)

	Lee and Colley 1990	Wood and Jones 1991	Lee and Brown 1992	Lee *et al.* 1994	Jones 1995	Barker and Wood 1999	DoE 1996
Sample size	12	24	83	47	40	24	50
1988–89	25	37	34	17			36
1989–90			48				
1990–91			60	47			
1991–92					'just over half'	58	
1992–93							60
1993–94							
1994–95						66	
1995–96							

* Satisfactory means marks of A, B or C based on the Lee and Colley criteria (1990 or 1992)

Other studies analysed the quality of specific EIS environmental components, for instance, landscape/visual (e.g. Mills 1994) and socio-economic impacts (e.g. Hall 1994). These studies also broadly suggested that EIS quality was not very good, but improving.

We are not aware of similarly formal, large scale recent studies of UK EIS quality, but indications are that EIS quality has continued to improve since then, albeit not consistently:

> Consultants working on large or controversial projects have had to improve the quality of their work substantially in recent years ... That has been one benefit of increased scrutiny of ESs on the part of statutory stakeholders and groups representing local residents and the public ... but the consensus seems to be that although the quality of ESs prepared for large and/or controversial projects has gone up, overall quality remains highly variable. 'Patchy' is the word most frequently used to describe current standards, both in terms of the quality of ESs themselves and the scrutiny they are given by local authorities. (ENDS Directory 2007)

8.4.2 Quality for whom?

These findings must, however, be considered in the wider context of 'quality for whom?' Academics may find that an EIS is of a certain quality, but the relevant planners or consultees may perceive it quite differently. For instance, the DoE (1996) study, Radcliff and Edward-Jones (1995), and Jones (1995) found little agreement about EIS quality between planners, consultees and the researchers; the only consistent trend was that consultees were more critical of EIS quality than planners were.

In interviews conducted by the Impacts Assessment Unit (DoE 1996), planning officers thought EISs were intended to gain planning permission and minimize the implication of impacts. Just over 40 per cent felt that EIS quality had improved, although this improvement was usually only marginal. Most of the others felt that this was difficult to assess when individual officers see so few EISs and when those they do see tend to be for different types of project, which raises different issues. A lack of adequate scoping and discussion

of alternatives was felt to be the major problem. EISs were seen to be getting 'better but also bigger'. Some officers linked EIS quality with the reputation of the consultants producing them, and believed that the use of experienced and reputable consultants is the best way to achieve good quality EISs.

Statutory consultees differed about whether EIS quality was improving. They generally felt that an EIS's objectivity and clear presentation were important and were improving, yet still wanting. LPAs, developers, consultants and consultees generally thought the key EIS criteria of comprehensiveness, objectivity and clear information were improving but still generally not good. Developers and consultants linked EIS quality with ability to achieve planning permission. Consultants felt that developers were increasingly recognizing the need for environmental protection and starting to bring in consultants early in project planning, so that a project could be designed around that need. One reason for this improvement may be that pressure groups were becoming more experienced with EIA, and thus had higher expectations of the process (DoE 1996).

8.4.3 Determinants of EIS quality

Several factors affect EIS quality, including the type and size of a project, and the nature and experience of various participants in the EIA process. Certain types of *project* have been associated with higher quality EISs. For instance, Schedule 1 projects, which generally have a high profile and attract substantial attention and resources, are likely to have better EISs (Lee and Brown 1992; DoE 1996). This trend is likely to continue under the rigorous pre-application requirements of the UK's National Infrastructure Unit of the Planning Inspectorate.

Regarding the *nature and experience of the participants* in the EIA process, EISs produced in-house by developers were generally of poorer quality than those produced by outside consultants: the DoE (1996) study, for instance, showed that EISs prepared in-house had an average mark of D/E, while those prepared by consultants averaged C/D, and those prepared by both B/C. Lee and Brown's (1992) analysis of 83 EISs concluded that 57 per cent of those prepared by environmental consultants were satisfactory, compared with only 17 per cent of those prepared in-house. Similarly, EISs prepared by independent applicants have tended to be better (C/D) than those prepared by local authorities for their own projects (D/E) (DoE 1996).

The experience of the developer, consultant and competent authority also affects EIS quality. For instance, Lee and Brown (1992) showed that of EISs prepared by developers (without consultants) who had already submitted at least one EIS, 27 per cent were satisfactory, compared with 8 per cent of those prepared by developers with no prior experience; Kobus and Lee (1993) cited 43 and 14 per cent respectively. A study by Lee and Dancey (1993) showed that of EISs prepared by authors with prior experience of four or more, 68 per cent were satisfactory compared with 24 per cent of those with no prior experience. The DoE (1996) study showed that of the EISs prepared by consultants with experience of five or fewer, about 50 per cent were satisfactory, compared with about 85 per cent of those prepared by consultants with experience of eight or more. EISs prepared for local authorities with no prior EIS experience were just over one-third satisfactory, compared with two-thirds for local authorities with experience of eight or more (DoE 1996). This suggests that EIS quality should improve over time simply by dint of practitioners gaining more experience.

Other determinants of EISs' quality include the availability of EIA guidance and legislation, with more guidance (e.g. DETR 2000; DoT 1993; local authority guides such as that of the Essex Planning Officers' Association 2007) leading to better EISs; the stage in project planning at which the development application and EIA are submitted, EISs for detailed planning applications generally being better than those for outline applications; and issues related to the interaction between the parties involved in the EIA process, including commitment to EIA, the resources allocated to the EIA and communication between the parties.

Environmental impact statement length also shows some correlation with EIS quality. For instance, Lee and Brown (1992) showed that the percentage of satisfactory EISs rose from 10 for EISs less than 25 pages long to 78 for those more than 100 pages long. In the DoE (1996) study, quality was shown to rise from an average of E/F for EISs of less than 20 pages to C for those of over 50 pages. However, as EISs became much longer than 150 pages, quality became more variable: although the very large EISs may contain more information, their length seems to be a symptom of poor organization and coordination. IEMA (2011) found the main text of many EISs to be more than 350 pages long, with those for nationally significant infrastructure projects typically being longer still. It noted that:

> many practitioners are frustrated with the length of ESs and have concerns about the value these documents give to consenting authorities, let alone wider groups such as the public . . . 25% of respondents [to an online survey] consider that the current length of ESs reduces the value of the assessment's findings to all audiences, even those with specialist environmental knowledge, such as the Environment Agency. Respondents indicate that this situation is worse in relation to less technical audiences. More than two fifths of respondents (42%) suggested that long ESs regularly reduce the value of an EIA's findings to stakeholders in non-statutory bodies and nearly two thirds (66.5%) believing the current length of the documents reduces the value of EIA to local communities. (IEMA, 2011)

8.5 The post-submission EIA process

After a competent authority receives an EIS and application for project authorization, it must review it, consult with statutory consultees and the public and come to a decision about the project. This section covers these points in turn.

8.5.1 Review

Planning officers generally see little difference between projects subject to EIA and other projects of similar complexity and controversy: once an application is lodged, the development process takes over. Competent authorities usually review EISs using their own knowledge and experience to pinpoint limitations and errors: the review is carried out primarily by reading through the EIS, consulting with other officers in the competent authority, consulting externally and comparing the EIS with the relevant regulations (DoE 1996).

Despite the ready availability of the Lee and Colley (1992) review criteria, only about one-third of local authorities use any form of review methods at all, and then usually as indicative criteria, to identify areas for further investigation, rather than in a formal way. About 10–20 per cent of EISs are sent for review by external consultants or by IEMA; but even when outside consultants are hired to appraise an EIS, it is doubtful whether the appraisal will be wholly unbiased if the consultants might otherwise be in competition with each other. There are also problems involved in getting feedback from the reviewing consultants quickly enough, given the tight timetable for making a project determination (DoE 1996). An innovative approach being used by some developers requires consultants who are bidding to carry out an EIA to include as part of their bid an 'independent' peer reviewer or 'critical friend' who will check and guarantee the quality of the consultants' work.

In the early days of EIA implementation in the UK, planning authorities required additional EIA information in about two-thirds of cases (e.g. Jones 1995; Lee *et al*. 1994; Weston 1995). This was usually done informally, without invoking the regulations. Circular 2/99 supports this by noting that '. . . if a developer fails to provide enough information to complete the ES, the application can be determined only by a refusal' (Regulation 3, DETR 1999b). We are not aware of similar more recent studies, although it is clear that planning authorities continue to require additional EIA information where they feel that the EISs do not provide adequate information.

8.5.2 Post-submission consultation and public participation

Competent authorities are required to send EISs to statutory and non-statutory consultees, and make them available to the public for comment. Public participation in the UK EIA system is typically limited to a few weeks following EIS submission, and notice of an EIS is normally in the form of an advertisement in a local newspaper, a site notice, and notification of neighbours. Increasingly, EISs are placed on the Internet, as well as being made available in hard copy form in council offices or libraries, and being available for purchase at a 'reasonable cost' as required by legislation.

Planning officers 'place great reliance on the consultees to review, verify and summarize at least parts of ESs' (Kreuser and Hammersley 1999). Local interest groups are often particularly active at this stage, reviewing and commenting on EIS quality as well as the planning application. Where the EIS contains insufficient information about a specific environmental component, competent authorities may put the developer and consultee in direct contact with each other rather than formally require further information themselves (DoE 1996).

The formal EIS may be only one of several similar documents presented as part of a planning application. IEMA (2011) note that

> In many of the UK's current development consent regimes there is considerable duplication of information between the Environmental Statement and other documents submitted alongside the application. A good example of this inefficiency can be seen in one of the UK's newest consent regimes, which was specifically designed to operate in a streamlined manner: applications for [Nationally Significant Infrastructure Projects]. Of the first few applications accepted by the Commission, a number have included an ES. However, included within these submissions were several additional assessment reports, addressing the predicted effects of the developments on: flood risk, sustainability, health, transport, carbon emissions, historic environment, landscape, waste and natural features. All of these issues were included within the ESs themselves and are regularly addressed in EIA practice.

The planning application process, including the consideration of EIA information, may also be only one of several consent regimes, diluting the amount of time and energy that the statutory consultees will put into it. For instance, Bird (1996) noted that the Environment Agency (which was formed in 1996 out of several agencies including HMIP):

requires impact assessments to be supplied with pollution permit applications. Therefore in their role as statutory planning EIS consultees, [they] are unlikely to waste time complaining about the poorly detailed designs given in a planning EIS, if they will be receiving another type of EIA document which precisely covers their area of concern. The Didcot B case study showed that even though HMIP considered the EIS to be satisfactory, they later demanded major design changes. [In the case of the Hamilton Oil gas terminal project in Liverpool Bay] HMIP raised no objectives to the EIS, but then rejected the [Integrated Pollution Control] authorization . . .

This problem of duplicate authorization procedures and the issues relating to discussion between EIA participants will be discussed further in case studies in Chapter 9.

8.5.3 Decision-making

As we noted in Chapter 1, one of the main purposes of EIA is to help to make better decisions, and it is therefore important to assess the performance of EIA in relation to this purpose. It is also important to remember that all decisions involve trade-offs. These include trade-offs in the EIA process between simplification and complexity, comprehensiveness and focus, urgency and the need for better information, facts and values, and certainty and uncertainty (Wood 2003; IEMA 2011). There are also trade-offs of a more substantive nature, in particular between the socio-economic and biophysical impacts of projects – sometimes reduced to the 'jobs vs. the environment' dilemma – and between groups who would win and lose from a project. Box 8.1 illustrates these trade-offs in relation to the UK government's decision to cancel a third runway at Heathrow Airport.

PLANNED THIRD RUNWAY AT HEATHROW IS SCRAPPED

Plans to build a third runway to increase capacity at London's overstretched Heathrow Airport will be cancelled by the new Coalition government. The text of the pact between the Conservatives and Liberal Democrats specifically identifies 'the cancellation of the third runway at Heathrow' as one of the parties' agreed environmental measures. It also pledges to refuse extra runways at Gatwick and Stansted.

But business representatives immediately warned the new government that restricting London's transport capacity would hit the capital's competitiveness and was a 'bad way to start'. The decision will also be a blow to the airport's operator, BAA. London First, which represents big businesses in the capital, said the government must come up with a 'plan B' if it was ruling out airport expansion, and insisted that high speed rail was no substitute for adequate international air links. It said: 'Given that Heathrow is currently at 99 per cent capacity, this is one of the principal factors affecting the competitiveness of London.'

Business groups had long argued that the expansion of Heathrow, which was approved by the former Labour government, was critical to supporting the growth of London as an international financial centre. Frequent business travellers have regularly complained about 'Heathrow hassle' in recent years, typified by long queues in the wake of terror alerts, overcrowding and outdated facilities.

The expansion had been bitterly opposed by councils, residents and environmental groups. Both the Tories and Liberal Democrats had pledged to scrap the scheme in their manifestos. John Stewart, chairman of anti-Heathrow expansion group Hacan CleanSkies, said: 'The third runway is dead in the water. Residents under the flight path are delighted and people who stood to lose their homes are relieved. It is also good for London as a whole as it would have been bad for the environment and it was not needed for the city's economic well-being.' Norman Baker, the Lib Dem MP who is an outspoken opponent of Heathrow expansion, said the move was 'the first fruit of the agreement' for people in London.

Source: Financial Times 2010

Box 8.1 Socio-economic and biophysical impact trade-offs – the third Heathrow runway, UK

Some impacts may be more tradeable in decision making than others. Sippe (1994) provides an illustration for both socio-economic and biophysical categories, of negotiable and non-negotiable impacts (Table 8.7). Sadler (1996) identified such trade-offs as the core of decision-making for sustainable development.

In the UK, the most obvious decision that is influenced by the EIA process is the competent authority's planning approval decision. The EIS may inform a planning officer's report, a planning committee's decision, and modifications and conditions to the project before and after submission. But the impact of EIA on decision-making may be much wider than this, influencing, for example, the alternatives under consideration, project design and redesign, and the range of mitigation measures and monitoring procedures (Glasson 1999). Indeed, the very presence of an effective EIA system may lead to the withdrawal of unsound projects and the deterrence of the initiation of environmentally damaging projects.

In Chapter 3 the various participants in the EIA process were identified. These participants will have varying perspectives on EIA in decision-making. A local planning officer may be concerned with the *centrality* of EIA in decision-making (does it make a difference?), central government might be concerned about *consistency* in application to development proposals across the country, and

whether they help to deliver *sustainable development* in an *efficient* manner; pressure groups may also be concerned with these criteria, but also with *fairness* (in providing opportunities for participation) and *integration* in the project cycle and approval process (to what extent is EIA easily bypassed?). A number of studies have attempted to determine whether EIA and associated consultations have influenced decisions about whether and how to authorize a project.

Early surveys of local planning officers (Kobus and Lee 1993; Lee *et al.* 1994) suggested that EISs were important in the decision in about half of the cases. Interviews with a wider range of interest groups (DoE 1996) found that about 20 per cent of respondents felt that the EIS had 'much' influence on the decision, more than 50 per cent felt that it had 'some' influence, and the remaining 20–30 per cent felt that it had little or no influence. Jones (1995) found that about one-third of planning officers, developers and public interest groups felt that the EIS influenced the decision, compared with almost half of environmental consultants and only a very small proportion of consultees. For planning decisions, it is the members of the planning committees who make the final decision. Interviews suggest that they are not generally interested in reading the EIS, but instead rely on the officer's report to summarize the main issues (DoE 1996). According to Wood

Table 8.7 Judging environmental acceptability – trade-offs

	Non-negotiable impacts	Negotiable impacts*
Ecological (physical and biological systems components)	• Degrades essential life support systems • Degrades the conservation estate • Adversely effects ecological integrity • Loss of biodiversity	• No degradation beyond carrying capacity • No degradation of productive systems • Wise use of natural resources
Human (humans as individuals or in social groupings)	• Loss of human life • Reduces public health and safety unacceptably • Unreasonably degrades quality of life where people live	• Community benefits and costs and where they are borne • Reasonable apportionment of costs and benefits • Reasonable apportionment of inter-generational equity • Compatibility with defined environmental policy goals

Source: Sippe (1994)

* In terms of net environmental benefits

and Jones (1997), planning committees followed officers' recommendations in 97 per cent of the cases they studied. The consultations related to the EIS are generally seen to be at least as important as the EIS itself (Jones 1995; Kobus and Lee 1993; Lee *et al.* 1994; Wood and Jones 1997). On the other hand, many non-statutory bodies feel excluded from the decision-making process, and one national non-statutory wildlife body complained that if a statutory consultee did not object, then their own objections went largely ignored (DoE 1996).

While studies of early EISs (e.g. Kobus and Lee 1993; Lee *et al.* 1994) suggested that material considerations were slightly more important than environmental considerations in the final decision on a project's authorization, a later study (Jones 1995) suggested that the environment was the principal factor influencing the decision, with planning policies given slightly less weight. Wood and Jones (1997) reported that the environment was seen to be the overriding factor influencing the decisions in 37 per cent of the cases they studied. However, only in very few cases would the final decision have been different in the absence of an EIS. Weston's (2002) study of planning appeal cases concludes:

> Procedurally EIA is much stronger today in the UK than it was in the early years of its implementation – yet the influence that EIA has on the actual decisions made by LPAs and planning inspectors remains weak, as those decisions are based on a complex web of factors that had evolved long before EIA was introduced ... Local authorities in England and Wales deal with around 450,000 applications for planning consent per year. The decisions on those applications are made on the basis of 'material considerations' including the local development plan, national planning policy guidance and the results of a formal consultation process. EIA cases make up less than 0.1% of those applications and for the most part the actual decision-making process for those cases will be little different to the other 99.9%.

Overall, then, in the UK project applications with EISs are not treated much differently from those without EISs. Although environmental issues are addressed more formally, in a discrete document, the final decision-making process is not changed much by EIA. The main procedural difference brought about by EIA is the need to consult people about the EIS, and the broader scope for public participation (not often used in practice) that it brings. The main substantive differences come in the form of modifications to projects and mitigation measures designed in early on, possibly additional or different conditions on the project, and generally a more comprehensive consideration of environmental issues by the competent authority.

•••

8.6 Legal challenges

A key driver behind recent improvements to EIA quality, including the 2011 EIA regulations and guidance, has been the threat of legal challenge, either on the basis that the project should have been subject to EIA but wasn't, or that the EIA process was inadequate. Legal challenges are important in that they interpret aspects of EIA legislation, set precedents for subsequent EIAs and, over time, have tended to strengthen EIA requirements. A consultant from a major environmental consultancy noted that:

> 'Recent case law has had a profound impact on our EIA work ... It's easy for objectors to criticise the EIA process on the basis of case law, to stand up at public inquiries and say the process has not been followed correctly. Scrutiny comes far more frequently and intensely than it used to, at least on the type of projects we're working on.' Mr Hewitt isn't pointing the finger at a single legal dispute that suddenly opened the floodgates to further legal challenges, rather he's arguing that the cumulative effect of EIA-related case law has been to make the raising of objections easier ... Continuously referring back to case law in a bid to construct ESs that comprehensively take account of all relevant legal judgments is a laborious process, but one that experienced clients have come to

view as a good investment, says Mr Hewitt. Anything that improves the chance of being granted planning approval and/or increasing the speed with which approval is granted is worth paying for. (ENDS Directory 2007)

This rather lengthy section reviews a selection of UK judicial review cases, to give the reader an idea of the kinds of issues that arise during such a legal challenge. It includes some of the key recent court cases that are triggering changes in UK EIA guidance (Baker, Mellor); key older cases that have influenced past guidance and subsequent court cases (Berkeley, Rochdale); and a few other cases that illustrate specific themes in EIA law. They are presented in the rough sequence within the EIA process in which the issue occurs, starting with the screening process and concluding with mitigation. They include quite lengthy quotes from the legal judgements, to give a flavour of the logic and arguments used by the courts, and to show how EIA legislation is used and interpreted.

The UK courts system is complex, with multiple layers and players. For the purposes of this section, however, only limited information about the system and main players is needed. First, the claimant (the person or organization initiating the legal challenge, also known as the plaintiff or in some cases the appellant) must have 'standing' to bring a legal challenge, in that they must be sufficiently affected or harmed by the decision that they are challenging. Claimants in EIA cases are typically local residents affected by a planning decision to allow a project, or developers affected by a competent authority's decision to require EIA. The defendant is the person or organization against which the claimant is making the legal challenge. Finally, where a public authority's decision is being judicially reviewed – as is the case for all of the legal challenges presented in this section – the UK courts use the test of 'Wednesbury unreasonableness', which is based on a completely unrelated court decision of 1947 involving operation of a cinema. A decision is 'Wednesbury unreasonable' if it is so unreasonable that no reasonable authority could have decided that way.

8.6.1 Environmental assessment is required even if it would not change a planning decision

Berkeley vs. Secretary of State for the Environment and others (2000) UKHL 36; (2000) 3 All ER 897; (2000) 3 WLR 420

The 'Berkeley 1' case involved a 1994 planning application for redevelopment of the Fulham Football Club. The local planning authority did not ask for an EIS (and none was prepared), but it did consult with a wide range of organizations, and carefully weighed up the advantages and disadvantages of the proposed scheme. In August 1995, the Secretary of State called in the application. He also did not require an EIS. He granted permission in August 1996.

Lady Berkeley, who lived near the site, challenged this planning permission, arguing that an EIA should have been carried out. Her appeal was dismissed, with the judge agreeing with the football club that upon the true construction of the regulations, no EIA was required. The judge also noted that, even if an EIA had been required, in his opinion the absence of the EIA 'had no effect on the outcome of the inquiry and could not possibly have done so'. A Court of Appeal decision of 1998 found that the judge was wrong to determine that no EIA was required, but upheld his decision on the basis of the EIA's lack of effect on the outcome of the inquiry. Lady Berkeley challenged the Court of Appeal decision, and the 'Berkeley 2' case came before the House of Lords in 2000.

The counsel for the Secretary of State this time accepted that the fact that an EIA would have made no difference to the outcome of a planning decision is not a sufficient reason for the courts not to quash that decision. Instead he argued that there had been substantial compliance with the requirements of the Directive.

The House of Lords concluded first that redevelopment of the football club could arguably be considered an 'urban development project' within paragraph 10(b) of Schedule 2; that its effect on ecology of the River Thames meant that it was likely to have significant environmental effects; and that in these circumstances individuals affected by the proposed development had a directly enforceable right to have the need for an EIA considered by the Secretary of State prior to him granting planning permission and not afterwards by a judge.

It also ruled that the EIA process goes beyond simply informing a planning decision, and so matters even if the EIA would not have changed the decision:

> The directly enforceable right of the citizen which is accorded by the Directive is not merely a right to a fully informed decision on the substantive issue. It must have been adopted on an appropriate basis and that requires the inclusive and democratic procedure prescribed by the Directive in which the public, however misguided or wrongheaded its views may be, is given an opportunity to express its opinion on the environmental issues.

It also dismissed the Secretary of State's argument that an equivalent of an EIS had been prepared:

> [The Secretary of State's counsel] says that the equivalent of the applicant's environmental statement can be found in its statement of case under the Inquiry Procedure Rules, read (by virtue of cross-referencing) with the planning authority's statement of case, which in turn incorporated the comprehensive officers' report to the planning sub-committee, which in turn incorporated the background papers such as the letters from the National Rivers Authority and the London Ecology Unit and was supplemented by the proofs of evidence made available at the inquiry. Members of the public had access to all these documents and the right to express their opinions upon them at the inquiry . . . I do not accept that this paper chase can be treated as the equivalent of an environmental statement . . . The point about the environmental statement contemplated by the Directive is that it constitutes a single and accessible compilation, produced by the applicant at the very start of the application process, of the relevant environmental information and the summary in non-technical language.

The planning permission was quashed.

8.6.2 Screening out on grounds that planning conditions can make the project's impacts insignificant

R on the application of Lebus vs. South Cambridgeshire DC (2003)[1]

The 'Lebus case' concerned a February 2000 planning application for an egg production unit for 12,000 free range chickens in a 1,180 m² building, and an associated dwelling for an agricultural worker. In April 2000, the claimants' solicitor wrote to South Cambridgeshire District Council claiming that the application required an EIA. The planning officer wrote back promptly, noting that the proposal did not require EIA under Schedule 1 of the 1999 EIA regulations since it housed less than 60,000 hens, but that it was a Schedule 2 proposal as the building would be more than 500 m². However the planning officer also noted that:

> consideration has to be given to each proposal on whether it would have significant effects on the environment by virtue of factors such as its location, impact, nature and size . . . When considering the need for an Environmental Assessment the above factors as well as issues such as: Airborne pollution; Dirty water and litter disposal; Ecology; Highways and access; and Landscape were taken into account. The Council did not wish to be drawn into requesting an Environmental Statement purely to get information it should rightfully expect anyway. It was considered all the above points could be covered in sufficient detail without formally requesting an Environmental Statement.

South Cambridgeshire granted planning permission in January 2002.

Justice Sullivan concluded that the local authority had not prepared any document that could be sensibly described as a screening opinion for the project. He then also noted that:

> in so far as the statutory question was addressed, it was addressed upon the basis that planning conditions would be imposed and management obligations would be enforceable under section 106. The question was not asked whether the development as

described in the application would have significant environmental effects, but rather whether the development as described in the application subject to certain mitigation measures would have significant environmental effects ... the underlying purpose of the Regulations in implementing the Directive is that the potentially significant impacts of a development are described together with a description of the measures envisaged to prevent, reduce and, where possible, offset any significant adverse effects on the environment. Thus the public is engaged in the process of assessing the efficacy of any mitigation measures. It is not appropriate for a person charged with making a screening opinion to start from the premise that although there may be significant impacts, these can be reduced to insignificance as a result of the implementation of conditions of various kinds. The appropriate course in such a case is to require an environmental statement setting out the significant impacts and the measures which it is said will reduce their significance.

Similar considerations applied in Bellway Urban Renewal Southern vs. John Gillespie [2003] EWCA Civ 400, where the Secretary of State gave permission for the redevelopment of a former gasworks into residential units, on the basis that the scheme would bring a contaminated site back into beneficial use, and that decontamination of the site could be secured through a planning condition. The claimant successfully argued that the Secretary of State had not considered the project's unmitigated effects, but rather had inappropriately assessed the effects only assuming that mitigation had been put in place.

These cases do not suggest that remediation measures must be totally ignored when decisions are made about the likely significant effects of a proposed development, but they do suggest that care and judgement has to be exercised. Well-established and uncontroversial remedial measures may well be taken into account, but for more complex projects, or where the proposed remediation measures are complex or less well understood, this may be less appropriate. Furthermore, the offer of remediation measures should not be used to

frustrate the purpose of the EIA Directive or substitute for its requirements.

8.6.3 Screening where there are cumulative impacts with previous phases

R oao Baker vs. Bath and North East Somerset Council ([2009] EWHC 595)[2]

The 'Baker case' involved a 2005 application by Hinton Organics (Wessex) Limited for an extension to a 2.1 ha composting site called Charlton Fields, which it had been operating since 2000. The application was to compost wood waste and cardboard, as well as green waste, at Charlton Fields, and to expand operations to another smaller (less than 0.5 ha) site about 1 kilometre away from Charlton Fields, named Lime Kiln. Partly composted waste from Charlton Fields would be transported to Lime Kiln, where the composting process would finish. The planning authority granted planning permission in 2006 without requiring EIA. This was challenged by the plaintiff.

The planning authority argued that no EIA was required for the Lime Kiln application because of the wording of the Town and Country Planning (Environmental Impact Assessment (England and Wales) Regulations 1999 that required EIA for 'Any change to or extension of development listed in this Schedule where such a change or extension meets the thresholds, if any, or description of development set out in this Schedule.' The relevant schedule for the disposal of waste included as thresholds: '(ii) the area of the development exceeds 0.5 of a hectare ... the thresholds and criteria ... applied to the change or extension (and not to the development as changed or extended).'

Mr Justice Collins ruled in favour of the plaintiff. Referring to two European court cases – Liege Airport (C-2/07) and Madrid ring road (C-142/07) – he noted that

> As far as the Lime Kiln application is concerned ... there is an issue as to whether that should be regarded as cumulative in the sense that it goes along with the other project, or whether in itself, albeit smaller than the threshold because it covers an area less than half an hectare, there is a likelihood of environmental damage ... there should have been, at the very least, consideration as to

whether, notwithstanding the threshold had not been crossed, it was, indeed, an EIA development, whether or not it was to be regarded as cumulative . . .

I have come to the conclusion that the regulations do not in the passage in parenthesis ['(and not to the development as changed or extended)'] properly implement the Directive. This is because they seek to limit consideration for the purposes of screening to consideration of the change or extension on its own. That is, in my view, contrary to the purpose of and the language of the Directive and the approach that should be adopted as set out by the court.

As a result of this ruling, the UK government is now applying the thresholds in Schedule 2.13 to the whole of the development once modified, and not just to the change or extension; and has added a new provision that will require any change or extension to an existing or approved Schedule 1 project to be screened for the need for EIA (DCLG 2011a).

A similar early EIA case, R. vs. Swale BC ex p RSPB [1991] 1 PLR 6, 16, concerned the construction of a storage area for cargo that would require the infill of Lappel Bank, a mudflat important for its wading birds. Justice Simon Brown concluded that:

> The proposals should not then be considered in isolation if, in reality, it is properly to be regarded as an integral part of an inevitably more substantial development. This approach appears to me appropriate to the language of the Regulations, the existence of the smaller development of itself promoting the larger development and thereby likely to carry in its wake the environmental effects of the latter . . . developers could otherwise defeat the object of the Regulations by piecemeal development proposals.

8.6.4 Screening for demolition

R (SAVE Britain's Heritage) vs. Secretary of State for Communities and Local Government, [2011] EWCA Civ 334[3]

The 'SAVE case' involved a decision by Lancaster City Council to permit the demolition of the historic Mitchell's Brewery building without requiring an EIA. Both parties agreed that the demolition would have a significant impact on cultural heritage. In May 2010, the High Court ruled that demolition was not a 'project' within the scope of the EIA Directive and so did not require EIA. The pressure group SAVE Britain's Heritage took the case to the Court of Appeals. In a judgement of March 2011 that reflected the recent case of Commission vs. Ireland C-50/09, Lord Justices Toulson and Sullivan took as a basis the EIA Directive's definition of 'project', namely:

> – the execution of construction works or of other installations or schemes,
> – other interventions in the natural surroundings and landscape including those involving the extraction of mineral resources . . . (Article 1.2).

[The defendant] readily accepted the proposition that the Directive must be interpreted in a purposive manner. If it is accepted that works are capable of having significant effects on the environment, the definition of 'project' in Article 1.2 should, if possible, be construed so as to include, rather than exclude, such works. Applying this approach to the first limb of the definition in Article 1.2, it seems to me that the execution of demolition works falls naturally within 'the execution of . . . other . . . schemes' . . . [But] it is unnecessary to give Article 1.2 a broad and purposive construction in order to reach the conclusion that, in ordinary language, demolition works which leave a site on completion in a condition which protects the public and preserves public amenity are capable of being a 'scheme' for the purposes of Article 1.2 . . .

I would not accept the premise underlying the Respondent's submission: that 'landscape' in the second limb must be a reference to a rural landscape. For the purposes of the Directive 'landscape' is something other than 'natural surroundings'. In the context of a Directive the purpose of which is to ensure that significant environmental effects are properly assessed before projects proceed, I do not see why 'landscape' in Article 1.2 should be confined to rural landscapes . . .

[The defendant] submitted that demolition could not fall within the Directive, even if it fell within the definition of project in Article 1.2, because it was not included in the lists of projects in Annexes I and II to the Directive. [But] the lists of projects include 'projects' that do not necessarily involve construction works; see eg. the list of 'Agriculture, silviculture and aquaculture' projects, and some of the 'Food Industry' projects. [The Commission vs. Ireland C-50/09 case concluded] that the Annexes refer to sectoral categories of projects, and do not describe the precise nature of the works which may comprise such a project. If demolition is capable of being a 'scheme' for the purposes of Article 1.2, it is also capable of being an 'urban development project' within paragraph 10 (b) of Annex II, even though the project comprises only demolition and restoration of the site.

8.6.5 Need for a screening statement where a project is 'screened out'

R vs. Secretary of State for the Environment, Transport and Regions and Parcelforce ex parte Marson [1998] EWHC Admin 351;[4] and R oao Mellor and Secretary of State for Communities and Local Government [2010] Env LR 2[5]

The 'Marson case' involved a 1996 planning application by Parcelforce to develop a 17 hectare site near Coventry Airport for sorting and handling of parcels. A group of local residents and parish councils sought a direction from the Secretary of State that environmental assessment was required. In a letter of February 1998, the Secretary of State noted that the development fell within 10(a) of Schedule 2, but would not be likely to have significant environmental effects, and that no EIA would be required. The applicants challenged this decision, suggesting that reasons must be given for declining to require an EIA. Lord Justices Nourse, Pill and Mummery comprehensively disagreed, citing inter alia the lack of a stated legal duty to do so, the discretion afforded to the Secretary of State, the applicant's opportunity to influence the planning process through other means.

This finding held for many years, but has recently been called into question by the 'Mellor case'. The Mellor Case involved a 2004 planning application by Partnerships in Care (PIC) for a medium secure hospital at HSM Forest Moor. In July 2006, PIC's consultants asked Harrogate Borough Council for a screening opinion. Nearby residents, including Mr Mellor, wrote to the council arguing that an EIA was needed, and in October the council determined that an EIA was required. PIC referred the matter to the Secretary of State, who decided in December 2006 that EIA was not required.

The matter was referred to the European Court of Justice. There, Advocate General Kokott concluded that, although the EIA Directive does not require a negative screening opinion to include reasons, third parties should be able to satisfy themselves that the competent authority has come to its determination in a legal robust manner. In sum, she determined that (1) a negative screening opinion does not need to contain reasons; but (2) the planning authority has a duty to provide further information and relevant documents on the negative screening decision if this is requested by an interested party; but in turn that (3) further information can be brief and does not have to be formal. These requirements are are also included in recent changes to UK EIA regulations (DCLG 2011a).

8.6.6 EIA may be required at the detailed consent stage even if it was not required at the outline consent stage

R oao Diane Barker vs. LB Bromley, C-290/03, [2007] Env LR 2

The 'Barker case' involves a two-stage planning application by London & Regional Properties Ltd for first outline and then detailed consent to develop a leisure complex in Crystal Palace Park. The London Borough of Bromley did not require an EIS for the first application, and granted outline planning consent in March 1998, reserving certain matters for subsequent approval before development started. The developer applied to the council for final determination of these reserved matters in January 1999, and the council issued a notice of approval in May 1999.

A nearby resident, Ms Barker, challenged the second permission and ended up bringing her challenge to the European Court of Justice. Broadly the challenge can be boiled down to the question: if a UK planning authority has decided that EIA is not required at the outline planning permission stage because they believe that the project would not have significant environmental effects, and if at the detailed planning permission stage it emerges that the project could have significant environmental effects, can and must they the planning authority require EIA at the detailed stage? Note that there is a distinction between 'can' and 'must', since LB Bromley argued that UK national legislation did not allow them to do this even if they had wanted to do it.

Advocate General Léger ruled in favour of Ms Barker:

> Article 1 (2) of Directive 85/337 defines 'development consent' for the purposes of the directive as the decision of the competent authority or authorities which entitles the developer to proceed with the project. It is apparent from the scheme and the objectives of Directive 85/337 that this provision refers to the decision (involving one or more stages) which allows the developer to commence the works for carrying out his project. Having regard to those points, it is therefore the task of the national court to verify whether the outline planning permission and decision approving reserved matters which are at issue in the main proceedings constitute, as a whole, a 'development consent' for the purposes of Directive 85/337 ...
>
> [W]here national law provides for a consent procedure comprising more than one stage, one involving a principal decision and the other involving an implementing decision which cannot extend beyond the parameters set by the principal decision, the effects which a project may have on the environment must be identified and assessed at the time of the procedure relating to the principal decision. It is only if those effects are not identifiable until the time of the procedure relating to the implementing decision that the assessment should be carried out in the course of that procedure. [In such

a legal context] it follows that the competent authority is, in some circumstances, obliged to carry out an environmental impact assessment in respect of a project even after the grant of outline planning permission, when the reserved matters are subsequently approved ... This assessment must be of a comprehensive nature, so as to relate to all the aspects of the project which have not yet been assessed or which require a fresh assessment.

> [So] Articles 2 (1) and 4 (2) of Directive 85/337 are to be interpreted as requiring an environmental impact assessment to be carried out if, in the case of grant of consent comprising more than one stage, it becomes apparent, in the course of the second stage, that the project is likely to have significant effects on the environment by virtue *inter alia* of its nature, size or location.

The UK government changed the Town and County Planning (EIA) (England) Regulations in 2008 to reflect these points (DCLG 2010).

8.6.7 EIA for outline planning applications and in other cases where there is uncertainty about the project

The 'Rochdale envelope'

Two legal challenges to planning permissions by Rochdale Metropolitan Borough Council have established the concept of the 'Rochdale envelope'.

R vs. Rochdale Metropolitan Borough Council ex parte Tew and others (1999)[6] – 'Rochdale 1' – concerned an outline planning application made in early 1999 by Wilson Bowden Properties Limited and English Partnership for a 213 hectare business park. Rochdale MBC had a long-standing policy that the area should be developed as a business park. The planning application was accompanied by an indicative land use schedule and floor space figures, and the accompanying letter noted that 'The master plan has been prepared for illustrative purposes ... [It] aims to demonstrate the general form of development, showing the integration of the access proposals, principal highways alignment, and possible patterns of land use ... ' Rochdale

MBC gave planning permission for the project subject to a range of conditions, including

- Condition 1.3: 'The development shall be carried out in accordance with the mitigation measures set out in the Environmental Statement submitted with the application, unless otherwise agreed in writing by the Local Planning Authority ... '
- Condition 1.7: 'No development shall be commenced until a scheme (the Framework Document) has been submitted to and approved by the Local Planning Authority showing the overall design and layout of the proposed Business Park, including details of the phasing of development and the timescale of that phasing. The Framework Document shall show details of the type and disposition of development and the provision of structural landscaping within and on the perimeters of the site. The Business Park shall be constructed in accordance with the approved Framework Document unless the Local Planning Authority consents in writing to a variation or variations.'
- Condition 1.11: 'This permission shall not be construed as giving any approval to the illustrative Masterplan accompanying the application.'

The plaintiffs argued that the EIS was inadequate because it did not provide adequate information as to the 'design and size or scale of the project', and that this information was necessary to identify the proposed development's main environmental effects. They also argued that, not only was the outline planning permission not tied to the illustrative masterplan on which the EIS was based, but that it expressly envisaged that a different layout and composition of users would emerge as part of the development of the Framework Document. They argued that a planning decision for an EIA project must be taken in the full knowledge of the project's likely environmental effects, and that it is not sufficient that full knowledge will be obtainable at a later stage.

The council, in turn, argued that the kind of detailed requirements envisaged by the plaintiffs would make it difficult, and possibly completely impractical, to seek planning permission for large

projects; and that Circular 15/88 expressly allowed outline planning permission to be sought for projects requiring EIA. Justice Sullivan, however, agreed with the plaintiffs in a judgement of May 1999:

> Condition 1.3 ... ties the mitigation measures to the Environmental Statement (unless otherwise agreed), but those measures were a response to the environmental impacts of development in accordance with the illustrative Masterplan. Recognising, as I do, the utility of the outline application procedure for projects such as this, I would not wish to rule out the adoption of a Masterplan approach, provided the Masterplan was tied, for example by the imposition of condition, to the description of the development permitted. If illustrative floor space or hectarage figures are given, it may be appropriate for an Environmental Assessment to assess the impact of a range of possible figures before describing the likely significant effects. Conditions may then be imposed to ensure that any permitted development keeps within those ranges.
>
> The fundamental difficulty in the present case is that ... the outline planning permission was not tied in any way to either of those documents. Conditions 1.7 and 1.11 dispensed with the Masterplan and replaced it with the Framework Document to be submitted and approved in due course. The reason given for the imposition of condition 1.11 explains that the Masterplan was submitted for illustrative purposes only and that it gave insufficient detail on which to determine the layout of the site. If it was inadequate for that purpose, it is difficult to see how it could have been an adequate description for the purposes of paragraph 2(a) of Schedule 3 to the Assessment Regulations.

The Rochdale saga promptly continued as 'Rochdale 2', R vs. Rochdale Metropolitan Borough Council ex parte Milne (2000).[7] After the results of Rochdale 1, the developers re-applied for outline planning permission for the business park, including a schedule of development, development framework and masterplan. Details of landscape and design were reserved (not provided), as were transport arrangements for most of the plots on the site. The planning application was accompanied by a comprehensive EIS.

Rochdale MBC again gave planning permission for the proposal in December 1999, but this time the planning conditions were much more closely tied to the EIS. For instance Condition 1.7 stated that:

'The development on this site shall be carried out in substantial accordance with the layout included within the Development Framework document', because 'The layout of the proposed Business Park is the subject of an Environmental Impact Assessment and any material alteration to the layout may have an impact which has not been assessed by that process.'

Condition 1.11 required that 'The development shall be carried out in accordance with the mitigation measures set out in the Environmental Statement submitted with the application unless provided for in any other condition attached to this permission.'

The plaintiff again challenged the planning permission, arguing that, despite the changes made to the planning application, it still did not provide 'a description of the development proposed'. The reserved matters – design and access arrangements – could significantly affect the environmental impacts of the project, for instance by the materials used or whether the development included a particularly striking 'landmark' building. He suggested that, to comply with the requirements of Schedule 3, the development must be described in enough detail to ensure that nothing is omitted that may be capable of having a significant environmental effect; and that outline planning applications are thus fundamentally inconsistent with the requirement for EIA. In this case, Justice Sullivan sided with the local authority and dismissed the application for judicial review:

If a particular kind of project, such as an industrial estate development project . . . is, by its very nature, not fixed at the outset, but is expected to evolve over a number of years depending on market demand, there is no reason why 'a description of the project' for

the purposes of the directive should not recognize that reality. What is important is that the environmental assessment process should then take full account at the outset of the implications for the environment of this need for an element of flexibility . . . It is for the authority responsible for granting the development consent . . . to decide whether the difficulties and uncertainties are such that the proposed degree of flexibility is not acceptable in terms of its potential effect on the environment.

Any major development project will be subject to a number of detailed controls, not all of them included within the planning permission. Emissions to air, discharges into water, disposal of the waste produced by the project, will all be subject to controls under legislation dealing with environmental protection. In assessing the likely significant environmental effects of a project the authors of the environmental statement and the local planning authority are entitled to rely on the operation of those controls with a reasonable degree of competence on the part of the responsible authority . . . The same approach should be adopted to the local planning authority's power to approve reserved matters.

The Rochdale judgements have significant implications for outline planning applications and for cases where there is uncertainty about details of the proposed project:

- Applications for 'bare' outline permissions with all matters reserved for later approval are very unlikely to comply with EIA requirements.
- Developers can have flexibility, but for EIA purposes they need to consider the range of possible parameters within which the project might evolve, and these must be detailed enough to allow a proper assessment of the likely environmental effects and proposed mitigation.
- The flexibility should not be abused, and does not give developers an excuse to provide inadequate descriptions of their projects. The planning authority must satisfy itself that, given the nature of the project, it has 'full knowledge' of its likely environmental effects.

- The outline planning application should specify clearly defined parameters within which the project may evolve, in the form of conditions and obligations. These should be 'tied' to the environmental information of the ES – the range of these parameters is the 'Rochdale envelope'.
- Implementation of reserved matters consents granted for matters that are not in the outline consent will be unlawful (IPC 2011).

8.6.8 Themes in judicial review findings

Until recently, judicial reviews of competent authority decisions have been limited by the courts' relatively narrow interpretation of the duties of competent authorities under the EIA regulations. However, a series of high-profile recent cases – including Baker, Mellor, Barker and SAVE – suggests that the courts are now taking a more proactive and wider view of the EIA Directive's requirements. Several conclusions can be drawn from these legal judgements:

- The EIA Directive is interpreted by the courts as having a 'wide scope and broad purpose', in line with the Kraaijveld (Dutch Dykes) Case C- 72/95.
- A project cannot be automatically excluded from EIA requirements simply because it is not listed in the EIA Directive or implementing regulations. Furthermore, because projects can be described in different ways, for EIA screening purposes it is probably better to consider the project's scope and purpose rather than its label.
- Where aspects of a project are uncertain, the EIA must provide enough information to allow a decision to be made taking into account these uncertainties.
- Provision of information equivalent to that in an EIS is not equivalent to EIA, since the public participation requirements of EIA are also important.
- The courts have clarified that EISs do not have to consider alternatives, even if the planning authority thinks that they should have been considered or if the alternatives would have a less severe impact than the proposed project.

- The imposition of planning conditions to the point where the project would no longer have significant environmental impacts is also not equivalent to EIA. The distinction between EIA screening (not including mitigation) and impact assessment (which can include mitigation) is important. 'A purposive approach might be as follows. Would an open minded adviser to the competent authority or member of the public concerned about the potential [significant environmental effect] want the systematic assembly of the EIA data to judge how effective the proposed [mitigation measure] would be? If so EIA is required' (McCracken 2010).

8.7 Costs and benefits of EIA

Much of the early resistance to the imposition of EIA was based on the idea that it would cause additional expense and delay in the planning process. EIA proponents refuted this by claiming that the benefits of EIA would well outweigh its costs. This chapter concludes with a discussion of the costs and benefits of EIA to various parties in the UK.

8.7.1 Costs of EIA

Environmental impact assessment has slightly increased the cost to *developers* of obtaining planning permission. An EIS generally costs between 0.01 and 5 per cent of project costs, with 0.1 to 1 per cent being a rough average for the UK (GHK 2010). Weston's (1995) survey of consultants showed that consultancies received on average £34,000 for preparing a whole EIS, £40,000 for several EIS sections, and £14,750 for one section: this itself highlights the variability of the costs involved. In 1997, the (former) DETR suggested £35,000 as a median figure for the cost of undertaking an EIA (DETR 1997b), and in 2010 DCLG suggested an average cost of almost £90,000 (€100,000): it is unclear whether this difference is due to a strong rise in the actual costs of EIA, or to some other factor.

There has been some concern that competition and cost-cutting by consultancies, an increase in 'cowboy' consultancies and the tendency for developers to accept the lowest bid for preparing an EIS may affect the quality of the resulting EIAs by limiting the consultants' time, expertise or equipment. Consultants note that 'on all but the largest developments there is always a limited budget – an EA expands to fill the available budget, and then some' (Radcliff and Edward-Jones 1995). However, Fuller (1992) argued that cost-cutting may not be helpful to a developer in the long run:

> A poor-quality statement is often a major contributory factor to delays in the system, as additional information has to be sought on issues not addressed, or only poorly addressed, in the original . . . Therefore reducing the cost of an environmental assessment below the level required for a thorough job is often a false economy.

The cost of EIA to *competent authorities* is much more difficult to measure and has until now been based on interviews rather than on a more systematic methodology. UK planning decisions for the kinds of large projects that require EIA have always taken a long time, often years. They consistently take considerably more time than do decisions for projects that do not require EIA (DoE 1996), but then they tend to be larger, more complex and more politically sensitive.

An early study (Lee and Brown 1992) found that about half the planning officers interviewed felt that the EIS had not influenced how long it took to reach a decision; the rest were about evenly split between those who felt that the EIA had speeded up or slowed down the process. In later interviews (DoE 1996), many planning officers felt that dealing with the EIS and the planning application were one and the same, and 'just part of the job'. Estimates for reviewing the EIS and associated consultation ranged from 5 hours to 6–8 months of staff time! Planning officers handling EIS cases tend to be development control team leaders and above, so staff costs would generally be higher than for standard planning applications. In some cases, planning officers also hire consultants to help them review and comment on EISs, adding to their costs.

The time taken to decide planning applications has recently been the focus of several studies (e.g.

National Audit Office 2008; DCLG 2008; Ball *et al.* 2008), none of which identified EIA as a factor leading to delays. Only Killian Pretty's 170 page review of planning applications (DCLG 2008) mentioned EIA at all, and then only very briefly to imply that their length should be shortened. Some consultants feel that EIA slows down the decision-making process and is a means through which LPAs can make unreasonable demands on developers to provide detailed information on issues 'which are not strictly relevant to the planning decision' (Weston 1995). However others feel that EIA does not necessarily slow things down: 'The more organised approach makes it more efficient and in some cases it allows issues to be picked up earlier. The EIS can thus speed up the system' (DoE 1996).

The Planning Act 2008, the primary aim of which was to speed up the planning system, set up a new system of National Policy Statements to provide policy guidance on energy, transport, water, wastewater and waste developments. It also established a parallel decision-making stream for major infrastructure projects, to help speed up their delivery. Early indications are that the pre-application stage – including preparation of EISs – for these projects is lengthening; it is not yet clear whether the government's aim of then deciding on the projects within a year of application will be met in practice (see also Section 3.5.7).

In 20 case studies, the time spent by *consultees* on EIA ranged from four hours to one-and-a-half days for statutory consultees, and from one hour to two weeks for non-statutory consultees. Although some consultees, like planning officers, argued that 'this is what we are here for', others suggested that they needed to prioritize what developments they got involved in because of time and resource constraints (DoE 1996). This may well be even more of a problem in today's more straightened circumstances.

8.7.2 Benefits of EIA

The benefits of EIA are mostly unquantifiable, so a direct comparison with the costs of EIA is not possible. Perhaps the clearest way to gauge whether EIA helps to reduce a project's environmental impacts is to determine whether a project was modified as a result of EIA. Early studies on EIA effectiveness (e.g. Kobus and Lee 1993; Tarling 1991; Jones 1995) showed that modifications to the project as a result of the EIA process were required in almost half the cases, with most modifications regarded as significant. More recently, the European Commission (2009) reported that EIAs led to improvements for most projects, although this was based on information from Member States other than the UK.

Environmental impact assessment can have other benefits in addition to project modification. A survey of *environmental consultants* (Weston 1995) showed that about three-quarters of them felt that EIA had brought about at least some improvements in environmental protection, primarily through the incorporation of mitigation measures early in project design and the higher regard given to environmental issues. However, other consultants felt that the system is 'often a sham with EISs full of platitudes' (Weston 1995), and some *developers* felt that 'the preparation of the ES had cost them too much time and money, and that the large amounts of work involved in EA often yielded few tangible benefits in terms of the actual planning decision reached' (Pritchard *et al*. 1995). Jones *et al*. (1998) found that only one-fifth of developers and consultants felt that there had been no benefits associated with EIA. Presumably this view has not significantly changed in the interim.

Competent authorities generally feel that projects and the environment benefit greatly from EIA (Jones 1995; Lee *et al*. 1994). EIA is seen as a way to focus the mind, highlight important issues, reduce uncertainty, consider environmental impacts in a systematic manner, save time by removing the need for planning officers to collect the information themselves, and identify problems early and direct them to the right people (DoE 1996; Jones 1995; Pritchard *et al*. 1995; Weston 2002). One planning officer noted: 'when the system first appeared I was rather sceptical because I believed we had always taken all these matters into account. Now I am a big fan of the process. It enables me to focus on the detail of individual aspects at an early stage' (DoE 1996).

Consultees broadly agree that EIA creates a more structured approach to handling planning applications, and that an EIS gives them 'something to work from rather than having to dig around for information ourselves'. However, when issues are not covered in the EIS, consultees are left in the same position as with non-EIA applications: some of their objections are not because the impacts are bad but because they have not been given any information on the impacts or any explanation of why a particular impact has been left out of the assessment. Consultees feel that an EIA can give them data on sites that they would not otherwise be able to afford to collect themselves, and that it can help parties involved in an otherwise too often confrontational planning system to reach common ground (DoE 1996).

8.8 Summary

In summary, all the parties involved agree that EIA as practised in the UK helps to improve projects and protect the environment, although the system could be much stronger: EIA is thus at least partly achieving its main aims. There are time and money costs involved, but there are also tangible benefits in the form of project modifications and more informed decision-making. When asked whether EIA was a net benefit or cost, 'the overwhelming response from both planning officers and developers/consultants was that it had been a benefit. Only a small percentage of both respondents felt that EIA had been a drawback' (Jones 1995).

Some stages in EIA – particularly early scoping, good consultation of all the relevant parties, and the preparation of a clear and unbiased EIS – are consistently cited as leading to clear benefits and cost-effectiveness (e.g. DoE 1996; IEMA 2011). Chapter 9 provides a set of primarily UK case studies that seek to exemplify some of the issues of and responses to particular aspects of the EIA process. Suggestions for future directions in EIA in the UK and beyond are discussed in Chapter 12.

SOME QUESTIONS

The following questions are intended to help the reader focus on the key issues of this chapter.

1 Reviewing the nature of UK EIS activity displayed in Figures 8.1 and 8.2, how might you explain the changing patterns of activity?

2 What might explain the changes in the predominant sectors of UK EIS activity since 2000, compared with before 2000, as set out in Figure 8.3?

3 From Table 8.2, are there any indications of notable differences in approaches to screening in relation to amount of practitioner EIA experience?

4 Compare and contrast the information in Tables 8.4 and 8.5. Identify and seek to explain any differences in content in relation to the importance of various environmental components in EIA scoping activity.

5 Given the information from Section 8.4.3 about determinants of EIS quality, if you were managing an EIA process for the first time, how would you try to optimize the quality of the resulting EIS?

6 Using the third runway at Heathrow (Box 8.1) as an example, what do you think are negotiable and non-negotiable impacts of an airport (Table 8.7)?

7 Do you agree with the judge in the Berkeley case (Section 8.6.1) who felt that no EIA should be required where the absence of an EIA would have 'no effect on the outcome of the inquiry and could not possibly have done so'? Why or why not?

8 In your words, what is the 'Rochdale envelope' (Section 8.6.7) and why is it important for EIA practice?

9 Section 8.7 suggests that the costs of EIA can be quantified, but its benefits cannot. How could you determine whether the costs of an EIA outweigh its benefits? Do you think that they do?

Notes

1 www.bailii.org/ew/cases/EWHC/Admin/2002/2009.html.

2 www.bailii.org/ew/cases/EWHC/Admin/2010/373.html.

3 www.bailii.org/ew/cases/EWCA/Civ/2011/334.html.

4 www.bailii.org/ew/cases/EWHC/Admin/1998/351.html.

5 www.bailii.org/eu/cases/EUECJ/2009/C7508.html.

6 www.bailii.org/ew/cases/EWHC/Admin/1999/409.html (Ground 2).

7 www.bailii.org/ew/cases/EWHC/Admin/2000/650.html.

References

Ball, M., Allmendinger, P. and Hughes, C. 2008. Housing supply and planning delay in the South of England. research funded by Economic and Social Research Council, grant RES-000–22–2115, Reading: University of Reading.

Barker, A. and Wood, C. 1999. An evaluation of EIA system performance in eight EU countries. *Environmental Impact Assessment Review* 19, 387–404.

Bird, A. 1996. *Auditing environmental impact statements using information held in public registers of environmental information*. Working Paper 165. Oxford: Oxford Brookes University, School of Planning.

CEC (Commission of the European Communities) 1993. *Report from the Commission of the Implementation of Directive 85/337/EEC on the assessment of the effects of certain public and private projects on the environment*. COM (93), 28, final. Brussels: CEC.

Davison, J.B.R. 1992. *An evaluation of the quality of Department of Transport environmental statements*. MSc dissertation, Oxford Brookes University.

DCLG (Communities and Local Government) 2008. The Killian Pretty review: planning applications – a faster and more responsive system: final report. Available at: www.communities.gov.uk/publications/planningandbuilding/killianprettyfinal.

DCLG 2010. The Town and Country Planning (EIA) Regulations: Consultation on draft regulations. Available at: www.communities.gov.uk/documents/planningandbuilding/pdf/1682192.pdf.

DCLG 2011a. Guidance on the Environmental Impact Assessment (EIA) Regulations 2011 for England. London: DCLG.

DCLG 2011b. Personal communication with Environmental Assessment Division on throughput of UK EISs.

DETR (Department of Environment, Transport and the Regions) 1997b. *Consultation paper: implementation of the EC Directive (97/11/EC) – determining the need for environmental assessment*. London: DETR.

DETR 1999a. *Town and Country Planning (EIA) Regulations*. London: HMSO.

DETR 1999b. *Town and Country Planning (EIA) Regulations*. Circular 2/99 London: HMSO.

DETR 2000. *Environmental impact assessment: a guide to the procedures*. London: DETR.

DETR (Department of Environmental, Transport and the Regions) 2000. Environmental impact assessment: A guide to the procedures. Available at: www.communities.gov.uk/documents/planningandbuilding/pdf/157989.pdf.

DoE 1996. *Changes in the quality of environmental impact statements*. London: HMSO.

DoT (Department of Transport) 1993. Design manual for roads and bridges, vol. 11, *Environmental assessment*. London: HMSO.

ENDS 2007. *Directory of Environmental Consultants 2006/2007*. London: Environmental Data Services.

Essex Planning Officers' Association 2007. *The Essex guide to Environmental Impact Assessment*. Chelmsford: Essex County Council. Available at: www.essex.gov.uk/Environment%20Planning/Planning/Minerals-Waste-Planning-Team/Planning-Applications/Application-Forms-Guidance-Documents/Documents/eia_spring_2007.pdf.

European Commission 2009. Study concerning the report on the application and effectiveness of the EIA Directive. Brussels: EC. Available at: ec.europa.eu/environment/eia/pdf/eia_study_june_09.pdf.

Ferrari, C. 1994. Environmental assessment: our client's perspective. Environmental Assessment: RTPI Conference, 20 April. Andover.

Financial Times 2010. Planned third runway at Heathrow is scrapped. *Fnancial Times*. Available at: www.ft.com/cms/s/0/9b278458–5ddb-11df-8153–00144feab49a.html#axzz1Ki8xefJV.

Fuller, K. 1992. Working with assessment. In *Environmental assessment and audit: a user's guide*, 14–15. Gloucester: Ambit.

Glasson, J. 1999. Environment impact assessment – impact on decisions. In *Handbook of environmental impact assessment*, J. Petts (ed), vol. 1, Oxford: Blackwell Science.

GHK 2010. Collection of information and data to support the impact assessment study of the review of the EIA Directive. London: GHK.

Gosling, J. 1990. *The Town and Country (assessment of environmental effects) regulations 1988: the first year of application*. Proposal for a working paper, Department of Land Management and Development, University of Reading.

Gray, I.M. and Edward-Jones, G. 1999. A review of the quality of environmental assessmsents in the Scottish forest sector, *Forestry* 72 (1), 1–10.

Hall, E. 1994. *The environment versus people? A study of the treatment of social effects in environmental impact assessment* (MSc dissertation, Oxford Brookes University).

IAU (Impacts Assessment Unit) 2003. *Screening decision making under the Town and Country Planning (EIA) (England and Wales) regulations 1999*. IAU: Oxford Brookes University.

IEMA (Institute of Environmental Management and Assessment) 2011. *The state of environmental impact assessment practice in the UK.* Lincoln: IEMA.

IPC (Infrastructure Planning Commission) 2011. Advice note 9: using the 'Rochdale Envelope'. Available at: www.infrastructure.independent.gov.uk/wp-content/uploads/2011/02/Advice-note-9.-Rochdale-envelope-web.pdf.

Jones, C.E. 1995. The effect of environmental assessment on planning decisions, *Report*, special edition (October), 5–7. Jones, C.E., Lee, N. and Wood, C. 1991. *UK environmental statements 1988–1990: an analysis*, Occasional Paper no. 29. EIA Centre, University of Manchester.

Jones, C.E., Lee, N. and Wood, C. 1991. *UK environmental statements 1988–1990: an analysis.* Occasional Paper 29. Manchester: EIA Centre, University of Manchester.

Jones, C., Wood, C. and Dipper, B. 1998. Environmental assessment in the UK planning process. *Town Planning Review* 69, 315–19.

Kobus, D. and Lee, N. 1993. The role of environmental assessment in the planning and authorisation of extractive industry projects. *Project Appraisal* 8 (3), 147–56.

Kreuser, P. and Hammersley, R. 1999. Assessing the assessments: British planning authorities and the review of environmental statements. *Journal of Environmental Assessment Policy and Management* 1, 369–88.

Lee, N. and Brown, D. 1992. Quality control in environmental assessment. *Project Appraisal* 7 (1), 41–5.

Lee, N. and Colley, R. 1990 (updated 1992). *Reviewing the quality of environmental statements*, Occasional Paper no. 24. University of Manchester.

Lee, N. and Dancey, R. 1993. The quality of environmental impact statements in Ireland and the United Kingdom: a comparative analysis. *Project Appraisal* 8 (1), 31–6.

Lee, N., Walsh, F. and Reeder, G. 1994. Assessing the performance of the EA process. *Project Appraisal* 9 (3), 161–72.

Leu, W.-S., Williams, W.P. and Bark, A.W. 1993. An evaluation of the implementation of environmental assessment by UK local authorities. *Project Appraisal* 10 (2), 91–102.

McCracken, R. QC 2010. EIA, SEA and AA, present position: where are we now?, *Journal of Planning Law* 12, 1515–32.

Mills, J. 1994. The adequacy of visual impact assessments in environmental impact statements. In *Issues in environmental impact assessment*, Working Paper no. 144. School of Planning, Oxford Brookes University, 4–16.

National Audit Office 2008. Planning for homes: speeding up planning applications for major housing development in England. Available at: www.nao.org.uk/publications/0809/planning_for_homes_speeding.aspx.

Petts, J. and Hills, P. 1982. *Environmental assessment in the UK.* Nottingham: Institute of Planning Studies, University of Nottingham.

Pritchard, G., Wood, C. and Jones, C.E. 1995. The effect of environmental assessment on extractive industry planning decisions. *Mineral Planning* 65 (December), 14–16.

Radcliff, A. and Edward-Jones, G. 1995. The quality of the environmental assessment process: a case study on clinical waste incinerators in the UK. *Project Appraisal* 10 (1), 31–8.

Rodriguez-Bachiller, A. with J. Glasson 2004. *Expert systems and geographical information systems.* London: Taylor and Francis.

Sadler, B. 1996. *Environmental assessment in a changing world: evaluating practice to improve performance.* Final report of the international study on the effectiveness of environmental assessment, Canadian Environmental Assessment Agency.

Sadler, B. 2012. Latest EA effectiveness study (not available at time this book went to press).

Scottish Government 2007. Environmental impact assessment directive: questions and answers. Available at: www.scotland.gov.uk/Publications/2007/11/26103828/1.

Sheate, W. 1994. *Making an impact: a guide to EIA law and policy.* London: Cameron May.

Sippe, R. 1994. *Policy and environmental assessment in Western Australia: objectives, options, operations and outcomes.* Paper for International Workshop, Directorate General for Environmental Protection, Ministry of Housing, Spatial Planning and the Environment, The Hague, The Netherlands.

Tarling, J.P. 1991. *A comparison of environmental assessment procedures and experience in the UK and the Netherlands* (MSc dissertation, University of Stirling).

Weston, J. 1995. Consultants in the EIA process. *Environmental Policy and Practice* 5 (3), 131–4.

Weston, J. 1996. Quality of statement is down on the farm. *Planning* 1182, 6–7.

Weston, J. 2000. EIA, decision-making theory and screening and scoping in UK practice. *Journal of Environmental Planning and Management* 43 (2), 185–203.

Weston, J. 2002. From Poole to Fulham: a changing culture in UK environmental impact decision making?

Journal of Environmental Planning and Management 45 (3), 425–43.

Wood, C. 1991. *Environmental impact assessment in the United Kingdom*. Paper presented at the ACSP-AESOP Joint International Planning Congress, Oxford Polytechnic, Oxford, July.

Wood, C. 1996. Progress on ESA since 1985 – a UK overview. In *The proceedings of the IBC Conference on Advances in Environmental Impact Assessment*, 9 July. London: IBC UK Conferences.

Wood, C. 2003. *Environmental impact assessment: a comparative review*, 2nd edn. Harlow: Prentice Hall.

Wood, C. and Jones, C. 1991. *Monitoring environmental assessment and planning*, DoE Planning and Research Programme. London: HMSO.

Wood, C. and Jones, C. 1997. The effect of environmental assessment on local planning authorities. *Urban Studies* 34 (8), 1237–57.

Wood, G. and Bellanger, C. 1998. *Directory of environmental impact statements July 1988–April 1998*. Oxford: IAU, Oxford Brookes University.

Zambellas, L. 1995. *Changes in the quality of environmental statements for roads*. MSc dissertation, Oxford Brookes University.

9 Case studies of EIA in practice

●●

9.1 Introduction

This chapter builds on the analysis in Chapter 8 by examining a number of case studies of EIA in practice. The selected case studies mainly involve EIA at the project level, although examples of SEA are also included. Links between EIA and other types of assessment are also examined, including a case study of the 'appropriate assessment' process required under the European Union Habitats Directive and an example of health impact assessment. The selected case studies are largely UK-based and cover a wide range of project and development types, including energy (offshore wind energy, gas-fired power stations and overhead electricity transmission lines), transport (road projects and airports), waste (municipal waste incinerator and wastewater treatment works) and other infrastructure projects (port development and flood defence works).

The case studies have been selected to illustrate particular themes or issues relevant to EIA practice, and some are linked to specific stages of the EIA process. These are:

- project definition in EIA and the effect of divided consent procedures on EIA (Wilton power station, Section 9.2);
- EIA, European protected habitats and appropriate assessment (N21 link road, Section 9.3);

- approaches to public participation in EIA (Portsmouth incinerator, Section 9.4);
- assessment of cumulative impacts (Humber Estuary schemes, Section 9.5);
- health impact assessment (Stansted airport second runway, Section 9.6);
- mitigation in EIA (Cairngorm mountain railway, Section 9.7);
- SEA at the national level (UK offshore wind energy development, Section 9.8); and
- SEA at the local level (Tyne and Wear local transport plan, Section 9.9).

It is not claimed that the selected case studies represent examples of best EIA practice – indeed two of the cases were the subject of formal complaints to the European Commission regarding the inadequate assessment of environmental impacts. However, the examples do include some innovative or novel approaches towards particular issues, such as towards the assessment of cumulative effects (Humber Estuary) and the treatment of public participation and risk communication (Portsmouth incinerator). The case studies also draw attention to some of the practical difficulties encountered in EIA, the limitations of the process in practice, plus opportunities for the future. This reinforces some of the criticisms of UK EIA practice made in Chapter 8, and pre-empts new directions identified in Chapters 11 and 12.

The selected case studies are largely based on original research either by the authors or by colleagues in the IAU at Oxford Brookes University (the exception is the power station case study in Section 9.2, which was researched by William Sheate, Reader in Environmental Assessment at Imperial College, University of London, and published in 1995).

....

9.2 Wilton power station case study: project definition in EIA

9.2.1 Introduction

This case study, originally documented by Sheate (1995), illustrates the problems of project definition in EIA, particularly in cases in which consent procedures for different elements of an overall scheme are divided. The case highlights the failure of the EIA process to fully assess the impacts of a proposed UK power station development. In particular, the EIA process failed to identify prior to the power station consent decision the environmental implications of the extensive electricity transmission lines required to service the new development.

The case study highlights a basic problem within EIA for UK energy sector projects caused by the splitting of consent procedures for electricity generation and transmission. This situation arose after the privatization of the UK electricity supply industry by the 1989 Electricity Act. The case illustrates how the division of consent procedures for individual components of the same overall project can result in conflicts with the EIA Directive's requirement to assess the direct, indirect and secondary effects of development projects. Although the case study relates to early EIA practice in the UK and EU (in the early 1990s), the issues raised remain largely unresolved and are still relevant to current practice in the UK and elsewhere.

9.2.2 The Wilton power station project

Early in 1991, newspaper reports began to identify the environmental consequences of proposed high-voltage electricity transmission lines necessary to connect a new power station on Teesside, northeast England, to the National Grid system. To many, it was astonishing that these impacts had not been identified at the time the power station itself was proposed. Close inspection of the environmental statement (ES) produced for the power station revealed that such issues had barely been identified at the time and therefore did not feature in the consent process for the power station. Following considerable public uproar over the proposed power lines, in April 1991 the Council for the Protection of Rural England (CPRE) lodged a formal complaint with the European Commission (EC) in Brussels against the UK Secretary of State for Energy (Sheate 1995).

This state of affairs could hardly be regarded as an example of good EIA practice, but how did it come about? The complaint concerned the EIA for a large new gas-fired power station at Wilton, near Middlesbrough on Teesside, proposed by Teesside Power Limited. CPRE argued that consent had been granted for the power station without the full environmental impacts of the proposal having been considered. Because of its size (1875 MW), the power station was an Annex I project and EIA was mandatory. However, the overall 'project' consisted of a number of linked components, in addition to the power station itself, including:

- a new natural gas pipeline;
- a gas reception and processing facility;
- a combined heat and power (CHP) fuel pipeline from the processing facility to the CHP facility; and
- new 400 kV overhead transmission lines and system upgrades (75–85 km in length, running from the power station site to Shipton, near York).

It was the implications of the transmission connections required to service the new power station that were of particular concern, although the other project components also had the potential for environmental impacts. Cleveland County Council (CC), in whose area the power station was located, expressed the view that a full assessment of the implications of all project components should be undertaken before the consent decision on the power station was taken. The County Planning Officer commented:

My council wanted the power station [consent decision] deferred until all the implications could be fully considered. But the Secretary of State [for Energy – the consenting authority for schemes of this type at the time] wasn't prepared to do this. The result is that different features of the scheme, which includes pipelines and a gas cleaning plant as well as the main station and its transmission lines, come up at different stages with different approval procedures. An overall view hasn't been possible.

Despite these concerns, consent for the power station was granted by the Secretary of State for Energy in November 1990. The decision was based on the information contained in the ES for the power station, and without the benefit of a public inquiry. However, crucially, the ES did not include a description or assessment of the effects of the other elements of the overall 'project', including the pipelines, gas processing facility and transmission lines, which were seen to be the responsibility of other companies under separate consent and EIA procedures. Although separate EIA procedures were in place for these other project components, so that their environmental impacts would subsequently be considered, CPRE in its complaint to the EC argued that, under the EIA Directive, the EIA for the power station should have included the main environmental effects of its associated developments. The failure to do so resulted in a piecemeal approach to EIA which, it was argued, contravened the requirement in the EIA Directive that all direct, indirect and secondary effects of a project should be assessed prior to consent being granted.

Sheate (1995) summarizes the argument made by CPRE:

Concern was expressed that the Secretary of State did not see fit to require further information on these aspects [the impacts of associated developments], as he is entitled to do under the UK's own implementing legislation. [The developer] had successfully received consent for the power station even though the major impacts on the environment of the electricity transmission lines, the gas pipeline, the gas processing facility and the CHP pipeline did not feature in the

accompanying documentation provided to the Secretary of State for Energy. Since the relevant information was not available to the Secretary of State – nor did he request such information – it was argued that his decision might not have been the same had all the relevant information been available to him. Since the information was not contained in the ES, neither the public nor interest groups had been alerted to these consequential impacts, which might otherwise have caused a public inquiry to be held where the issue would inevitably have been aired.

At the time of the case study, responsibility for new transmission lines in England rested with the National Grid Company (NGC), not the developer of the power station. NGC had an obligation to connect a new electricity generator into the national grid, and – if significant environmental impacts were likely – it was required to undertake its own EIA for new overhead lines or major upgrades of existing lines. EIA would therefore take place for new transmission lines (and for other types of associated development). However, this EIA process was undertaken after the power station had been given consent, and it was therefore unable to influence the decision over whether the power station should have been built in the first place, either in that location or somewhere closer to the existing transmission network, hence minimizing the adverse visual impacts of new overhead lines.

Essentially, the Wilton case revolved around the way in which 'projects' are defined for the purposes of EIA. The ES for Wilton power station referred to the 'overall project' as including both the power station and its associated developments, such as transmission lines. However, because of the fact that different elements of this overall project were subject to separate consent procedures, the project was divided into separate 'sub-projects', with the environmental impacts of each being assessed separately and at different time periods depending on the timescale of the various consent procedures. CPRE argued that, under the Directive, it was not appropriate to assess the impacts of associated developments in isolation from (and after) the main development, including the implications of the latter's location.

In their response to CPRE's complaint, the EC agreed in principle that, in such cases, combined assessment was necessary and that splitting of a project in this way was contrary to the EIA Directive:

I can confirm that it remains the Commission's view that, as a general principle, when it is proposed to construct a power plant together with any power lines either (a) which will need to be constructed in order to enable the proposed plant to function, or (b) which it is proposed to construct in connection with the proposals to construct the power plant, *combined assessment of the effects of the construction of both the plant and the power lines in question will be necessary* under Articles 3 and 5 of Directive 85/337/EEC when any such power lines are likely to have a significant impact on the environment. (Letter from EC to CPRE, 11 November 1993; emphasis added)

The UK government had argued that the proposed transmission lines in the Wilton case were not required primarily to service the new power station, since the proposed upgrading would allow NGC to increase exports of electricity from Scotland to England. However, evidence presented by NGC to the subsequent public inquiry into the power line proposals appeared to contradict this view. Although the upgrading would have some wider benefits for NGC, it was clear that the primary justification for the proposals, and indeed for the specific routes proposed, was the needs of Wilton power station. The government also argued that the Directive allowed for separate EIA procedures for power stations and transmission lines, since the former tend to be Annex I projects while the latter fall within Annex II of the Directive (for which EIA is required only if significant effects are likely). However, the Directive requires an assessment of *direct and indirect* effects, which cannot be ensured for a power station scheme unless the transmission implications are included within the EIA. The Commission's response clearly supported this interpretation of the Directive.

Despite this clarification of the purpose and intention of the Directive, the EC decided against taking infringement action against the UK govern-

ment in this case. Earlier, action had been taken by the EC in connection with EIA for the Channel Tunnel rail link and Kings Cross terminal 'project'. In that case, the EC had argued that these two projects were indivisible, because of the effect of each on the choice of site or route of the other:

The effect of dividing the London–Channel Tunnel project into the rail link on the one hand, and the terminal on the other, leads to the circumvention of Directive 85/337/EEC, since the siting of the rail link in London is no longer capable of being assessed and – for instance by the choice of another site for the terminal – its effects minimized during the consideration of the rail link route. Terminal and link are, because of the impact of the choice of the terminal site on the link, or the link on the site, indissociable. The intention to assess the link once the assessment of the impact of the terminal is [completed] does not therefore make acceptable the assessment of the terminal . . ., which failed, contrary to Article 3 of the Directive, to take into account the effects of its siting on the choice of [route for] the rail link. (Letter from the Environment Commissioner to the UK government, 17 October 1991)

The same argument seems to apply in the Wilton example. The power station and transmission lines were also indivisible, since the power lines would not have been required were it not for the new power station, and the location of the power station was critical to any subsequent decisions on the route of the power lines.

9.2.3 The Lackenby–Shipton power lines public inquiry

As noted above, the installation of power lines to service the new power station was the responsibility of a separate developer (the NGC) and was subject to separate – later – consent and EIA procedures. In the event, five alternative routing proposals were considered concurrently at a public inquiry, which started in May 1992 – some 18 months after consent had been given for the power station; indeed, by this stage, construction of the power station had already begun.

The proposed power line routes started in Lackenby, adjacent to the Wilton power station site, and then proceeded south to Picton, via alternative southern and northern routes. From Picton, alternative western, eastern and central routes ran south to Shipton, northwest of York (Figure 9.1). The total length of new power lines and system upgrades required was between 75 and 85 km, depending on the route options selected. The NGC itself expressed a preference for the shorter southern route from the power station to Picton, and for the western route option from Picton to Shipton. All of the proposed routes passed through or adjacent to (and visible from) important protected landscapes, including the North York Moors National Park and the Howardian Hills, an Area of Outstanding Natural Beauty (AONB). Key objectors to the proposals at the public inquiry included the local authorities through which the proposed routes ran (North Yorkshire CC,

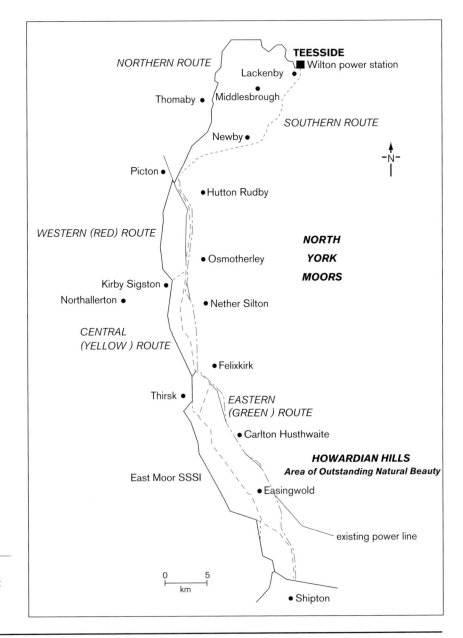

Figure 9.1

Alternative route options considered at the North Yorkshire power lines inquiry

Cleveland CC and others), the Country Landowners Association, the National Farmers Union and CPRE, as well as many individuals, including farmers and local residents. The principal issues considered at the inquiry included the visual impact of the pylons and overhead lines, potential health risks from electromagnetic radiation, issues of need and alternatives and effects on farming operations.

CPRE argued at the inquiry that the visual impacts of the proposals were unacceptable and should have been foreseen at a much earlier stage. It urged that the inquiry inspectors 'should not feel obliged to grant consent for the power lines simply because consent for the power station had already been granted and it was already being built' (Sheate 1995). It also invited the inspectors to comment on the inadequacy of the existing EIA procedures in such cases, in which consent for electricity generation is divided from consent for electricity transmission.

The inquiry ended in December 1992 and, after a long delay, the inspectors' report was published in May 1994. It recommended approval of NGC's preferred route options – the southern route from Lackenby to Picton and the western route from Picton to Shipton, subject to various detailed modifications to minimize the environmental impacts (e.g. around East Moor, a Site of Special Scientific Interest, SSSI). However, the inspectors agreed with CPRE's views on the EIA procedures in such cases:

> It seems to us that to site power stations without taking into account all relevant factors, including transmission to the areas of consumption, is likely to lead to the extension of high voltage power lines through areas currently not affected and the reinforcement of lines in areas already affected. It is not disputed that in the view of the scale and form of the towers these lines are inevitably highly intrusive and damaging to almost any landscape and as a result are unwelcome.
>
> It appears to us that there is a strong case for consideration to be given to the introduction of procedures to ensure that consents for future power stations take account of the resulting transmission requirements, and the environmental impacts of any necessary extension or reinforcement of the National

Grid, between the proposed generating plant and areas of consumption. (Inspectors' conclusions, 23 September 1993)

The failure of the EIA for Wilton power station to address the implications of transmission connections resulted in a situation in which 'Teesside Power Limited [the developer] neither had to demonstrate the full implications of the siting and development of the power station, nor to bear the full economic and environmental costs' (Sheate 1995). This was because there were limits on the costs that could be recouped by NGC for the provision of transmission connections to individual generating projects. This meant that NGC was under commercial pressure to develop the cheapest options, since any additional costs incurred to minimize the environmental impact of power lines – such as taking a longer route through less sensitive areas or placing all or part of the route underground – would be borne by NGC rather than the power station developer.

9.2.4 Lessons for EIA

Sheate (1995) argues that the Wilton power station case provides powerful evidence that, at the time, the procedures for consent approval in the electricity supply industry ran counter to the letter and spirit of the EIA Directive. According to Sheate, the situation could have been remedied by an amendment to the Electricity and Pipeline Works EIA Regulations. The suggested amendment read as follows:

> An environmental statement shall include information regarding the overall implications for, and impact of, power transmission lines and other infrastructure associated with the generating station where these are likely to have significant effects on the environment. (CPRE, letter to DTI, 22 February 1993)

The effect would be that, in cases where power lines or other associated infrastructure were likely to have a significant effect on the environment, these impacts should be material considerations in whether consent for the power station should be given and the Secretary of State for Energy should be aware of these before giving consent.

The consequence of such an amendment would be to ensure that power station proponents were forced to consider the transmission implications of their proposals, and that they would form part of the EIA and of any subsequent public inquiry. It would begin to reduce the difficulties that arise over the definition of projects and programmes. (Sheate 1995)

The case also highlights a wider problem within the EIA Directive concerning its ambiguous definition of the term 'project'. As we have seen, this is a particular issue for projects in the electricity supply industry, but it also applies to other infrastructure projects such as road, rail and other transport schemes. It has resulted in a number of complaints to the EC about whether a larger project can be split into a number of smaller schemes for the purposes of consenting and (therefore) EIA. The problem is that EIA in the UK – as in most EU Member States – has been implemented as part of existing consent procedures, and if these are divided for a project, then so is the requirement for EIA. This so-called 'salami-slicing' of projects runs counter to the purposes of the Directive, which states 'effects on the environment [should be taken] into account at the earliest possible stage in all the technical, planning and decision-making processes' (Preamble to Directive 85/337/EEC). As the case study illustrates, this purpose cannot be achieved if EIA is applied only to individual project components rather than to the project as a whole.

The issues raised by this case study remain relevant to current EIA practice. The issue of ambiguous project definition has not been resolved in the subsequent amendments to the EU EIA Directive, and consent procedures for electricity generation and transmission projects in the UK remain divided.

• •

9.3 N21 link road, Republic of Ireland: EIA and European protected habitats

9.3.1 Introduction

This case study, researched by Weston and Smith (1999), concerns a proposed road improvement scheme in County Kerry, Republic of Ireland. The proposed route of the road passed through part of a European protected habitat, a residual alluvial forest known as Ballyseedy Wood. Although the proposal was not subject to EIA (largely because the ecological status of the site was not known at the time), it was later subjected to a related procedure known as 'appropriate assessment' (or Habitats Regulation Assessment, HRA), which operates under the EU Habitats Directive. The Habitats Directive requires that projects likely to have a detrimental impact on a European priority habitat must be subject to an assessment of that impact. This assessment involves a series of sequential tests that must be passed for the project to be allowed to proceed. The case study examines the nature and interpretation of these tests, and demonstrates the high level of protection afforded to designated habitats in the EU (Weston and Smith 1999).

9.3.2 The proposals

Improvements to the N21 main road into Tralee, County Kerry, in the west of Ireland, had been an objective of the local authority, Kerry County Council, since the late 1960s. However, it was not until the prospect of European funding for these improvements emerged during the mid-1990s that substantial progress was made in advancing the scheme. The route was included in the Irish government's Operational Transport Programme for Ireland (OTP) in 1994. In the same year, the OTP was adopted for co-funding by the EC as part of the EU's Community Support Framework for Ireland. Under this Framework, the EU agreed to provide 85 per cent of the funding for the proposed improvements to the N21 link.

The proposed project comprised improvements to 12.5 km of the existing N21 highway between Castleisland and Tralee, including a short (2.4 km) new section of dual carriageway between Ballycarty and Tralee (Figure 9.2). The dual carriageway section of the scheme ran to the south of the existing highway and through Ballyseedy Wood, which was later discovered to be a priority habitat under the EU Habitats Directive. Following the announcement of European co-funding in July 1994, Kerry CC, as the local highways authority, began design work on the proposed scheme.

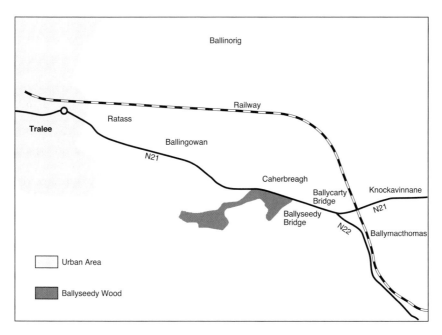

Figure 9.2

Map of the existing N21/N22 road network

9.3.3 The planning and EIA process

The N21 road improvement scheme was an Annex II project, for which EIA is required only if there are likely to be significant environmental effects. Like most EU Member States, at the time Ireland employed a series of size thresholds to help determine whether Annex II projects should be subject to EIA. In the case of road schemes of the type proposed (rural dual carriageways), EIA was required for schemes in excess of 8 km in length or if there were considered to be significant environmental effects. In such cases, EIA was carried out by the local highways authority and submitted to the DoE. After a period of consultation and a public inquiry (if one was held), the Minister for the Environment made a decision on the application. For Annex II schemes falling below the size threshold (less than 8 km in length) and not considered likely to cause significant environmental impacts, EIA was not required and the proposal was dealt with under normal planning legislation. This allowed for a period of public consultation, with the final decision as to whether to approve the scheme resting with the relevant local authority. For road schemes, it was the developer of the project, in this case the County Council as local highways authority, who determined whether or not EIA was required.

After commissioning a report from environmental consultants into the proposed scheme, Kerry CC decided that an EIA was not required in this case. This decision was based on the length of the dual carriageway section of the scheme (at 2.4 km, well below the 8 km threshold for such schemes) and on the belief that there were unlikely to be any significant environmental effects. However, following the publication of the proposals, the Council received a number of objections, mainly regarding the impact of the new dual carriageway on Ballyseedy Wood. After considering these objections and the subsequent report to the Council on the scheme prepared by the authority's officers, the Council's elected members decided to proceed with the proposals. However, this was not the end of the authorization process, since the compulsory purchase orders (CPOs) necessary for the scheme to proceed still had to be served and considered at a public inquiry (the CPO inquiry). Under the Irish system, members of the public and interested parties were allowed to give evidence at the CPO inquiry on environmental issues. However, the inquiry and the subsequent decision (including any alterations to the alignment of the route) was based solely on land acquisition, rights of way and access issues. The CPO inquiry for the N21 scheme was held in March 1996.

Following the Council's decision to go ahead with the scheme, a local organization objecting to the proposals commissioned an ecological assessment of Ballyseedy Wood. This assessment concluded that the wood comprised an area of residual alluvial forest that, although currently lacking protected status, complied with the description of a priority habitat as set out in the EU Habitats Directive of 1992. These conclusions were accepted both by the relevant Irish national authorities and Kerry CC, and the site was subsequently proposed as a Special Area of Conservation under the terms of the Directive. The revelation of the important ecological status of Ballyseedy Wood resulted in a number of formal complaints being submitted to the EC concerning its co-funding of the proposed scheme. It was argued that the Commission should re-consider its decision to co-finance the project, given its potentially damaging impacts upon a habitat of recognized European-wide importance. As a result of these complaints, the EC commissioned an independent study to provide advice on whether there was a need to re-consider the co-funding of the scheme.

9.3.4 The EU Habitats Directive

The EU Habitats Directive (92/43/EEC) requires all Member States to designate sites hosting important habitat types and species as Special Areas of Conservation. Together with Special Protection Areas (SPAs) designated under the Birds Directive (79/409/EEC), it is intended that these sites will form a network of European protected habitats known as 'Natura 2000'. The Habitats Directive is designed to protect the integrity of this European-wide network of sites, and includes provisions for the safeguarding of Natura 2000 sites and priority habitats.

In cases in which a project is likely to have a significant impact on a protected site, the Directive states that there must be an 'appropriate assessment of the implications for the site in view of [its] conservation objectives'. Under the terms of the Directive, consent can only be granted for such a project if, as a result of this appropriate assessment, either (a) it is concluded that the integrity of the site will not be adversely affected, or (b) where an adverse effect is anticipated, there is shown to be an absence of alternative solutions and imperative reasons of overriding public interest that the project should go ahead. The overall intention of the Directive is 'to prevent the loss of existing priority habitat sites whenever possible by requiring alternative solutions to be adopted' (Weston and Smith 1999). Projects that have a negative impact on the integrity of a priority habitat, but which are able to satisfy both the absence of alternatives and overriding-reasons tests, can go ahead. However, in such cases, the developer must provide compensatory measures to replace the loss of priority habitat. Huggett (2003) discusses the development of such measures in relation to a range of port-development proposals in the UK (see also Chapter 12).

The tests set out in the Directive are not absolute and require a degree of interpretation. For example, a literal interpretation of the 'absence of alternative solutions' test could be taken to imply that any alternative that is less damaging to the protected habitat than the proposed scheme should be selected, regardless of cost or impacts on other interests. European case law provides some indication as to the appropriate interpretation of the Directive's tests, and this is reviewed by Weston and Smith (1999). They conclude that both the 'absence of alternatives' and 'reasons of public interest' tests should be interpreted stringently, in view of the intention of the Directive to provide a significant level of protection to priority habitats. The application of these tests to the N21 link road proposal is now explored.

9.3.5 Appropriate assessment of the N21 link road proposals

Under Article 6 of the Habitats Directive, the appropriate assessment of the N21 project involved a series of sequential tests, concerning:

- the impact of the scheme on the integrity of the priority habitat;

- the presence or absence of alternative solutions; and
- the existence of imperative reasons of overriding public interest that the scheme should go ahead.

Each of these tests is examined, drawing on the results of the independent study commissioned by the EC, as reported in Weston and Smith (1999).

Impact on the integrity of the priority habitat

Ballyseedy Wood covers 41 ha, although the priority habitat that was the subject of assessment represented only a very small part of this overall area. A small area in the northern corner of the wood accorded with the definition in the Habitats Directive of a residual alluvial forest; it consists of alder and ash and is subject to regular flooding. Wet woodland of this type is the least common type of Irish forest, and the surviving examples tend to be small in area; the priority habitat area covered less than half a hectare. It was this northern edge of the wood that was to be lost to the proposed dual carriageway, including the areas of greatest ecological interest.

The direct land take of the proposed scheme involved the loss of only 3 per cent of the total area of the priority habitat. However, this does not necessarily mean that the effect on the integrity of the habitat would be insignificant. The independent study concluded that:

> On the basis of the assessments carried out by a number of environmental consultants and the evidence presented to the CPO inquiry, the loss of habitat could not be objectively assessed as being of no significance to the integrity of the habitat as a whole. There will be change caused to the habitat as a result of the removal of trees, the change in the hydrological regime and the re-routing of the river [another element of the scheme]. Evidence to the CPO inquiry suggested that areas of the wood, outside of the land take, would also be affected by this change. As part of EU policy the precautionary principle also needs to be applied to the assessment of the impact of a project on a priority habitat. In applying that principle

> it must be concluded that there is a risk that the integrity of the [habitat] will be significantly diminished by the proposed road. (Weston and Smith 1999)

It was therefore concluded that the impact on the priority habitat would be negative. Nevertheless, the project could still go ahead if it satisfied both of the remaining two tests; the first concerned the absence of alternative solutions.

The absence of alternative solutions

The County Council's identification of the preferred route alignment for the proposed scheme, and possible alternative routes, was based partly on a constraint mapping exercise in which areas with various environmental constraints (such as archaeological remains) were identified. Cost factors also featured in the choice of the preferred route, and a form of cost-benefit analysis (CBA) was carried out. The Council prepared a Design Report, which set out the need for the scheme and the alternatives considered. This reveals that the Council had identified and investigated a number of alternatives. Weston and Smith (1999) identify a total of six main alternatives to the proposed scheme, including a do-minimum option. Most of the alternatives considered completely avoided Ballyseedy Wood, generally by following more northerly route alignments. However, other adverse impacts arose from some of these alternative schemes, such as the demolition of residential properties, farm severance and the relocation of Ballyseedy Monument, a local war memorial. Notwithstanding these impacts, a number of viable alternative route options were clearly available to meet the objectives of the proposed scheme.

The CC tested the various route options against their ability to provide the best solution 'in terms of human safety, capacity and economic viability'. However, there appears to have been no systematic attempt to test the alternatives against the need to avoid the loss of priority habitat, even after the Council became aware of the importance of Ballyseedy Wood. The conclusion of the independent study was that '[the] alternatives were not examined to the same rigour or degree as the preferred route and appear to have been rejected without clearly defined and quantified justification' (Weston and Smith 1999).

An issue that appears not to have been considered by the CC in its route selection was the need to serve those areas where future development growth was planned. In this case this was the northern edge of Tralee, which was the location of a new Regional Technical College and of allocated industrial areas. This suggests that a more northerly route alignment for the dual carriageway – which would have avoided the impacts on Ballyseedy Wood – may have been better placed than the proposed scheme to accommodate the growth in traffic generated by these planned developments. The proposed scheme would have involved traffic serving these planned growth areas passing through the town centre of Tralee. This would have added to existing traffic problems in the town, and may have resulted in the time benefits derived from the improved N21 being lost because of increased congestion in Tralee. The independent study comments:

> It is surprising therefore that an alternative alignment for both the N22 and N21, which links the infrastructure to the areas of Tralee where future development is planned, has not been more fully investigated. A northern route proposed by private individuals, which could be of dual carriageway standard, was not adequately assessed in terms of the strategic objectives of the Operational [Transport] Programme or in terms of its benefits such as avoiding Ballyseedy Wood and maintaining the existing distinctive quality of the area around the Ballyseedy Monument. There are other possible alignments that appear not to have been fully considered, such as routes south or north of the railway line [which runs to the north of the existing N21]. Although the Council's Design Report rejects such routes because of the problems of crossing the railway line, farm severance and the impact on property, there appear to have been insufficient investigations and assessment on which to base such an outright rejection of such options.

Overall, there is little to suggest that the Council's alternatives have been tested to the same degree as the preferred option. The alternatives considered were not subjected to detailed costings, surveys, time-saving considerations, their ecological impacts or indeed their ability to meet the strategic objectives of Structural Funding. In the absence of the rigorous testing of all alternatives against clear objectively determined criteria it cannot, in this case, be concluded that the objectives of the [OTP] cannot be achieved with an alternative solution to that which would damage the priority habitat. (Weston and Smith 1999)

The second test, an absence of alternative solutions, was therefore failed. Under the terms of the Habitats Directive, the project could not therefore proceed, since a number of viable alternative solutions were shown to have been available in this case. It was not therefore necessary to carry out the third test, the existence of imperative reasons of overriding public interest in favour of the scheme. However, it is useful to do so, since this demonstrates how this test is applied in practice in the appropriate assessment process.

Public interest issues

The third test involves the balancing of the loss of priority habitat against other imperative public interest issues. Public interest issues would outweigh the loss of habitat if they resulted in 'far greater adverse impacts than does the loss of habitat' (Weston and Smith 1999). So, for example, if only a minor impact on the habitat was anticipated and the alternative options would result in extreme economic or other public interest disbenefits, then the public interest issues could be said to outweigh the loss of habitat. Conversely, if the impact on the habitat was great or uncertain, and the impact on the public interest issues was small, then the interests of the habitat would take precedence.

European case law provides some guidance on the type of public interest issues that can be considered to be 'imperative' reasons. Examples include the public interest of economic and social cohesion, human health, public safety and other environmental concerns. However, for such public interest reasons to out-weigh the loss of habitat they must be of a similar scale in importance [as the protection of the priority habitat] – that is of interest to the [European] Community as a whole – and be demonstrable. (Weston and Smith 1999)

In the case of the N21 scheme, it was the view of the CC that a number of public interest issues were relevant and that, when combined, the sum total of these issues outweighed the loss of the priority habitat at Ballyseedy Wood. The public interest issues arising in the case included:

- the strategic objectives of the wider OTP (of which the scheme was a component);
- the cost of alternative solutions;
- loss of family homes;
- road safety issues;
- heritage impacts on the Ballyseedy Monument;
- farm severance; and
- impacts on archaeology.

The independent study into the scheme concluded that none of these issues could be regarded as both imperative (that is, of equal importance as the loss of habitat) and overriding (that is, sufficiently damaging to override the protection of the habitat), and therefore this third test was also failed. The reasons for this conclusion included:

- *The existence of alternative solutions.* The fact that a range of alternative route options were available made it difficult to argue that the public interest issues arising in the case were unavoidable. For example, there was considerable local concern about the need to relocate the Ballyseedy Monument, a local war memorial, should one of the alternative routes be adopted. However, the need to relocate the Monument arose only with one of the six main alternatives considered and could therefore have been avoided by the adoption of one of the other alternative solutions.
- *The alternatives would not necessarily result in greater adverse impacts than the proposed scheme.* For example, there was no evidence that, apart

from one of the route options, any alternative solution would result in the loss of more family homes than the proposed scheme.

- *Some of the public interest issues were not demonstrable, due to a lack of data.* For example, no quantified data was produced on the road safety implications of alternative routes, compared with the proposed scheme. Evidence from the CC at the CPO inquiry suggested that all alternatives examined by the Council were equally safe. Also, it was not possible to argue that the proposed scheme was necessarily the most cost-effective, since the costs of all the alternative route options had not been worked out in detail. Indeed, it was suggested 'that an alternative route may be cheaper to construct because of the decreased disruption to existing road users, the impact of construction on properties in the existing corridor and the reduction of some mitigation costs' (Weston and Smith 1999). Another issue raised was the impact of alternative routes on farm severance. Again, however, 'there is little hard evidence to show that this is an area that has either been examined in any great detail, been quantified in any way or has been comparatively assessed against the [proposed] scheme' (Weston and Smith 1999).
- *The loss of habitat was a superior interest compared to most of the public interest issues raised.* Most of the public interest issues arising in the case were not equivalent in importance to the loss of priority habitat, and could not therefore be regarded as 'overriding' interests. Examples include the loss of family homes and farm severance. Although important issues at a local scale, these cannot be seen as equal in importance to the need to protect the priority habitat, given the status of the latter in the EU Habitats Directive. Similarly, in relation to archaeological impacts, in order to be of 'overriding' public interest, the archaeological feature affected would need to rank higher than the priority habitat on a European scale. There was no evidence that such impacts would arise with any of the alternative routes.

One public interest issue that appeared to be of greater importance was the need to relocate the Ballyseedy Monument, which arose with one of the alternative route options.

> The Council and the local community generally consider the relocation of the Monument to be unacceptable as it is considered one of the most important modern monuments in Ireland. The Monument, however, has no national or local statutory protection, whereas [Ballyseedy Wood] has statutory protection [at European level] through the [Habitats] Directive . . . On that basis, the relocation of the Monument, while clearly a very important public interest issue, cannot be seen as an 'overriding' public interest in terms of the presumption established by the Directive to protect the priority habitat. (Weston and Smith 1999)

Having failed all three of the tests required under the 'appropriate assessment' process, EU funding for the proposed N21 link road scheme was withdrawn.

9.3.6 Summary

The case study demonstrates that the process of appropriate assessment under the Habitats Directive, once a negative impact on a priority habitat has been established, is an exacting one. In particular, few projects are likely to have a genuine absence of viable alternatives, especially if the search for possible alternatives is widely defined. Also, to outweigh the loss of priority habitat, public interest reasons must be of equal or greater weight than the protection of priority habitats at European level. This means that issues of only local or even national importance would not be sufficient. Finally, as illustrated above, the absence of alternatives and imperative reasons tests are inextricably linked. 'While there remains the possibility of alternative solutions there are unlikely to be "imperative reasons of overriding public interest" to justify the preferred solution' (Weston and Smith 1999). Further guidance on the appropriate assessment process is provided in EC (2000, 2001, 2007) and Chapter 12.

9.4 Portsmouth incinerator: public participation in EIA

9.4.1 Introduction

This case study involves an innovative approach to public participation within the EIA process for a proposed municipal waste incinerator in Portsmouth, Hampshire, UK. The approach adopted by the developer in this case provided an opportunity for members of the public to take part in structured discussions about the project proposals and their environmental impacts before the submission of the planning application and environmental statement. This approach to extended public participation, beyond that required in the EU EIA Directive, has been used in a number of cases in the UK waste sector in recent years, not only at project level (as in this case) but also at more strategic levels in the development of local waste management strategies and plans (Petts 1995, 2003).

The increasing use of these methods reflects the perceived inadequacy of more traditional forms of public participation in the highly contentious arena of waste facility planning. However, questions remain about the effectiveness of such methods in providing genuine opportunities for the public and other interested stakeholders to participate in the EIA and wider development processes. The case described here is based largely on research carried out by Chris Snary as part of his PhD studies with the IAU at Oxford Brookes University (previously documented as Snary 2002), with additional material from Petts (1995, 2003).

9.4.2 Public participation and EIA

The wider context to the case study is the almost universal opposition towards proposed waste management facilities among those who live near proposed sites. Such public opposition is often dismissed simply as a NIMBY reaction or as being based on unjustified and irrational fears about potential impacts, particularly in relation to emissions and associated health risks. This is contrasted with the scientifically based technical assessments of impact and risk carried out by EIA practitioners. However, Snary (2002) points out that recent studies indicate that public opposition to such facilities is often based on a much wider range of considerations, including 'concern about the appropriateness of the waste management option, the trustworthiness of the waste industry and the perceived fairness of the decision-making process'.

Reflecting this improved understanding of the nature of public opposition, a number of commentators have called for better communication with the public at all stages of the waste management facility planning process (ETSU 1996; IWM 1995; Petts 1999). Such communication can take a variety of forms, ranging from a one-way flow of information from developer to public, through different levels of consultation and participation (in which there is a two-way exchange of views between the public and the developer and/or consenting authority, and the public's views are a legitimate input into the decision-making process). All of these types of communication are seen to be important components in the planning and EIA process for incinerators and other waste facilities, as Snary (2002) explains:

> Concerns about health risks require comprehensive information on the [predicted] emissions and a consultation process through which the public's views can affect the decision-making process. Concerns about the ability of the waste industry and regulators to manage risk competently require participation in a process through which their concerns can be openly addressed and conditions of competency discussed. Debate concerning fundamental policy issues and the legitimacy of the waste planning process [also] requires a public participation process through which a consensus may be built [at the plan-making stage of the waste incinerator planning process].

The search for improved methods of public participation is also linked to the growing social distrust of science and experts noted by a number of commentators (see, for example, House of Lords 2000; Petts 2003; Weston 2003).

9.4.3 Background to the proposed scheme

Hampshire is a county on the south coast of England, with a population of around 1.6 million. By the end of the 1980s, the county was faced with the problem of increasing volumes of household waste, set against a background of an ageing stock of incinerator plants (which failed to meet the latest emission standards) and growing difficulties in finding new and environmentally acceptable landfill sites. In response, the County Council's Waste Management Plan (1989) advocated an integrated approach to waste management, supporting recycling and waste minimization initiatives and emphasizing the need for a reduced reliance on landfill. Government financial regimes in operation at the time (the Non-Fossil Fuel Obligation) also provided cost incentives for the development of energy-from-waste schemes rather than landfill. It was also recognized that significant economies of scale could be obtained by developing a single large plant in the county rather than several smaller ones. As a result, following a tendering process, an application was submitted at the end of 1991 for a large energy-from-waste incinerator in Portsmouth, in the south of the county on a site selected by the CC (Petts 1995). The capacity of the plant was 400,000 tonnes per annum, which represented two-thirds of the household waste arising in the county (Snary 2002). The proposed location was on the site of one of the county's redundant incinerators, which had been closed in 1991 after failing to meet the latest emission standards.

The proposal met with much local opposition, from both local residents and ultimately the relevant local authority, Portsmouth City Council. Objections focused on a number of environmental issues, including the health risks posed by emissions from the plant; visual, noise and traffic impacts; and the close proximity of the site to residential areas. Policy concerns were also raised, in particular that, by concentrating on incineration as the preferred waste option, the promotion of recycling and waste minimization in the county would be adversely affected. In the event, the CC (the consenting authority for this type of project at the time) decided that it could not support the application, on the grounds that the proposal was too large and did not form part of a more integrated waste management strategy for the area (Snary 2002). The failure to gain approval for the proposed scheme resulted in a change of approach from the County Council, as Petts (1995) explains:

> By the summer of 1992 the County Council had failed to gain approval for the plant and was facing an urgent task to find a solution to the waste disposal problem. The traditional approach had failed. While the [county's waste management] plan which had supported the need for [energy-from-waste] had been subject to public consultation with relatively little adverse comment, this was now regarded as too passive a process and it seemed that the real concerns and priorities of the community had not been recognized by the County [Council]. There had not been strong support of the need for an integrated approach to waste management and there had been little recognition of the need to 'sell' [energy-from-waste] to the public. The proponents had been overly optimistic about their ability to push the project through with the standard, information-based approach to public consultation.

Faced with these problems, the CC embarked on the development of a more integrated and publicly acceptable household waste management strategy (Snary 2002). The Council's new approach involved an extensive proactive public involvement programme, launched in 1993, to examine the various options for dealing with household waste in the county. The aim was to attempt to establish 'a broad base of public support for a strategy which could be translated into new facilities' (Petts 1995). As part of this process, Community Advisory Forums were established in the three constituent parts of the county, based on the model of citizens' panels. Membership included a mix of people with different interests and backgrounds, including those with little prior knowledge of waste issues. At the end of the process (which lasted for six months), the forums presented their conclusions to the CC. The broad consensus reached was that:

- greater efforts should be made in waste reduction and recycling;

- energy-from-waste schemes would be needed as part of an integrated waste management strategy, but there was considerable concern about their environmental effects and the monitoring of plant; and
- landfill was the least preferred option (Petts 1995).

The public participation exercise in Hampshire resulted in the inclusion in the county's revised waste strategy (1994) of plans to build three smaller energy-from-waste incinerators (each with a capacity of 100,000–165,000 tonnes), rather than the single large incinerator originally proposed. The new plants were to be located in Portsmouth (on the same site as the earlier application), Chineham, near Basingstoke, and Marchwood, near Southampton. EIA work for these proposed developments began in 1998 (Petts 2003). It is the first of these plants that is the focus of this case study.

9.4.4 The contact group process

The EIA process for each of the three proposed incinerators in Hampshire involved a method of public participation known as the 'contact group' process. This involved an extended process of public questioning during the preparation of the ES for each site through a contact group involving a range of key local interests. These contact groups were established by the developer, Hampshire Waste Services (HWS), and were part of the contractual requirements placed on the company by the CC (Petts 2003). This approach had the potential to enable the public's views to result in reassessment of issues dealt with in the ES, and to changes in the project proposals and mitigation measures, prior to the submission of the ES to the competent authority.

The terms of reference for the Portsmouth contact group stated that it was designed (a) to allow key members of the public to develop informed decisions about waste issues and the proposal; and (b) to assist the developer (HWS) in ensuring that it understood and responded to the views of the members of the local community (Snary 2002). The arrangements for extended public participation in this case go beyond the legal requirements under the UK EIA Regulations (discussed in Chapter 6), and were the first time that such methods had been used in the UK EIA process for a waste incinerator (Snary 2002).

In the Portsmouth incinerator case, 10 members of the public were included in the contact group – they were selected by HWS to represent a range of local interests, and included a representative from the local school, the local branch of Friends of the Earth (FOE), and the Portsmouth Environmental Forum, plus seven representatives from the six neighbourhood forums in closest proximity to the project site. Group members were encouraged to network with the local residents in their neighbourhood. It was made clear to participants that membership did not imply support for the proposals, and indeed almost all of the participants were opposed to the development.

The contact group met once a week over a six-week period immediately prior to the submission of the planning application and ES in August 1998. Issues covered by the contact group at these meetings included:

- waste-to-energy incinerators and EIA;
- design of the plant;
- noise and traffic assessments;
- visual and ecological issues;
- alternative sites and noise issues; and
- air quality issues and health risk assessment.

Information was provided on these issues by HWS and by its consultants at the meetings. During discussions, the participants were able to make their views known by raising questions, concerns and suggestions. Answers to questions were provided on the day and in written form at the next meeting. There was also a closing meeting to discuss the conclusions of the ES. An independent chairperson was appointed by HWS 'to ensure that all participants had an equal opportunity to contribute to the meetings and that issues were fairly addressed' (Snary 2002).

9.4.5 Evaluation of the process

How effective were the methods of public participation employed in this case, and what were the views of the various participants in the process? Snary (2002) has assessed the success of the contact group process in the Portsmouth case, based on interviews with those involved; the process has also been evaluated by Petts (2003), drawing on observation of all three contact groups. Key findings are summarized below, focusing in particular on the limitations of the process in practice.

- *The contact group process took place too late in the EIA process.* The contact group meetings started only six weeks prior to the submission of the ES, and by this stage the majority of the EIA work had been completed. The opportunity for the group to influence the way in which impacts were defined, assessed and evaluated was therefore very limited. This was particularly true of the health risks posed by emissions, which were discussed only at the last meeting of the group. The process would have been more effective if it had started during the scoping stage of the EIA. However, the scoping exercise was restricted to consultation with the local planning authority and statutory consultees, with no public involvement (Snary 2002).

- *Insufficient time was allowed for the process.* A number of participants commented that the meetings were attempting to cover too much information – often of a complex nature – in too short a time. Again, this suggests that the process should have been started earlier to allow the wide range of issues involved to be dealt with adequately.

- *Criticisms were made of the EIA consultants.* Participant criticisms included the view that assessments were based too much on desk studies and that the consultants lacked detailed knowledge of the locality; that the consultants did not always provide adequate answers to questions; and that the EIA work should have been undertaken and presented by independent consultants (i.e. not employed by the developer).

- *Participants were generally better informed about the proposals.* Almost all participants stated that they felt better informed about the issues relating to the proposal as a result of attending the meetings. This is hardly surprising, but the developer's project manager also argued that the process had 'informed key members of the public better than the traditional methods of public involvement could ever have done'

(Snary 2002). However, doubts were expressed about the complex nature of the information provided about the health risks posed by the development. One participant commented: 'I am not a scientist and I found it very difficult to understand. I felt as though they were trying to blind me with figures and technical terms. The residents that I have spoken to who went to have a look at the environmental statement felt exactly the same; they didn't really understand the assessment.' These criticisms are partly related to the tight timescale for the contact group process, although non-experts will always need to have a degree of trust in those providing technical information in EIA. Snary suggests that such trust could have been increased by the use of independent consultants or an independent third party to summarize and validate the information presented.

- *Limited impact on the development proposals.* The project manager for the development stated that the process had resulted in changes to the architecture of the scheme (in particular the colour of the buildings) and improvements to the traffic assessment. However, apart from these relatively minor changes, many participants were sceptical about how else the views of the group had affected the proposals. These findings are not surprising, given the fact that the meetings took place at such a late stage in the planning, design and EIA work for the scheme.
- *Low levels of trust in the developer and consultants.* Reasons included a feeling that the developer was bound to be biased because its aim was to gain planning permission, a view that group members were only being provided with part of the information about health risks and concerns over the competency of the EIA consultants.
- *The process failed to resolve fundamental concerns about the proposal.* All but one of the participants still had relatively strong risk-related concerns about the proposal at the end of the contact group process. Therefore, although the contact group was able to better inform key local stakeholders about the risks posed by emissions, it was unable to convince the majority of the group that the risks were

acceptable and that waste-to-energy incineration was an appropriate waste management solution (Snary 2002). This is despite the fact that the Portsmouth incinerator proposal emerged as part of a county-wide waste strategy that was developed through an extensive and innovative public involvement exercise. Snary attributes this to inadequacies in the earlier strategic-level consultation exercise, which had failed to reach a consensus on the appropriate role of waste-to-energy incineration in the county's waste strategy and which most of the contact group members had been unaware of prior to joining the group. It was also unclear how the views expressed in the strategic consultation had influenced the county's developing waste strategy.

In her evaluation of the Hampshire contact group process, Petts (2003) reaches broadly similar conclusions:

> While the process did open up the environmental assessment to detailed questioning by a small but representative group of the public, it arguably started too late in the limited regulatory process to allow the Contact Group members to frame and define the problems to be considered and assessed. During the author's own observation and evaluation of the process, it was evident that questions about the assessment methods were able to be raised (for example, the Portsmouth Contact Group identified deficiencies in the transport assessment based upon knowledge of cycling on the local roads). Some reassessment did take place as a result of such a public quality assurance mechanism. However, this was limited. Participants valued the opportunity provided to them to review the assessment but were suspicious that outcomes had already been decided.

9.4.6 Summary

This case study has illustrated the use of extended methods of public consultation in EIA, which go beyond the minimum legal requirements in the EU EIA Directive. These methods are not without their practical difficulties, and these have been highlighted. The main weakness in this case appears to have been that the contact group meetings started too late in the overall EIA process. Public involvement at the scoping stage of the EIA may have helped to avoid some of the problems encountered. As a postscript, after a public inquiry was held in 2000, planning permission for the Portsmouth incinerator was finally granted in October 2001 – some 10 years after the initial application for an incinerator on the site had been submitted.

9.5 Humber Estuary development: cumulative effects assessment

9.5.1 Introduction

This case study provides an example of an attempt to assess the cumulative impacts of a number of adjacent concurrent projects in the Humber Estuary, Humberside, UK, undertaken in the late 1990s. This type of cumulative effects assessment (CEA), which was undertaken collaboratively by the developers involved in the various projects, is relatively uncommon in EIA. However, a number of other examples do exist, for example, in wind energy development cases in which several wind farms have been proposed in the same area. More generally, the assessment of cumulative impacts is widely regarded as one of the weak elements in project-level EIA (see, for example, Cooper and Sheate 2002; also Chapter 12).

Cumulative effects assessment studies of the type described here present a number of difficulties, and the case study examines how and to what extent these were overcome. The benefits derived from the CEA process are also discussed, from the viewpoint of the various stakeholders involved. This case study is based on research carried out by Jake Piper as part of her PhD studies with the IAU, Oxford Brookes University, and has previously been documented as Piper (2000). The Humber Estuary case study, together with a number of other examples of cumulative effects assessment in the UK, is also examined in Piper (2001a, b, 2002).

9.5.2 The Humber Estuary CEA

This case study involved a cluster of adjacent projects, proposed at around the same time by different developers. Each of the proposed projects required EIA, and because of the variety of project types, more than one consenting authority was involved in approving the projects. However, the developers concerned agreed to collaborate in the preparation of a single CEA of their combined projects, which was presented to each of the consenting authorities simultaneously.

In 1996–97, five separate developments were proposed along the north bank of the Humber Estuary, within a distance of 5 km of each other. The projects included:

- a new wastewater treatment works serving the city of Hull;
- a 1200 MW gas-fired power station;
- a roll-on/roll-off sea ferry berth;
- reclamation works for a ferry terminal; and
- flood defence works.

The five proposed projects involved four separate developers and five consenting authorities. The environment in the vicinity of the projects was a sensitive one, with a European site for nature conservation – an SPA designated for its bird interest under the EU Birds Directive and EU Habitats Directive – located within a short distance of the developments. It was the presence of this site, and the almost concurrent timing of the projects, that prompted the CEA study in this case. Indeed, the CEA was designed to satisfy the requirements for an 'appropriate assessment' of the effects of the proposed schemes on the SPA, under the terms of the Habitats Directive (similar to the process described in Section 9.3). It was also hoped that the CEA would help to avoid lengthy delays in securing approval for the projects, as Piper (2000) explains:

> The strategy adopted assumed that, by providing a common assessment to answer the needs of each of five competent authorities involved . . ., the amount of interplay and discussion required between these authorities would be reduced, avoiding lengthy delays . . . The strategy means, however, that any

insoluble problems associated with any one project could tie up all consent applications simultaneously.

In order to guide the CEA process, a steering group was established consisting initially of the developers and the two local authorities concerned. Other key statutory consultees, including the Environment Agency and English Nature, joined the steering group later, but non-governmental environmental organizations and the public were not directly involved.

A single environmental consultancy prepared the CEA, acting equally on behalf of all four developers. Draft reports were prepared in consultation with the statutory consultees and developers, with opportunities for review and comment. Close liaison with EN (the statutory body responsible for nature conservation) was an important element in the process, given the need to specifically address the potential impacts on the SPA. It was important to ensure that the document presented to the local authorities and other consenting authorities also fulfilled the requirements of this statutory consultee.

The steering group was involved in determining the scope of the CEA, but no public participation was arranged for this stage of the study. The scoping exercise identified those issues where there was potential for cumulative effects to occur. These included, during the construction phase, effects on bird species on the SPA site and on traffic, and during the operational phase, effects on estuary hydrodynamics, water quality and aquatic ecology. Data was made available for the study by the developers, including information from existing EIA work already undertaken; some additional modelling work was also carried out. The information provided included the probable timing of activities within the construction programmes for each project, the manpower requirements for these activities and associated traffic movements. Existing baseline data available included the range of bird species present at different times of year in the SPA, and their vulnerability to disturbance (Piper 2000). Prediction of cumulative impacts was assisted by the production of a series of tables and matrices, which brought together the levels and timing of impacts identified for each project. These included:

- a combined timetable of major construction works;
- bird disturbance potential (sensitivity in each month of the year);
- timetable of construction work potentially affecting birds, and monthly sensitivity;
- potential aquatic impacts of the developments; and
- predicted traffic patterns (vehicles per day, for each month of the construction works).

In arriving at predictions, it was decided to use the developers' best estimates, rather than a worst-case scenario approach (Piper 2001a).

As a result of the cumulative impacts predicted, a number of additional mitigation measures were proposed (in addition to those measures that would have been considered had the schemes been assessed separately). Examples included the scheduling of certain noise-generating construction activities such as piling outside sensitive periods (e.g. bird roosting), and the introduction of staggered working hours to reduce peak traffic volumes. It was also proposed that the design of adjacent projects should be integrated in such a way as to minimize environmental impacts. An example was revisions to the design of the ferry berth structure to complement the design of the outfall from the water treatment works, and so enhance mixing of water in the estuary. Finally, recommendations were made for continued monitoring of the cumulative effects on birds and the aquatic environment. Responsibility for funding this work was shared among a sub-group of the developers involved in the proposed schemes (Piper 2000).

9.5.3 Costs and benefits of the CEA process

Piper (2000) has assessed the costs and benefits associated with the Humber Estuary CEA study, drawing on a series of interviews with those involved in the process, including the developers, the relevant local authorities, other consenting authorities and statutory consultees. The views of these different stakeholders are summarized below, beginning with the developers of the proposed schemes.

Views of developers

- *Greater understanding of the area and potential development impacts.* Three of the four developers felt that the CEA process had increased their understanding of the estuary and the potential impacts of the proposed developments. For example, the power station developer referred to better understanding of the impacts to the mudflats and birds and potential traffic impacts, while the dock developer emphasized greater understanding of the hydrodynamics and morphology of the estuary and the relationship between the schemes and the SPA.
- *Other benefits.* These included the development of local relationships, including closer working relationships with the other developers, LPAs and statutory consultees; the establishment of a consistent basis for mitigation and monitoring; the opportunity to share the costs of ongoing monitoring work in the estuary; and – for one of the developers – the fact that the CEA process had facilitated the rapid achievement of planning approval.
- *Financial costs of the CEA process.* The financial cost of undertaking the CEA was relatively low for all of the developers, although the majority of the cost was in fact borne by a single developer (the water utility company). The cost of the CEA to this company represented around 5 per cent of the total cost of the EIA work for its proposed scheme. Costs were much lower for the other developers.
- *Changes to the project proposals and additional mitigation.* The CEA process resulted in some changes to the original project proposals and additional mitigation measures, which would not have occurred if the projects had been assessed separately. Examples included changes to piling operations during the power station construction to minimize noise impacts, modifications to the ferry berth construction to compensate for loss of bird habitats elsewhere in the estuary, changes to the timing of certain construction activities and staggering of working hours to minimize peak traffic flows. All the developers indicated that the additional mitigation prompted by the CEA had added relatively little to the costs

of the overall development. This may reflect the ability to share the costs of mitigation measures between the developments. Without this opportunity, mitigation might have been less effective or more costly (Piper 2000).

- *Delays caused by the CEA process.* Views differed about whether the CEA process had resulted in a saving or loss of time in obtaining consent for the proposed schemes. In part, this reflected the stage in the planning approval process reached by each developer at the start of the CEA process. Delays ranged from one to two months for the water utility company to six months for the dock developer (this last delay was attributed to the late involvement of a statutory consultee, despite an earlier invitation to join the study); the power station developer felt that its timetable had not been affected. Some delay may have been caused by the fact that the CEA process began after the bulk of the initial consultation and assessment work on some of the schemes had been completed. This resulted in some duplication of effort.
- *Other issues.* One developer noted the problem of distinguishing between those changes that resulted from the CEA process and those that would have occurred anyway through the proper consideration of each scheme in isolation. A further issue concerned the appropriate treatment of new projects that may come forward in the area after the initiation of the CEA. Should such projects be incorporated into the CEA process, implying an open-ended timescale for the process, or should a new CEA be started for the next group of schemes?

Views of local planning authorities and consenting authorities

The two local planning authorities responsible for the area in which the developments were located were supportive of the CEA study and identified a number of benefits from the process:

The study was found to be helpful in assessing the overall impact of several major projects proposed for a relatively small geographic area. The study was very helpful in its technical assessment of impacts. The study was definitely of great value for both [councils] in understanding likely impacts. [It] was probably of equal value in demonstrating the likely impacts to the developers themselves, making them fully aware of the potential consequences of their proposals. (Comments from local authority representatives, quoted in Piper 2000.)

The point was made that local planning authorities lack the technical expertise and resources to carry out detailed review of environmental assessments, and therefore rely on the integrity of ES authors and consultants to identify areas of potential concern. In this respect, 'a major factor in favour of the CEA [process] is that the advisers of each scheme proponent help "to monitor the others", thus "producing a more balanced product"' (Piper 2000). Both authorities commented on the lack of public participation in the CEA study. One noted that, partly due to the tight timescales involved, there had been little or no public consultation, and that this represented the main weakness in the process.

Other consenting authorities included three government departments (DTI, DETR and MAFF). The DTI commented that the study had facilitated decision-making, stating that 'without the CEA, the power station project would have been refused' (quoted in Piper 2000). The CEA approach would be recommended in similar cases of multiple projects elsewhere.

Views of statutory consultees

English Nature, as the statutory body responsible for nature conservation, was the principal consultee in this case and was involved in the CEA process from an early stage. It was necessary for the CEA to satisfy the requirements of EN, given its responsibilities under the Habitats Directive to ensure the protection of the SPA. These requirements were expressed in a number of planning conditions attached to the consents for the various schemes:

The conditions covered the mitigation of construction works (via measures to reduce disturbance of birds, a code of practice for

personnel and compliance with a programme of works designed to take account of other CEA-related construction projects) and the monitoring of construction. A monitoring scheme was outlined which will last throughout construction and for 5 years subsequently and will observe the movements and ranges of population of waterfowl. Provided these stipulated conditions are met, English Nature was of the opinion that the various projects would not, individually or [in combination], adversely affect the conservation objectives of the Special Protection Area. (Piper 2000)

English Nature commented that a number of factors – some of which were unique to this case – had assisted the completion of the CEA. These included the relatively small geographical area covered by the schemes; the fact that all schemes were at an early stage of development at the start of the process, although some project-specific EIA work had already been completed; the absence of direct competition between the developers to be the first to obtain planning consent; and the willingness of one of the developers (the water utility) to take the initiative in getting the study underway (Piper 2000). The latter was seen as particularly important, given that responsibility for undertaking the 'appropriate assessment' under the Habitats Directive properly rested with the consenting authority. As we have seen, in this case there were no fewer than five different consenting authorities. It was suggested that:

it would have been problematic to sort out exactly where responsibility lay, had the CEA strategy not been devised by the water utility and its advisers. For these reasons English Nature indicated that, whilst CEA was 'an excellent solution' [in this particular case], it is not a method of immediate and general applicability but depends upon the circumstances encountered in each case. (Piper 2000)

9.5.4 Summary

The consideration of cumulative effects is widely regarded as one of the weak areas in EIA, both at project level (see Section 12.4) and in some SEA studies (see Sections 9.8 and 9.9). This case study has demonstrated a novel approach to the assessment of cumulative effects, in this case associated with the impacts of a number of adjacent proposed developments. The assessment process was made possible by a number of factors, including the willingness of one of the developers to take the initiative in starting the CEA study and the fact that the developers involved were not directly in competition with each other. These circumstances may not apply in all such cases. Nevertheless, CEA studies of the type described have a number of benefits, for developers, consenting authorities and other key stakeholders, and – at least based on the evidence in this case – appear to involve relatively little additional cost.

9.6 Stansted airport second runway: health impact assessment

9.6.1 Introduction

This case study provides an example of health impact assessment for expansion proposals at a major airport in the southeast of England. Health impact assessment (HIA) is frequently undertaken as a parallel process alongside EIA and there are close links and partial overlaps between the two processes. The purpose of HIA is to identify and assess the potential health effects (adverse and beneficial) of a proposed project, plan or programme, and to provide recommendations that maximize beneficial health effects and reduce or remove adverse health impacts or inequalities (see also Chapter 12). At the time of the case study, HIA was not a regulatory requirement in the UK planning process. However, relevant government policy on air transport indicated that both EIA and HIA would be expected for major airport expansion proposals.

The case study concerns proposals for a second runway at Stansted airport in Essex. It provides an interesting example of the application of HIA to a major project proposal and reveals the close linkages between HIA and EIA. The Stansted

HIA was an example of 'comprehensive HIA', characterized by extensive stakeholder engagement and assessment methodologies based on a detailed review of the scientific literature. Weaker aspects of the assessment included the scoping out of certain health effects and a failure to adequately consider the cumulative effects of the airport's overall planned growth. There was also no consideration of alternatives in the assessment and as a result the overall level of influence of the HIA on the project proposals appears to have been limited.

9.6.2 Background to the proposals

Stansted airport is located in Essex, around 35 miles north east of central London. It is the third busiest airport in the UK, after Heathrow and Gatwick, with almost 19 million passengers in 2010. The second runway proposals at Stansted date from the mid-2000s. At this time, passenger numbers at the airport had experienced very rapid growth during the previous decade and the capacity of the existing single runway was expected soon to be reached. Further impetus for the proposals was provided by a government White Paper, 'The future of air transport', published in 2003 (DfT 2003). The White Paper set out a national, strategic policy framework for the development of UK airport capacity for the next 30 years. In relation to Stansted Airport and the wider southeast region, the government concluded that:

- there was an urgent need for additional runway capacity in the southeast;
- the first priority was to make best use of the existing runways, including the remaining capacity at Stansted and Luton;
- provision should be made for two new runways in the southeast by 2030; and
- the first new runway should be at Stansted, to be delivered as soon as possible.

The government invited airport operators to bring forward plans for increased airport capacity in the light of the White Paper's conclusions. The White Paper also stated that, in all cases where development was envisaged, full EIA would be required when specific proposals were brought forward. Operators would also be expected to undertake 'appropriate health impact assessment' (DfT 2003).

In response to the White Paper's support for expansion at Stansted, the airport's operator, BAA, brought forward proposals for two future phases of development. The first of these phases was known as Generation 1 (or G1), followed by Generation 2 (or G2). The G1 and G2 proposals were submitted as separate planning applications and were subject to separate EIA/HIA processes (ERM 2006, 2008). The G1 proposals sought to lift existing planning conditions limiting the annual number of passengers and flight movements at the airport (from 25 to 35 million passengers and from 241,000 to 264,000 air traffic movements per annum). This was to be achieved by making maximum use of the capacity of the existing runway, along with limited physical development (e.g. expanded terminal buildings). The G1 planning application was submitted in 2006. Permission was refused by the local planning authority, but BAA appealed against this refusal and the proposals were considered at a public inquiry held in 2007. Following the inquiry, planning permission was granted by the government in October 2008.

The G2 development involved proposals for a second runway and associated rail and road improvements in the immediate vicinity. Expanded passenger and aircraft handling infrastructure was also proposed, including a new terminal building, hotels, catering and car parks. Unlike the G1 development, the proposals also involved a substantial extension to the perimeter of the airport. A four year construction project was envisaged, with the second runway becoming operational in 2015. The additional capacity provided was expected to result in an increase in passenger numbers to 68 million by 2030. The G2 planning application was submitted in March 2008. The application was 'called in' for determination by central government following a public inquiry. However, before the start of the inquiry, the election of a new coalition government signalled a change in national airport policy. The new government announced in May 2010 that it would refuse permission for additional runways at Stansted and Gatwick. Consequently, on the basis that there was no longer government support for the proposals, BAA withdrew its application.

9.6.3 Aims and scope of the HIA

The Stansted second runway development proposals were subject to EIA. Health impact assessment was undertaken as a separate process, although there were important links between the EIA and HIA work. The overall objectives of the HIA were agreed between BAA and Essex Strategic Health Authority as to:

- identify the potential local health effects (positive and negative) from the G2 project;
- assess the likelihood and scale of the key local health effects; and
- make evidence based recommendations, which maximize positive effects and minimize negative effects and, as appropriate, recommend local requirements for monitoring local health effects.

The HIA was undertaken by consultants ERM, with support and advice from a Health Topic Group comprising representatives from local and regional public health organizations, the local planning authority and the applicant (BAA). HIA is normally categorized as either 'rapid HIA' or 'comprehensive HIA', depending on the time taken to complete the assessment and the extent of consultation undertaken. The Stansted HIA was an example of comprehensive HIA, reflected in the range and complexity of the methods used to predict the health consequences of the project and the extensive stakeholder engagement undertaken. The assessment also adopted a broad definition of health, encompassing physical, mental and social well-being. The scope of the HIA included the health effects on local residents arising from project-induced changes in the following:

- air quality;
- noise (air and ground noise);
- transport;
- employment and income;
- social capital;
- involuntary relocation;
- visual effects and light pollution; and
- health care and community facilities.

Certain aspects of the project and associated developments outside the airport were excluded from the HIA scope. These included the following issues:

- expansion associated with development in the M11 corridor (as this was addressed in the regional planning strategy);
- health service infrastructure planning for population expansion around the airport (as this was being considered separately by the local Primary Care Trust through its strategic and operational plans);
- any implications for emergency plans (as it was assumed that these would be addressed through existing emergency planning processes); and
- the effects of climate change on human health (as this was regarded as a wider than local impact and was therefore deemed to be outside the scope of the HIA).

The health effects of the Stansted G1 development proposals, which had yet to be approved at the time of the assessment, were also excluded (this is discussed further in Section 9.6.7).

The geographical scope of the assessment was confined to those communities adjacent to the airport. In practice, this area covered four local authority districts in Essex and Hertfordshire which were closest to the airport and considered most likely to experience health effects. A smaller inner zone within this area was also defined for the consideration of certain health effects (e.g. based on predicted pollutant concentrations and aircraft noise contours).

The assessment consisted of the following key stages:

- project profile;
- community profile;
- sakeholder engagement;
- development of the assessment methodology;
- assessment of health impacts; and
- mitigation/enhancement and monitoring.

Each of these key stages is discussed in more detail in the remainder of the case study.

9.6.4 Project profile

This first stage of the assessment was designed to identify the main routes or pathways through which the project might have implications for health. Identification of these 'health pathways' involved an examination of the characteristics of the development proposals and identification of their potential influence on health determinants. The key health pathways identified were associated with the following project features or activities:

- Construction: implications for exposure to environmental influences (e.g. increased noise, dust and traffic movements).
- Land take: implications for the functioning of and networking within communities ('social capital'), and access to health care and transport services.
- Increased aircraft, rail and road traffic movements: implications for increased exposure to noise and air pollutants, accessibility and the potential for injury.
- Changes to local roads: implications for community severance, access and social capital.
- Increased employment opportunities: implications for improved socio-economic well-being, reductions in unemployment and reduced inequalities.

It was also acknowledged that the development may influence additional pathways not associated with physical changes but reflecting intangible and/or perceived effects. These could include effects on social networks, community identity, access and accessibility and well-being. Most of the identified pathways were taken forward for detailed assessment in the HIA, although some minor health pathways were scoped out at this stage. These pathways were judged to have insufficient influence on health determinants to have health outcomes of consequence. Examples included the generation of dust, odour, fuel dumping, disruption to utilities and the visual effect of additional vehicles.

9.6.5 Community profile

A community profile was drawn up to provide a description of the communities that might be affected by the project. The profile was based primarily on information for the four immediate local authority districts. However, a more detailed study area was also defined, comprising those parishes most likely to be directly affected by the development. This area was defined using four main criteria:

- Land take: defined by the proposed boundary of the expanded airport.
- Aircraft noise: defined as the 54 dBA noise contour for the proposed development, based on air traffic predictions for 2030. This contour represented the lowest threshold noise level at which community annoyance was considered likely to be experienced.
- Visual impacts: defined as the zone of visual influence, from which the expanded airport would be visible.
- Secondary socio-economic effects: defined as those areas most likely to be affected by secondary effects associated with the construction workforce for the development and the services and facilities needed.

The resulting study area was not simply a circular zone defined by a radius from the airport, but a more complex area reflecting the likely distribution of key health effects. This area comprised 26 parishes in a zone extending to the south-west and north-east of the airport. This distribution largely reflected the orientation of flight paths and the resulting noise contours with the expanded airport.

The community profile was based on existing secondary data sources and provided information on a range of indicators, including population, education, employment and income, housing, crime and health. Areas with relatively high levels of deprivation or poor existing health were identified. The identification of such areas was important as these communities are more likely to be susceptible to health effects. Overall, the communities surrounding the existing airport were found to be relatively affluent and there were no severely deprived neighbourhoods within the study area. Performance on most health indicators was also significantly better than the national average.

9.6.6 Stakeholder engagement

A stakeholder engagement programme was undertaken as part of the HIA. This sought the views on potential health effects of those interested in or affected by the proposed development. More specifically, the engagement process sought to identify:

- stakeholder concerns regarding the project and its potential effects on health and well-being, and how to minimize such effects;
- stakeholder perception of the benefits that could arise from the project and how such benefits could be enhanced; and
- the priority issues and concerns of the stakeholder and what recommendations they would like to see noted within the HIA.

The geographic scope of engagement was similar but not identical to that used for the HIA community profile. Inner and outer engagement zones were defined. The boundaries of the inner zone were based on three main factors: (a) predicted aircraft noise contours for the expanded airport; (b) areas that could experience air quality changes; and (c) areas affected by the surface access development (traffic and construction effects). The outer engagement zone covered a wider area that also included those settlements that were expected to supply the bulk of the workforce for the expanded airport.

Engagement mechanisms included stakeholder interviews, workshops and a questionnaire survey of local residents. The interviews and workshops were carried out with key stakeholders representing organizations with strategic responsibilities in relation to health, housing, education, business, transport and other relevant areas. Open community workshops were not undertaken, as these had attracted a low level of interest from the public during the engagement process for the earlier Stansted G1 HIA (although groups opposing the development argued that the low response was due to a lack of advance publicity). Members of the public were engaged instead through a questionnaire survey. This was distributed to a sample of around 9,300 households in the inner and outer engagement zones. The content of the questionnaire was subject to a process of review by the

HIA team, BAA, the Health Topic Group and expert reviewers.

Key issues of concern to emerge from the stakeholder engagement included:

- air quality (particularly the potential health effects on vulnerable groups, including children and the elderly);
- air traffic noise;
- road traffic/congestion;
- effects on the 'social capital' of the area (more rapid pace of neighbourhood change; loss of identity);
- socio-economic issues (employment opportunities; inward migration of construction workers; effects on existing housing provision); and
- healthcare and community facilities (adequacy of existing capacity; effects on emergency services; effects on healthcare recruitment).

There was some overlap in the issues raised with those addressed in the EIA, particularly with respect to employment and wider socio-economic issues.

9.6.7 Assessment of health impacts

The HIA report included a series of detailed 'methodology statements' for each of the health pathways identified in the project profile. These methodology statements describe the methods used in the HIA to determine the likely scale of health outcomes, based on a review of the relevant scientific evidence (e.g. on the health effects of specific air pollutants) and the stakeholder engagement. In most cases, the methods were dependent on input data from the EIA studies, such as predictions of the concentrations of specific air pollutants or of air noise contours with and without the proposed development. This interdependence means that any weaknesses in the EIA's predictive methodologies or assumptions will also have been reflected in the HIA work (see Stop Stansted Expansion 2006 for a more detailed discussion of these issues). Most of the predicted health effects were quantified, generally by estimating the number of people likely to experience specific health outcomes. However, some impacts were discussed only qualitatively, in cases where the scientific evidence on health effects was less certain and did not allow quantified estimates to be made. Uncertainties, data limitations and other practical difficulties encountered were clearly outlined in the method statements.

The health effects considered in the assessment included the following:

- Air quality: health effects associated with increases in particulate matter and NO_2 concentrations (e.g. years of life lost; respiratory and other hospital admissions; GP consultations for asthma).
- Air noise: annoyance; sleep disturbance; cognitive effects on schoolchildren.
- Ground noise: annoyance; sleep disturbance.
- Transport: injuries and fatalities from road and rail accidents.
- Employment and income: positive effects of additional employment and income, including effects on mental health (e.g. depression), self-rated 'good health' (well-being), long-term limiting illness and mortality.
- Social capital: changes in civic participation, social networks and support, social participation, reciprocity and trust, and satisfaction with the area (e.g. associated with inward migration of construction workers and land take), and consequent health/well-being effects.
- Involuntary relocation: stress, anxiety and reduced well-being for those moving from existing residential properties due to land take.
- Visual effects and light pollution: reduction in well-being.
- Health care and community facilities: effects on existing facilities (e.g. due to inward migration of construction workforce; accidents; transmission of infectious diseases).

There was some degree of overlap with the impacts considered in the EIA, although the approach adopted in the HIA was rather different, with a greater emphasis on identifying the magnitude of effects and less focus on the evaluation of significance. For example, in relation to aircraft noise, whereas the EIA sought to identify the significance of changes in noise exposure, the HIA placed much more emphasis on quantifying the numbers of people likely to experience specific health outcomes. These quantified estimates were compared with the prevalence of the relevant health outcomes in the local population, where such data was available. However, the significance of the estimated health outcomes was not directly assessed. The HIA report stated that this was due to a lack of recognized significance assessment criteria for these effects.

In assessing the impacts of the second runway (G2) proposals, the HIA considered the health outcomes arising in the following scenarios:

- Base case with no G2 development (in 2015 and 2030): annual passenger numbers were assumed to be 35 million in this scenario, in both 2015 and 2030.
- With G2 development, in 2015: this was the date at which the second runway was expected to become operational.
- With G2 development, in 2030: at this date the enlarged airport was expected to have reached its capacity of 68 million passengers per annum.

Health effects arising during the construction of the second runway were also assessed. It is important to note that the base case for the assessment did not represent the situation at the time of the second runway application. Instead it was a projected baseline, which assumed that the earlier G1 planning application, to expand the capacity of the existing runway, would be approved. This resulted in a base case of 35 million passengers per annum rather than the actual baseline at the time of assessment in 2008, which was only 22 million (without approval of the G1 development, annual passenger numbers would have been limited to no more than 25 million in both 2015 and 2030, and therefore a figure of 25 million might also have been used as an alternative base case). The overall increase in passenger numbers assumed in the second runway HIA was therefore 33 million (from 35 to 68 million); this represented a 94 per cent increase in annual passenger numbers compared with the base case.

An alternative approach would have been to consider the G1 and G2 development proposals as two parts of a larger planned expansion of the airport. In this case, the resulting increase in passenger numbers would be significantly larger,

from a baseline of 22 (or 25) million to 68 million by 2030 (or an increase of 172–209 per cent). The resulting health effects would also be larger than for the G2 development alone. A consideration of the combined effects of the G1 and G2 proposals in the HIA would therefore have been useful. There was in fact no attempt to assess the combined health impacts of the G1 and G2 proposals as a whole. The health effects of the G1 development were therefore ignored in the HIA for the second runway development. Similarly, the health effects of the second runway had been ignored in the earlier HIA for the G1 development proposals. This use of separate assessment processes also applied to the EIA's for both planning applications. This approach was supported by the Planning Inspector at the public inquiry into the G1 proposals, when he concluded that 'for the purposes of the EIA Regulations, I accept BAA's view that the G1 proposals are not an integral part of an inevitably more substantial development' and that 'the lack of consideration of the combined impacts of the G1 and G2 proposals in the current ES does not frustrate the aims of the EIA Regulations and Directive' (The Planning Inspectorate 2008). Even if this view is accepted with respect to the G1 development, it seems less tenable for the later G2 proposals as these clearly did now represent part of a 'more substantial development'.

The failure to include an assessment of the effects of the combined G1 and G2 expansion proposals means that identification of cumulative health effects was likely to have been deficient. The issues raised here are similar to those highlighted in the earlier case study on Wilton power station in Section 9.2; in both cases the use of divided project consent and assessment procedures resulted in a failure to adequately address incremental and cumulative impacts.

9.6.8 Mitigation and enhancement of impacts

The HIA report provided a list of recommendations to BAA, the airport's operators, for the mitigation and enhancement of health effects. Feasible options for mitigation and enhancement measures were identified from the results of the assessment phase and the suggestions made by stakeholders.

These options were then subjected to a review by the Health Topic Group and an expert panel, before arriving at the final list of recommended measures.

The recommended mitigation measures in the HIA were relatively narrow in focus and did not include substantive changes to the actual project proposals. These were taken as a 'given' in the HIA. As the HIA notes, 'some of the effects are associated with features of the G2 project that cannot be adjusted without changing the purpose of the development itself . . . Inevitably, this means that some effects are more amenable to management than are others' (ERM 2008). A number of the proposed mitigation measures involved suggestions for improved communication about the scale of health effects with local communities; it was also recommended that monitoring of noise levels might be better undertaken by an independent third party rather than BAA. A number of generic mitigation measures to reduce emissions and noise at source were also recommended, including, for example, introduction of increasingly stringent technical standards, improved operational practices and the progressive withdrawal of the noisiest and dirtiest aircraft. It could be argued that such measures would have been implemented even in the absence of the proposed development, and should therefore be regarded as part of the 'no-development' future baseline rather than as project-specific mitigation.

The HIA did not identify whether, and in what ways, the earlier planning and EIA work on the project had incorporated an explicit consideration of health impacts into the development of the project proposals and of the mitigation measures recommended in the environmental statement. The HIA report simply states that 'many of the effects on the environment (and by extension, health) have been considered very thoroughly at the planning stage where options for runway location and mode of operation were evaluated' (ERM 2008). Further information on how health effects were taken into account in the evaluation of these options, and in what ways mitigation of health effects had been incorporated into the final project proposals, would have been useful.

These limitations partly reflected the timing of the HIA work, which was undertaken following the project design and EIA studies. This was necessary since the HIA's assessment methods were heavily dependent on data inputs from the EIA predictions, for example in relation to the predicted changes in air quality and noise levels. However, this raises questions about the overall ability of the HIA to influence the final project proposals. The timing of the assessment also explains the failure of the HIA to include any evaluation of alternative options; only the health effects of the final proposals, as detailed in the planning application, were assessed in the HIA. There was no consideration of the comparative health effects of alternative designs or modes of operation. It is therefore difficult to assess whether the chosen options delivered more favourable health effects (or smaller adverse effects) for the local communities than other feasible alternatives.

9.6.9 Summary

This case study has provided an example of the application of health impact assessment to a major project proposal. HIA is increasingly undertaken as a parallel process alongside EIA and is often dependent on the EIA for critical data inputs. The Stansted HIA was an example of a comprehensive HIA process. Extensive stakeholder engagement was undertaken and the assessment methodology was based on a detailed review of the relevant scientific evidence. Although a wide definition of health and well-being was adopted, the focus of the assessment was restricted to effects on the local communities adjacent to the airport. This resulted in the exclusion of important issues such as the effects of climate change on health. Other issues were also scoped out of the assessment on the basis that they were the responsibility of other organizations and would be addressed in their evolving plans and strategies. By focusing only on the second runway proposals and ignoring other aspects of the Stansted expansion plans, the assessment failed to adequately consider the incremental and cumulative health effects of the airport's planned future growth. There was also no consideration of the comparative health effects of alternative project options (other than the no-development baseline), and as a result the overall level of influence of the HIA on the project proposals appears to have been limited.

9.7 Cairngorm mountain railway: mitigation in EIA

9.7.1 Introduction

It is appropriate that one of our case studies includes a tourism project, for tourism is the world's largest industry, it is growing apace and it contains within itself the seeds of its own destruction. That tourism can destroy tourism has become increasingly recognized over the last 30 years or so, with a focus of concern widening from initially largely economic impacts to a now wider array that includes social and biophysical impacts (see Glasson *et al.* 1995; Hunter and Green 1995; Mathieson and Wall 2004). Mountain areas can be particularly sensitive to tourism impacts, including from walking, skiing and associated facilities. This case study takes a particularly controversial project, the Cairngorm mountain railway, in the Highlands of Scotland, which was opened in 2001 after a long and protracted debate about its impacts and their management. This brief case study focuses on the latter aspect as an example of approaches to mitigation and monitoring in EIA.

9.7.2 The project

The Cairngorm Ski Area is one of five ski areas in Scotland. It developed rapidly in the 1960s and 1970s in combination with the adjacent settlement of Aviemore. Chairlift facilities were built to take skiers to the higher slopes in winter, and also to carry walkers in other times of the year. However, the industry has been vulnerable to climate/ weather trends and to the quality of the infrastructure. In 1993 the Cairngorm Chairlift Company published a Cairngorm Ski Area Development Plan designed to upgrade facilities, to give better access to reliable snow-holding in the area, to reduce vulnerability to adverse weather conditions, to improve the quality of visitor experience and to improve economic viability, while ensuring that all relevant environmental considerations were taken fully into account. The Cairngorm Funicular Railway was a key element in the plan.

The Cairngorm Funicular is the UK's highest and fastest mountain railway. It is approximately 2 km in length and takes visitors in eight minutes from the existing chairlift station/car park base at Coire Cas (610 m) to the Ptarmigan top station (1100 m). It comprises two carriages (or trains of carriages) running on a single-line railway track between two terminal points (see Figure 9.3). The carriages, which start at opposite ends of the track, are connected by a hauling rope. As one carriage descends the track, the other travels upwards and they pass each other at a short length of double track midway. The track is carried on an elevated structure, a minimum of 1 m and a maximum of 6 m above ground level. The final 250 m runs in a 'cut and cover' tunnel. The development has also included a major remodelling of the existing chairlift base station, and replacement of the existing top station with a new development, which includes catering facilities for about 250 people, and a new interpretative centre, including various displays and an outdoor viewing terrace. The previous chairlift and towers have been removed as part of the development. It was anticipated that the railway would carry approximately 300,000 visitors a year, with two-thirds in the non-skiing months. This would represent a three- to fourfold increase over 1990s numbers reaching the top station by the chairlift, and a doubling of numbers from the early 1970s.

9.7.3 The EIA and planning process

The original planning application for the Funicular Railway was submitted in 1994, with an ES (Land Use Consultants 1994). Revised proposals and a supplementary ES were submitted in early 1995. The scheme was very controversial, with much opposition. Particular concerns focused on the potential impact of improved visitor access to the sensitive environment of the summit plateau, which is recognized as a European candidate Special Area of Conservation and an SPA. As a condition of the planning approval, it was necessary for the developer to satisfy Scottish Natural Heritage (SNH, the statutory body responsible for nature conservation in Scotland) that a visitor management plan (VMP) and other mitigation measures would be put in place that would avoid adverse impacts on the summit plateau.

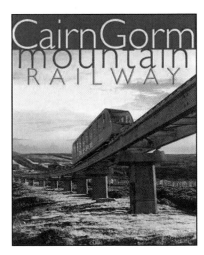

(a)

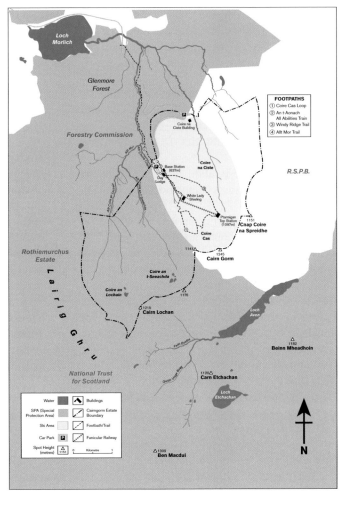

(b)

Figure 9.3

(a) Cairngorm mountain railway; (b) the wider environment

Source: HIE 2005

The planning application was approved by the Highland Council (the consenting authority) in 1996. This was subject to a Section 50 (now Section 75) planning agreement to create, in partnership with the SNH and in agreement with the developer/authority, a regime for visitor and environmental monitoring and management. Amended designs for the station buildings were approved in 1999, and construction work finally began in August 1999. The railway opened in December 2001, following the approval of the proposed VMP by SNH.

9.7.4 Visitor management, mitigation and monitoring measures

The Section 50 agreement attached to the planning approval is a legally binding agreement between the planning authority, in partnership with SNH, and the developer/operator and landowner. The agreement provides for:

• a baseline survey of current environmental conditions and visitor usage in the wider locality;
• an implementation plan providing details of the timing and means of implementation

of the development with particular reference to reinstatement following construction;

- an annual monitoring regime to identify changes and establish causes and consequences;
- an annual assessment by the operator of any actions necessary to ensure acceptable impacts to the European designated conservation sites on the summit plateau;
- fall-back responsibilities in the event of default; and
- eventual site restoration if public use of the development ceases (Highland Council 2003).

The Cairngorm Funicular Railway VMP was produced in the context of this agreement. The objective of the VMP is to protect the integrity of the adjacent areas that have been designated or proposed under the European Habitats and Birds Directives from the potential impacts of non-skiing visitors as a direct consequence of the funicular development. The VMP went through several stages and was subject to a short period of public consultation in 2000. Many issues were raised, including the innovative or repressive (according to your perspective) 'closed system', and the associated monitoring arrangements (SNH 2000).

The closed system, whereby non-skiing visitors are not allowed access to the Cairngorm plateau from the Ptarmigan top station, is a key feature of the VMP. Instead visitors must be content with a range of inside interpretative displays and access to an outside viewing terrace – plus, of course, shopping, catering and toilet facilities! This system proved very contentious, and received considerable criticism, in the public consultation on the VMP. Some saw it as violating the freedom to roam; for others, it was a cynical device for extracting economic benefit in shops and catering outlets. Others considered it unnecessary, given the recent improved pathway from the Ptarmigan top station to the summit of Cairngorm, as noted by one respondent: 'For years I have been advocating stone paths. People use the paths and the ground round about recovers. Now that the path up to the summit is pretty well complete most people will be barred from using it!' (SNH 2000). Another issue has been how to allow ingress to the facilities of the top station from non-railway-using walkers on the plateau, while preventing egress from non-walkers. Alternatives were suggested at the time to the

closed system including ranger-led walks and time-limited access, but the system was put in place and is part of a 25-year agreement. The guide leaflet for the funicular users includes the following:

> Protecting the Mountain Environment: large areas of the fragile landscape and habitats of the Cairngorms are protected under European Law. Cairngorm Mountain Limited is committed to ensuring that recreational activities are environmentally sustainable. For this reason the Railway cannot be used to access the high mountain plateau beyond the ski area at any time. Outwith the ski season, visitors are required to remain within the Ptarmigan building and viewing terrace, returning to the base station using the railway. Mountain walkers are welcome to walk from the car park and use the facilities at the Ptarmigan, but may not use the railway for their return journey and are asked to sign in and out of the building at the walkers' entrance.

Monitoring can support effective mitigation measures. For this project, monitoring covers all topics subject to baseline surveys – including visitor levels and behaviour, habitats, birds, soils and geomorphology. It uses the limits of acceptable change (LAC) method, whereby indicators and levels of acceptable change are identified, monitored and, when levels are reached, management responses can be triggered (see Glasson et al. 1995). In response to a concern about the independence of the monitoring activity, the annual monitoring reports are presented to the SNH and the Highlands Council by an independent reporting officer jointly appointed by them.

9.7.5 Conclusions

The Cairngorm Funicular has been operational for over 10 years. Visitor numbers have been less than the predictions in the ES, but still represent a substantial increase on previous levels in the 1990s. Conditions have been complied with, the Section 50 (75) agreement has been secured, and a good working partnership has been established between public authorities and the operator; there is access for all abilities to the Ptarmigan top station, an improved footpath system and the old White Lady chairlift system has been removed. Recently provision has been made for small groups of up to 10 visitors, including mountain railway passengers, to enjoy a 90 minute guided walk on a mountain trail path to the summit, outside the skiing season, every day between May and September.

9.8 SEA of UK offshore wind energy development

9.8.1 Introduction

This case study provides an example of the application of SEA to plans and programmes at a national level. It concerns the SEA of the UK government's plans for the future development of offshore wind energy. The SEA was carried out during 2002–03, prior to the implementation of the EU SEA Directive (2001/42/EC). Further information on the requirements of this Directive, and on SEA more generally, can be found in Chapter 11.

The context for this particular example of SEA was ambitious government targets for renewable energy generation, linked to the achievement of the UK's commitments in the Kyoto Protocol to significantly reduce CO_2 emissions. At the time of the SEA (2002–03), the UK government was committed to supplying 10 per cent of electricity needs from renewable sources by 2010, rising to 20 per cent by 2020. Offshore wind energy was seen as a major contributor towards these targets (DTI 2003a), and the UK government wished to see rapid development of the industry. But it was also committed to an SEA process, which was intended to influence decisions on which areas of the sea should be offered to developers (and which should be excluded), as well as to guide decisions on bids for development licences submitted by individual developers. At the time, offshore wind energy was a new industry undergoing rapid development, and there were therefore many uncertainties about environmental impacts, including potential cumulative effects. This presented difficulties for the SEA work.

9.8.2 Development of offshore wind energy in the UK

The development of offshore wind energy in the UK involves separate licensing and consent systems. The licensing system is operated by the Crown Estate, in its role as landowner of the UK sea bed. Licensing takes place under a competitive tendering process in which developers submit bids for potential wind farm sites. It is left to the developers themselves to identify potential sites, from within broad areas defined by the Department of Energy and Climate Change (DECC, previously DTI). The developers submitting successful bids are then offered an option on their proposed site. Detailed technical studies, consultation and EIA work on the site is then undertaken by the developer, prior to the submission of a consent application. The necessary planning consents are granted by DECC and DEFRA, following consultation with the LPAs most closely affected, statutory consultees and the public. Once the necessary consents have been obtained, developers are granted a lease of 40–50 years on the site and can then begin construction of the wind farm.

In the UK, the Crown Estate's first invitation to developers for site leases for offshore wind development (Round 1 of licensing) took place in 2001. This resulted in 18 planned developments, each of up to 30 turbines. Most of these schemes obtained planning consent in 2002–03 and were installed from 2003 onwards. After this first round of licensing, the government published 'Future offshore', a document setting out its plans for the second licensing round (DTI 2002). This envisaged much larger developments than in the previous round, and stated that future development was to be focused in three 'strategic areas' – the Thames Estuary, the Greater Wash and Liverpool Bay (Figure 9.4). These areas were selected as having the greatest development potential, based on the potential wind resource available, the bathymetry of the offshore area, proximity to existing grid connections and initial expressions of interest from developers (DTI 2003b); however, environmental constraints appeared to have had less influence on the choice of strategic areas.

A three-month consultation period on the 'Future offshore' document started at the end of 2002. The SEA of the government's plans for Round

2 licensing, which is the focus of this case study, started at the same time, with the resulting SEA Environmental Report submitted in May 2003 (for a 28-day consultation period). Despite this SEA process, the government was keen to maintain the pace of development in the offshore wind energy industry, and the deadline for developers to submit expressions of interest for Round 2 site leases to the Crown Estate was the end of March 2003 (i.e. prior to the completion of the SEA Environmental Report or the receipt of consultation responses on this report).

The successful bids for Round 2 developments were finally announced in December 2003. These included 15 projects with a total capacity of between 5.4 and 7.2 GW – this compares with the 1.2 GW consented under Round 1, and so represented a step change in the development of the industry in the UK. Some of the selected sites soon proved controversial, with concerns about the potential impacts on important bird habitats raised by the RSPB (2003).

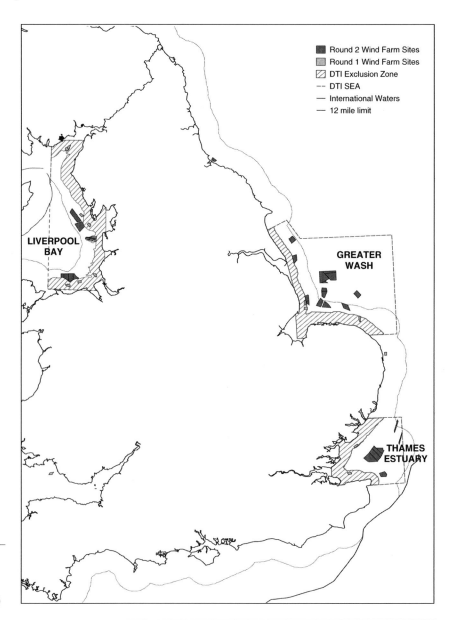

Figure 9.4

Map of the three strategic areas for offshore wind farm development (Round 2)

9.8.3 The SEA approach

The SEA in this case was of the UK government's draft programme for the second licensing round of offshore wind energy development. The SEA was commissioned by the DTI voluntarily, in accordance with the requirements of the EU SEA Directive (although this had not yet been implemented at the time). The timescale under assessment was from 2003 until 2020, with separate assessments undertaken of development up to 2010 and 2020 (DTI 2003a). Two potential development scenarios ('likely' and 'maximum credible') were considered and their likely impacts assessed. The 'likely' scenario envisaged the development of 4.0 GW of capacity by 2010, while the 'maximum credible' scenario envisaged 7.5 GW. By 2020, these figures were expected to increase to 10.2 and 17.5 GW respectively. A no-development option was also considered.

A steering group was used to guide the SEA process, with membership drawn from specialists in coastal/marine environmental issues, wind energy development and SEA. Steering group members included representatives from relevant government departments (DTI, DEFRA, ODPM); the Crown Estate; the British Wind Energy Association (BWEA), the body representing the UK wind energy industry; government and non-governmental environmental organizations, such as the RSPB, Joint Nature Conservancy Council (JNCC), Countryside Council for Wales, and EN; and the IEMA, the body representing the UK EIA 'industry'.

Consultation was undertaken on the scope and design of the SEA. A scoping workshop was held towards the end of 2002 and a scoping report was produced. Some changes to the scope of the SEA were introduced as a result of the consultation responses received, for example by including a wider range of socio-economic impacts that had been identified as important by a number of consultees (DTI 2003a). The environmental report produced at the end of the SEA process provided information on:

- The nature and extent of the technical, environmental and socio-economic constraints that may preclude or be affected by wind farm development.

- The identification of locations within the three strategic areas (the Thames Estuary, the Greater Wash and Liverpool Bay) with the lowest levels of constraint.
- The significance of the environmental and socio-economic impacts arising from different realistic scales of wind farm development in those areas with the lowest levels of constraint.
- Recommendations for managing the impacts of wind farm development in the three strategic areas.

Overall, it was concluded that:

The likely development scenario, to 2010, is achievable for each Strategic Area without coming into significant conflict with the main significant impact risks, namely areas of high sensitivity to visual impact, concentrations of sensitive seabirds, designated and potentially designated conservation sites, MoD Practice and Exercise Areas and main marine traffic areas.

[However], the 2020 likely development scenario would only be achievable subject to resolving the uncertainties concerning impacts on: physical processes, birds, elasmobranchs (shark, skate and ray species) and cetaceans.

The maximum credible scenario for all Strategic Areas, particularly the Greater Wash and Thames Estuary, for 2020, may be compromised by constraints, particularly cumulative impacts and conflict with marine traffic (commercial and recreational navigation); and large scale development could exclude fisheries from significant areas of fishing grounds, particularly if it were to coincide with severance areas associated with other offshore activities. (DTI 2003a)

In order to minimize environmental impacts, the following broad strategic approach was recommended:

- The development of fewer large wind farms, of around 1 GW (1,000 MW) or more capacity, located further offshore is generally preferable to several small-scale developments, though the latter would be preferable for development closer to the coast.

- In all strategic areas, avoid the majority of development within the zone of high visual sensitivity close to the coast.
- Where development might occur close to the coast, preferentially select low constraint areas and consider small-scale development.
- Pending the outcome of monitoring studies, avoid development in shallow water where birds such as common scoter and red-throated diver, and other species (including marine mammals) are known to congregate (particularly in Liverpool Bay and the Greater Wash).
- Address the uncertainties of large-scale impacts, particularly cumulative effects, at a strategic level (DTI 2003a).

The environmental report was subject to a short period of public consultation (28 days). The government argued that the report and the comments received would be 'a significant input to government decision-making on the nature of the second licensing round' (DTI 2003a).

9.8.4 SEA methods

It must be accepted that, in an SEA, the level of detail that can be analysed and presented, in respect of both baseline data and quantification of impacts, is less than in a project-level EIA. This was true of this particular SEA, which 'focuses more on assessing constraints, sensitivities and risks instead of detailed analysis of the characteristics of specific impacts' (DTI 2003a). The methods used in the SEA included a GIS-based spatial analysis (constraint mapping exercise), followed by a risk-based analysis of the likely impacts of the selected development scenarios (including the cumulative implications). Each of these methods is described briefly below, with selected examples included to illustrate the approach used.

Spatial analysis

The spatial analysis made use of electronic overlay mapping of a variety of technical, socio-economic and environmental features to identify areas of the sea with high or low constraints within each of the three strategic areas. Examples of the main features mapped are listed below:

Technical constraints to wind farm development:

- existing and planned licensed areas for aggregate extraction, waste disposal and military operations;
- oil and gas structures (pipelines) and safety zones;
- cultural heritage sites (wrecks and other sea bed obstructions);
- cables;
- existing shipping/navigation lanes; and
- proposed wind farm sites from the first round of licensing.

Socio-economic constraints:

- shipping;
- fishing effort; and
- shell-fishery areas.

Environmental constraints:

- marine habitats of conservation interest (designated and potentially designated);
- seascape sensitivity;
- fish spawning areas; and
- fish nursery areas.

Because of baseline data limitations, not all relevant constraints could be mapped within the relatively tight timescale of the SEA. In particular, it was not possible to map a number of important environmental constraints, such as the distribution of certain bird and fish species and migration routes. Whether these omissions invalidate the conclusions drawn from the constraint mapping exercise is open to question (see below for a summary of consultation responses on this issue). However, those factors that could not be mapped were considered in the later risk-based analysis of impacts.

A scoring system was used in the mapping of constraints, in which each area was awarded a score between 0 and 3 for each mapped constraint (with higher scores indicating greater constraints). The scoring system allowed the identification of locations within each of the three strategic areas that had several constraints (a high total score) and those with fewer overall constraints (a lower overall score), subject to the qualification that not all relevant constraints could be mapped (see Table 9.1). Broad conclusions from the spatial analysis are summarized below, for each strategic area (DTI 2003a):

- *Liverpool Bay.* Overall, the greater amount of constraint and sensitivities occured in the southern part of this strategic area, due to the presence of bird interests, marine habitats of conservation interest, seascape, fisheries and marine traffic. Seascape constraints in the north of the area were significant.
- *Greater Wash.* The Greater Wash had the largest area of low constraint in comparison with the other strategic areas and offered the greatest potential capacity for wind farm development. Inshore areas, particularly in the southern part of the area, had the greatest amount of constraint and sensitivity, particularly with respect to visual impacts, inshore fisheries, marine mammals, birds and offshore habitats of conservation interest.
- *Thames Estuary.* This region included areas of low constraint on its eastern boundary, and had fewer environmental constraints than the other strategic areas. However, several estuaries and marshes were important bird habitats. Commercial activities (e.g. aggregate extraction) and recreational navigation were other important constraints.

Risk-based analysis of impacts

For each strategic area, the likely impacts of the two development scenarios ('likely' and 'maximum credible') were assessed. This analysis incorporated factors that were mapped as part of the earlier spatial analysis, plus specific receptors that could not be mapped, such as particular bird species. Impacts were quantified wherever possible, or otherwise described qualitatively, and their significance evaluated using a risk-based approach. This was based on an assessment of (a) the likelihood of the impact occurring, and (b) the expected consequences (impact on the receptor). As with the spatial analysis, a scoring system was used in the evaluation of impact significance, as shown in Tables 9.2 and 9.3 (DTI 2003a).

The impact significance scores for each impact were calculated as the product of the consequence and likelihood scores, ranging from 1 (minor consequence and unlikely) to 25 (serious consequence and certain).

9.8.5 Issues raised in consultation responses

The environmental report produced at the end of the SEA process was subject to a short period of consultation. An analysis of the consultation

Table 9.1 Scores for mapping of constraints

Scores for fishing effort

0	None
1	Low (less than 500 hours per annum)
2	Medium (500–5,000 hours per annum)
3	High (over 5,000 hours per annum)

Scores for designated habitats of conservation interest

0	Designated habitats are absent
1	Not applicable
2	Nationally important habitats are present (including those not yet designated)
3	Internationally important habitats are present (including those not yet designated)

Scores for seascape

0	No sensitivity
1	Low sensitivity
2	Medium sensitivity
3	High sensitivity

Table 9.2 Scores for impact consequence

5	Serious (e.g. impacts resulting in irreversible or long-term adverse change to key physical and/or ecological processes; direct loss of rare and endangered habitat or species and/or their continued persistence and viability)
3	Moderate (e.g. impacts resulting in medium-term (5–20 years) adverse change to physical and ecological processes; direct loss of some habitat (5–20 per cent); crucial for protected species' continued persistence and viability in the area and/or some mortality of species of conservation significance)
1	Minor (e.g. impacts resulting in short-term adverse change to physical and ecological processes; temporary disturbance of species; natural restoration within two years requiring minimal or no intervention)
0	None (e.g. impact absorbed by natural environment with no discernible effects; no restoration or intervention required)
+	Positive (e.g. activity has net beneficial effect resulting in environmental improvement)

Table 9.3 Scores for impact likelihood

5	Certain (the impact will occur)
3	Likely (impact is likely to occur at some point during the wind farm life cycle)
1	Unlikely (impact is unlikely to occur, but may occur at some point during wind farm life cycle)

responses reveals a number of key issues that were raised by interested stakeholders. These include a range of concerns about the quality and effectiveness of the SEA process, and its influence on decisions for the next phase of wind energy developments. Many of these concerns arose from the tight timescale for the SEA work and the resulting practical difficulties encountered. The main points raised in consultation are highlighted briefly below (a fuller discussion can be found in DTI, 2003b). Many of the issues raised are interlinked; for example, weaknesses in baseline data may be due to limited consultation or a tight timescale in which to complete the SEA.

- *Pre-selection of the three strategic areas, and lack of a national-level SEA.* The three strategic areas in which Round 2 development was to be focused were selected as having the greatest development potential, based on the potential wind resource available, the bathymetry of the offshore area, proximity to existing grid connections and initial expressions of interest from developers (DTI 2003b). However, the selection did not appear to have taken explicit account of environmental constraints, and this was a cause of concern to a number of respondents.
- *The tight timescale for the sea and uncertainty over the influence of the SEA process on decision-making for future developments.* The timescale for the SEA was considered too tight to allow effective stakeholder engagement and consultation, or to allow additional baseline data to be collected. The fact that developer bids for Round 2 sites were invited before the completion of the SEA Environmental Report was also a source of concern.
- *Concern over the rapid development of offshore wind energy, prior to the proper consideration of*

potential impacts. Some respondents argued that the development of the offshore wind energy industry was too rapid and premature; greater efforts should be made to understand the impacts of the smaller Round 1 developments before allowing large-scale expansion of the industry.

- *The need for clearer locational guidance.* There was felt to be a need for clearer recommendations on suitable and unsuitable locations for future offshore wind energy development (including the definition of exclusion zones or 'no-go' areas), and it was considered that these had not emerged sufficiently from the SEA process.
- *Concerns about the scope and methodology of the SEA.* Most respondents were supportive of the overall methodology of the SEA, including the risk-based approach to the assessment of impact significance, but there was some disagreement over the detailed scores awarded to specific receptors or geographical areas.
- *Weaknesses in the available baseline data.* A recurrent theme in the consultation responses was limitations in the baseline data available to the SEA study. This included missing data for certain important environmental constraints (which could not be mapped) and areas in which the data used in the SEA was not the most accurate or appropriate. Some respondents thought that these data limitations were sufficiently serious as to invalidate the identification of areas of high and low constraints in the SEA. Data gaps and uncertainties about impacts also led respondents to urge a precautionary approach; the need for such an approach was also strengthened by ongoing delays in the designation of offshore areas of conservation interest under the EU Habitats Directive. Other uncertainties included doubts about whether the impacts of smaller wind farms (from the first round of licensing) could necessarily be extrapolated to larger wind farms further offshore.
- *Limited consultation with certain stakeholders.* According to some respondents, the SEA had involved only limited consultation with certain stakeholders (e.g. fisheries and recreational boating interests). This lack of consultation, again partly linked to the tight

timescale for the exercise, helped to explain some of the data weaknesses on certain issues in the SEA.

- *Insufficient attention to cumulative and indirect effects.* It was considered that insufficient attention was given to the impact of related onshore development in the SEA, such as transmission connections. This concern echoes the issues highlighted in the first case study in Section 9.2. More attention also needed to be devoted to cumulative impacts in the environmental report. There was no indication in the report of the carrying capacity of each of the strategic areas, and it was therefore difficult to assess the significance of the cumulative impacts arising under the two development scenarios.
- *Overlaps with project-level EIA.* There was some disagreement over the level of detail needed in the SEA, and which issues could be left to project-level EIA for individual sites. For example, bird distribution data was considered to be one area in which survey data could reasonably be collected at a more strategic level.
- *Responsibility for future SEA studies.* Some respondents requested clarification about who would be responsible for progressing further studies arising from the SEA, including additional data collection to fill existing data gaps and ongoing monitoring. Arrangements for the sharing of such data were felt to be important.

9.8.6 Summary

This case study of SEA was undertaken voluntarily, prior to the implementation of the EU SEA Directive. It provides an example of how SEA can be applied, within the context of a new, rapidly developing industry. The UK government's commitment to large-scale development of offshore wind energy to meet international obligations to reduce CO_2 emissions dictated a tight timescale for this SEA. However, the resulting limitations in baseline data, and restricted timescale for stakeholder consultation and feedback, were identified as particular weaknesses in this case.

9.9 SEA of Tyne and Wear local transport plan

9.9.1 Introduction

This case study concerns the SEA of the Local Transport Plan for Tyne and Wear, a metropolitan sub-region in the northeast of England. The case study is interesting in that it provides an example of an integrated form of assessment, in which an attempt was made to incorporate the results of various other types of assessment into the SEA process. These include health impact assessment (HIA), equality impact assessment (EqIA) and habitats regulation assessment (HRA). The assessment of alternative options is an important feature of SEA and this is therefore also a particular focus of the case study.

Local transport plans (LTPs) were introduced as a statutory requirement in England by the Transport Act 2000. This required local transport authorities to prepare a Local Transport Plan every five years and to keep it under review. Under the terms of the Act, LTPs are required to set out the authority's policies 'for the promotion and encouragement of safe, integrated, efficient and economic transport facilities and services to, from and within their area'. LTPs cover all forms of transport (passenger, freight and pedestrian; public and private) and include strategic policies and an associated implementation or delivery plan outlining more detailed proposals.

The case study concerns the third local transport plan (LTP3) for the Tyne and Wear metropolitan area. The LTP comprises a strategy covering 2011–21, supported by a delivery plan for the first three years of this period (Tyne and Wear Integrated Transport Authority 2011). The plan was prepared during 2010–11, with a parallel SEA process undertaken (Tyne and Wear Joint Transport Working Group 2011a, b). SEA of LTPs is a statutory requirement under the UK's SEA Regulations. Guidance from the UK Department for Transport (DfT) also indicates that there is a requirement for HIA and EqIA for LTPs (DfT 2009a, b). For the Tyne and Wear LTP, an attempt was made to integrate these assessments within the SEA.

9.9.2 Background to the plan

Tyne and Wear is a city-region in the northeast of England, encompassing an urban core plus a more rural hinterland. The area includes the major urban centres of Newcastle-upon-Tyne, Gateshead and Sunderland, and has a population of 1.1 million. Tyne and Wear has suffered from historic economic weaknesses and this is currently reflected in high levels of unemployment, below average income levels, deprivation, and related social and health problems. There are relatively low levels of car ownership in the area and higher than average levels of public transport use. Two main trunk roads, the A1 and A19, serve the region. Public transport includes the Tyne and Wear Metro (light rail) system, an extensive bus network, the North Shields to South Shields cross-Tyne ferry and local rail services to the Gateshead MetroCentre (a major retail and leisure complex) and Sunderland.

The LTP was intended to help address key challenges facing the area. These included the need for economic development and regeneration, the need to meet climate change targets for emissions reductions, the need for safe and sustainable communities, and protection and enhancement of the natural environment. In response to these challenges, the plan adopted a strategic framework based on three broad intervention types: (1) managing the demand for travel (including encouragement of modal shift towards more sustainable travel modes); (2) management and further integration of existing networks (with a particular focus on the encouragement of active travel modes and public transport); and (3) targeted new investment in key schemes (including, for example, investment in electric vehicles, bus corridor improvements and new park and ride schemes).

9.9.3 Overview of the SEA process

The SEA of the local transport plan was undertaken by consultants Atkins for the Tyne and Wear Integrated Transport Authority, the local transport authority responsible for the Tyne and Wear subregion. Key stages in the process included:

- Scoping, baseline studies and SEA methods: this involved determining and consulting on

the scope of the SEA; baseline and contextual studies; and development of the SEA methodology, including the identification of a set of appropriate SEA objectives to be used in the assessment.
- Assessment of alternatives: the development of strategic alternatives and their appraisal against the SEA objectives.
- Assessment of the effects of the draft plan: assessment of the effects of the policies in the draft plan; recommendations for mitigation or enhancement of impacts; and publication of the results of the assessment in an Environmental Report.
- Consultation on the draft plan and Environmental Report: followed by revisions to the draft plan as appropriate and publication of the final plan.
- Monitoring the effects of plan implementation.

An interesting feature of the SEA was its attempt to integrate other types of assessment within the SEA process. These included HIA, EqIA and HRA. Relevant government guidance states that HIA and EqIA are required for LTPs, although these assessments do not necessarily need to be formally incorporated within the SEA (DfT 2009a). HRA is an additional statutory requirement in cases in which a plan contains proposals that are likely to have a significant effect on a Special Protection Area or Special Area of Conservation (collectively known as Natura 2000 sites).

Impacts on human health are identified in the SEA Directive as one of the environmental topics to be considered in SEA. The requirement for a specific HIA in the government guidance on LTPs reflects the understanding that LTP policies and proposals may impact on factors influencing the health of communities and individuals. This could include for example changes in the accessibility and affordability of transport, levels of physical activity, air and noise pollution, personal safety (or perception of safety) and community severance. For the Tyne and Wear LTP, a separate HIA process was not undertaken; health considerations were instead fully integrated within the SEA process. This integration of health considerations took place at all stages in the SEA process and included, for example:

- involvement of the local NHS Primary Care Trust and other relevant public health organizations in the consultation on the scope and methods of the SEA;
- inclusion of health-related plans and programmes in the review of the policy context for the plan and in the identification of key sustainability issues;
- inclusion of relevant health indicators in the baseline data collection; and
- inclusion of a specific SEA objective on health ('to improve health and well-being and reduce inequalities in health').

EqIA involves an assessment of the impact of policies, strategies or plans on different social groups. Its purpose is to ensure that the plan does not discriminate against particular groups and where possible promotes greater equality. The EqIA of the Tyne and Wear LTP was undertaken as a parallel exercise to the SEA and its results were reported separately (Tyne and Wear Joint Transport Working Group 2011c). However, equalities issues were also fully integrated into the various stages of the SEA in the same ways as for health considerations. A specific SEA objective on equality was also included in the SEA Framework ('to promote greater equality of opportunity for all citizens, with the desired outcome of achieving a fairer society'; the SEA Framework is discussed further in Section 9.9.5).

The Tyne and Wear LTP was also subject to HRA screening. As with the EqIA, this was undertaken as a parallel process to the SEA and reported separately, although the findings were incorporated in the SEA environmental report. The impact on Natura 2000 sites was also included as a specific SEA objective ('to protect and where possible enhance the European sites').

9.9.4 Scoping and baseline studies

The topics assessed in the SEA were based on the list of factors identified in the SEA Directive. These included impacts on biodiversity, population, human health, fauna and flora, soil, water, air, noise, climatic factors, material assets, cultural heritage and landscape. As part of the scoping stage, a Scoping Report was produced and comments invited from statutory and other consultees

(including those representing public health, equality and diversity interests). The Scoping Report included contextual information on other plans, policies and programmes relevant to LTP3, initial baseline information, a summary of key environmental, social and health issues emerging from the initial work and a preliminary framework of objectives to be used in the SEA assessment process. A scoping workshop was also held in order to gather additional information and discuss the key issues and proposed SEA objectives (these objectives are discussed further in Section 9.9.5).

Baseline studies for the SEA included a review of the policy context, collection of a detailed evidence base on the state of the environment and identification of key environmental issues. Establishing the policy context to the LTP involved a review of other relevant plans and programmes, including those related to health and equality issues. This allowed identification of key themes and policy objectives, for environmental, health and equality-related issues. Detailed baseline information was collected on the current state of the environment and its likely evolution without the implementation of the plan. Baseline data collected included both environmental and social indicators, the latter including data on health, inequality, connectivity and accessibility.

Baseline data gaps and limitations were not explicitly identified in the SEA Environmental Report. It was therefore not clear whether potential indicators had been excluded due to a lack of baseline data. Consultation responses to the draft Environmental Report from one of the statutory consultees also included some criticism of the completeness and consistency of baseline data (including data on biodiversity, agricultural land quality and flood risk zones). The SEA consultants acknowledged these deficiencies, but stated that they could not be addressed due to 'budgetary constraints'. For a number of baseline indicators, there was also an unavoidable reliance on somewhat dated sources of information (e.g. 2001 Census data, which was almost 10 years out of date at the time of the assessment).

The baseline information and review of the policy context was used to identify a list of key environmental issues for the plan area. These covered a wide range of economic and social sustainability issues (e.g. the historic economic weakness of the sub-region and related social issues, including deprivation, child poverty, low incomes and low levels of car ownership), as well as environmental issues (e.g. poor air quality, noise, water quality, climate change, biodiversity threats, heritage and landscape character change). Problems of general health and health inequalities were also identified as key issues. Other issues were directly related to transport (e.g. congestion, accessibility and road safety).

9.9.5 SEA method and objectives

A key part of the assessment methodology was the development of an 'SEA framework'. This framework comprised a series of SEA objectives and associated indicators that were used in the assessment of the effects of the draft plan and of alternative options. The SEA objectives were developed through an iterative process, based on the review of relevant plans and programmes, the evolving baseline information, the key sustainability issues identified and consideration of which of these issues could potentially be addressed by the LTP. The list of objectives incorporated specific health, equalities and habitats issues. This was designed to ensure the integration of the HIA, EqIA and HRA screening processes within the SEA, while also meeting the requirements of the SEA Directive. A final list of 16 SEA objectives was drawn up, covering air quality, biodiversity, European sites, climate change, flood risk, resource use and waste, water quality, use of land, historic and cultural heritage, landscape and townscape quality, accessibility and community severance, noise and light pollution, health and well-being, equality, road safety and crime. For each of these objectives, the SEA framework provided a set of associated indicators (to measure performance against the objective) and a list of assessment 'prompt questions' (to guide the assessment of the effect of LTP policies or proposals on this objective). An example of these prompt questions and indicators, for the SEA objective on local air quality, is provided in Table 9.4.

Where possible, the indicators in the SEA framework were similar to those used in the earlier baseline studies. Analysis of the baseline situation for these indicators provided a means of summarizing current environmental conditions and predicted future trends (without implementation of the plan). This analysis was carried out for each of the SEA objectives using a simple three-point normative scale to describe both current conditions (good, moderate or poor) and expected future trends (improving, stable or declining). The overall conclusion was that, without the implementation of the plan, performance against a number of the SEA objectives was predicted to decline. These objectives included those relating to air quality, transport related CO_2 emissions, noise and light pollution, the resistance of transport infrastructure to climate change and flood risk, and crime levels.

9.9.6 Identification and assessment of alternatives

The SEA Directive requires a consideration of 'reasonable alternatives taking into account the objectives and the geographical scope of the plan or programme' and 'an outline of the reasons for selecting the alternatives dealt with'. For the Tyne and Wear LTP SEA, three broad strategic alternatives were considered. These comprised a 'do-minimum' scenario, a so-called 'realistic' scenario and an 'optimistic' (or aspirational funding) scenario. These alternative scenarios were developed by the LTP team in response to the identified local transport objectives and challenges. The main differences between the alternative options are summarized below.

Do-minimum scenario:

- no additional interventions in public transport, highway management, cycling and walking or freight and ports;
- highway capacity schemes that are already underway or have confirmed funding to go ahead;
- bus and metro fares to increase;
- rail and metro refurbishment; and
- workplace and school travel planning to remain at current levels.

Realistic scenario:

- emphasis on highway capacity schemes (mainly junction improvements);
- development of three new park and ride schemes;

Table 9.4 Extract from SEA framework for Tyne and Wear LTP3 SEA

Prompt questions for air quality SEA objective: will LTP proposals	Suggested indicators to measure performance against SEA objective
– Reduce traffic levels and promote more sustainable transport patterns across the area, particularly focusing on areas with low air quality (e.g. Air Quality Management Areas)?	– Levels of main pollutants for national air quality targets
	– Number of residential properties within AQMAs
– Promote walking and cycling and improve infrastructure for these forms of travel?	– Number of Euro engine buses operating in AQMAs/future AQMAs in Tyne and Wear
– Encourage Green Travel Plans and school travel plans?	– Effective use of awareness and marketing campaigns - percentage of the population reached by awareness campaigns
– Promote operation of the most modern vehicles, including buses and private cars?	
– Recognize the importance of awareness and marketing campaigns promoting the issue of improving air quality in the region?	– Number of business and School Travel Plans
	– Reduction in NOx and primary PM10 emissions through local authority's estate and operations (National Indicator 194)
– Reduce congestion on the inter-urban trunk road network in large urban areas?	
– Instigate financial incentives and measures on the basis of the polluter pays principle (e.g. congestion charge, road pricing)?	
– Promote the use of public transport?	

- bus priority lanes to be provided at eleven locations;
- integrated 'smart' ticketing on public transport;
- electric vehicle charging points; and
- emphasis on walking and cycling initiatives.

Optimistic scenario (as for realistic scenario, plus the following):

- much greater emphasis on highway capacity schemes;
- development of a further eleven park and ride schemes;
- provision of an additional nine bus priority lanes;
- greater emphasis on rail and metro, including re-opening a number of rail lines; and
- no additional emphasis on walking and cycling initiatives.

The SEA Environmental Report provided only limited information on the reasons for the selection of these particular alternatives. For example, it was not clear whether other strategic options had been considered at an earlier stage in the plan preparation process and subsequently rejected. The realism of the optimistic scenario (based on aspirational funding levels) at a time of significantly reduced public funding for transport schemes could also be questioned.

In order to compare the impacts of these alternative strategies, a qualitative assessment was made of their performance against each of the objectives in the SEA framework. This assessment was based on the series of assessment 'prompt questions' defined in the framework. Use was also made of constraint mapping, with a range of maps produced showing relevant environmental constraints and selected schemes overlaid where specific locations were known (e.g. park and ride scheme locations). The assessment of the effects of the alternatives on the SEA objectives was a qualitative exercise, employing a simple seven point scale (large, moderate or slight beneficial effect; neutral or no effect; slight, moderate or large adverse effect). Moderate or large effects were deemed to be significant. The conclusions on the likely scale of effects on each SEA objective were supported by a detailed commentary or explanation in the environmental report. However, there was no use of explicit significance criteria to guide this process; such criteria have proved useful in other SEAs of local transport plans and would have helped to more clearly justify the conclusions on significance in this case (see TRL 2004 for an example of the application of such criteria).

Evaluation of significance is of course often difficult in SEA of strategic plans due to the lack of detail about specific schemes, locations and timescales. In this case, there was also a difficulty in balancing the short-term and longer-term effects of the different strategies. For a number of SEA objectives, there was expected to be a mix of short-term adverse effects (e.g. associated with the construction of new infrastructure schemes) and potential longer-term benefits (e.g. due to reduced traffic and congestion levels once the schemes were operational). The absence of explicit criteria with which to assess significance presented some difficulties in these circumstances, as it was difficult to see how these different effects had been balanced. The SEA also appeared to adopt an implicit assumption that the proposed measures or interventions would prove to be effective, for example in changing travel behaviour in the desired direction. There was no explicit consideration of the deliverability or risk associated with proposed measures.

The assessment of the alternative strategies concluded that, overall, the realistic scenario provided the best balance between adverse and beneficial effects (Table 9.5). This conclusion was not clearly explained in the environmental report, although it appeared to reflect the absence of beneficial effects with the do-minimum scenario and the larger number of more severe (i.e. large rather than moderate) adverse effects with the optimistic scenario. Overall, predicted effects against the SEA objectives were as follows:

- Do-minimum scenario: no significant beneficial effects; significant adverse effects against 3 SEA objectives (all moderate adverse).
- Realistic scenario: significant beneficial effects against two SEA objectives (both moderate beneficial); significant adverse effects against five SEA objectives (all moderate adverse).
- Optimistic scenario: significant beneficial effects against four SEA objectives (all moderate beneficial); significant adverse effects

against six SEA objectives (three moderate adverse and three large adverse).

The absence of explicit methods or criteria with which to sum or weigh these effects was a weakness in the SEA. For example, it was unclear whether all of the SEA objectives were regarded as of equal importance or weight in the overall assessment.

9.9.7 Effects of the plan and mitigation

Following the appraisal of strategic alternatives, the preferred option for the LTP was developed further by the plan team. The resulting strategy in the draft plan was based largely on the realistic scenario and included 45 separate policies. In order to simplify the assessment, the SEA grouped related policies into a smaller number of 'policy components'. Policies within these components were expected to have broadly similar effects. Six main policy components were identified in the draft plan, including those concerned with (1) improving safety; (2) maintaining and managing infrastructure; (3) promoting sustainable transport modes; (4) parking; (5) freight; and (6) major schemes. The effects of these policy components were assessed against each of the SEA objectives, in a similar way as for the assessment of strategic alternatives using the same seven-point qualitative scale.

Significant adverse effects were identified against three of the SEA objectives (to ensure resilience to the effects of climate change and flood risk; to ensure efficient use of land and maintain the resource of productive soil; and to reduce noise, vibration and light pollution). These adverse effects were associated with the draft plan's policies on parking, freight and major schemes. Based on the results of the assessment, recommendations to improve the overall sustainability performance of the plan were made in the environmental report. These included:

- Policies relating to major schemes should include a requirement for a Construction Environmental Management Plan (CEMP) and a Site Waste Management Plan for any scheme that requires construction.
- There was no consideration of climate change adaptation within any of the policies in the draft plan. Policies relating to major schemes

Table 9.5 Assessment summary of strategic alternatives for Tyne and Wear LTP

SEA Objective	Strategic Alternative 1 The 'Do Minimum' Scenario	Strategic Alternative 2 The Realistic Scenario	Strategic Alternative 3 The Optimistic Scenario
Environmental Objectives			
1	-	0	++
2	-	-	–
3	-	-	–
4	-	0	+
5	–	–	-
6	-	–	–
7	0	–	—
8	0	–	—
9	-	–	—
10	–	++	++
Social Objectives, Including Health and Inequality Issues			
11	0	+	++
12	0	0	-
13	–	++	+
14	-	+	++
15	0	+	+
16	0	+	+

Scale of Effect (SE)

+++ Large beneficial   ++ Moderate beneficial   + Slight beneficial

0 Neutral or no effects

— Large adverse   – Moderate adverse   - Slight adverse

Those effects which are either moderate or major are deemed to be significant

No.	SEA Objective
1	Ensure good local air quality for all
2	To protect and where possible enhance biodiversity, geodiversity and the multi-functional green infrastructure network
3	Protect and where possible enhance the European sites *(HRA specific objective)*
4	To mitigate against climate change by decarbonizing transport
5	To ensure resilience to the effects of climate change and flood risk
6	Promote prudent use of natural resources, waste minimization and movement up the waste hierarchy
7	Protect and enhance the quality of the area's ground, river and sea waters
8	To ensure efficient use of land and maintain the resource of productive soil
9	Maintain and enhance the quality and distinctiveness of the area's historic and cultural heritage
10	Protect and enhance the character and quality of landscape and townscape
11	To improve accessibility to services, facilities and amenities for all and avoid community severance
12	Reduce noise, vibration and light pollution
13	Improve health and well-being and reduce inequalities in health *(HIA specific objective)*
14	To promote greater equality of opportunity for all citizens, with the desired outcome of achieving a fairer society *(EqIA specific objective)*
15	Improve road safety
16	Reduce crime and fear of crime and promote community safety

Source: Tyne and Wear Joint Transport Working Group 2011a

and maintaining infrastructure should be updated to include reference to climate change adaptation.

- Policies on identifying suitable sites for off-road lorry parking provision and freight consolidation centres should include reference that the site would not be located in a sensitive location for biodiversity/geodiversity and would minimize land take and loss of productive land.
- Policies on parking should include a reference to the fear of crime that may occur in car parks, particularly out of town car parks; suitable lighting and security presence may be appropriate forms of mitigation.
- Policies on parking should also make reference to the consideration of noise and light pollution that may be introduced at out of town car parks.

Most of these suggested amendments to the draft plan were incorporated into the policies in the final plan. As a result of these amendments, the performance of the final plan against the SEA objectives was improved, with fewer significant adverse effects identified than for the draft plan. Significant adverse effects were identified only for the major schemes policy component of the final plan, against two of the SEA objectives (resilience to climate change and flood risk and the efficient use of productive land). Further mitigation measures were recommended in the final environmental report in order to minimize these effects; these emphasized the need to avoid the location of major schemes in flood risk areas and to minimize the loss of agricultural land in the design of such schemes. A number of generic mitigation measures were also recommended (e.g. environmental management best practice measures to be adopted during construction projects).

9.9.8 Summary

This case study has examined the application of SEA to local transport plans. UK government guidance indicates that LTPs should be subject to HIA and EqIA, in addition to the requirement for SEA. LTPs also require screening for potential impacts on European protected habitats (habitats regulation assessment). In the case of the Tyne and Wear local transport plan, an attempt was made to integrate these different types of assessment within the SEA. This was achieved by incorporating health, equalities and habitats issues in the scoping and baseline stages of the SEA, and by the inclusion of specific objectives on these issues in the SEA assessment framework. Despite this innovative approach, the case study also reveals some weaknesses in the SEA process, particularly in relation to the identification and assessment of alternative options and in the evaluation of significance. The use of more explicit criteria with which to assess the significance of predicted effects and to compare alternatives would have helped to improve the clarity of the assessment.

9.10 Summary

This chapter has examined a number of case studies of EIA in practice. Most of the cases involve EIA at individual project level, although examples of SEA have also been discussed. Links with other related types of assessment, such as health impact assessment and appropriate assessment under the Habitats Directive, have also been explored. While it is not claimed that the selected case studies represent examples of best EIA practice, they do include examples of some novel and innovative approaches towards particular issues in EIA, such as extended methods of public participation and the treatment of cumulative effects. But the case studies have also drawn attention to some of the practical difficulties encountered in EIA, and to some of the limitations of the process in practice. Chapters 11 and 12 provide further discussion of a number of the new approaches considered in the case studies.

SOME QUESTIONS

The following questions are intended to help the reader focus on the key issues raised by the EIA and SEA case studies in this chapter.

1   The assessment of incremental and cumulative effects is revealed to be a weak area in a number of the case studies (Section 9.2 and 9.6). Why is assessment of these impacts often problematic in project-level EIA, and what solutions might you suggest to remedy the problem?

2   What factors accounted for the more successful treatment of cumulative effects in the Humber Estuary case study in Section 9.5?

3   For projects affecting European priority habitats, summarize the tests that must be carried out as part of the 'appropriate assessment' process (as discussed in Section 9.3). What guidance is available on the interpretation of these tests?

4   What were the main strengths and weaknesses of the public participation approaches adopted in the Portsmouth incinerator case study (Section 9.4)? How could the effectiveness of the public participation process have been improved?

5   Summarize the key similarities and differences between the HIA and EIA processes, as revealed by the Stansted airport case study (Section 9.6). In what ways are the two processes linked?

6   Summarize the main weaknesses in the SEA for UK offshore wind energy, as revealed in the stakeholder consultation (Section 9.7). How might these stakeholder concerns have been more effectively addressed?

7   Comment on the approach used to assess and compare alternatives in the SEA of the Tyne and Wear Local Transport Plan (Section 9.8). How could this element of the SEA have been improved?

· ·

References

Cooper, L.M. and Sheate, W.R. 2002. Cumulative effects assessment – a review of UK environmental impact statements. *Environmental Impact Assessment Review* 22 (4), 415–39.

DfT (Department for Transport) 2003. *The future of air transport – White Paper*. December 2003.

DfT 2009a. *Guidance on Local Transport Plans*. July 2009.

DfT 2009b. *Transport analysis guidance 2.11D: strategic environmental assessment for transport plans and programmes. Draft guidance*, April 2009.

DTI (Department for Trade and Industry) 2002. *Future offshore – a strategic framework for the offshore wind industry*.

DTI 2003a. *Offshore wind energy generation – phase 1 proposals and environmental report*. Report prepared by BMT Cordah for the DTI. April 2003.

DTI 2003b. *Responses to draft programme for future development of offshore windfarms and the accompanying environmental report – summary of comments, and DTI response*. June 2003.

EC (European Commission) 2000. *Managing Natura 2000 sites: the provisions of Article 6 of the 'Habitats' Directive 92/43/EEC*.

EC 2001. *Assessment of plans and projects significantly affecting Natura 2000 sites: methodological guidance on the provisions of Article 6.3 and 6.4 of the Habitats Directive 92/43/EEC*.

EC 2007. *Guidance document on Article 6(4) of the 'Habitats Directive' 92/43/EEC: clarification of the concepts of alternative solutions, imperative reasons of overriding public interest, compensatory measures, overall coherence: opinion of the Commission*.

ERM (Environmental Resources Mangement) 2006. *Health impact assessment of Stansted Generation 1: final report*. June 2006.

ERM 2008. *The Stansted Generation 2 project: a health impact assessment*. April 2008.

ETSU (Energy Technology Support Unit) 1996. *Energy from waste: a guide for local authorities and private* sector developers of municipal solid waste combustion and related projects. Harwell: ETSU.

Glasson, J., Godfrey, K. and Goodey, B. 1995. *Towards visitor impact management*. Aldershot: Avebury.

HIE (Highlands and Islands Enterprise) 2005. *Cairngorms estate management plan: 2005–2009*. Inverness: HIE.

House of Lords Select Committee on Science and Technology 2000. *Science and society*. Third report. London: HMSO.

Huggett, D. 2003. *Developing compensatory measures relating to port developments in European wildlife sites in the UK*.

Hunter, C. and Green, H. 1995.*Tourism and the environment: a sustainable relationship?* London: Routledge.

IWM (Institute of Waste Management) 1995. *Communicating with the public: no time to waste*. Northampton: IWM.

Land Use Consultants 1994. *Cairngorm Funicular Project—Environmental Statement (and Appendices)*. Glasgow: LUC.

Mathieson, A. and Wall, G. 2004. *Tourism: economic, physical and social impacts*. London: Longmans.

Petts, J. 1995. Waste management strategy development: a case study of community involvement and consensus-building in Hampshire. *Journal of Environmental Planning and Management* 38 (4), 519–36.

Petts, J. 1999. Public participation and environmental impact assessment. In *Handbook of environmental impact assessment*, J. Petts (ed), vol. 1, Process, methods and potential. Oxford: Blackwell Science.

Petts, J. 2003. Barriers to deliberative participation in EIA: learning from waste policies, plans and projects. *Journal of Environmental Assessment Policy and Management* 5 (3), 269–93.

Piper, J.M. 2000. Cumulative effects assessment on the Middle Humber: barriers overcome, benefits derived. *Journal of Environmental Planning and Management* 43 (3), 369–87.

Piper, J.M. 2001a. Assessing the cumulative effects of project clusters: a comparison of process and methods in four UK cases. *Journal of Environmental Planning and Management* 44 (3), 357–75.

Piper, J.M. 2001b. Barriers to implementation of cumulative effects assessment. *Journal of Environmental Assessment Policy and Management* 3 (4), 465–81.

Piper, J.M. 2002. CEA and sustainable development – evidence from UK case studies. *Environmental Impact Assessment Review* 22 (1), 17–36.

The Planning Inspectorate 2008. *Stansted G1 Inquiry: Inspector's Report*. January 2008.

Report to the Department for Transport and Somerset County Council, July 2004.

RSPB (Royal Society for the Protection of Birds) 2003. *Successful offshore wind farm bids raise serious concerns for birds*. RSPB press release, 18 December.

Sheate, W. R. 1995. Electricity generation and transmission: a case study of problematic EIA implementation in the UK. *Environmental Policy and Practice* 5 (1), 17–25.

Snary, C. 2002. Risk communication and the waste-to-energy incinerator environmental impact assessment process: a UK case study of public involvement. *Journal of Environmental Planning and Management* 45 (2), 267–83.

SNH (Scottish Natural Heritage) 2000. *Cairngorm Funicular Railway – Visitor Management Plan*. Paper presented to the SNH Board. SNH 100/5/7.

Stop Stansted Expansion 2006. *SSE response to BAA health impact assessment*. August 2006.

TRL (Transport Research Laboratory) 2004. *Strategic environmental assessment guidance for transport plans and programmes: Somerset County Council local transport plan SEA pilot: Alternatives and significance*. July.

Tyne and Wear Integrated Transport Authority 2011. *LTP3: The third Local Transport Plan for Tyne and Wear: strategy 2011–2021*. March 2011.

Tyne and Wear Joint Transport Working Group 2011a. *Local Transport Plan 3: strategic environmental assessment – environmental report*. April 2011.

Tyne and Wear Joint Transport Working Group 2011b. *Local Transport Plan 3: strategic environmental assessment – SEA statement*. April 2011.

Tyne and Wear Joint Transport Working Group 2011c. *LTP3 Equality impact assessment: final report*. April 2011.

Weston, J. 2003. Is there a future for EIA? Response to Benson. *Impact Assessment and Project Appraisal* 21 (4), 278–80.

Weston, J. and Smith, R. 1999. The EU Habitats Directive: making the Article 6 assessments. The case of Ballyseedy Wood. *European Planning Studies* 7 (4), 483–99.

10 Comparative practice

●●

10.1 Introduction

Most countries in the world have EIA regulations and have had projects subject to EIA. However the regulations vary widely, as do the details of how they are implemented in practice. This is due to a range of political, economic and social factors.

Environmental impact assessment is also evolving rapidly worldwide. When the second edition of this book was being written in 1999, for instance, many African countries and countries in transition had only recently enacted EIA regulations; by now, some of these countries have had considerable experience with EIA, and are developing more detailed guidelines and regulations. Just since the last edition of 2005, the EIA systems of three of the seven countries discussed in that edition – Peru, Poland and Canada – have undergone major changes, and half of the international organizations discussed at Section 10.9 have updated their EIA guidance.

This chapter aims to illustrate the range of existing EIA systems and act as comparisons with the UK and EC systems discussed earlier. It starts with an overview of EIA practice in the various continents of the world, and some of the factors that influence the development of EIA worldwide. It then discusses the EIA systems of countries in six different continents, focusing in each case on specific aspects of the system:

- Benin has one of the most advanced EIA systems in Africa, with good transparency, considerable public participation, integration of environmental concerns with national planning and robust administrative and institutional tools.

- Peru's EIA system is typical of many South American countries in its sector-specific orientation, relative lack of public participation and transparency, and late timing in project planning.

- Poland resembles several other countries in transition in that its EIA system has changed dramatically since the early post-communist days. In 2000, Poland enacted radical new regulations, which brings its EIA system in line with EU requirements.

- China's EIA system is discussed because of the worldwide effect that any Chinese environmental policy is likely to have in the future. China's environmental policies are restricted by the need to harmonize them with plans for economic development.

- Canada is known for its progressive environmental policies. Its federal EIA system has good procedures for mediation and public participation. Significant changes are currently being made to this system.

- Australia's EIA system, like Canada's, is split between the federal and state governments. The state of Western Australia provides a particularly interesting example of a good state system with many innovative features.

The chapter concludes with a discussion of the role of international institutions in developing and spreading good EIA practice for the projects and programmes they fund and support.

10.2 EIA status worldwide

Table 10.1 and Figure 2.2 show, to the authors' best knowledge, the status of EIA regulations worldwide in mid-2011. Box 10.1 gives an initial list of sources of information about EIA worldwide. More than 140 countries have some form of EIA regulation.

However, EIA practice is not even across different countries worldwide. Figure 10.1 summarizes the evolution of EIA in a typical country: it begins with an initial limited number of EIAs carried out on an ad hoc basis in response to public concerns, donor requirements or industries based in a country with EIA requirements carrying out EIAs of their activities in the country without EIA requirements. Over time, the country institutes EIA guidelines or regulations. These may prompt a rapid surge in the number of EIAs carried out in that country, as was the case in most EU countries. However, the regulations may apply to only a limited number of projects, or may be widely ignored, leading to only a small increase. Over time, the regulations may be fine-tuned or added to, the number of EIAs carried out annually levels off or may even shrink, and the EIA system is effectively 'mature'. The current status of EIA in different countries can be roughly charted on this continuum. Figure 10.2 broadly shows this status by continent, though individual countries may vary from this.

The situation in *Africa* is changing rapidly, with many countries having recently instituted EIA-specific regulations to complement earlier framework regulations. This development has been brought about by a range of initiatives including the 1995 African Ministerial Conference on Environment that committed African environment ministers to formalize the use of EIA; and the establishment of several organizations that aimed to improve EIA capacity and collaboration between African countries (e.g. Capacity Development and Linkages for Environmental Impact Assessment in Africa, Partnership for Environmental Assessment in Africa, and several African branches of the International Association for Impact Assessment). On the other hand, EIA in Africa is still beset by a lack of trained personnel, cost, concern that EIA

Although some of these references are countrty-specific, they discuss wider issues related to the region in question.

General: Lee and George (2000), Wood (2003); websites of affiliates and branches of the International Association for Impact Assessment (www.iaia.org/affiliatesbranches), EIA Wiki (eia.unu.edu/wiki/index.php/EIA_Systems) publications by the OECD, UNEP and World Bank; and articles in e.g. *Environmental Impact Assessment Review*, *Impact Assessment and Project Appraisal* and the *Journal of Environmental Assessment Policy and Management*.

Western Europe: EC (2009), GHK (2010), Wood (2003).

Central and Eastern Europe: Kovalev *et al*. (2009), Rzeszot (1999), Unalan and Cowell (2009), World Bank (2002).

Australia, New Zealand: Elliott and Thomas (2009), Wood (2003).

Asia: Briffett (1999), Vidyaratne (2006), World Bank (2006).

North America: Wood (2003).

South America: Brito and Verocai (1999), Chico (1995), CISDL (2006), Kirchhoff (2006).

Africa and Middle East: Almagi *et al*. (2007), Appiah-Opoku (2005), Bekhechi and Mercier (2002), Economic Commission for Africa (2005), El-Fadl and El-Fadel (2004), Kakonge (1999), Marara *et al*. (2011), Southern African Institute for Environmental Assessment (2003).

Box 10.1 Some references of EIA systems worldwide

Table 10.1 Existing EIA systems worldwide (with date of original implementation)

Country	Implementation	Country	Implementation	Country	Implementation
Western Europe		**Africa and Middle East**		**Americas**	
Austria	1993, 2000	Algeria	1983, 1990	Argentina	1994–6
Belgium	1985–92	Angola	2004	Belize	1995
Denmark	1989, 1999	Bahrain	?	Bolivia	1995
Finland	1994, 2004	Benin	2001	Brazil	1986, 1997
France	1976	Botswana	2005	Canada	1992
Germany	1990, 2005–06	Burkina Faso	1997	Chile	1997
Greece	1986, 2002	Cameroon	2005	Colombia	1997–2005
Iceland	2000, 2005	Comoros	1994	Costa Rica	1998 (partial)
Ireland	1989–2000	Cote d'Ivoire	1996	Cuba	1999
Italy	1986–96	Dem. Rep. of Congo	2002 (partial)	Dominican Rep.	2002
Luxembourg	1994	Egypt	1995	Ecuador	1999
Netherlands	1987, 2002	Ethiopia	2002	El Salvador	1998
Norway	1990	Gabon	1979	Guatemala	2003
Portugal	1987	Gambia	2005?	Guyana	1996
Spain	1986, 2008	Ghana	1999	Honduras	1993
Sweden	1987–91	Guinea	1987	Mexico	1988
Switzerland	1985	Iran	1994–2005	Nicaragua	1994
United Kingdom	1988	Iraq	1997 (partial)	Panama	2000
Central and Eastern Europe		Israel	1982, 2003	Paraguay	1994
		Jordan	1995	Peru	2009
Albania	2004	Kenya	2002–03	Uruguay	1994
Armenia	1995	Kuwait	1990, 1995–6	USA	1969
Azerbaijan	1996	Lebanon	in development	Venezuela	1976
Belarus	1992	Lesotho	2003		
Bosnia and Herzeg.	2003	Liberia	2003	**Asia**	
Bulgaria	2002, 2009	Madagascar	1997, 2004	Afghanistan	2007
Croatia	2006	Malawi	1997 (guidance)	Bangladesh	1995
Czech Rep.	1991, 2001	Mali	2008	Bhutan	2000
Estonia	1993, 2005	Mauritania	2004 (partial)	Cambodia	1999 (partial)
Georgia	2002	Mauritius	2002	China	2002
Hungary	2005	Morocco	2003	Hong Kong	1998
Kazakhstan	1997	Mozambique	1998	India	1994
Kosovo	2009	Namibia	2011	Indonesia	1999
Kyrgyzstan	1997	Niger	1998	Japan	1997
Latvia	2004	Nigeria	1992	Korea	1977–2000
Lithuania	1996–2005	Oman	1982, 2001	Lao PDR	2000
Macedonia	2005	Palestinian Auth.	2000	Malaysia	1987
Moldova	1996	Rwanda	2005	Mongolia	1998
Montenegro	2005	Qatar	2002	Nepal	1997
Poland	1990–2008	Senegal	2001	Pakistan	1997, 2000
Romania	1995	Seychelles	1994	Papua New Guinea	1978 (partial)
Russian Fed.	2000 (partial)	Sierra Leone	2008	Philippines	2003
Serbia	2004	South Africa	1997	Sri Lanka	1988
Slovakia	1994	Swaziland	2002	Taiwan	1994–2003
Slovenia	1996	Syria	2002, 2008	Thailand	1992
Tajikistan	2006	Tanzania	2004–05	Vietnam	1994
Turkey	1983, 1997	Togo	1988		
Turkmenistan	2001	Tunisia	1988, 1991	**Australia et al.**	
Ukraine	1995	Uganda	1998	Antarctica	1991
Uzbekistan	2000	United Arab Em.	1993, 2009	Australia	1999
		Yemen	1995	New Zealand	1991
		Zambia	1997		
		Zimbabwe	1997 (partial)		

Note: This list represents, to the best of our knowledge, the current status of original EIA legislation worldwide, but we cannot confirm its accuracy. Many EIA regulations have been updated or fine-tuned since the last edition of this book, and in other cases specific EIA regulations have supplemented more general framework regulations. This accounts for many of the changes in this list since 2005.

Sources: Badr 2009; CISDL 2009; Economic Commission for Africa 2005; World Bank 2006; and many other Internet sites and journal articles.

Figure 10.1

Evolution of EIA systems

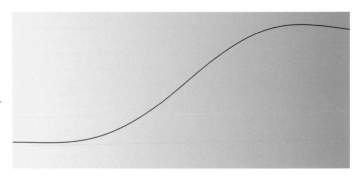

Number
of
EIAs/year

| Early EIAs, often donor funded | EIA regulations/ guidance enacted, increasing EIAs, quality variable | EIA mainstream, fine-tuning of regulations/ guidance |

Figure 10.2

Current status of EIA systems worldwide

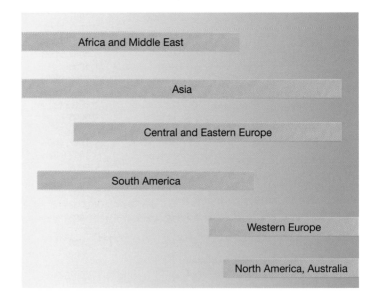

Africa and Middle East

Asia

Central and Eastern Europe

South America

Western Europe

North America, Australia

| Early EIAs, often donor funded | EIA regulations/ guidance enacted, increasing EIAs, quality variable | EIA mainstream, fine-tuning of regulations/ guidance |

might hold back economic development and lack of political will (e.g. Appiah-Opoku 2005; Kakonge 1999). Even where EIA legislation exists, this does not mean that it is put into practice, is carried out well, involves the public or is enforced (Okaru and Barannik 1996). As such, while some African countries such as Benin, the Seychelles and Tunisia have good regulations and considerable EIA practice, others such as Burundi and Guinea-Bissau remain on the far left of Figure 10.2.

Almost all countries in *South and Central America* have some form of legal system for environmental protection, including at least aspects of EIA. These systems vary widely, reflecting the countries' diverse political and economic systems: average income in some South American countries is more than ten times that in others. In general, the development of EIA in South America has been hampered by political instability, inefficient bureaucracy, economic stagnation and external debt (Brito and Verocai 1999). This may be changing recently – our example of Peru is an example of this – but EIA in South America is often still carried out centrally, with little or no public participation, and often after a project has already been authorized (Glasson and Salvador 2000).

Environmental impact assessment in *Asia* also varies widely, from very limited legislation (e.g. Cambodia) through to extensive experience with robust EIA regulation set within the context of SEA (e.g. Hong Kong). EIA regulations were established in many Asian countries in the late 1980s, and EIA is practised in all countries of the region through the requirements of donor institutions. On the other hand, Briffett (1999) suggests that many Asian EIAs are of poor quality, with poor scoping and impact prediction, and limited public participation. This is due in part to the perception that EIA may retard economic growth – symbolized by the wish, in some countries, to expose large buildings and infrastructure projects to show off the country's wealth (Briffett 1999). Many countries, like our case study of China, are in the process

of revising their early EIA systems in an attempt to deal with these problems.

Since the late 1980s, the *Central and Eastern European* countries ('countries in transition') have been going through the enormous change from centrally planned to market systems. This has included, in many cases, a move from publicly to privately owned enterprises. Many of these countries' economies were based on heavy industry, with concomitant high use of energy and resources, and many went through an economic crisis in the 1990s. Of the countries in transition, the Central and Eastern European countries have achieved (e.g. Poland) or are aiming towards (e.g. Turkey) EU accession, and are harmonizing their EIA legislation with the European EIA Directives. The Newly Independent States of the former Soviet Union all had similar systems, based on the 'state ecological expertise/review system' developed under the former Soviet Union. The countries of southeast Europe – Albania, Bosnia Herzegovina, Croatia, Yugoslavia and Macedonia – had relatively undeveloped EIA systems. The move from these

---

- In countries in or near tropical areas, environmental models, data requirements and standards from temperate regions may not apply.

- Socio-cultural conditions, traditions, hierarchies and social networks may be very different.

- The technologies used may be of a different scale, vintage and standard of maintenance, bringing greater risks of accidents and higher waste coefficients.

- Perceptions of the significance of various impacts may differ significantly.

- The institutional structures within which EIA is carried out may be weak and disjointed, and there may be problems of understaffing, insufficient training and know-how, low status and a poor co-ordination between agencies.

- EIA may take place late in the planning process and may thus have limited influence on project planning, or it may be used to justify a project.

- Development and aid agencies may finance many projects, and their EIA requirements may exert considerable influence.

- EIA reports may be confidential, and few people may be aware of their existence.

- Public participation may be weak, perhaps as a result of the government's (past) authoritarian character, and the public's role in EIA may be poorly defined.

- Decision-making may be even less open and transparent, and the involvement of funding agencies may make it quite complex.

- EIAs may be poorly integrated with the development plan.

- Implementation and regulatory compliance may be poor, and environmental monitoring limited or non-existent.

Box 10.2 Factors affecting the implementation of EIA in developing countries

systems to one aligned with the EIA Directives accounts for many of the recent EIA regulations in that region.

Box 10.2 summarizes some of the factors that affect the application of EIA in developing countries.

The EIA systems of *Western European* countries have already been amended at least twice, accounting for a multiplicity of EIA regulations in each Member State: Directive 85/337 was amended by Directives 97/11 and 2003/35/EC, and some countries already had EIA systems in place before the original Directive of 1985. A recent review of the status of EIA in EU Member States (GHK 2010) showed that EIAs are being carried out in all 27 European Member States, including the 12 'new' Member States, with a total of about 16,000 EIAs being carried out each year by the EU-27; and there has been a general increase in the number of EIAs carried out each year. However, even after three rounds of harmonization, EIA practice still varies widely across Europe.

Environmental impact assessment procedures in *North America, Australia* and *New Zealand* are still among the strongest in the world, with good provisions for public participation, consideration of alternatives and consideration of cumulative impacts. Several have separate procedures for federal and state/provincial projects. However, several of these systems are in the process of being streamlined – some would say weakened – in response to the economic recession and perceived problems of over-complexity and ponderousness.

The following sections discuss the EIA systems of different countries worldwide as examples of the concepts discussed above.

· ·

10.3 Benin

Benin, in West Africa, was once covered by dense tropical rainforest behind a coastal strip. This has largely been cleared and replaced by palm trees. Grasslands predominate in the drier north. Benin's main exports are cotton, crude oil, palm products and cocoa. Even compared to other nearby countries, Benin has a relatively low GDP per capita. However, it has had a fully functioning EIA

system since 1995, and was identified as one of three francophone African countries that is most advanced in EIA terms (d'Almeida 2001). Its EIA system is characterized by transparency, public participation, integration of environmental concerns with national planning and robust administrative and institutional tools (Baglo 2003).

Like many other African countries, Benin's early EIAs were carried out at the behest of funding institutions such as the World Bank and African Development Bank. Benin's constitution of December 1990 placed particular emphasis on environmental protection, and in 1993 the Environmental Action Plan was adopted. In 1995 the Benin Environmental Agency was created and made responsible for, *inter alia*, implementing national environmental policy, conducting and evaluating impact studies, preparing State of the Environment reports and monitoring compliance with environmental regulations. Although the Agency reports to the Ministry of the Environment, Habitat and Town Planning, it has corporate status and financial independence. The Agency subsequently developed regulations on EIA in 2001, as well as a range of EIA guides (e.g. on projects that require EIA, EIA for gas pipelines and irrigation projects; Baglo 2003). Benin also has a national association of EIA professionals.

Benin's EIA process is led by the Benin Environmental Agency. Although this has only two officers responsible for EIA, it can also draw on a forum of experts from public and private institutions to prepare or review specific EIAs. This approach allows the Agency to operate with minimal staff, ensures ongoing cooperation with other institutions and puts into practice the principle of broad participation in decision-making (Baglo 2003).

Figure 10.3 summarizes Benin's EIA process, which consists of:

- screening: this work is decentralized, with responsibility allocated to the ministries responsible for the proposed project's sector;
- project registration, scoping, and development of terms of reference for the EIA;
- preparation of a draft EIS, and 'publication' of the report primarily through the radio and non-government organizations (NGOs);
- if necessary, a public hearing to discuss the EIS, arranged by the Minister of Environment

through the creation of ad hoc Public Hearing Commissions;

- review of the EIS by the Agency: where the EIS is adequate, the Agency issues a certificate of environmental conformity;
- decision about the project by the ministry responsible for the sector concerned, taking into account the notice of environmental compliance, technical feasibility study and economic feasibility study; and
- follow-up assessment and audit.

Between 1997 and 2002, 78 EIAs were reviewed and 61 EISs were validated with certificates of environmental conformity (Yaha 2007). Projects that have been subject to EIA in Benin include livestock development projects, road improvements, drainage improvement in Cotonou following the 2010 floods, expansion of the Ouesse landfill site, urban and industrial development projects, and the West African Gas Pipeline. These have been paid for through a mixture of donor (e.g. World Bank), private and national government funds.

Environmental impact assessment practice in Benin, as in many other African countries, is limited by poor collaboration between some key ministries, a low level of public environmental awareness, illiteracy and poverty. Early problems with lack of indigenous expertise have been reduced through a range of EIA training courses run by the Benin Environmental Agency, the activities of its national association of EIA professionals and its participation in pan-African capacity-building activities (see Section 10.2).

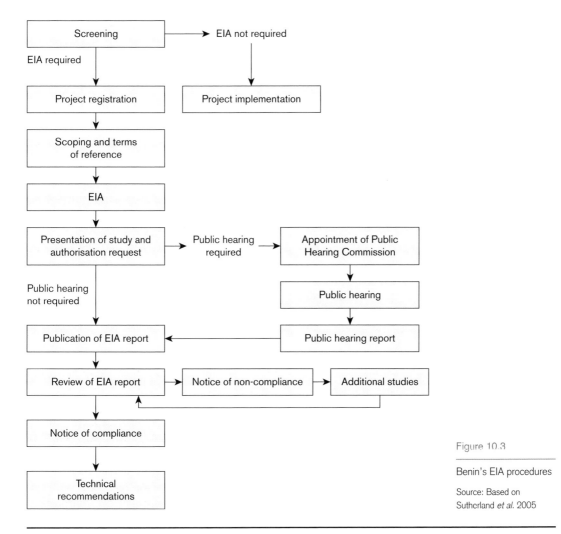

Figure 10.3

Benin's EIA procedures

Source: Based on Sutherland *et al.* 2005

10.4 Peru

Peru, the third largest country in South America, includes a thin dry strip of land along the coast, the fertile sierra of the Andean foothills and uplands, and the Amazon basin. Fishing, agriculture and mining are the main industries. A change in government in 1990 led to the reconstruction of the country after years of economic difficulties, and an extensive privatization programme – including the privatization of many of the state-owned mines – encouraged dramatic increases in foreign investment.

In September 1990, the Peruvian government enacted Decree 613–90, the Code of Environment and Natural Resources. This established EIA as a mandatory requirement for any major development project, but did not specify the EIA contents or legal procedures. The Ministry of Energy and Mining was the first ministry to put this decree into practice through Supreme Decree 016–93-EM, followed in 1994 and 1995 by separate but similar requirements by the ministries for fishing, agriculture, transport and communication, housing and building. Early indications were that EIS quality was quite high, but the discussions of mitigation measures were weak (Iglesias 1996), and public participation was limited.

Law 27,446 of 2001 – reaffirmed in October 2009 through Supreme Decree 019–2009-MINAM – replaced this disparate system of EIA with a unified national system that also applies to policies, plans and programmes. The remainder of this section focuses on this new system.

Annex II of Supreme Decree 019–2009-MINAM lists a wide range of projects and plans that require assessment, under headings that represent the relevant competent authority (e.g. agriculture ministry, energy and mining ministry). Any developer whose project is listed in Annex II, including modifications to pre-existing projects if these will have significant impacts, must prepare a preliminary evaluation. This includes details about the project, a plan for citizen participation, a brief description of the project's possible environmental impacts and mitigation measures. The competent authority must decide within 30 days whether the project is Category I (minor environmental impacts), II (moderate impacts), or III (significant impacts). An annex in the Supreme Decree lists the criteria that competent authorities must use in making this judgement: they include factors relating to human health, natural resources, designated areas, biodiversity and its components, and people's lifestyles.

If the project is Category I, then the preliminary evaluation becomes a 'declaration of environmental impact' and no further action is required. If, instead, the project is Category II or III, it requires, respectively, a semi-detailed or detailed EIS. The Supreme Decree details what information these EISs must contain, including an executive summary, project description, baseline data, information on how the public and statutory consultees were involved and any comments made at public meetings, impact assessment including comparison with environmental standards, and environmental management, contingency and closure plans. Only organizations on a register of institutions managed by the national environmental agency are allowed to prepare EISs. All EISs are public documents. The Supreme Decree supports public involvement in the EIA process but does not mandate specific techniques for this.

Once the EIS has been prepared, the developer submits it to the competent authority, who then has 40 (Category II) or 70 (Category III) days in which to review it and, if appropriate, consult the public on it. If necessary, the developer then has a limited time to comment on the review and provide further evidence, with a further 20 day resolution process. The EIA review process should take no longer than 30 days in total for Category I, 90 days for Category II and 120 days for Category III projects. At the end of the process, the competent authority can either provide or refuse to provide a certificate of EIS. Developers may only apply for other licenses or permits, and may only start project construction if they have received a certificate of EIS. The certificate also sets out specific obligations to prevent or mitigate potential environmental impacts.

Once a project is approved, the developer must carry out programmes of management, control and monitoring throughout the operations to ensure that the environmental management plan is adhered to. The environmental management plan, contingency plan, community relations plan, and/or decommissioning plan (as appropriate) must be updated five years after the project becomes operational, to ensure that they remain relevant and up to date.

Strengths of this new system include:

- The certificate system, which aims to deal with past problems of EISs in Peru being frequently prepared after the project construction has begun (Brito and Verocai 1999).
- The detailed requiremens for Category II and III EISs, which should help to ensure that the EISs are of good quality and provide the information necessary for the competent authorities to make informed decisions.
- The clearly stated and relatively limited time period for EIS review, which should prevent EISs from slowing down needed development.
- The emphasis on impact management, contingency planning and monitoring, which should help to ensure that project impacts are effectively managed.
- Weaknesses include the fact that the competent authorities charged with promoting certain types of development are also those that provide EIS certificates for those developments, leading to a potential 'poacher–gamekeeper' situation; and the lack of clear, forceful requirements for public participation in the EIA process.

10.5 China

Since 1978, China has been undergoing a rapid shift towards economic growth, decentralization of power, industrialization, private enterprise and urbanization. This has engendered many development projects with significant environmental impacts. China's EIA system has struggled to keep up, and to date has not managed to prevent some serious environmental harm (Moorman and Ge 2007). The system is still in a process of rapid evolution, with the strengthening in 2009 of its applications to plans and programmes.

EIA in China formally began with the enactment of the Provisional Environmental Protection Law of 1979, which was revised and finalized in 1989. Shortly after the law's introduction, several guidelines for its implementation were prepared, of which the central ones were the Management Rules on Environmental Protection of Capital Construction Projects of 1981. These were revised and formalized in 1986, with details on timing, funding, preparation, review and approval of EISs. Further, stronger ordinances were enacted in 1990 and December 1998, which required EIA for regional development programmes as well as individual projects, and strengthened legal liabilities and punishment for violation of EIA requirements.

At this stage, EIA still acted

> very much as a top-down administrative instrument, in response to serious environmental deterioration and external pressure from international funding organizations . . . [T]here was no preconceived notion that the public should be involved in the EIA process. (Wang *et al.* 2003)

Although tens of thousands of EISs or environmental impact forms were being prepared in China every year (Ortolano 1996), many projects that should have been subject to EIA were not, many EIAs were carried out post-construction, and the quality of EISs was variable (Mao and Hills 2002; China 1999).

Major changes to this system were brought about by the enactment of the EIA Law in October 2002. Table 10.2 lists existing EIA legislation and guidelines in China, and Figure 10.4 summarizes these new EIA procedures.

The competent authority for projects of national economic or strategic significance is the Ministry of Environmental Protection (MOEP, formerly the State Environmental Protection Agency). These projects are listed in MOEP Decree 5 and guidance of 2009, and include nuclear projects and projects crossing provincial boundaries. For projects of regional importance such as waste incinerators, smelters and chemical plants the competent authority is the provincial Environmental Protection Bureau (EPB); and for other types of project the provincial EPBs can determine whether the competent authority is the provincial, city or county/district EPBs. Usually district or county EPBs only examine EIA forms.

The EIA process begins when a developer asks the competent authority to determine whether or

Table 10.2 Chinese EIA regulations, governmental documents and guidelines

Name	Year
Regulations on Environmental Management of Construction Projects (State Council Decree 253)	1998
Circular on Relevant Issues of Executing EIA for Construction Projects (107 SEPA 1999)	1999
Forms for Environmental Impact Form and Environmental Impact Registration Form (draft) (178 SEPA 1999)	1999
Acceptance of Construction Project Environmental Protection Management Regulation (SEPA Decree 13)	2001
Law of the People's Republic of China on EIA (Presidential Decree 77)	2002
Provisions on Examination and Approval Procedure for EIA Documents of Construction Projects by the SEPA (SEPA Decree 29)	2005
Circular of Printing and Distributing 'Provisional Regulation for Public Participation in EIA' (28 SEPA 2006)	2006
Classified Directory for EIA of Construction Projects (MOEP Decree 2)	2008
Announcement on the Catalogue of Construction Projects with EIA Documents Directly Examined and Approved by the MOEP and Catalogue of Construction Projects with EIA Documents Examined and Approved by Provincial Environmental Bureaus as Entrusted by the MOEP (MOEP Announcement 7)	2009
Provision of Approval of EIA for Construction Projects by Categories (MOEP Decree 5)	2009

Source: Yang, personal communication

not a proposed action requires full EIA. As in Peru, three different levels of EIA apply in China. Projects with major potential environmental impacts require a full EIS, those with more limited impacts require an environmental impact form, and those with minimal impacts require only an environmental impact registration form with no further data provision. MOEP Decree 2 specifies what kind of EIA is needed for different projects, based on the project's impacts and the sensitivity of the receiving environment.

The competent authority personnel, sometimes assisted by outside experts, conduct a preliminary study and then makes a ruling. If an EIA is needed, the competent authority identifies those factors most likely to affect the environment and prepares a brief. The EIS's preparation is then entrusted to licensed, state-approved experts, who work to the brief. The expert analyses the relevant impacts and proposes mitigation measures. An EIS is then produced, which, according to the guidelines, needs to discuss:

- the general legislative background;
- the proposed project, including materials consumed and produced;
- the baseline environmental conditions and the surrounding area;

- the short-term and long-term environmental impacts of the project;
- impact significance and acceptability;
- a cost–benefit analysis of the environmental impacts;
- proposals for monitoring; and
- conclusions.

The public is to be given an opportunity to comment prior to the completion of a draft EIS, although the form of public participation is not prescribed. The organization that prepares the EIS must formally consider the opinions of relevant stakeholders, experts and the public, and include in the EIS their reasons for accepting or rejecting these opinions.

The EIS or environmental impact form is submitted to the competent authority, which checks the proposal against relevant environmental protection regulations and plans, confirms whether the area has the carrying capacity to cope with the project, considers whether the proposed mitigation measures are likely to be effective, and takes into account the comments of relevant experts before making a decision. For a controversial project, and projects that cross provincial boundaries, the document is submitted to the higher authority for examination and approval. If the project is

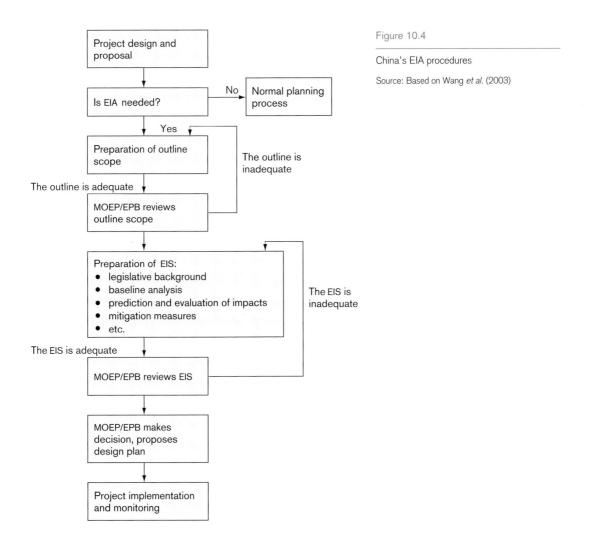

Figure 10.4

China's EIA procedures

Source: Based on Wang *et al.* (2003)

Project design and proposal

Is EIA needed? — No → Normal planning process

Yes

Preparation of outline scope

The outline is inadequate

The outline is adequate

MOEP/EPB reviews outline scope

Preparation of EIS:
- legislative background
- baseline analysis
- prediction and evaluation of impacts
- mitigation measures
- etc.

The EIS is inadequate

The EIS is adequate

MOEP/EPB reviews EIS

MOEP/EPB makes decision, proposes design plan

Project implementation and monitoring

approved, conditions for environmental protection may be included, such as monitoring and verification procedures. The competent authority must submit a report that states how the project will be carried out and how any required environmental protection measures will be implemented. Once this has been approved by the provincial authorities, a certificate of approval is issued.

The changes post-2002 certainly aimed to redress many of the problems of China's earlier EIA system. Developers are not permitted to begin construction until they have carried out EIA. The MOEP has used the law as the basis for carrying out several 'environmental storms' that have stopped projects whose construction had started before their EIA reports were approved. MOEP also announced in 2007 that no new projects would be approved in several cities with low environmental capacity to handle more pollutants (Yang 2008).

However, there is still often a conflict of interest between development-oriented local governments and the environmental protection agencies that they fund, and between people's priorities for environmental growth for improvement of their living standards. As such, local authorities are often unwilling to antagonize local leaders who strongly favour the proposed project, or impose constraints in the form of EIA (Mao and Hills 2002; Lindhjem *et al.* 2007). China's EIA process also continues to be criticized for its complexity, narrow historic focus on air, water and soil pollution, relatively low requirements for public participation, and lack of consideration of alternatives (Lindhjem *et al.* 2007; Wang *et al.* 2003; Yang 2008).

10.6 Poland

Poland, like other countries in transition, has undergone a rapid evolution in environmental policy, which is reflected in its EIA legislation and system.

In the latter days of communism, the communist regime was providing only the most basic services and environmental issues were being virtually ignored (Fisher 1992). Several areas of Poland were subject to severe pollution, causing widespread concern. In response to this, the government enacted the Environmental Protection Act (EPA) in 1980. This was subsequently strengthened through various amendments, the Land Use Planning Act of 1994, and an executive order of 1990 on developments exceptionally harmful to the environment. Under this system, an EIA began when a developer asked a local environmental authority whether an EIA was needed. If it was, the authority drew up a list of suitable consultants to carry out the work. Once the chosen consultant had completed the EIS, consultation with the public might be carried out but was not mandatory. If the EIS was accepted by the environmental authority, then the local planning authority could issue a 'location indication,' which listed alternative locations for the project. Based on this, the developer chose a site and continued to design the project, and the environmental consultants prepared a final EIS. The developer delivered the EIS along with a planning application to the local planning authority, which again consulted with the local environmental authority before making a decision about the project. Construction consent required yet a third EIS to accompany the technical design of the project.

This system was criticized for lacking screening criteria, being cumbersome and redundant with multiple EISs prepared for each project, having minimal procedures for public participation and for resource constraints on the commission that reviewed the EISs (Jendroska and Sommer 1994). It also could not deal with the huge social and economic changes that Poland went through after the overthrow of the Communist regime in late 1989:

There are no more economic plans and central planners, the currency is convertible and the best technology accessible, and the whole economy is being privatised. Moreover, administrative arrangements have been redesigned in order to create a strong central agency as an environmental watchdog ... [but] old industry is still operating. The observed improvement of environmental records since 1989 is only a side effect of the recession ... EIA law in Poland still reflects two characteristic features of the Communist regime: an aversion to getting the general public involved in decision-making, and a reluctance to developing procedural rules for dispute settlement. This means that this legislation not only is not efficient enough from the 'environmental' point of view, but also does not match the political and economic transformation towards an open and democratic society and a free market. (Jendroska and Sommer 1994)

In 1994, Poland became an associate partner of the EU, and it formally joined the EU in 2004. This process has required Poland to incrementally change its laws and statutes to progressively bring them in line with those of the EU. This process began with 1995 and 1998 amendments to the executive orders of 1990, and subsequently continued with three key EIA regulations: the 2000 Act on Access to Information on the Environment and its Protection and on EIA; the 2001 Environmental Protection Law (EPL), and the pithily named 2008 Act on Providing Information on the Environment and Environmental Protection, Public Participation in Environmental Protection and on Environmental Impact Assessment, which replaces the EPL.

Changes made over time to Poland's original EIA system include application of EIA to a wider range of projects; new requirements for screening, including two lists of projects requiring EIA that reflect Annexes I and II of the EIA Directive; greater emphasis on scoping; greater requirements for public consultation; requirements for transboundary impact assessment; and a concerted attempt to shift the emphasis of EIA from the preparation of a report to the process as a whole (Wiszniewska *et al.* 2002; Woloszyn 2004).

The new system is relatively typical of EIA in the EU, but includes some interesting variants (PIFIA 2008; EC 2009):

- It integrates the Habitat Directive's requirements for appropriate assessment into the EIA process. EIA is required not only for the equivalent to EIA Directive Annex I projects and Annex II projects that are likely to have significant environmental impacts, but also for projects that require appropriate assessment under the Habitat Directive. These EIAs must assess the impact of the project on Natura 2000 sites, and discuss alternatives and mitigation measures considered in relation to their impact on Natura 2000 sites.

- For projects that may have sigificant environmental impacts (Annex II equivalent), the developer must prepare an 'environmental information card' as a basis for the EIA screening stage. Where the competent authority decides that EIA is not required, the environmental information card serves as the basis for the official 'screening out' statement. Where EIA is required, the card serves as the basis for a mandatory scoping opinion.

- The EIS must include a description of analysed options, including the option favoured by the applicant, a rational alternative option, and the most advantageous option for the environment; and an analysis of probable social conflicts related to the project.

- A Decision on Environmental Conditions is required before any Annex I or II equivalent projects can get planning permission. The Decision on Environmental Conditions is based on the EIA or 'environmental information card', comments on the EIA from statutory consultees, the public, and other countries where relevant, and additional information such as land registry maps.

- If the EIA process shows that the project should be implemented according to a scenario other than that favoured by the applicant, the authorities issuing the Decision on Environmental Conditions are expected to specify that this scenario is the one that should be implemented. If the applicant does not agree to this, the authorities are expected to refuse permission for the project.

Depending on the source (EU 2009 or GHK 2010), approximately 2,200 to 4,000 EIAs are carried out in Poland every year. Of these, only a small proportion concern projects with transboundary impacts. However, because of the large initial number – GHK (2010) suggests that Poland might account for one third of all of the EIAs carried out in the 27 EU Member States – Poland has been involved in a high number of transboundary EIAs, including roads, railway lines and transmission lines. Poland has bilateral agreements with several other European Member States on applying EIA in a transboundary context, which regulate such issues as the translation of EIA documentation, timeframes, principles and formats of public participation, etc. (EU 2009).

10.7 Canada

Canada is an example of a country with a long-standing and strong EIA system that is currently in a state of flux. Canada's wealth of natural resources, which were originally plundered indiscriminately by the giant 'trusts' in coal, steel, oil and railroads, its lack of strong planning and land-use legislation, and the conflicting needs of its powerful provincial governments all prompted the development of a mechanism by which widespread environmental harm could be prevented. Canada's EIA system is characterized by a split between national and provincial procedures, quite complex routeing of different types of projects through different types of EIA processes, and innovative approaches to mediation and public participation in EIA.

Responsibility for EIA in Canada is shared between the federal and the provincial governments. The *federal* procedures apply to projects for which the government of Canada has decision-making authority. Early federal EIA guidelines were progressively strengthened throughout the 1970s and 1980s, and made legally binding in 1989. However concern over the limitations of this 'Environmental Assessment and Review Process' caused it, in turn, to be replaced in 1995 by the Canadian Environmental Assessment Act. Amendments to the act were made in 2001 and 2010. SEA of policy has been required since 1993, and SEA requirements were strengthened in 1999.

Gibson (2002) gives a useful review of the development of Canada's federal EIA system up to 2002.

The Canadian Environmental Assessment Agency (CEAA) administers the Canadian Environmental Assessment Act. An initial self-assessment by the responsible agency proposing the action determines whether the action requires EIA under the Act; that is, whether it:

- is a 'project' as defined by the Act;
- is not excluded by the Act's Exclusion List regulation;
- involves a federal authority; and
- triggers the need for an EIA under the Act.

The Exclusion List Regulation identifies projects for which EIAs are not required because their adverse environmental effects are not regarded as significant (e.g. simple renovation projects).

Once an EIA is determined to be required, a decision is made as to which of four EIA tracks to follow: screening, comprehensive study, mediation or review panel. Most projects require a 'screening' involving documentation of the project's environmental effects and recommended mitigation measures. 'Class screening' may be used to assess projects with known effects that can easily be mitigated. 'Model class screenings' provide a generic assessment of all projects within a class: the responsible authority uses a model report as a template, accounting for location- and project-specific information. 'Replacement class screenings' apply to projects for which no location – or project-specific information – is needed.

A small number of projects – typically less than one per cent – will require a fuller 'comprehensive study'. These projects are listed in the Comprehensive Study List Regulations and include, for instance, nuclear power plants, large oil and gas developments and industrial plants.

If a screening requires further review, it is referred to a mediator or review panel. Similarly, early in a comprehensive study, the Minister of the Environment must decide whether the project should continue to be assessed as a comprehensive study, or whether it should be referred to a mediator or review panel. Projects are normally referred to a mediator or review panel – essentially changing them from self-assessment by the responsible agency to independent, outside assessment –

where the significance of their impacts is uncertain, where the project is likely to cause significant adverse environmental effects and there is uncertainty about whether these are justified, or where public concern warrants it (CEAA 2003). A review panel is a group of experts approved by the Minister of the Environment, which reviews and assesses a project with likely adverse environmental impacts. The mediation option, new since 1995, is a voluntary process in which an independent mediator appointed by the Minister helps the interested parties to resolve their issues through a non-adversarial, collaborative approach to problem-solving. Very few projects go through the review panel or mediation route.

Any project requiring comprehensive study, mediation or a review panel must consider alternative means of carrying out the project, the project's purpose and its effects on the sustainability of renewable resources; and must include a follow-up programme. The responsible authority must take the results of the comprehensive study, or the mediator's or review panel's recommendations into account when making a decision on the project (CEAA 2003). Public comments must be considered at various stages of the EIA process, though it is more restricted for screenings. A participant-funding programme allows stakeholders to participate in comprehensive studies, panel reviews and mediation, and Aboriginal people have a specific consultation process (Sinclair and Fitzpatrick 2002).

The CEAA publishes many of its reports on the Web. Between 2006 and 2010, more than 22,000 federal EIAs were carried out: 99.6 per cent were screenings, but 97 comprehensive studies and 19 panel reports were also initiated during that time. The comprehensive studies included studies for pipelines, offshore oil and gas projects, mines, waste treatment centres, and decommissioning of a range of former projects (CEAA 2011).

Most of Canada's *provinces* have quite widely varying EIA regulations for projects under their own jurisdictions. These include Ontario's EA Act of 1976, very advanced at the time, but subsequently weakened in 1997; and Manitoba's sustainable development code of practice of 2001, which requires public officials to promote consideration of sustainability impacts in EIA. In early 1998, federal and provincial environment ministers signed an accord on EIA harmonization, which promotes cooperative use of existing processes to reduce duplication and inefficiency (Gibson 2002).

Concern over the duplication of functions between the federal and provincial levels, unclear leadership of EIAs where several government agencies are involved, and lengthy government processing led to changes to the Canadian Environmental Assessment Act in 2010, and to proposed regulations that would restrict the time that comprehensive studies can take. The changes to the act, which are widely perceived as weakening Canada's EIA process (e.g. Green Budget Coalition 2010), include delegation of the authority for EIA of major energy projects from the CEAA to the National Energy Board and Canadian Nuclear Safety Commission, exemption of many infrastructure projects from EIA, greater coordination functions being given to the CEAA, and powers being given to the Minister of the Environment to scope EIAs (with concerns that important impacts, or parts of projects, could be scoped out). A Parliamentary review of the Canadian Environmental Assessment Act, begun in autumn 2010, may well lead to further changes.

••

10.8 Australia and Western Australia

Like Canada, Australia also has a federal (Commonwealth) system with powerful individual states. Its environmental policies, including those on EIA, have some interesting features but are generally not as powerful as those of Canada. The Commonwealth EIA system was established as early as 1974 under the Environmental Protection (Impact of Proposals) Act. It applied only to federal activities. During the life of the Act (1974–2000) about 4,000 proposals were referred for consideration, but on average less than 10 formal assessments were carried out each year (Wood 2003). As such, the states put in place their own legislation or procedures to extend the scope of EIA to their own activities, and many of these state systems have become stronger and more effective than the national system.

Over time there has been concern about the variation in EIA procedures, and their implementation, between states in Australia and there have been attempts to increase harmonization (Australian and New Zealand Environment and Conservation Council – ANZECC 1991, 1996, 1997; see also Harvey 1998; Thomas 1998). In addition, a major review of Commonwealth EIA processes was undertaken in 1994, producing a set of very useful reports on cumulative impact and strategic assessment, social impact assessment, public participation, the public inquiry process, EIA practices in Australia and overseas comparative EIA practice (CEPA 1994). The review highlighted, among other issues, the need to reform EIA at the Commonwealth level – including a better consideration of cumulative impacts, social and health impacts, SEA, public participation and monitoring.

Following government changes and a further review of federal/state roles in environmental protection, Australia repealed its Commonwealth EIA legislation, and several other environmental statutes, to create the Environmental Protection and Biodiversity Conservation Act (EPBCA) in 1999. The EPBCA provides a lot more procedural detail than the original EIA legislation, and a range of documents has been produced to explain the processes (Environment Australia 2000). EIA is undertaken for matters of national environmental significance, defined as World Heritage properties, Ramsar wetlands, threatened and migratory species, the Commonwealth marine environment and nuclear actions. The Act promotes ecologically sustainable development; it also provides for SEA (IEMA 2002).

Padgett and Kriwoken (2001), Scanlon and Dyson (2001), and Marsden and Dovers (2002) provide early commentary on the Act and some developments in EIA and SEA in Australia. In its first year, the EPBCA did not appear to increase much the rate of Commonwealth EIA activity (Wood 2003), but by 2009–10 there had been a substantial increase to about 420 referrals in the year. The referrals were concentrated on proposals in the main resource development states of Queensland and Western Australia, and also Victoria, especially for mining and mineral exploration, and for residential development (Australian Government Department of Environment 2010). A review was undertaken of the first 10 years of operation of the EPBCA (Australian Government, Department of Environment 2009). Many positive features were noted, including: clear specification of matters of national environmental significance, the Environment Minister's role as decision-maker, public participation provisions, the explicit consideration of socio-economic issues, statutory advisory mechanisms and a strong compliance and enforcement regime. Important recommendations for change included: renaming it as the Australian Environment Act, establishing an independent Environment Commission to advise the government of project approvals, strategic assessments etc, provide for environmental performance audits, set up an Environmental Reparation Fund, and improve transparency in decision-making.

10.8.1 EIA in Western Australia

The Western Australia (WA) EIA system provides an interesting example of a good state system that includes many innovative features. Central to the success of the Western Australian system is the role of the EPA (Wood and Bailey 1994). The Environmental Protection Authority (EPA) was established by the WA Parliament as an Authority with the broad objective of protecting the State's environment and it is the independent environmental adviser that recommends to the WA government whether projects are acceptable. It is independent of political direction. The EPA determines the form, content, timing and procedures of assessment and can call for all relevant information; the advice it provides to the Minister for the Environment must be published. The EPA overrides virtually all other legislation, and the environmental decision (with conditions) is central to the authorization of new proposals. Other permits must await the environmental approval, based on the EIA.

Proposals may be referred to the EPA by any decision-making authority, the proponent, the Minister for the Environment, the EPA or any member of the public. The EPA determines the level of assessment. Until late 2010 there were five levels of assessment, the most comprehensive being the Public Environmental Review (PER) and the Environmental Review and Management Programme (ERMP). Under new procedures (WA EPA 2010), these have now been reduced to two: Assessment on Proponent Information with no public review, and Public Environmental Review with a public review period of generally 4–12 weeks. In practice this does not significantly alter

the EPA EIA procedures as the previous five levels of assessment could broadly be divided into either assessment without public review or assessment requiring a public review. Criteria for deciding the levels of assessment are set out in Table 10.3 (a).

Guidance is provided on scoping and on the content of the PER, as set out in Table 10.3 (b) and (c). The PER document is produced by the proponent, and it is subject to public review. The guidance on scoping for a PER contains interesting features, especially in relation to peer review and public consultation. The PER assessment pays particular attention to the regional setting, and seeks to highlight potential 'fatal flaws'. Waldeck et al. (2003) found that such EIA guidance influenced the practice of consultants and was perceived as effective in enhancing the outcomes of the EIA process – including increased certainty of outcome of the EIA process, and better design of proposals to meet environmental objectives from the outset.

The EPA then assesses the environmental acceptability of the proposals on the basis of the review document, public submissions, proponents' response, expert advice and its own investigations. The resulting EPA report to the Minister for the Environment pronounces on the environmental acceptability or otherwise of the proposal and on any recommended conditions to be applied to ministerial approval. Figure 10.5 provides an outline of the full procedure for PER assessment. The centrality of the EPA's review of the relevant environmental information to the Minister's decision, which itself has predominance, is the most remarkable aspect of the WA system, and one which highlights the significance of the EIA impact on decisions. The WA system also has a high level of public participation, especially in controversial EIAs. The central role of the EPA also ensures consistency.

However, the limited integration of the EIA and planning procedures and a biophysical focus to assessment have been weaker features of the WA procedures. Amendments in the mid-1990s were designed to secure better integration, improving the EIA of land-use schemes, but they did also reflect a shift of control away from the EPA to the Ministry of Planning. This was symptomatic of challenges faced by an effective system. Interestingly though, there is now provision for the EPA

Table 10.3 Some features of the Western Australian EIA system

(a) Criteria for deciding levels of assessment

For a proposal to be assessed at an API level, it must meet all of the following criteria:

- the proposal raises a limited number of significant environmental factors that can be readily managed, and for which there is an established condition-setting framework;
- the proposal is consistent with established environmental policy frameworks, guidelines and standards;
- the proponent can demonstrate that it has conducted appropriate and effective stakeholder participation; and
- there is limited, or local, interest only in the proposal.

If, based on the referral information, the EPA considers that the proposal is environmentally unacceptable, the chairman of the EPA will encourage the proponent to withdraw the referral or submit a new significantly modified proposal. The criteria for determining whether a proposal is unacceptable are set out in the Category 'B' of the accompanying Administrative Procedures (e.g. inconsistent with environmental poicy framework, likely to have significant impacts, proposal cannot be easily modified etc).

If a proposal meets *any* of the following criteria the EPA will apply a PER level of assessment:

- the proposal is of regional or WA state-wide significance;
- the proposal has several significant environmental issues or factors, some of which are considered to be complex or of a strategic nature;
- substantial and detailed assessment of the proposal is required to determine whether, and if so, how the environmental issues could be managed; or
- the level of interest in the proposal warrants a public review panel.

(b) A formal Environmental Scoping stage for PER

An Environmental Scoping Document (ESD) , designed to direct the proponent on key issues to address, and to identify impact predictions and information on the environmental setting, shall include:

- a concise description of the proposal and its environmental setting;
- the identification of the key environment factors and other environmental factors relevant to the proposal;
- the identification of the existing policy context relevant to each factor;
- the preliminary identification of the potential environmental impacts;
- a Scope of Works, setting out the proposed environmental studies and designed to identify or predict the direct and indirect environmental impacts of the proposal, including timeline for completion (the studies and investigations should be clearly linked to the identified environmental impacts and factors);
- the identification of an environmental management programme required;
- the identification of the spatial datasets, information products and databases required;
- a list of people, if necessary, proposed to provide peer review of the scope, methodologies, findings and/or conclusions of the surveys and investigations; and
- stakeholder consultation requirements.

(c) Guidance on the form and content of the assessment document for PER

The proponents should ensure that the PER document focuses on the environmental issues/factors of key significance. The document should include the following:

- a description of the proposal and alternatives considered, including alternative locations, with a view to minimizing environmental impacts;
- a description of the receiving environment, its conservation values and key ecosystem processes, and discussion of their significance in a regional setting – this should focus on those elements of the environment that may affect or be affected by the proposal;
- identification of the key issues (and list the environmental factors associated with these issues) and their potential 'fatal flaws';
- discussion and analysis of the direct and indirect impacts of the proposal, in a local and regional context, including cumulative impacts;
- findings of the surveys and investigations undertaken (and technical reports provided as appendices);
- identification of the measures proposed to mitigate significant adverse impacts;
- identification of any offsets, where appropriate, after all other steps in the mitigation sequence have been exhausted;
- environmental management programme;
- demonstration that the expectations for EIA identified elsewhere in the procedures have been carried out; and
- details of stakeholder and government agency consultation, how comments received have been responded to, and any subsequent modifications of the proposals.

Source: WA EPA 2010

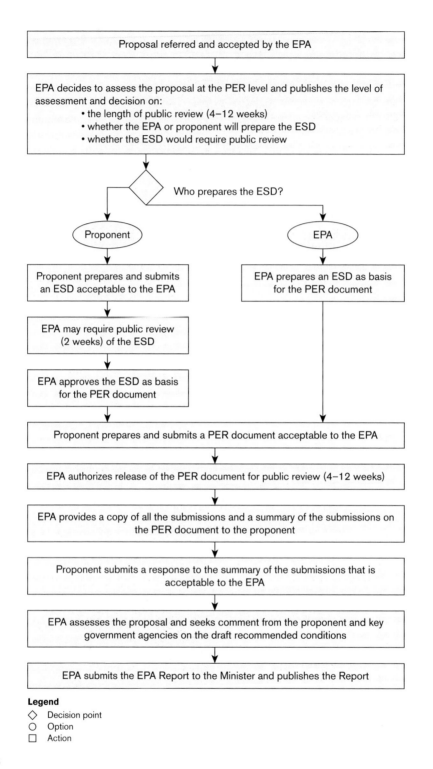

Legend

◇   Decision point
○   Option
□   Action

Figure 10.5

Outline of procedure for a PER assessment (Western Australia)

Source: Western Australia EPA (2010)

to assess strategic proposals, including policies, plans, programmes and developments. There is also provision for 'derived proposals' identified in assessed strategic proposals (which themselves have been agreed for implementation, and where environmental issues have been adequately addressed); in such cases the derived proposal would not require further assessment by the EPA except for checking on whether any implementation conditions relating to the proposal should change. With regard to socio-economic impacts, in 1993, WA lost its pioneering Social Impact Unit, which had provided expert advice on social impacts, and there is a continuing strong development lobby, in a state highly dependent on major energy and mineral projects, to further 'soften green laws'. However, for some recent high-profile and major energy and mineral developments in the north of the state, proponents and their consultants have been adopting more innovative environmental–social–economic approaches to assessment.

•••

10.9 International bodies

Many of the major international funding institutions and other international organizations have established EIA procedures. In several cases these have evolved over time, with some handbooks or guidance manuals now on their second or third edition, or with multiple updates.

The *European Bank for Reconstruction and Development*'s EIA requirements are typical of those of other lending institutions. The bank's environmental procedures of 1996 were updated in 2003 and have recently been widened out to environmental and social procedures (EBRD 2010). These aim to ensure that the environmental and social implications of potential bank-financed investment and technical co-operation projects are identified and assessed early in the bank's planning and decision-making process, and that environmental and social considerations – including potential benefits – are incorporated into the preparation, approval and implementation of projects.

The EBRD's assessment system is very much integrated into its project development process, as a process of due diligence. Main assessment steps involve:

- collection of preliminary information;
- project categorization to determine the level of EIA needed;
- impact assessment to inform due diligence considerations;
- disclosure of information; and
- characterization of environmental risks and opportunities, and risk management.

This is followed by Board approval, final negotiations and signing, implementation and monitoring (EBRD 2010).

Preliminary information includes the location of the project, historical and current land uses at the site, proposed construction activities, whether resettlement or economic displacement is likely to occur, characteristics of the local population including vulnerable groups, whether there are significant environmental and/or social issues of concern, who the main project stakeholders are, and the environmental and social reputation of the client. This information is used in screening discussions between the bank and the project sponsor to sort the proposed project into one of several categories:

- *Category A*: projects likely to cause significant adverse impacts, which, at the time of screening cannot readily be identified or assessed. A full EIA is required for these projects. Some types of projects automatically come under Category A; others are put into Category A on a case-by-case basis.
- *Category B*: projects likely to have less severe impacts than Category A projects. These require a less stringent environmental analysis. The scope of the environmental analysis is determined on a case-by-case basis.
- *Category C*: projects likely to result in minimal or no adverse impacts and that do not need analysis.
- *Category FI*: projects that will be developed through a financial intermediary. These require a variant on the EIA process discussed below.

Staff from the EBRD's Environment and Sustainability Department then establish terms of reference for the environmental and social assessment, including stakeholder engagement, and how compliance will be assessed. The client carries out these studies with support of EBRD staff. Measures to manage and mitigate a proposed project's impacts are typically set out in an Environmental and Social Action Plan. Public disclosure and consultation is required throughout the planning and assessment/analysis processes of Categories A and B projects. The EBRD sets environmental standards for each project. It may also specify an environmental and social action plan and/or monitoring to be carried out by the sponsor as a condition of investment. Prior to making a final decision about whether to lend money for the project, bank officials review the environmental due diligence information available, ensure that proposed mitigation measures are agreed with the project sponsor, highlight opportunities for environmental improvements, identify environmental monitoring requirements and any technical/environmental cooperation initiatives that should be undertaken and advise on whether the project complies with the Bank's environmental policy and procedures.

The *Asian Development Bank's Environmental Assessment Guidelines* (ADB 2003) have similar screening and assessment requirements. The guidelines give more detailed information about assessment of projects vs. programmes, a range of different sectors, equity investments, etc.; they also stress consultation.

The *World Bank* perceives EIA as one of its key environmental and social safeguard policies. Its Operational Policy/Bank Procedures 4.01 (most recently updated in 2007) require EIA for relevant lending operations, and its *Environmental assessment sourcebook* (World Bank 1991) and various updates explain the EIA process. EIA involves screening of the project into assessment categories by World Bank staff; preparation of an environmental assessment report by the proponent; review of the report by World Bank staff; an appraisal mission in which World Bank staff discuss and resolve environmental issues with the proponent; documentation of the findings; and supervision and evaluation during project implementation (World Bank 1999). Between 1989 and 1995, the World Bank screened over a thousand projects for their potential environmental impacts: of these 10 per cent were in Category A (primarily energy, agriculture and transport projects), 41 per cent in

Category B, and 49 per cent in Category C (World Bank 1997). Category A projects are those expected to have 'adverse impacts that may be sensitive, irreversible and diverse' (World Bank 1999), and they require a full EIA. For Category B projects, where impacts are 'less significant – not as sensitive, numerous, major or diverse', a full EIA is not required, but some environmental analysis is necessary. Category C projects have negligible or minimal direct disturbance on the physical setting, and neither EIA nor environmental analysis is required. Typical category C projects focus on education, family planning, health and human resource development.

Notable features of the World Bank process include a holistic environment definition, including physical, biological and socio-economic aspects, a high profile for public consultation and considerable focus on project implementation. A report (World Bank 1995) identified five main challenges ahead: moving EIA 'upstream' (into project design stages and at sectoral and regional levels); more effective public consultation; better integration of EIA into the project work programme (including mitigation, monitoring and management plans); learning from implementation (the 'feedback loop'); and engaging the private sector (especially financiers and project sponsors) to ensure that projects are subject to EIA of acceptable quality. Mercier (2003) reinforces the emphasis now placed on implementation of the mitigation, prevention and compensation measures contained in the EIA. Also, because many of the client countries now have their own EIA requirements and their own EIA staff and review mechanisms, the World Bank is increasingly involved in enhancing that capacity upfront during project preparation.

The *African Development Bank* (ADB 2003) and *European Investment Bank* (EIB 2007) have less comprehensive EIA guidance, but both require EIA to be carried out, promote public participation in the EIA process, and take account of these when deciding on whether to fund a project. The ADB guidance is for integrated environmental and social impacts.

Other organizations have also published EIA guidance. For instance UNEP's very useful *Environmental impact assessment training resources manual*, now in its second edition (UNEP 2002), includes case studies (primarily from developing countries), transparencies and detailed chapters on various stages of EIA. The UK Department for International Development and the Ministry of Foreign Affairs of Denmark have produced a similar guides (DFID 2003; Danida 2009). Of particularly increasing importance are the *Equator Principles*, based on both World Bank guidance, and on the International Finance Corporation (IFC) Performance Standards on social and environmental sustainability. Equator Principle Financial Institutions, now including over 70 major national and international banks, commit to not providing loans to projects (>US$10m value threshold) where the borrower will not, or is not able, to comply with domestic standards for EIA or international standards, whichever is the highest (IFC, 2006).

10.10 Summary

In 2002, Gibson suggested that EIA worldwide has been moving towards being:

- earlier in planning (beginning with purposes and broad alternatives);
- more open and participative (not just proponents, government officials and technical experts);
- more comprehensive (not just biophysical environment, local effects, capital projects, single undertakings);

- more mandatory (gradual conversion of policy-based to law-based processes);
- more closely monitored (by the courts, informed civil society bodies and government auditors);
- more widely applied (through law at various levels, but also in land-use planning, through voluntary corporate initiatives, and so on);
- more integrative (considering systemic effects rather than just individual impacts);
- more ambitious (overall sustainability rather than just individually 'acceptable' undertakings); and
- more humble (recognizing and addressing uncertainties, applying precaution).

Almost 10 years later, this chapter shows that these trends are still continuing a decade later. However, worldwide, EIA is still constrained by lack of political will, insufficient budget to implement proposed mitigation measures and lack of institutional capacity, as noted earlier by Goodland and Mercier (1999). Emerging trends in Canada, Australia, the Netherlands (GHK 2010) and elsewhere suggest that, even in developed countries, EIA also tends to be adapted – some might say watered down – where it is perceived to conflict with economic development.

Chapters 11 and 12 draw on some of the ideas discussed here, and elsewhere, to identify possibilities for the future, focusing primarily on the UK system, but set in the wider EU and global context.

SOME QUESTIONS

The following questions are intended to help the reader focus on the key issues of this chapter.

1   Figure 10.1 suggests that a greater number of EIAs are carried out in more evolved EIA systems than in less evolved systems. Does that, in turn, mean that one can tell how evolved a country's EIA system is on the basis of how many EIAs are carried out in that country? Explain your reasoning.

2   Compare two or three of the EIA systems described in this chapter with the UK system described at Chapter 3, or the US system of Section 2.2, in terms of:
    - which projects require EIA, and how screening is carried out;
    - what an EIS must contain;
    - who carries out the EIA;
    - public involvement; and
    - decision-making, including links to other licenses and permits.

3   Figure 10.2 suggests that more developed countries tend to have stronger EIA systems than less developed countries. However the EIA systems of Benin, Peru, China and Poland each have strong or innovative aspects that go beyond the UK or US systems. What are these aspects, and why might they have been instituted?

4   The countries discussed in this chapter have widely varying approaches to the consideration of alternatives in EIA. Which has the strongest approach? The weakest?

5   Peru and China allow only registered EIA experts to carry out EIA. What are the advantages and disadvantages of such an approach?

6   Peru's system can be criticised for having a 'poacher–gamekeeper' approach, where the ministry in charge of promoting certain projects is also responsible for the EIA process for those projects. Why is the term 'poacher–gamekeeper' used for such a scenario? Are there any other examples of 'poacher–gamekeeper' in this chapter?

7   The Western Australian EIA system is seen as one with many innovative features, which contribute to a good state system. What are these features? Are there also weaknesses?

8   Several of the international funding organisations require integrated environmental and social assessment. However individual countries' legislation focuses on environmental assessment. What might account for this discrepancy?

9   The World Bank and other funding organizations have played a key role in the application of EIA in many developing countries. What are possible reasons for these organizations' interest in EIA?

References

ADB (African Development Bank) 2003. *Integrated environmental and social impact assessment guidelines.*

ADB (Asian Development Bank) 2003. *Integrated environmental and social impact assessment guidelines.* Available at: www.adb.org.

Almagi, D., Sondo, V.A. and Ertel, J. 2007. Constraints to environmental impact assessment practice: a case study of Cameroon. *Journal of Environmental Assessment Policy and Management* 9 (3), 357–80.

ANZECC (Australia and New Zealand Environment and Conservation Council) 1991. *A national approach to EIA in Australia.* Canberra: ANZECC.

ANZECC (Australia and New Zealand Environment and Conservation Council) 1996. *Guidelines and criteria for determining the need for and level of EIA in Australia.* Canberra: ANZECC.

ANZECC (Australia and New Zealand Environment and Conservation Council) 1997. *Basis for a national agreement on EIA.* Canberra: ANZECC.

Appiah-Opoku, S. 2005. *The need for indigenous knowledge in environmental impact assessment: the case of Ghana.* New York: Edwin Mellen Press.

Australian Government Department of Environment 2009. *Independent review of the EPBC (1999) Act.* Canberra: Government of Australia.

Australian Government Department of Environment 2010. *Annual report 2009–2010.* Government of Australia.

Badr, E-S.A. 2009. Evaluation of the environmental impact asessment system in Egypt. *Impact Assessment and Project Appraisal* 27 (3), 193–203.

Baglo, M.A. 2003. *Benin's experience with national and international EIA processes.* Available at: www. ceaa.gc.ca/default.asp?lang=En&n=B4993348–1&offset=4.

Bekhechi, M.A. and J.-R. Mercier 2002. *The legal and regulatory framework for environmental impact assessments.* Available at: www.scribd.com/doc/16060372/The-Legal-and-Regulatory-Framework-for-Environmental-Impact-Assessments-A-Study-of-Selected-Countries-in-SubSaharan-Africa.

Briffett, C. 1999. Environmental impact assessment in East Asia. In *Handbook of environmental impact assessment*, J. Petts (ed), vol. 2, 143–67. Oxford: Blackwell Science.

Brito, E. and Verocai, I. 1999. Environmental impact assessment in South and Central America. In *Handbook of environmental impact assessment*, J. Petts (ed), vol. 2, Chapter 10, 183–202. Oxford: Blackwell Science.

CEAA (Canadian Environmental Assessment Agency) 2003. *Canadian environmental assessment act: an overview*. Ottawa: CEAA. www.ceaa.gc.ca.

CEAA (Canadian Environmental Assessment Agency) 2011. *Canadian environmental assessment agency*. Available at: www.ceaa.gc.ca.

CEPA 1994. *Review of Commonwealth environmental impact assessment*. Canberra: CEPA.

Chico, I. 1995. EIA in Latin America. *Environmental Assessment* 3 (2), 69–71.

China 1999 (in Chinese). *A summary of the environmental protection and management work of construction projects*. Available at: www.China-eia.com/chegxu/hpcx_main0.htm.

CISDL (Centre for International Sustainable Development Law) 2009. *Eco-health Americas law project*. Available at: www.cisdl.org/ecohealth/impact_assessment001.htm.

d'Almeida, K. 2001. *Cadre institutional législatif et réglementaire de l'évaluation environnementale dans les pays francophones d'Afrique et de l'Océan Indien*. Montréal, Canada: EIPF et Secrétariat francophone de l'AiEi/IAIA.

Danida 2009. *Danida environment guide: Environmental assessment for sustainable development*, 3rd edn. Copenhagen: Danida. Available at: www.danidadevforum.um.dk/NR/rdonlyres/3409F0D0-D7BA-4815-BF49-C7420D8DC9CF/0/DanidaGuidetoEnvironmentalAssessmentefternyAMG.pdf.

DFID (Department for International Development) 2003. *Environment guide*. London: DFID. Available at: www.eldis.org/vfile/upload/1/document/0708/DOC12943.pdf.

EBRD (European Bank for Reconstruction and Development) 2010. *Environmental and social procedures*. Available at: www.ebrd.com/downloads/about/sustainability/esprocs10.pdf.

EC (European Commission) DG ENV 2009. *Study concerning the report on the application and effectiveness of the EIA Directive*. Available at: ec.europa.eu/environment/eia/pdf/eia_study_june_09.pdf.

Economic Commission for Africa 2005. *Review of the application of environmental impact assessment in selected African countries*. Addis Ababa: ECA. www.uneca.org/eca_programmes/sdd/documents/eia_book_final_sm.pdf.

EIB (European Investment Bank) 2007. *EIB environmental assessment*. Luxembourg: European Investment Bank. Available at: www.eib.org/attachments/thematic/environmental-assessment.pdf.

El-Fadl, K. and El-Fadel, M. 2004. Comparative assessment of EIA systems in MENA countries: challenges and prospects. *Environmental Impact Assessment Review* 24 (6), 553–93.

Elliott, M. and Thomas, I. 2009. *Environmental impact assessment in Australia*, 5th edn. Annandale: The Federation Press.

Environment Australia 2000. *EPBC Act: various documents, including environmental assessment processes; administrative guidelines on significance; and frequently asked questions*. Canberra: Department of Environment and Heritage.

Fisher, D. 1992. *Paradise deferred: environmental policymaking in Central and Eastern Europe*. London: Royal Institute of International Affairs.

GHK 2010. *Collection of information and data to support the impact assessment study of the review of the EIA Directive*. Available at: www.ec.europa.eu/environment/eia/pdf/collection_data.pdf.

Gibson, R. 2002. From Wreck Cove to Voisey's Bay: the evolution of federal environmental assessment in Canada. *Impact Assessment and Project Appraisal* 20 (3), 151–60.

Glasson, J. and Salvador, N.N.B. 2000. EIA in Brazil: a procedures-practice gap. A comparative study with reference to EU, and especially the UK. *Environmental Impact Assessment Review* 20, 191–225.

Goodland, R. and Mercier, J.R. 1999. The evolution of environmental assessment in the World Bank: from 'Approval' to results, *World Bank environment department paper* no. 67, Washington, DC: World Bank.

Green Budget Coalition 2010. *Budget 2010: Environmental impact summary and analysis*. Available at: www.greenbudget.ca/pdf/Green%20Budget%20Coalition%27s%20Environmental%20Impact%20Summary%20and%20Analysis%20of%20Budget%202010%20%28July%202010%20.pdf.

Harvey, N. 1998. *EIA: procedures and prospects in Australia*. Melbourne: Oxford University Press.

IEMA (Institute of Environmental Management and Assessment) with EIA Centre (University of Manchester) 2002. *Environmental assessment yearbook* 2002. Manchester: EIA Centre, University of Manchester.

Iglesias, S. 1996. T*he role of EIA in mining activities: the Peruvian case*. MSc dissertation, Oxford Brookes University, Oxford.

International Finance Corporation (IFC) 2006. *Equator Principles*. Available at: www.equator-principles.com.

Jendroska, J. and Sommer, J. 1994. Environmental impact assessment in Polish law. the concept, development, and perspectives. *Environmental Impact Assessment Review* 14 (2/3), 169–94.

Kakonge, J.O. 1999. Environmental impact assessment in Africa. In *Handbook of environmental impact* assessment, J. Petts (ed), vol. 2, 168–82. Oxford: Blackwell Science.

Kirchhoff, D. 2006. Capacity building for EIA in Brazil: preliminary considerations and problems to be overcome. *Journal of Environmental Assessment Policy and Management* 8 (1), 1–18.

Kovalev, N., Köppel, J., Drozdov, A. and Dittrich, E. 2009. Democracy and the environment in Russia. *Journal of Environmental Assessment Policy and Management* 11 (2), 161–73.

Lee, N. and George, C. 2000. *Environmental assessment in developing and transitional countries: principles, methods and practice.* Chichester: Wiley.

Lindhjem, H., Hu, T., Ma, Z., Skjelvik, J.M., Song, G., Vennemo, H., Wu, J. and Zhang, S. 2007. Environmental economic impact assessment in China: problems and prospects. *Environmental Impact Assessment Review* 27 (1), 1–25.

Mao, W. and Hills, P. 2002. Impacts of the economic-political reform on environmental impact assessment implementation in China. *Impact Assessment and Project Appraisal* 29 (2), 101–11.

Marara, M., Okello, N., Kuhanwa, Z., Douven, W., Beevers, L. and Leentvaar, J. 2011. The importance of context in delivering effective EIA: case studies from East Africa, *Environmental Impact Assessment Review* 31 (3), 286–96.

Marsden, S. and Dovers, S. 2002. *Strategic Environmental Assessment in Australasia.* Annadale, New South Wales: Federation Press.

Mercier, J.R. 2003. Environmental assessment in a changing world at a changing world bank. In IEMA/EIA Centre 2003, *Environmental assessment outlook.* Manchester: EIA Centre, University of Manchester.

Moorman, J.L. and Ge, Z. 2007. Promoting and strengthening public particiaption in China's environmental impact assessment process: comparing China's EIA law and U.S. NEPA. *Vermont Journal of Environmental Law* 8, 281–335.

Okaru, V. and Barannik, A. 1996. Harmonization of environmental assessment procedures between the World Bank and borrower nations. In *Environmental assessment (EA) in Africa,* R. Goodland, J.R. Mercier and S. Muntemba (eds), 35–63. Washington, DC: World Bank.

Ortolano, L. 1996. Influence of institutional arrangements on EIA effectiveness in China. *Proceedings of the 16th annual conference of the international association for impact assessment,* 901–05. Estoril: IAIA.

Padgett, R. and Kriwoken, L.K. 2001. The Australian Environmental Protection and Biodiversity

Conservation Act 1999: what role for the Commonwealth in environmental impact assessment? *Australian Journal of Environmental Management* 8, 25–36.

PIFIA (Polish Information and Foreign Investment Agency) 2008. *Providing information on the environment and environmental protection, public participation in environmental protection and on environmental impact assessment.* Available at: www.paiz.gov.pl/polish_law/environmental_impact_assessment.

Rzeszot, U.A. 1999. Environmental impact assessment in Central and Eastern Europe. In *Handbook of environmental impact assessment,* J. Petts (ed), vol. 2, Chapter 7, 123–42. Oxford: Blackwell Science.

Scanlon, J. and Dyson, M. 2001. Will practice hinder principle? Implementing the EPBC Act. *Environment and Planning Law Journal* 18, 14–22.

Sinclair, A.J. and Fitzpatrick, P. 2002. Provisions for more meaningful public participation still elusive in proposed Canadian EA Bill. *Impact Assessment and Project Appraisal* 20 (3), 161–76.

Southern African Institute for Environmental Assessment 2003. *Environmental impact assessment in southern Africa.* Available at: www.saiea.com/saiea-book.

Sutherland, J.W., Agadzi, K.O. and Amekor, E.M.K. 2005. *Rationalising the environmental impact assessment procedures in ECOWAS Member Countries, Union of Producers, Transporters and Distributors of Electric Power in Africa.* Available at: www.updea-africa.org/updea/archiv/15CongresUPDEA%20EIA%20Presentation.pdf

Thomas, I. 1998. *EIA in Australia,* 2nd edn. New South Wales: Federation Press.

Unalan, D. and Cowell, R. 2009. Adoption of the EU SEA Directive in Turkey, *Environmental Impact Assessment Review* 29 (4), 243–51.

UNEP (United Nations Environment Programme) 2002. *UNEP Environmental Impact Assessment Training Resource Manual,* 2nd edn. Available at: www.unep.ch/etu/publications/EIAMan_2edition_toc.htm.

Vidyaratne, H. 2006. EIA theories and practice: balancing conservation and development in Sri Lanka. *Journal of Environmental Assessment Policy and Management* 8 (2), 205–22.

WA EPA (Western Australian Environmental Protection Authority) 2010. *Environmental impact assessment administrative procedures.* Perth: EPA.

Waldeck, S., Morrison-Saunders, A. and Annadale, D. 2003. Effectiveness of non-legal EIA guidance from the perspective of consultants in Western Australia. *Impact Assessment and Project Appraisal* 21 (3), 251–56.

Wang, Y., Morgan, R. and Cashmore, M. 2003. Environmental impact assessment of projects in the People's Republic of China: new law, old problem. *Environmental Impact Assessment Review* 23, 543–79.

Wiszniewska, B., Farr, J. and Jendroska, J. 2002. *Handbook on environmental impact assessment procedures in Poland*. Warsaw: Ministry of Environment.

Woloszyn, W. 2004. Evolution of environmental impact assessment in Poland: problems and prospects, *Impact Assessment and Project Appraisal* 22 (2), 109–19.

Wood, C. 2003. *Environmental impact assessment: a comparative review*, 2nd edn, Prentice Hall.

Wood, C. and Bailey, J. 1994. Predominance and independence in EIA: the Western Australian model. *Environmental Impact Assessment Review* 14 (1), 37–59.

World Bank 1991. *Environmental assessment sourcebook*. Washington, DC: World Bank. Available at: www.worldbank.org.

World Bank 1995. *Environmental assessment: challenges and good practice*. Washington, DC: World Bank.

World Bank 1997. *The impact of environmental assessment: a review of World Bank experience*. World Bank Technical Paper, no. 363, Washington, DC: World Bank.

World Bank 1999. *Environmental assessment*, BP 4.01, Washington, DC: World Bank.

World Bank 2002. *Environmental impact assessment systems in Europe and Central Asia Countries*. Available at: www.worldbank.org/eca/environment.

World Bank 2006. *Environmental impact assessment regulations and strategic environmental assessment requirements: practices and lessons learned in East and Southeast Asia. Environment and social development safeguard dissemination note no. 2.* Available at: www.vle.worldbank.org/bnpp/files/TF055249EnvironmentalImpact.pdf.

Yaha, P.Z. 2007. Benin: experience with results based management, in *Managing for development results*, Sourcebook 2nd edn, 131–42. Available at: www.mfdr.org/sourcebook/2ndEdition/4–5BeninRBM.pdf.

Yang, S. 2008. Public participation in the Chinese environmental impact assessment (EIA) system. *Journal of Environmental Assessment Policy and Management*, 10 (1), 91–113.

Part 4

· ·

Prospects

11 Widening the scope: strategic environmental assessment

●●

11.1 Introduction

EIA has increasingly been applied at the level of policies, plans and programmes (PPPs) as well as projects. In the USA, this so-called strategic environmental assessment (SEA) has been carried out in a relatively low-key manner since the 1970s as an extension of project EIA. In other countries, SEA roll-out has been slower but has caused more of a splash. The European SEA Directive of 2004 has led to significant changes in the planning system in some Member States, China has passed specific SEA legislation in 2009, and SEA is also a strong growth area in other parts of the world.

This penultimate chapter discusses the need for SEA and some of its limitations. It reviews the status of SEA in the USA, European Union, UNECE, and China. It then discusses in more detail how the European SEA Directive is being implemented in the UK. It concludes with the results of recent research into the effectiveness of the SEA Directive. By necessity this chapter must radically simplify many aspects of SEA. The reader is referred to Sadler *et al.* (2010) and Therivel (2010) for a more in-depth discussion. Chapter 9 presents two SEA case studies.

11.2 Strategic environmental assessment (SEA)

11.2.1 Definitions

Strategic environmental assessment can be defined as:

> a systematic process for evaluating the environmental consequences of proposed policy, plan or programme initiatives in order to ensure they are fully included and appropriately addressed at the earliest appropriate stage of decision making on par with economic and social considerations. (Sadler and Verheem 1996)

In other words, SEA is a form of EIA for PPPs, keeping in mind that evaluating environmental impacts at a strategic level is not necessarily the same as evaluating them at a project level.

Several things are important in Sadler and Verheem's definition. First, SEA is a process, not a snapshot or stapled-on addition at the end of a process. It should take place in parallel with the plan-making process, providing environmental information at all relevant stages. The definition also emphasizes the importance of integrating SEA in decision-making. Figure 11.1 shows the links between PPP-making and SEA.

Figure 11.1

Links between SEA
and the PPP-making
process

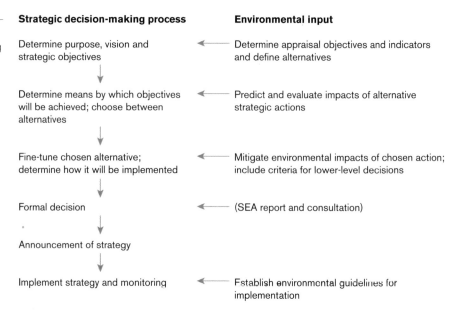

Strategic decision-making process	Environmental input
Determine purpose, vision and strategic objectives	← Determine appraisal objectives and indicators and define alternatives
Determine means by which objectives will be achieved; choose between alternatives	← Predict and evaluate impacts of alternative strategic actions
Fine-tune chosen alternative; determine how it will be implemented	← Mitigate environmental impacts of chosen action; include criteria for lower-level decisions
Formal decision	← (SEA report and consultation)
Announcement of strategy	
Implement strategy and monitoring	← Establish environmental guidelines for implementation

The definition distinguishes between policies, plans and programmes (PPPs). Although they are often lumped together in the SEA literature, PPPs are not the same things, and may require quite different forms of SEA. A policy is generally defined as an inspiration and guidance for action (e.g. 'to supply electricity to meet the nation's demands'), a plan as a set of co-ordinated and timed objectives for the implementation of the policy (e.g. 'to build X megawatts of new electricity generating capacity by 2020') and a programme as a set of projects in a particular area (e.g. 'to build four new combined cycle gas turbine power stations in region Y by 2020') (Wood 1991). PPPs can relate to specific sectors (e.g. transport, mineral extraction) or to all activities in a given area (e.g. land use, development or territorial plans).

In theory PPPs are tiered: a policy provides a framework for the establishment of plans, plans provide frameworks for programmes, programmes lead to projects. In practice, these tiers are amorphous and fluid, without clear boundaries. SEAs for these different PPP tiers can themselves be tiered, as shown in Figure 11.2, so that issues considered at higher tiers need not be reconsidered at the lower tiers. PPPs can also result in activities

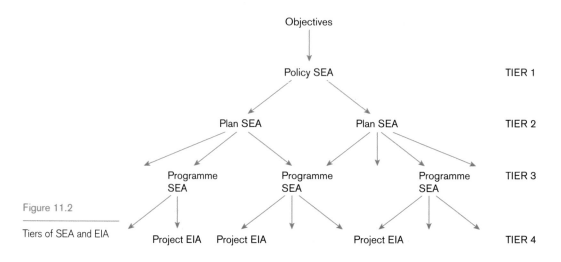

Figure 11.2

Tiers of SEA and EIA

Table 11.1 Main differences between SEA and EIA

	SEA	EIA
Nature of the action	Strategy, visions, plans	Construction/operation actions
Scale of impacts	Macro: global, national, regional	Micro: local, site
Timescale	Long to medium term	Medium to short term
Data	Mainly descriptive but mixed with quantifiable/mappable	Mainly quantifiable/mappable
Alternatives	Fiscal measures, economic, social or physical strategies, technologies, spatial balance of location	Specific alternative locations, design, timing
Assessment benchmarks	Sustainability criteria and objectives	Legal restrictions and best practice
Rigour/uncertainty	Less rigour, more uncertainty	More rigour, less uncertainty
Outputs	Broad brush	Detailed

Source: Based on Partidario (2003)

that have environmental impacts but are not development projects, such as privatization, different forms of land management, or indeed the revocation of a plan. Table 11.1 summarizes some of the major differences between EIA and SEA.

11.2.2 The need for SEA

Various arguments have been put forward for a more strategic form of EIA, most of which relate to *problems with the existing system of project EIA*. Project EIAs react to development proposals rather than anticipating them, so they cannot steer development towards environmentally robust areas or away from environmentally sensitive sites.

Project EIAs do not adequately consider the cumulative impacts caused by several projects, or even by one project's subcomponents or ancillary developments.[1] For instance, small individual mineral extraction operations may not need an EIA, but the total impact of several of these projects may well be significant. Section 9.5 provides another example. At present in most countries there is no legal requirement to prepare comprehensive cumulative impact statements for projects of these types.

Project EIAs cannot consider the impacts of potentially damaging actions that are not regulated through the approval of specific projects. Examples of such actions can include farm management practices, privatization and new technologies such as genetically modified organisms. Project

EIAs do not consider how much total development of a particular type is needed, and so they do not consider whether a given project is required at all. They also cannot fully address alternative types/modes and locations for developments, or the full range of possible mitigation measures, because these alternatives will often be limited by choices made at an earlier, more strategic level. In many cases a project will already have been planned quite specifically, and irreversible decisions taken at the strategic level, by the time an EIA is carried out.

Project EIAs often have to be carried out very quickly because of financial constraints and the timing of planning applications. This limits the amount of baseline data that can be collected and the quality of analysis that can be undertaken. For instance, the planning periods of many projects may require their ecological impact assessments to be carried out in the winter months, when it is difficult to identify plants and when many animals either are dormant or have migrated. The amount and type of public consultation undertaken in project EIA may be similarly limited.

By being carried out early in the decision-making process and encompassing all the projects or actions of a certain type or in a certain area, SEA can ensure that alternatives are better assessed, cumulative impacts are considered, the public is better consulted, and decisions about individual projects are made in a proactive rather than reactive manner.

Strategic environmental assessment can also help to *promote sustainable development*. In the UK, for instance, SEA is often expanded or integrated into sustainability assessment/appraisal. This not only involves broadening the scope of assessment to also consider social and economic issues, but also potentially setting sustainability objectives and testing whether the PPP will help to achieve them. In other words, sustainability assessment can test whether the PPP helps to promote a sustainability vision.

11.2.3 Problems with SEA

In the early days of SEA, lack of experience and appropriate techniques limited the quality of SEAs. As SEA practice has evolved, these problems have eased but others have emerged.

First, many PPPs are nebulous, and they evolve in an incremental and unclear fashion, so there is no clear time when their environmental impacts can be best assessed: 'the dynamic nature of the policy process means issues are likely to be redefined throughout the process, and it may be that a series of actions, even if not formally sanctioned by a decision, constitute policy' (Therivel *et al.* 1992). In practice, SEAs are often started late in the plan-making process, when major decisions have already been made. Second, where SEA is required only for programmes and/or plans but not policies, as is the case with the European SEA Directive, an environmentally unfriendly policy can lead to environmentally unfriendly plans: in such a case, the plan-level SEA can at best mitigate the plan's negative impacts, not consider more sustainable policy level alternatives.

Third, and as noted in Chapter 1, strategic levels of assessment of plans and programmes should provide useful frameworks for the more site specific project assessments, hopefully reducing workload and leading to more concise and effective EIAs. But the anticipated tiered relationship has proved to be more in theory than practice, leading to unnecessary and wasteful duplication of activity. Fourth, multiple PPPs often affect a single area or resource. For instance, energy and transport PPPs – and many others – affect climate change. Waste and minerals PPPs are often integrally interconnected, as are land-use and transport PPPs. As such, it is often difficult to assess a PPP on its own.

There has also been considerable uncertainty about whether SEA should be broadened out to also cover social and economic issues. Considering environmental issues separately from social and economic issues may give them an additional 'weight' in decision-making and helps to keep the integrity of the environmental assessment. On the other hand, sustainability appraisal (SA) more closely reflects actual decision-making, and is legally required for many UK PPPs anyway, so integrating the two procedures makes sense in terms of efficiency.

Finally, and most importantly, policy making is a political process. Decision-makers will weigh up the implications of a PPP's environmental impacts in the wider context of their own interests and those of their constituents. SEA does not make the final decision: it merely (sometimes maddeningly so) informs it.

11.3 SEA worldwide

Despite these problems, SEA has been increasingly carried out worldwide. For instance, the USA, European Union Member States, and China have all established SEA regulations; Canada requires SEA by cabinet decision; South Africa has guidance on SEA; and SEAs are regularly carried out in Hong Kong and elsewhere. This section discusses the SEA systems of the USA, the EU and UNECE because they are well developed and demonstrate a range of possible approaches. They differ in terms of whether they require or just encourage the preparation of SEAs; the types of strategic actions that require SEA; whether the SEAs consider only environmental issues or the full range of sustainability considerations; and the level of detail that they go into.

11.3.1 The USA

The USA has no separate SEA regulations. Instead, the National Environmental Policy Act of 1969 requires that

> all agencies of the Federal Government shall include in every recommendation or report on proposals for legislation and other major

Federal *actions* significantly affecting the quality of the human environment, a detailed statement by the responsible official on

- the environmental impact of the proposed action;
- any adverse environmental effects that cannot be avoided should the proposal be implemented;
- alternatives to the proposed action;
- the relationship between local short-term uses of man's environment and the maintenance and enhancement of long-term productivity; and
- any irreversible and irretrievable commitments of resources that would be involved in the proposed action should it be implemented. (42 USC §4332)

The term 'federal actions' has been interpreted through Council on Environmental Quality regulations (CEQ 1978) as meaning 'new and continuing activities, including projects and programs entirely or partly financed, assisted, conducted, regulated, or approved by federal agencies; new or revised agency rules, regulations, plans, policies, or procedures; and legislative proposals'. For such PPPs, federal agencies must prepare up to three stages of progressively more detailed assessment, until they can show that the next stage is not needed: (1) an intial analysis that includes a test of 'categorical exclusion' (a previous determination that the action would not result in significant environmental impacts); (2) environmental assessment; and (3) programmatic environmental impact statement (PEIS). If the environmental assessment stage determines that the action would not require a full PEIS, it instead concludes with a finding of no significant impact (FONSI) or a 'mitigated FONSI,' which shows that, with mitigation, the action would not have significant environmental impacts.

Hundreds of PEISs have been prepared to date under the NEPA, although these form only a small percentage of all the assessments carried out in the USA. Recent PEISs include those for wind energy development on western public lands (Bureau of Land Management), solar energy development in six southwestern states (Office of Energy Efficiency and Renewable Energy and others), radioactive

waste management (Department of Energy), and restoration of the impacts of the Deepwater Horizon oil spill (National Oceanic and Atmospheric Administration and others).

Only a few of the USA's 50 states have SEA regulations. Of these, the SEA system established by the California Environmental Quality Act of 1986 (State of California 1986) is the most well developed. 'Program environmental impact reports' (PEIRs) are required for series of actions that can be characterized as one large project and are related geographically, as logical parts in a chain of contemplated actions, in connection with the issuance of rules or regulations, or as individual activities carried out under the same authority and having generally similar environmental effects (CEQA 15168). Like project EIAs, PEIRs must include a description of the action, a description of the baseline environment, an evaluation of the action's impacts, a reference to alternatives, an indication of why some impacts were not evaluated, the organizations consulted, the responses of these organizations to the EIS and the agency's response to the responses.

In conjunction with the 40th anniversary of NEPA, the Council on Environmental Quality prepared draft guidance on aspects of SEA that they felt needed to be modernised and strengthened: when and how Federal agencies must consider greenhouse gas emissions and climate change in their proposed actions; the appropriateness of FONSIs and when environmental mitigation commitments need to be monitored; the use of categorical exclusions; and enhanced public tools for reporting on NEPA activities (CEQ 2010).

11.3.2 European Union and UNECE

It was initially intended that one European Directive would cover projects and PPPs, but by the time that Directive 85/337 was approved in 1985, its application was restricted to projects only. After 25 years of discussion and negotiations between the European Member States, the European Commission finally agreed on Directive 2001/42/EC 'on the assessment of the effects of certain plans and programmes on the environment' (EC 2001) on 21 July 2001. The full text of the Directive is given in Appendix 3. The Directive became operational on 21 July 2004. Like the EIA

Directive, the SEA Directive does not have a direct effect in individual European Member States, but instead needs to be interpreted into regulations in each Member State. Section 11.4 discusses how this has been done in England.

Directive 2001/42/EC requires SEA for plans and programmes (not policies) that:

1   are subject to preparation and/or adoption by an authority *and*
2   are required by legislative, regulatory or administrative provisions *and*
3   are likely to have significant environmental effects *and*
4   (a) are prepared for agriculture, forestry, fisheries, energy, industry, transport, waste management, water management, telecommunications, tourism, TC&P or land use *and* set the framework for development consent of projects listed in the EIA *or*
     (b) in view of the likely effect on sites, require an appropriate assessment under the Habitats Directive *or*
     (c) are other plans and programmes determined by Member States to set the framework for future development consent of projects.

Box 11.1 summarizes the SEA Directive's requirements. Draft plans and programmes must be accompanied by an 'environmental report' that discusses the current baseline, the likely effects of the plan or programme and reasonable alternatives, how the negative effects have been minimized and proposed monitoring arrangements. The public must be consulted on the proposed plan or programme together with the environmental report, and the authority preparing the plan or programme has to show how the information in the report and the comments of consultees have been taken on board. European guidance (EC 2003) gives more details on some aspects of the Directive.

In May 2003, the United Nations Economic Commission for Europe (UNECE) adopted an SEA Protocol similar to the European SEA Directive as a supplement to its 1991 Convention on EIA in a Transboundary Context (the Espoo Convention). The Protocol's requirements are broadly similar to, and compatible with, those of the EU Directive. Broadly, the same types of plans and programmes require SEA under the Protocol; the environmental

report required by the Protocol is similar to that required by the Directive, and the consultation requirements are similar. The Protocol is more focused on health impacts, makes more references to public participation, and addresses policies and legislation, although it only requires SEA of plans and programmes. Although negotiated under the UNECE (which covers Europe, the USA, Canada, the Caucasus and Central Asia), the Protocol is open to all UN members. It entered into force in July 2010, and currently (May 2011) has 38 signatories and 22 parties.

11.3.3 China

Compared with the US and Europe, SEA practice in China is still in its relatively early days. SEA has been required in China since the Environmental Impact Assessment Law, which applied to both plans and projects, became operational in September 2003. In August 2009, the Chinese government published new regulations, based on the EIA Law, but which apply specifically to plans.

Two types of plans require SEA in China. The shorter Type A process relates to land use plans, regional development plans, watershed and marine development plans, construction and utilization plans, and high-level conceptual plans. For such plans, the planning authority must prepare an environmental chapter or note that must be made publicly available, and must be submitted to the authorization authority alongside the draft plan.

The more rigorous Type B SEA process is required for a range of sectoral plans, for instance for industry, agriculture, energy and transport. Drafts of these plans must be accompanied by a full environmental impact report (EIR); the planning authority must seek the opinions of relevant institutions, experts and the general public on the draft plan and its EIR; it must arrange follow-up meetings with various parties if they have strongly divergent views; and it must include details in the final EIR of whether the opinions were adopted. The relevant environmental protection authority must form a review group that examines the EIR and submits its opinion, and the authorization authority must use this opinion as the main basis for its decision on the plan.

The Chinese SEA system has particular strengths: the quality check of Type B plans'

Preparing an environmental report in which the likely significant effects on the environment of implementing the plan, and reasonable alternatives taking into account the objectives and geographical scope of the plan, are identified, described and evaluated. The information to be given is (Article 5 and Annex I):

(a) An outline of the contents, main objectives of the plan, and relationship with other relevant plans and programmes.
(b) The relevant aspects of the current state of the environment and the likely evolution thereof without implementation of the plan.
(c) The environmental characteristics of areas likely to be significantly affected.
(d) Any existing environmental problems that are relevant to the plan including, in particular, those relating to any areas of a particular environmental importance, such as areas designated pursuant to Directives 79/409/EEC and 92/43/EEC.
(e) The environmental protection objectives, established at international, community or national level, which are relevant to the plan and the way those objectives and any environmental considerations have been taken into account during its preparation.
(f) The likely significant effects on the environment, including on issues such as biodiversity, population, human health, fauna, flora, soil, water, air, climatic factors, material assets, cultural heritage including architectural and archaeological heritage, landscape and the interrelationship between the above factors. (These effects should include secondary, cumulative, synergistic, short, medium and long-term permanent and temporary, positive and negative effects).
(g) The measures envisaged to prevent, reduce and as fully as possible offset any significant adverse effects on the environment of implementing the plan.
(h) An outline of the reasons for selecting the alternatives dealt with, and a description of how the assessment was undertaken including any difficulties (such as technical deficiencies or lack of know-how) encountered in compiling the required information.
(i) A description of measures envisaged concerning monitoring in accordance with Article 10.
(j) A non-technical summary of the information provided under the above headings.

The report must include the information that may reasonably be required taking into account current knowledge and methods of assessment, the contents and level of detail in the plan, its stage in the decision-making process and the extent to which certain matters are more appropriately assessed at different levels in that process to avoid duplication of the assessment (Article 5.2).

Consulting

- Authorities with environmental responsibilities, when deciding on the scope and level of detail of the information that must be included in the environmental report (Article 5.4).
- Authorities with environmental responsibilities and the public, to give them an early and effective opportunity within appropriate time frames to express their opinion on the draft plan and the accompanying environmental report before the adoption of the plan (Articles 6.1, 6.2).
- Other EU Member States, where the implementation of the plan is likely to have significant effects on the environment in these countries (Article 7).

Taking the environmental report and the results of the consultations into account in decision-making (Article 8)

Providing information on the decision:

When the plan is adopted, the public and any countries consulted under Article 7 must be informed and the following made available to those so informed:

- the plan as adopted;
- a statement summarising how environmental considerations have been integrated into the plan and how the environmental report of Article 5, the opinions expressed pursuant to Article 6 and the results of consultations entered into pursuant to Article 7 have been taken into account in accordance with Article 8, and the reasons for choosing the plan as adopted, in the light of the other reasonable alternatives dealt with; and
- the measures decided concerning monitoring (Article 9).

Monitoring the significant environmental effects of the plan's implementation (Article 10)

Source: EC 2001

Box 11.1 Requirements of the EU SEA Directive

EIRs, the formal requirement for authorization authorities to give considerable weight to SEA findings, and the emphasis on cumulative impacts and carrying capacities. A monitoring and follow-up process compares the actual impacts of implementing Type B plans against those predicted in the EIR. Weaknesses to date include SEAs not being carried out for relevant plans, or being carried out too late in the plan-making process to influence the plan; and the fact that most of the people who carry out SEA in China are project EIA experts, so the resulting SEAs often feel like modified EIAs (Therivel 2010).

11.4 SEA in the UK

The SEA Directive has had a huge influence on SEA practice in Europe, and, indirectly through the UNECE Protocol, worldwide. This section considers SEA practice in the UK as an example of this influence: the history and legislation of SEA and issues raised by these; typical steps involved in SEA; and effectiveness of SEA in the UK.

11.4.1 History and legislation

In the UK, in response to early government guidance, an abbreviated form of SEA – 'environmental appraisal' – was widely carried out from 1990. Environmental appraisal focused on testing the impacts of a draft plan against a 'framework' of environmental objectives. It required no collection of baseline evidence or policy context, consideration of alternatives, or monitoring. In 1999, new government guidance advised planning authorities to consider their plans' social and economic as well as environmental effects in a broader 'sustainability appraisal'. By October 2001 over 90 per cent of English and Welsh local authorities and all regional authorities had had some experience with appraisal. About half of the appraisals were 'environmental' and the other half 'sustainability' (Therivel and Minas 2002).

The implementation of the SEA Directive in 2004 led to much more formal, rigorous and detailed SEAs. In the UK, the SEA Directive is being implemented through different regulations in England, Wales, Scotland and Northern Ireland,

supported by a jointly agreed Practical Guide to the SEA Directive (ODPM *et al.*, 2006). Box 11.2 shows the SEA steps recommended in the Practical Guide: these clearly link to the requirements of the SEA Directive, but include some additional stages (A4, B1, D2, E2) which reflect the UK's plan-making process. Further guidance by other government bodies addresses how to consider specific topics such as climate change and biodiversity in SEA (e.g. Environment Agency 2011; CCW 2009), and how to carry out SEA for specific types of plans (e.g. PAS 2010; DfT 2009).

(A) Setting the context and objectives, establishing the baseline and deciding on the scope

(A1) Identifying other relevant plans, programmes and environmental protection objectives
(A2) Collecting baseline information
(A3) Identifying environmental problems
(A4) Developing SEA objectives
(A5) Consulting on the scope of SEA

(B) Developing and refining alternatives and assessing effects

(B1) Testing the plan or programme objectives against the SEA objectives
(B2) Developing strategic alternatives
(B3) Predicting the effects of the draft plan or programme, including alternatives
(B4) Evaluating the effects of the draft plan or programme, including alternatives
(B5) Considering ways of mitigating adverse effects
(B6) Proposing measures to monitor the environmental effects of plan or programme implementation

(C) Preparing the Environmental Report

(D) Consulting on the draft plan or programme and the Environmental Report

(D1) Consulting on the draft plan or programme and Environmental Report
(D2) Assessing significant changes
(D3) Decision making and providing information

(E) Monitoring implementation of the plan or programme

(E1) Developing aims and methods for monitoring
(E2) Responding to adverse effects

Source: ODPM *et al.* 2006

Box 11.2 SEA steps for development plans

Much of the discussion – still ongoing – about how to implement the SEA Directive in the UK has been about how SEA should relate to sustainability appraisal (SA). The Planning and Compulsory Purchase Act 2004, which was enacted only two months before the UK legislation implementing the SEA Directive, requires SA for regional and local level spatial plans in England and Wales, without specifying what these SAs should include or how they should relate to SEA. Subsequent guidance (ODPM 2006) suggested that joint SA/SEAs – essentially SEAs with a wider remit that also covers social and economic issues – should be prepared for such plans rather than, say, separate SEA and SA reports, or an 'SA addendum' to a central SEA report. Because regional and local level spatial plans account for a large proportion of all plans in England and Wales, UK authorities' past wider experience of SA, and government requirements regarding sustainable development, most other plan SEAs in England and Wales are also broadened out to SA/SEAs. The same does not hold true in Scotland and Northern Ireland, which require only SEA.

11.4.2 The SA/SEA process in practice

Prior to the SEA Directive, SAs of plans in the UK were mostly carried out in-house by the planners themselves. Post-Directive, some SA/SEAs are carried out completely in-house, some completely by consultants, and some by a mixture of consultants and in-house planners. There is no clear trend in who is carrying out SA/SEAs, nor what approach leads to the most changes to the plan or the most sustainable plan (Therivel and Walsh 2005; Sherston 2008). Very roughly, an SA/SEA will take 60–100 person days. The rest of this section discusses what carrying out a typical SA/SEA for a spatial plan would involve.

(A) Setting the context and objectives, establishing the baseline and deciding on the scope

The analysis of *other relevant plans, programmes and environmental objectives* is typically very comprehensive and seriously boring. It is usually presented as a long table that lists the other plan, what the other plan says, and what implications this has for the plan in question.

In the first few years after the SEA Directive was implemented, *baseline information* was also mostly presented in tables, which showed baseline data for the local authority, similar data at the regional and/or national level as a comparator, relevant targets, and data sources. The tables were quick to compile and allowed the authority to benchmark its baseline, but were difficult to read and provided no spatial information. More recently, SA/SEA baseline descriptions have become more descriptive and spatial, for instance showing maps of nature conservation areas or landscape designations, and in some cases providing overlay maps of constraints or opportunities. Figure 11.3 shows an example.

Part of the baseline description also includes predicting the *likely future situation in the absence of the plan*. For instance, air quality is expected to improve in the UK generally due to tightening European standards for vehicle emissions and the closure of some power stations as a result of the Large Combustion Plant Directive; and the marine areas around the UK are expected to be subject to many more impacts as a result of government policies on offshore energy production. This information allows the cumulative impacts of the plan – the plan plus other plans, projects and baseline trends – to be assessed.

Existing *environmental or sustainability problems* are often identified as a group exercise. Problems include where environmental targets are not achieved, environmental standards are exceeded, the plan area is doing worse than other similar areas, the situation is worsening over time, and things that local residents are unhappy about.

For objectives-led SA/SEAs, an *SA/SEA framework* of environmental, social and economic objectives and indicators would then be set up. This will act as an independent 'measuring stick' or series of questions against which the plan's impacts can be tested. The indicators are also useful for describing and monitoring the baseline environment. Table 11.2 shows part of a typical SA/SEA framework. For baseline-led SA/SEAs, no such framework would be prepared.

All of this information is collated into a scoping report, which is sent to the statutory consultees (in England these are the Environment Agency, Natural England and English Heritage) for five weeks, to allow them to comment on it.

(B) Developing and refining alternatives and assessing effects

The SEA Directive requires the environmental report to evaluate the effects of the plan 'and reasonable alternatives taking into account the objectives and the geographical scope of the plan'. Although guidance exists on *alternatives identification* (PAS 2008) and the quality of the alternatives being considered in SA/SEAs is generally improving, historically this stage has not been done well, and some SA/SEAs continue to limit their consideration of alternatives to a comparison of the proposed plan vs. no plan. Most of the successful SEA-related legal challenges in the UK have been around the development and assessment of alternatives. For instance, concerning a proposal in the East of England Regional Spatial Strategy to build housing on the Green Belt, Justice Mitting concluded that

[The SEA Directive] required that reasonable alternatives to the challenged policies be identified, described and evaluated before the choice was made. The environmental report produced by ERM did not attempt that task. It should have done so and the Secretary of State should not have decided to adopt the challenged policies until that had been done. The consequence of omitting to comply with the statutory requirement is demonstrated by the outcome. A decision has been made to erode the metropolitan green belt in a sensitive area without alternatives to that erosion being considered.[2]

Similarly, Justice Collins ruled in 2011 that:

It was not possible for the consultees to know from [the SEA for the Forest Heath Core Strategy] what were the reasons for rejecting any alternatives to the urban development where it was proposed or to know why the increase in the residential development made no difference. The previous reports did not

Table 11.2 Example of part of a typical SA/SEA framework

SA/SEA objective	Sub objective: will the plan	Indicators
1 Help deliver equality of opportunity and access for all	1 (a) Address existing imbalances of inequality, deprivation and exclusion 1 (b) Improve access to education, lifelong learning and training opportunities 1 (c) Improve accessibility to affordable housing and employment opportunities, particularly for disadvantaged sections of society	1.1 Percentage of areas in the most deprived 10% areas 1.2 Average house price compared to average annual salary 1.3 Number and percentage of affordable housing units provided per year 1.4 Number of homeless per 1000 households
2 Maintain and improve air quality	2 (a) Reduce the need to travel through the location and design of new development, provision of public transport infrastructure and promotion of cycling and walking 2 (b) Avoid locating new development where air quality could negatively impact upon peoples' health	2.1 Number of air quality management areas
3 Protect and enhance biodiversity, flora and fauna	3 (a) Maintain and achieve favourable condition of international and national sites of nature conservation importance 3 (b) Maintain the extent and enhance the quality of locally designated sites and priority habitats 3 (c) Maintain and enhance connectivity of corridors of semi-natural habitats	3.1 Number and extent (in hectares) of enhance designated sites of importance 3.2 Area of ancient woodland cover 3.3 Total extent (in hectares) of priority habitats 3.4 Percentage of features of internationally and nationally designated sites in favourable condition

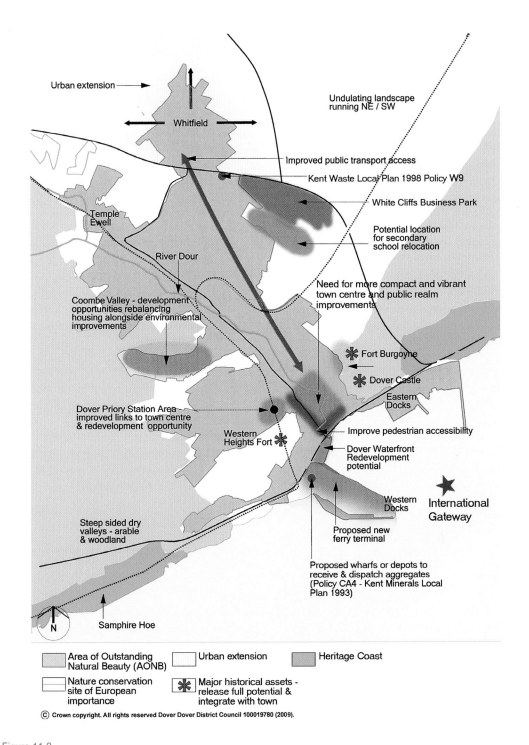

Figure 11.3

Example of a strategic level constraints map

Source: Dover District Council (2010)

properly give the necessary explanations and reasons and in any event were not sufficiently summarized nor were the relevant passages identified in the final report.[3]

The relevant parts of both plans were quashed.

Objectives-led *impact assessment* involves testing how well each plan alternative or sub-component fulfils each SA/SEA objective in the SA/SEA framework. Table 11.3 shows an example of how plan alternatives can be assessed and compared. In each case, the table cells are filled in, alternative by alternative or sub-component by sub-component, noting whether the alternative/sub-component:

- is clearly written: if not, it might be possible to rewrite it to make it clearer;
- has a negative impact (–): if so, this impact might be mitigated, for instance by rewriting the sub-component, adding a different sub-component, etc.;
- has a positive impact (+): if so, it might be possible to rewrite it to make it even more positive;
- has an uncertain impact (?): if so, it may be necessary to collect further information before the assessment can be completed, and the plan finalized;
- has an impact that depends on how the plan is implemented (I): if so, it may be possible to rewrite the plan to ensure that it is implemented positively; has no significant impact (0).

Baseline-led impact assessment, instead, involves comparing the expected 'with plan' situation against the expected 'without plan' situation, and determining whether the plan would change things for better or worse. Where the 'with plan' situation would be significantly worse than the 'without plan' situation, mitigation measures would be considered.

The focus of the assessment stage should not be on the symbol or the precise quantity of change, but rather on making appropriate changes to the plan: these are the *mitigation measures* required by the SEA Directive. The Directive implies a hierarchy of mitigation. Avoidance or prevention of impacts, for instance by moving proposed development away from a sensitive site or not allowing certain types of activities, is generally considered preferable to reduction or minimisation of impacts, for instance requiring developments to use certain technologies or achieve certain standards. Compensatory measures or offsets – allowing the impacts to happen to providing some kind of counterbalancing benefit – is the least preferable measure.

A given plan may require several rounds of impact assessment and mitigation, at different levels of detail, during the development of the plan:

- Broad strategic alternatives (e.g. whether housing should be at the edge of existing towns, scattered throughout an authority or in one large new town). These may need to be evaluated and compared early in the plan-making process before preferred alternative(s) can be agreed on.
- More detailed sub-components of the plan (e.g. plan policies on housing density and design). These may need to be evaluated and fine-tuned once the plan is closer to completion.
- Proposed locations for development (e.g. specific housing sites). These may need to be evaluated and fine-tuned at a level of detail close to that of project EIA.

(C) Preparing the Environmental Report

The findings of Stages A and B are published in an SA/SEA (or Environmental) Report alongside the draft plan, and made available to the public and statutory consultees. The Environmental Report also covers the remaining requirements of the SEA Directive, namely any problems faced in compiling the information in the report, and proposed monitoring arrangements.

(D) Consulting on the draft plan or programme and the Environmental Report

After the consultation responses have been received, they must be 'taken into account' in the final plan. Once the final plan has been agreed, it must be published alongside a statement that explains how the authority has taken the findings of the SA/SEA and the consultation responses into

Table 11.3 Example of part of a typical objectives-led assessment

SA/SEA objective	Alternative		
	Develop site X for employment	Develop site X for housing	Protect site X from development for the plan period
1 Help deliver equality of opportunity and access for all	– Takes up land that could potentially be used for housing	+	0 (no change)
2 Maintain and improve air quality	– – Would support employment that requires road access	– Would add to congestion, but could shorten the length and duration of some journeys	
3 Protect and enhance biodiversity, flora and fauna	? Status of biodiversity is unclear – requires further study		0 (no change)

account, and 'the reasons for choosing the plan . . . as adopted, in the light of the other reasonable alternatives dealt with'. The statement must also confirm the monitoring measures that will be carried out.

(E) Monitoring the implementation of the plan

Finally, the authority must monitor the significant environmental impacts of the plan's implementation.

11.4.3 SA/SEA effectiveness in the UK

A sequence of surveys of UK planners (Therivel and Minas 2002; Therivel and Walsh 2005; Sherston 2008; Yamane 2008) has given an indication of the effectiveness of the UK SA/SEA system, and changes to that system triggered by the SEA Directive. In terms of *direct effects*, more than 80 per cent of planners report that the SA/SEA process has led to some changes being made to their plan, with the SEA Directive leading to a noticeable increase in this. However most of these changes are limited to additions, deletions or rewording of individual plan policies, with only a limited number of plans being substantially changed as a result of SA/SEA (see Figures 11.4 and 11.5). This is confirmed by recent DCLG research which concludes that 'SA/SEA generally plays a "fine-tuning" rather than a "plan-shaping" role' (DCLG 2010).

Planners reported, however, that SA/SEA has considerable additional *indirect benefits*, including

greater understanding of their plan and of sustainability issues, more transparent plan-making, and inspiration for the next round of plan-making: see Figure 11.6. Planners also feel that the SA/SEA process, although itself biased slightly towards the environment, balances out the plan-making process that itself is biased in favour of social and economic concerns (Sherston 2008; Yamane 2008).

The DCLG (2010) research concluded with a range of recommendations for improving SA/SEA, many of which are also relevant for project-level EIA:

- Planning bodies should integrate the early, evidence gathering stages of the plan-making and SA/SEA processes in order to foster a more efficient and effective approach.
- The evidence base for SA/SEA should include a greater focus on sptaial information and reflect the spatial nature of the plan.
- The scope of the appraisal should reflect the alternatives being considered.
- Those undertaking the appraisal should not be afraid to omit from its scope issues that are not likely to be significant; however, this should be done transparently with a clear explanation.
- Plan-making should generate well thought out and clearly articulated alternatives.
- Plan impacts should be identified and evaluated with reference to the baseline situation.
- The level of detail the appraisal enters into should reflect the level of detail in the plan.

- The appraisal should consider the extent to which options and policies will be effectively delivered on the ground to help avoid unrealistic assessment results.
- Separate, understandable non-technical summaries of SA/SEA reports should be prepared to facilitate public engagement.
- There is further scope to engage the public in SA/SEA, particularly through the use of stakeholder events focused on options.
- Some topic-specific assessments can be integrated into the SA/SEA process, but Habitats

Regulations Assessment should be undertaken on a largely separate basis.
- Those undertaking the appraisal should ideally provide plan-makers with explicit recommendations to which they can respond.
- Links between SA/SEA and Annual Monitoring Reports should be strengthened with significant effects identified by the appraisal monitored through indicators included in the Annual Monitoring Reports. See Hanusch and Glasson (2008) for discussion of importance of monitoring in SEA/SA.

Figure 11.4

Proportion of plans changed as a result of SA/SEA in 2002, 2005 and 2008

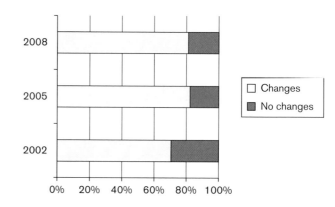

Figure 11.5

Type of changes, 2008

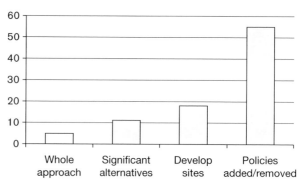

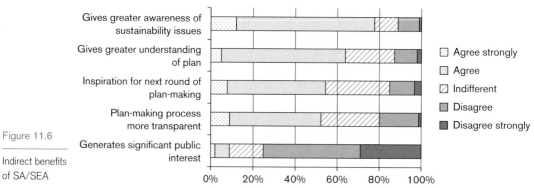

Figure 11.6

Indirect benefits of SA/SEA

11.5 Summary

SEA has spread and evolved rapidly over the last decade, and is likely to continue to do so for the foreseeable future. Its main limitation is, like that of EIA, that its findings only have to be 'taken into account'. In practice, this still leads to economic and social issues frequently being prioritized over environmental issues (Therivel *et al.* 2009).

However, impact assessment at the strategic rather than just the project level allows for an improved consideration of wider issues (such as climate change and deprivation), consideration of more strategic alternatives (such as how much development is needed and broadly where it should go) and better analysis of cumulative impacts. These all set a useful framework for project development and project-level EIA. These themes are taken further in the final chapter on prospects in EIA.

SOME QUESTIONS

The following questions are intended to help the reader focus on the key issues of this chapter, and to start building some understanding about SEA and the strategic level of assessment.

1   In the UK, SEAs are typically widened out to also consider social and economic topics. What are the advantages and disadvantages of such an approach?
2   One argument put forward for needing SEA is that EIAs do not adequately address cumulative impacts. Of the three SEA systems described in Section 11.3, do any clearly consider cumulative impacts?
3   Figure 11.3 shows a constraints map for an urban extension proposal. How is it different from the project-level constraints map of Figure 4.8? What might account for the differences?
4   Table 11.2 shows an example of a strategic level of impact assessment. How does this differ from the project-level techniques of Chapter 5? What might account for the differences?
5   Figure 11.6 shows that planners find that SEA helps them to have greater understanding of their plan. Why might that be the case?
6   Of the problems with EIA listed in Section 11.2.2, can you provide any specific examples from your own EIA practice, or find any in the rest of this book? Do you think that SEA, as described in this chapter, solves these problems?

Notes

1   See Section 12.3 for a discussion of cumulative impacts and Sections 9.8 and 9.9 for two UK case studies.
2   City and District Council of St. Albans vs. Secretary of State for Communities and Local Government, [2009] EWHC 1280 (Admin).
3   Save Historic Newmarket Ltd and others vs. Forest Heath District Council and others, [2011] EWHC 606 (Admin).

References

CCW (Countryside Council for Wales) 2009. SEA topic guidance for practitioners. Available at: www.ccw.gov.uk/landscape—wildlife/managing-land-and-sea/environmental-assessment/sea.aspx.

CEQ (Council on Environmental Quality) 1978. *Regulations for implementing the procedural provisions of the National Environmental Policy Act*, 40 Code of Federal Regulations 1500–1508.

CEQ 2010. New proposed NEPA guidance and steps to modernize and reinvigorate NEPA. Available at: www.whitehouse.gov/administration/eop/ceq/initiatives/nepa.

DCLG (Department for Communities and Local Government) 2010. Towards a more efficient and effective use of strategic environmental assessment and sustainability appraisal in spatial planning: summary. Available at: www.communities.gov.uk/documents/planningandbuilding/pdf/15130101.pdf.

DfT (Department for Transport) 2009. Strategic environmental assessment for transport plans and programmes, TAG Unit 2.11, 'in draft' guidance. Available at: www.dft.gov.uk/webtag/documents/project-manager/pdf/unit2.11d.pdf.

Dover District Council 2010. Whitfield Urban Extension Masterplan SPD Sustainability Appraisal. Available at: www.dover.gov.uk/pdf/WUE%20Masterplan%20SPD%20Draft%20SA%20Scoping%20Report%20REVISED.pdf.

EA (Environment Agency) 2011. *Strategic environmental assessment and climate change: guidance for practitioners.* Reading: Environment Agency.

EC (European Commission) 2001. *Directive 2001/42/ec on the assessment of the effects of certain plans and programmes on the environment.* Brussels: European Commission. Available at: www.europa.eu.int/comm/environment/eia/full-legal-text/0142_en.pdf.

EC 2003. *Implementation of Directive 2001/42 on the assessment of the effects of certain plans and programmes on the environment.* Brussels: European Commission. Available at: europa.eu.int/comm/environment/eia/030923_sea_guidance.pdf.

Hanusch, M. and Glasson, J. 2008. Much ado about SEA/SA monitoring: the performance of English Regional Spatial Strategies, and some German comparisons. *Environmental Impact Assessment Review.* 28, 601–617.

ODPM (Office of the Deputy Prime Minister), Scottish Executive, Welsh Assembly Government, and Department of the Environment, Northern Ireland 2006. A practical guide to the strategic environmental assessment directive. Available at: www.communities.gov.uk/documents/planningandbuilding/pdf/practicalguidesea.pdf.

Partidario. M.R. 2003. Strategic environmental assessment (SEA) IAIA'03 pre-meeting training course. Available at: www.iaia.org/publicdocuments/EIA/SEA/SEAManual.pdf.

PAS (Planning Advisory Service) 2008. *Local development frameworks: options generation and appraisal.* London: PAS.

PAS 2010. Sustainability appraisal: advice note. Available at: www.pas.gov.uk/pas/aio/627078.

Sadler, B. and Verheem, R. 1996. *SEA: status, challenges and future directions,* Report 53. The Hague, The Netherlands: Ministry of Housing, Spatial Planning and the Environment.

Sadler, B., Aschemann, R., Dusik, J., Fischer, T. and Partidario, M. (eds) 2010. *Handbook of strategic environmental assessment.* London: Earthscan.

Sherston, T. 2008. The effectiveness of strategic environmental assessment as a helpful development plan making tool. MSc dissertation, Oxford Brookes University.

State of California 1986. *The California environmental quality act.* Sacramento, CA: Office of Planning and Research.

Therivel, R. 2010. *Strategic environmental assessment in action,* 2nd edn. London: Earthscan.

Therivel, R. and Minas, P. 2002. Ensuring effective sustainability appraisal. *Impact Assessment and Project Appraisal* 19 (2), 81–91.

Therivel, R. and Walsh, F. 2006. The strategic environmental assessment directive in the UK: one year on. *Environmental Impact Assessment Review* 26 (7), 663–75.

Therivel, R., Wilson, E., Thompson, S., Heaney, D. and Pritchard, D. 1992. *Strategic environmental assessment.* London: RSPB/Earthscan.

Therivel, R., Christian, G. Craig, C. Grinham, R., Mackins, D., Smith, J., Sneller, T., Turner, R., Walker, D. and Yamane, M. 2009. Sustainability-focused impact assessment: English experiences. *Impact Assessment and Project Appraisal* 27 (2), 155–68.

Wood, C. 1991. EIA of policies, plans and programmes. *EIA Newsletter* 5, 2–3.

Yamane, M. 2008. Achieving sustainability of local plan through SEA/SA. MSc dissertation, Oxford Brookes University.

12 Improving the effectiveness of project assessment

•••

12.1 Introduction

Overall, the experience of EIA to date can be summed up as being like the proverbial curate's egg: good in parts. Current issues in the EIA process were briefly noted in Section 1.6: they include EIA methods of assessment, the quality and efficiency of the EIA process, the relative roles of the participants in the process, EIS quality, monitoring and post-decision, managing the widening scope and complexity of impact assessment activity, plus concern about its overall effectiveness. The various chapters on steps in the process have sought to identify best practice, and Chapter 8 provides an overview of the quantity and quality of UK practice to date. Detailed case studies of good practice and comparative international experience provide further ideas for possible future developments. The evolving, but still in some cases limited, experience in EIA among the main participants in the process – consultants, local authorities, central government, developers and affected parties – explains some of the current issues.

However, almost 25 years after the implementation of EC Directive 85/337, there is less scepticism in most quarters and a general acceptance of the value of EIA. There are still some substantial shortcomings, and there is considerable scope for improving quality, but practice and the underpinning knowledge and understanding have developed and EIA continues on its steep learning curve. The procedures, process and practice of EIA will undoubtedly evolve further, as evidenced by the comparative studies of other countries. The EU countries can learn from such experience and from their own experience since 1988.

This chapter focuses on the prospects for project-based EIA. The following section briefly considers the array of perspectives on change from the various participants in the EIA process. This is followed by a consideration of possible developments in some important areas of the EIA process and in the nature of EISs. The chapter concludes with a discussion of the parallel and complementary development of environmental management systems and audits. Together, these topics act as a kind of action list for future improvements to EIA.

•••

12.2 Perspectives on change

An underlying theme in any discussion of EIA is change. This has surfaced several times in the various chapters of this book. EIA systems and procedures are changing in many countries. Indeed, as O'Riordan (1990) noted (see Section 1.4), we should expect EIA to change in the face of shifting environmental values, politics and managerial capabilities. This is not to devalue the achievements of EIA; as the World Bank (1995) noted , 'Over the past decade, EIA has moved from the fringes of development planning to become a widely recognized tool for sound project decision making.'

The practice of EIA under the existing systems established in the EU Member States has also improved rapidly (see Chapters 2, 8 and 10). This change can be expected to continue in the future, as the provisions of the regularly amended EU EIA Directive work through, and even further amendments are introduced. Changes in EIA procedures, like the initial introduction of EIA regulations, can of course generate considerable conflict between levels of government: between federal and state levels, between national and local levels and, in the case of Europe, between the EU and its Member States. They also generate conflict between the other participants in the process: the developers, the affected parties and the facilitators (see Figure 3.1).

The *Commission of the European Communities* (CEC) is generally seen as positive and proactive with regard to EIA. The CEC welcomed the introduction of common legislation as reflected in Directive 85/337, the provision of information on projects and the general spread of good practice, but was concerned about the lack of compatibility of EIA systems across frontiers, the opaque processes employed, the limited access to the public and lack of continuity in the process. It pressed hard for amendments to the Directive, and has achieved some of its objectives in the various subsequent amendments. In addition the SEA Directive was implemented from 2004 (see Chapter 11). However, as noted in Section 2.8, there are some continuing and stubborn issues, including: variations in screening, transboundary issues, quality control, the absence of mandatory consideration of alternatives, lack of monitoring, and tiering issues between EIA and SEA (CEC 2009). The Commission is committed to reviewing and updating EIA procedures and there will no doubt be further changes. Other areas of attention

include, for example, cumulative assessment, public participation, economic valuation and EIA procedures for development aid projects. In contrast with the CEC, Member States tend to be more defensive and reactive. They are generally concerned about maintaining 'subsidiarity' with regard to activities involving the EU; this has been an ongoing issue with EIA (CEC 2009). Governments are also sensitive to increasing controls on economic development in an increasingly difficult, competitive and global economy.

For example, within the UK *government*, the DCLG (formerly ODPM; DETR; DoE) has been concerned to tidy up ambiguities in the project-based procedures, and to improve guidance and informal procedures for example, but is wary of new regulations. However, it has commissioned and produced research reports, for example on an EIA good practice guide, on the evaluation and review of environmental information and on mitigation in EIA, and its recent guidance and regulations reflect an acceptance of the value of EIA. *Local government* in the UK has begun to come to terms with EIA, and there is evidence that those authorities with considerable experience (e.g. Essex, Kent, Cheshire) learn fast, apply the regulations and guidance in user-friendly 'customized' formats to help developers and affected parties in their areas, and are pushing up the standards expected from project proponents. For example see the latest version of the very useful Essex Guide to EIA (Essex Planning Officers' Association, 2007) which can be freely downloaded.

Pressure groups – exemplified in particular in the UK by the Campaign to Protect Rural England (CPRE), the Royal Society for the Protection of Birds (RSPB) and Friends of the Earth (FoE) – and those parties affected by development proposals view project EIA as a very useful tool for increasing access to information on projects, and for advancing the protection of the physical environment in particular. They have been keen to develop EIA processes and procedures; see, for example, the reports by CPRE (1991, 1992) and RSPB (2000). Many *developers* are less enthusiastic about strengthening EIA procedures, but will welcome the government's recent clarification on ambiguities (DCLG 2011) – especially on whether EIAs are needed in the first place for their particular projects. For *facilitators* (consultants, lawyers, etc.), EIA has been a welcome boon; their interest in longer and wider procedures, involving more of their services, is clear.

Other participants in the process in the UK, such as the IEMA (see 12.3.2 below), academics and some environmental consultancies, are carrying out groundbreaking studies into topics such as best-practice guidelines, the use of monetary valuation and ecosystem services approaches in EIA and approaches to widening types of impact study. In addition, the production of several hundred EISs a year in the UK and in many other countries worldwide is generating a considerable body of expertise, innovative approaches and comparative studies. EISs are also becoming increasingly reviewed, and hopefully bad practice will be exposed and reduced. Training in EIA skills is also developing.

12.3 Possible changes in the EIA process: overviews of the future agenda

12.3.1 International studies of EIA effectiveness

Examples of recent key international studies of EIA effectiveness include those by the European Commission, as already noted above and in Chapter 2 (CEC 2009), and the 2011 update of the 1996 *International study of the effectiveness of environmental assessment* for the IAIA, by Sadler and colleagues (1996, 2011). As noted in Chapter 8, in a UK workshop discussion for the evolving international effectiveness study, Sadler (2010) identified an 'effectiveness triage' involving three clearance bars for EIA: *what must or should be done*, including legal and institutional framework and methodological realities; *what is done*, including cases of good practice; and *what is the outcome*, in particular the contribution to decision-making, and environmental benefits. He raises, for example, many questions about the second of the above, the nature of current practice. Is consultation a

procedural cornerstone or overrated and under-performing? Are screening and scoping focusing on the impacts that matter? Is the evaluation of significance based on adequate evidence? Are mitigation measures sufficiently tailored? Is monitoring still the weak link? Such points resonate with much of the content in the very useful summary of international best and worst case EIA performance contained in the earlier international effectiveness study (Sadler 1996; see Box 12.1).

But in particular, the 2010 workshop raised the issue of the rapidly changing context of EIA – as noted in Section 1.5.1. While climate change can be seen as reinforcing the importance of EIA, economic recession and severe financial challenges may be more counter-productive with the risk of weakening of support for green issues 'until we get the economy back on its feet!' FoE (2011) provides a UK example of this. Of course, there should be much mutual synergy through: for example, investment in green infrastructure, but this needs enlightened and far-seeing governance.

12.3.2 UK IEMA study of EIA effectiveness

The UK IEMA study (IEMA 2011) provides a very timely study on the state of UK EIA practice. While good progress has been made over 25 years, the study concludes that '(UK) EIA practice is not perfect and further improvements must be made if it is to continue to offer value in the 21st Century.' The study raises many significant issues about the UK EIA process, relating for example to issues in the approach to screening, scoping, assembling baseline data, assessment of significance, mitigation and enhancement, cumulative impacts, monitoring and adaptive EIA – many of which are also covered in the earlier chapters of this book. The IEMA study concludes with a vision for UK EIA: 'EIA must enable developments that work for the developer, community and environment and that getting this right will save resources at the same time as generating improved environmental outcomes.' Table 12.1 provides a set of six key areas for delivering that vision.

Best-case performance

The EA process:

- facilitates informed decision-making by providing clear, well-structured, dispassionate analysis of the effects and consequences of proposed actions;
- assists the selection of alternatives, including the selection of the best practicable or most environmentally friendly option;
- influences both project selection and policy design by screening out environmentally unsound proposals, as well as modifying feasible action;
- encompasses all relevant issues and factors, including cumulative effects, social impacts and health risks;
- directs (not dictates) formal approvals, including the establishment of terms and conditions of implementation and follow-up;
- results in the satisfactory prediction of the adverse effects of proposed actions and their mitigation using conventional and customized techniques; and
- preserves as an adaptive, organizational learning process in which the lessons experienced are fed back into policy, institutional and project designs.

Worst-case performance

The EA process:

- is inconsistently applied to development proposals with many sectors and classes of activity omitted;
- operates as a 'stand alone' process, poorly related to the project cycle and approval process and consequently is of marginal influence;
- has a non-existent or weak follow-up process, lacking surveillance and enforcement of terms and conditions, effects monitoring, etc.;
- does not consider cumulative effects or social, health and risk factors;
- makes little or no reference to the public, or consultation is perfunctory, substandard and takes no account of the specific requirements of affected groups;
- results in EA reports that are voluminous, poorly organized and descriptive technical documents;
- provides information that is unhelpful or irrelevant to decision-making;
- is inefficient, time consuming and costly in relation to the benefits delivered; and
- understates and insufficiently mitigates environmental impacts and loses credibility.

Source: Sadler 1996

Box 12.1 Summary of international best- and worst-case EA performances

Table 12.1 Key areas to deliver IEMA vision for EIA and to facilitate future success of UK EIA practice

1	**A focus on communicating the added value generated by EIA:** enhance the communication of the positive effects of EIA (e.g. EIA leading to improvements in project design)
2	**Realizing the efficiencies of effective EIA co-ordination:** recognize the value that a good EIA co-ordinator brings to the efficient running and effective application of the assessment
3	**Developing new partnerships to enhance the EIA process:** value effective partnerships with planners; legal advisers; design teams; and construction contractors, etc.,especially those involved in managing EIA outcomes
4	**Listening, communicating and engaging effectively with communities**
5	**Practitioners actively working together to tackle the difficult issues in EIA** to generate pragmatic solutions to difficult EIA issues
6	**Delivering environmental outcomes that work now and in the future:** recognize the importance of designing measures in a way that maximizes the chance of their being implemented effectively; plus effective monitoring

Source: Adapted from IEMA (2011)

12.4 Possible changes in the EIA process: more specific examples

So what might be done? A pragmatic approach to change could subdivide the future agenda into proposals to *improve* EIA procedures, usually sooner and maybe more easily than proposals to *widen* the scope of EIA, which are likely to come later and will probably be more difficult to implement. *Improvements to project EIA* cover some of the changes introduced by the various amendments to the EC Directive, including developments in approaches to screening, the mandatory consideration of alternatives and a strong encouragement to undertake scoping at an early stage in the project development cycle. There could also be more support for more transparent procedures, and encouragement for consultation, for the explanation and publication of decisions and for greater weight to be given to cumulative impacts and risk assessment.

The methods of assessment could also benefit from further attention. Uncertainty about the unknown may mean the EIA process starts too late and results in a lack of integration with the management of a project's life cycle. The EIA process and the resulting EISs may lack balance, focus on the more straightforward process of describing the project and its baseline environment and consider much less the identification, prediction and evaluation of impacts. The forecasting methods used in EIA are not explained in most cases (see Section 8.4). Practical advances in predicting the magnitude of impacts and determining their importance (including the array of multi-criteria and monetary evaluation techniques) would be beneficial. A good 'method statement', explaining how a study has been conducted – in terms of techniques, consultation, the relative roles of experts and others – should be a basic element of any EIS.

Widening the scope of eia includes, in particular, the development of tiered assessment through the introduction of SEA (as discussed in Chapter 11). Another important extension of the scope of EIA includes 'completing the circle' through the more widespread use of monitoring and auditing. Unfortunately, this vital step in the EIA process is still not mandatory after several amendments to the EC Directive. More wide-ranging changes include the move to a 'whole of environment' approach, with a more balanced consideration of both biophysical and socio-economic impacts. Such widening of scope should lead to more integrated EIA. There may also be a trend towards using EIA to identify environmental limits and environmental constraints on the project, rather than focusing only on identifying the project's impacts on the environment – through what might be termed environmental impact design. Testing a project's resilience to future changes and shocks could also become a component of EIA.

The following sections discuss possibilities for some of these short- and longer-term proposals: better consideration of cumulative impacts, widening the scope to include socio-economic impacts; embracing the growing areas of health impact assessment, equality impacts assessment, appropriate assessment and resilience thinking; building climate change centrally into EIA; developing integrated impact assessment and moving towards environmental impact design.

12.4.1 Cumulative impacts

Many projects are individually minor, but collectively may impose a significant impact on the environment. Activities such as residential development, farming and household behaviour normally fall outside the scope of conventional EIA. The ecological response to the collective impact of such activities may be delayed until a threshold is crossed, when the impact may come to light in sudden and dramatic form (e.g. flooding). Odum (1982) refers to the 'tyranny of small decisions' and the consequences arising from the continual growth of small developments; cumulative impacts can also be described as 'death by a thousand cuts'. While there is no particular consensus on what constitutes cumulative impacts, the categorization by the Canadian Environmental Assessment Research Council (CEARC) (Peterson *et al.* 1987) is widely quoted, and includes:

- time-crowded perturbations: which occur because perturbations are so close in time that the effects of one are not dissipated before the next one occurs;

- space-crowded perturbations: when perturbations are so close in space that their effects overlap;
- synergisms: where different types of perturbation occurring in the same area may interact to produce qualitatively and quantitatively different responses by the receiving ecological communities;
- indirect effects: those produced at some time or distance from the initial perturbation, or by a complex pathway; and
- nibbling: which can include the incremental erosion of a resource until there is a significant change/it is all used up.

Cumulative impact assessment is predicting and assessing all other likely existing, past and reasonably foreseeable future effects on the environment arising from perturbations which are time-crowded; space-crowded; synergisms; indirect; or, constitute nibbling. (CEPA 1994)

The need to include cumulative impact assessment in EIA has been long recognized. In the CEQA of 1970, significant impacts are considered to exist if 'the possible effects of a project are individually limited but cumulatively considerable'. Subsequent legislative reference is found in the 1991 Resource Management Act of New Zealand, which makes explicit reference to cumulative effects, and now also in the amended EU Directive, which refers to the need to consider the characteristics of projects having regard to 'the cumulation with other projects'. In Canada, which has been at the forefront in the development of 'cumulative effects assessment' (CEA), the consideration of cumulative effects is explicit and mandatory in legislation both federally and in several provinces. The UK guidance is for rather more limited consideration of cumulative effects:

Generally, it would not be sensible to consider the cumulative effects with other applications which have yet to be determined, since there can be no certainty that they will receive planning permission. However, there could be circumstances where two or more applications for development should be considered together. For example, where

the applications in question are not directly in competition with one another, so that both or all of them might be approved, and where the overall combined environmental impact of the proposals might be greater than the sum of the separate parts. (DCLG 2011)

However, it is in the practical implementation of the consideration of cumulative impacts that the problems and deficiencies become clear, and cases of good practice and, until recently, useful methodologies have been limited. In Australia, assessments have largely been carried out by regulatory authorities rather than by project proponents, and have focused on regional air quality and the quality and salinity of water in catchment areas (CEPA 1994). Figure 12.1 provides an example of a simple perturbation impact model developed by Lane and associates (1988). It is basically an 'impact tree' that links (a) the principal causes driving a development with, (b) the main perturbations induced with, (c) the primary bio-physical and socio-economic impacts and (d) the secondary impacts. The figure shows some of the potential cumulative impacts associated with a number of area-related tourism developments.

There are some significant examples of good practice guidance. In the US, the CEQ produced a practice guide *Considering cumulative effects* (CEQ 1997), based on numerous case studies. The guide consists of 11 steps for CEA, in three main stages (see also Chapter 2, Section 2.2.4). In Canada, a *Cumulative effects assessment practitioners guide* (CEAA 1999) provides a very useful overview and clarification of terms and fundamentals, of practical approaches to completing CEAs, and case studies of approaches used by project proponents. The guide provides some clear and simple definitions – 'Cumulative effects are changes to the environment that are caused by an action in combination with other past, present and future human actions. A CEA is an assessment of those effects.' Further Canadian work has sought to improve the practice of CEA (see Baxter *et al.* 2001). In the EU, there has also been an attempt to support practice in the area through the development of *Guidance for the assessment of indirect and cumulative impacts* (Hyder Consulting 1999). Piper (2000, 2001a, b) provides valuable evidence on the state of UK practice in

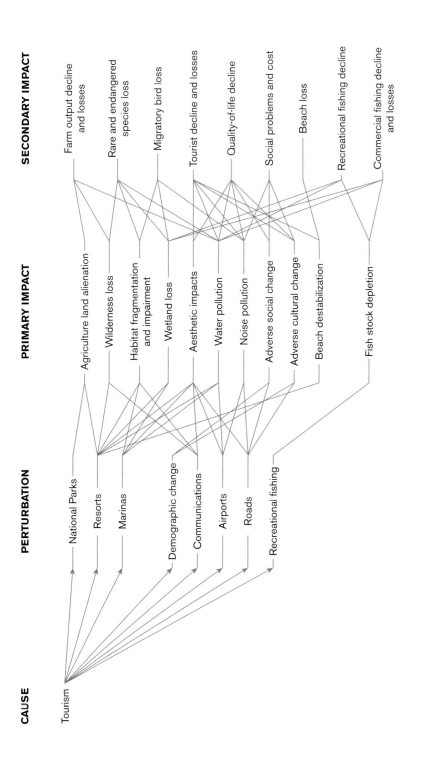

Figure 12.1

Cumulative impacts: perturbation impact model

Source: Lane and associates 1988

Table 12.2 Key steps in a CEAM framework

1	Initiate the CEA process by identifying the incremental direct and indirect effects of the proposed project (or policy, plan or programme) on selected VECs (valued ecosystem components) within the environs of the project location.
2	Identify other past, present, and reasonably foreseeable future actions within the space and time boundaries that have been, are, or could contribute to cumulative effects (stresses) on the VECs and their indicators.
3	For the selected VECs, assemble appropriate information on their indicators, and describe and assess their historical to current and even projected conditions.
4	'Connect' the proposed project (or other PPP) and other actions in the CEAM study study area to the selected VECs and their indicators.
5	Assess the significance of the cumulative effects on each VEC over the time horizon for the study.
6	For VECS or their indicators that are expected to be subject to negative incremental impacts from the proposed project and for which the cumulative effects are significant, develop appropriate action or activity-specific 'mitigation measures' for such impacts.

Source: Adapted (substantially simplified) from Canter and Ross (2010)

CEA, drawing on research on a number of case studies (see Section 9.5).

Between them, these guides and assessments of practice highlight some of the key process and organizational issues in considering cumulative impacts/effects. Process issues include, for example: establishing the geographic scope of the analysis (how wide should the impacts region be), establishing the time frame for the analysis (including not only present projects, but also those in the non-immediate time frame – past and reasonably foreseeable future) and determining the magnitude and significance of the effects. A key organizational question in the UK (see Piper 2001b) is 'Which organization has the responsibility to require or commission the CEA work?' This is complicated when, as is often the case in CEA, there is more than one competent authority involved (Piper 2001b; Therivel and Ross 2007).

Canter and Ross (2010) provide a recent state of play of CEAM (cumulative effects assessment and management); the inclusion of 'M' in the term reflects the increasing attention being given to the management and mitigation of cumulative effects. They identify a six-step framework, as set out in Table 12.2. They also discuss the good, bad and ugly lessons of the practice of CEAM. 'Good', for example, includes: adoption of a valued ecosystem component (VEC)-based perspective; agency/proponent and public context scoping; use of scenarios where reasonably forseeable future actions are uncertain; and dissemination of good

practice. Examples of 'bad' lessons include: over focus on biophysical environmental components at the expense of socio-economic; vague terms of reference for studies; inadequate guidance; lack of expertise and overcomplex studies. Downright 'ugly' include for example: minimal attention to CEAM; lack of commitment by key decision makers; lack of multi-stakeholder collaboration and – on occasion – an attitude that CEAM cannot be done. In this context, Canter *et al.* (2010) conclude: 'By all accounts, cumulative effects continue to be a persistent analytical challenge, although there is evidence of progress towards better practice.'

12.4.2 Socio-economic impacts

Widening the scope of EIA to include socio-economic impacts in a much better way is seen as a particularly important item for the agenda. Although most of the environmental receptors listed in EC and UK regulations are still biophysical in nature, the inclusion of 'human beings' as one of the receptors to be considered in EIA does imply a wider definition of 'the environment', encompassing its human (i.e. social, economic and cultural) dimensions. The inclusion of socio-economic impacts can help to better identify all of the potential biophysical impacts of a project, because socio-economic and biophysical impacts are interrelated (Newton 1995). Early inclusion of socio-economic considerations in the EIA can provide an opportunity to modify project design or implementation to minimize adverse socio-economic effects and to maximize beneficial effects (Chadwick 2002). It also allows a more complete picture of a project's impacts, in a consistent format, in a publicly available document. Failure to include such impacts can lead to delays in the EIA process, since the competent authority may request further information on such matters.

While there are varying interpretations of the scope of socio-economic or social impacts, over time a number of reports have highlighted the importance of this area (see, for example, CEPA 1994; IAIA 1994; Vanclay 2003; Glasson 2009). SIA has been defined by Burdge (1999) as 'the systematic analysis, in advance, of the likely impacts a proposed action will have on the life of individuals and communities'. Most development decisions involve trade-offs between biophysical and socio-economic impacts. Also, development projects affect various groups differently; there are invariably winners and losers. Yet the consideration of socio-economic impacts is very variable in practice, and often very weak. Some countries have useful practice and associated legislative impetus for SIA (for example, the USA, Canada and some states of Australia). International funding institutions are also increasingly giving a high profile to such impacts, as shown at Section 10.9.

However, in Europe the profile is lower, and the consideration of socio-economic impacts has continued to be the poor relation (Chadwick 2002; Glasson 2009). The uncertain status of such impacts, plus the lack of best-practice guidance on their assessment, has resulted in a partial approach in practice. When socio-economic impacts are included, there tends to still be a focus on the more measurable direct employment impacts. The consideration of the social–cultural impacts (such as severance, alienation, social polarization, crime and health) is often very marginal. Although there is now increasing momentum behind the assessment of health impacts, the important area of crime and safety has had a much lower profile. Glasson and Cozens (2011) provide an update on some key issues for advancing the better consideration of these topics in EIA practice including: the need to employ meaningful data, including 'fear of crime' considerations; the consideration of innovative approaches to the use of indicators;

and use of evidence and concepts from the field of environmental criminology.

However, the fuller and better consideration of socio-economic impacts does raise issues and challenges, for example about the types of impact, their measurement, the role of public participation and their position in EIA. One categorization of socio-economic impacts is into: (a) quantitatively measurable impacts, such as population changes, and the effects on employment opportunities or on local financial implications of a proposed project, and (b) non-quantitatively measurable impacts, such as effects on social relationships, psychological attitudes, community cohesion, cultural life or social structures (CEPA 1994). Such impacts are wide-ranging; many are not easily measured, and direct communication with people about their perceptions of socio-economic impacts is often the only method of documenting such impacts. There is an important symbiotic relationship between developing public participation approaches and the fuller inclusion of socio-economic impacts. SIA can establish the baseline of groups that can provide the framework for public participation to further identify issues associated with a development proposal. Such issues may be more local, subjective, informal and judgemental than those normally covered in EIA, but they cannot be ignored. Perceptions of the impacts of a project and the distribution of those impacts often largely determine the positions taken by various groups on a given project and any associated controversy.

12.4.3 Health impact assessment

Health impact assessment (HIA) is a major growth area in the field of impact assessment, as evidenced by the popularity in recent years of the HIA 'track' in the annual conference of the influential International Association for Impact Assessment. There has been a surge of academic papers, reviews, guidelines and websites relating to HIA (Ahmad 2004), but what is HIA, where is it best practised, how is it practised and how does it relate to EIA as discussed in this book?

'Health' includes social, economic, cultural and psychological well-being – and the ability to adapt to the stress of daily life (Health Canada 1999). Many environmental factors give rise to positive

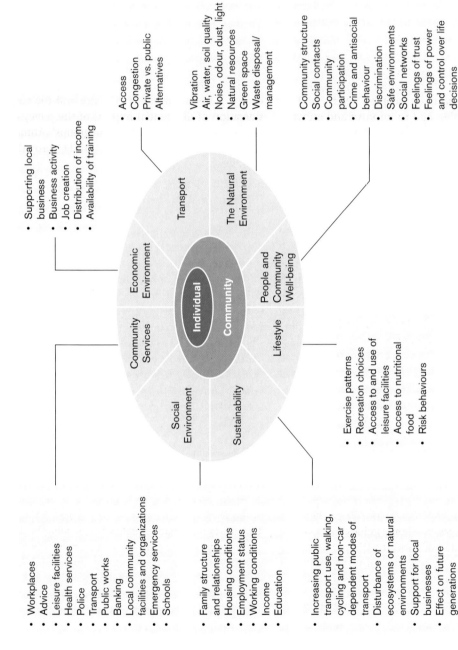

- Supporting local
  business
- Business activity
- Job creation
- Distribution of income
- Availability of training

- Access
- Congestion
- Private vs. public
- Alternatives

- Vibration
- Air, water, soil quality
- Noise, odour, dust, light
- Natural resources
- Green space
- Waste disposal/
  management

- Community structure
- Social contacts
- Community
  participation
- Crime and antisocial
  behaviour
- Discrimination
- Safe environments
- Social networks
- Feelings of trust
- Feelings of power
  and control over life
  decisions

- Workplaces
- Advice
- Leisure facilities
- Health services
- Police
- Transport
- Public works
- Banking
- Local community
  facilities and organizations
- Emergency services
- Schools

- Family structure
  and relationships
- Housing conditions
- Employment status
- Working conditions
- Income
- Education

- Increasing public
  transport use, walking,
  cycling and non-car
  dependent modes of
  transport
- Disturbance of
  ecosystems or natural
  environments
- Support for local
  businesses
- Effect on future
  generations

- Exercise patterns
- Recreation choices
- Access to and use of
  leisure facilities
- Access to nutritional
  food
- Risk behaviours

Transport

The Natural
Environment

Economic
Environment

People and
Community
Well-being

Community
Services

Individual

Community

Lifestyle

Social
Environment

Sustainability

Figure 12.2

Some of the many environmental determinants of health outcomes

Source: Western Australia Department of Health 2007

and negative health oucomes, as exemplified in Figure 12.2 from a very useful Western Australian publication on HIA (Western Australia Department of Health 2007). Health impact refers to a change in the existing health status of a population within a defined geographical area over a specified period of time. HIA is a combination of procedures and methods by which a policy, plan, programme or project may be judged as to the effects it may have on the health of a population. It provides a useful, flexible approach to helping those developing and delivering proposals to consider their potential (and actual) impacts on people's health, and on health inequalities, and to improve and enhance a proposal (Taylor and Quigley 2002; Taylor and Blair-Stevens 2002; WHO Regional Office for Europe 2003; Douglas 2003).

HIA is well advanced in a number of developed countries, particularly Canada, the Netherlands, in parts of Scandinavia, and more recently in Australia and the UK. Some developing countries are also finding it very relevant to their needs (see Phool-charaeon *et al.* 2003, for Thailand). Policy drivers can be found at various levels of government. In the UK, for example, see the Department of Health and the Association of Public Health Observatories websites. In the EU, the Directive on SEA specifically and very usefully refers to the impact of plans and programmes on human health (see Box 11.1).

The main stages in the HIA process are very similar to those used in EIA, including: screening, scoping, profiling (identifying the current health status of people within the defined spatial boundaries of the project using existing health indicators and population data), assessment (HIA stresses the importance of consultation with community groups to identify potential impacts), implementation and decision-making, and monitoring and continual review (Douglas 2003). There are now also many useful national guides; for example, for Ireland (IPHI 2009) and for Western Australia as previously noted. Appendix 6 provides further UK and international website gateways into the burgeoning HIA field.

The overlap between HIA and EIA in terms of process, and in terms of many categories of baseline data (Figure 12.2 indicates the potential wide coverage of HIA) does raise questions as to why HIA and EIA are not better integrated. Ahmad (2004) suggests an interesting list of reasons for

this, including the difficulty of establishing causality between population health and multiple pollutants; limitations on resources to carry out such assessments within the often tight timeframes of EIA; confidentiality of some health data; lack of mandatory legal framework requiring HIA; and bias among EIA professionals towards engineering and ecology backgrounds. However, he also concludes that there are many benefits to be gained from closer integration, in terms of shared experience, procedures, data and values. With regard to the last, HIA can bring to EIA 'values such as equity, transparent use of evidence and the consideration of differential impacts of the policy or project on various population subgroups' (Ahmad 2004). The SEA Directive 2001/42/EC provides an important milestone on the desirable path to a more integrated approach – a concept that is developed a little further in Section 12.4.8.

12.4.4 Equality impact assessment

It has been noted several times in this book that the distributional impacts of proposed developments rarely fall evenly on affected parties and areas and are mostly ignored in EIA. For example, a UK study by Walker *et al.* (2005), which examined the extent to which EIA, and impact assessment methodologies more generally, involved an assessment of the distribution of impacts likely to result from policy-making or project approval, found that the methodologies used provided no effective consideration of distributional or environmental justice concerns. Though a particular project may be assessed as bringing a general benefit, some groups and/or geographical areas may be receiving most of any adverse effects, the main benefits going to others elsewhere. Figure 4.9 shows a rare example of equality impact assessment in EIA. This raises important equality issues, and there is a growing literature on issues of environmental justice (or perhaps it should be environmental injustice), where certain sections/areas of the community receive increasing environmental burdens, become socially and environmentally more unacceptable places to live, and risk becoming trapped in a vicious circle of decline (Agyeman and Evans 2004; Downey 2005).

In recent years such issues have begun to be addressed, partly through the growth of equality impact assessment (EqIA). An early step was gender impact assessment; this received international prominence through the World Conference on Women at Beijing, which in 1995 called on governments to 'mainstream a gender perspective into all policies and programmes so that, before decisions are taken an analysis is made of the effects on women and men respectively.' This requirement was then built into the Treaty of Amsterdam, Articles 2 and 3, 1997. In the UK EqIAs were introduced first in Northern Ireland where legislation had made it unlawful to discriminate on the grounds of religious belief or political opinion. Disability equality requirements followed and since 2010, the Equality Act has provided the underpinning legal framework in the UK.

EqIA is about considering how projects, plans, programmes and policies may impact, either positively or negatively, on different sectors of the population in different ways. The key sectors typically considered include age, gender, race/ethnicity (including gypsies and travellers), religion, disability and sexual orientation, although other dimensions could include rural vs. urban, poor vs. rich, or people with vs. without access to cars. The steps in the process are also very similar to those used in EIA, and again there might be merit in the integration of the approach into the wider EIA process. It is important to identify the baseline equality characteristics and needs of the population likely to be affected by the development proposal. For example: is the workforce skewed towards male and young employees? Are some ethnic groups substantially under-represented in the workforce? Are various socio-economic issues concentrated in certain wards of particular towns? In England some of the spatial inequalities can be identified in some detail by using information from the Index of Multiple Deprivation (IMD 2011); relative levels of deprivation (for local authority areas, down to ward level) can be assessed by their rank position relative to all other English local authority areas; and regular updating of the IMD provides valuable trend data. The potential impacts of a proposed development on the baseline can be assessed and mitigation and enhancement measures can be introduced to hopefully improve the equality outcomes. Table 12.3 provides a summary example of equalities impacts in an EqIA that accompanied an ES for a large mixed-

use redevelopment of nearly 5000 homes of mixed tenure, along with associated health, community, leisure, education and retail facilities in inner London (Scott Wilson 2006).

12.4.5 Appropriate assessment

Appropriate assessment is a Europe-specific form of assessment that tests the impacts of a project or plan on the integrity of internationally important nature conservation sites: Special Protection Areas for birds, and Special Areas of Conservation for habitats and species.[1] Appropriate assessment is required through Articles 6.3 and 6.4 of the Habitats Directive:

6.3 Any plan or project not directly connected with or necessary to the management of the site but likely to have a significant effect thereon, either individually or in combination with other plans or projects, shall be subject to appropriate assessment of its implications for the site in view of the site's conservation objectives. In the light of the conclusions of the assessment of the implications for the site and subject to the provisions of paragraph 4, the competent national authorities shall agree to the plan or project only after having ascertained that it will not adversely affect the integrity of the site concerned and, if appropriate, after having obtained the opinion of the general public.

6.4 If, in spite of a negative assessment of the implications for the site and in the absence of alternative solutions, a plan or project must nevertheless be carried out for imperative reasons of overriding public interest, including those of social or economic nature, the Member State shall take all compensatory measures necessary to ensure that the overall coherence of Natura 2000 is protected. It shall inform the Commission of the compensatory measures adopted.

An entire book could be written just about appropriate assessment but, in short, it focuses on a very specific part of the environment (the integrity of SPAs and SACs), considers cumulative ('in combination') impacts, and is very precautionary (a plan or project may only be permitted

Table 12.3 Illustration of EqIA impacts

Issue	Affected group	Impact
(a) Summary of significant adverse impacts affecting specific equalities groups		
Health	Mental health sufferers, including among BME population	Temporary increase in stress as result of demolition and redevelopment
Community cohesion	BME groups, women, including lone parents, children, gay and lesbian people	Temporary or permanent disruption of existing social networks, increased isolation as result of rehousing/redevelopment
Community facilities	BME groups, particularly Turkish community	Permanent loss of facilities for social gatherings
Well-being	Older women	Temporary or permanent loneliness, isolation as result of decant process
Well-being	Disabled people	Temporary risk of individual needs being overlooked during decant and redevelopment process
Well-being	Older people	Temporary/permanent stress, disruption, anxiety increased as result of change, including change to established routine
Well-being	Children	Temporary/long-term disruption to living environment during childhood as a result of living on major redevelopment
Leisure and open spaces and well-being	Children and young people	Possible permanent impact of private courtyards actively excluding casual use by older children including teenagers – both on their well-being and courtyard cohesion
Leisure and open spaces	Children and young people	Temporary loss of access to open spaces, hang-outs in public spaces, play areas during construction
(b) Summary of significant beneficial impacts affecting specific equalities groups (housing, employment and skills only)		
Housing	BME households	Improved housing quality Reduced overcrowding New homes for young people Increased home ownership levels in affordable housing
	Women/ single parent households	More appropriate housing for young children
	Disabled people	More accessible homes to enable independent living
	Older people	Improved insulation and heating for warmer homes Lifetime homes support independent living
	Children	Reduced overcrowding More generous bedroom and storage provision for children in social rented sector
	All groups	More storage, less accidents around home
Employment and skills	BME	Target group for construction employment opportunities Targeted skills training
	Women	Children's centre facilitates women to seek employment
	Women	Target group for construction employment Targeted skills training

Source: Scott Wilson (2006)

if it will have no significant impact on site integrity or if other very tough tests are passed). Appropriate assessment is called 'appropriate' because the level of detail of the assessment, and when the assessment can stop, depends on the project/plan and relevant SPA/SACs. The European Commission (2000) has published guidance that explains how appropriate assessment can be carried out in up to four steps, with the findings of each step determining whether the next step is needed:

- *Screening*: Determine whether the plan, 'in combination' with other plans and projects, is likely to have a significant adverse impact on a European site.
- *Appropriate assessment*: Determine the impact on the integrity of the European site of the plan, 'in combination' with other projects or plans, with respect to the site's structure, function and conservation objectives. Where there are adverse impacts, assess the potential mitigation of those impacts. Where there aren't, then the plan can proceed as it is.
- *Assessment of alternatives solutions*: Where the plan is assessed as having an adverse effect (or risk of this) on the integrity of a European site, examine alternative ways of achieving the plan objectives that avoid adverse impacts on the integrity of the European site.
- *Assessment where no alternative solutions* remain and where adverse impacts remain: Assess compensatory measures where, in the light of an assessment of imperative reasons of overriding public interest, it is deemed that the plan should proceed.

A high-profile example of appropriate assessment was the extension to Rotterdam Harbour. The project would significantly affect about 3,000 hectares of marine and natterjack toad habitats, but there were no alternatives and it would create roughly 10,000 long-term jobs. The project was given permission on condition that compensation was provided in the form of a new marine reserve, 25,000 hectares of protected area, and new dunes. A contrasting case was a proposed container terminal (port) at Dibden Bay in southern England, which would have affected the integrity of the Solent and Southampton Water SPA. This proposal was refused on appropriate assessment grounds because alternatives were available in the form of other UK ports that could provide enough container capacity.

12.4.6 Climate change and EIA

Climate change presents a fundamental challenge for all countries worldwide. EIA (and SEA) would seem directly relevant and very appropriate as tools: to assess the impacts of development actions on climate change, and climate change impacts on those development actions, and to advance appropriate mitigation and adaptation measures. Annex IV of the EU EIA Directive does identify the following in the important information to be supplied by the developer:

> 3. A description of the aspects of the environment likely to be significantly affected by the propsed project, including in particular, population, fauna, flora, soil, water, air, *climatic factors*, material assets ... and the inter-relationships between the above factors. (author emphasis)

Further, the UK government (DCLG 2007) noted that 'LPAs should not require specific and standalone assessments (of climate change) where the requisite information can be provided through ... environmental impact assessments'. In 2009, a survey of EIA practitioners by the UK Institute of Environmental Assessment and Management (IEMA 2010a) found that 88 per cent felt that, where relevant, carbon emissions should be considered in the EIA and reported in the ES.

Yet recent practice suggests that EIA is not fulfilling its potential with regard to climate change. While the EIA Directive does mention climatic factors, the 2009 review of the EU EIA Directive (CEC 2009) notes that climate change issues are not expressly addressed in the Directive and that Member States recognize that they are not adequately identified and assessed within EIA practice. Wilson and Piper (2010) note similar experience from Canada, where a report by the Canadian Environmental Assessment Agency (CEEA 2003) found that climate change had not been well covered in most EAs. They suggest a number of reasons for this limited take-up including, for example, the often shorter term time

Table 12.4 IEMA principles for EIA mitigation of GHG emissions

Overarching principles

- The GHG emissions from all projects will contribute to climate change; the largest inter-related cumulative environmental effect.
- The consequences of a changing climate have the potential to lead to significant environmental effects on all topics in the EIA Directive – e.g. population, fauna, soil, etc.
- The UK has legally binding GHG reduction targets; EIA must therefore give due consideration to how a project will contribute to the achievement of these targets.
- GHG emissions have a combined environmental effect that is approaching a scientifically defined environmental limit; as such any GHG emissions or reductions from a project might be considered to be significant.
- The EIA process should, at an early stage, influence the design and location of projects to optimise GHG performance and limit likely contributions to GHG emissions.

More specific assessment principles

- During scoping, climate change and mitigation issues and opportunities should be considered alongside each other to ensure integration in project design.
- The scope of GHG emissions must consider the relevant policy framework (local to global) and should also review the relevant findings in any associated SA/SEA.
- When assessing alternatives, consideration of the relative GHG emissions performance of each option should be considered alongside a range of environmental criteria.
- Baseline considerations related to GHG emissions should refer to the policy framework and also include the current situation and, where possible, take account of the likely future baseline situation.
- Quantification of GHG emissions (e.g. carbon calculators) will not always be necessary within EIA; however where qualitative assessment is used (e.g. emissions trends related to construction practices) it must be robust, transparent and justifiable.
- The assessment should aim to consider whole life effects (e.g. embodied energy, and emissions related to construction, operation and decommissioning – as relevant).
- The significance of a projects's emissions should be based on its net GHG effects, which may be positive (reduced) or negative (additional).
- Where GHG emissions cannot be avoided, the EIA should aim to reduce the residual significance of a project's emissions at all stages – design, construction, operation, etc.
- Where GHG emissions remain significant, but cannot be reduced further, approaches to compensate the project's remaining emissions should be considered.

Source: IEMA (2010a)

horizons of EIA compared with climate change, difficulties in dealing with climate change uncertainty, some fragmentation of EIA (as noted in Chapter 1 of this book) and the difficulty of addressing interrelationships of factors (CEC 2009).

So what might be the way forward for EIA and climate change? The IEMA (2010a, b) has produced assessment principles relating to both climate change mitigation and adaptation; Table 12.4 sets out some over-arching principles, and more specific EIA assessment principles.

12.4.7 Resilience thinking

Project planning typically assumes that future changes will be gradual and predictable, whereas in reality they often come as sharp, unforeseen shocks: floods, volcanic eruptions, pandemics, economic crises, power outages etc. Resilience thinking is about how to deal with such shocks not by setting up systems to protect people and developments against all negative future change (as in risk assessment), but rather by making them able to cope with the shocks when they do come. It is the equivalent of teaching a child safe cycling and assertiveness rather than keeping them home from school for fear of accidents and bullying.

Some quite subtle and complex principles underlie resilience thinking, which can only be briefly summarized here. First is the *inevitability of change*, and the concept of adaptive cycles. All socio-economic systems go through an initial period of slow growth and accumulation, be it the formation of a woodland or a community group.

This is typically followed by a short sharp period of decline, precipitated by a shock, say a woodland fire or the death of a key member of the community group. Depending on the system's resilience, the end result can be a reorganization into an equally 'good' new state – say, a new young woodland – or a worse state like a charred unproductive field or the disbanding of the community group. The phase of decline might be delayed, for instance by putting out forest fires, but this simply delays and escalates the impacts of the change when it does occur.

The second is the *importance of thresholds or tipping points*. Socio-environmental systems have a certain ability to recover from impacts, but if they are tipped over a threshold, then they plunge into a new state, which is normally disproportionately hard to recover from. For instance, it is much harder to return a eutrophic lake to a healthy state than to prevent a healthy lake from becoming eutrophic.

Third is *the importance of 'slow variables'* like climate, soil, global economic systems, or social networks. These systems act as buffers and reservoirs for the regeneration of smaller, faster systems such as habitats, species, communities and individuals. However, when the slow variables themselves are worn away (e.g. through a drop-feed of greenhouse gases or soil erosion) then this buffer and regeneration function is also worn down.

What does this mean for the planning of major projects? Some types of development – both the types of projects and how they are designed and implemented – are more resilient than others. Resilient projects would:

Embrace variability rather than control it. Instead of increased flood defences, 'just in time' production and air conditioning, this would involve designing projects to cope with floods, having industrial processes that can cope with delayed parts, and having windows that open in offices and on public transport.

Build in redundancy or duplication, so that if one aspect fails the other one can take over. The Deepwater Horizon oil spill would have been a minor blip for BP if the oil platform had had a back-up blow-out preventer. Providing access to a development by both road and rail,

and putting emergency gates in the central reservation of major roads to allow cars to turn around, allows flexibility in case of accidents, flooding or congestion. Housing developments with 'spare' land can convert this to food production or temporary shelter if necessary.

Maintain some modularity or disconnectedness, since over-connected systems are susceptible to shocks and transmit them rapidly. In the Middle Ages, villages would shut themselves off during times of plague. Modern equivalents are dykes, bunds, security barriers/gates and other access controls.

Recognize the importance of slow variables. This would mean giving greater weight in project planning and planning decisions to things like loss of high-quality agricultural land, water cycles, emissions of greenhouse gases, loss of customs and languages, and resettlement of communities.

Create tighter feedback loops between human actions and environmental outcomes. Many of our impacts occur away from us: in other countries where our food is grown and our clothes are manufactured, or in other parts of the UK where our energy is produced and waste disposed. Examples of this approach include greater emphasis on local rather than centralized production (e.g. energy, water, food), the proximity principle in siting waste disposal projects, and community development and ownership of infrastructure projects.

Promote and sustain diversity in all forms (environmental, social and economic). This principle runs counter to the common approach to decision-making, which promotes efficiency, targets and guarantees, but it is diversity that allows different responses to shocks and provides a source of future options. Examples include protecting areas of ecological diversity, promoting pilot projects for new technologies (e.g. various forms of tidal energy or carbon storage), and protecting indigenous people's lifestyles (adapted from Walker and Salt 2006).

Table 12.5 shows how the results of resilience assessment might differ from the results of traditional project planning.

Table 12.5 Contrasting resilience and traditional project planning approaches

Scenario	Results of traditional project planning	Results of resilience thinking	Source on which this example was based
A very small-scale (three person) biodiesel producer in Barbados helps to reduce waste going to landfill and provides 'indigenous' fuel, but competes with others for limited waste cooking oil as fuel, and production costs are high due to the small scale nature of the operation	Increase the size of the operation, mechanize it, improve its efficiency	Develop a co-operative of small-scale biodiesel producers; develop biodiesel as a tourism project that provides tourism income as well as money from selling the diesel	Gadreau and Gibson (2010)
Two small villages in Tajikistan are facing water shortages due to ageing infrastructure and increasing population of humans and livestock	Build a new reservoir	Train local people to repair and maintain the existing water infrastructure, improve family planning, regulate water use through quotas and rules	Fabricius *et al.* (2009)
Increasing number of 'muddy floods' from agricultural run-off in England and Belgium cause millions of euros of damage each year	Improve flood defences	Improve 'institutional memory': value and maintain historical understanding of factors leading to these floods and how to manage the floods	Boardman and Vandaele (2010)

The Resilience Alliance has also developed a resilience assessment framework (RA 2010). This differs from EIA in that, *inter alia*, it places greater emphasis on uncertainty and disruptions (both past and future), considers higher scale actions and events that could affect the project scale, identifies thresholds of change and alternate states that could result from exceeding these thresholds, and focuses explicitly on the governance systems that manage changes. We are not aware of any cases where resilience assessment and EIA have been integrated, but clearly resilience assessment has the potential to strengthen EIA and make EIA projects better able to cope with future change, and we expect resilience thinking to be increasingly integrated into EIA.

12.4.8 Integrated impact assessment

As noted at the beginning of the book (Section 1.5.3), there has been an explosion of terms in relation to environmental assessment. One of these is that of integrated environmental assessment, which can relate to both environmental themes and techniques. In terms of themes, the preced-

ing discussion of widening of scope to include more clearly socio-economic, health, equality and resilience content, can lead to a more integrated impact assessment (IIA), with decisions based partly on the extent to which various biophysical, social and economic impacts can be traded (Figure 12.3). For example, decision-makers might be unwilling to trade critical biophysical assets (e.g. a main river system and the quality of water supply) for jobs or lifestyle, but willing to trade less critical biophysical assets. Integrated impact assessment differs from traditional EIA in that it is consciously multi-disciplinary, does not take citizens' participation or the ultimate users of EIA for granted and recognizes the critical role of complexity and uncertainty in most decisions about the environment (Bailey *et al.* 1996; Davis 1996). Hence it tolerates a much broader array of methods and perspectives (quantitative and qualitative, economic and sociological, computer modelling and oral testimony) for evaluating and judging alternative courses of action. However, integration is not without its problems, including limitations on the transferability of assessment methods (see *Project Appraisal* 1996). The Integrated Assessment

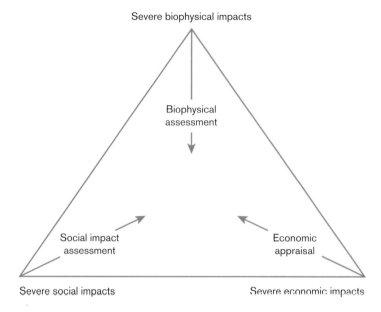

Severe biophysical impacts

Biophysical
assessment

Social impact
assessment

Economic
appraisal

Severe social impacts

Severe economic impacts

Figure 12.3

Integrated impact assessment

Workshop at the IAIA 2002 Conference highlighted the continuing problems of including social processes in integrated assessment (IAIA 2002).

Another equally important perspective is of the integration of relevant planning, environmental protection and pollution procedures. At the one extreme the UK still has multiple regulations for EIA, grafting the procedures into an array of relevant planning and other legislation; there is also parallel environmental protection and pollution legislation. At the other, there is the New Zealand 'one-stop shop' *Resource Management Act*. A better integration of relevant procedures represents another challenge for most EIA systems.

12.4.9 Extending EIA to project design: towards environmental impact design

An important and positive trend in EIA has been its application at increasingly early stages of project planning. For instance, while the DoT's 1983 *Manual of environmental appraisal* applied only to detailed route options, its later *Design manual for roads and bridges* requires a staged approach covering, in turn, broadly defined route corridors,

route options and the chosen route (Highways Agency 2011). National Grid also uses multiple levels of environmental analysis for its transmission lines, from broad feasibility studies to detailed design (National Grid 20xx). This application of EIA to the early stages of project planning helps to improve project design and to avoid the delayed and costly identification of environmental constraints that comes from carrying out EIA once the project design is completed.

McDonald and Brown (1995) suggest that the project designer must be made part of the EIA team:

> Currently, most formal administrative and reporting requirements for EIA are based on its original role as a stand alone report carried out distinct from, but in parallel with the project design . . . We can redress [EIA limitations] by transferring much of the philosophy, the insights and techniques which we currently use in environmental assessments, directly into planning and design activities.

A further evolution of this concept is to use EIA to identify basic environmental constraints

Figure 12.4

Art and development project combined: the Hundertwasser/Spittelau incinerator in Vienna

Source: Wikimedia Commons

before the design process is begun, but then allow designers freedom to design innovative and attractive structures as long as they meet those constraints. Figure 12.4 is an example of this approach: the magnificent Hundertwasser incinerator in Vienna, an incinerator that people might actually *want* to have in their city.

Holstein (1996) calls this postmodern approach 'environmental impact design' (EID), and distinguishes it from EIA's traditionally conservative, conservation-based focus.[2] The following paragraphs explain Holstein's view of EID.

> EIA as presently practised deconstructs a site: it takes an environment apart to highlight the different interacting components within it (e.g. soil, water, flora). EIA suggests that the site has another (environmental) function other than that for which it is being developed. Yet this relationship to deconstruction is only superficial because EIA is conservation based; it makes little challenge to the fixed hierarchies of modernism that underpin it,

such as development-induced growth and technological subservience. Environmental design within EIA is too often merely a byproduct of assessment or is even handed back to the developer to have another shot at the design themselves. It makes little use of artistic-based metaphors to provide any re-enchantment or return to human landscape values, it makes no attempt to rip apart environmental function and form, and creates no demand for the kind of relative individualism needed to reflect cultural sustainability to an uninterested-unless-aroused population (all characteristics of postmodernism). Through this passivity of EIA, time, space, communication, leadership – all the key elements of good flowing design are lost.

This said, initially it might be argued that true postmodernism is simply beyond the remit of an EIA that exists for objective assessment rather than artistic purposes. The above description should be called EID. EID emphasizes the artistic contribution

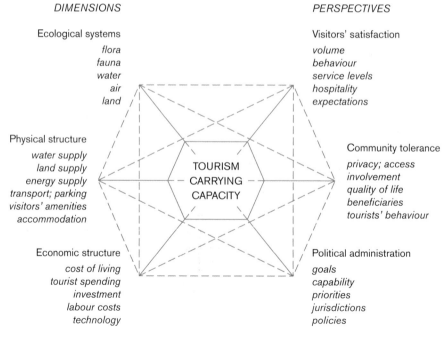

Figure 12.5

Carrying capacity: a tourism example

Source: Glasson *et al.* 1995

to EIA; it requires a different set of approaches (and probably personnel) than pure EIA, as well as creativity and elements of cultural vision. To an extent, some of the principles of EID are already being undertaken in EIA, in the mitigation sections of EISs, and especially within environmental divisions of the larger developers (e.g. the utilities) who often seem to see the formal EIA process as merely a lateral extension to their own design policies. Even so, rarely is it recognized as an artistic activity.

The key difference between EIA and EID lies in the concept of 'unmodifiable design'. Traditionally, EIAs are carried out on projects in which most of the structural elements have already been finalized. In more EID-oriented approaches, there is less unmodifiable design, and thus more scope for introducing environmentally sound design as mitigation measures. An even more radical path would be a postmodern EIA which aims to begin with so few unmodifiable design ideas that the EIA essentially becomes the leading player in design (adapted from Holstein 1996).

12.4.10 Complementary changes: enhancing skills and knowledge

The previous discussions indicate that EIA practitioners need to develop further their substantive knowledge of the wider environment. There is also an important role for 'State of the environment reports' and the development of 'carrying capacity and sustainability indicators' – if not interpreted too narrowly. Carrying capacity is multi-dimensional and multi-perspective (see Figure 12.5 for an example for tourism impact assessment). Carrying capacity is also an elastic concept, and the capacity can be increased through good management.

Practitioners also need to develop both 'technical' and 'participatory' approaches, using, for example, focus group, Delphi and mediation approaches. EIA has been too long dominated by the 'clinical expert' with the detached quantitative analysis. However, there is still a place for the sensible use of the rapidly developing technology – including expert systems and GIS (Rodriguez-Bachiller with Glasson 2004). There is also a need for more capacity building of EIA expertise, plus relevant research, including, for example,

more comparative studies and longitudinal studies (following impacts over a longer life cycle – moving towards adaptive EIA).

∙∙

12.5 Extending EIA to project implementation: environmental management systems, audits and plans

An environmental management system (EMS), like EIA, is a tool that helps organizations to take more responsibility for their actions, by determining their aims, putting them into practice and monitoring whether they are being achieved. However, in contrast with the orientation of EIA to future development actions, EMS involves the review, assessment and incremental improvement of an *existing organization*'s environmental effects. EMS can thus be seen as a continuation of EIA principles into the implementation stage of a project. In essence, EMS and EIA can be seen as environmental protection tools with complementary purposes, with EIA seeking to anticipate and mitigate/enhance impacts of proposed new projects at the planning and design stage, and EMS helping organizations to effectively manage the day to day impacts during the full life cycle of such projects (Palframan 2010).

EMS has evolved from environmental audits, which were first carried out in the 1970s by private firms in the USA for financial and legal reasons as an extension of financial audits. Auditing later spread to private firms in Europe as well and, in the late 1980s, to local authorities in response to public pressure to be 'green'. In the early 1990s environmental auditing was strengthened and expanded to encompass a total quality approach to organizations' operations through EMS. EMS is now seen as good practice and has mostly subsumed environmental auditing.

This section reviews existing standards on EMS, briefly discusses the application of EMS and environmental auditing by both private companies and local authorities, and concludes by considering the links between EMS and EIA, using environmental management plans (EMPs) and other vehicles.

12.5.1 Standards and regulations on EMS

Three EMS standards apply in the UK: the EC's Eco-Management and Audit Scheme (EMAS) of 1993, which was revised in 2001; the International Organization for Standardization's (ISO) series 14000; and the more recent British Standard (BS) 8555. The schemes are compatible with each another, but differ slightly in their requirements.

The EC's EMAS scheme was adopted by EC Regulation 1836/93 in July 1993 (EC 1993), and became operational in April 1995. It was originally restricted to companies in industrial sectors, but since the 1993 regulations were replaced in 2001 by Regulation 761/2001 (EC 2001a) it has been open to all economic sectors, including public and private services. It was most recently updated in 2009/10 by Regulation 1221/2009, which came into force in January 2010. It is a voluntary scheme and can apply on a site-by-site basis. To receive EMAS registration, an organization must:

- Establish an environmental policy agreed by top management, which includes provisions for compliance with environmental regulation, and a commitment to continual improvement of environmental performance.
- Conduct an environmental review that considers the environmental impacts of the organization's activities, products and services; its framework of environmental legislation; and its existing environmental management practices.
- Establish an EMS in the light of the results of the environmental review that aims to achieve the environmental policy. This must include an explanation of responsibilities, objectives, means, operational procedures, training needs, monitoring and communication systems.
- Carry out an environmental audit that assesses the EMS in place, conformity with the organization's policy and programme and compliance with relevant environmental legislation.
- Provide a statement of its environmental performance that details the results achieved against the environmental objectives, and steps proposed to continuously improve the organization's environmental performance. (EC 2001b)

The environmental review, EMS, audit procedure and environmental statement (ES) must be approved by an accredited eco management and audit scheme (EMAS) verifier. The validated statement must be sent to the EMAS competent body for registration and made publicly available before an organization can use the EMAS logo. In the UK the competent body is the IEMA. Although EMAS was originally oriented towards larger private organizations, it can also apply to local authorities and smaller companies.

The *International Organization for Standardization's ISO 14000* series was first discussed in 1991,

Table 12.6 Differences between EMAS and ISO14001

	EMAS	ISO 14001
Preliminary environmental review	Verified initial review	No review
External communication and verification	Environmental policy, objectives, EMS and details of organization's performance made public	Environmental policy made public
Audits	Frequency and methodology of audits of the EMS and of environmental performance	Audits of the EMS (frequency of methodology not specified)
Contractors and suppliers	Required influence over contractors and suppliers	Relevant procedures are communicated to contractors and suppliers
Commitments and requirements	Employee involvement, continuous improvement of environmental performance and compliance with environmental legislation	Commitment of continual improvement of the EMS rather than a demonstration of continual improvement of environmental performance

Source: EC 2001b

and a comprehensive set of EMS standards was published in September 1996. These include ISO 14001 on EMS specifications (ISO 1996a), ISO 14004 on general EMS guidance (ISO 1996b) and ISO 14010–14014, which give guidance on environmental auditing and review. EMAS and ISO 14001 are compatible, but have some differences. These are shown in Table 12.6.

In 2003 the UK government introduced a new EMS initiative – BS 8555 (*Guide to the implementation of an environmental management system including environmental performance evaluation*) – to assist organizations, in particular small and medium sized enterprises, to implement an environmental management system and subsequently achieve EMAS registration (DEFRA 2003). The standard includes guidance on how to develop indicators, so right from the start it is possible to know whether environmental impacts have been successfully reduced. The IEMA Acorn Scheme provides an officially recognized EMS standard recommended by the government. Acorn provides a route to EMS implementation, broken down into a series of logical, convenient, manageable phases using the British Standard BS 8555, plus a clearly defined route plan to ISO 14001 certification and/or EMAS registration.

12.5.2 Implementation of EMS and environmental auditing

By 2010, more than 130,000 organizations worldwide had gained ISO 14001 certification, with over 10,000 in the UK. In addition in the UK over 150 organizations have achieved the BS8555 and IEMA Acorn scheme, and another 500 are working through the scheme. Europewide, 4,500 organizations have participated in EMAS, with over 70 of these in the UK. Organizations perceive EMS as a way to reduce their costs through good management practices such as waste reduction and energy efficiency. They also see EMS as good publicity and, less directly, as a way of boosting employees' morale. However, private companies still have problems implementing EMS due to commercial confidentiality, legal liability, cost and lack of commitment. Smaller companies are especially affected by the cost implications of establishing EMS systems, and have been slower than the larger companies in applying it to their operations. The use of EMS by local authorities has been limited by cutbacks in central government funding, government reorganization and growing public concerns about economic rather than environmental issues.

12.5.3 Links between EMS and EIA

Environmental information

The growth in EMS is important to EIA for several reasons. First, EMS of both public sector and private sector organizations will increasingly generate environmental information that will also be useful when carrying out EIAs. For example, local authorities' State of the Environment Reports provide data on environmental conditions in areas that can be used in EIA baseline studies. Generally, such reports will contain information on such topics as local air and water quality, noise, land use, landscape, wildlife habitats and transport.

In contrast, private companies' environmental audit findings have traditionally been kept confidential, and it is noticeable from Section 12.5.2 that many more companies have opted for ISO 14001 accreditation – which requires only limited disclosure of information – than EMAS accreditation. Thus a private company's EMS is likely to be useful for EIA only if that company intends to open a similar facility elsewhere. However, environmental auditing information about levels of wastes and emissions produced by different types of industrial processes, the types of pollution abatement equipment and operating procedures used to minimize these by-products, and the effectiveness of the equipment and operating procedures will be useful for determining the impact of similar future developments and mitigation measures. Some of these audits are also likely to provide models of 'best practice', which other firms can aspire to in their existing and future facilities. Most interestingly, however, project EIAs are increasingly used as a starting point for their projects' EMSs. For instance, emission limits stated in an EIA can be used as objectives in the company's EMS, once it is operational. The EMS can also test whether the mitigation measures discussed in the EIA have been installed and whether they work effectively in practice. Overall, EMS is likely to increase the level of environmental monitoring, environmental

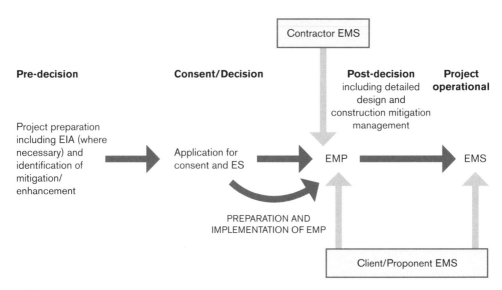

Figure 12.6

Linkages between EIA, EMPs and EMS

Source: IEMA 2008

Table 12.7 Benefits of preparing an EMP

1   Creates a framework for ensuring and demonstrating conformance with legislative requirements, conditions and mitigation set out in ESs.

2   Provide a continuous link or 'bridge' between the design phase of a project and the construction, and possibly operational, phase.

3   Ensures an effective communication or feedback system is in place between the operators on site, the contractor, the environmental manager (or consultant) and ultimately the regulator.

4   Preparing a draft EMP at an early stage demonstrates commitment to mitigation and can help reduce delays post-consent by showing how consultees and consenting authority concerns will be addressed.

5   Drives cost savings through improved environmental risk management.

Source: Adapted from IEMA 2008, 2011

awareness and the availability of environmental data; all of this can only be of help in EIA.

Environmental Management Plans

A very practical link between EIAs and EMSs can be provided by environmental management plans (EMPs) – to add yet another acronym! The aim of EMPs is to ensure that the effort put into the EIA process pre-application and consent is effectively delivered post-consent. This may involve overcoming a variety of perceived barriers linking EIA and EMS, including different consenting regimes, time periods and personnel, and lack of

resources (Palframan 2010). Recent experience of EMPs has been of a less formal, simpler, less bureaucratic, and *'EMS-lite'* approach (Marshall 2004). The IEMA has been a strong UK advocate of the EMP approach, and set out its position in its practitioner guide on *Environmental Management Plans* (IEMA 2008). An EMP is a document that: sets out the actions that are needed to manage environmental and community risks associated with the life cycle of a development, identifies what is needed, when, and who is responsible for its delivery. It is a bridge between the EIA process pre-consent and EMS operated by various stakeholders (e.g. project construction contractors,

Table 12.8 The building blocks for developing a successful EMP

1	Involvement of the proponent, construction teams and contractors during the formulation of mitigation when planning the development to ensure:

1   Involvement of the proponent, construction teams and contractors during the formulation of mitigation when planning the development to ensure:
  –   the mitigation is deliverable;
  –   costs of mitigation actions are factored into the detailed design stage, while the construction budget is still being developed; and
  –   there is buy-in and commitment when developing mitigation at the EIA stage, to increase likelihood of effective implementation.

2   Involvement of competent environmental professionals in the design and specification of mitigation actions to ensure:
  –   that the requirements are very clear; and
  –   to improve the chances of successful delivery.

3   Ensuring mitigation measures identified while planning the development have been formulated with the involvement of relevant stakeholders, or a clear timetable and process for further consultation post-consent is set out (where mitigation requires more detailed design post-consent).

4   Clearly identified and sufficiently detailed mitigation measures in the pre-consent phase (a framework or draft EMP prepared alongside an ES is helpful as it can set out additional detail in preparation for a full EMP).

5   Ensuring mitigation proposals are identifiable in documents accompanying the application for development consent;

6   Ensuring mitigation measures are presented as elements that the proponent would be willing to have included in the final consenting documentation.

Source: Adapted from IEMA 2008, 2011

project operation managers) post-consent. Figure 12.6 provides a simple illustration of this bridging role; Table 12.7 outline further reasons for using EMPs and the key building blocks for the approach.

The IEMA believes that EMPs will become increasingly common in UK practice; a practitioner survey found that almost 80 per cent of respondents agreed that a draft EMP should be required within the EIS (IEMA 2011). However, the format and name may vary. For example, all EISs produced by the Environment Agency for England and Wales include an environmental action plan (EAP). This acts as an interface between the EIA and the EMS and keeps the EIA as a 'live' document through the project life. Projects for other developers have included Construction Environmental Management Plans (CEMPs) which focus on implementation during the project construction stage; these are more limited, but are still valuable for this often very disruptive stage in a project's life (Palframan 2010).

12.6 Summary

As in a number of other countries discussed in Chapter 10, the practice of EIA for projects in

the UK, set in the wider context of the EU, has progressed rapidly up the learning curve. Understandably, however, practice has highlighted problems as well as successes. The resolution of problems and future prospects are determined by the interaction between the various parties involved. In the EU the various amendments to the EIA Directive have helped to improve some steps in the EIA process, including screening, scoping, consideration of alternatives and participation. However, some key issues remain unresolved, including the lack of support for mandatory monitoring. This chapter has identified an agenda for other possible changes, including cumulative impacts, socio-economic impacts and the linked areas of health impact and equalities impact assessment, appropriate assessment, resilience thinking, the key area of climate change, IIA and EID. Some of these will be easier to achieve than others, and there will no doubt be other emerging issues and developments in this dynamic area, and systems and procedures will continue to evolve in response to the environmental agenda and to our managerial and methodological capabilities.

There is also an urgent need to 'close the loop', to learn from experience. While the practice of mandatory monitoring is still patchy, notable progress has been made in the development of environmental management and auditing systems. Assessment can be aided by the development of EMSs for existing organizations, be they private-sector firms or local authorities. The information from such activities, plus the recent and important development of EMPs as a bridge between EIA and EMS activity, pre- and post-consent, could provide a significant improvement in the quality and effective implementation of EIAs.

As EIA activity spreads, more groups will become involved. Capacity building and training is vital both in the EIA process, which may have some commonality across countries, and in procedures that may be more closely tailored to particular national contexts. EIA practitioners also need to develop their substantive knowledge of the wider environment and to improve both their technical and participatory approaches in the EIA process.

SOME QUESTIONS

The following questions are intended to help the reader focus on the important issues of this chapter, and to start to consider potential approaches for improving the effectiveness of project assessment.

1   Change is a feature of EIA systems; what is driving such change?
2   Which stakeholders are more positive about further developing EIA systems and which are less so, and why?
3   Review the features of 'best-case' EA performance identified by Sadler in 1996; do those features still all apply today? Would you add any new features?
4   Consider possible explanations as to why the assessment of cumulative impacts has been such a challenging task for EIA?
5   What do you understand by 'environmental justice'?
6   Identify the potential key socio-economic impacts of a new major project with which you are familiar.
7   How might such impacts vary between the construction and operational stages of the project?
8   For the same project used in Question 6, consider the potential health impacts, again considering how such impacts might vary between the construction and operational stages of the project?
9   Similarly, for the same project again, consider the potential equality impacts.
10   Examine the case for integrating health and equality impacts within a socio-economic impact assessment as part of a more integrated approach to EIA that includes both biophysical and socio-economic impacts.
11   When does appropriate assessment apply in the EU? What do you understand by the term 'imperative reasons of overriding public interest'? Why might they have been significant for the Rotterdam Harbour extension, but not for Dibden Bay on Southampton Water?
12   Why has climate change not been well covered in many EIAs?
13   Review the specific climate assessment principles for EIA from Table 11.4; consider which might be most difficult to achieve.
14   What kind of resilience 'features' could one integrate into the design of an urban housing development? A rural landfill site?
15   What do you understand by the term 'environmental impact design'?
16   What is an EMS? Outline some of the differences between the EMAS and ISO 14001 EMS systems.
17   Discuss the potential value of environmental management plans for more effective EIA.

Notes

1   In practice, it is also applied to Ramsar wetland sites, candidate SACs, and European Marine Sites.
2   This term was originally coined for a slightly different context by Turner (1995).

References

Agyeman, J. and Evans, B., 2004. Just sustainability: the emerging discourse of environmental justice in Britain? *The Geographical Journal*, 170, 2, 155–64.

Ahmad, B. 2004. Integrating health into impact assessment: challenges and opportunities. *Impact Assessment and Project Appraisal* 22 (1), 2–4.

Bailey, P., Gough, P., Chadwick, C. and McGranahan, G. 1996. *Methods of integrated environmental assessment: research directions for the European Union.* Stockholm: Stockholm Environmental Institute.

Baxter, W., Ross, W. and Spaling, H. 2001. Improving the practice of cumulative effects assessment in Canada. *Impact Assessment and Project Appraisal* 19 (4), 253–62.

Boardman, J. and Vandaele, K. 2010. Soil erosion, muddy floods and the need for institutional memory. *Area* 42 (2), 502–13.

Burdge, R. 1999. The practice of social impact assessment – background. *Impact Assessment and Project Appraisal* 17 (2), 84–8.

Canter, L and Ross, W. 2010. State of practice of cumulative effects assessment and management: the good, the bad and the ugly. *Impact Assessment and Project Appraisal* 28 (4), 261–68.

CEAA (Canadian Environmental Assessment Agency) 1999. *Cumulative effects assessment: practitioners' guide.* Quebec: CEAA (www.ceaa.gc.ca).

CEC 2000. *Assessment of plans and programmes significantly affecting Natura 2000 sites: Methodological guidance on the provisions of Article 6(3) and (4) of the Habitats Directive 92/43/EEC.* Brussels: CEC.

CEC 2009. *Study concerning the report on the application and effectiveness of the EIA Directive: final report.* Brussels: DG Environment.

CEPA (Commonwealth Environmental Protection Agency) 1994. *Review of Commonwealth environmental impact assessment.* Canberra: CEPA.

CEQ (Council on Environmental Quality, USA) 1997. *Considering cumulative effects under the National Environmental Policy Act.* Washington, DC: Office of the President. Available at: www.ceq.eh.doe.gov/nepa/nepanet/htm.

Chadwick, A. 2002. Socio-economic impacts: are they still the poor relations in UK environmental statements? *Journal of Environmental Planning and Management* 45 (1), 3–24.

CPRE (Council for the Protection of Rural England) 1991. *The environmental assessment directive – five years on.* London: Council for Protection of Rural England.

CPRE 1992. *Mock directive.* London: Council for Protection of Rural England.

Davis, S. 1996. *Public involvement in environmental decision making: some reflections on West European experience.* Washington, DC: World Bank.

DCLG (Department of Communities and Local Government) 2007. *Planning Policy Statement: Planning and Climate Change. Supplement to PPS1.* London: DCLG.

DCLG 2011. *Guidance on the Environmental Impact Assessment (EIA) Regulations 2011 for England.* London: DCLG.

DEFRA 2003. *An Introductory Guide to EMAS.* London: DEFRA.

Douglas, C. H. 2003. Developing health impact assessment for sustainable futures. *Journal of Environmental Assessment Policy and Management* 5 (4), 477–502.

Downey, L. 2005. Assessing environmental inequality: How the conclusions we draw vary according to the definitions we employ. *Sociological Spectrum*, 25, 349–69.

EC (European Commission) 1993. *Regulation no. 1836/93 allowing voluntary participation by companies in the industrial sector in an eco-management and audit scheme.* Brussels: EC.

EC 2001a. *Regulation no. 761/2001 of the European Parliament and of the Council of 19 March 2001 allowing voluntary participation by organisations in a community eco-management and audit scheme (emas).* Brussels: EC.

EC 2001b. *EMAS and ISO/EN ESO 14001: differences and complementarities.* Available at: www.europa.eu.int/comm/environment/emas/pdf/factsheets.

Essex Planning Officers' Association 2007. *The Essex Guide to Environmental Impact Assessment.* Chelmsford: Essex County Council.

Fabricius, C., Quinlan, A. and Otambekov, A. 2009. *Resilience assessment in Roghun, Tajikistan.* Available at: www.nmmu.ac.za/documents/SRU/Resilience%20Assessment%20in%20Roghun%2017%20May.pdf.

FoE (Friends of the Earth) 2011. *The greenest government ever: one year on.* London: FoE.

Gadreau, K. and Gibson, R. 2010. Illustrating integrated sustainability and resilience based assessments: a small-scale biodiesel project in Barbados. *Impact Assessment and Project Appraisal* 28 (3), 233–43.

Glasson, J. 2009. Socio-economic impacts. In *Methods of environmental impact assessment.* 3rd edn, P. Morris and R. Therivel (eds), Chapter 2. London: Spon.

Glasson, J. and Cozens, P. 2011. Making communities safer from crime: an undervalued element in environmental assessment. *EIA Review* 31, 25–35.

Glasson, J., Godfrey, K. and Goodey, B. 1995. *Towards visitor impact management.* Aldershot: Avebury.

Health Canada 1999. *Canadian handbook of health impact assessment.* vol. 1: *The basics.* Ottawa: Health Canada.

Highways Agency 2011. *Design manual for roads and bridges,* London: the Stationery Office.

Holstein, T. 1996. *Reflective essay: postmodern EIA or how to learn to love incinerators.* Written as part of MSc course in Environmental Assessment and Management, Oxford Brookes University, Oxford.

Hyder Consulting 1999. *Guidelines for the assessment of indirect and cumulative impacts as well as impact interactions.* Brussels: CEC-DGXI. Available at: www.europa.eu.int/comm/environment/eia/eia_ support.htm).

IAIA (International Association for Impact Assessment) 1994. Guidelines and principles for social impact assessment. *Impact Assessment* 12 Summer.

IAIA 2002. Workshop on Integrated Assessment, in *IAIA Annual conference.* The Hague, The Netherlands: IAIA.

IEMA (Institute of Environment Management and Assessment) 2008. *Practitioner series No 12: environmental management plans.* Lincoln: IEMA.

IEMA 2010a. *IEMA Principles series:climate change mitigation and EIA.* Lincoln: IEMA.

IEMA 2010b. *IEMA Principles series:climate change adaptation and EIA.* Lincoln: IEMA.

IEMA 2011.*The state of environmental impact assessment practice in the UK.* Lincoln: IEMA.

IMD (Index of Multiple Deprivation) 2011. *The English indices of multiple deprivation 2010.* London: DCLG.

IPHI (Institute of Public Health in Ireland) 2009. *Health impact assessment guidance.* Dublin and Belfast: IPHI.

ISO (International Organization for Standardization) 1996a. *ISO 14001 Environmental management systems – specification with guidance for use.*

ISO 1996b. *ISO 14004 Environmental management systems – general guidelines on principles, systems and supporting techniques.*

Lane, P. and associates 1988. *A reference guide to cumulative effects assessment in Canada,* vol. 1, Halifax: P Lane and Associates/CEARC.

Marshall, R. 2004. Can industry benefit from participation in EIA follow up? in Morrison-Saunders, A. and J. Arts (eds). *Assessing impact: handbook of EIA and SEA follow-up.* London: Earthscan.

McDonald, G. T. and Brown, L. 1995. Going beyond environmental impact assessment: environmental input to planning and design. *Environmental Impact Assessment Review* 15, 483–95.

National Grid 2011. *Methodological guidence for options appraisal.* Warwick: National Grid.

Newton, J. 1995. *The integration of socio-economic impacts in EIA and project appraisal.* MSc dissertation, University of Manchester Institute of Science and Technology.

Odum, W. 1982. Environmental degradation and the tyranny of small decisions. *Bio Science* 32, 728–29.

O'Riordan, T. 1990. EIA from the environmentalist's perspective. VIA 4, March 13.

Palframan, L. 2010. *The integration of EIA and EMS systems: experiences from the UK.* 30th Annual Conference of IAIA Proceedings.

Peterson, E. *et al.* 1987. *Cumulative effects assessment in Canada: an agenda for action and research.* Quebec: Canadian Environmental Assessment Research Council (CEARC).

Phoolcharoen, W., Sukkumnoed, D. and P. Kessomboon 2003. Development of health impact assessment in Thailand: recent experiences and challenges. *Bulletin of the World Health Organization* 81 (6), 465–67.

Piper, J. 2000. Cumulative effects assessment on the Middle Humber: barriers overcome, benefits derived. *Journal of Environmental Planning and Management* 43 (3), 369–87.

Piper, J. 2001a. Assessing the cumulative effects of project clusters: a comparison of process and methods in four UK cases. *Journal of Environmental Planning and Management* 44 (3), 357–75.

Piper, J. 2001b. Barriers to implementation of cumulative effects assessment. *Journal of Environmental Assessment Policy and Management* 3 (4), 465–81.

Project Appraisal 1996. Special edition: *Environmental Assessment and Socio-economic Appraisal in Development* 11(4).

RA (Resilience Alliance) 2010. *Assessing resilience in social-ecological systems.* Workbook for Practitioners. Version 2.0. Available at: www. resalliance.org/index.php/resilience_assessment.

RSPB 2000. *Biodiversity and EIA: a good practice guide for road schemes*. RSPB,WWF, English Nature and Wildlife Trusts.

Rodriguez-Bachiller, A. with J. Glasson 2004. *Expert systems and geographical information systems for impact assessment*. London: Taylor and Francis.

Sadler, B. 1996 *International study in the effectiveness of environmental assessment*. Ottawa: Canadian Environmental Assessment Agency.

Sadler, B. 2012. Latest EA effectiveness study (not available at time this book went to press).

Scott Wilson (2006), *ES for Woodberry Down (London)*, London Borough of Hackney: Scott Wilson for Hackney Homes.

Taylor, L. and Blair-Stevens, C. 2002. *Introducing health impact assessment (HIA): informing the decision-making process*. London: Health Development Agency.

Taylor, L. and Quigley, R. 2002. *Health impact assessment: a review of reviews*. London: Health Development Agency.

Therivel, R. and Ross, B. 2007. Cumulative effects assessment: does scale matter?, *Environmental Impact Assessment Review* 27, 365–85.

Turner, T. 1995. *City as landscape: a post-postmodernist view of design and planning*. London: E&FN Spon.

Vanclay, F. 2003. International principles for social impact assessment. *Impact Assessment and Project Appraisal* 21 (1), 5–12.

Walker, B. and Salt, D. 2006. *Resilience thinking*. Washington, DC: Island Press.

Walker, G., Fay, H. and Mitchell, G. 2005. *Environmental justice impact assessment: an evaluation of requirements and tools for distributional analysis (A report for Friends of the Earth)*. Leeds: Institute for Environment and Sustainability Research, University of Leeds.

Western Australia Department of Health 2007. *Health impact assessment in WA: summary document*. Perth: Western Australia Department of Health.

WHO Regional Office for Europe 2003. *Health impact assessment methods and strategies*. Available at: www.euro.who.int/eprise/main/WHO/progs/HMS/home.

Wilson, E. and Piper, J. 2010. *Spatial planning and climate change*. Abingdon: Routledge.

World Bank 1995. *Environmental assessment: challenges and good practice*. Washington, DC: World Bank.

Appendix 1

● ●

Full text of the European Commission's EIA Directive
(the Consolidated EIA Directive)

Council Directive of 27 June 1985 on the assessment
of the effects of certain public and private projects on
the environment (85/337/EEC)

Amended by:
Council Directive 97/11/EC of 3 March 1997;
Directive 2003/35/EC of the European Parliament and of the
Council of 26 May 2003; and
Directive 2009/31/EC of the European Parliament and of the
Council of 23 April 2009.

Article 1

1   This Directive shall apply to the assessment of the environmental effects of those public and private projects that are likely to have significant effects on the environment.
2   For the purposes of this Directive: *'project' means*:
    –   the execution of construction works or of other installations or schemes;
    –   other interventions in the natural surroundings and landscape including those involving the extraction of mineral resources;
    'developer' means:
    –   the applicant for authorization for a private project or the public authority that initiates a project;

'development consent' means:
    –   the decision of the competent authority or authorities that entitles the developer to proceed with the project;
'public' means:
    –   one or more natural or legal persons and, in accordance with national legislation and practice, their associations, organizations or groups;
'public concerned' means:
    –   the public affected or likely to be affected by, or having an interest in, the environmental decision-making procedures referred to in Article 2(2); for the purposes of this definition, non-governmental organizations promoting environmental protection and meeting any requirements under national law shall be deemed to have an interest.

3 The competent authority or authorities shall be that or those that the Member States designate as responsible for performing the duties arising from this Directive.

4 Member States may decide, on a case-by-case basis if so provided under national law, not to apply this Directive to projects serving national defence purposes, if they deem that such application would have an adverse effect on these purposes.

5 This Directive shall not apply to projects the details of which are adopted by a specific act of national legislation, since the objectives of this Directive, including that of supplying information, are achieved through the legislative process.

Article 2

1 Member States shall adopt all measures necessary to ensure that, before consent is given, projects likely to have significant effects on the environment by virtue, *inter alia*, of their nature, size or location are made subject to a requirement for development consent and an assessment with regard to their effects. These projects are defined in Article 4.

2 The environmental impact assessment may be integrated into the existing procedures for consent to projects in the Member States, or, failing this, into other procedures or into procedures to be established to comply with the aims of this Directive.

2(a) Member States may provide for a single procedure in order to fulfil the requirements of this Directive and the requirements of Council Directive 96/61/EC of 24 September 1996 on integrated pollution prevention and control.[1]

3 Without prejudice to Article 7, Member States may, in exceptional cases, exempt a specific project in whole or in part from the provisions laid down in this Directive.
In this event, the Member States shall:
(a) consider whether another form of assessment would be appropriate;
(b) make available to the public concerned the information obtained under other forms of assessment referred to in point (a), the information relating to the exemption decision and the reasons for granting it;
(c) inform the Commission, prior to granting consent, of the reasons justifying the exemption granted, and provide it with the information made available, where applicable, to their own nationals.

The Commission shall immediately forward the documents received to the other Member States.

The Commission shall report annually to the Council on the application of this paragraph.

Article 3

The environmental impact assessment shall identify, describe and assess in an appropriate manner, in the light of each individual case and in accordance with Articles 4 to 11, the direct and indirect effects of a project on the following factors:

- human beings, fauna and flora;
- soil, water, air, climate and the landscape;
- material assets and the cultural heritage;
- the interaction between the factors mentioned in the first, second and third indents.

Article 4

1 Subject to Article 2 (3), projects listed in Annex I shall be made subject to an assessment in accordance with Articles 5 to 10.

2 Subject to Article 2 (3), for projects listed in Annex II, the Member States shall determine through:
(a) a case-by-case examination, or
(b) thresholds or criteria set by the Member State
whether the project shall be made subject to an assessment in accordance with Articles 5 to 10.

Member States may decide to apply both procedures referred to in (a) and (b).

3 When a case-by-case examination is carried out or thresholds or criteria are set for the purpose of paragraph 2, the relevant selection criteria set out in Annex III shall be taken into account.

4 Member States shall ensure that the determination made by the competent authorities under paragraph 2 is made available to the public.

Article 5

1 In the case of projects that, pursuant to Article 4, must be subjected to an environmental impact assessment in accordance with Articles 5 to 10, Member States shall adopt the necessary measures to ensure that the developer supplies in an appropriate form the information specified in Annex IV inasmuch as:
  (a) the Member States consider that the information is relevant to a given stage of the consent procedure and to the specific characteristics of a particular project or type of project and of the environmental features likely to be affected;
  (b) the Member States consider that a developer may reasonably be required to compile this information having regard *inter alia* to current knowledge and methods of assessment.

2 Member States shall take the necessary measures to ensure that, if the developer so requests before submitting an application for development consent, the competent authority shall give an opinion on the information to be supplied by the developer in accordance with paragraph 1. The competent authority shall consult the developer and authorities referred to in Article 6 (1) before it gives its opinion. The fact that the authority has given an opinion under this paragraph shall not preclude it from subsequently requiring the developer to submit further information.
  Member States may require the competent authorities to give such an opinion, irrespective of whether the developer so requests.

3 The information to be provided by the developer in accordance with paragraph 1 shall include at least:
  (a) a description of the project comprising information on the site, design and size of the project;
  (b) a description of the measures envisaged in order to avoid, reduce and, if possible, remedy significant adverse effects;
  (c) the data required to identify and assess the main effects that the project is likely to have on the environment,
  (d) an outline of the main alternatives studied by the developer and an indication of the main reasons for his choice, taking into account the environmental effects;
  (e) a non-technical summary of the information mentioned in the previous indents.

4 Member States shall, if necessary, ensure that any authorities holding relevant information, with particular reference to Article 3, shall make this information available to the developer.

Article 6

1 Member States shall take the measures necessary to ensure that the authorities likely to be concerned by the project by reason of their specific environmental responsibilities are given an opportunity to express their opinion on the information supplied by the developer and on the request for development consent. To this end, Member States shall designate the authorities to be consulted, either in general terms or on a case-by-case basis. The information gathered pursuant to Article 5 shall be forwarded to those authorities. Detailed arrangements for consultation shall be laid down by the Member States.

2 The public shall be informed, whether by public notices or other appropriate means such as electronic media where available, of

the following matters early in the environ-mental decision-making procedures referred to in Article 2 (2) and, at the latest, as soon as information can reasonably be provided:

(a) the request for development consent;

(b) the fact that the project is subject to an environmental impact assessment proce-dure and, where relevant, the fact that Article 7 applies;

(c) details of the competent authorities responsible for taking the decision, those from which relevant information can be obtained, those to which comments or questions can be submitted, and details of the time schedule for transmitting comments or questions;

(d) the nature of possible decisions or, where there is one, the draft decision;

(e) an indication of the availability of the information gathered pursuant to Article 5;

(f) an indication of the times and places where and means by which the relevant information will be made available;

(g) details of the arrangements for public participation made pursuant to paragraph 5 of this Article.

3 Member States shall ensure that, within reasonable time-frames, the following is made available to the public concerned:

(a) any information gathered pursuant to Article 5;

(b) in accordance with national legislation, the main reports and advice issued to the competent authority or authorities at the time when the public concerned is informed in accordance with paragraph 2 of this Article;

(c) in accordance with the provisions of Directive 2003/4/EC of the European Parliament and of the Council of 28 January 2003 on public access to environ-mental information,[2] information other than that referred to in paragraph 2 of this Article that is relevant for the decision in accordance with Article 8 and that only becomes available after the time the public concerned was informed in accordance with paragraph 2 of this Article.

4 The public concerned shall be given early and effective opportunities to participate in the environmental decision-making procedures referred to in Article 2 (2) and shall, for that purpose, be entitled to express comments and opinions when all options are open to the competent authority or authorities before the decision on the request for development consent is taken.

5 The detailed arrangements for informing the public (for example by bill posting within a certain radius or publication in local news-papers) and for consulting the public con-cerned (for example by written submis-sions or by way of a public inquiry) shall be determined by the Member States.

6 Reasonable time-frames for the different phases shall be provided, allowing sufficient time for informing the public and for the public concerned to prepare and participate effectively in environmental decision-making subject to the provisions of this Article.

....

Article 7

1 Where a Member State is aware that a project is likely to have significant effects on the environment in another Member State or where a Member State likely to be significantly affected so requests, the Member State in whose territory the project is intended to be carried out shall send to the affected Member State as soon as possible and no later than when informing its own public, *inter alia*:

(a) a description of the project, together with any available information on its possible transboundary impact;

(b) information on the nature of the decision that may be taken,

and shall give the other Member State a reasonable time in which to indicate whether it wishes to participate in the environmental decision-making procedures referred to in Article 2 (2), and may include the information referred to in paragraph 2 of this Article.

2 If a Member State that receives information pursuant to paragraph 1 indicates that it intends to participate in the environmental

decision-making procedures referred to in Article 2 (2), the Member State in whose territory the project is intended to be carried out shall, if it has not already done so, send to the affected Member State the information required to be given pursuant to Article 6 (2) and made available pursuant to Article 6 (3) (a) and (b).

3   The Member States concerned, each insofar as it is concerned, shall also:

(a)   arrange for the information referred to in paragraphs 1 and 2 to be made available, within a reasonable time, to the authorities referred to in Article 6 (1) and the public concerned in the territory of the Member State likely to be significantly affected; and

(b)   ensure that those authorities and the public concerned are given an opportunity, before development consent for the project is granted, to forward their opinion within a reasonable time on the information supplied to the competent authority in the Member State in whose territory the project is intended to be carried out.

4   The Member States concerned shall enter into consultations regarding, *inter alia*, the potential transboundary effects of the project and the measures envisaged to reduce or eliminate such effects and shall agree on a reasonable time frame for the duration of the consultation period.

5   The detailed arrangements for implementing this Article may be determined by the Member States concerned and shall be such as to enable the public concerned in the territory of the affected Member State to participate effectively in the environmental decision-making procedures referred to in Article 2 (2) for the project.

Article 8

The results of consultations and the information gathered pursuant to Articles 5, 6 and 7 must be taken into consideration in the development consent procedure.

Article 9

1   When a decision to grant or refuse development consent has been taken, the competent authority or authorities shall inform the public thereof in accordance with the appropriate procedures and shall make available to the public the following information:

(a)   the content of the decision and any conditions attached thereto,

(b)   having examined the concerns and opinions expressed by the public concerned, the main reasons and considerations on which the decision is based, including information about the public participation process,

(c)   a description, where necessary, of the main measures to avoid, reduce and, if possible, offset the major adverse effects.

2   The competent authority or authorities shall inform any Member State that has been consulted pursuant to Article 7, forwarding to it the information referred to in paragraph 1 of this Article.

The consulted Member States shall ensure that information is made available in an appropriate manner to the public concerned in their own territory.

Article 10

The provisions of this Directive shall not affect the obligation on the competent authorities to respect the limitations imposed by national regulations and administrative provisions and accepted legal practices with regard to commercial and industrial confidentiality, including intellectual property, and the safeguarding of the public interest.

Where Article 7 applies, the transmission of information to another Member State and the receipt of information by another Member State shall be subject to the limitations in force in the Member State in which the project is proposed.

Article 10(a)

Member States shall ensure that, in accordance with the relevant national legal system, members of the public concerned:

    (a) having a sufficient interest, or alternatively;

    (b) maintaining the impairment of a right, where administrative procedural law of a Member State requires this as a precondition;

have access to a review procedure before a court of law or another independent and impartial body established by law to challenge the substantive or procedural legality of decisions, acts or omissions subject to the public participation provisions of this Directive.

Member States shall determine at what stage the decisions, acts or omissions may be challenged.

What constitutes a sufficient interest and impairment of a right shall be determined by the Member States, consistently with the objective of giving the public concerned wide access to justice. To this end, the interest of any non-governmental organisation meeting the requirements referred to in Article 1 (2), shall be deemed sufficient for the purpose of subparagraph (a) of this Article. Such organisations shall also be deemed to have rights capable of being impaired for the purpose of subparagraph (b) of this Article.

The provisions of this Article shall not exclude the possibility of a preliminary review procedure before an administrative authority and shall not affect the requirement of exhaustion of administrative review procedures prior to recourse to judicial review procedures, where such a requirement exists under national law.

Any such procedure shall be fair, equitable, timely and not prohibitively expensive.

In order to further the effectiveness of the provisions of this article, Member States shall ensure that practical information is made available to the public on access to administrative and judicial review procedures.

Article 11

1   The Member States and the Commission shall exchange information on the experience gained in applying this Directive.

2   In particular, Member States shall inform the Commission of any criteria and/or thresholds adopted for the selection of the projects in question, in accordance with Article 4 (2).

3   Five years after notification of this Directive, the Commission shall send the European Parliament and the Council a report on its application and effectiveness. The report shall be based on the aforementioned exchange of information.

4   On the basis of this exchange of information, the Commission shall submit to the Council additional proposals, should this be necessary, with a view to this Directive's being applied in a sufficiently coordinated manner.

Article 12

1   Member States shall take the measures necessary to comply with this Directive within three years of its notification.[3]

2   Member States shall communicate to the Commission the texts of the provisions of national law that they adopt in the field covered by this Directive.

Article 14

This Directive is addressed to the Member States.

Notes

1   OJ No L 257, 10.10.1996, p. 26.
2   OJ L 41, 14.2.2003, p. 26.
3   This Directive was notified to the Member States on 3 July 1985.

Annex I

•••

Projects subject to article 4 (1)

1 Crude-oil refineries (excluding undertakings manufacturing only lubricants from crude oil) and installations for the gasification and liquefaction of 500 tonnes or more of coal or bituminous shale per day.

2 – Thermal power stations and other combustion installations with a heat output of 300 megawatts or more, and
   – Nuclear power stations and other nuclear reactors including the dismantling or decommissioning of such power stations or reactors[1] (except research installations for the production and conversion of fissionable and fertile materials, whose maximum power does not exceed 1 kilowatt continuous thermal load).

3 (a) Installations for the reprocessing of irradiated nuclear fuel;
   (b) Installations designed:
       – for the production or enrichment of nuclear fuel;
       – for the processing of irradiated nuclear fuel or high-level radioactive waste;
       – for the final disposal of irradiated nuclear fuel;
       – solely for the final disposal of radioactive waste;
       – solely for the storage (planned for more than 10 years) of irradiated nuclear fuels or radioactive waste in a different site than the production site.

4 – Integrated works for the initial smelting of cast-iron and steel;
   – Installations for the production of non-ferrous crude metals from ore, concentrates or secondary raw materials by metallurgical, chemical or electrolytic processes.

5 Installations for the extraction of asbestos and for the processing and transformation of asbestos and products containing asbestos: for asbestos-cement products, with an annual production of more than 20,000 tonnes of finished products, for friction material, with an annual production of more than 50 tonnes of finished products, and for other uses of asbestos, utilization of more than 200 tonnes per year.

6 Integrated chemical installations, i.e. those installations for the manufacture on an industrial scale of substances using chemical conversion processes, in which several units are juxtaposed and are functionally linked to one another and that are:
   (i)   for the production of basic organic chemicals;
   (ii) for the production of basic inorganic chemicals;
   (iii) for the production of phosphorous-, nitrogen- or potassium-based fertilizers (simple or compound fertilizers);
   (iv) for the production of basic plant health products and of biocides;

(v) for the production of basic pharmaceutical products using a chemical or biological process;

(vi) for the production of explosives.

7 (a) construction of lines for long-distance railway traffic and of airports[2] with a basic runway length of 2100 m or more;

(b) construction of motorways and express roads;[3]

(c) construction of a new road of four or more lanes, or realignment and/or widening of an existing road of two lanes or less so as to provide four or more lanes, where such new road, or realigned and/or widened section of road would be 10 km or more in a continuous length.

8 (a) Inland waterways and ports for inland-waterway traffic that permit the passage of vessels of over 1350 tonnes;

(b) Trading ports, piers for loading and unloading connected to land and outside ports (excluding ferry piers) that can take vessels of over 1350 tonnes.

9 Waste disposal installations for the incineration, chemical treatment as defined in Annex IIA to Directive 75/442/EEC[4] under heading D9, or landfill of hazardous waste (i.e. waste to which Directive 91/689/EEC[5] applies).

10 Waste disposal installations for the incineration or chemical treatment as defined in Annex IIA to Directive 75/442/EEC under heading D9 of non- hazardous waste with a capacity exceeding 100 tonnes per day.

11 Groundwater abstraction or artificial ground-water recharge schemes where the annual volume of water abstracted or recharged is equivalent to or exceeds 10 million cubic metres.

12 (a) Works for the transfer of water resources between river basins where this transfer aims at preventing possible shortages of water and where the amount of water transferred exceeds 100 million cubic metres/year;

(b) In all other cases, works for the transfer of water resources between river basins where the multi-annual average flow of the basin of abstraction exceeds 2000 million cubic metres/year and where the amount of water transferred exceeds 5 per cent of this flow.

In both cases transfers of piped drinking water are excluded.

13 Waste water treatment plants with a capacity exceeding 150,000 population equivalent as defined in Article 2 point (6) of Directive 91/271/EEC.[6]

14 Extraction of petroleum and natural gas for commercial purposes where the amount extracted exceeds 500 tonnes/day in the case of petroleum and 500,000 m^3/day in the case of gas.

15 Dams and other installations designed for the holding back or permanent storage of water, where a new or additional amount of water held back or stored exceeds 10 million cubic metres.

16 Pipelines with a diameter of more than 800 mm and a length of more than 40 km:
– for the transport of gas, oil, chemicals; and,
– for the transport of carbon dioxide (CO_2) streams for the purposes of geological storage, including associated booster stations.

17 Installations for the intensive rearing of poultry or pigs with more than:
(a) 85,000 places for broilers, 60,000 places for hens;
(b) 3,000 places for production pigs (over 30 kg); or
(c) 900 places for sows.

18 Industrial plants for the
(a) production of pulp from timber or similar fibrous materials;
(b) production of paper and board with a production capacity exceeding 200 tonnes per day.

19 Quarries and open-cast mining where the surface of the site exceeds 25 hectares, or peat extraction, where the surface of the site exceeds 150 hectares.

20 Construction of overhead electrical power lines with a voltage of 220 kV or more and a length of more than 15 km.

21 Installations for storage of petroleum, petro-chemical, or chemical products with a capacity of 200,000 tonnes or more.

22 Any change to or extension of projects listed in this Annex where such a change or extension in itself meets the thresholds, if any, set out in this Annex.

23 Storage sites pursuant to Directive 2009/31/EC of the European Parliament and of the Council of 23 April 2009 on the geological storage of carbon dioxide.[7]

24 Installations for the capture of CO_2 streams for the purposes of geological storage pursuant to Directive 2009/31/EC from installations covered by this Annex, or where the total yearly capture of CO_2 is 1.5 megatonnes or more.

....

Notes

1 Nuclear power stations and other nuclear reactors cease to be such an installation when all nuclear fuel and other radioactively contaminated elements have been removed permanently from the installation site.

2 For the purposes of this Directive, 'airport' means airports that comply with the definition in the 1944 Chicago Convention setting up the International Civil Aviation Organization (Annex 14).

3 For the purposes of the Directive, 'express road' means a road that complies with the definition in the European Agreement on Main International Traffic Arteries of 15 November 1975.

4 OJ No L 194, 25.7.1975, p. 39. Directive as last amended by Commission Decision 94/3/EC (OJ No L 5, 7.1.1994, p. 15).

5 OJ No L 377, 31.12.1991, p. 20. Directive as last amended by Directive 94/31/EC (OJ No L 168, 2.7.1994, p. 28).

6 OJ No L 135, 30.5.1991, p. 40. Directive as last amended by the 1994 Act of Accession.

7 OJ L 140, 5.6.2009, p. 114.

Annex II

• •

Projects subject to article 4 (2)

1 **Agriculture, silviculture and aquaculture**
   (a) projects for the restructuring of rural land holdings;
   (b) projects for the use of uncultivated land or semi-natural areas for intensive agricultural purposes;
   (c) water management projects for agriculture, including irrigation and land drainage projects;
   (d) initial afforestation and deforestation for the purposes of conversion to another type of land use;
   (e) intensive livestock installations (projects not included in Annex I);
   (f) intensive fish farming;
   (g) reclamation of land from the sea.

2 **Extractive industry**
   (a) quarries, open-cast mining and peat extraction (projects not included in Annex I);
   (b) underground mining;
   (c) extraction of minerals by marine or fluvial dredging;
   (d) deep drillings, in particular:
       – geothermal drilling,
       – drilling for the storage of nuclear waste material,
       – drilling for water supplies,
       with the exception of drillings for investigating the stability of the soil;
   (e) surface industrial installations for the extraction of coal, petroleum, natural gas and ores, as well as bituminous shale.

3 **Energy industry**
   (a) industrial installations for the production of electricity, steam and hot water (projects not included in Annex I);
   (b) industrial installations for carrying gas, steam and hot water; transmission of electrical energy by overhead cables (projects not included in Annex I);
   (c) surface storage of natural gas;
   (d) underground storage of combustible gases;
   (e) surface storage of fossil fuels;
   (f) industrial briquetting of coal and lignite;
   (g) installations for the processing and storage of radioactive waste (unless included in Annex I);
   (h) installations for hydroelectric energy production;
   (i) installations for the harnessing of wind power for energy production (wind farms);
   (j) installations for the capture of CO_2 streams for the purposes of geological storage pursuant to Directive 2009/31/EC from installations not covered by Annex I to this Directive.

4 **Production and processing of metals**
   (a) installations for the production of pig iron or steel (primary or secondary fusion) including continuous casting;
   (b) installations for the processing of ferrous metals:
       (i) hot-rolling mills;

(ii) smitheries with hammers;

(iii) application of protective fused metal coats;

(c) ferrous metal foundries;

(d) installations for the smelting, including the alloyage, of non-ferrous metals, excluding precious metals, including recovered products (refining, foundry casting, etc.);

(e) installations for surface treatment of metals and plastic materials using an electrolytic or chemical process;

(f) manufacture and assembly of motor vehicles and manufacture of motor-vehicle engines;

(g) shipyards;

(h) installations for the construction and repair of aircraft;

(i) manufacture of railway equipment;

(j) swaging by explosives;

(k) installations for the roasting and sintering of metallic ores.

5 **Mineral industry**

(a) coke ovens (dry coal distillation);

(b) installations for the manufacture of cement;

(c) installations for the production of asbestos and the manufacture of asbestos-products (projects not included in Annex I);

(d) installations for the manufacture of glass including glass fibre;

(e) installations for smelting mineral substances including the production of mineral fibres;

(f) manufacture of ceramic products by burning, in particular roofing tiles, bricks, refractory bricks, tiles, stoneware or porcelain.

6 **Chemical industry (Projects not included in Annex I)**

(a) treatment of intermediate products and production of chemicals;

(b) production of pesticides and pharmaceutical products, paint and varnishes, elastomers and peroxides;

(c) storage facilities for petroleum, petrochemical and chemical products.

7 **Food industry**

(a) manufacture of vegetable and animal oils and fats;

(b) packing and canning of animal and vegetable products;

(c) manufacture of dairy products;

(d) brewing and malting;

(e) confectionery and syrup manufacture;

(f) installations for the slaughter of animals;

(g) industrial starch manufacturing installations;

(h) fish-meal and fish-oil factories;

(i) sugar factories.

8 **Textile, leather, wood and paper industries**

(a) industrial plants for the production of paper and board (projects not included in Annex I);

(b) plants for the pretreatment (operations such as washing, bleaching, mercerization) or dyeing of fibres or textiles;

(c) plants for the tanning of hides and skins;

(d) cellulose-processing and production installations.

9 **Rubber industry**

Manufacture and treatment of elastomer-based products.

10 **Infrastructure projects**

(a) industrial estate development projects;

(b) urban development projects, including the construction of shopping centres and car parks;

(c) construction of railways and intermodal transshipment facilities, and of intermodal terminals (projects not included in Annex I);

(d) construction of airfields (projects not included in Annex I);

(e) construction of roads, harbours and port installations, including fishing harbours (projects not included in Annex I);

(f) inland-waterway construction not included in Annex I, canalization and flood-relief works;

(g) dams and other installations designed to hold water or store it on a long-term basis (projects not included in Annex I);

(h) tramways, elevated and underground railways, suspended lines or similar lines of a particular type, used exclusively or mainly for passenger transport;

(i) oil and gas pipeline installations and pipelines for the transport of CO_2 streams for the purposes of geological storage (projects not included in Annex I);

(j) installations of long-distance aqueducts;

(k) coastal work to combat erosion and maritime works capable of altering the coast through the construction, for example, of dykes, moles, jetties and other sea defence works, excluding the maintenance and reconstruction of such works;

(l) groundwater abstraction and artificial groundwater recharge schemes not included in Annex I;

(m) works for the transfer of water resources between river basins not included in Annex I.

11 **Other projects**

(a) permanent racing and test tracks for motorized vehicles;

(b) installations for the disposal of waste (projects not included in Annex I);

(c) waste-water treatment plants (projects not included in Annex I);

(d) sludge-deposition sites;

(e) storage of scrap iron, including scrap vehicles;

(f) test benches for engines, turbines or reactors;

(g) installations for the manufacture of artificial mineral fibres;

(h) installations for the recovery or destruction of explosive substances;

(i) knackers' yards.

12 **Tourism and leisure**

(a) ski-runs, ski-lifts and cable-cars and associated developments;

(b) marinas;

(c) holiday villages and hotel complexes outside urban areas and associated developments;

(d) permanent camp sites and caravan sites;

(e) theme parks.

13 – Any change or extension of projects listed in Annex I or Annex II, already authorized, executed or in the process of being executed, which may have significant adverse effects on the environment (change or extension not included in Annex I);

– Projects in Annex I, undertaken exclusively or mainly for the development and testing of new methods or products and not used for more than two years.

Annex III

• •

Selection criteria referred to in article 4 (3)

1   **Characteristics of projects**
The characteristics of projects must be considered having regard, in particular, to:
–   the size of the project;
–   the cumulation with other projects;
–   the use of natural resources;
–   the production of waste;
–   pollution and nuisances;
–   the risk of accidents, having regard in particular to substances or technologies used.

2   **Location of projects**
The environmental sensitivity of geographical areas likely to be affected by projects must be considered, having regard, in particular, to:
–   the existing land use;
–   the relative abundance, quality and regenerative capacity of natural resources in the area;
–   the absorption capacity of the natural environment, paying particular attention to the following areas:
(a) wetlands;
(b) coastal zones;
(c) mountain and forest areas;

(d) nature reserves and parks;
(e) areas classified or protected under Member States' legislation; special protection areas designated by Member States pursuant to Directive 79/409/EEC and 92/43/EEC;
(f) areas in which the environmental quality standards laid down in Community legislation have already been exceeded;
(g) densely populated areas;
(h) landscapes of historical, cultural or archaeological significance.

3   **Characteristics of the potential impact**
The potential significant effects of projects must be considered in relation to criteria set out under 1 and 2 above, and having regard in particular to:
–   the extent of the impact (geographical area and size of the affected population);
–   the transfrontier nature of the impact;
–   the magnitude and complexity of the impact;
–   the probability of the impact;
–   the duration, frequency and reversibility of the impact.

Annex IV

• •

Information referred to in article 5 (1)

1 Description of the project, including in particular:
   – a description of the physical characteristics of the whole project and the land-use requirements during the construction and operational phases;
   – a description of the main characteristics of the production processes, for instance, nature and quantity of the materials used;
   – an estimate, by type and quantity, of expected residues and emissions (water, air and soil pollution, noise, vibration, light, heat, radiation, etc.) resulting from the operation of the proposed project.
2 An outline of the main alternatives studied by the developer and an indication of the main reasons for this choice, taking into account the environmental effects.
3 A description of the aspects of the environment likely to be significantly affected by the proposed project, including, in particular, population, fauna, flora, soil, water, air, climatic factors, material assets, including the architectural and archaeological heritage, landscape and the inter-relationship between the above factors.

4 A description[1] of the likely significant effects of the proposed project on the environment resulting from:
   – the existence of the project;
   – the use of natural resources;
   – the emission of pollutants, the creation of nuisances and the elimination of waste; and
   – the description by the developer of the forecasting methods used to assess the effects on the environment.
5 A description of the measures envisaged to prevent, reduce and where possible offset any significant adverse effects on the environment.
6 A non-technical summary of the information provided under the above headings.
7 An indication of any difficulties (technical deficiencies or lack of know-how) encountered by the developer in compiling the required information.

• •

Notes

1 This description should cover the direct effects and any indirect, secondary, cumulative, short, medium and long-term, permanent and temporary, positive and negative effects of the project.

Appendix 2

· ·

Town and Country Planning (EIA) Regulations 2011 – Schedule 2 (Regulation 2.1)

· ·

Descriptions of development and applicable thresholds and criteria for the purposes of the definition of 'Schedule 2 development'

In the table below:

- 'area of the works' includes any area occupied by apparatus, equipment, machinery, materials, plant, spoil heaps or other facilities or stores required for construction or installation;

- 'controlled waters' has the same meaning as in the Water Resources Act 1991;[1]
- 'floorspace' means the floorspace in a building or buildings.

The table below sets out the descriptions of development and applicable thresholds and criteria for the purpose of classifying development as Schedule 2 development.

Column 1: Description of development	Column 2: Applicable thresholds and criteria
The carrying out of development to provide any of the following:	
1 Agriculture and aquaculture	
(a) Projects for the use of uncultivated land or semi-natural areas for intensive agricultural purposes;	The area of the development exceeds 0.5 hectares.
(b) Water management projects for agriculture, including irrigation and land drainage projects;	The area of the works exceeds 1 hectare.
(c) Intensive livestock installations (unless included in Schedule 1);	The area of new floorspace exceeds 500 square metres.
(d) Intensive fish farming;	The installation resulting from the development is designed to produce more than 10 tonnes of dead weight fish per year.
(e) Reclamation of land from the sea.	All development.

Column 1: Description of development	Column 2: Applicable thresholds and criteria
2 Extractive industry	
(a) Quarries, open-cast mining and peat extraction (unless included in Schedule 1); (b) Underground mining;	All development except the construction of buildings or other ancillary structures where the new floorspace does not exceed 1,000 square metres.
(c) Extraction of minerals by fluvial or marine dredging;	All development.

(d) Deep drillings, in particular:
    (i) geothermal drilling;
    (ii) drilling for the storage of nuclear waste material;
    (iii) drilling for water supplies;
with the exception of drillings for investigating the stability of the soil;
	(i) In relation to any type of drilling, the area of the works exceeds 1 hectare; or
	(ii) in relation to geothermal drilling and drilling for the storage of nuclear waste material, the drilling is within 100 metres of any controlled waters.

(e) Surface industrial installations for the extraction of coal, petroleum, natural gas and ores, as well as bituminous shale.	The area of the development exceeds 0.5 hectares.

Column 1: Description of development	Column 2: Applicable thresholds and criteria
3 Energy industry	
(a) Industrial installations for the production of electricity, steam and hot water (unless included in Schedule 1);	The area of the development exceeds 0.5 hectares.
(b) Industrial installations for carrying gas, steam and hot water;	The area of the works exceeds 1 hectare.
(c) Surface storage of natural gas; (d) Underground storage of combustible gases; (e) Surface storage of fossil fuels;	(i) The area of any new building, deposit or structure exceeds 500 square metres; or (ii) a new building, deposit or structure is to be sited within 100 metres of any controlled waters.
(f) Industrial briquetting of coal and lignite;	The area of new floorspace exceeds 1,000 square metres.
(g) Installations for the processing and storage of radioactive waste (unless included in Schedule 1);	(i) The area of new floorspace exceeds 1,000 square metres; or (ii) the installation resulting from the development will require the grant of an environmental permit under the Environmental Permitting (England and Wales). Regulations 2010([2]) in relation to a radioactive substances activity described in paragraphs 5 (2) (b), (2) (c) or (4) of Part 2 of Schedule 23 to those Regulations, or the variation of such a permit.
(h) Installations for hydroelectric energy production;	The installation is designed to produce more than 0.5 megawatts.
(i) Installations for the harnessing of wind power for energy production (wind farms);	(i) The development involves the installation of more than 2 turbines; or; (ii) the hub height of any turbine or height of any other structure exceeds 15 metres.
(j) Installations for the capture of carbon dioxide streams for the purposes of geological storage pursuant to Directive 2009/31/EC from installations not included in Schedule 1.	All development.

Column 1: Description of development	Column 2: Applicable thresholds and criteria
4 Production and processing of metals	

(a) Installations for the production of pig iron or steel (primary or secondary fusion) including continuous casting;
 (b) Installations for the processing of ferrous metals:
     (i) hot-rolling mills;
     (ii) smitheries with hammers;
     (iii) application of protective fused metal coats.
 (c) Ferrous metal foundries;
 (d) Installations for the smelting, including the alloyage, of non-ferrous metals, excluding precious metals, including recovered products (refining, foundry casting, etc.);
 (e) Installations for surface treatment of metals and plastic materials using an electrolytic or chemical process;
 (f) Manufacture and assembly of motor vehicles and manufacture of motor-vehicle engines;
 (g) Shipyards;
 (h) Installations for the construction and repair of aircraft;
 (i) Manufacture of railway equipment;
 (j) Swaging by explosives;
 (k) Installations for the roasting and sintering of metallic ores.
	The area of new floorspace exceeds 1,000 square metres.

Column 1	Column 2
5 Mineral industry	
(a) Coke ovens (dry coal distillation); (b) Installations for the manufacture of cement; (c) Installations for the production of asbestos and the manufacture of asbestos-based products (unless included in Schedule 1); (d) Installations for the manufacture of glass including glass fibre; (e) Installations for smelting mineral substances including the production of mineral fibres; (f) Manufacture of ceramic products by burning, in particular roofing tiles, bricks, refractory bricks, tiles, stonewear or porcelain.	The area of new floorspace exceeds 1,000 square metres.

Column 1: Description of development	Column 2: Applicable thresholds and criteria
6 Chemical industry (unless included in Schedule 1)	
(a) Treatment of intermediate products and production of chemicals; (b) Production of pesticides and pharmaceutical products, paint and varnishes, elastomers and peroxides;	The area of new floorspace exceeds 1,000 square metres.
(c) Storage facilities for petroleum, petrochemical and chemical products.	(i) The area of any new building or structure exceeds 0.05 hectares; or (ii) more than 200 tonnes of petroleum, petrochemical or chemical products is to be stored at any one time.
7 Food industry	
(a) Manufacture of vegetable and animal oils and fats; (b) Packing and canning of animal and vegetable products; (c) Manufacture of dairy products; (d) Brewing and malting; (e) Confectionery and syrup manufacture; (f) Installations for the slaughter of animals; (g) Industrial starch manufacturing installations; (h) Fish-meal and fish-oil factories; (i) Sugar factories.	The area of new floorspace exceeds 1,000 square metres.
8 Textile, leather, wood and paper industries	
(a) Industrial plants for the production of paper and board (unless included in Schedule 1); (b) Plants for the pre-treatment (operations such as washing, bleaching, mercerisation) or dyeing of fibres or textiles; (c) Plants for the tanning of hides and skins; (d) Cellulose-processing and production installations.	The area of new floorspace exceeds 1,000 square metres.
9 Rubber industry	
Manufacture and treatment of elastomer-based products.	The area of new floorspace exceeds 1,000 square metres.

Column 1: Description of development	Column 2: Applicable thresholds and criteria
10 Infrastructure projects	
(a) Industrial estate development projects; (b) Urban development projects, including the construction of shopping centres and car parks, sports stadiums, leisure centres and multiplex cinemas; (c) Construction of intermodal transshipment facilities and of intermodal terminals (unless included in Schedule 1);	The area of the development exceeds 0.5 hectares.
(d) Construction of railways (unless included in Schedule 1);	The area of the works exceeds 1 hectare.
(e) Construction of airfields (unless included in Schedule 1);	(i) The development involves an extension to a runway; or (ii) the area of the works exceeds 1 hectare.
(f) Construction of roads (unless included in Schedule 1);	The area of the works exceeds 1 hectare.
(g) Construction of harbours and port installations including fishing harbours (unless included in Schedule 1);	The area of the works exceeds 1 hectare.
(h) Inland-waterway construction not included in Schedule 1, canalisation and flood-relief works; (i) Dams and other installations designed to hold water or store it on a long-term basis (unless included in Schedule 1); (j) Tramways, elevated and underground railways, suspended lines or similar lines of a particular type, used exclusively or mainly for passenger transport;	The area of the works exceeds 1 hectare.
(k) Oil and gas pipeline installations and pipelines for the transport of carbon dioxide streams for the purposes of geological storage (unless included in Schedule 1); (l) Installations of long-distance aqueducts;	(i) The area of the works exceeds 1 hectare; or (ii) in the case of a gas pipeline, the installation has a design operating pressure exceeding 7 bar gauge.
(m) Coastal work to combat erosion and maritime works capable of altering the coast through the construction, for example, of dykes, moles, jetties and other sea defence works, excluding the maintenance and reconstruction of such works;	All development.
(n) Groundwater abstraction and artificial groundwater recharge schemes not included in Schedule 1; (o) Works for the transfer of water resources between river basins not included in Schedule 1;	The area of the works exceeds 1 hectare.
(p) Motorway service areas.	The area of the development exceeds 0.5 hectares.

Column 1: Description of development	Column 2: Applicable thresholds and criteria
11 Other projects	
(a) Permanent racing and test tracks for motorised vehicles;	The area of the development exceeds 1 hectare.
(b) Installations for the disposal of waste (unless included in Schedule 1);	(i) The disposal is by incineration; or (ii) the area of the development exceeds 0.5 hectare; or (iii) the installation is to be sited within 100 metres of any controlled waters.
(c) Waste-water treatment plants (unless included in Schedule 1);	The area of the development exceeds 1,000 square metres.
(d) Sludge-deposition sites; (e) Storage of scrap iron, including scrap vehicles;	(i) The area of deposit or storage exceeds 0.5 hectare; or (ii) a deposit is to be made or scrap stored within 100 metres of any controlled waters.
(f) Test benches for engines, turbines or reactors; (g) Installations for the manufacture of artificial mineral fibres; (h) Installations for the recovery or destruction of explosive substances; (i) Knackers' yards.	The area of new floorspace exceeds 1,000 square metres.

Column 1: Description of development	Column 2: Applicable thresholds and criteria
12 Tourism and leisure	
(a) Ski-runs, ski-lifts and cable-cars and associated developments;	(i) The area of the works exceeds 1 hectare; or (ii) the height of any building or other structure exceeds 15 metres.
(b) Marinas;	The area of the enclosed water surface exceeds 1,000 square metres.
(c) Holiday villages and hotel complexes outside urban areas and associated developments; (d) Theme parks;	The area of the development exceeds 0.5 hectares.
(e) Permanent camp sites and caravan sites;	The area of the development exceeds 1 hectare.
(f) Golf courses and associated developments.	The area of the development exceeds 1 hectare.

Column 1: Description of development	Column 2: Applicable thresholds and criteria
13 Changes and extensions	
(a) Any change to or extension of development of a description listed in Schedule 1 (other than a change or extension falling within paragraph 21 of that Schedule) where that development is already authorised, executed or in the process of being executed.	Either: (i) The development as changed or extended may have significant adverse effects on the environment; or (ii) in relation to development of a description mentioned in a paragraph in Schedule 1 indicated below, the thresholds and criteria in column 2 of the paragraph of this table indicated below applied to the change or extension are met or exceeded. *Paragraph in Schedule 1* — *Paragraph of this table* 1 — 6 (a) 2 (a) — 3 (a) 2 (b) — 3 (g) 3 — 3 (g) 4 — 4 5 — 5 6 — 6 (a) 7 (a) — 10 (d) (in relation to railways) or 10 (e) (in relation to airports) 7 (b) and (c) — 10 (f) 8 (a) — 10 (h) 8 (b) — 10 (g) 9 — 11 (b) 10 — 11 (b) 11 — 10 (n) 12 — 10 (o) 13 — 11 (c) 14 — 2 (e) 15 — 10 (i) 16 — 10 (k) 17 — 1 (c) 18 — 8 (a) 19 — 2 (a) 20 — 6 (c)
(b) Any change to or extension of development of a description listed in paragraphs 1 to 12 of column 1 of this table, where that development is already authorised, executed or in the process of being executed.	Either— (i) The development as changed or extended may have significant adverse effects on the environment; or (ii) in relation to development of a description mentioned in column 1 of this table, the thresholds and criteria in the corresponding part of column 2 of this table applied to the change or extension are met or exceeded.
(c) Development of a description mentioned in Schedule 1 undertaken exclusively or mainly for the development and testing of new methods or products and not used for more than two years.	All development.

Notes

1   1991 c. 57. See section 104.

2   S.I. 2010/675.

Appendix 3

●●

Full text of the European Commission's SEA Directive

Directive 2001/42/EC of the European Parliament and of the Council of 27 June 2001 on the assessment of the effects of certain plans and programmes on the environment

Article 1: Objectives

The objective of this Directive is to provide for a high level of protection of the environment and to contribute to the integration of environmental considerations into the preparation and adoption of plans and programmes with a view to promoting sustainable development, by ensuring that, in accordance with this Directive, an environmental assessment is carried out of certain plans and programmes that are likely to have significant effects on the environment.

Article 2: Definitions

For the purposes of this Directive:

(a) 'plans and programmes' shall mean plans and programmes, including those co-financed by the European Community, as well as any modifications to them:
  – which are subject to preparation and/or adoption by an authority at national, regional or local level or which are prepared by an authority for adoption, through a legislative procedure by Parliament or Government, and
  – which are required by legislative, regulatory or administrative provisions;

(b) 'environmental assessment' shall mean the preparation of an environmental report, the carrying out of consultations, the taking into account of the environmental report and the results of the consultations in decision-making and the provision of information on the decision in accordance with Articles 4 to 9;

(c) 'environmental report' shall mean the part of the plan or programme documentation containing the information required in Article 5 and Annex I;

(d) 'The public' shall mean one or more natural or legal persons and, in accordance with national legislation or practice, their associations, organisations or groups.

Article 3: Scope

1 An environmental assessment, in accordance with Articles 4 to 9, shall be carried out for

plans and programmes referred to in paragraphs 2 to 4, which are likely to have significant environmental effects.

2   Subject to paragraph 3, an environmental assessment shall be carried out for all plans and programmes,

(a) which are prepared for agriculture, forestry, fisheries, energy, industry, transport, waste management, water management, telecommunications, tourism, town and country planning or land use and which set the framework for future development consent of projects listed in Annexes I and II to Directive 85/337/EEC, or

(b) which, in view of the likely effect on sites, have been determined to require an assessment pursuant to Article 6 or 7 of Directive 92/43/EEC.

3   Plans and programmes referred to in paragraph 2 that determine the use of small areas at local level and minor modifications to plans and programmes referred to in paragraph 2 shall require an environmental assessment only where the Member States determine that they are likely to have significant environmental effects.

4   Member States shall determine whether plans and programmes, other than those referred to in paragraph 2, which set the framework for future development consent of projects, are likely to have significant environmental effects.

5   Member States shall determine whether plans or programmes referred to in paragraphs 3 and 4 are likely to have significant environmental effects either through case-by-case examination or by specifying types of plans and programmes or by combining both approaches. For this purpose Member States shall in all cases take into account relevant criteria set out in Annex II, in order to ensure that plans and programmes with likely significant effects on the environment are covered by this Directive.

6   In the case-by-case examination and in specifying types of plans and programmes in accordance with paragraph 5, the authorities referred to in Article 6 (3) shall be consulted.

7   Member States shall ensure that their conclusions pursuant to paragraph 5, including the reasons for not requiring an environmental assessment pursuant to Articles 4 to 9, are made available to the public.

8   The following plans and programmes are not subject to this Directive:

–   plans and programmes the sole purpose of which is to serve national defence or civil emergency;

–   financial or budget plans and programmes.

9   This Directive does not apply to plans and programmes co-financed under the current respective programming periods[1] for Council Regulations (EC) No 1260/1999[2] and (EC) No 1257/1999.[3]

Article 4: General obligations

1   The environmental assessment referred to in Article 3 shall be carried out during the preparation of a plan or programme and before its adoption or submission to the legislative procedure.

2   The requirements of this Directive shall either be integrated into existing procedures in Member States for the adoption of plans and programmes or incorporated in procedures established to comply with this Directive.

3   Where plans and programmes form part of a hierarchy, Member States shall, with a view to avoiding duplication of the assessment, take into account the fact that the assessment will be carried out, in accordance with this Directive, at different levels of the hierarchy. For the purpose of, *inter alia*, avoiding duplication of assessment, Member States shall apply Article 5 (2) and (3).

Article 5: Environmental report

1   Where an environmental assessment is required under Article 3 (1), an environmental report shall be prepared in which the likely significant effects on the environment of

implementing the plan or programme, and reasonable alternatives taking into account the objectives and the geographical scope of the plan or programme, are identified, described and evaluated. The information to be given for this purpose is referred to in Annex I.

2   The environmental report prepared pursuant to paragraph 1 shall include the information that may reasonably be required taking into account current knowledge and methods of assessment, the contents and level of detail in the plan or programme, its stage in the decision-making process and the extent to which certain matters are more appropriately assessed at different levels in that process in order to avoid duplication of the assessment.

3   Relevant information available on environmental effects of the plans and programmes and obtained at other levels of decision-making or through other Community legislation may be used for providing the information referred to in Annex I.

4   The authorities referred to in Article 6 (3) shall be consulted when deciding on the scope and level of detail of the information that must be included in the environmental report.

Article 6: Consultations

1   The draft plan or programme and the environmental report prepared in accordance with Article 5 shall be made available to the authorities referred to in paragraph 3 of this Article and the public.

2   The authorities referred to in paragraph 3 and the public referred to in paragraph 4 shall be given an early and effective opportunity within appropriate time frames to express their opinion on the draft plan or programme and the accompanying environmental report before the adoption of the plan or programme or its submission to the legislative procedure.

3   Member States shall designate the authorities to be consulted that, by reason of their specific environmental responsibilities, are likely to be concerned by the environmental effects of implementing plans and programmes.

4   Member States shall identify the public for the purposes of paragraph 2, including the public affected or likely to be affected by, or having an interest in, the decision-making subject to this Directive, including relevant non-governmental organisations, such as those promoting environmental protection and other organisations concerned.

5   The detailed arrangements for the information and consultation of the authorities and the public shall be determined by the Member States.

Article 7: Transboundary consultations

1   Where a Member State considers that the implementation of a plan or programme being prepared in relation to its territory is likely to have significant effects on the environment in another Member State, or where a Member State likely to be significantly affected so requests, the Member State in whose territory the plan or programme is being prepared shall, before its adoption or submission to the legislative procedure, forward a copy of the draft plan or programme and the relevant environmental report to the other Member State.

2   Where a Member State is sent a copy of a draft plan or programme and an environmental report under paragraph 1, it shall indicate to the other Member State whether it wishes to enter into consultations before the adoption of the plan or programme or its submission to the legislative procedure and, if it so indicates, the Member States concerned shall enter into consultations concerning the likely transboundary environmental effects of implementing the plan or programme and the measures envisaged to reduce or eliminate such effects.

Where such consultations take place, the Member States concerned shall agree on detailed arrangements to ensure that the authorities referred to in Article 6 (3) and the public referred to in Article 6 (4) in the Member State likely to be significantly affected are informed and given an opportunity to forward their opinion within a reasonable time-frame.

3   Where Member States are required under this Article to enter into consultations, they shall agree, at the beginning of such consultations, on a reasonable timeframe for the duration of the consultations.

Article 8: Decision making

The environmental report prepared pursuant to Article 5, the opinions expressed pursuant to Article 6 and the results of any transboundary consultations entered into pursuant to Article 7 shall be taken into account during the preparation of the plan or programme and before its adoption or submission to the legislative procedure.

Article 9: Information on the decision

1   Member States shall ensure that, when a plan or programme is adopted, the authorities referred to in Article 6 (3), the public and any Member State consulted under Article 7 are informed and the following items are made available to those so informed:
   (a)   the plan or programme as adopted;
   (b)   a statement summarizing how environmental considerations have been integrated into the plan or programme and how the environmental report prepared pursuant to Article 5, the opinions expressed pursuant to Article 6 and the results of consultations entered into pursuant to Article 7 have been taken into account in accordance with Article 8 and the reasons for choosing the plan or programme as adopted, in the light of the other reasonable alternatives dealt with; and
   (c)   the measures decided concerning monitoring in accordance with Article 10.

2   The detailed arrangements concerning the information referred to in paragraph 1 shall be determined by the Member States.

Article 10: Monitoring

1   Member States shall monitor the significant environmental effects of the implementation of plans and programmes in order, *inter alia*, to identify at an early stage unforeseen adverse effects, and to be able to undertake appropriate remedial action.

2   In order to comply with paragraph 1, existing monitoring arrangements may be used if appropriate, with a view to avoiding duplication of monitoring.

Article 11: Relationship with other Community legislation

1   An environmental assessment carried out under this Directive shall be without prejudice to any requirements under Directive 85/337/EEC and to any other Community law requirements.

2   For plans and programmes for which the obligation to carry out assessments of the effects on the environment arises simultaneously from this Directive and other Community legislation, Member States may provide for coordinated or joint procedures fulfilling the requirements of the relevant Community legislation in order, *inter alia*, to avoid duplication of assessment.

3   For plans and programmes co-financed by the European Community, the environmental assessment in accordance with this Directive shall be carried out in conformity with the specific provisions in relevant Community legislation.

Article 12: Information, reporting and review

1   Member States and the Commission shall exchange information on the experience gained in applying this Directive.

2   Member States shall ensure that environmental reports are of a sufficient quality to meet the requirements of this Directive and shall communicate to the Commission any measures they take concerning the quality of these reports.

3   Before 21 July 2006 the Commission shall send a first report on the application and effectiveness of this Directive to the European Parliament and to the Council.

   With a view further to integrating environmental protection requirements, in accordance with Article 6 of the Treaty, and taking into account the experience acquired in the application of this Directive in the Member States, such a report will be accompanied by proposals for amendment of this Directive, if appropriate. In particular, the Commission will consider the possibility of extending the scope of this Directive to other areas/sectors and other types of plans and programmes.

   A new evaluation report shall follow at seven-year intervals.

4   The Commission shall report on the relationship between this Directive and Regulations (EC) No 1260/1999 and (EC) No 1257/1999 well ahead of the expiry of the programming periods provided for in those Regulations, with a view to ensuring a coherent approach with regard to this Directive and subsequent Community Regulations.

Article 13: Implementation of the Directive

1   Member States shall bring into force the laws, regulations and administrative provisions necessary to comply with this Directive before 21 July 2004. They shall forthwith inform the Commission thereof.

2   When Member States adopt the measures, they shall contain a reference to this Directive or shall be accompanied by such reference on the occasion of their official publication. The methods of making such reference shall be laid down by Member States.

3   The obligation referred to in Article 4 (1) shall apply to the plans and programmes of which the first formal preparatory act is subsequent to the date referred to in paragraph 1. Plans and programmes of which the first formal preparatory act is before that date and which are adopted or submitted to the legislative procedure more than 24 months thereafter, shall be made subject to the obligation referred to in Article 4 (1) unless Member States decide on a case by case basis that this is not feasible and inform the public of their decision.

4   Before 21 July 2004, Member States shall communicate to the Commission, in addition to the measures referred to in paragraph 1, separate information on the types of plans and programmes that, in accordance with Article 3, would be subject to an environmental assessment pursuant to this Directive. The Commission shall make this information available to the Member States. The information will be updated on a regular basis.

Article 14: Entry into force

This Directive shall enter into force on the day of its publication in the Official Journal of the European Communities.

Article 15: Addressees

This Directive is addressed to the Member States. Done at Luxembourg, 27 June 2001.

For the European Parliament
The President
N. FONTAINE
For the Council
The President
B. ROSENGREN

Notes

1   The 2000–06 programming period for Council Regulation (EC) No 1260/1999 and the 2000–06 and 2000–07 programming periods for Council Regulation (EC) No 1257/1999.

2   Council Regulation (EC) No 1260/1999 of 21 June 1999 laying down general provisions on the Structural Funds (OJ L 161, 26.6.1999, p. 1).

3   Council Regulation (EC) No 1257/1999 of 17 May 1999 on support for rural development from the European Agricultural Guidance and Guarantee Fund (EAGGF) and amending and repealing certain regulations (OJ L 160, 26.6.1999, p. 80).

Annex I

Information referred to in Article 5 (1)

The information to be provided under Article 5 (1), subject to Article 5 (2) and (3), is the following:

(a) an outline of the contents, main objectives of the plan or programme and relationship with other relevant plans and programmes;

(b) the relevant aspects of the current state of the environment and the likely evolution thereof without implementation of the plan or programme;

(c) the environmental characteristics of areas likely to be significantly affected;

(d) any existing environmental problems that are relevant to the plan or programme including, in particular, those relating to any areas of a particular environmental importance, such as areas designated pursuant to Directives 79/409/EEC and 92/43/EEC;

(e) the environmental protection objectives, established at international, Community or Member State level, which are relevant to the plan or programme and the way those objectives and any environmental considerations have been taken into account during its preparation;

(f) the likely significant effects[1] on the environment, including on issues such as biodiversity, population, human health, fauna, flora, soil, water, air, climatic factors, material assets, cultural heritage including architectural and archaeological heritage, landscape and the interrelationship between the above factors;

(g) the measures envisaged to prevent, reduce and as fully as possible offset any significant adverse effects on the environment of implementing the plan or programme;

(h) an outline of the reasons for selecting the alternatives dealt with, and a description of how the assessment was undertaken including any difficulties (such as technical deficiencies or lack of know-how) encountered in compiling the required information;

(i) a description of the measures envisaged concerning monitoring in accordance with Article 10;

(j) a non-technical summary of the information provided under the above headings.

Notes

1 These effects should include secondary, cumulative, synergistic, short, medium and long-term, permanent and temporary, positive and negative effects.

Annex II

· ·

Criteria for determining the likely significance of effects
referred to in Article 3 (5)

1   The characteristics of plans and programmes, having regard, in particular, to
    –   the degree to which the plan or programme sets a framework for projects and other activities, either with regard to the location, nature, size and operating conditions or by allocating resources;
    –   the degree to which the plan or programme influences other plans and programmes including those in a hierarchy;
    –   the relevance of the plan or programme for the integration of environmental considerations in particular with a view to promoting sustainable development;
    –   environmental problems relevant to the plan or programme;
    –   the relevance of the plan or programme for the implementation of Community legislation on the environment (e.g. plans and programmes linked to waste-management or water protection).

2   Characteristics of the effects and of the area likely to be affected, having regard, in particular, to
    –   the probability, duration, frequency and reversibility of the effects;
    –   the cumulative nature of the effects;
    –   the transboundary nature of the effects;
    –   the risks to human health or the environment (e.g. due to accidents);
    –   the magnitude and spatial extent of the effects (geographical area and size of the population likely to be affected);
    –   the value and vulnerability of the area likely to be affected due to:
        (i)   special natural characteristics or cultural heritage;
        (ii) exceeded environmental quality standards or limit values;
        (iii) intensive land-use;
    –   the effects on areas or landscapes that have a recognized national, Community or international protection status.

Appendix 4

· ·

The Lee and Colley review package

The Lee and Colley method reviews EISs under four main topics, each of which is examined under a number of sub-headings:

1   Description of the development, the local environment and the baseline conditions:
    • description of the development
    • site description
    • residuals
    • baseline conditions
2   Identification and evaluation of key impacts:
    • identification of impacts
    • prediction of impact magnitudes
    • assessment of impact significance
3   Alternatives and mitigation:
    • alternatives
    • mitigation
    • commitment to mitigation
4   Communication of results:
    • presentation
    • balance
    • non-technical summary

In outline, the content and quality of the environmental statement is reviewed under each of the subheads, using a sliding scale of assessment symbols A–F:

Grade A indicates that the work has generally been well performed with no important omissions.

Grade B is generally satisfactory and complete with only minor omissions and inadequacies.

Grade C is regarded as just satisfactory despite some omissions or inadequacies.

Grade D indicates that parts are well attempted but, on the whole, just unsatisfactory because of omissions or inadequacies.

Grade E is not satisfactory, revealing significant omissions or inadequacies.

Grade F is very unsatisfactory with important task(s) poorly done or not attempted.

Having analysed each sub-head, aggregated scores are given to the four review areas, and a final summary grade is attached to the whole statement.

Appendix 5

• •

Environmental impact statement review package
(IAU, Oxford Brookes University)

Using the review packages

The IAU review package was developed for a research project into the changing quality of EISs that was funded by the DoE, the Scottish and Welsh Offices in 1995/96. The package is a robust mechanism for systematically reviewing EISs. The full review package has been updated to combine the requirements of the 2011 EIA Regulations, the DoE checklist, a review package developed by Manchester University, an EU review checklist as well as notions of best practice developed by the IAU. The package is divided into 8 sections and within each section are a number of individual review criterion. In all, the package assesses the quality of an EIS against 92 criteria, some of which are not necessarily relevant to all projects. Each criterion is graded on the basis of the quality of the material provided and each section is then awarded an overall grade. From the grades given to each section an overall grade for the EIS is arrived at. The IAU review grades are based upon the grading system developed by Manchester University for their review package. These grades are:

A = indicates that the work has generally been well performed with no important omissions;

B = is generally satisfactory and complete with only minor omissions and inadequacies;

C = is regarded as just satisfactory despite some omissions or inadequacies;

D = indicates that parts are well attempted but, on the whole, just unsatisfactory because of omissions or inadequacies;

E = is not satisfactory, revealing significant omissions or inadequacies;

F = is very unsatisfactory with important task(s) poorly done or not attempted.

These grades can be used to test an EIS's compliance with the relevant Regulations, with the pass/fail mark lying between grades 'C' and 'D'. By using this grading system the reviewer can more readily identify the aspects of the EIS that need completing and because the grades are well established the competent authority can confidently justify any requests for further information. The assessment of EIS quality against these grades is rather like the marking of an academic essay in that while the activity – i.e. review – is carried out independently, objectively and systematically, the attributing of individual grades to individual criterion is inherently subjective. One way of reducing the subjectivity of the review is for the EIS to be assessed by two independent reviewers on the basis of a 'double blind' approach. Here each reviewer assesses the EIS against the criteria and grades the EIS on the basis of 'A' to 'F' for each criterion and for the ES as a whole. The reviewers then compare results and agree grades.

In arriving at overall grades, from all of the individual grades, a decision must be made over whether, for example, an 'A' grade for one area outweighs a 'D' grade for another area. This will depend entirely on perspective, as an individual reviewer may consider some aspects to be more important than others and so it is not a simple matter of counting up all of the 'A', 'B' and 'Cs' and giving an overall grade based on the most common or average grade. In some cases a clear 'F' grade for one of the minimum regulatory requirements (e.g. non-technical summary) could be seen as resulting in an overall fail for the EIS because of the importance of that particular aspect. Other areas (e.g. consideration of alternatives) may be seen as less crucial where that aspect is not of particular relevance to the project in question. An 'F' grade for one such criteria, may not, in such cases, prevent an EIS being attributed a 'C' grade, or above, overall. Attributing the overall grade for an EIS through this process requires the reviewer to come to a judgement on the weight to be given to the individual review areas and is rather like attributing weight to planning considerations.

The success of EIS review relies a great deal on the experience of the reviewer and their ability to make a judgement on the quality of the EIS as a whole, based upon the systematic assessment of its parts. In reviewing the EIS a reviewer should come to a view on the information provided based upon a balance between:

- what it 'must' contain;
- what it could contain; and
- what it can be reasonably expected to contain.

Oxford Brookes University

Impacts Assessment Unit

Environmental Impact Statement Review Package

Name of Project:

EIS Submitted by:

Date Submitted:

Review Grades

A = Relevant tasks well performed, no important tasks left incomplete.

B = Generally satisfactory and complete, only minor omissions and inadequacies.

C = Can be considered just satisfactory despite omissions and/or inadequacies.

D = Parts are well attempted but must, as a whole, be considered just unsatisfactory because of omissions and/or inadequacies.

E = Not satisfactory, significant omissions or inadequacies.

F = Very unsatisfactory, important task(s) poorly done or not attempted.

NA = Not applicable in the context of the EIS or the project.

1 DESCRIPTION OF THE DEVELOPMENT

Criterion	Review grade	Comments
Principal features of the project		
1.1 Explains the purpose(s) and objectives of the development.		
1.2 Indicates the nature and status of the decision(s) for which the environmental information has been prepared.		
1.3 Gives the estimated duration of the construction, operational and, where appropriate, decommissioning phase, and the programme within these phases.		
1.4 **Provides a description of the development comprising information on the site, design and size of the development.**[1]		
1.5 **Provides diagrams, plans or maps and photographs to aid the description of the development.**		
1.6 Indicates the physical presence or appearance of the completed development within the receiving environment.		
1.7 Describes the methods of construction.		
1.8 Describes the nature and methods of production or other types of activity involved in the operation of the project.		
1.9 Describes any additional services (water, electricity, emergency services etc.) and developments required as a consequence of the project.		
1.10 Describes the project's potential for accidents, hazards and emergencies.		
Land requirements		
1.11 Defines the land area taken up by the development and/or construction site and any associated arrangements, auxiliary facilities and landscaping areas, and shows their location clearly on a map. For a linear project, describes the land corridor, vertical and horizontal alignment and need for tunnelling and earthworks.		
1.12 Describes the uses to which this land will be put, and demarcates the different land use areas.		
1.13 Describes the reinstatement and after-use of landtake during construction.		
Project inputs		
1.14 Describes the nature and quantities of materials needed during the construction and operational phases.		
1.15 Estimates the number of workers and visitors entering the project site during both construction and operation.		
1.16 Describes their access to the site and likely means of transport.		
1.17 Indicates the means of transporting materials and products to and from the site during construction and operation, and the number of movements involved.		
Residues and emissions		
1.18 Estimates the types and quantities of waste matter, energy (noise, vibration, light, heat, radiation etc.) and residual materials generated during construction and operation of the project, and rate at which these will be produced.		
1.19 Indicates how these wastes and residual materials are expected to be handled/treated prior to release/disposal, and the routes by which they will eventually be disposed of to the environment.		
1.20 Identifies any special or hazardous wastes (defined as . . .) which will be produced, and describes the methods for their disposal as regards their likely main environmental impacts.		
1.21 Indicates the methods by which the quantities of residuals and wastes were estimated. Acknowledges any uncertainty, and gives ranges or confidence limits where appropriate.		
Overall Grade for Section 1 = Comments		

1 Schedule 4 Part 2 Criteria (2011 EIA Regulations)

2 DESCRIPTION OF THE ENVIRONMENT

Criterion		Review grade	Comments
Description of the area occupied by and surrounding the project			
2.1	Indicates the area expected to be significantly affected by the various aspects of the project with the aid of suitable maps. Explains the time over which these impacts are likely to occur.		
2.2	Describes the land uses on the site(s) and in surrounding areas.		
2.3	Defines the affected environment broadly enough to include any potentially significant effects occurring away from the immediate areas of construction and operation. These may be caused by, for example, the dispersion of pollutants, infrastructural requirements of the project, traffic etc.		
Baseline conditions			
2.4	Identifies and describes the components of the affected environment potentially affected by the project.		
2.5	The methods used to investigate the affected environment are appropriate to the size and complexity of the assessment task. Uncertainty is indicated.		
2.6	Predicts the likely future environmental conditions in the absence of the project. Identifies variability in natural systems and human use.		
2.7	Uses existing technical data sources, including records and studies carried out for environmental agencies and for special interest groups.		
2.8	Reviews local, regional and national plans and policies, and other data collected as necessary to predict future environmental conditions. Where the proposal does not conform to these plans and policies, the departure is justified.		
2.9	Local, regional and national agencies holding information on baseline environmental conditions have been approached.		
Overall Grade for Section 1 = Comments			

3 SCOPING, CONSULTATION AND IMPACT IDENTIFICATION

Criterion		Review grade	Comments
Scoping and consultation			
3.1	There has been a genuine attempt to contact the general public, relevant public agencies, relevant experts and special interest groups to appraise them of the project and its implication. Lists the groups approached.		
3.2	Statutory consultees have been contacted. Lists the consultees approached.		
3.3	Identifies valued environmental attributes on the basis of this consultation.		
3.4	Identifies all project activities with significant impacts on valued environmental attributes. Identifies and selects key impacts for more intense investigation. Describes and justifies the scoping methods used.		
3.5	Includes a copy or summary of the main comments from consultees and the public, and measures taken to respond to these comments.		
Impact identification			
3.6	**Provides the data required to identify the main effects that the development is likely to have on the environment.**[1]		

Criterion	Review grade	Comments
3.7 Considers direct and indirect/secondary effects of constructing, operating and, where relevant, after-use or decommissioning of the project (including positive and negative effects). Considers whether effects will arise as a result of 'consequential' development.		
3.8 Investigates the above types of impacts in so far as they affect: human beings, flora, fauna, soil, water, air, climate, landscape, interactions between the above, material assets, cultural heritage.		
3.9 Also noise, land use, historic heritage, communities.		
3.10 If any of the above are not of concern in relation to the specific project and its location, this is clearly stated.		
3.11 Identifies impacts using a systematic methodology such as project specific checklists, matrices, panels of experts, extensive consultations, etc. Describes the methods/approaches used and the rationale for using them.		
3.12 The investigation of each type of impact is appropriate to its importance for the decision, avoiding unnecessary information and concentrating on the key issues.		
3.13 Considers impacts that may not themselves be significant but that may contribute incrementally to a significant effect.		
3.14 Considers impacts that might arise from non-standard operating conditions, accidents and emergencies.		
3.15 If the nature of the project is such that accidents are possible that might cause severe damage within the surrounding environment, an assessment of the probability and likely consequences of such events is carried out and the main findings reported.		
Overall Grade for Section 1 = Comments		

4 PREDICTION AND EVALUATION OF IMPACTS

Criterion	Review grade	Comments
Prediction of magnitude of impacts		
4.1 Describes impacts in terms of the nature and magnitude of the change occurring and the nature, location, number, value, sensitivity of the affected receptors.		
4.2 Predicts the timescale over which the effects will occur, so that it is clear whether impacts are short, medium or long term, temporary or permanent, reversible or irreversible.		
4.3 Where possible, expresses impact predictions in quantitative terms. Qualitative descriptions, where necessary, are as fully defined as possible.		
4.4 Describes the likelihood of impacts occurring, and the level of uncertainty attached to the results.		
Methods and data		
4.5 **Provides the data required to assess the main effects that the development is likely to have on the environment.**[1]		
4.6 The methods used to predict the nature, size and scale of impacts are described, and are appropriate to the size and importance of the projected disturbance.		

Criterion	Review grade	Comments
4.7 The data used to estimate the size and scale of the main impacts are sufficient for the task, clearly described, and their sources clearly identified. Any gaps in the data are indicated and accounted for.		
Evaluation of impact significance		
4.8 Discusses the significance of effects in terms of the impact on the local community (including distribution of impacts) and on the protection of environmental resources.		
4.9 Discusses the available standards, assumptions and value systems that can be used to assess significance.		
4.10 Where there are no generally accepted standards or criteria for the evaluation of significance, alternative approaches are discussed and, if so, a clear distinction is made between fact, assumption and professional judgement.		
4.11 Discusses the significance of effects taking into account the appropriate national and international standards or norms, where these are available. Otherwise the magnitude, location and duration of the effects are discussed in conjunction with the value, sensitivity and rarity of the resource.		
4.12 Differentiates project-generated impacts from other changes resulting from non-project activities and variables.		
4.13 Includes a clear indication of which impacts may be significant and which may not and provides justification for this distinction.		
Overall Grade for Section 4 = Comments		

5 ALTERNATIVES

Criterion	Review grade	Comments
5.1 **Provides an outline of the main alternatives studied and gives an indication of the main reasons for their choice, taking into account the environmental effects.**[1]		
5.2 Considers the 'no action' alternative, alternative processes, scales, layouts, designs and operating conditions where available at an early stage of project planning, and investigates their main environmental advantages and disadvantages.		
5.3 If unexpectedly severe adverse impacts are identified during the course of the investigation, which are difficult to mitigate, alternatives rejected in the earlier planning phases are re-appraised.		
5.4 The alternatives are realistic and genuine.		
5.5 Compares the alternatives' main environmental impacts clearly and objectively with those of the proposed project and with the likely future environmental conditions without the project.		
Overall Grade for Section 5 = Comments		

6 MITIGATION AND MONITORING

Criterion	Review grade	Comments
Description of mitigation measure		
6.1 **Provides a description of the measures envisaged in order to avoid, reduce and, if possible, remedy significant adverse effects.**		
6.2 Mitigation measures considered include modification of project design, construction and operation, the replacement of facilities/resources, and the creation of new resources, as well as 'end-of-pipe' technologies for pollution control.		
6.3 Describes the reasons for choosing the particular type of mitigation, and the other options available.		
6.4 Explains the extent to which the mitigation methods will be effective. Where the effectiveness is uncertain, or where mitigation may not work, this is made clear and data are introduced to justify the acceptance of these assumptions.		
6.5 Indicates the significance of any residual or unmitigated impacts remaining after mitigation, and justifies why these impacts should not be mitigated.		
Commitment to mitigation and monitoring		
6.6 Gives details of how the mitigation measures will be implemented and function over the time span for which they are necessary.		
6.7 Proposes monitoring arrangements for all significant impacts, especially where uncertainty exists, to check the environmental impact resulting from the implementation of the project and its conformity with the predictions made.		
6.8 The scale of any proposed monitoring arrangements corresponds to the potential scale and significance of deviations from expected impacts.		
Environmental effects of mitigation		
6.9 Investigates and describes any adverse environmental effects of mitigation measures.		
6.10 Considers the potential for conflict between the benefits of mitigation measures and their adverse impacts.		
Overall Grade for Section 6 = Comments		

7 NON-TECHNICAL SUMMARY

Criterion	Review grade	Comments
7.1 **There is a non-technical summary of the information provided under paragraphs 1 to 4 of Part 2 of Schedule 4.**[1]		
7.2 The non-technical summary contains at least a brief description of the project and the environment, an account of the main mitigation measures to be undertaken by the developer, and a description of any remaining or residual impacts.		
7.3 The summary avoids technical terms, lists of data and detailed explanations of scientific reasoning.		
7.4 The summary presents the main findings of the assessment and covers all the main issues raised in the information.		
7.5 The summary includes a brief explanation of the overall approach to the assessment.		
7.6 The summary indicates the confidence that can be placed in the results.		
Overall Grade for Section 7 = Comments		

8 ORGANISATION AND PRESENTATION OF INFORMATION

Criterion	Review grade	Comments
Organisation of the information		
8.1 Logically arranges the information in sections.		
8.2 Identifies the location of information in a table or list of contents.		
8.3 There are chapter or section summaries outlining the main findings of each phase of the investigation.		
8.4 When information from external sources has been introduced, a full reference to the source is included.		
Presentation of information		
8.5 Mentions the relevant EIA legislation, name of the developer, name of competent authority(ies), name of organisation preparing the EIS, and name, address and contact number of a contact person.		
8.6 Includes an introduction briefly describing the project, the aims of the assessment, and the methods used.		
8.7 The statement is presented as an integrated whole. Data presented in appendices are fully discussed in the main body of the text.		
8.8 Offers information and analysis to support all conclusions drawn.		
8.9 Presents information so as to be comprehensible to the non-specialist. Uses maps, tables, graphical material and other devices as appropriate. Avoids unnecessarily technical or obscure language.		
8.10 Discusses all the important data and results in an integrated fashion.		
8.11 Avoids superfluous information (i.e. information not needed for the decision).		
8.12 Presents the information in a concise form with a consistent terminology and logical links between different sections.		
8.13 Gives prominence and emphasis to severe adverse impacts, substantial environmental benefits, and controversial issues.		
8.14 Defines technical terms, acronyms and initials.		
8.15 The information is objective, and does not lobby for any particular point of view. Adverse impacts are not disguised by euphemisms or platitudes.		
Difficulties compiling the information		
8.16 Indicates any gaps in the required data and explains the means used to deal with them in the assessment.		
8.17 Acknowledges and explains any difficulties in assembling or analysing the data needed to predict impacts, and any basis for questioning assumptions, data or information.		
Overall Grade for Section 8 = Comments		

COLLATION SHEET
Minimum requirements of Schedule 4 Part 2 (2011 EIA Regulations)

Criterion	Overall Grade	Areas where more information required
(1) A description of the development comprising information on the site, design and size of the development.		
(2) A description of the measures envisaged in order to avoid, reduce and, if possible, remedy significant adverse effects.		
(3) The data required to identify and assess the main effects that the development is likely to have on the environment.		
(4) An outline of the main alternatives studied and an indication of the main reasons for their choice, taking into account the environmental effects.		
(5) A non-technical summary of the information provided under 1 to 4 above.		
Overall Grade (A–F):		
List of Information that is required to complete the EIS		

IAU Best Practice Requirements

Criterion	Overall Grade	Areas where more information required
Description of the development		
Description of the environment		
Scoping, consultation, and impact identification		
Prediction and evaluation of impacts		
Alternatives		
Mitigation and monitoring		
Non-technical summary		
Organisation and presentation of information		
Overall Grade (A–F):		
Comments		

Appendix 6

• •

Selected EIA journals and websites

Journals

Environmental Impact Assessment Review
    www.elsevier.com

The Environmentalist
    Institute of Environmental Management and
    Assessment (IEMA)
    www.iema.net

Impact Assessment and Project Appraisal
    www.iaia.org/publications/iapa-journal.aspx

*Journal of Environmental Assessment Policy and
    Management (JEAPM)*
    www.worldscinet.com/jeapm

Journal of Environmental Law
    www.jel.oxfordjournals.org

Journal of Environmental Management
    www.elsevier.com

Journal of Environmental Planning and Management
    www.tandf.co.uk/journals

Journal of Environmental Policy and Planning
    www.tandf.co.uk/journals

Journal of Planning and Environment Law
    www.sweetandmaxwell.co.uk

*Review of European Community and International
    Environmental Law*
    www.wiley.com

Websites

United Kingdom

Countryside Council for Wales
    www.ccw.gov.uk

Department for Communities and Local Government
    www.communities.gov.uk/planningandbuild
    ing/planningenvironment

Environment Agency
    www.environment-agency.gov.uk

*Institute of Environmental Management and
    Assessment (IEMA)*
    www.iema.net

Natural England
    www.naturalengland.org.uk

Royal Society for the Protection of Birds (RSPB)
    www.rspb.org.uk/ourwork/policy/planning/
    environmentalassessment

Scottish Environment Protection Agency (SEPA)
    www.sepa.org.uk

The Scottish Government
    www.scotland.gov.uk/Topics/Built-
    Environment/planning/National-Planning-
    Policy/themes/enviro-assessment

Scottish Natural Heritage
www.snh.gov.uk/planning-and-
development/environmental-assessment

Scotland and Northern Ireland Forum ofr
Environmental Research (SNIFFER)
www.seaguidance.org.uk

Strategic Environmental Assessment Information
Service
www.sea-info.net

Sustainable Development Commission
www.sd-commission.org.uk

Other European

Arctic Environmental Impact Assessment
www.arcticcentre.ulapland.fi/aria

European Centre for Nature Conservation
www.ecnc.org

European Commission
www.ec.europa.eu/environment/eia

European Environment Agency
www.eea.europa.eu

List of Ministries Responsible for EIA/SEA in EU
Member States
www.ec.europa.eu/environment/eia/contacts

Netherlands Commission for Environmental
Assessment
www.eia.nl

Regional Environmental Centre for Central and
Eastern Europe
www.rec.org

Russian Regional Environmental Centre
www.rusrec.ru/en

United Nations Economic Commission for Europe
(UNECE)
www.unece.org/env/eia

North America

British Columbia Environmental Assessment Office
www.eao.gov.bc.ca

Canadian Environmental Assessment Agency (CEAA)
www.ceaa.gc.ca

Environment Canada
www.ec.gc.ca

IAIA Western and Northern Canada
www.iaiawnc.org

Ontario Association for Impact Assessment
www.oaia.on.ca

United States Council on Environmental Quality
(CEQ)
www.whitehouse.gov/administration/
eop/ceq

United States Environmental Protection Agency (EPA)
www.EPA.gov

United States National Environmental Policy Act
(NEPA)
www.ceq.hss.doe.gov

Australia and New Zealand

Australian Government
www.environment.gov.au/epbc/assessments

New Zealand Association for Impact Assessment
www.nzaia.org.nz

New Zealand Ministry for the Environment
www.mfe.govt.nz

New Zealand Parliamentary Commissioner for the
Environment
www.pce.parliament.nz

Asia

Chinese Ministry of Environmental Protection
www.english.mep.gov.cn

Environment and Sustainable Development in
Central Asia and Russia
www.caresd.net

Hong Kong Environmental Protection Department
www.epd.gov.hk/epd/english/
environmentinhk/eia_planning

Indian EIA Division, Ministry of Environment and
Forests
www.envfor.nic.in/divisions/iass

Japanese Ministry of the Environment
www.env.go.jp/en/policy

Korean Society of Environmental Impact Assessment (KSEIA)
www.eia.or.kr/eng

Malaysian Department of Environment
www.doe.gov.my

Regional Environmental Centre for Central Asia (CAREC)
www.carecnet.org/en

Republic of Korea, Ministry of Environment
www.eng.me.go.kr

Africa

Eastern Africa Association for Impact Assessment
www.ira-eaaia.org

International Association for Impact Assessment (South Africa)
www.iaia.co.za

Southern African Institute for Environmental Assessment (SAIEA)
www.saiea.com

International organizations

African Development Bank
www.afdb.org/en/topics-sectors/sectors/environment

Asian Development Bank
www.adb.org/Environment

European Bank for Reconstruction and Development (EBRD)
www.ebrd.com/pages/project/eia

International Association for Impact Assessment (IAIA)
www.iaia.org

International Institute for Environment and Development
www.iied.org

Organisation for Economic Co-operation and Development (OECD)
www.oecd.org

United Nations Economic Commission for Europe (UNECE)
www.unece.org/env/eia

United Nations Environment Programme (UNEP)
www.unep.org/themes/assessment

World Bank
www.worldbank.org

Health impact assessment

Association of Public Health Observatories: HIA Gateway
www.apho.org.uk

IMPACT: International Health Impact Assessment Consortium
www.liv.ac.uk/ihia

London Health Commission
www.london.gov.uk/lhc/hia

World Health Organization
www.who.int/hia/en

Social impact assessment

International Association for Impact Assessment
www.iaia.org/iaiawiki/sia

SIA Hub for Social Impact Assessment practitioners
www.socialimpactassessment.net

Index

● ●